10 CLASSIC MYSTERY AND SUSPENSE PLAYS OF THE MODERN THEATRE

BOOKS AND PLAYS BY STANLEY RICHARDS

10 CLASSIC MYSTERY AND SUSPENSE PLAYS OF THE MODERN THEATRE

Edited with an introductory note and prefaces to the plays
by STANLEY RICHARDS

DODD, MEAD & COMPANY · NEW YORK

Copyright © 1973 by Stanley Richards
All rights reserved
ISBN: 0-396-06707-7
Library of Congress Catalog Card Number: 72-7755
Printed in the United States of America

FOR REGINALD DENHAM

CONTENTS

AN INTRODUCTORY NOTE

There is probably no successful play, whether it be drama, comedy, or melodrama, that does not have suspense as an integral part of its structure. Yet the term "suspense" has been standardized to identify a special genre of play—the thriller. It is a form of theatre that has its own specifications and its singular demands must be met by its creators in order to achieve the highest degree of chilling effectiveness.

The demands of course may vary somewhat from play to play, but according to Reginald Denham, who has been associated with some of the modern theatre's foremost mystery and suspense plays, there are *four* vital ingredients which are essential to their success. "First, there must be the leavening agent of humor—a large dollop of it. This is indispensable, so that the audience may get relief when the inner tension becomes too intense. Shakespeare knew this when he introduced the drunken, bawdy porter immediately after the Macbeths murdered Duncan. Humor must be cunningly introduced at those psychological moments when the suspense is well-nigh unbearable."

Then, as is true with all forms of drama, there must be audience identification. "The people in the theatre must say, 'This could happen to me, or to my family or to my friends.' In that way the impact on them is intensified. They do not feel they are merely looking from afar at some academic case history. Instead the particular dramatic happening is something that could occur to themselves the moment they leave the theatre, or perhaps it might actually be going on in their own homes while they are looking at the play."

Mr. Denham's third requisite for a successful melodrama perhaps is the one most indigenous to the genre—*audible* audience participation. "There must be some spot where the public exclaims vocally.

In *Angel Street*, when the detective left his hat behind in the room just as the villain was about to enter, the entire house shouted nightly, 'Your hat! Your hat!' In *Ladies in Retirement*, the point at which Ellen Creed is tricked by her nephew into thinking she sees the ghost of the friend she has baked in the oven, evoked a similar startled chorus. The gasps that greeted that moment were as regular nightly as those in *Night Must Fall*, when the inspector carried the decapitated head of the victim across the stage in a hatbox." These are moments that often can spell the difference between success and failure, and in just about every one of our classic thrillers there have been those few seconds of terror or anguish that effectively generated a vocal response from audiences.

Lastly, it is Mr. Denham's opinion that the end of a thriller should not be too tightly tied. "There should be an avenue for speculation after you have left the play; an intriguing area for discussion and argument wherein audience members may exercise the ingenuity of their minds."

Suspense and mystery plays have come a long way from what Mr. Denham describes as "the creaking-door dramas," such as *The Bat* and *The Cat and the Canary*, "wherein shudders flapped, windows banged, clutching hands came out of bookcases, door hinges groaned, lights went on and off for no logical reason and characters were puppets without psychology or truth."

The signal for the demise of "the creaking-door drama" came in 1929 with the arrival of Patrick Hamilton's thriller, *Rope*, which brought to the theatre "another sort of shudder, based on real psychology." Hamilton showed us "the unhinged creak in a human mind and the clutching hand of fear destroying a human soul." This triumph of realism over meretricious theatricalism was so revolutionary that *Rope* became the pattern for all modern suspense plays.

In the introductory note to my preceding collection, *Best Mystery and Suspense Plays of the Modern Theatre*, I wrote: "The fact that the plays found within these pages enjoyed enormous audience popularity on stage and in various metamorphoses in other media has proven unequivocally that they have fulfilled one of the theatre's major functions, which is to entertain." The same statement can be applied to the plays in this anthology. Each of the ten selections has to a degree become a classic of its kind and period, and not only have they all succeeded in fulfilling their entertainment quota on stages in many parts of the world, but they also were successfully converted into motion pictures that brought pleasure to millions of moviegoers and television viewers.

I am quite confident that they now will provide many hours of equally chilling entertainment for the reader.

STANLEY RICHARDS

10 CLASSIC MYSTERY AND SUSPENSE PLAYS OF THE MODERN THEATRE

Ten Little Indians

AGATHA CHRISTIE

Agatha Christie

In *Ten Little Indians,* one of her most ingenious and
popular mystery plays, Agatha Christie (who, in 1971, was
created a Dame of the Order of the British Empire by
Queen Elizabeth II) adeptly employed a familiar nursery rhyme as
a framework for her suspenseful plot. And while the audience, early
on, is made aware of the fact that the murderer is fastidiously following the rhyme, providing a general idea of what will come next,
Dame Agatha dexterously keeps us guessing as to just *how* the murderer will continue to dovetail each succeeding crime with the progression of the rhyme. It is a work of superior design, and although
intricately patterned, there is no concealment of vital facts. It is this
honest procedure that has placed her so high in the ranks of the
world's foremost purveyors of fictional crime and detection. A wily
mistress of criminal ceremonies, she is like a perfect hostess serving
hemlock at a cocktail party, and as the London *Daily Express* com-
mented, "no one brews shuddering suspense better than Agatha
Christie."

Ten Little Indians also has proved to be one of Dame Agatha's
most durable properties. Originally published in 1939 as a novel, *Ten
Little Niggers,* the author's own dramatization (utilizing the same
title) opened in London in 1943 and immediately became one of the
West End's leading thrillers. It ran for 260 performances, a not
inconsiderable feat considering that the world was still in the throes
of a devastating war. In 1944, the play, now retitled *Ten Little
Indians,* opened on Broadway and surpassed the success of the British
presentation by playing for 426 performances. Later, it found equal
favor on the road, and even today it remains a prime staple of stock
and repertory companies, here and in England.

Two film versions were made of the play; the first, released in 1945 under the title *And Then There Were None* was performed by an exceptional cast headed by Walter Huston, Judith Anderson, and Barry Fitzgerald. The second screen transmutation (1965) reverted to the play's original New York title and although it featured such capable character actors as Stanley Holloway and Wilfrid Hyde-White, it didn't nearly measure up to the excellence of the 1945 film, mainly because it veered too far from the Christie original.

Earlier in her career, Dame Agatha largely relied upon collaborators (or adaptors) to help fashion plays from her stories, but for a number of years now she has been the sole chatelaine of her work. As Peter Saunders, producer of her record-breaking *The Mousetrap*, has said: "Agatha Christie can condense a novel into a play with an amazing theatre sense. She has an instinct for writing lines which sound natural and actors find them remarkably easy to learn."

Saunders knows whereof he speaks for in order to keep the performance of this rare theatrical mint (now in its twenty-first year in London) as fresh as it was at the beginning, he engages a new cast each year, thereby avoiding any risk of actors giving jaded performances through endless repetition year after year. *The Mousetrap*, which opened on November 25, 1952, is the longest-running play in world theatre history—an attainment that no other dramatist, from Aristophanes on, can match.

Fifty-two years after she revolutionized detective fiction with her first published novel, *The Mysterious Affair at Styles*—which introduced her immortal character, Hercule Poirot, to the world—Dame Agatha Christie remains supreme in her realm. Her more than eighty books, translated into many languages, have enjoyed worldwide sales of over 350 million copies. Yet, with all due consideration to her prodigious reputation as a mystery novelist, it must be acknowledged that she is a formidable figure in the modern theatre as well. Since 1928, when *Alibi*, the Michael Morton dramatization of her classic, *The Murder of Roger Ackroyd*, ran for 250 performances at the Prince of Wales Theatre in London, Agatha Christie has been represented on stage by approximately twenty plays that either she herself has written or that have been adapted by others from her stories. During one period, 1953–1954, she became England's first distaff playwright to have three offerings running concurrently in the West End: *The Mousetrap; Spider's Web;* and *Witness for the Prosecution.* The latter also made contemporary stage history by winning the 1954–1955 New York Drama Critics' Circle Award as the year's best foreign play—the only mystery and suspense drama ever accorded this accolade.

Agatha Christie's other plays include: *Verdict; Hidden Horizon; Towards Zero; The Hollow; The Unexpected Guest; Rule of Three; Appointment with Death; Black Coffee; Go Back for Murder;* and *Love From a Stranger,* which she dramatized with Frank Vosper. Her newest thriller, *Fiddlers Five,* presently is establishing box-office records on its tour of the British provinces prior to opening in the West End.

Her theatre pieces, and approximately fifteen motion pictures culled from her works, amply justify the observation of the distinguished British critic, Ivor Brown: "Nowadays we live, not only as readers, but as play and filmgoers, in a whirl of Christie criminology."

Agatha Mary Clarissa Miller was born in 1890 in Torquay, Devonshire, the English countryside that has served as the setting for many of her stories. In her youth she studied piano and voice in Paris, and with the encouragement of her mother and the novelist-dramatist Eden Phillpotts, a Devon neighbor, began to write what she has described as "stories of unrelieved gloom, where most of the characters died." (A somewhat prophetic preamble to an extraordinary career!) In 1914 she married Archibald Christie, and although the marriage was dissolved fourteen years later, she retained the Christie name professionally. Her second husband is the noted archaeologist, Sir Max Mallowan, whom she married in 1930, and she often has served as his assistant on expeditions in the Middle East. The couple maintain two residences, a home near Oxford and an estate in Devonshire.

In 1972, Dame Agatha Christie celebrated her eighty-second year with the publication of her eighty-second novel, *Elephants Can Remember.*

Ten Little Indians was first produced under the title *Ten Little Niggers* at the St. James's Theatre, London, on November 17, 1943. The cast was as follows:

ROGERS	*William Murray*
FRED NARRACOTT	*Reginald Barlow*
MRS. ROGERS	*Hilda Bruce-Potter*
VERA CLAYTHORNE	*Linden Travers*
PHILIP LOMBARD	*Terence de Marney*
ANTHONY MARSTON	*Michael Blake*
WILLIAM BLORE	*Percy Walsh*
GENERAL MACKENZIE	*Eric Cowley*
EMILY BRENT	*Henrietta Watson*
SIR LAWRENCE WARGRAVE	*Allan Jeayes*
DR. ARMSTRONG	*Gwyn Nicholls*
Directed by	Irene Hentschel
Décor by	Clifford Palmer

Ten Little Indians was first presented in the United States at the Broadhurst Theatre, New York, on June 27, 1944, by the Messrs. Shubert and Albert de Courville. The cast was as follows:

ROGERS	*Neil Fitzgerald*
MRS. ROGERS	*Georgia Harvey*
FRED NARRACOTT	*Patrick O'Connor*
VERA CLAYTHORNE	*Claudia Morgan*
PHILIP LOMBARD	*Michael Whalen*
ANTHONY MARSTON	*Anthony Kemble Cooper*
WILLIAM BLORE	*J. Pat O'Malley*
GENERAL MACKENZIE	*Nicholas Joy*
EMILY BRENT	*Estelle Winwood*
SIR LAWRENCE WARGRAVE	*Halliwell Hobbes*
DR. ARMSTRONG	*Harry Worth*

Directed by	Albert de Courville
Setting by	Howard Bay

SCENE: *The living room of a house on Indian Island, off the coast of Devon, England.*

ACT ONE

A summer evening in August.

ACT TWO

SCENE 1: *The following morning.*
SCENE 2: *The same day. Afternoon.*

ACT THREE

SCENE 1: *The same night.*
SCENE 2: *The following afternoon.*

ACT ONE

The scene is the living room of a house on Indian Island. It is a very modern room, and luxuriously furnished. It is a bright sunlight evening. Nearly the whole of the back of the stage is a window looking directly out to sea. French doors are open in center to balcony. It should give the impression of being like the deck of a liner, almost overhanging the sea. There is a chair out on the balcony and the main approach to the house is presumed to be up steps on the left side of the balcony. There is also presumed to be steps on the right of the balcony, but these are not the direct way up from the landing stage, but are supposed to lead around the house and up behind it, since the house is supposed to be built against the side of a steep hill. The French doors are wide so that a good area of the balcony is shown.

In the left wall, near windows, is a door to dining room. Downstage left is a door communicating with hall. Pull cord below this door.

Up right is a door to study. Middle stage right is fireplace. Over it hangs the reproduction of the "Ten Little Indians" nursery rhyme. On the mantelpiece are a group of ten china Indian figures. They are not spaced out, but clustered so that the exact number is not easily seen.

Center are two sofas with space between. Chair and small table up left. Club chair with tabouret right and above it, down left, where there is also a bookcase. There is a window seat up right and cocktail cabinet below mantelpiece. Tabouret down right. Before fireplace is a big white bearskin rug with a bear's head. There is an armchair and

*tabouret right center. A square ottoman at lower end of
fireplace. A settee with table left of it in front of window
at back.*

When the curtain rises, ROGERS *is busy putting final touches
to room. He is setting out bottles on cocktail cabinet.*
ROGERS *is a competent, middle-aged manservant. Not a
butler, but a house-parlorman. Quick and deft. Just a
trifle specious and shifty. There is a noise of seagulls.
Motorboat horn heard off.* MRS. ROGERS *enters from dining
room. She is a thin, worried, frightened-looking woman.*
NARRACOTT *enters center, carrying a market basket filled
with packages.*

NARRACOTT: First lot to be arriving in Jim's boat. Another lot not far
behind.

MRS. ROGERS: Good evening, Fred.

NARRACOTT: Good evening, Mrs. Rogers.

MRS. ROGERS: Is that the boat?

NARRACOTT: Yes.

MRS. ROGERS: Oh, dear, already? Have you remembered everything?

NARRACOTT: [*Giving her basket*] I think so. Lemons. Slip soles.
Cream. Eggs, tomatoes and butter. That's all, wasn't it?

MRS. ROGERS: That's right. So much to do I don't know where to
start. No maids till the morning, and all these guests arriving today.

ROGERS: [*At mantel*] Calm down, Ethel, everything's shipshape now.
Looks nice, don't it, Fred?

NARRACOTT: Looks neat enough for me. Kind of bare, but rich folks
like places bare, it seems.

MRS. ROGERS: Rich folks is queer.

NARRACOTT: And he was a queer sort of gentleman as built this place.
Spent a wicked lot of money on it he did, and then gets tired of
it and puts the whole thing up for sale.

MRS. ROGERS: Beats me why the Owens wanted to buy it, living on
an island.

ROGERS: Oh, come off it, Ethel, and take all that stuff out into the
kitchen. They'll be here any minute now.

MRS. ROGERS: Making that steep climb an excuse for a drink, I suppose. Like some others I know.

[*Motorboat horn heard off*]

NARRACOTT: That be young Jim. I'll be getting along. There's two gentlemen arriving by car, I understand. [*Goes up to balcony*]

MRS. ROGERS: [*Calling to him*] I shall want at least five loaves in the morning and eight pints of milk, remember.

NARRACOTT: Right.

[MRS. ROGERS *puts basket on floor; exits to hall*]

ROGERS: Don't forget the oil for the engine, Fred. I ought to charge up tomorrow, or I'll have the lights running down.

NARRACOTT: [*Going off*] 'Twas held up on railway. It's at the station now. I'll bring it across the first thing tomorrow.

ROGERS: And give a hand with the luggage, will you?

NARRACOTT: Right.

MRS. ROGERS: [*Enters with list*] I forgot to give you the list of guests, Tom.

ROGERS: Thanks, old girl. [*Looks reflectively at list*] H'mm, doesn't look a very classy lot to me. [*Refers to list*] Miss Claythorne. She'll probably be the secretary.

MRS. ROGERS: I don't hold much with secretaries. Worse than hospital nurses, and them giving themselves airs and graces and looking down on the servants.

ROGERS: Oh, stop grousing, Ethel, and cut along to that lovely up-to-date expensive kitchen of yours.

MRS. ROGERS: [*Picks up basket; going out*] Too many new-fangled gadgets for my fancy!

[*Voices of* VERA *and* LOMBARD *heard outside.* ROGERS *stands at center doors ready to receive them. He is now the well-trained, deferential manservant.* VERA *and* LOMBARD *enter from balcony. She is a good-looking girl of twenty-five. He is an attractive, lean man of thirty-four, well tanned, with a touch of the adventurer about him. He is already a good deal taken with* VERA]

LOMBARD: [*Gazing round room, very interested*] So this is it!

VERA: How perfectly lovely!

ROGERS: Miss Claythorne!

VERA: You're—Rogers?

ROGERS: Yes. Good evening, miss.

VERA: Good evening, Rogers. Will you bring up my luggage and Captain Lombard's?

ROGERS: Very good, miss. [*He exits*]

VERA: [*To* LOMBARD] You've been here before?

LOMBARD: No—but I've heard a lot about the place.

VERA: From Mr. and Mrs. Owen?

LOMBARD: No, old Johnny Brewer, a pal of mine, built this house— it's a sad and poignant story.

VERA: A love story?

LOMBARD: Yes, ma'am—the saddest of all. He was a wealthy old boy and fell in love with the famous Lily Logan—married her—bought the island and built this place for her.

VERA: Sounds most romantic.

LOMBARD: Poor Johnny! He thought by cutting her off from the rest of the world—without even a telephone as a means of communication—he could hold her.

VERA: But of course the fair Lily tired of her ivory tower—and escaped?

LOMBARD: U'huh. Johnny went back to Wall Street, made a few more millions, and the place was sold.

VERA: And here we are. [*Moving as if to go out of door*] Well, I ought to find Mrs. Owen. The others will be up in a minute.

LOMBARD: [*Stopping her*] It would be very rude to leave me here all by myself.

VERA: Would it? Oh, well, I wonder where she is?

LOMBARD: She'll come along when she's ready. While we're waiting. [*Nodding towards cabinet*] Do you think I could have a drink? I'm very dry. [*Starts preparing drinks*]

VERA: Of course you could.

LOMBARD: It's certainly warm after that steep climb. What's yours?

VERA: No, thanks, not for me— Not on duty.

LOMBARD: A good secretary is never off duty.

VERA: Really. [*Looking round room*] This is exciting!

LOMBARD: What?

VERA: All this. The smell of the sea—the gulls—the beach and this lovely house. I am going to enjoy myself.

LOMBARD: [*Smiling. Coming to her*] I think you are. I think we both are. [*Holding up drink*] Here's to you—you're very lovely.

[ROGERS *enters with two suitcases*]

VERA: [*To* ROGERS] Where is Mrs. Owen?

ROGERS: Mr. and Mrs. Owen won't be down from London until tomorrow, miss. I thought you knew.

VERA: Tomorrow—but—

ROGERS: I've got a list here of the guests expected, miss, if you would like to have it. The second boatload's just arriving. [*Holds out list*]

VERA: Thank you. [*Takes list.* ROGERS *goes into hall*] How awful —I say, you will be sweet and help me, won't you?

LOMBARD: I won't move from your side.

VERA: Thank you. [*She reads list*] It seems silly to have brought only us in the first boat and all the rest in the second.

LOMBARD: That, I'm afraid, was design, not accident.

VERA: Design? What do you mean?

LOMBARD: I suggested to the boatman that there was no need to wait for any more passengers. That and five shillings soon started up the engine.

VERA: [*Laughing*] Oh, you shouldn't have done that!

LOMBARD: Well, they're not a very exciting lot, are they?

VERA: I thought the young man was rather nice-looking.

LOMBARD: Callow. Definitely callow. And very, very young.

VERA: I suppose you think a man in his thirties is more attractive.

LOMBARD: I don't think, my darling—I know.

[MARSTON *enters. Good-looking young man of twenty-three or so. Rich, spoiled—not very intelligent*]

MARSTON: [*Coming down to them*] Wizard place you've got here.

[*Prepares to greet* VERA *as his hostess.* LOMBARD *stands beside her like a host*]

VERA: [*Shakes hands*] I'm Mrs. Owen's secretary. Mrs. Owen has been detained in London, I'm afraid, and won't be down until tomorrow.

MARSTON: [*Vaguely*] Oh, too bad.

VERA: May I introduce Captain Lombard, Mr.—er—

MARSTON: Marston, Anthony Marston.

LOMBARD: Have a drink?

MARSTON: Oh, thank you.

[BLORE *comes up on balcony. Middle-aged, thickset man. Is wearing rather loud clothes and is giving his impression of a South African gold magnate. His eyes dart about, making notes of everything*]

LOMBARD: What will you have? Gin, whiskey, sherry—?

MARSTON: Whiskey, I think.

[*They go down to cabinet*]

BLORE: [*Seizing* VERA'S *hand and wringing it heartily*] Wonderful place you have here.

VERA: I'm Mrs. Owen's secretary. Mrs. Owen has been detained in London, I'm afraid, and won't be down until tomorrow.

LOMBARD: Say when!

MARSTON: Oh, wizard!

BLORE: How are you? [*Makes for cocktail cabinet*]

LOMBARD: My name's Lombard. Have a drink, Mr.—

BLORE: Davis. Davis is the name.

LOMBARD: Mr. Davis—Mr. Marston!

[VERA *sits on sofa*]

BLORE: How are you, Mr. Marston? Pleased to meet you. Thanks, Mr. Lombard. I don't mind if I do. Bit of a stiff climb up here. [*He goes up to balcony*] But whew! What a view and what a height! Reminds me of South Africa, this place.

LOMBARD: [*Staring at him*] Does it? What part?

BLORE: Oh—er—Natal, Durban, you know.

LOMBARD: Really? [*Hands him drink*]

BLORE: Well, here's to temperance. Do you—er—know South Africa?

LOMBARD: Me? No.

BLORE: [*With renewed confidence*] That's where I come from. That's my Natal state—ha-ha.

LOMBARD: Interesting country, I should think.

BLORE: Finest country in the world, sir. Gold, silver, diamonds, oranges, everything a man could want. Talk about a land flowing with beer and skittles.

[GENERAL MACKENZIE *arrives on balcony. Upright, soldierly old man, with a gentle, tired face*]

MACKENZIE: [*Hesitating courteously*] Er— How do you do?

[VERA *rises; meets him*]

VERA: General MacKenzie, isn't it? I'm Mrs. Owen's secretary. Mrs. Owen has been detained in London, I'm afraid, and won't be down until tomorrow. Can I introduce Captain Lombard—Mr. Marston and Mr.—

BLORE: [*Approaching him*] Davis, Davis is the name. [*Shakes hands*]

LOMBARD: Whiskey and soda, sir?

MACKENZIE: Er—thanks. [*Studies* LOMBARD] You in the service?

LOMBARD: Formerly in the King's African Rifles. Too tame for me in peace time. I chucked it.

MACKENZIE: Pity. [*As* LOMBARD *pours out soda*] When.

[MISS EMILY BRENT *arrives. She is a tall, thin spinster, with a disagreeable, suspicious face*]

EMILY: [*Sharply to* VERA] Where is Mrs. Owen? [*Puts case on sofa*]

VERA: Miss Brent, isn't it? I'm Mrs. Owen's secretary. Mrs. Owen has been detained in London, I'm afraid.

LOMBARD *and* VERA: And won't be down until tomorrow.

[*They tail off, rather embarrassed*]

EMILY: Indeed. Extraordinary. Did she miss the train?

VERA: I expect so. Won't you have something? May I introduce Captain Lombard—General MacKenzie—Mr. Marston. I think you all met on the boat. And Mr.—

BLORE: Davis, Davis is the name. May I take your case?

LOMBARD: Do let me give you a drink? A dry Martini? A glass of sherry? Whiskey and soda?

EMILY: [Coldly] I never touch alcohol.

LOMBARD: You never touched alcohol!

EMILY: [She picks up case] I suppose you know, young man, that you left us standing there on the wharf?

VERA: I'm afraid, Miss Brent, I was to blame for that. I wanted to—

EMILY: It seems to me most extraordinary that Mrs. Owen should not be here to receive her guests.

VERA: [Smiling] Perhaps she's the kind of person who just can't help missing trains.

BLORE: [Laughs] That's what I reckon she is.

EMILY: Not at all. Mrs. Owen isn't the least like that.

LOMBARD: [Lightly] Perhaps it was her husband's fault.

EMILY: [Sharply] She hasn't got a husband. [VERA stares. ROGERS enters] I should like to go to my room.

VERA: Of course. I'll take you there.

ROGERS: [To VERA] You'll find Mrs. Rogers upstairs, miss. She will show you the room.

[VERA and EMILY exit left, followed by ROGERS. WARGRAVE enters from balcony]

LOMBARD: [Comes forward] I'm afraid our host and hostess haven't arrived, sir. My name's Lombard.

WARGRAVE: Mine's Wargrave. How do you do?

LOMBARD: How do you do? Have a drink, sir?

WARGRAVE: Yes, please. A whiskey.

BLORE: [Crosses to WARGRAVE] How are you? Davis, Davis is the name. [LOMBARD gets his drink. Affably to WARGRAVE] I say, wonderful place you've got here. Quite unique.

WARGRAVE: As you say— Quite unique.

BLORE: Your drink, sir.

[WARGRAVE *puts coat on sofa, takes his drink and sits. Watches proceedings from there*]

MARSTON: [*To* LOMBARD] Old Badger Berkeley rolled up yet?

LOMBARD: Who did you say?

MARSTON: Badger Berkeley. He roped me in for this show. When's he coming?

LOMBARD: I don't think he is coming. Nobody of the name of Berkeley.

MARSTON: [*Jaw drops*] The dirty old double-crosser! He's let me down. Well, it's a pretty wizard island! Rather a wizard girl, that secretary. She ought to liven things up a bit. I say, old man, what about dressing for dinner if there's time?

LOMBARD: Let's go and explore.

MARSTON: Oh, wizard!

LOMBARD: Things are a bit at sixes and sevens with the Owens not turning up.

MARSTON: Tricky, what? I say, wizard place for a holiday, what?

[MARSTON *and* LOMBARD *exit left.* BLORE *wanders out on balcony, looks back sharply into room and presently exits right on balcony as* GENERAL MACKENZIE *and* WARGRAVE *talk.* WARGRAVE *continues to sit like a Buddha. He observes* MACKENZIE, *standing looking rather lost, absent-mindedly pulling his moustache.* MACKENZIE *is carrying a shooting-stick. He looks at it wistfully, half opens and closes it*]

WARGRAVE: Aren't you going to sit down?

MACKENZIE: Well, to tell you the truth, you seem to be in my chair.

WARGRAVE: I am sorry. I didn't realize you were one of the family.

MACKENZIE: Well, it's not that exactly. To tell you the truth, I've never been here before. But you see I live at the Benton Club— have for the last ten years. And my seat is just about there. Can't get used to sitting anywhere else.

WARGRAVE: It becomes a bit of a habit. [*He rises*]

MACKENZIE: Yes, it certainly does. Thank you— [*Sits*] Well, it's not quite as good as the club's, but it's a nice chair. [*Confidentially*] To tell you the truth, I was a bit surprised when I got this invitation. Haven't had anything of the kind for well over four years. Very nice of them, I thought.

ROGERS: [*Enters. Picks up* WARGRAVE's *coat from sofa*] Can I have your keys, sir?

WARGRAVE: Is Lady Constance Culmington expected here, can you tell me? [*Gives him keys*]

ROGERS: [*Surprised*] Lady Constance Culmington? I don't think so, sir. Unless she's coming down with Mr. and Mrs. Owen.

WARGRAVE: Oh.

ROGERS: Allow me, sir. [*Takes* GENERAL MACKENZIE's *coat*] Can I have your keys, sir?

MACKENZIE: [*Rising*] No, thanks. I'll unpack for myself.

ROGERS: Dinner is at eight o'clock, sir. Shall I show you to your room?

MACKENZIE: Please.

[MACKENZIE *goes to door left, which* ROGERS *holds open for him.* WARGRAVE *follows more deliberately, looking round room in an unsatisfied fashion.* ROGERS *follows them out. Sound of seagulls, then* DR. ARMSTRONG *arrives upon balcony, followed by* NARRACOTT *carrying his suitcase.* ARMSTRONG *is a fussy, good-looking man of forty-four. He looks rather tired*]

NARRACOTT: Here you are, sir. I'll call Rogers. [*Exits*]

[ARMSTRONG *looks round; nods approval; looks out at sea. Then* NARRACOTT *returns.* ARMSTRONG *tips him.* NARRACOTT *exits.* ARMSTRONG *sits.* BLORE *comes along balcony; pauses at sight of* ARMSTRONG]

BLORE: How are you? Davis. Davis is the name.

ARMSTRONG: Mine's Armstrong. [*Rises*]

BLORE: Doctor Armstrong, I believe.

ARMSTRONG: Yes.

BLORE: Thought so. Never forget a face.

ARMSTRONG: Don't tell me I've forgotten one of my patients!

BLORE: No, no, nothing like that, but I once saw you in court giving expert evidence.

ARMSTRONG: Oh, really? Are you interested in the Law?

BLORE: Well, you see, I'm from South Africa. Naturally, legal processes in this country are bound to interest a colonial.

ARMSTRONG: Oh, yes, of course.

BLORE: Have a drink?

ARMSTRONG: No, thanks. I never touch it.

BLORE: Do you mind if I do? Mine's empty.

ARMSTRONG: Not a bit.

BLORE: [Pours himself a drink] I've been having a look round the island. It's a wonderful place, isn't it?

ARMSTRONG: Wonderful. I thought as I was coming across the mainland what a haven of peace this was.

BLORE: [Putting his face close to his] Too peaceful for some, I daresay.

ARMSTRONG: Wonderfully restful. Wonderful for the nerves. I'm a nerve specialist, you know.

BLORE: Yes, I know that. Did you come down by train?

ARMSTRONG: No, I motored down. Dropped in on a patient on the way. Great improvement—wonderful response.

BLORE: Best part of two hundred miles, isn't it? How long did it take you?

ARMSTRONG: I didn't hurry. I never hurry. Bad for the nerves. Some mannerless young fellow nearly drove me into the ditch near Amesbury. Shot past me at about eighty miles an hour. Disgraceful bit of driving. I'd like to have had his number.

BLORE: [Comes to him] Yes, and if only more people would take the numbers of these young road hogs.

ARMSTRONG: Yes. You must excuse me. I must have a word with Mr. Owen. [He bustles out]

BLORE: Oh, but—Mr. Owen isn't coming down—

> [BLORE rings bell. Finishes drink; puts glass on sofa. ROGERS enters almost immediately]

ROGERS: You rang, sir?

BLORE: Yes, take my hat, will you? [*Hands him his cap*] What time's supper?

ROGERS: Dinner is at eight o'clock, sir. [*Pauses*] In a quarter of an hour. I think tonight dressing will be optional.

BLORE: [*Familiarly*] Got a good place, here.

ROGERS: [*Draws himself up rather stiffly*] Yes, thank you, sir.

BLORE: Been here long?

ROGERS: Just under a week, sir.

BLORE: Is that all? [*Pause*] So I don't suppose you know much about this crowd that's here?

ROGERS: No, sir.

BLORE: All old friends of the family?

ROGERS: I really couldn't say, sir.

BLORE: Oh, well— Oh, Rogers—

ROGERS: Yes, sir?

BLORE: Rogers, do you think you could put some sandwiches and a bottle of beer in my room at night? I get an 'ell of an appetite with this sea air.

ROGERS: I'll see what I can do, sir.

BLORE: Rogers—I'll see you won't lose by it. Where's my room?

ROGERS: I'll show you, sir.

BLORE: [*As they go out*] Good. I can do with a wash and brush up straightaway. [*Exits with ROGERS*]

> [MRS. ROGERS *enters. She picks up glass from sofa and from table and takes them down to cocktail cabinet.* ROGERS *returns with tray of eight glasses*]

MRS. ROGERS: [*She takes glasses off tray and* ROGERS *puts on dirty ones*] Oh, there you are, Rogers. You ought to clear these dirty glasses. You're always leaving the dirty work to me. Here I am with a four-course dinner on my hands and no one to help me. You might come and give me a hand with the dishing up. . . . Who was it that you were talking to, by the way?

ROGERS: Davis, South African gentleman. No class if you ask me—and no money either.

MRS. ROGERS: I don't like him— Don't like any of 'em much. More like that bunch we had in the boarding house, I'd say.

ROGERS: Davis gives out he's a millionaire or something. You should see his underwear! Cheap as they make 'em.

MRS. ROGERS: Well, as I said, it's not treating us right. All these visitors arriving today and the maids not coming till tomorrow. What do they think we are?

ROGERS: Now, then— Anyway, the money's good.

MRS. ROGERS: So it ought to be! Catch me going into service again unless the money was good.

ROGERS: Well, it is good, so what are you going on about?

MRS. ROGERS: Well, I can tell you this, Rogers. I'm not staying any place where I'm put upon. Cooking's my business! I'm a good cook—

ROGER: [*Placating her*] First-rate, old girl.

MRS. ROGERS: But the kitchen's my place and housework's none of my business. All these guests! I've a good mind to put my hat and coat on and walk out now and go straight back to Plymouth.

ROGERS: [*Grinning*] You can't do that, old girl.

MRS. ROGERS: [*Belligerently*] Who says I can't? Why not, I should like to know?

ROGERS: Because you're on an island, old girl. Had you forgotten that?

MRS. ROGERS: Yes, and I don't know as I fancy being on an island.

ROGERS: Don't know that I do, either, come to that. No slipping down to a pub, or going to the pictures. Oh, well, it's double wages on account of the difficulties. And there's plenty of beer in the house.

MRS. ROGERS: That's all you ever think about—beer.

ROGERS: Now, now, stop your nagging. You get back to the kitchen or your dinner will be spoilt.

MRS. ROGERS: It'll be spoilt anyway, I expect. Everybody's going to be late. Wasted on them, anyway. Thank goodness, I didn't make a soufflé. [VERA *enters*. MRS. ROGERS *goes to door*] Oh, dinner won't be a minute, miss. Just a question of dishing up. [*Exits*]

VERA: Is everything all right, Rogers? Can you manage between the two of you?

ROGERS: Yes, thank you, miss. The missus talks a lot, but she gets it done. [*Exits*]

[VERA *goes to window.* EMILY *enters, having changed*]

VERA: What a lovely evening!

EMILY: Yes, indeed. The weather seems very settled.

VERA: How plainly one can hear the sea.

EMILY: A pleasant sound.

VERA: Hardly a breath of wind—and deliciously warm. Not like England at all.

EMILY: I should have thought you might feel a little uncomfortable in that dress.

VERA: [*Not taking the point*] Oh, no.

EMILY: [*Nastily*] It's rather tight, isn't it?

VERA: [*Good-humored*] Oh, I don't think so.

EMILY: [*Sits; takes out gray knitting*] You'll excuse me, my dear, but you're a young girl and you've got your living to earn—

VERA: Yes?

EMILY: A well-bred woman doesn't like her secretary to appear flashy. It looks, you know, as though you were trying to attract the attention of the opposite sex.

VERA: And would you say I do attract them?

EMILY: That's beside the point. A girl who deliberately sets out to get the attention of men won't be likely to keep her job long.

VERA: [*Laughing at her*] Ah! Surely that depends on who she's working for?

EMILY: Really, Miss Claythorne!

VERA: Aren't you being a little unkind?

EMILY: [*Spitefully*] Young people nowadays behave in the most disgusting fashion.

VERA: Disgusting?

EMILY: [*Carried away*] Yes. Low-backed evening dresses. Lying half naked on beaches. All this so-called sun-bathing. An excuse for immodest conduct, nothing more. Familiarity! Christian names —drinking cocktails! And look at the young men nowadays. Decadent! Look at that young Marston. What good is he? And that Captain Lombard!

VERA: What do you object to in Captain Lombard? I should say he was a man who'd led a very varied and interesting life.

EMILY: The man's an adventurer. All this younger generation is no good—no good at all.

VERA: You don't like youth—I see.

EMILY: [*Sharply*] What do you mean?

VERA: I was just remarking that you don't like young people.

EMILY: [*Rises*] And is there any reason why I should, pray?

VERA: Oh, no— [*Pauses*] but it seems to me that you must miss an awful lot.

EMILY: You're very impertinent.

VERA: [*Quietly*] I'm sorry, but that's just what I think.

EMILY: The world will never improve until we stamp out immodesty.

VERA: [*To herself*] Quite pathological.

EMILY: [*Sharply*] What did you say?

VERA: Nothing.

[EMILY *sits.* ARMSTRONG *and* LOMBARD *enter, talking*]

LOMBARD: What about the old boy—

ARMSTRONG: He looks rather like a tortoise, don't you think so?

LOMBARD: All judges look like tortoises. They have that venomous way of darting their heads in and out. Mr. Justice Wargrave is no exception.

ARMSTRONG: I hadn't realized he was a judge.

LOMBARD: Oh, yes. [*Cheerfully*] He's probably been responsible for sending more innocent people to their death than anyone in England. [WARGRAVE *enters and looks at him*] Hello, you. [*To* VERA] Do you two know each other? Mr. Armstrong—Miss Claythorne. Armstrong and I have just decided that the old boy—

VERA: Yes, I heard you and so did he, I think.

[WARGRAVE *moves over to* EMILY. EMILY *rises as she sees*
WARGRAVE *approaching*]

EMILY: Oh, Sir Lawrence.

WARGRAVE: Miss Brent, isn't it?

EMILY: There's something I want to ask you. [*Indicating she wants to talk to him on the balcony*] Will you come out here?

WARGRAVE: [*As they go*] A remarkably fine night! [*They go out*]

[MARSTON *enters with* BLORE. *They are in conversation*]

MARSTON: Absolutely wizard car—a super-charged Sports Mulatti Carlotta. You don't see many of them on the road. I can get over a hundred out of her.

[VERA *sits on sofa*]

BLORE: Did you come from London?

MARSTON: Yes, two hundred and eight miles and I did it in a bit over four hours. [ARMSTRONG *turns and looks at him*] Too many cars on the road, though, to keep it up. Touched ninety going over Salisbury Plain. Not too bad, eh?

ARMSTRONG: I think you passed me on the road.

MARSTON: Oh, yes?

ARMSTRONG: You nearly drove me into the ditch.

MARSTON: [*Unmoved*] Did I? Sorry.

ARMSTRONG: If I'd seen your number, I'd have reported you.

MARSTON: But you were footling along in the middle of the road.

ARMSTRONG: Footling? Me footling?

BLORE: [*To relieve atmosphere*] Oh, well, what about a drink?

MARSTON: Good idea. [*They move toward the drinks*] Will you have one, Miss Claythorne?

VERA: No, thank you.

LOMBARD: [*Sitting beside* VERA *on sofa*] Good evening, Mrs. Owen.

VERA: Why Mrs. Owen?

LOMBARD: You'd make the most attractive wife for any wealthy business man.

VERA: Do you always flirt so outrageously?

LOMBARD: Always.

VERA: Oh! Well, now we know. [*She turns half away, smiling*]

LOMBARD: Tell me, what's old Miss Brent talking to the Judge about? She tried to buttonhole him upstairs.

VERA: I don't know. Funny—she seemed so definite that there wasn't a Mr. Owen.

LOMBARD: You don't think that Mrs. Owen—I mean that there isn't—that they aren't—

VERA: What, married you mean?

[ROGERS *enters, switches on lights, draws curtains and exits to study.* MARSTON *comes to sofa.* LOMBARD *rises*]

MARSTON: Damn shame we didn't know each other. I could have given you a lift down.

VERA: Yes, that would have been grand.

MARSTON: Like to show you what I can do across Salisbury Plain. Tell you what—maybe we can drive back together?

[WARGRAVE *and* EMILY *return.* MACKENZIE *enters; sits*]

VERA: [*Surprised*] But I— [*Rising*]

MARSTON: But it seems damn silly. I've got an empty car.

LOMBARD: Yes, but she likes the way she's going back and—

VERA: [*Crosses to fireplace*] Look! Aren't they sweet? Those ten little china Indians. [MARSTON *and* LOMBARD *scowl at each other*] Oh, and there's the old nursery rhyme.

LOMBARD: What are you talking about? What figures? What nursery rhyme?

VERA: [*She points at the figures and rhyme—reading*] "Ten little Indian boys going out to dine,
One choked his little self, and then there were nine—"
[ROGERS *enters.* VERA *continues reading nursery rhyme.* BLORE *crosses up to below her;* EMILY *to above her*]
"Nine little Indian boys sat up very late,
One overslept himself, and then there were eight."

BLORE: "Eight little Indian boys traveling in Devon.
One got left behind, and then there were seven—"

VOICE: [*Very slowly and clearly from off up right*] Ladies and gentlemen, silence, please! [*All rise. Everybody stops talking and stares round at each other, at the walls. As each name is mentioned that person reacts by a sudden movement or gesture*] You are charged with these indictments: that you did respectively and at divers times commit the following: Edward Armstrong, that you did cause the death of Louisa Mary Clees. William Henry Blore, that you brought about the death of James Stephen Landor. Emily Caroline Brent, that you were responsible for the death of Beatrice Taylor. Vera Elizabeth Claythorne, that you killed Peter Ogilvie

Hamilton. [VERA *sits on sofa*] Philip Lombard, that you were guilty of the deaths of twenty-one men, members of an East African tribe. John Gordon MacKenzie, that you sent your wife's lover, Arthur Richmond, to his death. [MACKENZIE *sits down*] Anthony James Marston, that you were guilty of the murder of John and Lucy Combes. Thomas Rogers and Ethel Rogers, that you brought about the death of Jennifer Brady. Lawrence John Wargrave, that you were guilty of the murder of Edward Seton. Prisoners at the bar, have you anything to say in your defense?

[*There is a momentary paralyzed silence. Then there is a scream outside door left.* LOMBARD *springs across the room to it. Indignant murmur breaks out as people recover from first shock. Door left opens to show* MRS. ROGERS *in a fallen heap.* MARSTON *springs across to* LOMBARD. *They pick up* MRS. ROGERS *and carry her in to sofa.* ARMSTRONG *comes to her*]

ARMSTRONG: It's nothing much. She's fainted, that's all. She'll be round in a minute. Get some brandy—

BLORE: Rogers, get some brandy.

[ROGERS, *shaking all over, goes out*]

VERA: Who was that speaking? It sounded—

MACKENZIE: [*His hands shaking, pulling at his moustache*] What's going on here? What kind of practical joke was that?

[BLORE *wipes face with handkerchief.* WARGRAVE *stands in middle of room near sofas, thoughtfully stroking chin, his eyes peering suspiciously from one to the other*]

LOMBARD: Where the devil did that voice come from? [*They stare all round. He goes into study*] Here we are.

VOICE: You are charged with these indictments—

VERA: Turn it off! Turn it off! It's horrible!

[LOMBARD *switches it off.* MRS. ROGERS *groans*]

ARMSTRONG: A disgraceful and heartless practical joke!

WARGRAVE: [*With significance*] So you think it's a joke, do you?

ARMSTRONG: What else could it be?

[EMILY *sits down*]

WARGRAVE: [*With significance*] At the moment I'm not prepared to give an opinion.

[ROGERS *returns with brandy and glass on tray. Puts it on table*]

MARSTON: Who the devil turned it on, though? And set it going?

WARGRAVE: We must enquire into that. [*He looks significantly at* ROGERS]

[LOMBARD *enters with record; puts it on chair.* MRS. ROGERS *begins to move and twist*]

MRS. ROGERS: Oh, dear me! Oh, dear me!

[*The others move nearer, obscuring table where the brandy is. Attention is focused on* MRS. ROGERS]

ROGERS: Allow me, madam. [*To* ARMSTRONG] Allow me, sir. If I speak to her— Ethel—Ethel— [*His tone is urgent and nervous*] It's all right. All right, do you hear? Pull yourself together.

[MRS. ROGERS *begins to gasp and moan. She tries to pull herself up. Her frightened eyes stare round the room*]

ARMSTRONG: [*Taking wrist*] You'll be all right now, Mrs. Rogers. Just a nasty turn.

[BLORE *pours out brandy*]

MRS. ROGERS: Did I faint, sir?

ARMSTRONG: Yes.

MRS. ROGERS: It was the voice—the awful voice—like a judgment—

[ROGERS *makes anxious movement.* MRS. ROGERS' *eyelids flutter. She seems about to collapse again*]

ARMSTRONG: Where's the brandy? [*They draw back a little, disclosing it.* BLORE *gives glass to* VERA, *who gives it to* ARMSTRONG. VERA

sits on edge of sofa, holding cushion under MRS. ROGERS' *head*]
Drink this, Mrs. Rogers.

MRS. ROGERS: [*She gulps a little. Revives. She sits up again*] I'm
all right now. It just—gave me a turn.

ROGERS: [*Quickly*] Of course it did. Gave me a turn, too. Wicked
lies it was! I'd like to know—

> [WARGRAVE *deliberately clears his throat. It stops* ROGERS,
> *who stares at him nervously.* WARGRAVE *clears his throat
> again, looking hard at* ROGERS]

WARGRAVE: Who was it put the record on the gramophone? Was it
you, Rogers?

ROGERS: I was just obeying orders, sir, that's all.

WARGRAVE: Whose orders?

ROGERS: Mr. Owen's.

WARGRAVE: Let me get this quite clear. Mr. Owen's orders were—what
exactly?

ROGERS: I was to put a record on the gramophone in the study. I'd
find the records in the drawer in there. I was to start with that
one, sir. I thought it was to give you all some music.

WARGRAVE: [*Skeptically*] A very remarkable story.

ROGERS: [*Hysterically*] It's the truth, sir! Before heaven, it's the
truth! I didn't know what it was—not for a moment. It had a
name on it. I thought it was just a piece of music.

> [WARGRAVE looks toward LOMBARD, *who examines record*]

WARGRAVE: Is there a title?

LOMBARD: [*Grinning*] A title? Yes, sir. It's entitled "Swan Song."

> [*It amuses him, but some of the others react nervously*]

MACKENZIE: The whole thing is preposterous—preposterous! Slinging
accusations about like this. Something must be done about it.
This fellow Owen, whoever he is—

EMILY: That's just it. Who is he?

WARGRAVE: [*With authority*] That is exactly what we must go into
very carefully. I should suggest that you get your wife to bed,
Rogers. Then come back here.

ROGERS: Yes, sir.

ARMSTRONG: I'll give you a hand.

VERA: [*Rising*] Will she be all right, Doctor?

ARMSTRONG: Yes, quite all right.

> [ARMSTRONG *and* ROGERS *help* MRS. ROGERS *up and take her out*]

MARSTON: [*To* WARGRAVE] Don't know about you, sir, but I feel I need another drink.

WARGRAVE: I agree.

MARSTON: I'll get them.

MACKENZIE: [*Muttering angrily*] Preposterous—that's what it is—preposterous. [*Sits*]

MARSTON: Whiskey for you, Sir Lawrence?

EMILY: [*Sits*] I should like a glass of water, please.

VERA: Yes, I'll get it. I'll have a little whiskey, too.

> [VERA *takes glass of water to* EMILY, *then sits with her own drink. They sip drinks without speaking, but they eye each other.* ARMSTRONG *returns*]

ARMSTRONG: She'll be all right. I've given her a sedative.

BLORE: Now, then, Doctor, you'll want a drink after all this.

ARMSTRONG: No, thank you. I never touch it. [*Sits*]

BLORE: Oh, so you said. You have this one, General? [*Crosses to* MACKENZIE]

> [MARSTON *and* LOMBARD *refill their glasses.* ROGERS *enters.* WARGRAVE *takes charge.* ROGERS *stands near door. He is nervous. Everyone focuses attention on him*]

WARGRAVE: Now, then, Rogers, we must get to the bottom of this. Tell us what you know about Mr. Owen.

ROGERS: He owns this place, sir.

WARGRAVE: I am aware of that fact. What I want you to tell me is what you yourself know about the man.

ROGERS: I can't say, sir. You see, I've never seen him.

> [*Faint stir of interest*]

MACKENZIE: What d'you mean, you've never seen him?

ROGERS: We've only been here just under a week, sir, my wife and I. We were engaged by letter through a registry office. The Regina, in Plymouth.

BLORE: That's a high-class firm. We can check on that.

WARGRAVE: Have you got the letter?

ROGERS: The letter engaging us? Yes, sir. [*Hunts for it and hands it to* WARGRAVE, *who runs through it*]

WARGRAVE: Go on with your story.

ROGERS: We arrived here like the letter said, on the 4th. Everything was in order, plenty of food in stock and everything very nice. Just needed dusting and that.

WARGRAVE: What next?

ROGERS: Nothing, sir. That is, we got orders to prepare the room for a house party—eight. Then yesterday, by the morning post, I received another letter saying Mr. and Mrs. Owen might be detained and, if so, we was to do the best we could, and it gave the instructions about dinner and putting on the gramophone record. Here it is, sir. [*Hands over letter*]

WARGRAVE: H'mm. Headed Ritz Hotel and typewritten.

[BLORE *steps up to him and takes letter out of his hands.* MARSTON *goes to left of* BLORE. MACKENZIE *rises; looks over* WARGRAVE'S *shoulder*]

BLORE: Coronation machine Number Five. Quiet now. No defects. Ensign paper—most common make. We shan't get much out of this. We might try it for fingerprints, but it's been handled too much.

LOMBARD: Quite the little detective.

[WARGRAVE *turns and looks at him sharply.* BLORE'S *manner has completely changed, so has his voice.* MACKENZIE *sits again.* LOMBARD *sits on sofa*]

MARSTON: [*Taking letter*] Got some fancy Christian names, hasn't he? Ulick Norman Owen. Quite a mouthful.

WARGRAVE: [*Takes letter from* MARSTON] I am obliged to you, Mr.

Marston. You have drawn my attention to a curious and suggestive point. [*He looks round in his court manner*] I think the time has come for all of us to pool our information. It would be well for everybody to come forward with all the information they have regarding our unknown host. We are all his guests. I think it would be profitable if each one of us were to explain exactly how that came about.

[*There is a pause*]

EMILY: [*Rising*] There's something very peculiar about all this. I received a letter with a signature that was not very easy to read. It purported to be from a woman whom I had met at a certain summer resort two or three years ago. I took the name to be Ogden. I am quite certain that I have never met or become friendly with anyone of the name of Owen.

WARGRAVE: Have you got that letter, Miss Brent?

EMILY: Yes. I will fetch it for you. [*Goes out*]

WARGRAVE: Miss Claythorne?

VERA: [*Rises*] I never actually met Mrs. Owen. I wanted a holiday post and I applied to a secretarial agency, Miss Grenfell's in London. I was offered this post and accepted.

WARGRAVE: And you were never interviewed by your prospective employer?

VERA: No. This is the letter. [*Hands it to him. Sits again*]

WARGRAVE: [*Reading*] "Indian Island, Sticklehaven, Devon. I have received your name from Miss Grenfell's Agency. I understand she knows you personally. I shall be glad to pay you the salary you ask, and shall expect you to take up your duties on August 8th. The train is the 12:10 from Paddington and you will be met at Oakbridge Station. I enclose five pounds for expenses.

Yours truly,
Una Nancy Owen."

[MARSTON *starts to go*] Mr. Marston?

MARSTON: Don't actually know the Owens. Got a wire from a pal of mine, Badger Berkeley. Told me to roll up here. Surprised me a bit because I had an idea the old house had gone to Norway. I haven't got the wire.

WARGRAVE: Thank you. Doctor Armstrong?

ARMSTRONG: [*After a pause, rising*] In the circumstances, I think I may admit that my visit here was professional. Mr. Owen wrote me that he was worried about his wife's health—her nerves, to be precise. He wanted a report without her being alarmed. He therefore suggested that my visit should be regarded as that of an ordinary guest.

WARGRAVE: You had no previous acquaintance with the family?

ARMSTRONG: No.

WARGRAVE: But you had no hesitation in obeying the summons?

ARMSTRONG: A colleague of mine was mentioned and a very handsome fee suggested. I was due for a holiday, anyway.

[*EMILY reenters and hands letter to* WARGRAVE, *who unfolds it and reads.* EMILY *sits down*]

WARGRAVE: "Dear Miss Brent: I do hope you remember me. We were together at Bell Haven guest house in August some years ago and we seemed to have so much in common. I am starting a guest house of my own on an island off the coast of Devon. I think there is really an opening for a place where there is good plain English cooking, and a nice old-fashioned type of person. None of this nudity and gramophones half the night. I shall be very glad if you could see your way to spending your summer holiday on Indian Island—as my guest, of course. I suggest August 8th, 12:40 from Paddington to Oakbridge.

Yours sincerely,
U.N."

H'm, yes, the signature *is* slightly ambiguous.

LOMBARD: [*Rises; crosses to* VERA. *Aside to her*] I like the nudity touch!

WARGRAVE: [*Takes letter from pocket*] Here is my own decoy letter. From an old friend of mine, Lady Constance Culmington. She writes in her usual vague, incoherent way, urges me to join her here and refers to her host and hostess in the vaguest of terms.

LOMBARD: [*With sudden excitement, staring at* BLORE] Look here, I've just thought of something—

WARGRAVE: In a minute.

LOMBARD: But I—

WARGRAVE: We will take one thing at a time, if you don't mind, Captain Lombard. General MacKenzie?

[BLORE *sits*]

MACKENZIE: [*Rather incoherently, pulling at moustache*] Got a letter—from this fellow Owen—thought I must have met him sometime at the club—mentioned some old cronies of mine who were to be here—hoped I'd excuse informal invitation. Haven't kept the letter, I'm afraid. [*Sits*]

WARGRAVE: And you, Captain Lombard?

LOMBARD: Same sort of thing. Invitation mentioning mutual friends. I haven't kept the letter either.

[*Pause.* WARGRAVE *turns his attention to* BLORE. *He looks at him for some minutes. When he speaks, his voice is silky and dangerous*]

WARGRAVE: Just now we had a somewhat disturbing experience. An apparently disembodied voice spoke to us all by name, uttering certain definite accusations against us. We will deal with those accusations presently. At the moment I am interested in a minor point. Amongst the names received was that of William Henry Blore. But as far as we know, there is no one named Blore amongst us. The name of Davis was not mentioned. What have you to say about that, Mr. Davis?

BLORE: [*Rises*] Cat's out of the bag, it seems. I suppose I'd better admit my name isn't Davis.

WARGRAVE: You are William Henry Blore?

BLORE: That's right.

LOMBARD: I will add something to that. Not only are you here under a false name, Mr. Blore, but in addition I've noticed this evening that you're a first-class liar. You claim to have come from Natal, South Africa. I know South Africa and Natal well, and I'm prepared to swear that you've never set foot there in your life.

[*All turn toward* BLORE. ARMSTRONG *goes up to window*]

BLORE: You gentlemen have got me wrong. I'm an ex-C. I. D. man.

LOMBARD: Oh, a copper!

BLORE: I've got my credentials and I can prove it. I run a detective agency in Plymouth. I was put onto this job.

WARGRAVE: By whom?

BLORE: Why, Mr. Owen. Sent a very nice money order for expenses, and said I was to join the house party, posing as a guest. He also sent a list of all your names and said I was to keep an eye on you all.

WARGRAVE: Any reason given?

BLORE: Said Mrs. Owen had got some valuable jewels. [*Pause*] Mrs. Owen, my foot! I don't believe there's any such person.

WARGRAVE: [*Sits*] Your conclusions are, I think, justified. [*Looks down at letters*] Ulick Norman Owen. Una Nancy Owen. Each time, that is to say, U. N. Owen. Or, by a slight stretch of fancy, Unknown.

VERA: But it's fantastic! Mad!

WARGRAVE: [*Rises. Quietly*] Oh, yes, I've no doubt in my own mind that we have been invited here by a madman—probably a dangerous homicidal lunatic.

[*There is an appalled silence*]

ROGERS: Oh, my gawd!

WARGRAVE: Whoever it is who has enticed us here, that person has taken the trouble to find out a great deal about us. [*Pause*] A very great deal. And out of his knowledge concerning us, he has made certain definite accusations.

BLORE: It's all very well to make accusations.

MACKENZIE: A pack of damn lies! Slander!

VERA: It's iniquitous! Wicked!

ROGERS: A lie—a wicked lie—we never did, neither of us—

MARSTON: Don't know what the damned fool was getting at—

[*Everybody more or less speaks at once*]

WARGRAVE: [*Raises a hand for silence*] I wish to say this. Our unknown friend accuses me of the murder of one Edward Seton. I remember Seton perfectly well. He came up before me for trial in June, 1930. He was charged with the murder of an elderly woman. He was very ably defended and made a good impression on the jury in the witness box. Nevertheless, on the evidence he was certainly guilty. I summed up accordingly and the jury brought in a verdict of guilty. In passing sentence of death, I fully concurred with this verdict. The appeal was lodged on the grounds of misdirection. The appeal was dismissed and the man was duly executed. [*Pause*] I wish to say before you all that my conscience is perfectly clear on the matter. I did my duty and nothing more. I passed sentence on a rightly convicted murderer.

[*There is a pause*]

ARMSTRONG: Did you know Seton at all? I mean, personally.

WARGRAVE: [*Looks at him. He hesitates a moment*] I knew nothing of Seton previous to the trial.

LOMBARD: [*Low to* VERA] The old boy's lying. I'll swear he's lying.

MACKENZIE: [*Rises*] Fellow's a madman. Absolute madman. Got a bee in his bonnet. Got hold of the wrong end of the stick all round. [*To* WARGRAVE] Best really to leave this sort of thing unanswered. However, feel I ought to say—no truth—no truth whatever in what he said about—er—young Arthur Richmond. Richmond was one of my officers. I sent him on reconnaissance in 1917. He was killed. Also like to say—resent very much—slur on my wife. Been dead a long time. Best woman in the world. Absolutely— Caesar's wife. [*He sits down again*]

MARSTON: I've just been thinking—John and Lucy Combes. Must have been a couple of kids I ran over near Cambridge. Beastly bad luck.

WARGRAVE: [*Acidly*] For them or for you?

MARSTON: Well, I was thinking—for me—but, of course, you're right, sir. It was damned bad luck for them, too. Of course, it was pure accident. They rushed out of some cottage or other. I had my license suspended for a year. Beastly nuisance.

ARMSTRONG: This speeding's all wrong—all wrong. Young men like you are a danger to the community.

MARSTON: [*Wanders to window; picks up his glass, which is half-full*] Well, I couldn't help it. Just an accident.

ROGERS: Might I say a word, sir?

LOMBARD: Go ahead, Rogers.

ROGERS: There was a mention, sir, of me and Mrs. Rogers, and of Miss Jennifer Brady. There isn't a word of truth in it. We were with Miss Brady when she died. She was always in poor health, sir, always from the time we came to her. There was a storm, sir, the night she died. The telephone was out of order. We couldn't get the doctor to her. I went for him, sir, on foot. But he got there too late. We'd done everything possible for her, sir. Devoted to her, we were. Anyone will tell you the same. There was never a word said against us. Never a word.

BLORE: [*In a bullying manner*] Came into a nice little something at her death, I suppose. Didn't you?

ROGERS: [*Stiffly*] Miss Brady left us a legacy in recognition of our faithful service. And why not, I'd like to know?

LOMBARD: [*With meaning*] What about yourself, Mr. Blore?

BLORE: What about me?

LOMBARD: Your name was on the list.

BLORE: I know, I know. Landor, you mean? That was the London and Commercial Bank robbery.

WARGRAVE: [*Crosses to mantelpiece. Lights pipe*] I remember the name, though it didn't come before me. Landor was convicted on your evidence. You were the police officer in charge of the case.

BLORE: I was, my Lud.

WARGRAVE: Landor got penal servitude for life and died in Dartmoor a year later. He was a delicate man.

BLORE: He was a crook. It was him put the night watchman out. The case was clear from the start.

WARGRAVE: [*Slowly*] You were complimented, I think, on your able handling of the case.

BLORE: I got my promotion. [*Pause*] I was only doing my duty.

LOMBARD: [*Sits*] Convenient word—duty. [*There is a general suspicious movement.* VERA *rises, moves as if to cross left, sees* EMILY, *turns. She sits again.* WARGRAVE *moves up to window seat.* ARMSTRONG *to window*] What about you, Doctor?

ARMSTRONG: [*Shakes his head good-humoredly*] I'm at a loss to understand the matter. The name meant nothing to me—what was it? Close? Close? I really don't remember having a patient of that name—or its being connected with a death in any way. The thing's a complete mystery to me. Of course, it's a long time ago. [*Pause*] It might possibly be one of my operation cases in hospital. They come too late, so many of these people. Then, when the patient dies, it's always the surgeon's fault.

LOMBARD: And then it's better to take up nerve cases and give up surgery. Some, of course, give up drink.

ARMSTRONG: I protest! You've no right to insinuate such things. I never touch alcohol.

LOMBARD: My dear fellow, I never suggested you did. Anyway, Mr. Unknown is the only one who knows all the facts.

WARGRAVE: Miss Claythorne?

VERA: [*Starts. She has been sitting, staring in front of her. She speaks unemotionally and without feeling of any kind*] I was nursery governess to Peter Hamilton. We were in Cornwall for the summer. He was forbidden to swim out far. One day, when my attention was distracted, he started off—as soon as I saw what happened I swam after him. I couldn't get there in time—

WARGRAVE: Was there an inquest?

VERA: [*In the same dull voice*] Yes, I was exonerated by the coroner. His mother didn't blame me, either.

WARGRAVE: Thank you. Miss Brent?

EMILY: I have nothing to say.

WARGRAVE: Nothing?

EMILY: Nothing.

WARGRAVE: You reserve your defense?

EMILY: [*Sharply*] There is no question of defense! I have always acted according to the dictates of my conscience. [*Rises*]

[BLORE *goes to fireplace*]

LOMBARD: What a law-abiding lot we seem to be! Myself excepted—

WARGRAVE: We are waiting for your story, Captain Lombard.

LOMBARD: I haven't got a story.

WARGRAVE: [*Sharply*] What do you mean?

LOMBARD: [*Grinning and apparently enjoying himself*] I'm sorry to disappoint all of you. It's just that I plead guilty. It's perfectly true. I left those natives alone in the bush. Matter of self-preservation.

[*His words cause a sensation.* VERA *looks at him unbelievingly*]

MACKENZIE: [*Rises. Sternly*] You abandoned your men?

[EMILY *moves to window seat*]

LOMBARD: [*Coolly*] Not quite the act of a pukka sahib, I'm afraid. But after all, self-preservation's a man's first duty. And natives don't mind dying, you know. They don't feel about it as Europeans do—

[*There is a pause.* LOMBARD *looks round at everyone with amusement.* WARGRAVE *clears throat disapprovingly*]

WARGRAVE: Our inquiry rests there. [ROGERS *crosses to door*] Now, Rogers, who else is there on this island besides ourselves and you and your wife?

ROGERS: Nobody, sir. Nobody at all.

WARGRAVE: You're sure of that?

ROGERS: Quite sure, sir.

WARGRAVE: Thank you. [ROGERS *moves as if to go*] Don't go, Rogers. [*To everybody*] I am not yet clear as to the purpose of our unknown host in getting us to assemble here. But in my opinion he's not sane in the accepted sense of the word. He may be dangerous. In my opinion, it would be well for us to leave this place as soon as possible. I suggest that we leave tonight.

[*General agreement.* MACKENZIE *sits*]

ROGERS: I beg your pardon, sir, but there's no boat on the island.

WARGRAVE: No boat at all?

ROGERS: No, sir.

WARGRAVE: Why don't you telephone to the mainland?

ROGERS: There's no telephone. Fred Narracott, he comes over every morning, sir. He brings the milk and the bread and the post and the papers, and takes the orders.

MARSTON: [Picks up drink from window seat and crosses down to sofa. Raising his voice] A bit unsporting, what? Ought to ferret out the mystery before we go. Whole thing's like a detective story. Positively thrilling.

WARGRAVE: [Acidly] At my time of life, I have no desire for thrills.

MARSTON: [Grins; stretches out his legs] The legal life's narrowing. I'm all for crime. [Raises his glass] Here's to it. [Drinks it off at a gulp, appears to choke, gasps, has a violent convulsion and slips onto sofa. Glass falls from his hand]

ARMSTRONG: [Runs over to him, bends down, feels pulse, raises eyelid] My God, he's dead!

[The others can hardly take it in. ARMSTRONG sniffs lips, then sniffs glass. Nods]

MACKENZIE: Dead? D'you mean the fellow just choked and—died?

ARMSTRONG: You can call it choking if you like. He died of asphyxiation, right enough.

MACKENZIE: Never knew a man could die like that—just of a choking fit.

EMILY: [With meaning] In the middle of life we are in death. [She sounds inspired]

ARMSTRONG: A man doesn't die of a mere choking fit, General MacKenzie! Marston's death isn't what we call a natural death.

VERA: Was there something in the whiskey?

ARMSTRONG: Yes. By the smell of it, cyanide. Probably potassium cyanide. Acts pretty well instantaneously.

LOMBARD: Then he must have put the stuff in the glass himself.

BLORE: Suicide, eh? That's a rum go.

VERA: You'd never think he'd commit suicide. He was so alive. He was enjoying himself.

[EMILY *comes down and picks up remains of Indian from behind chair*]

EMILY: Oh! Look—here's one of the little Indians off the mantel-piece—broken! [*Holds it up*]

CURTAIN

ACT TWO

The same. The following morning.

The windows are open and the room has been tidied. It is a fine morning. There are only eight Indians on the mantelpiece.

Suitcases are piled up on the balcony. All are waiting for the boat to arrive. MACKENZIE *is sitting in his chair, looking definitely a little queer.* EMILY *is sitting, knitting, with her hat and coat on.* WARGRAVE *is sitting in the window seat, a little apart, and is thoughtful. His manner is judicial throughout scene.* VERA, *by window, is restless. She comes into the room as if to speak, no one takes any notice, goes down left and sits.*

ARMSTRONG *and* BLORE *come up on balcony.*

ARMSTRONG: We've been up to the top. No sign of that boat yet.

VERA: It's very early still.

BLORE: Oh, I know. Still the fellow brings the milk and the bread and all that. I should have thought he'd have got here before this. [*Opens door and looks in*] No sign of breakfast yet— Where's that fellow Rogers?

VERA: Oh, don't let's bother about breakfast—

WARGRAVE: How's the weather looking?

BLORE: The wind has freshened a bit. Rather a mackerel sky. Old boy in the train yesterday said we were due for dirty weather. Shouldn't wonder if he wasn't right—

ARMSTRONG: [*Nervously*] I wish that boat would come. The sooner we get off this island the better. It's absurd not keeping a boat on the island.

BLORE: No proper harbor. If the wind comes to blow from the southeast, a boat would get dashed to pieces against the rocks.

EMILY: But a boat would always be able to take us to the mainland?

BLORE: No, Miss Brent—that's just what it wouldn't.

EMILY: Do you mean we should be cut off from the land?

BLORE: Yes. Condensed milk, ryvita and tinned stuff till the gale had blown itself out. But you needn't worry. The sea's only a bit choppy.

EMILY: I think the pleasures of living on an island are rather overrated.

ARMSTRONG: [*Restless*] I wonder if that boat's coming. Annoying the way the house is built slap up against the cliff. You can't see the mainland until you've climbed to the top [*To* BLORE] Shall we go up there again?

BLORE: [*Grinning*] It's no good, Doctor. A watched pot never boils. There wasn't a sign of a boat putting out when we were up there just now.

ARMSTRONG: What can this man Narracott be doing?

BLORE: [*Philosophically*] They're all like that in Devon. Never hurry themselves.

ARMSTRONG: And where's Rogers? He ought to be about.

BLORE: If you ask me, Master Rogers was pretty badly rattled last night.

ARMSTRONG: I know. [*Shivers*] Ghastly—the whole thing.

BLORE: Got the wind up properly. I'd take an even bet that he and his wife did do that old lady in.

WARGRAVE: [*Incredulous*] You really think so?

BLORE: Well, I never saw a man more scared. Guilty as hell, I should say.

ARMSTRONG: Fantastic—the whole thing—fantastic.

BLORE: I say, suppose he's hopped it?

ARMSTRONG: Who, Rogers? But there isn't any way he could. There's no boat on the island. You've just said so.

BLORE: Yes, but I've been thinking. We've only Rogers' word for that. Suppose there is one and he's nipped off in it the first thing.

MACKENZIE: Oh! No. He wouldn't be allowed to leave the island.
[*His tone is so strange they stare at him*]

BLORE: Sleep well, General?

MACKENZIE: I dreamed—yes, I dreamed—

BLORE: I don't wonder at that.

MACKENZIE: I dreamed of Lesley—my wife, you know.

BLORE: [*Embarrassed*] Oh—er—yes—I wish Narracott would come.
[*Turns up to window*]

MACKENZIE: Who is Narracott?

BLORE: The bloke who brought us over yesterday afternoon.

MACKENZIE: Was it only yesterday?

BLORE: [*Determinedly cheerful*] Yes, I feel like that, too. Batty
gramophone records—suicides—it's about all a man can stand. I
shan't be sorry to see the back of Indian Island, I give you my
word.

MACKENZIE: So you don't understand. How strange!

BLORE: What's that, General?

[MACKENZIE *nods his head gently.* BLORE *looks question-
ingly at* ARMSTRONG, *then taps his forehead significantly*]

ARMSTRONG: I don't like the look of him.

BLORE: I reckon young Marston's suicide must have been a pretty
bad shock to him. He looks years older.

ARMSTRONG: Where is that poor young fellow now?

BLORE: In the study—put him there myself.

VERA: Doctor Armstrong, I suppose it was suicide?

ARMSTRONG: [*Sharply*] What else could it be?

VERA: [*Rises*] I don't know. But suicide— [*She shakes her head*]

BLORE: You know, I had a pretty funny feeling in the night. This
Mr. Unknown Owen, suppose he's on the island. Rogers mayn't
know. [*Pause*] Or he may have told him to say so. [*Watches*
ARMSTRONG] Pretty nasty thought, isn't it?

ARMSTRONG: But would it have been possible for anyone to tamper
with Marston's drink without our seeing him?

BLORE: Well, it was standing up there. Anyone could have slipped
a dollop of cyanide in it if they'd wanted to.

ARMSTRONG: But that—

ROGERS: [*Comes running up on balcony. He is out of breath. Comes straight to* ARMSTRONG] Oh, there you are, sir. I've been all over the place looking for you. Could you come up and have a look at my wife, sir?

ARMSTRONG: Yes, of course. [*Goes toward door*] Is she feeling under the weather still?

ROGERS: She's—she's—[*Swallows convulsively*]

ARMSTRONG: You won't leave the island without me?

[*They go out*]

VERA: I wish the boat would come. I hate this place.

WARGRAVE: Yes. I think the sooner we can get in touch with the police the better.

VERA: The police?

WARGRAVE: The police have to be notified in a case of suicide, you know, Miss Claythorne.

VERA: Oh, yes—of course.

BLORE: [*Opening door left*] What's going on here? No sign of any breakfast.

VERA: Are you hungry, General? [MACKENZIE *does not answer. She speaks louder*] Feeling like breakfast?

MACKENZIE: [*Turns sharply*] Lesley—Lesley—my dear.

VERA: No—I'm not—I'm Vera Claythorne.

MACKENZIE: [*Passes a hand over his eyes*] Of course. Forgive me. I took you for my wife.

VERA: Oh!

MACKENZIE: I was waiting for her, you see.

VERA: But I thought your wife was dead—long ago.

MACKENZIE: Yes. I thought so, too. But I was wrong. She's here. On this island.

LOMBARD: [*Comes in from hall*] Good morning.

BLORE: Good morning, Captain Lombard.

LOMBARD: Good morning. Seem to have overslept myself. Boat here yet?

BLORE: No.

LOMBARD: Bit late, isn't it?

BLORE: Yes.

LOMBARD: [*To* VERA] Good morning. You and I could have had a swim before breakfast. Too bad all this.

VERA: Too bad you overslept yourself.

BLORE: You must have good nerves to sleep like that.

LOMBARD: Nothing makes me lose my sleep.

[VERA *goes to mantlepiece*]

BLORE: Didn't dream of African natives, by any chance, did you?

LOMBARD: No. Did you dream of convicts on Dartmoor?

BLORE: [*Angrily*] Look here, I don't think that's funny, Captain Lombard.

LOMBARD: Well, you started it, you know. I'm hungry. What about breakfast? [*Sits*]

BLORE: The whole domestic staff seems to have gone on strike.

LOMBARD: Oh, well, we can always forage for ourselves.

VERA: [*Examining Indian figures*] Hullo, that's strange.

LOMBARD: What is?

VERA: You remember we found one of these little fellows smashed last night?

LOMBARD: Yes— That ought to leave nine.

VERA: That ought to leave nine. I'm certain there were ten of them here when we arrived.

LOMBARD: Well?

VERA: There are only eight.

LOMBARD: [*Looking*] So there are. [*He goes to mantelpiece*]

[*They look at each other*]

VERA: I think it's queer, don't you?

LOMBARD: Probably only were nine to begin with. We assumed there were ten because of the rhyme. [ARMSTRONG *enters. He is upset, but striving to appear calm. Shuts door and stands against it*] Hullo, Armstrong, what's the matter?

ARMSTRONG: Mrs. Rogers is dead.

[WARGRAVE *rises*]

BLORE *and* VERA: No? How?

ARMSTRONG: Died in her sleep. Rogers thought she was still under the influence of the sleeping draught I gave her and came down without disturbing her. He lit the kitchen fire and did this room. Then, as she hadn't appeared, he went up, was alarmed by the look of her and went hunting for me. [*Pause*] She's been dead about five hours, I should say. [*Sits down*]

BLORE: What was it? Heart?

ARMSTRONG: Impossible to say. It may have been.

BLORE: After all, she had a pretty bad shock last night.

ARMSTRONG: Yes.

WARGRAVE: She might have been poisoned, I suppose, Doctor?

ARMSTRONG: It is perfectly possible.

WARGRAVE: With the same stuff as young Marston?

ARMSTRONG: No, not cyanide. It would have to have been some narcotic or hypnotic. One of the barbiturates, or chloral. Something like that.

BLORE: You gave her some sleeping powders last night, didn't you?

ARMSTRONG: [*Rises, crossing to cabinet for drink of water*] Yes, I gave her a mild dose of Luminal.

BLORE: Didn't give her too much, did you?

ARMSTRONG: Certainly not. What do you mean?

BLORE: All right—no offense, no offense. I just thought that perhaps if she'd had a weak heart—

ARMSTRONG: The amount I gave her could not have hurt anyone.

LOMBARD: Then what exactly did happen?

ARMSTRONG: Impossible to say without an autopsy.

WARGRAVE: If, for instance, this death had occurred in the case of one of your private patients, what would have been your procedure?

ARMSTRONG: [*Sits down*] Without any previous knowledge of the woman's state of health, I could certainly not give a certificate.

VERA: She was a very nervous-looking creature. She had a bad fright last night. Perhaps it was heart failure.

ARMSTRONG: Her heart certainly failed to beat—but what caused it to fail?

EMILY: [*Firmly and with emphasis*] Conscience.

[*They all jump and look at her.* WARGRAVE *moves to right*]

ARMSTRONG: What exactly do you mean by that, Miss Brent?

EMILY: You all heard— She was accused, together with her husband, of having deliberately murdered her former employer—an old lady.

BLORE: And you believe that's true, Miss Brent?

EMILY: Certainly. You all saw her last night. She broke down completely and fainted. The shock of having her wickedness brought home to her was too much for her. She literally died of fear.

ARMSTRONG: [Doubtfully] It is a possible theory. One cannot adopt it without more exact knowledge of her state of health. If there was a latent cardiac weakness—

EMILY: Call it, if you prefer, An Act of God.

[EVERYONE is shocked]

BLORE: Oh, no, Miss Brent. [Moves up left]

[LOMBARD goes to window]

EMILY: [Emphatically] You regard it as impossible that a sinner should be struck down by the wrath of God? I do not.

WARGRAVE: [Strokes his chin. His voice is ironic] My dear lady, in my experience of ill doing, Providence leaves the work of conviction and chastisement to us mortals—and the process is often fraught with difficulties. There are no short cuts.

BLORE: Let's be practical. What did the woman have to eat and drink last night after she went to bed?

ARMSTRONG: Nothing.

BLORE: Nothing at all? Not a cup of tea? Or a glass of water? I'll bet you she had a cup of tea. That sort always does.

ARMSTRONG: Rogers assures me she had nothing whatever.

BLORE: He might say so.

LOMBARD: So that's your idea?

BLORE: Well, why not? You all heard that accusation last night. What if it's true? Miss Brent thinks it is, for one. Rogers and his missus did the old lady in. They're feeling quite safe and happy about it—

VERA: Happy?

BLORE: [Sits] Well—they know there's no immediate danger to

them. Then, last night some lunatic goes and spills the beans. What happens? It's the woman cracks. Goes to pieces. Did you see him hanging round her when she was coming to? Not all husbandly solicitude? Not on your sweet life. He was like a cat on hot bricks. And that's the position. They've done a murder and got away with it. But if it's all going to be raked up again now, it's the woman will give the show away. She hadn't got the nerve to brazen it out. She's a living danger to her husband, that's what she is, and him—he's all right. He'll go on lying till the cows come home, but he can't be sure of her. So what does he do? He drops a nice little dollop of something into a nice cup of tea, and when she's had it, he washes up the cup and saucer and tells the doctor she ain't had nothing.

VERA: Oh, no. That's impossible. A man wouldn't do that—not to his wife.

BLORE: You'd be surprised, Miss Claythorne, what some husbands would do. [Rises]

ROGERS: [Enters. He is dead-white and speaks like an automaton. Just the mask of the trained servant. To VERA] Excuse me, miss. I'm getting on with breakfast. I'm not much of a hand as a cook, I'm afraid. It's lunch that's worrying me. Would cold tongue and gelatine be satisfactory? And I could manage some fried potatoes. And then there's tinned fruit and cheese and biscuits.

VERA: That will be fine, Rogers.

BLORE: Lunch? Lunch? We shan't be here for lunch! And when the hell's that boat coming?

EMILY: Mr. Blore! [Picks up her case and marches up to window seat—sits]

BLORE: What?

ROGERS: [Fatalistically] You'll pardon me, sir, but the boat won't be coming.

BLORE: What?

ROGERS: Fred Narracott's always here before eight. [Pause] Is there anything else you require, miss?

VERA: No, thank you, Rogers.

[ROGERS goes out]

BLORE: And it's not Rogers! His wife lying dead upstairs and there he's cooking breakfast and calmly talking about lunch! Now he says the boat won't be coming. How the 'ell does he know?

EMILY: Mr. Blore!

BLORE: What?

VERA: Oh, don't you see? He's dazed. He's just carrying on automatically as a good servant would. It's—it's pathetic, really.

BLORE: He's pulling a fast one, if you ask me.

WARGRAVE: The really significant thing is the failure of the boat to arrive. It means that we are being deliberately cut off from help.

MACKENZIE: That's very little time—very little time—

BLORE: What's that, General?

MACKENZIE: [*Rising*] Very little time. We mustn't waste it talking about things that don't matter.

[*He turns to window. All look at him dubiously before resuming*]

LOMBARD: [*To* WARGRAVE] Why do you think Narracott hasn't turned up?

WARGRAVE: I think the ubiquitous Mr. Owen has given orders.

LOMBARD: You mean, told him it's a practical joke or something of that kind?

BLORE: He'd never fall for that, would he?

LOMBARD: Why not? Indian Island's got a reputation for people having crazy parties. This is just one more crazy idea, that's all. Narracott knows there's plenty of food and drink on the island. Probably thinks it's all a huge joke.

VERA: Couldn't we light a bonfire up on the top of the island? So that they'd see it?

LOMBARD: That's probably been provided against. All signals are to be ignored. We're cut off all right.

VERA: [*Impatiently*] But can't we *do* something?

LOMBARD: Oh, yes, we can do something. We can find the funny gentleman who's staged this little joke, Mr. Unknown Owen. I'll bet anything you like he's somewhere on the island, and the sooner we get hold of him the better! Because, in my opinion, he's mad as a hatter. And as dangerous as a rattlesnake.

WARGRAVE: Hardly a very good simile, Captain Lombard. The rattlesnake at least gives warning of its approach.

LOMBARD: Warning? My God, yes! [*Indicating nursery rhyme*] That's our warning. [*Reading*]
"Ten little Indian boys—"
There were ten of us after Narracott went, weren't there?
"Ten little Indian boys going out to dine,
One choked his little self-"
Marston choked himself, didn't he? And then—
"Nine little Indians sat up very late,
One overslept himself"—overslept himself—
The last part fits Mrs. Rogers rather well, doesn't it?

VERA: You don't think—? Do you mean that he wants to kill us all?

LOMBARD: Yes, I think he does!

VERA: And each one fits with the rhyme!

ARMSTRONG: No, no, it's impossible. It's coincidence. It must be coincidence!

LOMBARD: Only eight little Indian boys here. I suppose that's coincidence too. What do you think, Blore?

BLORE: I don't like it.

ARMSTRONG: But there's nobody on the island.

BLORE: I'm not so sure of that!

ARMSTRONG: This is terrible!

MACKENZIE: None of us will ever leave this island.

BLORE: Can't somebody shut up grandpa?

LOMBARD: Don't you agree with me, Sir Lawrence?

WARGRAVE: [*Slowly*] Up to a point—yes.

LOMBARD: Then the sooner we get to work the better. Come on, Armstrong. Come on, Blore. We'll make short work of it.

BLORE: I'm ready. Nobody's got a revolver, by any chance? I suppose that's too much to hope for.

LOMBARD: I've got one. [*Takes it out of pocket*]

BLORE: [BLORE's *eyes open rather wide. An idea occurs to him—not a pleasant one*] Always carry that about with you?

LOMBARD: Usually. I've been in some tight places, you know.

BLORE: Oh. Well, you've probably never been in a tighter place than you are today. If there's a homicidal maniac hiding on this island, he's probably got a whole arsenal on him—and he'll use it.

ARMSTRONG: You may be wrong there, Blore. Many homicidal maniacs are very quiet, unassuming people.

WARGRAVE: Delightful fellows!

ARMSTRONG: You'd never guess there was anything wrong with them.

BLORE: If Mr. Owen turns out to be one of that kind, we'll leave him to you, Doctor. Now, then, let's make a start. I suggest Captain Lombard searches the house while we do the island.

LOMBARD: Right. House ought to be easy. No sliding panels or secret doors [Goes toward study]

BLORE: Mind he doesn't get you before you get him!

LOMBARD: Don't worry. But you two had better stick together— Remember—"One got left behind."

BLORE: Come on, Armstrong.

[They go along and out up right]

WARGRAVE: [Rises] A very energetic young man, Captain Lombard.

VERA: Don't you think he's right? If someone is hiding on the island, they'll be bound to find him. It's practically bare rock.

WARGRAVE: I think this problem needs brains to solve it. Rather than brawn. [Goes toward balcony]

VERA: Where are you going?

WARGRAVE: I'm going to sit in the sun—and think, my dear young lady. [Goes up right on balcony]

EMILY: Where did I put that skein of wool? [Gets up]

VERA: Did you leave it upstairs? Shall I go and see if I can find it?

EMILY: No, I'll go. I know where it's likely to be. [Goes out]

VERA: I'm glad Captain Lombard has got a revolver.

MACKENZIE: They're all wasting time—wasting time—

VERA: Do you think so?

MACKENZIE: Yes, it's much better to sit quietly—and wait.

VERA: Wait for what? [Sits]

MACKENZIE: For the end, of course. [There is a pause. MACKENZIE rises, opens and shuts both doors left] I wish I could find Lesley.

VERA: Your wife?

MACKENZIE: Yes. I wish you'd known her. She was so pretty. So gay—

VERA: Was she?

MACKENZIE: I loved her very much. Of course, I was a lot older than she was. She was only twenty-seven, you know. [*Pause*] Arthur Richmond was twenty-six. He was my A. D. C. [*Pause*] Lesley liked him. They used to talk of music and plays together, and she teased him and made fun of him. I was pleased. I thought she took a motherly interest in the boy. [*Suddenly to* VERA, *confidentially*] Damn fool, wasn't I? No fool like an old fool. [*A long pause*] Exactly like a book the way I found out. When I was out in France. She wrote to both of us, and she put the letters in the wrong envelope. [*He nods his head*] So I knew—

VERA: [*In pity*] Oh, no.

MACKENZIE: [*Sits*] It's all right, my dear. It's a long time ago. But you see I loved her very much—and believed in her. I didn't say anything to him—I let it gather inside—here— [*Strikes chest*] a slow, murderous rage— Damned young hypocrite—I'd liked the boy—trusted him.

VERA: [*Trying to break spell*] I wonder what the others are doing?

MACKENZIE: I sent him to his death—

VERA: Oh—

MACKENZIE: It was quite easy. Mistakes were being made all the time. All anyone could say was that I'd lost my nerve a bit, made a blunder, sacrificed one of my best men. Yes, it was quite easy— [*Pause*] Lesley never knew. I never told her I'd found out. We went on as usual—but somehow nothing was quite real any more. She died of pneumonia. [*Pause*] She had a heart-shaped face— and grey eyes—and brown hair that curled.

VERA: Oh, don't.

MACKENZIE: [*Rises*] Yes, I suppose in a way—it was murder. Curious, murder—and I've always been such a law-abiding man. It didn't feel like that at the time. "Serves him damn well right!" that's what I thought. But after— [*Pause*] Well, you know, don't you?

VERA: [*At a loss*] What do you mean?

MACKENZIE: [*Stares at her as though something puzzles him*] You don't seem to understand—I thought you would. I thought you'd be glad, too, that the end was coming—

VERA: [*Draws back, alarmed. Rises; backs down left*] I— [*She eyes him warily*]

MACKENZIE: [*Follows her—confidentially*] We're all going to die, you know.

VERA: [*Looking round for help*] I—I don't know.

MACKENZIE: [*Vaguely to* VERA] You're very young—you haven't got to that yet. The relief! The blessed relief when you know that you've done with it all, that you haven't got to carry the burden any longer. [*Moves up right*]

VERA: [*Follows him—moved*] General—

MACKENZIE: Don't talk to me that way! You don't understand. I want to sit here and wait—wait for Lesley to come for me. [*Goes out on balcony and draws up chair and sits. The back of his head down to shoulders is visible through window. His position does not change throughout scene*]

VERA: [*Stares after him. Her composure breaks down. Sits*] I'm frightened— Oh! I'm frightened—

[LOMBARD *comes in up right*]

LOMBARD: All correct. No secret passage—one corpse.

VERA: [*Tensely*] Don't!

LOMBARD: I say, you do look low. How about a drink to steady your nerves?

VERA: [*Rises, flaring up*] A drink! Two corpses in the house at nine o'clock in the morning and all you say, "Have a drink"! An old man going quite crackers—"Have a drink"! Ten people accused of murder—that's all right—just have a drink. Everything's fine so long as you have a drink.

LOMBARD: All right. All right.—Stay thirsty.

VERA: Oh, you—you're nothing but a waster—an adventurer—you make me tired. [*Moves to fireplace*]

LOMBARD: [*Crossing to her*] I say, you are het up. What's the matter, my sweet?

VERA: I'm not your sweet!

LOMBARD: I'm sorry. I rather thought you were.

VERA: Well, you can think again.

LOMBARD: Come now—you know you don't really feel like that. We've got something in common, you and I. Rogues and murderers can't fall out. [*He takes her hand—she draws away*]

VERA: Rogues and murderers—!

LOMBARD: Okay. You don't like the company of rogues and murderers—and you won't have a drink. I'll go and finish searching— [*Exits*]

[EMILY *returns.* VERA *moves up to window*]

EMILY: Unpleasant young man! I can't find it anywhere. [*Sees* VERA's *face*] Is anything the matter?

VERA: [*Low*] I'm worried about the General. He really is ill, I think.

EMILY: [*Looks from* VERA *to* MACKENZIE, *then goes out on balcony and stands behind him. In loud, cheerful voice, as though talking to an idiot child*] Looking out for the boat, General? [MACKENZIE *does not answer.* EMILY *waits a minute, then comes slowly in. Unctuously*] His sin has found him out.

VERA: [*Angrily*] Oh, don't!

EMILY: One must face facts.

VERA: Can any of us afford to throw stones?

EMILY: [*Sits*] Even if his wife was no better than she should be— and she must have been a depraved woman—he had no right to take judgment into his own hands.

VERA: [*Coldly angry*] What about—Beatrice Taylor?

EMILY: Who?

VERA: That was the name, wasn't it? [*Looks at her challengingly*]

EMILY: You are referring to that absurd accusation about myself?

VERA: Yes.

EMILY: Now that we are alone, I have no objection to telling you the facts of the case— Indeed I should like you to hear them. [VERA *sits*] It was not a fit subject to discuss before gentlemen— so naturally I refused to say anything last night. That girl, Beatrice Taylor, was in my service. I was very much deceived by her. She had nice manners and was clean and willing. I was very pleased with her. Of course, all that was sheerest hypocrisy. She was a loose girl with no morals. Disgusting! It was some time before I found out that she was what they call "in trouble." [*Pause*] It was a great shock to me. Her parents were decent folks, too, who had brought her up strictly. I'm glad to say they didn't condone her behavior.

VERA: What happened?

EMILY: [*Self-righteously*] Naturally, I refused to keep her an hour under my roof. No one shall ever say I condoned immorality.

VERA: Did she drown herself?

EMILY: Yes.

VERA: [*Rises*] How old was she?

EMILY: Seventeen.

VERA: Only seventeen.

EMILY: [*With horrible fanaticism*] Quite old enough to know how to behave. I told her what a low depraved thing she was. I told her that she was beyond the pale and that no decent person would take her into their house. I told her that her child would be the child of sin and would be branded all its life—and that the man would naturally not dream of marrying her. I told her that I felt soiled by ever having had her under my roof—

VERA: [*Shuddering*] You told a girl of seventeen all that?

EMILY: Yes. I'm glad to say I broke her down utterly.

VERA: Poor little devil!

EMILY: I've no patience with this indulgence toward sin.

VERA: And then, I suppose, you turned her out of the house?

EMILY: Of course.

VERA: And she didn't dare go home— What did you feel like when you found she'd drowned herself?

EMILY: [*Puzzled*] Feel like?

VERA: Yes. Didn't you blame yourself?

EMILY: Certainly not. I had nothing with which to reproach myself.

VERA: I believe—I believe you really feel like that. That makes it even more horrible. [*Turns away, then goes up to center windows*]

EMILY: That girl's unbalanced! [*Opens bag and takes out a small Bible. Begins to read it in a low mutter*] "The heathen are sunk down in the pit that they made—" [*Stops and nods her head*] "In the net which they hid is their own foot taken." [ROGERS *enters.* EMILY *stops and smiles approvingly*] "The Lord is known by the judgment He executeth, the wicked is snared in the work of his own hand."

ROGERS: [*Looks doubtfully at* EMILY] Breakfast is ready.

EMILY: "The wicked shall be turned into hell." [*Turns head sharply*] Be quiet!

ROGERS: Do you know where the gentlemen are, miss? Breakfast is ready.

VERA: Sir Lawrence Wargrave is sitting out there in the sun. Doctor Armstrong and Mr. Blore are searching the island. I shouldn't bother about them. [*She comes in*]

[ROGERS *goes out to balcony*]

EMILY: "Shall not the isles shake at the sound of the fall, when the wounded cry, when the slaughter is made in the midst of thee?"

VERA: [*Coldly. After waiting a minute or two*] Shall we go in?

EMILY: I don't feel like eating.

ROGERS: [*To* MACKENZIE] Breakfast is ready. [*Goes off right on balcony*]

EMILY: [*Opens Bible again*] "Then all the princes of the sea shall come down from their thrones, and lay away their robes, and put off their 'broidered garments." [BLORE *enters up right*] "They shall clothe themselves with trembling, they shall sit upon the ground, and shall tremble at every moment, and be astonished at thee." [*Looks up and sees* BLORE, *but her eyes are almost unseeing*]

BLORE: [*Speaks readily, but watches her with a new interest*] Reading aloud, Miss Brent?

EMILY: It is my custom to read a portion of the Bible every day.

BLORE: Very good habit, I'm sure.

[ARMSTRONG *comes along balcony and in*]

VERA: What luck did you have?

ARMSTRONG: There's no cover in the island. No caves. No one could hide anywhere.

BLORE: That's right. [LOMBARD *enters*] What about the house, Lombard?

LOMBARD: No one. I'll stake my life there's no one in the house but ourselves. I've been over it from attic to cellar.

[ROGERS *enters from balcony.* WARGRAVE *comes along balcony, slowly, and in*]

ROGERS: Breakfast is getting cold.

[EMILY *is still reading*]

LOMBARD: [*Boisterously*] Breakfast! Come on, Blore. You've been yelping for breakfast ever since you got up. Let's eat, drink and be merry, for tomorrow we die. Or who knows, perhaps, even today!

[VERA *and* ARMSTRONG *cross to door*]

EMILY: [*Rises; drops knitting.* BLORE *picks it up*] You ought to be ashamed of such levity, Captain Lombard!

LOMBARD: [*Still in the same vein, with determination*] Come on, General, can't have this. [*Calls*] Breakfast, I say, sir— [*Goes out on balcony to* MACKENZIE. *Stops—stoops—comes slowly back and stands in window. His face is stern and dangerous*] Good God! One got left behind— There's a knife in MacKenzie's back.

ARMSTRONG: [*Goes to him*] He's dead—he's dead!

BLORE: But he can't be— Who could have done it? There's only us on the island.

WARGRAVE: Exactly, my dear sir. Don't you realize that this clever and cunning criminal is always comfortably one stage ahead of us? That he knows exactly what we are going to do next, and makes his plans accordingly? There's only one place, you know, where a successful murderer could hide and have a reasonable chance of getting away with it.

BLORE: One place—where?

WARGRAVE: Here in this room—Mr. Owen is one of us!

CURTAIN

SCENE 2

There is a storm; the room is much darker—the windows closed and beating rain and wind. WARGRAVE *comes in from left, followed by* BLORE.

BLORE: Sir Lawrence?

WARGRAVE: Well, Mr. Blore?

BLORE: I wanted to get you alone. [*Looks over shoulder at dining room*] You were right in what you said this morning. This damned murderer is one of us. And I think I know which one.

WARGRAVE: Really?

BLORE: Ever hear of the Lizzie Borden case? In America. Old couple killed with an axe in the middle of the morning. Only person who could have done it was the daughter, a respectable, middle-aged spinster. Incredible. So incredible that they acquitted her. But they never found any other explanation.

WARGRAVE: Then your answer to the problem is Miss Emily Brent?

BLORE: I tell you that woman is as mad as a hatter. Religious mad, I tell you—she's the one. And we must watch her.

WARGRAVE: Really? I had formed the impression that your suspicions were in a different quarter.

BLORE: Yes— But I've changed my mind, and I'll tell you for why— she's not scared and she's the only one who isn't. Why? Because she knows quite well she's in no danger—hush—

[VERA *and* EMILY *enter.* VERA *is carrying coffee tray*]

VERA: We've made some coffee. [*She puts tray on tabouret*] Brr— it's cold in here.

BLORE: You'd hardly believe it when you think what a beautiful day it was this morning.

VERA: Are Captain Lombard and Rogers still out?

BLORE: Yes. No boat will put out in this—and it couldn't land, anyway.

VERA: Miss Brent's. [*Hands coffee cup to* BLORE]

[EMILY *comes down, sits on left sofa*]

WARGRAVE: Allow me. [*Takes cup and hands it to* EMILY]

VERA: [*To* WARGRAVE] You were right to insist on our going to lunch—and drinking some brandy with it. I feel better.

WARGRAVE: [*Returns to coffee tray—takes his own coffee; stands by mantelpiece*] The court always adjourns for lunch.

VERA: All the same, it's a nightmare. It seems as though it can't be true. What—what are we going to do about it?

[BLORE *sits*]

WARGRAVE: We must hold an informal court of enquiry. We may at least be able to eliminate some innocent people.

BLORE: You haven't got a hunch of any kind, have you, Miss Claythorne?

WARGRAVE: If Miss Claythorne suspects one of us three, that is rather an awkward question.

VERA: I'm sure it isn't any of you. If you ask me who I suspected, I'd say Doctor Armstrong.

BLORE: Armstrong?

VERA: Yes. Because, don't you see, he's had far and away the best chance to kill Mrs. Rogers. Terribly easy for him, as a doctor, to give her an overdose of sleeping stuff.

BLORE: That's true. But someone else gave her brandy, remember.

[EMILY *goes up left and sits*]

WARGRAVE: Her husband had a good opportunity of administering a drug.

BLORE: It isn't Rogers. He wouldn't have the brains to fix all this stunt—nor the money. Besides you can see he's scared stiff.

[ROGERS *and* LOMBARD, *in mackintoshes, come up on balcony and appear at windows.* BLORE *goes and lets them in. As he opens the window, a swirl of loud wind and rain comes in.* EMILY *half screams and turns around*]

LOMBARD: My God, it's something like a storm.

EMILY: Oh, it's only you—

VERA: Who did you think it was? [*Pause*] Beatrice Taylor?

EMILY: [*Angrily*] Eh?

LOMBARD: Not a hope of rescue until this dies down. Is that coffee? Good [*To* VERA] I'm taking to coffee now, you see.

VERA: [*Takes him a cup*] Such restraint in the face of danger is nothing short of heroic.

WARGRAVE: [*Crosses to down left; sits*] I do not, of course, profess to be a weather prophet. But I should say that it is very unlikely that a boat could reach us, even if it knew of our plight, under twenty-four hours. Even if the wind drops, the sea has still to go down.

[LOMBARD *sits.* ROGER *pulls off his shoes*]

VERA: You're awfully wet.

BLORE: Is anyone a swimmer? Would it be possible to swim to the mainland?

VERA: It's over a mile—and in this sea you'd be dashed on the rocks and drowned.

EMILY: [*Speaking like one in a trance*] Drowned—drowned—in the pond— [*Drops knitting*]

WARGRAVE: [*Rising; startled, moves up to her*] I beg your pardon, Miss Brent. [*He picks it up for her*]

BLORE: After dinner nap.

[*Another furious gust of wind and rain*]

VERA: It's terribly cold in here.

ROGERS: I could light the fire if you like, miss?

VERA: That would be a good idea.

LOMBARD: [*Crossing*] Very sound scheme, Rogers. [*He sits on fender; puts on shoes*]

ROGERS: [*Goes toward door—is going through but comes back and asks*] Excuse me, but does anybody know what's become of the top bathroom curtain?

LOMBARD: Really, Rogers, are you going bats, too?

BLORE: [*Blankly*] The bathroom curtain?

ROGERS: Yes, sir. Scarlet oilsilk. It's missing.

[*They look at each other*]

LOMBARD: Anybody seen a scarlet oilsilk curtain? No good, I'm afraid, Rogers.

ROGERS: It doesn't matter, sir, only I just thought as it was odd.

LOMBARD: Everything on this island is odd.

ROGERS: I'll get some sticks and a few knobs of coal and get a nice fire going. [Goes out]

VERA: I wonder if he would like some hot coffee. He's very wet.

[Runs out after him, calling "Rogers"]

LOMBARD: What's become of Armstrong?

WARGRAVE: He went to his room to rest.

LOMBARD: Somebody's probably batted him one by now!

WARGRAVE: I expect he had the good sense to bolt his door.

BLORE: It won't be so easy now that we're all on our guard. [Lights cigarette at mantelpiece]

[A rather unpleasant silence]

WARGRAVE: I advise you, Mr. Blore, not to be too confident. I should like shortly to propose certain measures of safety, which I think we should all adopt.

LOMBARD: Against whom?

WARGRAVE: Against each other. We are all in grave danger. Of the ten people who came to this island, three are definitely cleared. There are seven of us left—seven little Indian boys.

LOMBARD: One of whom is a bogus little Indian boy.

WARGRAVE: Exactly.

BLORE: Well, in spite of what Miss Claythorne said just now, I'd say that you, Sir Lawrence, and Doctor Armstrong are above suspicion. He's a well-known doctor, and you're known all over England.

WARGRAVE: [Interrupts him] Mr. Blore, that proves nothing at all. Judges have gone mad before now. So have doctors. [Pause] So have policemen.

LOMBARD: Hear, hear. [VERA returns] Well, does he want some coffee?

VERA: [Crossing to tabouret, lightly] He'd rather make himself a nice cup of tea! What about Doctor Armstrong? Do you think we ought to take him up a cup?

WARGRAVE: I will take it up if you like.

LOMBARD: I'll take it. I want to change.

VERA: Yes, you ought to. You'll catch cold.

WARGRAVE: [*Smiling ironically*] I think Doctor Armstrong might prefer to see me. He might not admit you, Captain Lombard. He might be afraid of your revolver.

BLORE: Ah, that revolver. [*Meaningly*] I want a word with you about that—

VERA: [*To* LOMBARD] Do go and change.

> [WARGRAVE *takes cup from her and, passing behind, goes out*]

LOMBARD: [*To* BLORE] What were you going to say?

BLORE: I'd like to know why you brought a revolver down here on what's supposed to be a little social visit.

LOMBARD: You do, do you? [*After a momentary pause*] I've led a rather adventurous life. I've got into the habit of taking a revolver about with me. I've been in a bit of a jam once or twice. [*Smiles*] It's a pleasant feeling to have a gun handy. [*To* BLORE] Don't you agree?

> [ARMSTRONG *enters and stands at left*]

BLORE: We don't carry them. Now, then, I want the truth about this gun—

LOMBARD: What a damned suspicious fellow you are, Blore!

BLORE: I know a fishy story when I hear one.

ARMSTRONG: If it's about that revolver, I'd like to hear what you've got to say.

LOMBARD: Oh, well, I got a letter, asking me to come here as the guest of Mr. and Mrs. Owen— It would be worth my while. The writer said that he had heard I'd got a reputation for being a good man in a tight place. There might be some danger, but I'd be all right if I kept my eyes open.

BLORE: I'd never have fallen for that.

LOMBARD: Well, I did. I was bored. God, how I was bored back in this tame country. It was an intriguing proposition, you must admit.

BLORE: Too vague for my liking.

LOMBARD: That was the whole charm. It aroused my curiosity.

BLORE: Curiosity killed the cat.

LOMBARD: [*Smiling*] Yes, quite.

VERA: Oh, do go and change, please!

LOMBARD: I'm going, my sweet, I'm going. The maternal instinct I think it's called.

VERA: Don't be ridiculous—

[VERA *collects* EMILY'S *cup.* LOMBARD *exits*]

BLORE: That's a tall story. If it's true, why didn't he tell it to us last night?

ARMSTRONG: He might have thought that this was exactly the emergency for which he had been prepared.

VERA: Perhaps it is.

ARMSTRONG: [*Puts down cup on tabouret*] I hardly think so. It was just Mr. Owen's little bit of cheese to get him into the trap with the rest of us. He must have known him well enough to rely on his curiosity.

BLORE: If it's true, he's a wrong 'un, that man. I wouldn't trust him a yard.

VERA: Are you such a good judge of truth?

[WARGRAVE *enters*]

ARMSTRONG: [*With a sudden outburst*] We must get out of here— we must before it is too late. [*He is shaking violently*]

[BLORE *sits down*]

WARGRAVE: The one thing we must not do is to give way to nerves.

ARMSTRONG: [*Sits on fender*] I'm sorry. [*Tries to smile*] Rather a case of "Physician, heal thyself." But I've been overworked lately and run down.

WARGRAVE: Sleeping badly?

ARMSTRONG: Yes. I keep dreaming—hospital—operations— A knife at my throat— [*Shivers*]

WARGRAVE: Real nightmares.

ARMSTRONG: Yes. [*Curiously*] Do you ever dream you're in court—sentencing a man to death?

WARGRAVE: [*Sits; smiling*] Are you by any chance referring to a man called Edward Seton? I can assure you I should not lose any sleep over the death of Edward Seton. A particularly brutal and cold-blooded murderer. The jury liked him. They were inclined to let him off. I could see. However— [*With quiet ferocity*] I cooked Seton's goose.

[*Everyone gives a little shiver*]

BLORE: Brr! Cold in here, isn't it? [*Rises*]

VERA: I wish Rogers would hurry up.

BLORE: Yes, where is Rogers? He's been a long time.

VERA: He said he'd got to get some sticks.

BLORE: [*Struck by the word*] Sticks? Sticks? My God, sticks!

ARMSTRONG: My God! [*Rises, looking at mantelpiece*]

BLORE: Is another one gone? Are there only six?

ARMSTRONG: [*Bewildered*] There are only five.

VERA: Five?

[*They stare at each other*]

WARGRAVE: Rogers and Lombard? [*Rises*]

VERA: [*With a cry*] Oh, no, not Philip!

[LOMBARD *enters; meets* BLORE *rushing out calling* "Rogers"]

LOMBARD: Where the hell is Blore off to like a madman?

VERA: [*Running to him*] Oh, Philip, I—

WARGRAVE: Have you seen Rogers?

LOMBARD: No, why should I?

ARMSTRONG: Two more Indians have gone.

LOMBARD: Two?

VERA: I thought it was you—

[BLORE *returns, looking pretty awful*]

ARMSTRONG: Well, what is it?

BLORE: [*Only just able to speak. His voice quite unlike itself*] In the—scullery.

VERA: Is he—?

BLORE: Oh, yes, he's dead all right—

VERA: How?

BLORE: With an axe. Somebody must have come up behind him whilst he was bent over the wood box.

VERA: [*Wildly*] "One chopped himself in half—then there were six." [*She begins laughing hysterically*]

LOMBARD: Stop it, Vera— Stop it! [*Sits her on sofa. Slaps her face. To the others*] She'll be all right. What next, boys? Bees? Do they keep bees on the island? [*They stare at him as if not understanding. He keeps his nonchalant manner up with a trace of effort*] Well, that's the next verse, isn't it?

"Six little Indian boys playing with a hive,
   A bumblebee stung one, and then there were five."

[*He moves round the room*]

ARMSTRONG: My God! He's right. There are only five.

LOMBARD: A bumblebee stung one— We all look pretty spry, nothing wrong with any of us. [*His glance rests on* EMILY] My God, you don't think— [*He goes slowly over to her, bends down, touches her. He then picks up a hypodermic syringe, and turns to face the others*] A hypodermic syringe.

WARGRAVE: The modern bee-sting.

VERA: [*Stammering*] While she was sitting there—one of us—

WARGRAVE: One of us.

[*They look at each other*]

ARMSTRONG: Which of us?

CURTAIN

ACT THREE

SCENE 1

Some hours later, the same night.

The curtains are drawn and the room is lit by three candles. WARGRAVE, VERA, BLORE, LOMBARD *and* ARMSTRONG, *who is dirty and unshaven, are sitting in silence. From time to time they shoot quick, covert glances at each other.* VERA *watches* ARMSTRONG; BLORE *watches* LOMBARD; LOMBARD *watches* WARGRAVE; ARMSTRONG *watches* BLORE *and* LOMBARD *alternately.* WARGRAVE *watches each in turn, but most often* VERA *with a long, speculative glance. There is silence for some few minutes. Then* LOMBARD *speaks suddenly in a loud, jeering voice that makes them all jump.*

LOMBARD:

"Five little Indian boys sitting in a row,
Watching each other and waiting for the blow."

New version up to date! [*He laughs discordantly*]

ARMSTRONG: I hardly think this is a moment for facetiousness.

LOMBARD: Have to relieve the gloom. [*Rises*] Damn that electric plant running down. Let's play a nice round game. What about inventing one called "Suspicions"? A suspects B, B suspects C—and so on. Let's start with Blore. It's not hard to guess whom Blore suspects. It sticks out a mile. I'm your fancy, aren't I, Blore?

BLORE: I wouldn't say no to that.

LOMBARD: You're quite wrong, you know. Abstract justice isn't my line. If I committed murder, there would have to be something in it for me.

BLORE: All I say is that you've acted suspiciously from the start.

You've told two different stories. You came here with a revolver. Now you say you've lost it.

LOMBARD: I have lost it.

BLORE: That's a likely story!

LOMBARD: What do you think I've done with it? I suggested myself that you should search me.

BLORE: Oh! You haven't got it on you. You're too clever for that. But you know where it is.

LOMBARD: You mean I've cached it ready for the next time?

BLORE: I shouldn't be surprised.

LOMBARD: Why don't you use your brains, Blore? If I'd wanted to, I could have shot the lot of you by this time, pop, pop, pop, pop, pop.

BLORE: Yes, but that's not the big idea. [*Points to rhyme*]

LOMBARD: [*Sits*] The crazy touch? My God, man, I'm sane enough!

BLORE: The doctor says there are some lunatics you'd never know were lunatics. [*Looks around at everyone*] That's true enough, I'd say.

ARMSTRONG: [*Breaking out*] We—we shouldn't just sit here, doing nothing! There must be something—surely, surely, there is something that we can do? If we lit a bonfire—

BLORE: In this weather?

WARGRAVE: It is, I am afraid, a question of time and patience. The weather will clear. Then we can do something. Light a bonfire, heliograph, signal.

ARMSTRONG: [*Rises*] A question of time—time? [*Laughs in an unbalanced way*] We can't afford time. We shall all be dead.

WARGRAVE: I think the precautions we have now adopted will be adequate.

ARMSTRONG: I tell you—we shall all be dead. All but one— He'll think up something else—he's thinking now— [*Sits again*]

LOMBARD: Poor Louise—what was her name—Clees? Was it nerves that made you do her in, Doctor?

ARMSTRONG: [*Almost mechanically*] No, drink. I used to be a heavy drinker. God help me, I was drunk when I operated— Quite a simple operation. My hand shaking all over the place— [*Buries his face in his hands*] I can remember her now—a big, heavy, countrified woman. And I killed her!

LOMBARD: [*Rises*] So I was right—that's how it was?

ARMSTRONG: Sister knew, of course, but she was loyal to me—or to the hospital. I gave up drink—gave it up altogether. I went in for a study of nervous diseases.

WARGRAVE: Very successfully. [*Rises*]

ARMSTRONG: One or two lucky shots. Good results with one or two important women. They talked to their friends. For the last year or two I've been so busy I've hardly known which way to turn. I'd got to the top of the tree.

LOMBARD: Until Mr. Unknown Owen—and down will come cradle and doctor and all.

ARMSTRONG: [*Rises*] Will you stop your damnable sneering and joking?

WARGRAVE: [*Comes between* ARMSTRONG *and* LOMBARD] Gentlemen, gentlemen, please. We can't afford to quarrel.

LOMBARD: That's okay by me. I apologize.

ARMSTRONG: It's this terrible inactivity that gets on my nerves. [*Sits*]

WARGRAVE: [*Sits*] We are adopting, I feel convinced, the only measures possible. So long as we remain together, all within sight of each other, a repetition of the tragedies that have occurred is—must be—impossible. We have all submitted to a search. Therefore, we know that no man is armed either with firearms or a knife. Nor has any man got cyanide or any drug about his person. If we remain, as I say, within sight of each other, nothing can happen.

ARMSTRONG: But we can't go on like this—we shall need food—sleep—

BLORE: That's what I say.

WARGRAVE: Obviously, the murderer's only chance is to get one of us detached from the rest. So long as we prevent that we are safe.

ARMSTRONG: Safe—?

LOMBARD: You're very silent, Vera?

VERA: There isn't anything to say— [*Pause.* WARGRAVE *rises*] I wonder what the time is. It's this awful waiting—waiting for the hours to go by and yet feeling that they may be the last. What is the time?

LOMBARD: Half past eight.

VERA: Is that all?

LOMBARD: Pretty awful light, this. How are the candles holding out?

BLORE: There's a whole packet. Storm's dying down a bit, what do you think, sir? [Rises; goes up to window]

WARGRAVE: Perhaps. We mustn't get too optimistic.

ARMSTRONG: The murderer's got everything on his side. Even the weather seems to be falling in with his plans.

[WARGRAVE sits on sofa. Long pause]

BLORE: [Rising] What about something to eat?

VERA: [Rises] If you like, I'll go out and open some tongue and make some coffee. But you four stay here. [To WARGRAVE] That's right, isn't it?

WARGRAVE: Not quite. You see, Miss Claythorne, it might be inadvisable to eat or drink something that you had prepared out of our sight.

VERA: Oh! [Slowly] You don't like me, do you?

WARGRAVE: It's not a question of likes or dislikes.

[VERA sits down]

LOMBARD: There are very few tricks that will get past you, Sir Lawrence. You know, if you won't be offended at my saying so, you're my fancy.

WARGRAVE: [Rises, looking at him coldly through his spectacles in the best court manner] This is hardly the moment, Captain Lombard, for any of us to indulge in the luxury of taking offense.

LOMBARD: I don't think it's Blore, [To Blore] I may be wrong, but I can't feel you've got enough imagination for this job. All I can say is, if you are the criminal, I take my hat off to you for a damned fine actor.

BLORE: Thank you, for nothing. [Sits]

LOMBARD: [Pause. Looks at ARMSTRONG] I don't think it's the Doctor. I don't believe he's got the nerve. [Looks at VERA] You've got plenty of nerve, Vera. On the other hand, you strike me as eminently sane. Therefore, you'd only do murder if you had a thoroughly good motive.

VERA: [Sarcastically] Thank you.

ARMSTRONG: [*Rises*] I've thought of something.

LOMBARD: Splendid. Animal, vegetable, or mineral?

ARMSTRONG: That man [*Points to* BLORE] says he's a police officer. But we've no proof of that. He only said so after the gramophone record, when his name had been given. Before that he was pretending to be a South African millionaire. Perhaps the police officer is another impersonation. What do we know about him? Nothing at all.

LOMBARD: He's a policeman all right. Look at his feet.

BLORE: [*Rises and sits again*] That's enough from you, Mr. Lombard!

[ARMSTRONG *sits*]

LOMBARD: Well, now we know where we are. By the way, Miss Claythorne suspects you, Doctor. Oh, yes, she does. Haven't you seen her shoot a dirty look from time to time? It all works out quite prettily. I suspect Sir Lawrence. Blore suspects me. Armstrong suspects Blore. [*To* WARGRAVE] What about you, sir?

WARGRAVE: Quite early in the day, I formed a certain conclusion. It seemed to me that everything that had occurred pointed quite unmistakably to one person. [*Pause. He looks straight ahead*] I am still of the same opinion.

VERA: Which one?

WARGRAVE: Well—no, I think it would be inadvisable to mention that person's name at the present time.

LOMBARD: Inadvisable in the public interest?

WARGRAVE: Exactly.

[*Everyone looks at each other*]

BLORE: What about the food idea?

ARMSTRONG: No, no, let's stay here. We're safe here.

VERA: I can't say I'm hungry.

LOMBARD: I'm not ravenous myself. You can go out and have a guzzle by yourself, Blore.

BLORE: Tell you what. Suppose I go and bring in a tin of biscuits? [*Rises*]

LOMBARD: Good idea.

[BLORE *starts to go*]

LOMBARD: Oh, Blore.

BLORE: Eh?

LOMBARD: An *unopened* tin, Blore.

[BLORE *takes candle from bookcase; goes out. A pause. Everybody watches door. A gust of wind—the curtains rattle.* VERA *rises.* WARGRAVE *sits*]

LOMBARD: It's only the wind—making the curtains rattle.

VERA: I wonder what happened to the bathroom curtain? The one that Rogers missed.

LOMBARD: By the wildest stretch of imagination, I cannot see what any homicidal maniac wants with a scarlet oilsilk curtain.

VERA: Things seem to have been disappearing. Miss Brent lost a skein of knitting wool.

LOMBARD: So the murderer, whoever he or she is, is a kleptomaniac, too.

VERA: How does it go? "Five little Indian boys—"

LOMBARD:

> "Going in for law,
>   One got in Chancery—"

VERA: In Chancery, but how could that apply? Unless, of course— [*She looks at* WARGRAVE]

WARGRAVE: Precisely, my dear young lady. That's why I'm sitting right here.

LOMBARD: Ah! But I'm casting you for the role of murderer—not victim.

WARGRAVE: The term can apply to a boxer.

LOMBARD: [*To* VERA] Maybe we'll start a free fight. That seems to let you out, my dear.

VERA: That awful rhyme. It keeps going round and round in my head. I think I'll remember it till I die. [*She realizes what she has said and looks around at the others. Pause*] Mr. Blore's a long time.

LOMBARD: I expect the big bad wolf has got him.

WARGRAVE: I have asked you once before to try and restrain your rather peculiar sense of humor, Captain Lombard.

LOMBARD: Sorry, sir. It must be a form of nervousness.

[BLORE *returns with a tin of biscuits.* WARGRAVE *rises, takes tin and opens it*]

WARGRAVE: Put your hands up. Search him.

[ARMSTRONG *and* LOMBARD *cross to search* BLORE. ARMSTRONG *offers biscuits to* VERA]

VERA: [*Sits*] No, thank you.

[BLORE *sits*]

LOMBARD: Come now—you've had no dinner.

VERA: I couldn't eat anything.

LOMBARD: I warn you—Blore will wolf the lot.

BLORE: I don't see why you need be so funny about it. Starving ourselves won't do us any good. [*Sadly*] How are we off for cigarettes?

LOMBARD: [*Takes out his case and opens it; sighs ruefully*] I haven't got any.

ARMSTRONG: I've run out, too.

WARGRAVE: Fortunately, I'm a pipe smoker.

VERA: [*Rousing herself. Crossing to hall door*] I've got a whole box upstairs in my suitcase. I'll get them. I could do with a cigarette myself. [*Pauses at door*] See that you all stay where you are. [*Goes out, carrying a candle from bookcase*]

[WARGRAVE *goes to door, looking after her, leaving tin on sofa*]

BLORE: [*Rises; fetches tin from sofa—eating solidly*] Not bad, these biscuits.

LOMBARD: What are they, cheese?

BLORE: Cheese and celery.

LOMBARD: That girl ought to have had some.

ARMSTRONG: Her nerves are in a bad state.

WARGRAVE: I don't know that I'd agree with you there, Doctor. Miss

Claythorne strikes me as a very cool and resourceful young lady— quite remarkably so.

LOMBARD: [*Looking curiously at* WARGRAVE] So that's your idea, is it? That she's the fox in the woodpile?

ARMSTRONG: Hardly likely—a woman!

WARGRAVE: You and I, Doctor, see women from slightly different angles.

BLORE: What does anyone say to a spot of whiskey?

LOMBARD: Good idea, providing we tackle an unopened bottle.

[*An appalling and bloodcurdling shriek of utter terror comes from overhead and a heavy thud. All four men start up.* LOMBARD *and* BLORE *snatch up candles.* BLORE *takes candle from mantelpiece. All four rush to hall door and out in this order:* LOMBARD, BLORE, ARMSTRONG *and* WARGRAVE—*the latter is slow getting under way, owing to age. Stage is quite dark as soon as* LOMBARD *and* BLORE *have gone through door and before* WARGRAVE *reaches door. Confused noises off. Then, on stage,* WARGRAVE'S *voice calls out,* "Who's that?" *Sound of a shot. A confused moving about on the stage; voices off also; off faint—then come nearer. Dining room door opens. Then hall door.* BLORE *heard swearing off. Also* ARMSTRONG'S VOICE]

VERA: [*Coming in from dining room, stumbling about*] Philip, Philip, where are you? I've lost you.

LOMBARD: [*Coming in from hall*] Here I am.

VERA: Why can't we have some light? It's awful in the dark. You don't know where you are. You don't know where anyone is. [*Sits on sofa*]

LOMBARD: It's that damned draught on the stairs—blowing all the candles out. Here, I've got a lighter. [*Lights his and her candle. Sits next to her*]

VERA: Where's Doctor Armstrong?

ARMSTRONG: [*From hall*] I'm hunting for the matches.

LOMBARD: Never mind matches—get some more candles.

VERA: I was horrified to death—it went right round my throat—

LOMBARD: What did?

VERA: The window was open in my room. It blew out the candle as I opened the door. And then a long strand of seaweed touched my throat. I thought, in the dark, that I was being strangled by a wet hand—

[*Murmur off left*]

LOMBARD: I don't wonder you yelled.

VERA: Who hung that seaweed there?

LOMBARD: I don't know. But when I find out, he'll be sorry he was ever born.

[ARMSTRONG *comes quietly in from hall*]

VERA: [*Sharply*] Who's that?

ARMSTRONG: It's all right, Miss Claythorne. It's only me.

BLORE: [*In hall*] Here we are. [*A faint glow through door as he lights candles. He comes in carrying candle*] Who fired that shot?

[VERA *rises; turns and screams. Light reveals* WARGRAVE *set upright on window seat, red oilsilk curtain draped around shoulders. Grey skein of wool plaited into wig on his head. In center of forehead is round dark mark with red trickling from it. Men stand paralyzed.* VERA *screams.* ARMSTRONG *pulls himself together, waves others to stand back and goes over to* WARGRAVE. *Bends over him; straightens up*]

ARMSTRONG: He's dead— Shot through the head—

VERA: [*Leans against window*] "One got in Chancery—and then there were four—"

ARMSTRONG: Miss Claythorne.

LOMBARD: Vera.

VERA: You got me out of the way! You got me to go upstairs for cigarettes! You put that seaweed there— You did it all so that you could kill that helpless old man in the dark—you're mad—all of you—crazy! [*Her voice is low and full of horror*] That's why you wanted the red curtain and the knitting wool— It was all planned —long ago—for *that*— Oh, my God, let me get out of here—! [*She edges to the hall door and rushes out, as:*]

CURTAIN

SCENE 2

The following afternoon.

It is brilliant sunshine. The room is as it was the night before.

BLORE, LOMBARD *and* VERA *are sitting on the left sofa, eating tinned tongue on tray.*

LOMBARD:

> "Three little Indian boys,
> Sitting in a row,
> Thinking as they guzzle
> Who's next to go?"

VERA: Oh, Philip!

BLORE: That's all right, Miss Claythorne. I don't mind joking on a full stomach.

VERA: I must say I was hungry. But all the same, I don't think I shall ever fancy tinned tongue again.

BLORE: I was wanting that meal! I feel a new man.

LOMBARD: We'd been nearly twenty-four hours without food. That does lower the morale.

VERA: Somehow, in the daylight, everything seems different.

LOMBARD: You mustn't forget there's a dangerous homicidal lunatic somewhere loose on this island.

VERA: Why is it one doesn't feel jittery about it any more?

LOMBARD: Because we know now, beyond any possible doubt, who it is, eh, Blore?

BLORE: That's right.

LOMBARD: It was the uncertainty before—looking at each other, wondering which.

VERA: I said all along it was Doctor Armstrong.

LOMBARD: You did, my sweet, you did. Until, of course, you went completely bats and suspected us all.

VERA: [*Rises to mantelpiece; takes three cigarettes out of box*] It seems rather silly in the light of day.

LOMBARD: Very silly.

BLORE: Allowing it is Armstrong, what's happened to him?

LOMBARD: We know what he wants us to think has happened to him.

VERA: [*Gives* BLORE *and* LOMBARD *cigarettes*] What exactly did you find?

LOMBARD: One shoe—just one shoe—sitting prettily on the cliff edge. Inference—Doctor Armstrong has gone completely off his onion and committed suicide.

BLORE: [*Rises*] All very circumstantial—even to one little china Indian broken over there in the doorway.

VERA: I think that was rather overdoing it. A man wouldn't think of doing that if he was going to drown himself.

LOMBARD: Quite so. But we're fairly sure he didn't drown himself. But he had to make it appear as though he were the seventh victim all according to plan.

VERA: Supposing he really is dead?

LOMBARD: I'm a bit suspicious of death without bodies.

VERA: How extraordinary to think that there are five dead bodies in there, and here we've been eating tinned tongue.

LOMBARD: The delightful feminine disregard for facts—there are six dead bodies and they are not all in there.

BLORE: Oh, no, no. She's right. There are only five.

LOMBARD: What about Mrs. Rogers?

BLORE: I've counted her. She makes the fifth.

LOMBARD: [*Rises. A little exasperated*] Now look here: Marston, one. Mrs. Rogers, two. General MacKenzie, three. Rogers, four. Emily Brent, five, and Wargrave, six.

[VERA *takes tray to table*]

BLORE: [*Counting themselves*] Seven, eight, nine—Armstrong, ten. That's right, old man. Sorry. [*Sits*]

LOMBARD: [*Sits*] Don't you think it would be an idea if we brought Mrs. Rogers downstairs and shoved her in the morgue, too?

BLORE: I'm a detective, not an undertaker.

VERA: [*Sits*] For heaven's sake, stop talking about bodies! The point is Armstrong murdered them.

LOMBARD: We ought to have realized it was Armstrong straightaway.

BLORE: How do you think Armstrong got hold of your revolver?

LOMBARD: Haven't the slightest idea.

VERA: Tell me exactly what happened in the night?

LOMBARD: Well, after you threw a fit of hysterics and locked yourself in your room, we all thought we'd better go to bed.

BLORE: So we all went to bed—and locked ourselves in our rooms.

LOMBARD: About an hour later, I heard someone pass my door. I came out and tapped on Blore's door. He was there all right. Then I went to Armstrong's room. It was empty. That's when I tapped on your door and told you to sit tight—whatever happened. Then I came down here. The window on the balcony was open—and my revolver was lying just beside it.

BLORE: But why the devil should Armstrong chuck that revolver away?

LOMBARD: Don't ask me—either an accident or he's crazy.

VERA: Where do you think he is?

LOMBARD: Lurking somewhere, waiting to have a crack at one of us.

VERA: We ought to search the house.

BLORE: What—and walk into an ambush?

VERA: [Rises] Oh—I never thought of that.

LOMBARD: Are you quite sure you heard no one moving about after we went out?

VERA: Oh, I imagined all sorts of things—but nothing short of setting the house on fire would have got me to unlock my door.

LOMBARD: I see—just thoroughly suspicious.

BLORE: [Rises] What's the use of talking? What are we going to do?

LOMBARD: If you ask me—do nothing. Sit tight and take no risks.

BLORE: Look here, I want to go after that fellow.

LOMBARD: What a dog of the bulldog breed you are, Blore. By the way, between friends and without prejudice, you did go in for that little spot of perjury, didn't you?

[VERA sits]

BLORE: [Sits. Hesitating] Well, I don't suppose it makes any odds now. Landor was innocent, all right. The gang squared me and between us we put him away for a stretch. Mind you, I wouldn't admit it now if it wasn't that—

LOMBARD: You think we're all in the same boat?

BLORE: Well, I couldn't admit it in front of Mr. Justice Wargrave, could I?

LOMBARD: No, hardly.

BLORE: [Rises] I say, that fellow Seton, do you think he was innocent?

LOMBARD: I'm quite sure of it. Wargrave had a reason for wanting him out of the way. Well, Blore, I'm delighted you've come off your virtuous perch. I hope you made a tidy bit out of it?

BLORE: [Injured] Nothing like what I ought to have done. They're a mean lot, that Benny gang. I got my promotion, though.

LOMBARD: And Landor got penal servitude and died in jail.

BLORE: I couldn't tell he was going to die, could I?

LOMBARD: No, that was your bad luck.

BLORE: His, you mean.

LOMBARD: Yours, too. Because as a result of that fact you may get your life cut short unpleasantly soon.

BLORE: What? Me? By Armstrong? I'll watch it.

LOMBARD: You'll have to. Remember there are only three Indians there.

BLORE: Well, what about you?

LOMBARD: I shall be quite all right, thank you. I've been in tight places before and I've got out of them. And I mean to get out of this one. [Pause] Besides, I've got a revolver.

BLORE: Yes—that revolver. Now listen. You said you found it lying down there. What's to prove you haven't had it all the time?

LOMBARD: Same old gramophone record! No room in your head for more than one idea at a time, is there?

BLORE: No, but it's a good idea.

LOMBARD: And you're sticking to it.

BLORE: And I would have thought up a better story than that, if I were you.

LOMBARD: I only wanted something simple that a policeman could understand.

BLORE: What's wrong with the police?

LOMBARD: Nothing—now that you've left the Force.

BLORE: Now look here, Captain Lombard, if you're an honest man, as you pretend—

LOMBARD: Oh, come, Blore, we're neither of us honest.

BLORE: If you're telling the truth for once, you ought to do the square thing and chuck that revolver down there.

LOMBARD: Don't be an ass!

BLORE: I've said I'll go through the house looking for Armstrong, haven't I? I'm willing to do that, will you lend me that revolver?

LOMBARD: [Rises] No, I won't! That revolver's mine. It's my revolver and I'm sticking to it.

BLORE: [Angrily] Then do you know what I'm beginning to think?

LOMBARD: You're not beginning to think it, you square-headed flattie. You thought it last night, and now you've gone back to your original idea. I'm the one and only U. N. Unknown Owen. Is that it?

BLORE: I won't contradict you.

LOMBARD: Well, think what you dammed well please! But I warn you—

VERA: [Incisively] I think you are both behaving like a pair of children.

[They both look at her rather sheepishly]

LOMBARD: Sorry, Teacher.

VERA: [To BLORE, scornfully] Of course, Captain Lombard isn't the unknown. The Unknown Owen is Armstrong—and I'll tell you one very good proof of it.

BLORE: Oh, what?

VERA: Think of the rhyme. "Four little Indian boys—going out to sea. A red herring swallowed one, and then there were three." Don't you see the subtlety of it? A red herring? That's Armstrong's pretended suicide, but it's only a red herring—so really he isn't dead!

BLORE: That's very ingenious.

VERA: To my mind, it's absolute proof. You see, it's all mad because he's mad. He takes a queer, childish, crazy pleasure in sticking to the rhyme and making everything happen in that way. Dressing up the Judge, killing Rogers when he was chopping sticks; using a hypodermic on Miss Brent, when he might just as well have drugged her. He's got to make it all fit in.

BLORE: And that might give us a pointer. Where do we go from here?

[Goes up to mantelpiece and reads]

"Three little Indian boys walking in the zoo.
   A big bear hugged one, and then there were two."
[*He laughs*] He'll have a job with that one. There's no zoo on this island! [*His laughter is cut short as he sees the big bear rug on which he is standing. He edges off the rug and turns to* LOMBARD]

BLORE: I say, Captain Lombard, what about a nice bottle of beer?

LOMBARD: Do stop thinking about your stomach, Blore. This craving for food and drink will be your undoing.

BLORE: But there's plenty of beer in the kitchen.

LOMBARD: Yes, and if anyone wanted to get rid of you, the first place they'd think of putting a lethal dose would be in a nice bottle of beer.

[*From outside comes the sound of a motorboat hooter*]

BLORE: What's that? A boat! A boat!

[*All rush to balcony.* BLORE *rushes out onto balcony. There is a scream, then a crash and thud*]

VERA: Oh, God! [*Puts hands over eyes*]

[LOMBARD, *revolver in hand, rushes to window, looks out, then returns slowly to room.* VERA *sits down*]

LOMBARD: Blore's got his.

VERA: How?

LOMBARD: A booby trap—all set—a wire across the door attached to something above.

VERA: Is he?

LOMBARD: Yes. Crushed. Head stove in. That great bronze bear holding a clock, from the landing.

VERA: A bear? Oh, how ghastly! It's this awful childishness!

LOMBARD: I know. God, what a fool Blore was!

VERA: And now there are two.

LOMBARD: Yes, and we'll have to be very careful of ourselves.

VERA: We shan't do it. He'll get us. We'll never get away from this island!

LOMBARD: Oh, yes, we will. I've never been beaten yet.

VERA: Don't you feel—that there's someone—now—in this room—watching us, watching and waiting?

LOMBARD: That's just nerves.

VERA: Then you do feel it?

LOMBARD: [*Fiercely*] No, I don't!

VERA: [*Rises*] Please, Philip, let's get out of this house—anywhere. Perhaps if that was a boat, they'll see us.

LOMBARD: All right. We'll go to the top of the island and wait for relief to come. It's sheer cliff on the far side and we can see if anyone approaches from the house.

VERA: Anything's better than staying here.

LOMBARD: Won't you be rather cold in that dress?

VERA: I'd be colder if I were dead.

LOMBARD: Perhaps you're right. [*Goes to window*] A quick reconnaissance.

VERA: Be careful, Philip—please! [*Follows him to window*]

LOMBARD: I'm not Blore. There's no window directly above. [*He goes out on balcony and looks down. He is arrested by what he sees*] Hullo, there's something washed up on the rocks.

VERA: What? [*She joins him*] It looks like a body.

LOMBARD: [*In a strange new voice*] You'd better wait in there. I'm going to have a look.

> [*He exits to left on balcony.* VERA *wanders back into room. Her face is full of conflicting emotions*]

VERA: Armstrong—Armstrong's body—

LOMBARD: [*Comes in very slowly*] It's Armstrong drowned—Washed up at high water mark.

VERA: So there's no one on the island—no one at all, except us two.

LOMBARD: Yes, Vera. Now we know where we are.

VERA: Now we know where we are?

LOMBARD: A very pretty trick of yours, with that wire. Quite neat. Old Wargrave always knew you were dangerous.

VERA: You—

LOMBARD: So you did drown that kid after all.

VERA: I didn't! That's where you're wrong. Please believe me. Please listen to me!

LOMBARD: I'm listening. You'd better make it a good story.

VERA: It isn't a story! It's the truth! I didn't kill that child. It was someone else.

LOMBARD: Who?

VERA: A man. Peter's uncle. I was in love with him.

LOMBARD: This is getting quite interesting.

VERA: Don't sneer. It was hell! Absolute hell. Peter was born after his father's death. If he'd been a girl, Hugh would have got everything.

LOMBARD: Well-known tale of the wicked uncle.

VERA: Yes—he was wicked—and I didn't know. He said he loved me, but that he was too poor to marry. There was a rock far out that Peter was always wanting to swim to. Of course, I wouldn't let him. It was dangerous. One day we were on the beach and I had to go back to the house for something I'd forgotten. When I got back to the rock, I looked down and saw Peter swimming out to the rock. I knew he hadn't a chance, the current had got him already. I flew towards the beach and Hugh tried to stop me. "Don't be a fool," he said. "I told the little ass he could do it."

LOMBARD: Go on. This *is* interesting.

VERA: I pushed past him—he tried to stop me, but I got away and rushed down. I plunged into the sea and swam after Peter. He'd gone before I could get to him.

LOMBARD: And everything went off well at the inquest. They called you a plucky girl, and you kept discreetly quiet about Hugh's part in the business.

VERA: Do you think anyone would have believed me? Besides, I couldn't! I really was in love with him.

LOMBARD: Well, it's a pretty story. And then I suppose Hugh let you down?

VERA: Do you think I ever wanted to see him again?

LOMBARD: You certainly are an accomplished liar, Vera.

VERA: Can't you believe the truth when you hear it?

LOMBARD: Who set the trap that killed Blore? *I* didn't—and Armstrong's dead. I've broken most of the Commandments in my time—and I'm no saint. But there's one thing I won't stand for and that's murder!

VERA: You won't stand for murder! What about those natives you left to die in Africa?

LOMBARD: That's what's so damn funny—I didn't.

VERA: What do you mean?

LOMBARD: For once—just once, mark you, I played the hero. Risked my life to save the lives of my men. Left them my rifle and ammunition and all the food there was—and took a chance through the brush. By the most incredible luck it came off—but it wasn't in time to save them. And the rumor got around that I'd deliberately abandoned my men. There's life for you!

VERA: Do you expect me to believe that? Why, you actually admitted the whole thing.

LOMBARD: I know. I got such a kick out of watching their faces.

VERA: You can't fool me with a stupid lie like that!

LOMBARD: [Completely losing his temper] Blast you!

VERA: Why didn't I see it before? It's there in your face—the face of a killer—

LOMBARD: You can't fool me any longer!

VERA: Oh— [She sways forward as if fainting. LOMBARD runs to catch her. She wrests the revolver from him] Now!

LOMBARD: [Backing away] You cunning little devil!

VERA: If you come one step nearer, I'll shoot!

LOMBARD: You—young, lovely, and quite, quite mad.

[LOMBARD makes a movement to VERA. She shoots. He falls down. She goes over to him, her eyes full of horror, as she realizes what she has done. The revolver falls from her hand. Suddenly she hears a low laugh coming from the study door. She turns her head slowly in that direction. The laughter grows louder, the door slowly opens and WARGRAVE enters. He carries a rope in his hand]

WARGRAVE: It's all come true. My Ten Little Indian plan— My rhyme—my rhyme—

VERA: Ah! [Stifled scream]

WARGRAVE: [Angrily] Silence in court! [Looks around suspiciously] If there is any more noise, I shall have the court cleared. It's all right, my dear. It's all right. Don't be frightened. This is a

Court of Justice. You'll get justice here. [*Crosses and locks dining room and hall doors. Confidentially*] You thought I was a ghost. You thought I was dead. Armstrong said I was dead. That was the clever part of my plan. Said we'd trap the murderer. We'd fix up my supposed death so I should be free to spy upon the guilty one. He thought it an excellent plan—came out that night to meet me by the cliff without any suspicion. I sent him over with a push—so easily. He swallowed my red herring all right. [VERA *is petrified with horror. In a confidential manner*] You know, Vera Claythorne, all my life I've wanted to take life,—yes, to take life. I've had to get what enjoyment I could out of sentencing the guilty to death. [VERA *moves to revolver*] I always enjoyed that—but it wasn't enough. I wanted more— I wanted to do it myself with my own hands— [WARGRAVE *follows* VERA. VERA *leans against hall door. Suddenly curbs excitement and speaks with severe dignity*] But I'm a Judge of the High Court. I've got a sense of justice. [*As if listening to an echo*] As between our Sovereign Lord the King and the prisoner at the Bar—will true deliverance make— Guilty, my Lord. Yes. [*Nods head*] Guilty. You were all guilty, you know, but the law couldn't touch you, so I had to take the law into my own hands! [*Holds up hands in a frenzy of delight*] Into my own hands! Silence in the court! [VERA *hammers on door.* WARGRAVE *takes her arm and drags her to sofa*] Anthony Marston first. Then Mrs. Rogers. Barbitone in the brandy. MacKenzie—stabbed. Got Rogers with an axe when he was chopping sticks. Doped Emily Brent's coffee so she couldn't feel the hypodermic. Booby trap for Blore. [*Confidentially*] Blore was a fool. I always knew it would be easy to get Blore. Returning that revolver was a clever touch. Made the end interesting. I knew you two would suspect each other in the end. The question was, who'd win out? I banked on you, my dear. The female of the species. Besides, it's always more exciting to have a girl at the end. [*He steps onto sofa, and* VERA *falls to the floor*] Prisoner at the Bar, have you anything to say why sentence should not be passed on you? Vera Elizabeth Claythorne, I sentence you to death—

VERA: [*With a sudden outcry*] Stop! Stop! I'm not guilty! I'm not guilty!

WARGRAVE: Ah, they all say that. Must plead not guilty. Unless, of course, you're going all out for a verdict of insanity. But you're not mad. [*Very reasonably*] I'm mad, but you're not.

VERA: But I *am* innocent!! I swear it! I never killed that child. I never wanted to kill him. You're a judge. You know when a person is guilty and when they're innocent. I swear I'm telling the truth!

WARGRAVE: So you didn't drown that boy after all? Very interesting. But it doesn't matter much now, does it?

VERA: What— [*Makes inarticulate sounds as the rope swings in front of her*]

WARGRAVE: I can't spoil my lovely rhyme. My ten little Indian boys. You're the last one. One little Indian boy left all alone. He went and hanged himself. I must have my hanging—my hanging—

[LOMBARD *comes slowly to, picks up revolver and shoots.* WARGRAVE *falls back off the sofa*]

VERA: Philip—Philip—!

[BOTH *are on floor in front of sofa*]

LOMBARD: It's all right, darling! It's all right!

VERA: I thought you were dead! I thought I'd killed you.

LOMBARD: Thank God, women can't shoot straight. At least, not straight enough.

VERA: I shall never forget this!

LOMBARD: Oh, yes, you will. You know there's another ending to that Ten Little Indian rhyme:

"One little Indian boy, left all alone,
He got married—and then there were none!"

[*Takes rope and puts his head in noose, too. He kisses her*]

[*There is the sound of a motorboat hooter*]

CURTAIN

The
Desperate Hours

JOSEPH HAYES

Based on the novel by Joseph Hayes

Joseph Hayes

It is a rare occasion indeed when a writer can parlay a single property into an outstanding success in three mediums—novel, play, and film—and this is exactly what Joseph Hayes did with *The Desperate Hours*.

A chilling suspense story about three escaped convicts who terrorize an Indiana home, it was described on publication as "a novel of nerve-shattering impact." A leading best seller for many months and a major book club selection, the novel aroused heated interest among Broadway producers and various film-makers who recognized its dramatic potentials. But Mr. Hayes had had a previous experience in the theatre that taught him a valuable lesson. His first Broadway play, *Leaf and Bough*, opened in 1949 and ignominiously expired after three performances. According to Mr. Hayes, "Everybody had a hand in it except the author. I learned then that an author has to fight to keep control of his work." And he did just that with *The Desperate Hours*.

Ignoring solicitous offers of assistance, he did his own dramatization, and as additional protective insurance, he coproduced (with Howard Erskine) the Broadway presentation of the play. *The Desperate Hours* reached the stage on February 10, 1955, and it promptly became a sellout attraction. The reviewer for *The New Yorker* called it "the season's great dramatic hit and perhaps even a historic one. This is quite as it should be, because it is a very rare thing, an almost perfect melodrama—fast, tight, logical, combining sentiment with gunfire in exactly the right proportions." Walter Kerr considered it "a slam-bang melodrama with a glowering figure behind every door and a nervous finger on every trigger." He concluded that Joseph Hayes "had made a lightning-paced thriller out of his novel about an ordinary household invaded by killers. It's a beaut!"

It ran for 212 performances in New York and won the Antoinette Perry (Tony) Award as the outstanding play of the season. It also earned an additional Tony for its director, Robert Montgomery, who was cited for the season's most distinguished job of staging. The universality of the play subsequently was proved by productions in many leading foreign cities, including London, Paris, Rome, and Stockholm.

Hollywood was the next destination for the property, and here again Mr. Hayes succeeded in holding the author's reins by doing his own screenplay. Ably guided by producer-director William Wyler, the movie (with Humphrey Bogart, Fredric March, and Martha Scott) won the 1955 Mystery Writers of America award for best motion picture in the suspense category.

After *The Desperate Hours*, Mr. Hayes had two additional Broadway successes. In 1956 he coproduced and directed Kyle Crichton's period comedy, *The Happiest Millionaire*, which restored Walter Pidgeon to the stage; and in 1962 his suspense drama, *Calculated Risk* (based on a London corporate melodrama by George Ross and Campbell Singer) attracted theatregoers for 221 performances.

Joseph Hayes was born in Indianapolis, Indiana, in 1918. When he was thirteen, he entered a Benedictine monastery, but after two years left it to rejoin the world. He completed his high school education, then hitchhiked around the country, supporting himself by doing odd jobs. Later, he attended Indiana University where he met his wife, Marrijane. They were married in their sophomore year and in 1941 moved to New York where he took a job in the editorial department of a play publishing house. During this period, he and his wife wrote many plays for amateur production and he also turned out several television scripts and short stories for magazines. The plays in particular were profitable enough for the young couple to buy a house in Brookfield, Connecticut, where the author and his family have lived for a number of years.

Joseph Hayes' other published novels include: *The Third Day, Don't Go Away Mad,* and *The House After Midnight.*

The Desperate Hours was first produced at the Ethel Barrymore Theatre, New York, on February 10, 1955, by Howard Erskine and Joseph Hayes. The cast was as follows:

TOM WINSTON	*Judson Pratt*
JESSE BARD	*James Gregory*
HARRY CARSON	*Kendall Clark*
ELEANOR HILLIARD	*Nancy Coleman*
RALPHIE HILLIARD	*Malcolm Brodrick*
DAN HILLIARD	*Karl Malden*
CINDY HILLIARD	*Patricia Peardon*
GLENN GRIFFIN	*Paul Newman*
HANK GRIFFIN	*George Grizzard*
ROBISH	*George Mathews*
CHUCK WRIGHT	*Fred Eisley*
MR. PATTERSON	*Wyrley Birch*
LT. CARL FREDERICKS	*Rusty Lane*
MISS SWIFT	*Mary Orr*

Directed by	Robert Montgomery
Setting and Lighting by	Howard Bay
Costumes by	Robert Randolph

The Desperate Hours was first presented in England on April 19, 1955, at the London Hippodrome. The cast was as follows:

TOM WINSTON	*Denis Shaw*
JESSE BARD	*Patrick Allen*
HARRY CARSON	*Gordon Tanner*
ELEANOR HILLIARD	*Diana Churchill*
RALPHIE HILLIARD	*David Hannaford*
DAN HILLIARD	*Bernard Lee*
CINDY HILLIARD	*Jacqueline Ellis*
GLENN GRIFFIN	*Richard Carlyle*
HANK GRIFFIN	*Barry Foster*
ROBISH	*George Margo*
CHUCK WRIGHT	*William Russell*
MR. PATTERSON	*Charles Rolfe*
LT. CARL FREDERICKS	*Donald Stewart*
MISS SWIFT	*Dorothy Baird*

Staged by	Howard Erskine
Setting by	Howard Bay
Production supervised by	Robert Montgomery

SCENE: *The City of Indianapolis.*

TIME: *The present.*

ACT ONE
A day in autumn.

ACT TWO
Later.

ACT THREE
Later.

SCENE

The action throughout the play alternates between two sets on stage. In the first two acts, the Hilliard home is at stage right and the Sheriff's office is at stage left. In Act Three, the Hilliard home is at stage right, and at stage left is a corner of an attic room. The action shifts back and forth between the two sets by the use of blackouts and sliding black curtains which mask the set that is not in focus.

The Hilliard home is the principal set. This consists of various rooms, all blended together by fluid action; lights focus the attention in the various rooms, as the action of the play requires.

On the ground floor level of the house, there are two rooms in view at all times: the living room and a back hall or pantry. In the living room, there is an outside door in the rear wall; next to this door are stairs rising to the up-stairs level. At right a door gives access to a den or library, offstage. At left, facing downstage, there is another door; this door, presumably, leads into a dining room; the dining room is adjacent to a kitchen; the kitchen door opens into the pantry or back hall. In this manner, a character leaving the living room exits through the dining room door and in a moment reappears in the pantry. This pantry is a small room in itself. In addition to the kitchen door, there is an exterior side door of the house itself opening off the pantry at stage left. Back stairs descend along the exterior wall at left: a narrow passageway gives access to the upper floor. The entire ground floor, then, consists of a living room with front stairs curving up, a front door, a door to the den and a door to the dining room; a pantry with a door to the kitchen, an exterior side door, shelves, and a *narrow stairway going up. In addition, a portion of the side yard is visible at left.*

The upper level—constructed above the ground floor level described above—consists of two bedrooms and an upstairs hall between; this hall gives access to the downward flow of the front stairway. The bedroom at stage right is the master bedroom, containing twin beds, windows right and up center, and a bureau. The bedroom at stage left is a boy's bedroom, with a bunk, various shelves with toys, and a window overlooking the side yard. Between the two bedrooms is a small hall: downstage is a small table with a telephone.

At far left stage, during the first two acts, is the Sheriff's office on ground level, a bare sort of room with a wall-clock, a desk, various files, and radio and intercom apparatus. In the last act, a corner of an attic appears at stage left; this is constructed above the Sheriff's office, and in Act Three the office is completely masked.

ACT ONE

SHERIFF'S OFFICE

The curtain rises, morning light fades in on the Sheriff's office. WINSTON, *a deputy sheriff inclined to matter-of-fact laziness, sits at desk, speaking on the telephone. On the desk are an intercom, radio apparatus, sheafs of papers, and so forth. The wall-clock reads 8:10.*

WINSTON: [*Plaintively*] Baby . . . didn't I just tell you? I can't leave till Bard gets here. [*He listens*] Listen, baby—this night shift gets my goat as much as it does yours. You think I wouldn't like to be in that nice warm bed? [*There is a buzz from the intercom on the desk*] Hold it. [*He speaks into the intercom*] Yeah, Dutch?

DUTCH'S VOICE: Winston . . . Bard's going to want those Terre Haute reports right away.

WINSTON: [*Irascibly, into intercom*] What do you think I'm gonna do with 'em . . . eat 'em for breakfast? [*He flips off the intercom, returns to the phone*] Hello, baby . . . [*Listens*] Yeah, that's what I said, isn't it? In that nice warm bed *with you*. Who'd you think I . . . [*Listens*] Okay, okay, baby . . . go back to sleep and wait for papa. [*Hangs up, shakes head, pleased; speaks with gusto*] Give me a jealous woman every time!

> [BARD *enters.* WINSTON *is sleepy and glad to be relieved.* BARD *takes off jacket, removes gun from shoulder-holster through the following. All very casual and commonplace at first*]

BARD: [*As he enters*] Morning, Tom.

WINSTON: [*Stretching*] Well! About time.

BARD: [*Stows gun in drawer of file*] Overslept. Sorry.

WINSTON: [*Rising slowly*] You got a lovely excuse.

BARD: I'll tell her you think so. [*Above desk, riffles reports*] Quiet night?

WINSTON: [*Preparing to go*] If kids'd stay out of cars and off motorcycles, we'd soon be out of jobs around here.

BARD: Not another burglary in Speedway City? [*Laughs*] This guy's getting tiresome.

WINSTON: A real sex-nut, that one. Same old story . . . all he took was diamonds and women's panties. What the hell's the connection.

BARD: You figure it out, Tom. [*Then tensing . . . so that from now on the pace and tone change*] What's this?

WINSTON: [*Yawns, looking over* BARD'S *shoulder*] Federal prison break . . . Terre Haute. None of our concern.

BARD: When'd it come in?

WINSTON: [*Ready to leave*] Hours ago. The three of 'em busted out some time before dawn. . . .

BARD: [*Sits at desk, snaps button on intercom*] Why didn't you call me?

WINSTON: Call you? Why?

DUTCH'S VOICE: Yes, Jesse?

BARD: [*Into intercom*] Dutch . . . get me Lieutenant Fredericks, State Police.

WINSTON: Jesse . . . remember what your Irish wife threatened last time I routed you out of the nest . . .

BARD: Terre Haute's only seventy miles away. They could've walked here by now!

FREDERICKS' VOICE: [*On intercom—crisp, middle-aged, cynical*] I wondered when you'd start yipping, Bard.

BARD: [*Quickly*] Fredericks . . . anybody sitting on anything?

FREDERICKS' VOICE: I'm sitting on just what you're sitting on, Deputy. Only mine ain't sweatin'.

BARD: Griffin's woman . . . Helen Laski . . . any dope on her?

FREDERICKS' VOICE: Not a trace. Chicago . . . Cleveland . . . St. Louis. All we know is she was here in town three weeks ago.

BARD: Just don't let any cop touch her. She's the beacon'll lead us straight . . .

FREDERICKS' VOICE: Bard . . . it's an FBI case anyway. The city police've ripped whole buildings apart. We got the highways blocked. We're working through all the dives . . .

BARD: If Glenn Griffin wants to come here, no roadblock's gonna stop him. And he's too sharp to hole up any place you'd think of looking.

FREDERICKS' VOICE: Look, lad . . . get the chip off your shoulder. [*Shortly*] You want Griffin so bad, go get him!

>[BARD *flips off the intercom.* WINSTON *reluctantly removes his coat*]

WINSTON: Glenn Griffin . . . is he the one you . . . ?

BARD: [*Thoughtfully*] Yeah . . . he's the one. [*Studying reports*] Glenn Griffin . . . his brother, Hank . . . and . . . who's the third one? Samuel Robish.

WINSTON: Life-termer. A three-time loser. And nasty. [*As* BARD *picks up the phone and dials,* WINSTON *returns his coat to the hanger*] You're not going to get any sleep today, are you, Winston? No, I'm not going to get any sleep today. I'm going to sit on the teletype machine like a good little boy scout . . .

>[BARD *smiles a bit as* WINSTON *exits. Then he speaks into the telephone in contrasting gentle tones*]

BARD: Hello, Katie. Did I wake you? . . . I've just had an idea . . . why don't you go over to my mother's for the day? [*Laughs—but the urgency comes through*] Oh, stop groaning . . . how often do I ask you to *let* her talk your arm and leg off? . . . No, not this afternoon. *Now!* . . . And Katie . . . don't mention where you're going, huh? . . . To the neighbors, anyone . . . Good. . . . Right away. Take a taxi. . . . Sure, splurge.

>[BARD *hangs up, sits thinking, with the smile fading.* WINSTON *enters, with* CARSON, *who is youthful, businesslike, rather studious-looking.* WINSTON *places a teletype message on desk before* BARD]

WINSTON: It had to break, Jesse. [*Then with a touch of sarcasm as* BARD *reads*] Oh—this is Mr. Carson, FBI.

BARD: [*Briskly*] How are you? Look, it says they beat up a farmer south of the prison before daybreak. How come we're just getting it?

CARSON: They left him in his barn, out cold . . . ripped out his phone. He just staggered into a general store and reported his car stolen . . . [*With a touch of good-natured irony*] How are *you?*

BARD: Have you put this on the air?

CARSON: Deputy, I've been in touch with Sheriff Masters by telephone.

BARD: I hope he's enjoying his extended vacation . . . he sure picked a fine time to leave me in charge here . . .

CARSON: The way I understand it, you know this Glenn Griffin fellow better than any police officer in the area. How about your taking over this section?

[*Pause. The whole weight falls on* BARD. *He accepts it . . . slowly. Then:*]

BARD: Okay . . . *Okay* . . . Let's find that car! [*He goes into action —hands teletype to* WINSTON] Tom, put this description on the air. Tell 'em to repeat it every half hour.

WINSTON: [*Protesting*] We'll be flooded with calls. Every crackpot in five states . . .

BARD: [*Sitting at desk*] We'll follow up every tip!

WINSTON: [*To* CARSON—*groaning*] I hope you know what you just did!

[WINSTON *exits.* CARSON *moves to desk and offers* BARD *a cigarette*]

CARSON: Any ideas where they might dig in?

BARD: [*Shaking his head*] All I know is . . . just as long's Glenn Griffin's running around free and safe—with that prison guard's .38 in his paw—well, it's not free or safe for anyone else. No decent people anywhere—whether they've ever . . . [*The lights begin to dim*] heard of Glenn Griffin or not . . .

HILLIARD HOME

Lights rise slowly. We see the complete outline of a typical house in the suburbs: pleasant, comfortable, undistinguished. ELEANOR HILLIARD, *an attractive woman in her*

*early forties, enters from the dining room, moves to front
door, opens it and looks out. The morning light outside is
bright and cheerful. Not finding the morning paper, she
closes the door as* RALPHIE *enters from dining room.*
RALPHIE, *aged ten, is dressed for school and carries a half-
empty glass of milk, which he stares at balefully as he sits.*
ELEANOR, *who is extremely neat, is arranging pillows on the
sofa.*

ELEANOR: [*Gently*] Ralphie, you left your bike outside all night
again.

RALPHIE: [*As though this answers her*] It didn't rain.

ELEANOR: Well, it's not going to rain today, either. But you're going
to put it in the garage before you go to school.

> [DAN HILLIARD *enters from dining room and crosses to front
> door to look out. He is a typical, undistinguished but im-
> mediately likable man in his forties*]

DAN: [*Calling up the stairs as he passes*] Cindy! It's eight-thirty.

CINDY: [*Off, in her room upstairs*] Can't a girl straighten her girdle
in peace?

DAN: [*Surprised*] Girdle? . . . Girdle! [*Goes to* ELEANOR] Ellie,
can a twenty-year-old child with a figure like Cindy's . . .

ELEANOR: [*Smiling*] It's a joke, Dan.

DAN: Oh. Thank the Lord. She has to have a solid hour for primping
and then she complains all the way downtown because we don't
live in the city limits.

RALPHIE: Ain't love disgusting?

ELEANOR: Don't say "ain't."

DAN: [*To* RALPHIE—*firmly*] Don't say "love," either. [*There is a
thud of a newspaper thrown against the front door.* DAN *steps
swiftly to the door. He and* ELEANOR *have a slight collision. She
moves downstage and he opens the door and goes off onto the
porch*] Hey! Hey!

ELEANOR: [*Teasing*] Try holding your nose and gulping it, Ralphie.

RALPHIE: It tastes sour.

ELEANOR: [*Picking up her small pad and pencil from coffee table*] Yesterday it tasted like chalk.

> [*She sits and starts making her shopping list.* DAN *returns, picks up the* Indianapolis Star, *and enters the room, closing the door*]

DAN: [*A suggestion of grouchiness*] Some day I'm going to catch up with that paper boy and we're going to have a lawsuit on our hands.

ELEANOR: Dan, you have time for a second cup of coffee.

DAN: [*Glances at his watch and then up the stairs*] In half a minute she'll come prancing down those stairs and start urging *me* to hurry.

> [DAN *exits into the dining room.* RALPHIE *takes a long drink of the milk but cannot finish it.* CINDY *comes down the stairs in time to see him*]

CINDY: Well, *today* you are a man! [*She goes to the closet, gets her coat and bag*]

RALPHIE: If cows only knew how I hated 'em!

ELEANOR: What would they do?

CINDY: [*To* ELEANOR] Where's dad? What was he shouting at me?

ELEANOR: What does he shout every morning at eight-thirty?

CINDY: He shouts it's eight-thirty.

ELEANOR: You win the kewpie doll.

> [CINDY *moves swiftly toward the dining room as* DAN *appears in the door with a cup of coffee*]

CINDY: [*To* DAN *as she swings past him*] Say, you'd better hurry!

DAN: [*Looks after* CINDY, *then to* ELEANOR *as he sits on sofa*] What'd I tell you?

> [DAN *sets his cup of coffee on the table and picks up the newspaper and reads*]

RALPHIE: Dad . . . Why did the moron lock his father in the refrigerator?

DAN: [*His attention on the newspaper*] Ralphie, do I have to answer that one?

RALPHIE: [*Brightly*] Because he liked cold pop! [*There is an escape of breath from* DAN *which might or might not pass as a laugh*] Well, why don't you laugh?

DAN: I laughed. What do you want me to do . . . roll on the floor?

RALPHIE: You *almost* rolled on the floor last night when I told you why the moron ate dynamite.

ELEANOR: [*Shakes her head warningly but continues writing*] Ralphie . . .

RALPHIE: My name is Ralph. R-a-l-p-h. There's no Y on the end of it. I looked up my birth certificate.

ELEANOR: Sorry.

[*Through the following,* RALPHIE *rises and, with glass in hand, moves to the chair by front door to pick up his jacket and football; he rather elaborately manages to conceal the half-glass of milk on the floor out of sight in the process*]

RALPHIE: Big game after school today. Fourth grade versus fifth grade. [*Having achieved his purpose; with a sigh of relief*] We'll slaughter 'em! [*Kisses* ELEANOR]

ELEANOR: 'Bye, darling.

[DAN *leans back to be kissed, but* RALPHIE *brushes past him and goes to dining room door, where* DAN's *voice stops him*]

DAN: Hey! Aren't you forgetting something?

RALPHIE: [*Embarrassed and uncertain*] Oh. [*He then returns to* DAN, *who leans for a kiss; instead,* RALPHIE *extends his hand and shakes* DAN's *hand with grave formality*] So long, dad. I hope you have a very pleasant day at the office. [*He turns and goes into the dining room, leaving* DAN *staring after him, then reappears in the pantry on his way to the side door*] So long, dream-witch. I hope Chuck Wright doesn't even notice your new dress.

CINDY: [*Steps into pantry with glass of orange juice in her hand*] 'Bye. Flunk geography, will you, pest?

RALPHIE: [*As he goes out the side door*] *Mister* Pest to you.

ELEANOR: [*Calling from living room*] Ralphie! Your bicycle!

DAN: What do you suppose that was all about?

ELEANOR: [*Toying with her pad and pencil*] Our son Ralph . . .

spelled R-a-l-p-h . . . considers himself too old to kiss a man . . . that's you . . . good-bye or good night.

DAN: [*Covering his hurt*] Oh.

ELEANOR: He said last night he hoped you'd understand.

DAN: [*With an empty smile*] I was hoping maybe he just didn't like my shave lotion. [*As* ELEANOR *unconsciously touches his hair*] Ellie, what's happening to both of them lately? This . . . this young lawyer Cindy works for . . . she can't be *serious*, can she?

ELEANOR: [*Sits*] She hasn't confided in me, Dan . . . which could mean she is.

DAN: She's only twenty years old!

ELEANOR: I was nineteen.

DAN: You had some sense.

ELEANOR: Sure. I married you.

DAN: [*As though he has proved a point*] Well, I didn't drive a Jaguar!

[CINDY *enters from the dining room and goes to put on her coat*]

CINDY: Chuck and I find his Jaguar a very comfortable little surrey. Come climb into my Ford coupé, dad . . . and don't whisper when I'm in the next room. It's not polite.

DAN: [*As he rises and moves to closet*] Now she'll speed.

ELEANOR: [*Automatically*] Careful now, Dan.

CINDY: [*Satirically—chidingly*] Mother . . . you say that every morning of the world. What could possibly happen to a man in the personnel office of a department store? [*She exits, closing the door*]

DAN: [*Pointing at closed door*] That's what I mean! That's not Cindy. Those are Chuck Wright's ideas. Last night on the way home, she asked me point-blank if I didn't think I led a pretty dull life.

ELEANOR: What'd you say?

DAN: [*Firmly*] I said I didn't like Chuck Wright, either.

[DAN *goes to the door, and* ELEANOR *follows him*]

ELEANOR: Dan . . . at Chuck's age . . . you were going to be another

Richard Halliburton, remember? Climb the Matterhorn . . . swim at midnight in the Taj Mahal. My father threatened to throw you . . .

[*Outside,* CINDY *taps horn impatiently*]

DAN: I'm going to be late. [*They kiss: casual, without meaning, habit*] If you're going to use the car today, buy some gas first. *Before* you have to walk a mile for it this time.

[DAN *exits.* ELEANOR *closes the door.* ELEANOR *leans against the door a second, utters an almost silent "Whew," puts her shopping list and pencil on the telephone table, pushes her hair back from her forehead, pushes up her sleeves and prepares to begin the day. She moves to sofa, folds the newspaper and straightens the cushions. Then she goes upstairs, casually humming, and into* RALPHIE'S *room. She shakes her head and begins to gather up the soiled clothes. She flips on a small portable radio and takes the clothes down the hall, presumably to the bathroom, disappears*]

NEWSCASTER'S VOICE: . . . five-state alarm. Police authorities have requested all citizens to be on the lookout for a 1941 Dodge sedan . . . gray . . . mud-spattered . . . bearing Indiana license plates number HL6827 . . . that is HL6827. . . . One of the convicts is wearing a pair of faded blue farmer's overalls which were . . .

[ELEANOR *has returned and flips the radio to music. The music plays through the scene.* ELEANOR *starts to make* RALPHIE'S *bed. The door chimes sound*]

ELEANOR: Wouldn't you know it . . . every time . . . [*The chimes sound again, insistently. She comes down the stairs, but before she reaches the last step the chimes are heard for the third time. She crosses to the door and opens it*] Yes? [*The young man who stands there . . . still out of sight . . . is in his mid-twenties and wears faded blue farmer's overalls. He is tall with—at the moment—a rather appealing boyish expression on his handsome face*]

GLENN: Sorry to bother you, ma'am, but it looks like I lost my way. [*As he speaks,* ROBISH *and* HANK GRIFFIN *appear outside and enter the house by the side door, stealthily*] Could you kindly direct me to the Bowden Dairy? I know it's somewhere in the neighborhood, but I must have the wrong . . .

> [HANK GRIFFIN—*who is younger than* GLENN, *shorter, not so handsome, with a confused, hard, but somehow rather sensitive face—remains in the pantry, looking out the window of the side door.* ROBISH *is large, bull-like, slow, with a huge head sunk between two bulky upthrust shoulders. He goes into the kitchen at once and reappears in the dining room door. Both wear prison garb. The following action has a cold, machinelike precision about it*]

ELEANOR: [*Her back to the room*] Let me see. I've seen that sign. But there are no dairies very close. You see, this is a residential . . .

> [ROBISH *now stands in the room.* ELEANOR *becomes conscious of his presence. She breaks off and turns. In that moment* GLENN *whips out the gun, forces his way into the room, pushing* ELEANOR. *He slams the door and locks it, then moves down to* ELEANOR]

GLENN: Take it easy, lady. [*As her mouth trembles open*] Easy, I said. You scream, the kid owns that bike out there'll come home an' find you in a pool of blood. [GLENN *only nods to* ROBISH, *who stumps up the stairs and through the following looks into* CINDY's *room,* RALPHIE's *room, then enters the master bedroom and searches*] You there, Hank?

HANK: [*Speaking as he moves into the living room*] All clear out back. Lincoln in garage . . . almost new. Garage lock broken.

> [ELEANOR *looks at* HANK, *who returns her stare boldly. A shudder goes through her. Through the following,* GLENN's *swagger suggests a deep insecurity. Above,* ROBISH *is examining and discarding various of* DAN's *clothes in the bedroom . . . creating havoc.* GLENN *steps to* ELEANOR]

GLENN: I'll take the keys to the Lincoln now, lady . . .
ELEANOR: Keys? . . . [*Conquering shudders*] Keys? . . .
GLENN: Lady, when I talk, you snap. Snap fast!

ELEANOR: Top of . . . top of refrigerator . . . I think . . . I always misplace the . . . [*As* GLENN *nods to* HANK, *who goes into dining room then into pantry with the keys and out the side door and off*] Take it . . . you only want the car . . . take it and go . . .

GLENN: [*Shouts toward the stairs*] What're you doin' up there, Robish—takin' a bath?

ROBISH: Nobody home but the missus. [*He goes into upstairs hall, with* DAN's *clothes*]

GLENN: I figured it. [*He examines the house . . . looks into the den*] Good-lookin' family you got, lady. I seen 'em leavin'. [*As* ROBISH *descends*] How many bedrooms up there, Robish?

ROBISH: Four. An' two complete cans, for Chrissake . . .

[*The sound of a car door being slammed startles* ELEANOR]

GLENN: Don't be so jumpy, lady. Only the kid brother takin' care of the cars.

ROBISH: [*Holding up* DAN's *suit*] Th' sonofabitch's got five suits up there. [*He tosses the suit over the back of a chair and goes into the dining room . . . to reappear a few moments later searching the shelves in the pantry*]

GLENN: Class, all the way . . . [*To* ELEANOR] I guess you're tumbling to the idea, ain't you, lady?

ELEANOR: [*Picks up her purse from sofa*] You want money . . . here . . . take it . . . anything . . .

GLENN: [*Takes purse and dumps contents on sofa*] Pretty. [*Holds up a locket*] Gold? [*As* ELEANOR *nods wordlessly, he slips it into his pocket*] I got a gal with a yen for gold a mile wide. [*Picks up the money*] This all the dough you got in the house?

ELEANOR: [*With difficulty*] Yes . . . yes . . . my husband always says . . . too much cash in . . .

GLENN: [*Grins*] Old man's right. Ain't ever safe to have too much cash layin' around. [*He pockets the money*] Gives people ideas.

[ROBISH *returns, disgruntled*]

ROBISH: [*To* GLENN] My gut's growlin'.

GLENN: We heard it.

ROBISH: [*To* ELEANOR] Missus, where you keep th' liquor?

ELEANOR: [*Backing away from him to chair, sits*] We don't have . . . I don't think we . . .

    [HANK *enters the side door, locks it*]

GLENN: [*Gesturing to den*] Robish . . . park your butt'n there'n keep your eyes peeled that side-a th' house.

ROBISH: [*Aggressively; to* ELEANOR] I ain't had me a drink'n eighteen years.

GLENN: Robish, you don't hear so good. It's a kinda library. Improve your mind.

    [HANK *enters from dining room*]

HANK: Gray job's in the garage, outta sight. Lincoln's ready in the driveway . . . headin' out. But she's low on gas.

    [*He hands the car keys to* GLENN, *who pockets them*]

ROBISH: [*Stolidly*] I need me a gun. [GLENN *nods to* HANK, *who turns and runs upstairs. Through the following, he looks into* CINDY'S *room,* RALPHIE'S *room, and enters the master bedroom, where he searches through the top bureau drawer, tossing out handkerchiefs and other odds and ends of clothing*] I don't like none of it.

GLENN: [*Calling up the stairs*] Hey, Hank, Robish don't like it. After them hard bunks . . . them concrete floors!

HANK: Tell 'im to lump it.

GLENN: Lump it. Robish. [*Gestures to den*] In there.

ROBISH: I don't feel right without a gun.

GLENN: Tell you what, Robish . . . Let's you'n me go out an' stick up a hardware store!

ROBISH: Now you're talkin'!

GLENN: [*Sardonically*] Sure . . . Come'n, Robish. Every copper'n the state's waitin' for us to pull a job like that! [*Moves to door*] What're you stallin' for? [HANK *finds an automatic in the drawer and pockets it and starts back downstairs*] Come on!

ROBISH: [*Turning away—growling, inwardly seething*] Awwww . . . don't do me no favors. [*For the first time,* GLENN *laughs.* HANK, *watching* ROBISH, *joins in.* ELEANOR *stares.* ROBISH'S *face hardens*

and, scowling, he makes a sudden movement toward HANK]
What're yuh yakkin' at, yuh . . .

> [*But* GLENN *moves. The laughter dies. He grabs* ROBISH,
> *whips him about*]

GLENN: [*In low hard tones*] Lissen! How many times I gotta tell
you? Keep your mitts off the kid, you don't wanna get your skull
laid open. [*Pause.* ROBISH *and* GLENN *face each other. Then*
ROBISH *turns sullenly and grabs suit of clothes, growling.* GLENN,
*having asserted his total control, laughs, takes cigar from humidor
on coffee table and tosses it to* ROBISH] Here . . . make yourself
sick on a good cigar.

> [ROBISH, *seething, doesn't attempt to catch it; it falls to
> the floor. Then, defiantly,* ROBISH *steps on it, grinding it
> into the carpet*]

GLENN: Robish, you gonna give the lady the idea we ain't neat.
ROBISH: [*He picks up the humidor*] Coupla brothers! Shoulda
knowed better. Ain't neither one dry back-a the ears yet. [*Exits
into the den*]
ELEANOR: [*Who has been watching in horror*] What . . . what do
you . . . ?
GLENN: [*Ignoring her, crosses to* HANK] What'd you find? [HANK,
keeping his eyes on ELEANOR, *takes the automatic out of his pocket
and hands it to* GLENN, *who examines it.* GLENN, *to* ELEANOR]
Lady, now I ask you . . . is that a nice thing to keep aroun' the
house? [*He hands the automatic to* HANK, *whispering*] Put it in
your pocket and keep it there. Family secret, huh? What Robish
don't know, don't hurt nobody . . . okay? [GLENN *laughs, gives*
HANK *a playful push and goes to chair in high spirits*] Let 'em
comb the dives!
HANK: [*Sits on sofa; jubilantly*] You foxed 'em good, Glenn.
GLENN: Came aroun' their roadblocks like we was flyin' a airplane!
Everything's chimin'! [*He sits in the armchair, becomes conscious
of the comfort. He raises himself by the arms and sinks again into
the chair, delighted*] Foam rubber, I betcha. Foam rubber, lady?

[ELEANOR *nods*] I seen the ads. [*He squirms in the seat, enjoying it*] Melts right into your tail!

HANK: [*Takes a cigarette from the box on the coffee table, lights it with the table lighter and, rising, hands it to* GLENN] Christ, what a place to take the stir-taste outta your mouth! Freezer full-a meat! Carpet makes you want to take your shoes off!

ELEANOR: How long do you intend to . . .

GLENN: [*Casually*] Be outta here by midnight, lady.

HANK: Midnight? I thought you said Helen was waiting . . .

GLENN: Not in town, Hank. We don't make it so easy for 'em. She left three weeks ago.

HANK: [*Laughs, grabs a fistful of cigarettes from the box on the coffee table, picks up the lighter, and flips it several times in her face*] I don't care if we never leave. [*He exits into the dining room and reappears in the pantry, where he stands looking out the window of the side door*]

GLENN: [*Rises*] Now, lady . . . you think you can talk on the phone without bustin' into tears?

ELEANOR: [*Rises with great difficulty, takes a feeble step, then gets control of herself, straightens, and walks with dignity and determination to the phone table, turns to face* GLENN] Whom do you want me to call?

[GLENN *laughs*]

GLENN: I always go for a gal with guts! That's *whom* we're gonna call—a gal with real guts. Person to person . . . Mr. James calling Mrs. James . . . Atlantic 6-3389 . . . in Pittsburgh. Pittsburgh, P.A.

BLACKOUT

SHERIFF'S OFFICE

Lights rise swiftly. CARSON *sits near desk, writing on small note pad. The clock reads 5:32.* BARD *is finishing a telephone conversation, a note of exultation in his voice.*

BARD: [*Into phone*] Yeah . . . okay . . . good deal! [*He replaces*

the phone] Pittsburgh! They've located Helen Laski. Avalon
Hotel, Pittsburgh. We'll have a record of any calls to or from . . .
in a few minutes now.

CARSON: Bard . . . stop me if I'm out of line . . . but what's this
thing to you? You, personally?

BARD: [*Slowly rubbing his chin*] You've heard of that first law of
the jungle . . . haven't you, Carson? [*The light on the radio
flashes.* BARD *presses the button, snaps*] Deputy Bard!

WINSTON'S VOICE: Jess . . . this is Winston. Car three.

BARD: What've you got, Tom?

WINSTON'S VOICE: That hardware store holdup on the south side . . .

BARD: [*Eagerly*] Yeah? Yeah?

WINSTON'S VOICE: [*Wearily*] No guns stolen. All they took was fishing rods.

[BARD *presses the button and looks at* CARSON]

CARSON: They'd be too shrewd to pull a stunt like that.

BARD: Look, Carson . . . do me a favor. It's almost time for supper.
All I've heard since morning is how damn wise those rats are. I'm
up to here with it.

CARSON: Where're they getting their clothes?

BARD: My theory is they're running around naked so nobody'll
notice 'em. [*The telephone rings.* BARD *picks it up*] Deputy
Bard . . . Yeah . . . [*Disappointment*] Yeah. Okay. [*Hangs
up*] Helen Laski checked out of the Avalon Hotel last night. No
phone calls, no messages of any kind received today . . . [CARSON
rises and with a look at BARD *goes to the window.* BARD *bursts out*]
I know! I know! They'd be too smart to make a call to a hotel.
They used somebody in between!

CARSON: [*At the window*] I didn't say a word.

BARD: You know where that leaves us, don't you? Beating our
tails ragged over nothing around here.

CARSON: Only you don't believe it.

BARD: Sure I believe it. I'm a trained police officer. I go by the
facts, not crazy hunches. I reckon they're not here.

CARSON: [*Turns*] Why don't you put some more patrol cars on the
streets, anyway? Just in case?

BARD: [*Rises and paces*] That damn jalopy's been reported in every state in the union . . . sixty times in Indiana alone! The earth won't open up and swallow it! Okay, let's try anything! [*He picks up phone, dials . . . as the lights dim*] Where is that beat-up gray car?

HILLIARD HOME

It is dark outside and dim throughout the house, except for the living room, which is brilliantly lighted. ELEANOR *sits on the sofa, staring ahead.* HANK *is in the pantry sitting in a chair that is obviously from the breakfast nook; he holds the portable radio from* RALPHIE'S *room in his lap with the music playing—a loud jazzy tune, in contrast to the soft gentleness of the morning music.* HANK *wears a dark red shirt with a cardigan sweater over it and the prison trousers. He smokes fairly steadily.*

The ravages of the afternoon are everywhere apparent; the atmosphere of invasion hangs over the entire house. There is an open box of cigars on the coffee table with some of the cigars scattered on the table. There is a carton of cigarettes, with the top ripped back, on the table. A coffee cup is also on the table and another is on the table beside the armchair. There are odds and ends of food. The ashtrays are filled to overflowing.

In the living room, GLENN, *at window, is filled with a sense of triumph; he is almost gay, and his enjoyment of what follows is clear.* GLENN *wears a pair of* DAN'S *slacks and a sport shirt.* ELEANOR, *alert in every fiber, is pale, haggard, stiff.* ROBISH *is entering from the den; he is wearing a full suit including shirt and tie—*DAN'S *best, and it does not quite fit. A cigar is jammed in the corner of his mouth.*

ROBISH: What if this joker gets suspicious . . . that gray car parked right in his own garage?

GLENN: [*Casually*] Can it, Robish.

ROBISH: [*To* ELEANOR] Why ain't he here? You said quarter to six.

ELEANOR: The traffic may be heavy . . . or Cindy may have had to work late . . . or . . . anything . . . *anything!*

> [HANK *suddenly rises and looks out the window in the side door. He moves up toward the kitchen door and calls:*]

HANK: Glenn! Black coop just turned in the driveway.

GLENN: Turn off the clatter back there, Hank.

> [HANK *turns off the radio and places it on the back stairs*]

HANK: [*Looking out the side door*] You want me to grab 'em?

GLENN: Not with all them cars goin' by out there.

HANK: Woman comin' around to the front door, Glenn.

> [ELEANOR *places her hand at her mouth.* GLENN *unlocks the door*]

GLENN: [*To* ELEANOR] You don't have to do nothin' but keep your trap shut. [*He turns the gun to cover the front door. There is a brief pause. The front door opens and* CINDY *enters, casually, swiftly, a trifle breathless. She stops dead when she sees* GLENN] Come right in, redhead. [CINDY *backs away, pulling the door closed, but she suddenly stops, frozen in the door. The reason she stops is simply that* GLENN *has turned the gun toward* ELEANOR'S *head*] We still got the old lady, sis. [ROBISH *is standing at den door . . . dull, brutish . . . with his little eyes roving over* CINDY. CINDY *closes the door and stands in front of it.* GLENN *grins*] That's bein' real sensible.

CINDY: [*Planting her feet slightly*] Mother . . . how long have these animals been here?

> [ELEANOR *starts, as though she would warn* CINDY. GLENN'S *grin flickers, fades, and a hardness comes into his face . . . but not into his tone*]

GLENN: Spitfire, too. You watch out, redhead.

HANK: [*At side door, calls*] Glenn! He's lookin' in the garage.

GLENN: [*Calling to* HANK—*confident, knowing*] He'll come in. [*He grabs* CINDY *and pushes her toward chair*] Sit down now, sweetie . . . and no talking. Not a goddam word.

HANK: [*In pantry*] He's coming around now—fast.

> [GLENN *moves into position near front door. Pause. Then the door opens, and* DAN *enters, evening paper in hand*]

DAN: Ellie, whose car is that in the . . .

> [GLENN *slams door shut behind* DAN, *and* DAN *breaks off, staring in bewilderment at* GLENN, *then at the gun*]

GLENN: [*In flat cold tones*] It's loaded. Now lock the door . . . [*Sardonically*] Please.

> [*Unable to speak yet, his eyes on* GLENN, DAN *turns and locks the door. Then:*]

DAN: [*Baffled; softly*] What're you . . . why . . . I don't . . .

GLENN: You never know what's comin', do you, pop?

> [DAN *then turns to* ELEANOR]

DAN: Ellie? . . .

ELEANOR: I'm all right, Dan.

DAN: [*Looking about the room, glances toward stairs*] Where's Ralphie?

ELEANOR: Not home yet.

HANK: [*Calls from pantry*] Driveway ain't blocked, Glenn.

CINDY: The house is crawling with them, dad.

GLENN: [*Sizing her up*] Don't get me jumpy, redhead, this thing's liable to explode.

DAN: [*Flatly, glancing at newspaper in his hand*] Glenn Griffin.

GLENN: [*Laughs, takes paper*] Lotsa people heard-a me, didn't they? [*In satisfaction*] Front page. [*Disgusted*] They always gotta use the same goddam picture. [*He tosses the paper to the floor*]

DAN: Griffin . . . you fire that thing . . . and you'll have the whole neighborhood in here in two minutes.

GLENN: I don't want to take that chance, Hilliard . . . any more'n you want me to.

ROBISH: You dumb, mister?

GLENN: [*Sizing up Dan*] Naw, he ain't dumb, Robish. He's a smart-eyed bastard, this guy . . .

DAN: What're you . . . I don't understand . . . what do you *want*?

GLENN: Take it easy, pop.

DAN: [*Controlling himself with effort*] What do you want here?

GLENN: [*Takes a step toward DAN*] I don't want nobody to get hurt. . . . What do *you* want, pop?

DAN: That's . . . what I want, too. [*Then, shrewdly*] That's what you're depending on, isn't it?

GLENN: You got it, Buster. First try.

DAN: But . . . why *here?* Why *my* house?

GLENN: Your break, pop. I like the location. Those empty lots'n both sides. The bike parked on the nice lawn. I like suckers with kids . . . they don't take no chances.

DAN: Anyone who could think up a scheme like that is . . .

GLENN: [*Cutting in*] . . . is smart, pop.

ELEANOR: [*Quickly*] Dan! They've done nothing.

GLENN: Now I'm gonna explain the facts-a-life to you, Hilliard. You listen, too, redhead . . . listen good. You can get brave . . . any one of you . . . just about any time you feel up to it. Might even get away with it. *But* . . . that ain't sayin' what'll happen to the others . . . the old lady here . . . the redhead . . . the little guy owns the bike . . . [*Slight pause*] Okay, pop, you got it all the way now.

> [*Another pause.* DAN *moves to sofa and drops his hat on it.* ELEANOR'S *hand and his meet, briefly clasping.* DAN *turns to* GLENN]

DAN: [*Taking a deep breath*] How long?

GLENN: [*Grinning*] Now that's the kinda sensible talk a guy likes to hear.

DAN: [*Firmly*] How long?

GLENN: Matter of hours . . . before midnight . . . maybe sooner. Meantime, everything goes on just like normal.

DAN: Why midnight?

GLENN: [*Almost politely*] None-a your goddam business.

ELEANOR: They have a friend coming . . . with money.

DAN: What if . . .

GLENN: [Speaking at the same time; stops DAN] Lady, you speak when I tell you.

DAN: The police are looking everywhere for you. What if . . .

GLENN: They ain't looking here, pop. They show here, it ain't gonna be pretty.

DAN: They could trail your friend . . .

GLENN: Let's get one thing straight, pop. [Gesturing to the window] Any red lights show out there . . . you folks get it first. [There is a slight pause. DAN crosses to the window and peeks out between the drawn curtains. GLENN laughs] Gives you a funny feelin', don't it? You don't know what's happenin' . . . or where . . . or what it adds up to . . . for you. Ever had that feelin' before, pop? Me, I get it all the time. Even kinda like it. But you and me . . . we ain't much alike, are we, pop?

CINDY: [A breath] Thank God.

DAN: [Turns from window] Griffin . . . if you . . . what if I could get you the same amount of money you're waiting for? Now. Before midnight.

ROBISH: Hey, that don't sound like a bad . . .

GLENN: Hilliard, you maybe think you're a big shot . . . fifteen thousand a year. But I had me a look at your bankbooks. Two hundred lousy bucks in the kitty. Hell, I had more'n fifteen grand in my hands at one time, pop . . . and I ain't twenty-five yet.

CINDY: I hope it helped pass your time in jail . . . counting it.

DAN: I could raise more. I could . . .

ROBISH: What about that? We could blow outta here right away! This joker's usin' his brain.

GLENN: [Sharply] Use yours, Robish. Helen's on her way here.

ROBISH: To hell with that! Why should me and the kid risk our necks . . . just so you can get some copper knocked off!

GLENN: [Dangerously now—low and intense] Go spill your guts somewhere else!

ROBISH: [Shouting] What do I care who busted your goddam jawbone?

GLENN: [Topping him] I'll bust yours if . . .

[*They are now shouting at each other across* DAN]

ROBISH: This guy talks sense! Don't I have nothin' to say? . . .

GLENN: NO! You ain't got a goddam stinkin' thing to say! [ROBISH *retreats slightly.* GLENN *turns on* DAN *more quietly but with force*] You, Hilliard . . . I seen what you been up to. Robish here, he ain't got a brain. *But* . . . he ain't got a gun, either. Don't try to get in between, you smart-eyed sonofabitch! Clickey-clickety-click. [*He makes a gesture at* DAN's *temple*] I can see them wheels goin' around in there, pop. *Don't ever try that again!* [*He backs away, eyes on* DAN; *speaks softly now—to* ELEANOR] Now, lady . . . serve us up that chicken you been thawin' out.

DAN: My wife's not your servant.

GLENN: [*Thinly, daring* DAN *to protest*] I always wanted me a servant . . .

ELEANOR: [*Begins to rise*] I don't mind, Dan.

DAN: [*Firmly*] I do. Sit down, Ellie.

GLENN: [*Exploding wildly*] Lissen, Hilliard! I . . . [*Then he stops; sizing* DAN *up, forcing control. Almost quietly at first, building in intensity*] I had a old man like you. Always callin' the tune. Outside his house, nobody. Inside, Mister God! Little punk went to church every Sunday . . . took it from everybody . . . licked their shoes . . . tried to beat it into Hank'n me . . . be a punk, be a nobody . . . take it from you shiny-shoed, down-your-noses sonsabitches with white handkerchiefs in your pockets! [*He snatches the handkerchief from* DAN's *breast pocket, spits into it, and throws it on the floor*] You remember, pop . . . I could kill you just for kicks. [*Pause. Without taking his eyes off* DAN *he again gestures to* ELEANOR, *speaks coldly again*] Now, lady . . . get out there'n cook it.

[ELEANOR *starts to rise, but* HANK's *voice stops her*]

HANK: [*Turning from window in side door*] Kid comin' up the driveway . . . walkin' . . .

[GLENN *starts for the front door*]

DAN: Griffin . . . you've got to let me explain to Ralphie first . . .

[ROBISH *grabs* DAN *by the shoulders and shoves him against the window*]

GLENN: I don't got to do nothin'. You pull anything now, you can sit'n watch me kick the kid's face in.

HANK: [*Calling again from the side door*] Comin' to the front door . . .

GLENN: [*At front door, unlocks it*] You got to learn to take orders from other people now, pop . . .

[*The front door opens and* RALPHIE *enters, whistling.* GLENN *slams the door behind him and locks it.* RALPHIE *stops*]

RALPHIE: [*Bewildered*] Hey . . . what is . . . [ROBISH *takes a single step*] Who are you? [*He turns to the door, sees* GLENN. *A split second. Then he turns and runs to the dining room . . . as* HANK *appears in the dining room door*] Get out of . . .

[RALPHIE *whirls and dashes to the front door, evading* GLENN]

DAN: [*Quickly*] Ralphie, it's all right! It's . . .

[ROBISH *grabs* RALPHIE *at the door. He shakes him by the shoulders roughly, venting on the child the spleen that* GLENN *has stirred in him*]

ROBISH: Where ya think you're goin? Don't you know who's boss 'roun' here? Ya gotta take orders from Griffin. Griffin's the big shot 'roun' here. . . .

[*As* RALPHIE's *head snaps back and forth,* DAN *moves. He grabs* ROBISH, *whips him around.* RALPHIE *breaks away and runs, fighting tears, to* ELEANOR *on the sofa. She takes him in her arms as he sits, clutching her.* DAN *slams* ROBISH *against the window and draws back for a blow, his mind gone blank; he is propelled blindly by jungle atavistic urges beyond his control. But* GLENN *steps in*]

GLENN: It ain't gonna be like this! Not like this, see! [*In the scuffle the table near the chair is overturned.* ELEANOR *stifles a scream as* GLENN *brings the gun down on* DAN's *shoulder.* DAN *goes down.* ROBISH *recovers and starts toward* DAN, *but* GLENN *steps in between]* You hear me, Robish? *Nothin's gonna screw this up!*

ROBISH: *[Blinking owlishly at the gun in* GLENN's *hand]* You think I'm gonna let that . . .

GLENN: *[An order—low, intense]* Get outta here!

ROBISH: *[Glaring, goes to dining room door]* My gut's growlin' again.

> *[*ROBISH *kicks open the dining room door and exits.* DAN, *his tie askew, manages to sit in chair, holding his shoulder.* GLENN *regains his familiar swagger]*

GLENN: Give the old lady a hand, redhead. Out there . . . if you please.

> *[*CINDY *and* ELEANOR *rise,* ELEANOR *going into dining room]*

CINDY: Where do we keep that rat poison?

> *[As* CINDY *follows* ELEANOR, HANK *steps into her path, blocking her way.* GLENN *laughs and crosses to foot of stairs;* CINDY *is trapped between them]*

GLENN: *[Goading* DAN*]* She's a honey, ain't she, Hank?

HANK: *[Arrogantly]* I don't go for redheads.

DAN: *[Sensing danger for* CINDY*]* Griffin . . .

CINDY: *[With a sharpness, to* HANK*]* For God's small favors, make me eternally grateful.

> *[*HANK *drops his arm and* CINDY *exits into the dining room.* HANK *follows her with his eyes and gives a low whistle.* GLENN *turns to* DAN*]*

GLENN: Kid's been in stir for three years, pop. Don't cost nothin' to look.

DAN: *[His eyes still on* HANK*]* Just don't try changing your mind, young fellow.

GLENN: Hilliard, you're a funny gink. You don't know when you're licked, do you? . . . Now just one thing—you got a gun in the house?

RALPHIE: [*Too quickly, as he kneels on sofa*] No . . . we don't.

GLENN: [*Enjoying himself*] Well, pop?

DAN: You heard the boy. I don't have a gun.

GLENN: That's right. You don't. Show him, Hank. [*After* HANK *displays the automatic*] There for a minute I thought you was gonna lie to me, pop.

DAN: Griffin . . . listen to me . . .

GLENN: I'll do the talkin'. You listen, Hilliard! That dough's halfway here now and nothin's gonna foul this up, see. You pull any of that muscle-stuff again . . .

DAN: That won't happen again . . .

GLENN: . . . and I'm gonna let Robish work you over . . .

DAN: . . . I went blank there for a . . .

GLENN: . . . after that, you ain't gonna know what happens to the others. That the way you want it?

DAN: Griffin . . . [*Very softly . . . with strength now*] *hands off!*

GLENN: I don't go for threats . . .

DAN: Hands off, that's all I know! If one of you touches one of us again . . .

GLENN: Don't talk tough to me, Hilliard . . .

DAN: . . . I can't promise what'll happen. . . . I can't promise *any-thing* . . . if one of you touches one of us again. I don't *know* what I'll do. Can't you understand that, you half-baked squirt? I'll make you use that gun, Griffin. So help me. We're done for then, but so are you. [*Drops voice*] It won't matter then whether your friend gets here or not . . .

BLACKOUT

SHERIFF'S OFFICE

The clock reads 7:03. WINSTON, *his feet propped up on desk, is trying to sleep. The radio signal is flickering.* BARD *flips on radio.*

CARSON'S VOICE: Bard . . . this is Carson.

BARD: [*Wearily*] I'm still here, Carson.

CARSON'S VOICE: Helen Laski's been spotted.

BARD: [*Changing—alert and eager*] Where?

CARSON'S VOICE: She's heading west from Pittsburgh. On U.S. 40. Driving very slow and careful. Approaching Columbus, Ohio. Heading west!

BARD: [*With satisfaction*] West!

CARSON'S VOICE: Ought to be here about eleven or twelve tonight.

BARD: [*An excited throb in his voice*] Okay. Now listen. Don't let anyone tail her. I don't want her picked up, or alerted. But I want her clocked. Every town she goes through . . . every village. I want to know every time she stops to get gas, go to the can, anything.

CARSON'S VOICE: Looks like your hunch is paying off, Bard.

BARD: Could be, Carson. *Could be!* [BARD *flips off the radio and slaps* WINSTON's *feet off the desk*] I told you they were homing pigeons, Tom! They do it every time . . . right back to the womb that spewed 'em.

WINSTON: Okay, they're pigeons. You're an owl. I'm sleepy.

BARD: They're layin' low here now . . . thinkin' how clever they been . . . getting Laski out of town so she could backtrack to 'em. Clever! *Not so damned!*

WINSTON: Jess, you're raving. How long since you ate solid food?

DUTCH'S VOICE: [*On intercom*] Jess . . .

BARD: [*Flips intercom button*] Yeah, Dutch?

DUTCH'S VOICE: Your wife called again. She says she's still at your mother's but drowning in a sea of words . . . whatever that means.

BARD: [*With a laugh*] Tell her to stay there all night, Dutch. Tell her I said it's . . . uh . . . Be-Kind-to-Talkative-Mothers-Week. [*He flips off the intercom, turns to* WINSTON *exultantly*] About twenty miles out of town, we'll put a real tag on Miss Helen Laski and she'll breeze right in and lead us straight to the hole! How many hours till midnight, Tom?

WINSTON: By my watch . . . [*The lights begin to dim*] too goddamned-many.

BLACKOUT

HILLIARD HOME

The living room lights are on; the rest of the house is in dimness. HANK *is in the chair in the pantry, smoking. In the living room the family is arranged in a pattern within view of the windows. The curtains are slightly open.* ROBISH *is sitting on the stairs.* GLENN *is lounging in a chair near the windows.* DAN *looks at his watch.*

GLENN: Pop, that's a good-looking timepiece you got there. [*He extends his hand*] I'll take it. [DAN *rises, pauses, then slips the wrist watch band off his wrist. He crosses and hands the watch to* GLENN, *who examines it*] Fancy. [*He slips it on his own wrist*] D'you snitch this from that department store, pop?

DAN: [*Quietly, with dignity*] My wife gave it to me . . . on our twentieth anniversary. [*He returns to seat*]

GLENN: [*Winding the watch*] Now ain't that real touchin'? [*To* RALPHIE] Hey, Buster . . . ain't it time for you to hit the sack? You want to grow up, be a big man like pop here, don't you?

[RALPHIE *kisses* ELEANOR *good night, then crosses directly to* GLENN]

RALPHIE: Half-baked squirt!

[ROBISH *laughs.* GLENN *grabs the front of* RALPHIE'S *shirt but releases him after a moment with a laugh.* RALPHIE *turns and goes upstairs and into his own room and sits on the bed*]

GLENN: [*As* RALPHIE *goes*] Some brat you got there, missus. Some day he's gonna get his head knocked off.

[DAN *rises and crosses to the stairs,* ROBISH *stands up and blocks his way*]

ROBISH: What you think you're gonna do . . . go to the toilet for him?

GLENN: It's his house, Robish. Hilliard don't want that kid hollering out a window up there any more'n we do. [ROBISH *steps down from the stairs and* DAN *goes up to* RALPHIE'S *room.* ROBISH *moves toward the window.* GLENN *flips off the living room lights and jumps up, closing the window curtains*] How many times I gotta tell you—stay outta the way-a them windows. [*He motions* ROBISH *toward the den*] Get in there and turn on the telvision.

ROBISH: [*Protesting*] Listen, Griffin . . .

GLENN: And keep it lit so it looks natural from out front.

> [ROBISH *stomps angrily into the den. The living room is now in dimness.* DAN *turns on light in* RALPHIE'S *room, stands a moment without speaking.* RALPHIE *studies his father a second*]

RALPHIE: Dad . . . they're not so tough.

DAN: [*Still facing the door, abstracted*] Don't you fool yourself, Ralphie.

RALPHIE: You could've licked the big guy if that Griffin hadn't . . .

DAN: [*Turning to the boy*] Ralphie, we can't lick them . . . at least not that way. I lost my temper, that's all. I . . . can't let that happen again.

RALPHIE: [*Not daring to believe it*] Dad . . . are you scared?

DAN: Of course not. Why, you ought to know . . . [*He suddenly sits on the bed, facing the boy*] Ralphie, listen to me. Those two guns they have down there . . . they're loaded. Those are real bullets. When a gun goes off, it doesn't only make a sound. Those bullets can kill people. Do you understand that, son?

RALPHIE: I've been thinking . . . I could climb out Cindy's window . . . out across the porch roof . . . I could get to the Wallings. Get help . . .

DAN: [*Patience running thin*] Ralphie . . .

RALPHIE: The porch isn't much higher'n the garage roof. I've jumped off the garage roof a lot of times.

DAN: Ralphie, how many times have I told you to stay off the garage roof?

RALPHIE: *You* could, though. I'll *bet* you could.

DAN: Look, Ralphie . . . Listen, Ralph . . . Ralph. You want me to call you Ralph, don't you? You want to be considered a grown-up boy in this house? Then you've got to behave like one . . . *think* like one . . . beginning right now!

RALPHIE: I've got a better idea. I could wait till that young one goes into the living room, sometime, then sneak down the back stairs . . .

DAN: [*Anger rising*] Ralphie, didn't you hear them? If you got out of here . . . even if you brought the police . . . do you know what would happen? They would shoot your mother and your sister . . . and y,ou . . . *you'd* be the reason they did it.

RALPHIE: You *are* scared.

DAN: No, no, of course not . . . It's only . . . [*Suddenly changes*] Yes, son . . . yes, I'm scared. But I'm not ashamed of being scared. . . . Sometimes it's better to be scared. You think about that now. You think hard about that, hear?

RALPHIE: Well, I'm not. And Cindy's not either.

DAN: [*Rising, urgently*] You'd better . . .

> [*The telephone in the house rings.* DAN *stops. Immediate tension . . . there is a pause until the second ring starts.* GLENN *rises and turns on the living room lights.* HANK *runs up the back stairs and to the phone extension in the upstairs hall.* ROBISH *appears in the door of the den*]

GLENN: Hank! [*To* CINDY] Okay, redhead . . . you get the pleasure. [CINDY *rises from the sofa and crosses toward telephone*] If it's for Mr. James, I'll take it. Anyone else, let 'em talk . . . except the brat.

> [*The telephone continues to ring—insistently, mechanically.* HANK *picks up the phone in the upstairs hall with his hand on the circuit breaker in the cradle until he hears* CINDY *speak. Then he opens the circuit and listens.* DAN *stands behind the door to* RALPHIE'S *room . . . alert, waiting*]

HANK: [*When he is ready at the phone*] Okay, Glenn.

GLENN: [*Beside* CINDY *at the phone table*] Like any other night, see. Normal.

[CINDY *picks up the phone with her left hand.* GLENN *grabs the instrument and puts it in her right hand so he can try to listen, too*]

CINDY: [*Into phone*] Hello? . . . Oh . . . No, I can't . . . not to-night . . . I simply can't, that's all. . . . Nothing's the matter, I . . .

[*She slowly replaces the phone. Upstairs,* HANK *replaces the extension and starts down the stairs into the living room.* DAN *opens the door of* RALPHIE'S *room and comes down a few steps on the stairs*]

GLENN: [*To* CINDY—*impatiently*] Well? *Well?*

CINDY: [*Bleakly*] I flunked.

GLENN: Who was it?

HANK: [*Descending stairs*] His name's Chuck. And he's coming, anyway. For a date.

[*Pause,* HANK'S *eyes on* CINDY. GLENN *takes a few steps, thinking furiously*]

GLENN: You ain't's wise's I thought you was, spitfire.

HANK: She couldn't help it. He was in a drugstore around the corner. Wouldn't even listen. Wants her to go dancing.

GLENN: [*Turns to* CINDY] Okay. You be ready, cutie. When boy friend stops out front, you duck out . . .

[*Pause: general amazement*]

ROBISH: Griffin . . . you off your rocker?

GLENN: [*Calling*] Hilliard . . . get down here. [*To* ELEANOR] You stick with the brat, he don't get no ideas.

[ELEANOR *rises and starts up the stairs, passing* DAN *as he descends*]

DAN: [*To* ELEANOR, *in a low voice*] Lock the door.

[GLENN *flips on radio, then crosses to* CINDY *as the music rises*]

GLENN: You wanna dance, redhead? You shoulda told Hank. [*To

HANK] C'mon kid, you want a dance, take a dance. [*To* CINDY, *who moves slightly away*] Give the kid a break, spitfire.

> [DAN *watches tensely . . . as* HANK *looks* CINDY *over, with arrogance, but the longing clear in his face. Then* HANK *moves, crossing toward* CINDY, *passing her, flipping off the radio. In silence, he walks with dignity, inwardly disturbed, toward the dining room door, exits. A moment—while* GLENN *stares after* HANK, *amazed, frowning. Above,* ELEANOR *enters* RALPHIE'S *bedroom, closes and locks door, turns off bedroom light*]

GLENN: [*Baffled, almost to himself*] Oughta see Hank dance. Has all the babes groggy.

> [HANK *appears in pantry, oddly shaken*]

HANK: [*In whisper*] Dammitohell . . .

GLENN: [*Recovering, turning to* DAN] Hilliard . . . the gas is low in that fancy buggy of yours. Fill'er up'n check the battery'n oil.

ROBISH: You ain't lettin' 'em *both* out?

> [*In the pantry,* HANK *sinks into the chair, sits quietly*]

GLENN: The kid'n the missus stay. Him or the redhead pull something, they know what'll happen here. Pop here's a smart cookie. He don't want no coppers settin' up machine guns on his nice smooth lawn . . . throwin' tear gas through his windows. [*Moves closer to* DAN, *threateningly*] 'Cause that happens, you know who's gonna get it, don't you, Hilliard? Not you. [*He gestures upstairs*] Them. I'm gonna see to it personal. [*Slowly*] An' you're gonna stay alive to remember it the rest of your life.

> [*There is a pause. Then* DAN *steps toward* CINDY]

DAN: You hear that, Cindy? [*Crosses to closet and gets his coat and* CINDY'S]

CINDY: I'll do *anything* to get away from that voice.

ROBISH: Okay, everybody's gone nuts. Gimme some liquor.

DAN: No, no liquor.

GLENN: This time the old man's right, Robish.

ROBISH: [*Shrewdly—striking the weak spot*] You lettin' this joker give the orders?

GLENN: [*Tricked*] Nobody gives me orders. Not ever again! [*To* DAN] Make it bourbon, pop. Bonded. [*To* CINDY] You . . . bring back some late-edition papers. [*He sits*]

CINDY: [*Getting into her coat—scathingly*] Would you like a scrap-book and a jar of paste?

[HANK, *suddenly alert in pantry, looks out window of side door*]

HANK: [*Calling*] Car stoppin' at the curb. Little low-slung job. Foreign make, some kind.

CINDY: [*To* GLENN] It's a Jaguar. You should know what a jaguar is . . . it's a fierce jungle animal . . . very brave against smaller, less ferocious animals. But it's a snarling coward when trapped.

[*She goes to the door.* DAN *follows, stops her*]

DAN: Cindy! [*She turns to him; slight pause; then gently*] You . . . you be careful, hear?

[*As* DAN *opens the door,* GLENN *rises quickly and steps to the dining room door, out of sight of the front door.* HANK *watches out the window of the side door*]

GLENN: If that spitfire tries anything!

DAN: Griffin . . . what if the police track you down? Sooner or later . . . through no fault of ours . . . what if . . .

GLENN: [*Smugly—in control*] I'd never know who done it, pop.

DAN: But you couldn't blame *us*!

GLENN: [*Slowly*] Hilliard, I got news for you. I—can—do—anything —I—want. Nice family you got here, pop. You love that woman of yours, you ain't gonna reach for no phone in that filling station. Them coppers're after *me*, y'know. They don't give a hoot in hell about you. Or your family. [*He crosses to the door*] Clickety-clickety-click . . . give you something to think about, pop.

[GLENN *opens the door and gestures* DAN *to go.* DAN *goes out, setting his shoulders. Above,* ELEANOR *watches out* RALPHIE'S *window*]

ROBISH: [As GLENN *closes and locks the door*] Jeez, I'm gettin' up a thirst all of a sudden.

> [*He exits into den.* GLENN, *after a short pause, turns out the living room lights and goes through the dining room door and into the pantry where he joins* HANK, *who stares moodily out the window of the side door*]

GLENN: Kid, everythin's chimin'! Told you I'd shack you up in style, didn't I?

HANK: [*Noncommital*] Yeah . . .

GLENN: Hey . . . what's eatin' you, anyway?

HANK: Y'know something, Glenn? I never had a "date" in my life.

GLENN: Date? Hell, you laid enough babes to . . .

HANK: Naw, I mean a *date.* Y'know . . . ordinary things like that.

GLENN: [*Scornfully*] Malted milks? Hot dogs at a drive-in?

HANK: Maybe . . .

GLENN: You got it comin', kid . . . all the babes you can handle and still walk straight up.

HANK: Babes like Helen?

GLENN: [*Astonished*] Yeah. . . . What's the matter with Helen?

HANK: She's a tramp.

> [HANK *goes to the kitchen door and disappears.* GLENN *stares after him, puzzled*]

BLACKOUT

SHERIFF'S OFFICE

> [BARD *is at the desk, working over various reports.* CARSON *enters briskly. Clock: 8:56.*]

CARSON: Bard . . . hold onto your hat. She's not coming.

BARD: What're you talking about . . . not coming? She's halfway . . .

CARSON: [*Shaking his head*] Helen Laski's not coming. She made one simple mistake. She ran a red light on the outskirts of Columbus. A patrol car gave chase.

BARD: [*Rising, outraged*] Carson . . . are you telling me they arrested Helen Laski for a traffic violation? Good God, they had orders! It's been on every teletype for hours . . . *do not arrest!*

CARSON: They didn't arrest her. She gave them the slip . . . in downtown Columbus. Abandoned the convertible. Swallowed up. Presto! [*He shrugs*] These mistakes are bound to happen.

BARD: You can't afford mistakes against a mind like Glenn Griffin's! [*He sits at the desk and flips the button on the intercom*] Dutch! I want every long distance telephone call and a record of every telegram from Columbus, Ohio, to Indianapolis from . . .

[*He looks at* CARSON]

CARSON: Eight.

BARD: From eight o'clock to now . . . and straight through the night. As fast as they get 'em. Any number to any number. Names, addresses, the works. [*Flips off the intercom, sits back*] Imagine those greedy sonsabitches in Columbus trying to pick her off for a lousy fifteen-buck fine!

CARSON: [*Sits and picks up the deck of cards on the desk*] She has to contact him . . . wherever he is. All we can do is wait. How about a game of double solitaire?

BARD: [*Rising and pacing*] Wait . . . wait . . . wait.

DIMOUT

HILLIARD HOME

The lights are dim throughout the house. ELEANOR *is moving from the window to the door in* RALPHIE'S *room.* RALPHIE *is asleep on his bed.* HANK *is in the pantry watching out the window of the side door.* ROBISH *is turning from the window in the living room.* GLENN *is leaving the pantry to appear in the living room.*]

ROBISH: Tired-awaitin'. I been thinkin' about a snort of whisky for eighteen years.

GLENN: [*As he enters from the dining room*] Shut up, he's comin' in. [*He gestures for* ROBISH *to turn on the living room lights.*

ROBISH *turns on the lights and unlocks and opens the front door.* DAN *enters, the fury and frustration packed solid through his whole frame. A new fear has taken root in him now, and he speaks flatly, quietly.* GLENN *says:*] C'mere, pop. [*As* DAN *crosses and* ROBISH *closes and locks the front door*] You mind takin' your hands outta your pockets? [DAN *obliges*] Thank you kindly. . . .

ROBISH: Where the hell you been?

[DAN *faces* ROBISH. GLENN *frisks him expertly*]

DAN: The service stations close early in this neighborhood. . . . [GLENN *is circling* DAN] I don't have a gun, Griffin.

[GLENN *brings the whisky bottle out of* DAN's *coat pocket. It is in a paper bag which he removes and drops on the floor*]

ROBISH: [*Outraged, seeing the bottle*] Chrissake, a pint!

DAN: You didn't specify any particular amount.

GLENN: [*Laughs, looking at the bottle*] Kentucky Tavern . . . nothing but the best for pop! [*As* ROBISH *snatches the bottle*] Robish, go'n out'n check the car over. [*He sits on the sofa, putting his feet up*]

ROBISH: [*Working with the bottle*] Maybe he's got coppers stashed in the back seat. Let Hank check it.

GLENN: [*Dismissing it—lifts voice*] Hank! Check the car.

HANK: [*Bitterly*] Yeh . . . me. [*He rises from the chair and opens the door as he calls*] Okay, Glenn.

[*He exits through the side door, closing it.* DAN *goes to the stairs, begins to mount*]

GLENN: You didn't get any ideas out there, did you, Hilliard?

ROBISH: [*Struggling with bottle*] Kee-rist . . . eighteen years an' then you can't get it open! [*Succeeds, takes a long swig from bottle*]

DAN: [*On second step of stairs, calls*] Ellie . . .

ELEANOR: [*Comes out of room to the head of the stairs*] We're all right, Dan. Cindy's not back yet.

GLENN: Pop, when I ask you a question, you answer!

DAN: [*Turns, flatly*] No. No ideas.

> [*Above,* ELEANOR *returns to* RALPHIE'S *room and closes the door.* HANK *re-enters the pantry and speaks as he crosses toward the living room*]

HANK: Car's okay. [*He enters the living room through the dining room door*] I didn't try the motor. [*A glance at* DAN] Looks like the whole street's gone to sleep.

GLENN: See, Robish. Hank ain't yellow. Taught him how not to be yellow, didn't I, Hank?

HANK: You taught me everything.

> [*The strange twist of bitterness in his tone causes* GLENN *to look at him sharply.*]

DAN: [*Haunted by his new fear*] Griffin . . .

GLENN: [*Briskly; unpleasantly now*] Your woman's waitin'. Go to bed.

DAN: [*Firmly*] Griffin . . . when you do leave tonight, we're staying in this house. My family. All of us.

GLENN: [*Eyes on* HANK] Yeh, yeh. You give me a fair shake, I give you a fair shake. [*Pause.* DAN *stands, thinking.* HANK *crosses to take the bottle from* ROBISH; *drinks.* GLENN *rises, glaring at* DAN. DAN *turns and goes upstairs.* GLENN *stops* HANK *as he returns the bottle to* ROBISH *and turns to leave the room.* GLENN *presses on, puzzled*] I did teach you everything, didn't I, Hank?

HANK: [*Meeting his brother's gaze: levelly*] Yeh. Everything . . . except maybe how to live in a house like this.

> [HANK *goes swiftly to dining room door and exits. He enters the pantry and sits in the chair. Above,* DAN *enters the master bedroom, takes off topcoat, and sits in the dimness on the bed, facing the door, alone.* GLENN, *after a pause follows* HANK *into the pantry*]

ROBISH: Ahhh . . . my gut's beginnin' to burn good!

> [ROBISH *turns off the living room lights, then sits, drinking*]

GLENN: [*In the pantry; baffled*] Live here? We ain't gonna *live* here.

HANK: No. Or any place like it. Ever.

GLENN: Hank, what the hell's . . .

HANK: When Helen gets here, we gonna give Hilliard a fair shake?

GLENN: [*Angrily*] Anybody ever give *you* a fair shake?

HANK: Who the hell ever had a chance?

GLENN: [*An idea*] The redhead! She got you goin', kid? [*Laughs and kneels facing* HANK; *with warm comradeship*] Tell you what, kid . . . when we leave, we'll take her along. Just for you.

HANK: [*After a pause—bitterly*] Fair shake!

GLENN: [*Anger again*] What you think I'm gonna do? [*Trying to sell* HANK *the idea*] Nobody's gonna be suspicious if we got two women'n the car. We'll take 'em both. [*He gives* HANK *a playful punch*] You give me the idea yourself!

> [GLENN *rises and leaves the pantry through the kitchen door. He appears in the living room, pauses for a moment, looking back, and then crosses and exits into the den. Above,* ELEANOR *rises and leaves* RALPHIE'S *room, leaving the door ajar. She crosses the hall and enters the master bedroom, turns on the lights. She gazes a moment at* DAN]

ELEANOR: [*Not quite a question*] Dan . . .

DAN: [*Still sitting on the bed*] I did what they told me. I saw the Wallings coming home from the movies. I could've . . . [*Bursting out rebelliously*] What *should* I have done, Ellie?

ELEANOR: Nothing. If the police come, Dan . . . it could be worse.

DAN: And if they don't? . . . You can't deal with boys like that. With guns in their hands. Stone walls! If you could just *talk* to them . . . *reason* . . . be sure he means what he . . .

ELEANOR: Dan . . . it won't be long now . . .

DAN: [*Rises*] It makes no sense! You open a door . . . a door you've opened thousands of times . . . and wham, all of a sudden the whole world makes no sense!

ELEANOR: [*Moves to him, puts her hand on his shoulder*] Dan, some day we'll look back on these hours and . . .

DAN: [*Quietly*] Ellie, there is no *some day*. They've all been smashed now . . . [*He sinks into chair*] broken off . . .

ELEANOR: They can't do this to you! I won't allow them to . . .

DAN: My brain's like a stone in my head. All this must've started months ago . . . maybe years . . . when that kid down there started hatching this scheme in his cell . . . before we ever even heard his name. . . .

ELEANOR: Dan, it's such a short, *short* time. Any minute now. All they'll have is the car. Even that's insured . . . isn't it silly, the things you think of? As soon as they've gone, you'll pick up the phone . . .

[*The expression on* DAN's *face stops her. Across the hall,* RALPHIE *rises from his bed and stands at his door, listening*]

DAN: [*Turning away—flatly*] Just like that . . .

ELEANOR: [*Sitting on bed, facing* DAN] Dan . . . what are you thinking?

DAN: I'm thinking a man could be haunted forever . . . afterwards . . . by the thought that if he'd done just this at just the right time . . . or that at just the proper moment . . . he might have prevented it all.

ELEANOR: No, no, something else. When they leave you'll pick up the phone and . . . [*Stops; realizing*] They won't let you do that, will they?

DAN: [*Rising; speaks reassuringly now*] Of course they will, darling . . .

ELEANOR: No!

DAN: Shh . . .

ELEANOR: How can they stop it?

DAN: They can't. There's no way to . . .

ELEANOR: [*Finally*] I know, Dan. I know.

DAN: Don't imagine things, Ellie!

ELEANOR: [*Hollowly*] They'll have to take someone along . . .

DAN: [*Turned away*] No, Ellie, no. The thought never occurred to me. . . . I . . . I hope Cindy doesn't stay out too late, that's all.

ELEANOR: She won't take any chances, Dan.

DAN: [*Turning, sees* RALPHIE, *who has crossed into the room and stands at the door*] Hey, skipper . . . what're you doing up this late?

> [*He knows* RALPHIE *has heard, stops.* ELEANOR *rises and goes to* RALPHIE]

RALPHIE: [*To* DAN, *their eyes locked*] Are you going to let them . . . what you just said? . . .

DAN: Ralphie, I just explained to your mother . . .

ELEANOR: [*Her arms around* RALPHIE'S *shoulders*] Dear, your mother had a wild idea, that's all. Those men haven't even thought of that.

RALPHIE: I don't want them to take me along with them.

DAN: [*Kneeling across the bed, takes* RALPHIE'S *shoulders*] I wouldn't let them do that, Ralphie. You ought to *know* I wouldn't let them do that!

RALPHIE: [*Backs away, turns and goes to the door*] How are you going to stop them?

> [RALPHIE *turns away and goes to his door. He looks back at* DAN *and* ELEANOR, *then goes into his room and closes the door and sinks onto the bed.* DAN *and* ELEANOR *look at each other, helplessly. The sound of an approaching motorcar is heard. There is immediate tension.* DAN *steps to the window. Below,* HANK *leaps to the side door, looks out the window, gun ready*]

ELEANOR: Cindy?

DAN: Yes, dear . . . Cindy.

> [ELEANOR *turns off the bedroom lights and she and* DAN *sit in the darkness on the bed. The car motor stops and two car doors slam. In pantry,* HANK *steps back from the side door. In the headlight beams from the car,* CINDY *appears outside, followed by* CHUCK, *who is a rather ordinary-appearing young man in his mid-twenties. He wears a sports coat and an expression of amazed bewilderment*]

CHUCK: [*Catching up with her*] Cindy . . . are you going in like this?

CINDY: [*At the step*] Please, Chuck!

CHUCK: Look, I know I bowled you over. I've bowled myself over, too. But when a fellah proposes to a girl, he kind of expects an answer . . . like yes or no . . . not: "Take me home, Chuck!"

CINDY: [*Her mind elsewhere*] Was . . . was that a proposal?

CHUCK: Well, it wasn't much of one, but it was the best I could manage . . . with you off on another planet somewhere. I don't mind admitting you've got me so balled-up tonight, I . . . [*Shakes his head as* CINDY *fumbles in her pocket for her keys. He touches her arm*] Look . . . redhead . . .

CINDY: [*Whirling on him; sharply*] Don't call me that!

CHUCK: But I always call you . . . All *right!* One minute you act like you hate me . . .

CINDY: Oh, no . . .

CHUCK: . . . and the next . . .

CINDY: Chuck . . .

CHUCK: [*Hopefully*] Yes? . . .

CINDY: Chuck . . . listen.

CHUCK: Well? . . .

CINDY: [*Abruptly changing her mind*] I'll tell you tomorrow . . . at the office.

CHUCK: You'll tell me one thing right now . . .

CINDY: [*Tensely, turns away*] It doesn't concern you, Chuck.

CHUCK: [*Turns her around, takes her hands*] If it concerns you, it concerns me. There. That's all I've been trying to say all evening. You've done something to me, Cindy. I've known a lot of girls . . . but . . . but you've opened doors . . . in me . . . in the world. So I've got to know . . . now . . . have I been kidding myself? Are you closing the doors? [*Suddenly,* CINDY *throws her arms around his neck and kisses him, in desperation, deeply touched, clinging to him. He slips his arms around her waist. Inside,* HANK *is watching . . . turns away. They break the kiss slowly and* CINDY *lays her head against his chest*] Cindy . . . you're trembling all over. [*He lifts her chin*] You'd better tell me.

CINDY: Yes . . .

CHUCK: Your family? . . . [*She nods*] Cindy, you can't fret about it. If it's them. Because . . . look . . . it's *you.* You're the one I want to take care of now. *Only, you.* [*She stares, realizing that she cannot tell him*] Well, Cindy?

> [CINDY *shakes her head. She turns to the door, taking out her keys*]

CINDY: [*With finality*] No! Good night, Chuck.

CHUCK: [*Off on another tangent*] Your father doesn't like me. He thinks I've helled around too much, maybe. . . .

CINDY: Please, Chuck . . .

CHUCK: Let's go in and talk it over with him. I . . .

CINDY: [*Turning on him—in desperation*] Please . . . please . . . please!

> [CHUCK, *with mingled disgust and defeat, takes the keys from her hand and unlocks the door.* HANK, *in the pantry, holds the automatic in readiness.* CINDY *pushes past* CHUCK *and blocks the door as he lets it swing open, the keys still in the lock*]

CHUCK: All right, Cindy. I'm not coming in. . . .

> [CINDY *closes the door in his face and leans limply against it, facing* HANK. CHUCK *stands for a moment staring at the door. Then, he turns away; suddenly he turns back and takes the keys from the lock and is about to call to* CINDY. *He thinks better of it, looks at the keys, then at the house, and turns and walks away, putting the keys in his pocket. There is the sound of one car door slam and the motor starts and the car drives away . . . the headlights dimming out quickly. Inside,* CINDY *moves toward the back stairs*]

HANK: [*His voice sardonic, aping* GLENN'S *manner*] Use the other stairs, redhead. Glenn'll want to know you're home.

> [CINDY *turns and leaves the pantry through the kitchen door. Above,* DAN *leaves the bedroom and goes to the head of the stairs. In the living room* ROBISH *turns on the lights. He is now quite drunk, his voice heavier and louder than before. As* CINDY *enters from the dining room, he leans*

across the stairs with his hand against the wall, blocking her way]

ROBISH: Have fun, sweetie? Parkin' with the boy friend? [HANK *appears in the dining room door, the gun out of view*] He gettin' any, that guy?

[*Above,* DAN *turns on the light in the upstairs hall.* ELEANOR *comes to the door of the bedroom*]

DAN: Cindy? . . .

HANK: [*Eyes on* ROBISH] Get on upstairs, miss.

[DAN *descends the stairs and* ELEANOR *comes to the head of the stairs, leaning over the railing*]

ROBISH: [*Voice blurred*] Aw naw, aw naw. Ain't been searched yet. Got to search her first.

DAN: [*Taking in the situation swiftly, barks*] Griffin!

ROBISH: Searched the ol' man, didn't we?

HANK: Get out of her way, Robish!

[GLENN *appears in the door of the den, immediately alert, throwing off sleep*]

DAN: Griffin, if you intend to let him get away with this . . .

GLENN: [*Revolver in hand now*] Stay where you are, Hilliard!

ROBISH: Pretty little gal might try to sneak a gun in . . .

DAN: Griffin, you don't want to have to use that gun of yours, do you?

GLENN: [*Grabs* ROBISH] You goddam lunkhead . . .

ROBISH: [*With one swing of his arm throws* GLENN *back*] Everybody givin' me orders! [*Steps toward* CINDY] Lift your arms, baby.

DAN: [*Coming down between* ROBISH *and* CINDY] A shot'll be heard, Griffin. . . .

[*But* HANK *steps in with the automatic drawn on* ROBISH *and pushes* DAN *back onto the stairs. There is a pause.* ROBISH *stands blinking owlishly at the automatic*]

GLENN: [*A breath*] Hank . . . you damn fool!

ROBISH: [*Incredulously*] Where'd ya get that?

HANK: [*Still covering* ROBISH] You going up to bed now, miss?

ROBISH: [*Bawling*] Where'd yuh get that gun?

GLENN: [*Shoves* ROBISH *toward dining room*] Go sleep it off, Robish!

ROBISH: [*Turns at the dining room door*] Turnin' on me, huh? All of yuh. [*Drunkenly maudlin*] Turnin' on your ol' pal Robish. Okay. Ya wait. Ya-*all* wait . . .

> [*He goes into the dining room. Above, for the first time,* RALPHIE *moves: cautiously he opens the door of his room.* ROBISH *appears in the pantry, staggering*]

GLENN: What's it to you, Hank?

HANK: [*Muttering defensively*] It ain't safe to touch the women.

GLENN: Yeah? . . .

CINDY: Thank you . . . Hank . . .

HANK: [*After the briefest sort of pause*] Get the hell to bed.

GLENN: [*Crosses toward* CINDY] Don't get the idea you ain't gonna be searched, redhead!

> [*At this point* ROBISH *goes out the side door, slamming it behind him. The significance of* ROBISH's *exit reaches* GLENN *in the living room. He springs into action*]

GLENN: Christ! [*He runs through the dining room door as he speaks*] Cover 'em, Hank. Let 'em have it if you have to!

> [*He goes through the pantry and out the side door, slamming it as he goes.* DAN *is tense all through, and uncertain*]

HANK: Don't get the idea I won't . . .

ELEANOR: [*On stairs above*] Dan?

DAN: Stay up there, Ellie . . . hear?

HANK: [*A warning*] Don't get any ideas now . . .

DAN: [*To* CINDY] Cindy! You look . . . [*He glances at* HANK, *then back to* CINDY] Are you sick?

CINDY: No, I . . .

> [CINDY *turns to* DAN. *Their eyes meet. Pause. And then* CINDY *collapses.* DAN *takes a step toward her. She holds onto the back of the chair and sinks into it*]

ELEANOR: Cindy!

HANK: Don't move, mister!

DAN: Dammit, this child's sick! If there's any decency in you at all . . .

[RALPHIE *appears in the pantry, coming down the back stairs. He listens a moment, then goes to the side door and opens it*]

HANK: If you're trying to . . . [RALPHIE *slams the side door as he goes out into the darkness*] Glenn? . . . [*There is no reply.* HANK, *utterly bewildered, motions* DAN *into the corner and moves cautiously to* CINDY] She's just scared, I guess . . . [*He bends over* CINDY] Miss . . . no need to be . . .

[CINDY *moves with animal swiftness. She grasps* HANK'*s arm and sinks her teeth into his wrist, hard.* HANK *drops the automatic on the floor in front of* CINDY. *He utters a cry of pain and surprise and straightens up, holding his wrist.* DAN *moves in with his right arm encircling* HANK'*s shoulders, pinning his hands to his chest.* CINDY *picks up the automatic and stands ready.* DAN *drags* HANK *to the front door and opens it.* HANK *calls for "Glenn," but* DAN *succeeds in pushing him out the door.* DAN *closes and locks the door as* CINDY *runs across the room to the light switch. She turns off the living room lights. There is only the light flooding down the stairs from the upstairs hall*]

DAN: Ellie! Get on the phone up there! [CINDY *crosses to hand* DAN *the automatic*] Cindy . . . lock the back door!

[*Above,* ELEANOR *goes down the hall and notices the door to* RALPHIE'*s room open. She steps in and calls. Then she goes into the master bedroom and calls*]

ELEANOR: Ralphie! . . . Ralphie!

[CINDY *goes through the dining room on the run and into the pantry, where she locks the side door and returns to the living room*]

DAN: Ellie, for God's sake, get on the phone! Stay away from the windows, hear! [*He impatiently picks up the phone and dials the operator*]

ELEANOR: [*In master bedroom*] Dan! [*She runs to the head of the stairs*]

DAN: Operator. *Operator!*

[CINDY *returns to the living room and starts up the front stairs*]

ELEANOR: Don't, Dan . . . for God's sake! [*Screams*] Dan, don't! *Ralphie's not in the house!*

[CINDY *freezes on the stairs, looks at* DAN. DAN *stands with the phone in his hand*]

OPERATOR: [*On phone*] Operator. Operator. This is your operator. Your call, please? Your call, please? . . .

[DAN *replaces the phone*]

DAN: [A *whisper*] God Almighty!

CINDY: Maybe he got away.

[*Another pause, shorter; then* GLENN *appears outside at the side door with* RALPHIE. GLENN *has* RALPHIE's *arm pinned behind him and holds the boy as a shield. They move to the steps, out of sight of the door*]

GLENN: Hilliard! Can you hear me in there, Hilliard?

RALPHIE: [*Plaintively*] Dad! Dad, he's hurting my arm.

ELEANOR: [*In terror*] Dan, was that Ralphie? *Was that Ralphie?*

DAN: Stay up there, Ellie! [*Calling slightly louder*] Don't shout out there, Griffin! [*Then, lower*] Cindy, take your mother to her room. If you hear a shot . . . make the call!

[DAN *goes through the dining room door and on into the pantry.* CINDY *goes up the front stairs.* ELEANOR *goes into the master bedroom and stands near the door.* CINDY *picks up the extension phone in the upstairs hall, but keeps her hand on the circuit breaker. She is tense, waiting, her attention turned toward the stairs.* DAN *is in the pantry*]

GLENN: [*A loud whisper*] We go now, Hilliard . . . they find the brat in a ditch. [DAN *unlocks and opens the side door*] Turn on the light. And toss out the automatic.

DAN: Let the boy come in, Griffin.

GLENN: Lights first. Then the gun. [DAN *turns on the pantry light. Then he tosses the automatic out.* GLENN *pushes* RALPHIE *up the steps and into the pantry before him*] You're both covered, pop.

RALPHIE: [*Still defiant*] I . . . I tried.

DAN: [*Gently*] So did I. Go up to your mother now.

> [RALPHIE *slips behind the open door and mounts the rear stairs.* HANK *appears outside and picks up the automatic*]

GLENN: [*Casually, to* HANK] Get the lunkhead inside.

> [GLENN *faces* DAN]

HANK: [*Off*] On your feet, Robish.

GLENN: Couldn't wait, could you, pop? Less'n a hour an' you couldn't wait.

> [HANK *appears, the gun in hand, urging a staggering* ROBISH, *who is groggy, holding his head.* HANK *guides him through the pantry and into the living room*]

ROBISH: [*As he passes through the pantry*] Wha' happened? What . . .

HANK: Shut up!

> [ROBISH *and* HANK *appear in the living room.* ROBISH *flops on the sofa.* HANK *stands at the foot of the stairs.* GLENN *closes the side door*]

GLENN: I hadda put Robish on ice for a while, pop . . . 'cause he couldn't learn who was runnin' things aroun' here. I guess I gotta learn you, too.

> [GLENN *strikes* DAN'S *left shoulder with his left fist, violently. Then* GLENN *strikes him a stomach blow with the pistol in his right hand.* DAN *crumples and falls.* GLENN *kneels over him and strikes three violent blows with the pistol.* DAN *doesn't move. All this is very silent.* GLENN *rises, turns and*]

locks the side door . . . and steps over DAN'S *body, goes through the kitchen door and into the living room through the dining room door.* HANK *follows him with his eyes as* GLENN *crosses slowly to sit in the chair at the window. He looks up at* HANK. *Their eyes meet.* HANK *sits slowly on the stairs. The lights begin to dim slowly]*

VERY SLOW CURTAIN

ACT TWO

SHERIFF'S OFFICE

Outside the window, night. The clock reads 12:04. CARSON *seated at desk, plays solitaire.* WINSTON *sits curled up awkwardly on chair.* BARD *leans against files, thumbing through telephone reports. A long pause.* CARSON *glances at his watch.*

CARSON: It's another day . . . in case anyone's interested.

BARD: There's a full moon, too. So what? [*Holding up the reports*] Collect calls . . . person-to-person . . . pay stations. Would you believe this many people sit up talking on the telephone at night? Why the hell don't they go to bed? [*Drops the reports on the desk.*]

WINSTON: Why don't we?

CARSON: [*Picking up the reports*] You've got all the reasons right here. . . . Sickness . . . impulse . . . birth . . . death . . . drunkenness . . . love . . . hate . . .

BARD: What the hell're you . . . a poet or something?

CARSON: It'll break, Bard. You can stretch a wire just so tight.

DUTCH'S VOICE: [*On intercom*] Jess . . . that 11:02 person-to-person from Columbus to Blackstone 2726 . . .

BARD: [*Flipping intercom button*] Yeah, yeah?

DUTCH'S VOICE: It was the daughter calling to say the honeymoon was already a huge success.

BARD: Great!

DUTCH'S VOICE: My theory is this Helen Laski found another guy and climbed in the hay.

[BARD *flips off the intercom.* WINSTON *rises sleepily*]

WINSTON: I'll be in the file room, flat on my face. My theory is this Helen Laski don't believe in telephones. Uses carrier pigeons. Has a secret compartment in her brassiere.

[WINSTON *exits. Outside, a police siren is heard fading in and coming to a stop*]

CARSON: [*Shuffling cards*] You'd find double solitaire kind of restful.

BARD: Carson, you deal me just one of those cards and I'm gonna report you to the FBI. [*Shaking head but smiling faintly*] Isn't it just my luck to meet up with a character like you on a night like this?

CARSON: You're not such hot company yourself. . . . Ten bucks says they're in Denver . . . or New Orleans . . . or Nome, Alaska, by now.

BARD: They're here.

CARSON: Who told you . . . that monkey on your back?

BARD: I say they're here, Carson, because Glenn Griffin's got all kinds of dark pockets in his mind . . . all kinds of weird twists. [*Pacing*] He's always acting, for one thing . . . trying to live up to some phony picture he carries around in that snarled-up brain of his . . . some stupid, childish image of what a really clever criminal should be.

CARSON: [*Shrugs*] Well, that's a good reason. It doesn't explain why he's in town, but it's a good reason. Any others?

BARD: [*Sits*] Carson, did you ever look into the eyes of one of those crazy kids . . . and hear him say, "You got yours coming, copper"? Between his teeth . . . with his broken jaw wired up tight . . . "I'll get you." *That's* why I know he's here and that's why *I'm* going to get to him before he gets to *me*. [*Rises*] Any objections, Carson?

CARSON: No objections, Bard. But if we catch up with him . . . our job's to arrest, if possible.

BARD: You remindin' me who's actually in charge here, Carson?

CARSON: Something like that. My friends call me Harry. [*He goes back to his cards*]

BARD: Well, I'll tell you right now . . . I'm making no promises . . . Harry.

DIMOUT

HILLIARD HOME

Dimness over all the house. GLENN *is at the living room window, smoking. The window curtains are parted slightly.* HANK *is in the pantry, sitting on the back stairs.* CINDY *sits in* RALPHIE'S *bedroom.* RALPHIE *is on the bed asleep. In the master bedroom,* DAN *is stretched out on the bed with a damp towel folded and placed over his forehead.* ELEANOR *sits on the twin bed, facing him, with a dry towel in her hands.*

ELEANOR: [*Softly*] Darling . . . can you hear me? I want you to promise . . .

DAN: What? Oh . . . I must've dozed off. Isn't that . . . remarkable?

ELEANOR: You needed it. I slipped off myself several times . . . but I heard every sound . . . every car that went by.

> [DAN *stirs*]

DAN: What time is it?

> [ELEANOR *reaches out and turns on the lamp on the night table between the beds. She looks at the clock on the table*]

ELEANOR: After one . . .

DAN: [*Trying to sit up*] Midnight. He said mid . . .

ELEANOR: Shhh. Don't move. Listen. What you did—what you tried —that was a foolish and terrible and wonderful thing . . . [*Shakes her head as though trying to clear it*] No, no, that's not what I meant to say. Dan, you must never do anything like that again. Ever. You . . . you might have been killed. I want you to promise me now. Dan, are you listening?

DAN: What're they doing down there? Why haven't they gone?

ELEANOR: Dan, please. Nobody knows anything about what's happening here. Nobody in the world. We're all alone in this. Dan, I'm pleading with you. . . .

DAN: Ellie . . . how long has it been since I said I love you?

ELEANOR: Dan . . .

DAN: Why shouldn't a man say it? Why didn't I say it all the time . . . over and over?

ELEANOR: You didn't need . . .

DAN: Ellie, why'm I so grouchy in the mornings? No, that's not what I mean . . . I mean . . . what's the matter, people don't laugh more? Waking up . . . seeing the sun . . . That . . . that was a funny joke Ralphie told . . . about the moron and the icebox.

ELEANOR: [*Smiling wanly*] Not very . . .

DAN: All right, it was lousy. Is that any reason not to laugh? [*In awe*] God . . . this morning. How many hours ago? It's . . . it's like looking back on something that happened . . . a whole lifetime ago. [*Reaches out his right hand to her face*] Your face . . . darling, you're beautiful. Do you know that? I must've been deaf, dumb, and blind. For years.

ELEANOR: [*Takes his hand in hers*] Dan . . . you haven't promised.

[DAN *sits up with difficulty*]

DAN: Ellie . . . I can't. I'm feeling along a blank wall. In the dark. If I find a hole . . . or even a crack . . . I've got to explore it. There's light behind that wall, Ellie. I never knew how much. There was light there once and there's got to be light again!

ELEANOR: Dan, look at yourself. Your head. Next time . . . you don't know. *You don't know.* He'll kill you.

DAN: [*Grimly*] He won't kill me as long as he needs me. [*Suddenly*] You look so *tired.* Damn them! [*Gently*] When this is over, we're going to have a maid here. A full-time maid.

ELEANOR: You wouldn't really like it, Dan. None of us like having strangers in the . . .

[*She breaks off, realizing what she is saying. Their eyes meet. Pause. Then, there is the sound of a branch cracking off a tree and brushing down the side of the house. She starts and crumples.* DAN *holds her. Below,* GLENN *looks out the living room window.* HANK *rises and looks out the window in the side door*]

DAN: It's all right, dear. It's all right. Only one of those dead branches off the oak. [*He takes her into his arms*] My God, Ellie . . . it's a jungle. We jump at nothing. That's how you slept, isn't it . . . like an animal in the . . .

[*The telephone rings, cutting him off. In the living room,* GLENN *quickly steps to the phone and turns on the hall light.* HANK *runs up the back stairs to the extension phone in the upstairs hall.* CINDY *rises and opens the door of* RALPHIE'S *room.* RALPHIE *doesn't stir.* DAN *opens the bedroom door*]

GLENN: I'll take it, Hank.

HANK: [*Ready at the phone upstairs*] I'm here, Glenn.

[HANK *takes up the phone after* GLENN *answers and stands staring at* CINDY *in the door of* RALPHIE'S *room as he listens*]

GLENN: [*Picks up the phone downstairs*] Hello? . . . Put her on. . . . Yeah, this is Mr. James. *Put her on!* . . . Hi, doll, what's up? . . . Where are you? . . . Mmm—okay, get this. That stuff you're carrying . . . put it in a envelope . . . an' take down this address . . . Daniel C. Hilliard . . .

[GLENN *continues, but his voice is under the following dialogue so that the address is not heard*]

HANK: [*To* CINDY, *harshly*] Stay inside an' shut the door, redhead.

[CINDY, *in defiance, doesn't move*]

ELEANOR: Dan, what is it?

DAN: Shhh . . .

GLENN: [*Under above dialogue*] . . . 243 North Central Avenue. . . . Soon's I get it, we'll make tracks, doll. . . . See you Louisville. You know where.

[GLENN *hangs up.* HANK *replaces the extension phone and comes down the front stairs and is about to go into the dining room. He stops in door when* DAN *comes downstairs*]

ELEANOR: [*Follows* DAN *to the bedroom door*] Dan!

DAN: [*As he comes down the stairs*] Griffin! Who was that? What's happening?

GLENN: [*Casually*] Tell you in the morning, pop . . . after breakfast.

DAN: [*Shocked*] After break— You'll tell me now!

GLENN: [*Angry*] What's another day, pop? Get some shuteye. You're gonna need it.

[GLENN *turns his back on* DAN *and walks toward the window.* DAN *starts toward* GLENN]

HANK: Glenn! Watch it!

[GLENN *whirls.* DAN *stops, looks at* HANK, *then at* GLENN, *and turns and goes up the stairs.* ELEANOR *moves into bedroom and stands waiting for* DAN. CINDY, *who has been waiting at the head of the stairs, goes into her room and closes the door.* GLENN *goes to the window, picks up the road map from the table, and stands in the window, studying it.* HANK *goes into the pantry and stands looking out the window of the side door*]

ELEANOR: [*As* DAN *comes into the bedroom*] Well? . . .

DAN: [*Flatly, low*] They're not going.

ELEANOR: Oh, Dan, no!

DAN: [*Suddenly the violence in him mounts to a determined grimness*] They're going!

[DAN *turns to the door.* ELEANOR *stops him. The following builds in intensity until they are almost snarling at each other*]

ELEANOR: Dan, you promised, you promised!

DAN: [*Erupting slightly*] Ellie, don't tie my hands! I'm tied up enough already!

ELEANOR: [*Desperately*] If you go down there now, something terrible is going to happen. I know it. I *feel* it.

DAN: How long can we go on sitting on top of a volcano?

ELEANOR: [*Takes his hand, tugging at him*] Dan, you're going to lie down now! I'm telling you!

DAN: [*Shouting, throws her off*] You're not telling me what to do! [*Pause. They are appalled. They stand looking at each other for a moment. Then they go into each other's arms.* DAN *says, almost whispering*] Ellie, what're we doing? What're we *doing*? [*Slight pause*] How can he know, that scum down there . . . how can he know how to do this? A boy who never loved anyone in his life.

[ELEANOR *turns out the bed lamp and sits on the bed.* DAN *sits beside her and puts his arms around her. Below,* CLENN *flicks the map with his fingers and exits; goes into the pantry.* HANK *turns away from the door*]

HANK: Glenn . . . we gotta get outta here. What if they trace that call?

GLENN: [*Grinning*] You ever hear of a burg called Circleville, Ohio? It's nineteen miles south-a Columbus. Them dumb coppers might be tracin' calls outta Columbus, Hank, but not outta no jerk town like Circleville.

HANK: [*Turns back to the window*] We'd be better off anywhere but here.

GLENN: It can't be nowhere else but here. With that much dough . . . in this town . . . I can have that copper put on ice for good.

HANK: [*Shaking his head*] That one idea . . .

GLENN: Yeah, that one idea. Kid, you gotta stick with me on this. You're . . . Hank, you're all I got. You know that. It's you'n me against 'em all!

HANK: [*Trapped: conflicting emotions. He turns to the window*] I know, I know . . .

[GLENN *grabs him, turns him around*]

GLENN: You know . . . you know! You don't know nothin'! I gotta get this outta my brain. I gotta sleep again. You didn't lay in that bed . . . pain twistin' down in your gut . . . months . . . jaw clamped up in a vise . . . eatin' that slop through a tube . . . months . . . Till pretty soon there ain't nothin' in your mind but the face-a the guy that done it. Me with my hands up . . . tossin' out my gun . . . and that bastard walkin' up'n cloutin' me. I can still hear the way the bone cracked . . . *An' me with my hands up!*

BLACKOUT

SHERIFF'S OFFICE

Clock: 6:15. Early morning. CARSON *is seated.* BARD *is rising from behind the desk.*

BARD: Yeah, he had his hands up. Trying to surrender. *After* he'd plugged one of the best damn cops ever walked. While Jerry was laying there twisting and screaming in the gutter . . . with a bullet in a nerve . . . *then* Griffin throws out his empty gun and steps out of the doorway of that hotel, big as life. Only I didn't let him get away with it. I let him have it. One crack . . . right in that grinning face of his. [*Rubbing his fist*] If I'd only arrested him . . . or shot him before he gave up . . . he'd probably've forgotten it. But according to *his* warped code, *I* double-crossed *him.*

CARSON: [*Quietly*] Under the circumstances . . . police code, too.

BARD: [*Leans over desk*] Listen! That kid's as ruthless as they come! He'd as soon kill a human being as step on a bug.

CARSON: All right . . . so civilization didn't take. In his case. But we've climbed a long way out of the slime, Jess. Maybe that slime still clings to some of us. *Them.* But you're a police officer, Jess . . . and civilized men can't let the slime on *them* drag *us* back down. If we don't live by the rules, the rules will soon disappear. Then . . . [*Shrugs*] we're all right back where we started.

BARD: Rules! He was sentenced to ten years. He'd have been out again anyway inside of three more.

CARSON: Which only proves it's a pretty ramshackle system. But it's all we've got. You had no right to break his jaw. And if we find him, you've no right to kill him unless it's the only way to stop him.

BARD: [*Sits on edge of desk; bitterly*] Sure, send him back to that cardboard prison . . . so he can start all over again.

CARSON: No choice, Jess. Unless you want to become just like him.

In that case, he wins, anyway. [*Rises*] I'm ready for breakfast. How about you?

[BARD, *thoughtful for a moment, looks at* CARSON, *rises*]

BARD: Yeah.

DIMOUT

HILLIARD HOME

It is morning. ELEANOR *is seated on the sofa,* RALPHIE *beside her.* HANK *stands at the window, smoking.* DAN *is entering from the dining room, followed by* GLENN. GLENN *picks his teeth with finger and wipes hand on sofa*]

GLENN: Lady, that 'as a goddam good breakfast. [*Takes* HANK'S *cigarette, turns to* DAN] Hilliard, you ever broke, your woman can support you good. Cookin'. [*Takes a drag on the cigarette and returns it to* HANK]

DAN: [*Sitting in chair*] How much longer, Griffin?

GLENN: Hell, you don't have any worse headache'n Robish 'n there . . . [*Gestures into the den*] and he's nursin' a hangover to boot.

DAN: [*Level and insistent*] How long?

GLENN: Till I get a certain envelope in the mail. Meantime . . . everything goes on just like before aroun' here. You'n the redhead go to work.

HANK: Glenn, if he's gonna be gone all day outta the house . . .

GLENN: You don't trust Hilliard, Hank? Now me—I trust the old gink. You know why? I got him where the hair's short, that's why. Junior here gets a break. He misses a day of school. [CINDY *comes out of her room and down the stairs*] Won't hurt you none, kid. Missed a few myself.

CINDY: [*At foot of stairs; scornfully*] And look at you.

RALPHIE: [*Kneeling on sofa*] I'd just as soon go . . .

GLENN: [*Crosses to* CINDY] Yeah, you're lookin', sis. Pass you on the street, you'd look right through us both. You're seein' us now, redhead.

CINDY: No comment.

GLENN: [*To* DAN] Now, get the lead outta your . . . [*The thud of the newspaper is heard against the front door. The* HILLIARDS *are not startled but* GLENN *and* HANK *jump into action.* HANK, *drawing the automatic, moves up to the door.* GLENN, *with the .38 ready, covers the family.* HANK *unlocks and opens the door a crack. He kneels down and reaches out with his left hand to bring in the paper.* HANK *rises, closing the door, and hands the paper to* GLENN. GLENN *unfolds the paper.* HANK *locks the door.* RALPHIE, *who has been watching it all, snickers. After a split-second pause*] Get your kicks young, kid. [*To* DAN] You don't want to be late for that time-clock, pop.

[ELEANOR *rises and crosses to* GLENN, *fire in her eyes*]

ELEANOR: Why do you want to go on torturing my husband? You know what he'll be thinking . . . wondering . . . imagining . . . in that office! You take pleasure in torturing him, don't you?

GLENN: [*Easily*] Lady, I take pleasure in looking out for my own skin . . . and Hank's.

DAN: [*In warning*] Ellie . . .

ELEANOR: No, no, it's some sort of cruel, inhuman, sadistic game with you! You're playing a *game!*

[*Abruptly, she explodes into violence; slaps* GLENN *full across the face.* DAN *steps in, grabs her and swings her around to the far end of the sofa, then turns to look at* GLENN. *The family is in a small group, defiant. Long pause, while* GLENN *rubs his jaw*]

GLENN: [*Quietly, sitting*] Whole family gettin' tough this morning. Nothin' personal, ma'am.

DAN: [*Grimly, knowing*] It's personal all right! In some strange mixed-up way.

GLENN: Clickety-click. Don't get ulcers tryin' to dope it, pop. [*To* CINDY] You, redhead. Keep that pretty mouth shut today, see. Or that boy friend of yours ain't gonna want to take you on no more rides. Not after Robish gets done with you.

[*Pause*]

DAN: [*Deciding*] I'm not leaving this house today!

GLENN: [*Hardening*] You ain't learned yet who's runnin' it?

HANK: [*Steps near* GLENN] Glenn, I think . . .

GLENN: [*Rising; exploding*] You think! With what? I'm lookin' out for you, you slobberin' pukin' little bastard. Now get in there and turn on the news reports! [GLENN *turns to* DAN] You ain't had nothin', pop. Nothin' like what you deserve.

DAN: Deserve? . . .

GLENN: Yeah . . . deserve! You'n your fancy carpet and your big lawn'n your goddam snazzy car!

DAN: [*Takes a step toward* GLENN] Griffin . . . [ELEANOR *touches* DAN's *arm to restrain him but he pulls away and continues*] you're not going to take it out on me and my family because you hate the world! I've worked for every cent I ever made . . . worked hard . . . for this house, that car . . . and I'm proud of it! That table you've scarred with your whisky . . . the furniture you've wiped your filthy hands on . . . the carpet you've burnt holes in. Proud because I *did* work for it!

GLENN: [*Spits on carpet with contempt*] Sucker! Just like our old man, ain't he, Hank?

DAN: I pity the poor man!

GLENN: Don't waste your time. He kicked off while we was in reform school. He was a *proud* bastard, too. Now get outta here!

DAN: I'm staying right here!

GLENN: [*Violent*] Hilliard, I told you . . . [*Changes—shrugs*] Okay . . . [*Sits*] Okay . . . You stay . . . an' we stay. 'Cause we ain't gonna beat it outta here till we get that dough. An' that dough's in a letter . . . addressed to you . . . at your office. [*Pause. The fight goes out of* DAN] We don't want no Federal men tracin' anything up to your front door here, do we? . . . See, pop, I'm thinkin' of you.

[ELEANOR *takes* DAN's *arm*]

ELEANOR: He'll go. He's going. [*As* CINDY *moves to closet and gets her own coat and brings* DAN's *coat to him*] Dan, I'll be upstairs with Ralphie. If one of them starts up the stairs, I'll scream so loud they'll *have* to use their guns. That'll be the end of it. For them, too. Now I'll get your coat. It's getting colder every minute . . .

[CINDY *already stands waiting with* DAN'S *coat*]

DAN: I . . . I can hold my own coat, Cindy.

CINDY: Maybe I'd *like* to hold your coat.

[DAN *climbs into coat, then turns to* ELEANOR]

ELEANOR: Careful now, Dan . . . I know, I say that every morning of the world, don't I?

[DAN *takes* ELEANOR *in his arms. They kiss . . . with great meaning and tenderness, in sharp contrast to yesterday morning's casual good-bye.* GLENN *makes a kissing sound with his mouth, then makes a pop with his finger in his mouth.* HANK *takes a step down as* GLENN *laughs mockingly*]

HANK: What's so funny? [*As* GLENN *frowns, the laughter dying*] I don't see nothin' so funny, you should break your neck laughin'.

GLENN: I laugh when I feel like it. You don't have a goddam thing to say about it! That right? . . . That right, Hank?

HANK: I never had nothin' to say about anything.

[HANK *turns on his heel and goes through the dining room door and into the pantry.* CINDY *steps down to* RALPHIE, *and tousles his hair*]

CINDY: [*Softly*] Mister pest to you.

GLENN: You, Hilliard. That nick on your head—you got a story ready? 'Cause it wouldn't take much of a slip today, pop. Just a little one and . . . you're gonna wish you never come back through that door.

DAN: [*Quietly, with dignity and force*] Griffin . . . you're staying here now for only one reason. To get a man killed. A man who did something to you. I couldn't understand that before. Now I can. I understand it because I'm more like you now than you know. If any harm comes to anyone in this house, Griffin, I'm going to kill you. Me. No matter what it takes . . . whether the police capture you first or not . . . if it takes my whole life, Griffin, I'll find you and I'll kill you. Do you understand that?

GLENN: [*Impressed but attempting swagger*] Pop . . . you're a regular comedian.

DAN: *Do you understand that?*

GLENN: Sure, pop . . . I got you. All the way.

DAN: And if not you, Griffin . . . your brother.

GLENN: [*Immediately tense, violent; leaps up*] You come near Hank and . . .

DAN: [*Firmly*] That's the deal, Griffin. That's the deal. You've turned me into your kind of animal now.

> [GLENN *does not move.* DAN *turns, takes a long look at* RALPHIE, *then* ELEANOR. CINDY *opens the door.* DAN *follows* CINDY *out, closing the door behind him*]

GLENN: [*Moving up to the door*] Lady . . . you didn't know what a tough old bird you married, did you?

ELEANOR: [*Softly*] No. No, I didn't. [*She sits quietly*]

GLENN: [*Calls*] Robish! [*As* GLENN *moves into the dining room,* ROBISH *enters from the den and sits. He is suffering from a hangover and from last night's violence.* GLENN *appears in the pantry.* HANK *is now standing at the window of the side door, watching* DAN *and* CINDY *drive away.* GLENN *stands for a moment, looks down at the radio, bends down and turns it on. Music rises*] You ain't interested in the news?

HANK: Same old stuff. That car. That's all they got. [*Faces* GLENN *suddenly*] Glenn . . . why're you crowdin' it? Why go on takin' these chances?

GLENN: You don't take chances, you might as well be dead.

> [*The sound of an old truck approaching fades in*]

HANK: That's what we're gonna be . . . all of us . . . this keeps up.

GLENN: You start yammerin' again, I'm gonna give you a belt across the . . . [*They hear the truck. Immediate tension.* GLENN *tries to see out the window of the side door, then rushes into the living room.* ELEANOR *has risen and crossed up to the window.*

HANK *stays looking out the window of the side door*] Who is it, lady?

ELEANOR: Only Mr. Patterson. He . . . he hauls away the trash.

GLENN: Okay, let him get it and clear out.

ELEANOR: Only . . . he'll . . . this is the end of the month. He'll come to the door to collect.

GLENN: [*Calls*] Hank! [HANK *leaves the pantry and comes into living room*] Okay, pay him. [ELEANOR *goes to pick up her checkbook from sofa.* GLENN *turns to* RALPHIE] Upstairs, kid. And not a squeak. [RALPHIE, *on sofa, folds arms, doesn't move*] Take him up, Hank, and keep his mouth shut.

> [HANK *lifts* RALPHIE *off the sofa, sets him on his feet and pushes him upstairs.* ELEANOR *goes into the pantry.* MR. PATTERSON *appears outside and knocks at the side door. Above,* HANK *stands at the door of* RALPHIE's *room, listening.* RALPHIE *sits on the bed*]

ROBISH: [*Miserable*] My gut's growling.

GLENN: Knock off!

ROBISH: Jeez, I forgot what a headache feels like . . .

GLENN: Shut up!

> [ELEANOR *opens the side door and admits* MR. PATTERSON *to the pantry*]

ELEANOR: Just a minute. Mr. Patterson, while I . . . You stay here, please . . .

PATTERSON: [*Pushes right in*] Don't mind if I do . . . [ELEANOR *returns to the living room*] Wind always puts a nasty nip in the air . . . raises merry . . . [*He sees that* ELEANOR *has gone, raises his voice*] . . . raises merry Cain with my arthritis.

> [PATTERSON, *through the following, notices with interest the small radio, the stacked cigarette butts, the chair. He gathers up the newspapers and places them on the chair, glancing with some interest at the headlines. In the living room,* ELEANOR *sits on the sofa and writes the check on the coffee table.* GLENN *leans over the back of the sofa, watching her*]

GLENN: [*Whispers*] You always pay the old gink with a check?

ROBISH: Who the hell is it?

[GLENN *silences* ROBISH *with a gesture*]

ELEANOR: Yes, yes, my husband . . . [*Then firmly*] . . . my husband thinks it's not safe to have cash in the house. [*Signs*] That's funny, isn't it?

PATTERSON: You speaking to me, Mrs. Hilliard?

ELEANOR: [*Rises*] No, Mr. Patterson, I'm coming.

[GLENN *stops* ELEANOR, *takes the check and examines it*]

GLENN: Hank's upstairs with the brat. Be careful!

[*He returns the check to* ELEANOR, *who goes into the pantry*]

ROBISH: [*Rises*] Who is that out . . .

GLENN: [*At dining room door, listening*] Shut up!

[ROBISH *and* GLENN *listen,* GLENN *holding the dining room door slightly open*]

PATTERSON: [*As* ELEANOR *enters the pantry*] You . . . uh . . . got company, Mrs. Hilliard?

ELEANOR: Company?

PATTERSON: Well . . . I notice things, y'know. Always have. [*Takes the check from* ELEANOR'S *hand*] Thank you, thank you! [*Peering*] You feelin' yourself, Mrs. Hilliard?

ELEANOR: [*Desperate to get him out*] Only . . . I've got a slight cold. Nothing . . .

PATTERSON: [*Turns and opens the door*] We-ell, lotta colds around. Flu, too. Bad year for the flu, y'know. [*In the doorway, he turns back*] Your daughter buy herself another one of them secondhand cars?

ELEANOR: [*Holding the door open for him*] No. No!

[*In panic, she closes the door in his face, leans against it.* GLENN *rushes into the pantry, followed by* ROBISH. HANK *looks out the window of* RALPHIE'S *room.* PATTERSON,

after a look back at the house, disappears. GLENN *pushes*
ELEANOR *upstage and looks out the window of the side
door]*

ROBISH: He's snoopin' around the garage.

ELEANOR: Oh, no, he's only taking the trash from the containers
alongside.

ROBISH: Up on his toes lookin' in the windows!

ELEANOR: On Thursday mornings he always . . .

HANK: [*Leaving* RALPHIE's *room to run down back stairs*] Glenn!
He wrote something down.

ROBISH: Griffin, that joker wrote down the license. I seen him! Fork
over the gun.

ELEANOR: I'm sure he . . .

GLENN: [*Locked in indecision*] Dry up, both-a-you, I'm thinkin'.

ROBISH: He's climbin' in the cab of the truck. *Gimme the gun!* I
can hop on the back.

HANK: [*At foot of back stairs*] Glenn . . . we don't want a murder
rap ridin' us!

[GLENN *meets* HANK's *eyes, then, with a smile of defiance
and revenge, hands the gun to* ROBISH. *The truck door is
heard being slammed. Then, the motor starting and failing
—starting and failing under the following]*

GLENN: [*To* ROBISH] You call me on the phone. An' stay outta
sight till it's dark, see. I'll have Hilliard bring you back. Use your
head for a change!

ROBISH: [*Going out the side door on the run*] My head feels
better already.

[*As* ROBISH *disappears, the truck motor catches and we
hear it start up, shift, and drive away.* HANK *looks pale
and sick.* ELEANOR, *stunned, moves dazedly toward the living
room]*

ELEANOR: He . . . he knew nothing. [*Corrects self*] Knows nothing.
[*She goes into the living room and sinks onto the sofa slowly,
beginning to weep]*

HANK: Glenn, are you crazy? Hilliard won't bring Robish back in here.

GLENN: He will when I'm done with him on the phone. Pop don't want Robish picked up any more'n we do . . . an' tippin' the cops this address. [*Suddenly grabs* HANK, *pushes him against wall of the pantry*] What's the matter with you anyway, kid? You got a weak stomach after all? [HANK *turns his head away*] What're you stewin' about? You're free, ain't you?

HANK: [*Wrenches himself loose, starts for kitchen door*] I was free-er in that cell!

> [HANK *goes into the living room. After a second* GLENN *follows him.* HANK *ignores* GLENN *and goes to the den door with a side glance at* ELEANOR; *he slams the door.* GLENN *is baffled and angry*]

GLENN: [*To* ELEANOR] Lady! Shut up that wailin'! Go some place else'n cry!

> [ELEANOR *rises slowly and, with difficulty, mounts the stairs*]

ELEANOR: Poor man . . . that poor old man . . . he wouldn't hurt a fly.

DIMOUT

SHERIFF'S OFFICE

Darkness outside. WINSTON *is seated,* BARD *is pacing.*

BARD: Who'd want to pump three slugs in the back of an innocent old guy like that?

WINSTON: Who can say? Somebody settling an old score . . . old crony he cheated at cards . . .

BARD: Sixty-three years old, half-crippled with arthritis . . . wouldn't harm a fly. [BARD *looks up as* FREDERICKS *enters.* LT. FREDERICKS *is an older man, crisp and efficient, with a weathered face. He wears a State Police uniform*] Fredericks, are we going to get that stuff from the state's attorney's office or aren't we?

FREDERICKS: Carson's prying it out of them. Bard, why make so much of an old garbage man gettin' bumped?

BARD: He was killed by a .38. The prison guard at Terre Haute . . .

FREDERICKS: Sure, there's only one .38 in the state! Deputy, you got an obsession. You can't tie in *every* crime in the area with those three.

BARD: I reckon not, Lieutenant. Only *you* tell *me* why anybody'd . . . [*Breaks off as* CARSON *enters*] Well, Carson?

CARSON: [*Tearing the top off large manila envelope which he has brought in, emptying the contents on the desk during the following*] Claude Patterson died at the hands of person or persons unknown. All I've got is the junk the old man was carrying in his pockets when they found the body. [*Handling the items*] Checks . . . Seventeen one-dollar bills . . . Ball-point pen . . . A snuff box . . . Wallet . . . Usual stuff. Driver's license . . . Photograph of a younger girl, taken forty years ago, at least.

BARD: [*Examining checks*] Checks made out to Claude Patterson, some to cash. Thirteen for three dollars, two for six bucks.

WINSTON: The guy made more'n I do.

CARSON: Some scraps of paper . . .

[BARD *smoothes them out during the following*]

WINSTON: [*To* CARSON] How long ago do they figure it happened?

CARSON: Before noon, coroner said. Old man must've run into the woods from the truck. A hunter came across the body just before dusk. City police found the truck parked alongside a service station other side of . . .

BARD: [*Very, very quietly*] Hold it. [*Low whistle of amazement between teeth*] God! Look't this . . . [*As others examine the scrap of paper*] State's attorney's office examined this stuff?

CARSON: [*As he looks at paper*] That was my impression. [*Then softly, too*] Good Lord!

WINSTON: [*An excited whisper*] Patterson might've got just a quick glance. In a hurry, y'know . . .

FREDERICKS: [*Cynically*] He heard it on the radio . . . jotted it down just in case.

WINSTON: But if you change that 3 to a 8, you got it. Maybe his eyes . . . a old man like that . . .

BARD: [*Thoughtfully*] Or there was mud on the plate.

WINSTON: Jesse, if you change that 3 to a 8, you got it!

BARD: [*With throb in voice*] Just for a while . . . just for a little while now . . . we're *going* to change that 3 to an 8. We'll just kinda pretend Mr. Patterson didn't *own* a radio. We're gonna pretend he saw that license. Tom . . . these checks. Start working backwards! [*As* WINSTON *rises*] Names, addresses, telephone numbers, where they work. Everything!

FREDERICKS: Sure, let's go on a wild-goose chase . . . break the monotony.

BARD: Those were the last people saw him alive. These and whatever other customers live in that neighborhood. Let's find that neighborhood and let's scour it down with a wire brush.

WINSTON: Go ahead, Jess, say it.

BARD: I don't like to say it, Tom . . .

WINSTON: Say it, Jess. [*To* CARSON *as he exits*] He was right. . . . This is it!

BARD: God, it might be. Right here in town!

FREDERICKS: You want any more troopers on it, lemme know. My men got nothing else to do. [*He exits*]

BARD: [*Sitting at the desk*] Any bets now, Carson? Any bets that beat-up gray car isn't in that neighborhood somewhere? Any bets, Harry?

CARSON: No bets, Jess.

BARD: [*Flips intercom, speaks into it*] Dutch. Get me a city map in here. And a city directory! [*Flips off intercom. To* CARSON] Now. If only we can get to 'em before some other innocent citizen stumbles across their path . . .

BLACKOUT

HILLIARD HOME

Evening. Living room lights are on. Light in RALPHIE'S *room is on. The door chimes sound.* ELEANOR *stands facing the door.* GLENN *is moving from the window to the stairs.* HANK *is in door of den, automatic ready. Above,* RALPHIE *sits on his bed with a small toy. The door chime is heard a second time.*

GLENN: Okay, lady, answer it. But careful.

[*He goes up the stairs until he is out of sight of the front door.* ELEANOR *looks at* HANK, *then goes to the front door and unlocks and opens it slightly.* MISS SWIFT *barges right in and* HANK *ducks into the den and closes the door, leaving it open enough to hear and also cover the people in the room.* GLENN *moves around the bend of the landing and stands near the head of the stairs, listening.* MISS SWIFT *is youngish, pert*]

MISS SWIFT: [*As she pushes into the room*] Good evening, Mrs. Hilliard, I've come to see Ralph.

ELEANOR: [*Standing with the door open wide*] Oh . . . yes. [*Glances nervously upstairs*] Yes . . . [*Speaks for* GLENN'S *benefit*] Ralphie, it's your teacher. Miss Swift.

[ELEANOR *closes the door. Upstairs,* RALPHIE *opens the door of his room and starts down the hall; but, seeing* GLENN, *he returns to his room and stands listening at the door*]

MISS SWIFT: [*As she moves down*] You see, Ralph so rarely misses a day at school that I thought I'd drop by to . . . [*She stops, looking at the disordered room; her manner changes*] I . . . I daresay I should have telephoned first.

ELEANOR: [*Nervously*] Oh, no, no, that's perfectly all . . . [*Abruptly*] Please sit down.

MISS SWIFT: [*Sits on sofa*] I do hope that Ralph isn't seriously ill . . .

[*She realizes that she is sitting on an uncomfortable object, reaches back and brings out the empty whisky bottle, which she places on the coffee table*]

ELEANOR: [*With a valiant effort at control*] Only . . . just a cold. But we thought it best not to expose the other children.

[*Above,* RALPHIE *turns from the door of his room, picks up a composition book and a pencil from the bookshelves beside the bed. He sits in the chair writing in the composition book through the following*]

MISS SWIFT: My dear Mrs. Hilliard, there is no such thing as a cold. Have you had a doctor's opinion?

ELEANOR: No. That is, we thought we could doctor it ourselves. . . .

MISS SWIFT: Mrs. Hilliard, how could you *possibly* doctor it yourself if you're convinced it's a *cold*? One member of a class stays home one day, and whoosh, it goes through the entire room. Not the germs, you understand, but the *idea* of the germs. [*She rises and moves quickly to stairs*] Perhaps I'd better have a look at him myself.

[GLENN *quickly ducks out of sight and down the back stairs.* ELEANOR *moves fast and stops* MISS SWIFT *on the third step*]

ELEANOR: No, you can't!

RALPHIE: [*Calling from his room*] I'll be down in a minute, Miss Swift!

MISS SWIFT: Well, of course, if I've come . . .

RALPHIE: I'm just finishing my composition!

MISS SWIFT: [*Smiling*] Your son, Mrs. Hilliard, is going to be a brilliant author some day . . . [CINDY *enters through front door, followed by* DAN *and* ROBISH] You mark my . . . [*She breaks off as she sees* DAN] Mr. Hilliard?

[CINDY *stops.* ROBISH, *after one glance at* MISS SWIFT, *closes the door and stands against the frame with his back to her*]

ELEANOR: Dan, you . . . uh . . . remember Miss Swift. Ralphie's teacher! [DAN *glances from den to rear hall, immediately alert*] Ralphie, are you *coming*?

DAN: Sure I remember. How're you, Miss Swift?

ELEANOR: Miss Swift . . . dropped in to see how Ralphie was feeling.

[*As* MISS SWIFT *stares at* DAN, *he makes his decision. He is drunk! He immediately goes into a muted drunk act, turns to* ROBISH]

DAN: She did, did she? What do you think of that . . . Johnny? That's what I call a nice little old PTA practice. [*Ushering* ROBISH *toward the dining room*] You know where I keep it, Johnny. Help yourself. [MISS SWIFT *stares at* ROBISH *as he, keeping his face turned away from her, moves into the dining room. He turns, when out of her line of vision, and draws the .38 from his pocket as the dining room door closes.* DAN *grabs* MISS SWIFT *by the arm, turning her away from* ROBISH] Miss Swift! Met old pal Johnny at a . . . [*Turns to* CINDY] Cindy, say hello to Miss Swift. [CINDY *and* MISS SWIFT *exchange nods.* DAN *sits on sofa*] Whew, has Cindy been laying it to me! Leave it to Cindy to know where to find her old man.

[ROBISH *appears in pantry, speaks to* GLENN, *who is listening. Above,* RALPHIE *starts down the stairs*]

ROBISH: She seen me!

GLENN: *Clam up!*

DAN: [*Picks up whisky bottle from coffee table and upends it into coffee cup*] Where does the stuff go in this house? [*He lays the bottle flat on the coffee table*]

RALPHIE: [*On stair, one step above* MISS SWIFT] I . . . I finished my composition for this week, Miss Swift.

MISS SWIFT: [*Nonplused, takes composition book*] I'll . . . I'll see that you get full credit, Ralph.

[*She turns and steps down one step, but* DAN *stops her*]

DAN: [*In a commanding tone*] Miss Swift! [*He rises and goes to foot of stairs*] I'll take that, please. [*He takes the composition book from her hands rudely, opens it and reads, then looks up at* RALPHIE, *who turns and runs up the stairs and into his own room, where he stands listening at the partly closed door*] So . . . so this is what they call a composition nowadays. You . . . you encourage such drivel, Miss Swift?

MISS SWIFT: Mr. Hilliard . . . in all fairness . . . I don't think you're in any condition to discuss *anything* tonight.

DAN: In that case, I'll read it in the morning.

[MISS SWIFT *glances upstairs, then comes down and crosses to* ELEANOR, *places a hand on her arm*]

MISS SWIFT: Mrs. Hilliard, let me assure you that what I've seen here tonight will in no way affect my belief in Ralph.

[*After a glance back at* DAN, *she goes quickly to the front door, opens it, and marches out, closing the door. Immediately,* HANK *rushes in from the den and up to the front door and locks it, then moves to the window and stands looking out.* ELEANOR *crosses toward* DAN, *who sinks into the chair.* ROBISH *enters from the dining room, followed by* GLENN]

ELEANOR: Oh, Dan . . . Dan, how did you ever? . . .

ROBISH: Griffin, we gotta stop that dame!

HANK: Sure, Robish . . . shoot up the whole town!

ROBISH: She seen *me!*

DAN: She wasn't looking at you!

GLENN: Old guy's right, Robish. Hilliard took her mind offa you. Stand up, pop! [DAN *rises and* GLENN *frisks him*] Gotta hand it to you, Hilliard. You had that dame in a real stew. You'd of made a great con man. [*To* ELEANOR] Get up there with that smart brat.

[ELEANOR *turns and goes up the stairs*]

HANK: Glenn . . . this is goin' on too long.

GLENN: [*Ignoring* HANK] Robish, did you get that piece of paper outta the old guy's pocket?

ROBISH: Couldn't. He jumped outta the truck.

GLENN: You dumb goddam . . .

ROBISH: [*Displaying the pistol*] He didn't get far.

GLENN: [*Reaching for it*] I'll take the .38 now, Robish.

ROBISH: [*Holds it away*] I kinda like th' feel of it.

[*Pause; a silent duel*]

GLENN: [*An effort to hold his command*] Get on the back door!

ROBISH: Get on the back door yourself, Griffin! Stuff it!

[ROBISH *laughs defiantly, pockets the gun and sits*]

DAN: Griffin . . . the money didn't come to the office today.

GLENN: [*His mind on* ROBISH *and the gun*] Dope it yourself, pop, you're so smart.

DAN: You didn't really expect it.

GLENN: Mail takes time. You should-a thought of that. It wasn't mailed till early this mornin'. [*Grinning, turns to* DAN] Ought to get here some time tomorrow.

[*Pause. General shock*]

HANK: [*Bleakly*] Tomorrow?

DAN: [*To* GLENN, *angrily*] Why, you young . . .

GLENN: Take it easy, pop . . . 'n stay healthy. [*To* HANK] Yeah . . . tomorrow. What's one more night?

HANK: [*Low*] Christ!

DAN: Griffin, I've played your filthy game up to now . . . but by bringing that ape back here after he killed a man . . .

ROBISH: [*Threatening, under his breath*] Who you callin' a ape?

DAN: . . . we're accessories now.

GLENN: That's right, Hilliard. You're on our side now. [*To* HANK] I'll take the automatic, kid.

HANK: [*Takes a backward step away from* GLENN] I'm hanging onto it.

[HANK *turns and exits through the dining room door and goes into the pantry, where he stands looking out the window of the side door.* GLENN *steps to the dining room door, stops, and turns back to* DAN]

GLENN: How you like that, pop? They both got the guns. [*Raises his voice so* HANK *can hear in the pantry*] Only they ain't got half a brain between 'em. Without me, they're cooked . . . an' they know it! [GLENN *turns on* CINDY, *moving toward her*] You didn't feel like blabberin' to the boy friend, did you, sweetie?

CINDY: [*Holding her ground*] I felt like it! But I didn't. I'll explain it the night you take your walk to the electric chair!

[GLENN'S *tension has been growing. He explodes.* HANK *turns from the pantry window and rushes into the living room*]

GLENN: [*Threateningly, to* CINDY, *who backs away*] There're ways of shuttin' that pretty face of yours, redhead!

HANK: [*As he enters the living room*] What's the boy friend doin' drivin' past the house out there . . . slow?

GLENN: [*Pushing her shoulder, forces her against window*] If you pulled a fast one, spitfire . . .

HANK: [*In panic*] Glenn, listen!

GLENN: [*Turning back into room*] Lemme think, willya?

HANK: Glenn! They're not gonna stop comin' to the door!

GLENN: [*Crossing to him*] Yellow, Hank?

HANK: Yeah . . . okay . . . yellow! *They're not gonna stop coming to the door!*

BLACKOUT

SHERIFF'S OFFICE

Clock: 8:25. There is a map of Indianapolis on the wall and an area has been marked off with heavy crayon. FRED-ERICKS *is studying the map.* BARD *is speaking over the radio.*

BARD: I'm looking at a map of the neighborhood, Tom. Where are you?

WINSTON'S VOICE: Parked behind a service station. Corner of Kessler Boulevard and Keystone. [*As* BARD *marks an X on the map location*] The main roads are covered. The other cars're just where you put 'em. It's a high-toned sort of neighborhood, Jesse.

BARD: Okay. Now. Let's start knocking on a few high-toned doors!

FREDERICKS: Bard . . . there're over two hundred houses in that area. It'll take all night and part of tomorrow . . .

BARD: [*Ignoring* FREDERICKS] Every one of the trashman's customers. Begin with those. And Tom . . . especially the garages, you got me?

[CARSON *enters*]

WINSTON'S VOICE: We're on it, Jess . . .

[BARD *switches off the radio*]

CARSON: [*Holding out letter*] This, my friend, was brought into the city police station during the noon hour.

BARD: [*Taking the letter*] Noon!

CARSON: A bellhop's given six different descriptions of the man who tipped him five bucks to deliver it. All we know for sure is the man had two arms, two legs and presumably one head.

BARD: [*Takes letter out of envelope, glances at it*] It's not signed.

CARSON: Go ahead, read it . . . you'll understand why.

BARD: [*Begins to read briskly and tone changes to a hushed whisper*] "To the Police . . . innocent people will be in the house or automobile with the three fugitives you want. If you shoot, you will be responsible for taking the lives of people who have done no harm. Any attempt to trace this letter will only endanger my family . . ." [*Pause.* BARD *holds letter up to light*] Handwriting disguised . . . no watermarks.

FREDERICKS: It's a blind.

BARD: [*Whispers, touched*] The idiot.

CARSON: That letter's no blind!

BARD: But he ought to *know!* God, doesn't he know? Carson, isn't there some way to get word to this guy, whoever he is, that you can't play ball with savages like that?

CARSON: How? Without tipping them he wrote that?

BARD: *You* take a shot in the dark, Federal man! They'll tear that poor guy to ribbons, inside and out, before they're done. You can't cooperate with scum like that!

CARSON: No? . . . What would *you* do, Jesse? I'd say he was smart to write that. Might keep some itchy-fingered officer from shooting his wife or child.

BARD: Itchy-fingered like *me*, Carson?

CARSON: You got more sense. That's what's eating you, friend. You know what a spot the man's on. What *would* you do, Jesse . . . under the circumstances?

BARD: [*After a moment*] I'd play ball. [BARD *flips on intercom and speaks into it*] Dutch, get me car nine . . . Deputy Winston. [*Flips off the intercom. Quietly*] Yeah, I reckon I'd do just that. An' maybe pray a little.

[BARD *switches on radio circuit light*]

WINSTON'S VOICE: Car nine . . .

BARD: Tom . . . stop 'em up there.

WINSTON'S VOICE: [*Incredulously*] *Stop* 'em . . . ?

BARD: You heard me. I'm countermanding the orders. Bury those prowl cars, *bury* 'em.

FREDERICKS: You can't put off a showdown, lad.

BARD: Nobody wants a showdown any more'n I do . . . but not if it means getting some poor slob's family massacred! [*Into mike*] You hear me, Tom? Keep those patrols off the streets! Stash 'em!

WINSTON'S VOICE: You're callin' it, Jess . . . Listen—that sporty little foreign car I reported a while ago . . . he just went by the corner again.

BARD: [*Considers a moment*] Okay. Bring him in, Tom. Who knows? But quiet up there! No sirens, no red lights.

WINSTON'S VOICE: It'll be a pleasure to arrest *any*body!

[BARD *switches off the radio*]

FREDERICKS: You call that police work?

BARD: What do you propose . . . alert 'em, force their hand?

FREDERICKS: That letter pretty well establishes they're in that neighborhood. I'll tell you what I propose—tear gas.

BARD: Anybody wonder why this guy didn't sign his name? Why he doesn't trust the police to help him?

FREDERICKS: Tear gas and riot guns. I'll have some moved up there . . . just in case you begin to see the light!

[FREDERICKS *exits. Pause*]

CARSON: [*Quietly*] Changing your tune, Jess? . . .

[BARD *moves to the desk, puzzled at himself and his feelings, ignores* CARSON. *He rereads the letter in silence*]

BARD: Those guys wouldn't try to use a sports car for a getaway. Probably some fresh kid out trying to pick up a girl. . . .

BLACKOUT

HILLIARD HOME

The living room lights are on, the rest of the house dim. ELEANOR *is with* RALPHIE *in his room.* DAN *is seated in the living room.* ROBISH *is at door of den.* CINDY *is on the second step of the stairs.* HANK *is at the window.* GLENN *is at the front door, which is very slightly ajar so that he can look out through the crack.*

HANK: He knows somethin's up . . .

CINDY: Chuck knows nothing. Naturally, he's puzzled . . . he . . .

GLENN: [*Closes and locks the door*] Knock off, I'm thinkin'.

HANK: Glenn . . .

GLENN: [*Abstracted*] Don't let it get you, kid.

HANK: Glenn . . . I've had it!

GLENN: What're you talkin' about?

HANK: The old man with the trash . . . the teacher . . . now this guy goin' by out there . . . over'n over. I've had it! [*He goes into the dining room and to the pantry, where he stands looking out the window of the side door*]

GLENN: [*Moving fast to the dining room*] Robish, cover 'em!

[ROBISH *rises and glances out window*]

GLENN: [*Enters the pantry, grabs* HANK's *arm*] What the hell does that mean? "I've had it"?

HANK: What're we waitin' for, Glenn?

GLENN: Don't start that again! I gotta dope this . . .

HANK: We're accessories now.

[DAN *rises and leaves the living room by the dining room door.* CINDY *moves to the dining room door, listening*]

GLENN: You're learnin' big words aroun' this house, ain't you?

HANK: Glenn . . . I ain't going to the chair 'cause that ape in there got trigger happy.

GLENN: We're pullin' stakes tomorrow . . . *after* we get the dough.

[DAN *appears in the pantry*]

HANK: [*Shouting*] What good's the dough gonna do you in the death house?

GLENN: [*Intensely*] I gotta pay Flick to take care of Bard, don't I? [*Turns, following* HANK'*s gaze, sees* DAN] What're you gapin' at?

HANK: I'm goin', Glenn. By myself.

GLENN: [*Whirling on him*] You leave here without me, they'll have you back'n stir'n less'n a hour!

HANK: I can take care of myself.

GLENN: Since when?

HANK: [*Firmly*] Since right now!

[GLENN *is baffled, angry, frightened, unable to cope*]

GLENN: *Listen,* you yellow little punk . . . you're gónna do what I tell you!

HANK: Not any more, Glenn.

DAN: Hank, I don't advise your leaving here alone. . . .

HANK: They won't catch me, Mr. Hilliard. Don't worry about that.

GLENN: [*Between them*] Look who's tellin' who not to worry! You're talkin' like Hilliard was our old man. [*Faces* DAN] If Hilliard was our old man, he'd have something coming to him from way back! [HANK *unlocks the door and* GLENN *whips about . . . changing: pleading now, helpless, slightly pathetic*] Listen, Hank . . . you can't duck out on me. Christ, kid . . . it's always been *us.* You'n me! Listen . . . without you . . . without you . . .

HANK: Come along, Glenn?

GLENN: [*Wildly*] Goddammit, *I'm* callin' the tune! You're gonna listen to me, I took care of you, I . . .

[GLENN *breaks off because* HANK *has taken the automatic from his pocket.* GLENN *stares*]

HANK: You ain't stoppin' me . . . either one of you! [*Pause*] I'll take the girl's coop.

[CINDY, *who has been standing at the dining room door, now slips out, heading for the pantry*]

DAN: [*Quickly*] They could trace that license in ten minutes.

HANK: Okay, Mr. Hilliard . . . I can pick up a car anywhere.

ROBISH: [*Calls to* GLENN] Griffin . . . redhead's gettin' nosy!

[CINDY *appears in the pantry.* HANK *sees her, and on his face is the naked longing.* GLENN *turns, frowning; he sees* CINDY. *He taps his forehead with the heel of his hand, smiling*]

GLENN: I get it. Christ, kid, I get it now! [*He grabs* CINDY *and pulls her toward* HANK. DAN *puts his arm around her, holding* GLENN *off*] Ain't I always learned you? You want something, *take* it!

DAN: Your brother knows it's not that simple, Griffin!

GLENN: [*Fiercely*] I'll *make* it that simple! *Hank gets what he wants!*

[*Pause, while* HANK *looks at* CINDY]

HANK: [*In choked tones*] I doubt it, Glenn. I doubt if I ever will.

[HANK *suddenly opens the door, turns and goes out, slamming the door behind him. He quickly disappears.* GLENN *springs to the door and looks out the window. Stunned, muttering almost to himself, he sags in door*]

GLENN: You be careful, kid. . . . Take care of yourself, see . . . You . . . [*He turns and sees* CINDY *in* DAN's *arms, pulls up the swagger*] Good riddance. He was beginnin' to get on my nerves. [*Then, abruptly*] You satisfied, redhead?

DAN: Cindy had nothing to do with . . .

GLENN: *Satisfied?*

DAN: Go to your room, Cindy. [CINDY *slips up the back stairs.* DAN *turns to* GLENN, *who goes toward the living room, seething, growing more and more violent.* DAN *follows* GLENN] Griffin, you'd better get hold of yourself.

[*Above*, ELEANOR *has left* RALPHIE *and is now at the head of the stairs*]

ELEANOR: Dan, what is it? What . . .

GLENN: [*As he enters the living room*] All of you! All of you! [*Turns on* DAN] You satisfied now, you smart-eyed bastard? Clickety-click, you got at him, didn't you?

[*Above,* RALPHIE *joins* ELEANOR *at head of stairs*]

DAN: God, boy, you'd better . . .

GLENN: *Shut up, pop!* . . . Pop! If you was our pop . . .

DAN: Griffin, I don't know how much reason you've got left in that
head of yours, but you can't turn this on . . .

GLENN: [*Pacing like a maddened caged animal*] I can do anything
I *want!* You and your goddam house!

ROBISH: [*At window*] Stir-crazy!

GLENN: That goddam spitfire'n her fancy skirts swishin'!

DAN: I'd advise you to let loose of that idea!

GLENN: [*Grabs composition book from table and sweeps ashtray
to the floor*] That brat an' his "composition"!

DAN: [*Still at foot of stairs*] If you don't get hold . . .

[ELEANOR *comes down the stairs a few steps*]

GLENN: I got hold! I got hold good! [*Twisting the composition
book in his hands*] Now I'm gonna "advise" you, pop. You're
gonna go up there now an' you're gonna learn that kid we ain't
playin' cowboys-an'-Indians aroun' here. [*Taking pleasure in it*]
You're gonna give that brat a real old-fashioned lacin'!

DAN: We don't do things that way in this house!

GLENN: This house, this house! I got my gut-full-a this house! [*Eyes
on* DAN] Robish! How'd *you* like to show Hilliard how it's done?

ROBISH: Yeah . . . I ain't got nothin' else to do. [*Above,* RALPHIE
returns to his own room, stands by bed]

GLENN: [*Sadistically*] Okay, Robish . . . whale the tar outta that
brat!

[ROBISH *starts to the stairs.* DAN *moves up the stairs slowly.*
ROBISH *stops at foot of stairs*]

ELEANOR: [*Leaning on stair rail. To* GLENN] I hope they get your
brother! I hope they kill him!

GLENN: [*Calls up to* DAN] Let's hear him bawlin', pop! *Loud!*
My old man used a belt!

[DAN *enters* RALPHIE'S *room, closes the door and turns on
the light.* ELEANOR *mounts the stairs and goes into the*

master bedroom, where she stands listening behind the closed door. DAN *faces* RALPHIE]

DAN: [*Breathlessly*] Ralphie . . .

RALPHIE: Did Hank take your gun? Then there's only one gun now . . .

DAN: [*Gently, but urgently*] Son . . . you've got to help . . .

ROBISH: [*Starts up the stairs*] We don't hear nothin', Hilliard!

DAN: [*Swiftly, softly, suffering*] Ralphie . . . listen to me. No matter what you think now . . . no matter what you think of me . . . what names you give it . . . you've got to do what I tell you.

ROBISH: [*Rounding the landing*] What's goin' on in there?

DAN: Ralphie, listen! I want you to cry.

ROBISH: [*Coming down the hall*] What's the stall?

DAN: [*Almost a whisper*] Do you hear me? Ralphie . . . son . . . please . . . for God's sake do what I say now!

RALPHIE: I . . . I can't.

ROBISH: [*Outside the door*] You want some help, Hilliard?

[*Trapped,* DAN *lifts his hand and brings it down, in desperation, open-palmed: a stinging blow across the boy's face.* RALPHIE, *stunned, stands staring at his father.* DAN *goes sick and empty clear through. Then* DAN *sinks to bed, gathers* RALPHIE *in his arms, and* RALPHIE *begins to cry. He cries softly at first, then louder and louder. Below,* GLENN *hears the sounds and drops the composition book to the floor, as though he has found some small release inside*]

DIMOUT

SHERIFF'S OFFICE

Clock reads 8:59. WINSTON *stands to one side of* CHUCK, *who, bewildered, faces* BARD *across the desk.* BARD *is examining* CHUCK's *driver's license.*

BARD: What's your business, Mr. . . . [*Glances at license*] Wright?

CHUCK: Attorney, Swisshelm and Edwards. Circle Tower Building. . . . What's this all about?

BARD: Your firm handle criminal cases?

CHUCK: We're strictly corporation law. You haven't answered my question, Deputy.

WINSTON: Don't get fresh.

BARD: Empty out your pockets, Wright.

CHUCK: You've no right to . . .

BARD: Look, Wright . . . you're not in court! Empty out your pockets! [As CHUCK *complies*] What you been up to, last hour or so . . . in that . . . [Consults CHUCK's *registration*] . . . Jaguar of yours? Cruising 'round in circles?

WINSTON: You scoutin' for those rats, Wright?

CHUCK: What rats?

BARD: Let's not be cagey, kid . . . it makes me suspicious. [Picks up *newspaper from top of radio and hands it to* CHUCK, who reads the *headlines and begins to realize*] We know they're up there some-where . . . holed up in one of those nice houses . . . so . . . [Stops, frowning; studying expression on CHUCK's face] What's up, boy?

CHUCK: Nothing . . .

BARD: You know something? [When CHUCK shakes his head] Sus-pect something?

CHUCK: No . . .

BARD: [Rising] Dammit, don't lie to me! Your face looks like I just kicked you.

CHUCK: Well . . . it's just that . . . my girl lives . . . there.

BARD: Name?

CHUCK: Her name's . . . Allen [Firmly] Constance Allen.

WINSTON: [Consulting the list] No Allens on the list, Jess.

BARD: [Picks up DAN's letter, hands it to CHUCK] Here . . . read this. [BARD sits as CHUCK reads] Now. Let's have it, kid. What's the girl's name?

CHUCK: I . . . don't know.

BARD: [Gently probing now] She's in there . . . with those three. What's the address?

CHUCK: If . . . if he'd wanted you to know . . . [Tosses letter to the desk] . . . he'd have signed his name.

BARD: [Changing] Wright, that guy ought to know he can't crib-bage aroun' with the police like this. If he doesn't, you should!

CHUCK: What do you expect him to do? He's doing all he can! He's quite a guy!

BARD: [*Rising*] Kid . . . I honestly don't know what *I'd* do if I was in your shoes . . . but I'm in mine . . . and I want that name. Now spit it out or I'll slap you in the pokey so fast . . .

CHUCK: You've got no charges!

BARD: I've got sixty of 'em. Aidin' and abettin' . . . withholding evidence . . . accessory to murder! Or didn't you know they murdered a man this afternoon? Yeah, that's the kind of scum you're lettin' your girl spend the evening with.

> [*Pause.* CHUCK *sinks into chair.* BARD *sits on edge of desk.* CHUCK *swallows*]

CHUCK: I . . . I can't make that decision. For them. You'd better slap on one of those charges, Deputy. Because I don't know the name. I never said I did.

BARD: [*Rising*] Why, you young . . . [*He is interrupted by the intercom*]

DUTCH'S VOICE: Special Agent Carson, Jesse.

BARD: [*Switches on radio*] Yes, Carson?

CARSON'S VOICE: Deputy . . . it just blew wide open!

BARD: What? . . . What've you got?

CARSON'S VOICE: City policemen just caught Hank Griffin trying to steal a car. He decided to shoot it out. . . .

BARD: Killed?

CARSON'S VOICE: Killed.

BARD: [*In a different tone; very quietly*] Anything else?

CARSON'S VOICE: Plenty . . . The gun the boy was carrying—it was registered. [*As* BARD'S *eyes meet* CHUCK'S] In the name of Hilliard . . . Daniel C. Hilliard.

> [BARD *glances at* WINSTON, *who glances at list, looks up, nods*]

BARD: Just like that. Eleanor Hilliard wrote a check to Claude Patterson this morning.

WINSTON: [*Reading from list*] Hilliard, Daniel C. Wife, Eleanor.

One son age ten, Ralph. One daughter age twenty, Cynthia . . . called Cindy.

[CHUCK *has turned in the chair, watching* WINSTON. *Their eyes now meet*]

BARD: [*After a slight pause*] Okay. Carson . . . throw a cordon around the Hilliard house. Let no one in or out of that block. Only keep everything out of sight of the windows. I'll be up there in ten minutes. And Carson . . . have the newsboys got this?

CARSON'S VOICE: Not yet. Not even the death.

BARD: Well, for God's sake, keep 'em off it!

CARSON'S VOICE: We'll try, Jess.

[BARD *flips off the radio circuit light*]

WINSTON: [*Gets coat*] You call it, Jess.

CHUCK: [*Rising*] You can't move in! You read Mr. Hilliard's letter.

BARD: [*Taking his revolver out of desk drawer, checks it, Abstracted*] Get out of here now, kid.

CHUCK: [*Demanding*] What're you going to do?

BARD: What the sweet hell do you think I'm going to do . . . blow up the house?

[BARD *takes his jacket from back of chair and starts putting it on*]

CHUCK: [*Earnestly*] Deputy . . . what if you could sneak someone inside? With a gun. There are only two of them in there now.

WINSTON: [*Putting on coat*] This is police work, son. Stay out of it.

CHUCK: If somebody was in there . . . between them and the family . . . and if he could get 'em both at one crack . . .

BARD: [*Ignoring* CHUCK, *flips on intercom*] Dutch . . . get an ambulance up to Kessler and Keystone. Keep it out of sight. [*Flips off intercom. Turns to* CHUCK] You're out of it, Wright. Stay out!

CHUCK: I'm not out of it! Those're my people in there! [*To* BARD, *urgently*] You read the letter. There can't be any shooting when they come out, either. . . . *What are you going to do?*

BARD: [*Annoyed at the question*] Look! Will you get out of here!

CHUCK: May I have my things?

BARD: [*Shoving items across the desk*] Take 'em.

CHUCK: [*Picking up his things, putting them in pockets*] May I have those keys, Deputy?

BARD: [*Looks at keys, which he has unconsciously been holding in his hand since he went through* CHUCK's *belongings*] Here. [*He hands the keys to* CHUCK]

CHUCK: Thanks.

[CHUCK *goes out, as* WINSTON *returns with rifle*]

WINSTON: The boy's got a good question, Jess.

BARD: [*Thoughtfully; quietly*] A damn good question . . . I wish I had the answer. [*As they start out*] Well, let's get on it now. Let's get up there!

DIMOUT

CURTAIN

ACT THREE

DAN *is at the window of the master bedroom.* ELEANOR *is sitting on the bed. Across the hall,* RALPHIE *is asleep on his bed.* CINDY *is out of sight in her room.* ROBISH *is at the window in the living room.* GLENN *is in the pantry. As the lights dim up he is leaving the pantry and appears in the living room. Living room lights are on; the rest of the house is dim.*

ROBISH: [*Turning from the window as* GLENN *enters*] Griffin . . . somethin' funny goin' on. There ain't been no cars goin' by out there for a long time. [*Steps toward* GLENN] Griffin, you deef?

GLENN: [*Who has been pacing, stops*] Robish . . . let's grab the two women'n blow.

ROBISH: With no dough?

GLENN: [*Vacantly*] With no dough.

ROBISH: Okay. Ya wanna go . . . go. Wind up like the kid brother. In the morgue.

GLENN: Lay off, Robish.

ROBISH: On a slab. By this time they got 'im or shot 'im.

[*Above,* DAN *goes to other window in the bedroom*]

GLENN: [*Wildly*] Nothin' happens to Hank!

ROBISH: [*Chuckles heavily*] That's po'try, Griffin. Got 'im or shot 'im.

GLENN: [*Starting toward* ROBISH] You don't know nothin'! Goddam you, Robish . . .

[ROBISH *lifts the gun, almost casually. In this moment, the telephone shrills.* GLENN *stops*]

ROBISH: [*Shouting*] Hilliard! Answer that!

[DAN *turns on the bedroom lights, opens the door, and picks up the phone in the upstairs hall at the time that* GLENN, *below, is already answering it.* CINDY *has come out of her room and stands near the door to* RALPHIE'S *room.* DAN, *undecided as to what to do with the phone, looks at* CINDY]

GLENN: [*Leaping to the phone almost before the first ring is over*] Hank! [*Into instrument*] Hello! [*Then, sagging in disappointment, snarls*] Who? . . . [*He replaces the phone angrily*]

ROBISH: [*Approaching* GLENN] Christ, who is it?

GLENN: [*Vacantly, going through dining room door*] Something about . . . a night watchman . . .

ROBISH: [*Calling*] Hilliard!

DAN: [*Speaks into the extension*] Hello . . . this is Mr. Hilliard speaking. [*Suddenly alert*] Yes, Carl? . . . I'll be right down.

[DAN *replaces the phone and turns to the stairs*]

ROBISH: [*At foot of stairs*] Who was that? What's going on?

DAN: [*On stairs, calls down*] The money's here. It arrived special delivery at the store. I'll go get it.

[DAN *turns back up the stairs and enters the bedroom, where he faces* ELEANOR, *who is sitting on the bed.* CINDY *returns to her own room.* GLENN *has returned from the dining room during* DAN'S *last speech.* ROBISH *turns to him*]

ROBISH: [*Trying to penetrate* GLENN'S *preoccupation*] Griffin . . . the dough's here.

GLENN: [*Stands for a moment at foot of stairs*] How come that wasn't Hank on the phone?

ROBISH: You better snap out of it. [*As* GLENN *goes into the den*] Jeez, you're givin' me the willies. . . .

[*He stands looking after* GLENN. *In the bedroom above,* DAN *picks up his coat from over the back of the chair and paces with the coat in his hands.* ELEANOR *follows him with her eyes as she speaks*]

ELEANOR: I can't believe it. Now. Tonight! No more waiting. In an hour now . . . *Less* than an hour! [*Slight pause.* DAN *puts on his coat*] Dan . . . look at me. . . . [*Rises, fighting alarm*] Dan!

ROBISH: [*Shouting up the stairs*] Hilliard! That dough's waiting!

ELEANOR: Tell me. What are you planning, Dan?

[*Pause.* DAN *turns to face her*]

DAN: I can't wait any longer for the opportune moment, that's all.

ELEANOR: What do you mean?

DAN: I've got to . . . make the moment . . . for myself.

ELEANOR: [*Sinks down at foot of bed*] Dan, tell me. My blood's stopped. Dan . . .

DAN: There are only three bullets left in that gun down there.

ELEANOR: I'm going to scream!

DAN: No, you're not, you're going to listen.

ELEANOR: My heart's pushing up out of . . . Dan, *what do you mean?*

DAN: I'm going to force Robish to use those bullets.

ELEANOR: [*Whispers*] Use them . . . How?

DAN: [*Quietly*] On me.

ROBISH: Hilliard, what's the stall?

ELEANOR: [*Rising, to him*] Dan, this isn't you! They've driven you . . . Oh, God, *Dan!*

DAN: I've tried every other way, haven't I? *Haven't* I?

ELEANOR: [*Swiftly, in a whisper*] We know, we're not asking for more, we know what you've done. Even Ralphie . . .

DAN: If I can get Griffin out of the way before Robish even knows what's happening . . . [*Grimly; murderously*] And I *can.*

ELEANOR: Dan, no matter how much you want to kill Griffin . . .

DAN: There's no other way!

ELEANOR: There is. There has to be!

DAN: [*Gently, urgently*] Darling, you've got to face this with me. Griffin hates me. He hated me before he even saw me. I can't explain it. Every hour some new black hole appears in him. He's cracking up, Ellie. God knows what a mind like that will turn to . . . which one of us . . . Now. Do you see? We're no better off when I get the money. Do you see?

ELEANOR: All I see is one thing. One thing . . . *We're* not saved if *you* die.

DAN: Please, Ellie, don't make it so . . .

ELEANOR: All right . . . go down there. Kill Griffin. Make Robish shoot you. Do you imagine a man like that has to have *bullets* to . . . [DAN *turns to her*] . . . against Ralphie? . . . or Cindy? . . . or me? *Do* you?

DAN: [*Realizing that it was only panic, softly*] All right, Ellie.

ELEANOR: We're not saved if you die.

DAN: All *right*, Ellie!

ELEANOR: [*Sits on bed*] Oh, God, darling! [DAN *sinks into chair*] Dan . . . you're the hub . . . it all revolves around you. If anything . . .

DAN: Everything's blurred again. One minute it all looks sharp . . . clear . . .

ELEANOR: [*Places her hand on* DAN's] Dan. [*He looks at her*] We can't let them panic us now.

[*There is a moment of understanding between them*]

ROBISH: Hilliard! Get th' lead out!

[DAN *and* ELEANOR *break. He rises and opens the door, starting downstairs.* ELEANOR *rises and stands at the door*]

GLENN: [*Entering from den*] Ask 'em where they get the news on that damn thing.

[DAN *is coming down the stairs.* CINDY *comes out of her room and follows.* GLENN *sinks to chair*]

ROBISH: Goddam you, Hilliard, you don't get down here, I'm gonna . . . [*He sees* DAN *on the stairs*] We ain't gonna blow till we get that dough, Hilliard.

GLENN: Where's the redhead?

[DAN, *moving to the closet, turns to* CINDY *on stairs*]

DAN: Cindy, go to your room. Lock the door.

GLENN: Redhead goes along!

[CINDY *remains on the stairs*]

ROBISH: [*Turning to* GLENN] The gal stays right here.

GLENN: [*Ignoring* ROBISH; *a grotesque caricature of his old self*] Open the letter . . . take out two thousand dollars . . .

ROBISH: To hell with that!

GLENN: Redhead takes it to Lombardi's Grille . . .

DAN: [*Putting on coat*] Cindy is not going to deliver any . . .

GLENN: [*Turns in chair to face* DAN] Lombardi Grille. South Illinois Street.

ROBISH: To hell with that. Ain't got time now!

GLENN: She sits'n has a drink. A man sits down with her. Then . . .

ROBISH: Then nothin'! Yuh lissen to me. . . .

GLENN: [*Vaguely*] Then . . .

DAN: What then, Griffin?

GLENN: She gives him the dough. Two G's.

ROBISH: Yuh bring all that dough here, Hilliard . . . soon's yuh lay your mitts on it.

[DAN *goes to open the door*]

GLENN: We don't get outta here till I hear from Flick he's got his money.

[DAN, *with door open, now nods to* CINDY, *who comes down the stairs and goes out.* DAN *follows and closes the door*]

ROBISH: Wastin' time, wastin' time. I tell yuh the redhead stays. We gotta have . . . [*He hears the door close. Turns*] Now, how we gonna take two dames in the car? [*He locks the door as* GLENN *goes to the phone, dials*] Loco. Christ! Loco.

[ROBISH *goes into pantry, locks the back door*]

GLENN: [*On phone*] What? . . . Oh . . . Mr. Flick. Room . . . uh . . . 202.

[ROBISH *returns to the living room*]

ROBISH: [*In dining room door*] I lay my hands'n that dough, yuh can rot'n here, Griffin!

BLACKOUT

THE WALLINGS' ATTIC

The corner of an attic room that seems to be suspended
in darkness. The room has a cluttered look: discarded
furniture, an old iron bed-frame leaning against the wall.
A single small window overlooks the Hilliard house in the
distance. CARSON *is looking out the window through binoc-*
ulars. BARD *behind him, wearing hat.* FREDERICKS *is*
seated on an old trunk. On an old box is radio apparatus.
A rifle with a telescopic sight leans against the wall near
the window.

CARSON: [*Reporting, without lowering binoculars*] Jesse . . . a man
and a girl just came out the front door of the Hilliard house.

BARD: That'll be Hilliard and his daughter.

CARSON: They're getting into the black coupé in the driveway. [*He*
hands the glasses to BARD, *who looks through the window*]
Cocky, aren't they? Letting them both out of there even now.

BARD: Yeah . . . gettin' real cocksure.

FREDERICKS: [*Crisply*] Why not? They know they got us hog-tied
. . . 's long as we sit up here in the attic of the house next door.

BARD: [*Hands glasses back to* CARSON *and turns to* FREDERICKS]
Don't start riding me again, Fredericks.

[*There is a buzz from the radio apparatus.* BARD *flips a*
switch and picks up the microphone]

WINSTON'S VOICE: [*On radio*] Car nine—Winston.

BARD: [*Into mike*] Yeah, Tom?

WINSTON'S VOICE: Jesse . . . Hilliard and his daughter just turned
south on Keystone. You want me to pick 'em up?

BARD: No.

FREDERICKS: What the hell're we waiting for? We got the phone tap.
We know where he's going.

BARD: [*Annoyed—into mike*] Tom . . . let them get downtown to
that store. Then . . . when he's got his mail, whatever it is . . .
pick him up and bring him here to the Wallings' house. Come in

here from the north, though . . . and careful nobody in the Hilliard windows can see you.

WINSTON'S VOICE: What'll I tell the guy?

BARD: Nothing. [*Flips off radio, puts down mike*]

FREDERICKS: Bard, this is stupid as hell! I tell you, we got no choice now. Move in.

BARD: And I tell you I've got an animal gnawing away inside me tonight, Fredericks, and I don't need this crap from you! I'm aware of the alternatives. We could bust in there now . . . or try to bluff 'em out . . . or try to sneak in and flush 'em . . . but . . .

FREDERICKS: [*Rising*] Let's get one thing straight. There's going to be blood. There're only two people in that house now.

BARD: Two human beings.

FREDERICKS: Okay! Measure them against the just as innocent people those two can knock off if they bluff their way out of this trap.

BARD: The guy's wife and kid!

FREDERICKS: Lad, you're putting a weapon in the hands of every felon in the country, you let . . .

BARD: [*Overriding*] I didn't invent the scheme, dammit! I'm doing all I can. We've got sixty officers in those woods now . . . the streets are blocked off . . .

FREDERICKS: Bastards like them're wily.

BARD: [*Turning to* CARSON] Carson! Those're escapees from a Federal prison in there. You call it!

CARSON: [*Turns from window slightly*] I'll string along with you, Deputy . . . at least until we speak to Hilliard.

FREDERICKS: O-kay, lads. It's your baby. I'm just a sour old man hates to see frisky young slobs make fools of theirselves. [*Harshly*] But pity's a luxury your badge don't afford!

[*The radio buzzes.* BARD *flips switch, picks up mike*]

BARD: [*Into mike*] Deputy Bard . . .

DUTCH'S VOICE: We just got another telephone report, Jess. A man's voice, unidentified, *inside* the house called a downtown hotel . . . spoke to a man named Flick . . . told him to meet a red-headed girl at Lombardi Grille . . . South Illinois Street.

BARD: [*Lowers mike*] God Almighty, that's the daughter. [*Into mike*] Dutch . . . put a city detective in the Lombardi Grille. Have him pick up the man and the girl.

DUTCH'S VOICE: There's more. The one called Flick is supposed to call back to the Hilliard house . . . let the telephone ring three times, then hang up. Some sort of hanky-panky.

BARD: Thanks, Dutch. [*Flips off radio. Puts down mike*] Wonder what the devil that's all about.

CARSON: [*Quietly—looking through the glasses*] Bard . . . there's some sort of activity behind the Hilliard garage. You can barely make it out in the light from the window.

BARD: [*Takes glasses, looks*] Looks to me like somebody stretched out on the ground.

BLACKOUT

HILLIARD HOME

The lights are on in the living room and in the master bedroom. The rest of the house is dim. ELEANOR *and* RALPHIE *stand at the window of the master bedroom.* ROBISH *is in the window in the pantry, looking out the window of the side door.* GLENN *sits on the arm of the sofa in the living room, listening to the newscaster on the radio. Though* ROBISH *begins speaking as soon as the lights are up, the radio newscaster is heard all through the beginning of the scene until* GLENN *turns the radio off.*

RADIO NEWSCASTER: [*On speaker, under scene*] . . . see what the weather man has in store for us. Clear skies tomorrow, much colder, with brisk winds tomorrow and Sunday. No more rain is predicted for the Indianapolis area . . . but better dig out that overcoat because winter is almost here! This has been Kyle McGreevey, your ten-o'clock newscaster, now saying . . . good night and good cheer!

ROBISH [*As the lights come up*] Griffin! [GLENN *does not answer, his attention on radio*] Griffin, can yuh hear me? I seen somethin' out by the garage! [*Still no answer.* ROBISH *takes an uncertain step*

toward the kitchen, suddenly whirls and unlocks the side door,
opens it a crack, hiding behind it, gun ready, speaks in low, cau-
tious growl] Hey, out there? *Turns and calls into house; a plea*
for help, lost without his "leader"] Griffin! [*Out the door;*
slightly louder] Listen . . . anybody out there . . . coppers . . .
we'll blast the woman'n kid in here! [*Pause. The silence works on*
him; the uncertainty becomes turbulent] Christ! What am I gonna
. . . Christ! [ROBISH *closes and locks the side door, turns and goes*
through the kitchen door to appear in the living room. GLENN *rises*
from sofa and turns off the radio. There is a growing wildness in
him. Convinced now, deluding himself into thinking what he
wants to believe, he enters another phase in which nothing can
touch him. This is in sharp contrast to the stunned glassy fear of
the last scenes. He is gay, refusing reality, like a man with too many
drinks. ROBISH, *entering the living room, cannot reach him through*
the following] Griffin, yuh hear me?

GLENN: [*In soft disbelief*] He's okay.

ROBISH: I seen . . .

GLENN: [*Mounting joy*] Hank's okay, Robish.

ROBISH: To hell with the kid. He's in the clink. Lissen . . .

> [*During the following,* CHUCK *appears at the side door out-*
> *side. He lets himself in with* CINDY's *key and closes the door.*
> *He stands for a while in the pantry, listening. He moves to*
> *the pantry wall and stands with an ear against it. Then he*
> *goes up the back stairs and appears in the upstairs hall. He*
> *looks around cautiously into* RALPHIE's *room and closes the*
> *door, leaving it slightly ajar*]

GLENN: [*With violent relief*] They'd have had it on the news,
wouldn't they? Nothing. They're still lookin' for all of us. Not a
goddam word about Hank!

ROBISH: Lissen . . . we gotta change our ideas.

GLENN: [*At the stairs*] Ideas perkin' fine. Everythin's chimin'. *Hank*
made it! He's on his way to Helen!

ROBISH: [*Disgusted*] Who yuh tryin' to con? I tell yuh, I seen somethin' move out by the garage.

GLENN: [*High spirits. Laughs*] Goblins, Robish. Like on Hallow-

een when we was kids. God, how Hank used to go for that Hallow-
een crap! Dress up . . . burnt cork'n his face . . .

ROBISH: [*Looks out window*] Any coppers out there . . .

GLENN: We're snug, we're snug. Two hours now, we'll be in Louisville. Hank's with Helen.

ROBISH: They put that on the radio, did they? Any cops stick their
necks'n here, I blow up the whole goddam house.

[CHUCK *is in* RALPHIE'S *bedroom, his gun ready*]

BLACKOUT

THE WALLINGS' ATTIC

FREDERICKS *is still seated on the trunk.* BARD *has the glasses
and is looking out the window.* CARSON *stands by.*

FREDERICKS: If there's any shooting over there . . .

BARD: [*Hands glasses to* CARSON, *turns*] I'll give the signal to close
in. Satisfied, Lieutenant?

FREDERICKS: [*Rises as* CARSON *takes up the watch through the
window*] No, I'm not. There's another gun in that house now
. . . 'cause we waited.

BARD: [*Turning toward the window*] What I'd like to know is how
that kid got through the police lines.

FREDERICKS: Plenty of ways . . . you know the neighborhood well
enough.

CARSON: [*His first show of emotion*] A reckless muddlehead like
that could botch up everything if he startles them in there!

FREDERICKS: Why shouldn't he take it in his own hands?

CARSON: If only his gun's between those two and the family somehow . . .

BARD: My hunch is the boy's layin' low . . . not knowin' where everybody is . . . waitin' for someone to make a move . . . us or them.

FREDERICKS: Lads, you're up a creek.

CARSON: The boy's smart enough to know he's done for if he doesn't
get them both at the same time . . . and fast!

FREDERICKS: Lads, you're up a long, long creek and no paddles.

[*The radio buzzes.* BARD *flips switch, picks up mike*]

BARD: [*Into mike*] Deputy Bard . . .

WINSTON'S VOICE: [*On radio*] Jess . . . Hilliard's on his way upstairs. Tread easy now, you guys. This gentleman's had it.

[BARD *flips off radio, puts down mike. They all wait, looking at the stairs*]

FREDERICKS: [*As he turns*] Man plays with dynamite, he's going to get it.

[DAN *enters up the stairs, looks around, quietly terrified but determined*]

BARD: Evening, Mr. Hilliard. My name's Bard. Deputy Sheriff, Marion County . . . I received your letter, Mr. Hilliard.

DAN: I didn't write you any letter.

BARD: [*Taking letter out of his pocket*] Look, Mr. Hilliard . . . we wouldn't be here if we didn't have it all pretty straight. So let's not waste . . . [*Stops, staring into* DAN's *face; then, very gently*] Sorry. You want to sit down, Mr. Hilliard?

[BARD *helps* DAN *to box where he sits beside the radio equipment, back to audience*]

DAN: [*Flatly*] Where'd I slip up?

BARD: You didn't. Young Griffin's dead. He had your gun.

DAN: [*The name sinking in . . . recognition*] Bard . . . Bard . . . do you know a man named Flick?

BARD: I've heard the name.

DAN: My daughter's paying Flick two thousand dollars to kill you.

BARD: So . . . [*In wonder*] So that's the way he was going to do it. [*Briskly*] Well, Mr. Flick's being arrested, right about now . . . Lombardi Grille . . .

DAN: [*Rises, steps threateningly toward* BARD] You fool! You damned clumsy . . .

BARD: Okay, Hilliard. Let off steam. Take a swing. How'd I know what they'd send your girl into? I swear . . .

DAN: Swear? What can you swear to? That when I'm not back in there in time . . . when Flick doesn't call . . . they won't jump to the conclusion that . . . [*Breaks off*] What can anyone swear to?

BARD: Don't worry about Flick's call, Mr. Hilliard. We know the signal. We can handle it.

DAN: [*Picks up rifle with telescopic sight*] Are you planning to use this?

FREDERICKS: They both still in there?

DAN: Yes.

BARD: [*Takes rifle from* DAN, *replaces it*] How many guns?

DAN: [*Looks out window toward his own house*] One. With three bullets.

FREDERICKS: That helps!

DAN: [*Turns from window. Slowly*] Also . . . my wife and son.

FREDERICKS: Mr. Hilliard—if these two convicts get away with this scheme . . .

DAN: I don't care about that now. I don't want them . . . or you . . . to kill my wife or boy. That's first. *First.* God help me, that comes first!

BARD: Nobody's blaming you, Mr. Hilliard. Nobody in his right mind can raise a voice against what you've done . . . But I can't let you go back in there.

> [*Pause. Then, slowly,* DAN *takes the special delivery envelope containing money from his inside topcoat pocket. He hands it to* BARD, *who examines the contents*]

DAN: Until they get that . . . they're not coming out.

FREDERICKS: [*Crisply*] Then we move in.

DAN: [*Erupting*] What'm I supposed to do . . . *sit up here and watch it happen?*

FREDERICKS: It's plain suicide for you to go back in there now!

DAN: [*A look at the window*] That may be. There comes a time when that fact just doesn't enter in . . . You don't give a hang about a life or two . . . what's one more?

BARD: [*Drops envelope with money on box; he is having an inner struggle*] Mr. Hilliard . . . we're trying to help you.

DAN: [*Pleading forcefully, hopelessly*] Then clear out! Get away.

Take your men . . . your rifles . . . your floodlights . . . and *get away!*

[CARSON *steps in, picks up the envelope with the money and holds it out to* DAN]

CARSON: We can't do that, Mr. Hilliard. I'll give you ten minutes . . . from the time you walk through that door over there. Shortly after you're inside, we'll give them the telephone signal they're waiting for. If you need us, flicker a light. You've got ten minutes. It's on your shoulders.

[*Pause.* DAN *takes the envelope.* CARSON *steps back*]

BARD: Mr. Hilliard, you'd better have the whole picture. Charles Wright is in the house.

DAN: [*Amazed. Turns to* BARD] Chuck?

BARD: And he's armed. We couldn't prevent it. [*Slight pause*] Do you want a gun, Mr. Hilliard?

DAN: [*Quietly*] No . . . thanks.

[*He puts the envelope into his inside topcoat pocket*]

BARD: They search you when you come in? [DAN *nods slowly*] Good luck . . . sir.

[DAN *turns to the stairs, then stops, turns*]

DAN: I've changed my mind.

BARD: You want a gun?

DAN: Please.

[BARD *takes his own revolver from his holster and hands it to* DAN]

BARD: You know how to use it?

[DAN *looks at revolver, nods, breaks it and shakes the bullets into his hand, examines the empty chamber*]

FREDERICKS: [*Shocked*] Are you crazy?

DAN: Maybe. Only a crazy man'd go in there with an empty gun. Griffin doesn't think I'm crazy.

BARD: That's a pretty long shot, isn't it?

DAN: I don't have any short ones in sight. Do you?

> [DAN *firmly puts the bullets into* BARD's *hand. Then, he turns and goes down the stairs. Pause. Then* BARD *flips the switch on the radio, picks up mike*]

BARD: [*Into mike*] Car nine . . . Winston.

WINSTON'S VOICE: Parked in side drive, Jess.

BARD: Tom . . . take Mr. Hilliard back to his car. [BARD *puts down the mike, flips off the radio; thoughtfully*] How'd you like to be riding up to *your* door like that, Fredericks?

FREDERICKS: Just luck I'm not. Or you.

BARD: Yeah. They didn't happen to pick on us, that's all.

> [BARD *picks up binoculars from window sill.* CARSON *looks at his watch*]

BLACKOUT

HILLIARD HOME

The lights are on in the living room; the rest of the house is dim. ELEANOR *and* RALPHIE *are in the master bedroom at the window.* CHUCK *still stands in* RALPHIE's *room with the door open, listening, waiting.* GLENN *is at the window in the living room.* ROBISH *is turning from the window in the side door in the pantry.*

ROBISH: [*Calling as he moves toward living room*] Here he comes, Griffin!

GLENN: [*Exhilarated*] Only two hours now, Robish. Two lousy hours! I'll do the drivin', make it in less!

ROBISH: [*As he enters the living room*] The little gal ain't with him.

> [*Above,* CHUCK *steps into the upstairs hall, listening*]

GLENN: Who cares? Who gives a damn?

> [GLENN *steps to the door, unlocks and opens it.* DAN *stands*

in the doorway, his hands in his topcoat pockets. DAN *comes into the room.* GLENN *closes and locks the door and moves to* DAN. GLENN'S *mood is almost a travesty on his previous behavior.* DAN'S *manner is profoundly quiet, as he sizes up the situation, frowning at the strange change in* GLENN]

ROBISH: [*At foot of stairs*] Hand over the dough, Hilliard.

DAN: [*Ignores this, lifts voice*] Stay up there, Ellie. Keep the door locked.

ROBISH: Yuh hear me?

DAN: [*Flatly—almost a challenge*] I don't have it.

ROBISH: [*Roaring*] What?

GLENN: Now, pop . . . who you kiddin'? Take your hands outta your pockets . . . *please.*

[*This is what* DAN *wants. He does so, facing* GLENN. GLENN *frisks him, feels the gun in the pocket, reaches in*]

ROBISH: I'll take the cash, Griffin!

[GLENN *takes the gun out of* DAN'S *pocket with his right hand, looking into* DAN'S *eyes*]

GLENN: What'd you say, Robish? [*He whips the gun out, points it at* ROBISH *and pushes* DAN *around behind him*] I didn't hear you, Robish!

[ROBISH *stares at the gun, lowering his own*]

ROBISH: [*Steps toward* DAN] You lousy sonofa . . .

GLENN: [*Laughs*] Had it all doped, didn't you? [*He reaches with his left hand across his own body, keeping the aim on* ROBISH, *into* DAN'S *inside coat pocket, brings out the envelope*] This what you had in mind, Robish?

ROBISH: [*To* DAN] You bastard!

GLENN: [*Stepping toward* ROBISH, *who backs away*] Not pop. Not my old pal pops! [*Pockets the money*] Any objections, Robish?

ROBISH: Let's get outta here!

[*The telephone rings.* ROBISH *makes a move to answer it*]

GLENN: Stay away from it, Robish. [*They all stand and listen in frozen silence while the phone rings three times: spaced, automatic.* GLENN *waits after the third ring until he's sure that there won't be a fourth. He laughs*] Well, that takes care of Bard! Time to break up housekeeping.

> [*Above,* ELEANOR *moves to bedroom door, switches on the bedroom lights and opens the door. She sees* CHUCK *in the hall, gasps. He turns to her and signals her to silence. She closes and locks the door and stands with* RALPHIE, *who has come to her side*]

ROBISH: [*As action takes place above*] Let's get movin'.

DAN: Griffin . . . you'd better take me along. *Only* me!

ROBISH: Like hell. We gotta have a dame in the car.

> [GLENN *has stopped on the stair, looks at* DAN]

DAN: Griffin . . . I'm the only one who knows you hired a man named Flick to kill Bard.

GLENN: [*Makes the "clickety-click" gesture*] Right up to the very end!

DAN: You'd better take me along.

GLENN: Nothin' can touch me now, Hilliard! Everythin's goin' my way!

ROBISH: Come on. Them woods out there could be full-a Feds, all we know.

GLENN: And you . . . you, Hilliard, can come along, too. 'Cause it's like this, see—Hank's waitin'.

DAN: Waiting?

ROBISH: You're off your rocker!

GLENN: So I'm in a kinda hurry! [*He goes to the stairs and up.* CHUCK *steps into* RALPHIE's *room and closes the door*] Hey, missus, get the brat ready. We're goin' on a little picnic.

> [*He reaches the door of the bedroom.* ELEANOR *and* RALPHIE *move away from the door*]

ROBISH: [*Covers* DAN *with pistol*] He's gettin' some sense back.

[GLENN *tries the bedroom door*]

GLENN: Hey, folks, you don' wanna miss the fun. The ice cream'll be all et up! [*He knocks on the door*] Lady, you don' want me to have to kick in this nice shiny door, do you?

[GLENN *steps back, lifts his leg and kicks the door; it splinters. At the same moment,* CHUCK *opens the door of* RALPHIE's *bedroom and steps behind* GLENN, *lifting his gun. He brings it down with great force on* GLENN's *head behind the ear;* GLENN *spins and falls backward into* RALPHIE's *bedroom.* CHUCK *plunges down the stairs*]

ROBISH: No racket up there! No noise!

[DAN *sees* CHUCK *descending the stairs, gun in hand;* DAN *ducks into dining room door, as* ROBISH *catches sight of* CHUCK. ROBISH *fires, hitting* CHUCK, *whose gun explodes toward the floor.* CHUCK, *clutching his shoulder, falls across living room floor.* ROBISH, *out of control, unthinking now, throws open the front door. Above,* ELEANOR—*hearing the shots—runs out of the bedroom and comes down the stairs wildly, leaving* RALPHIE *alone in the bedroom. Outside, floodlights illuminate the whole house in a harsh cold light*]

ELEANOR: Dan? . . .

DAN: [*Shouting*] Stay there, Ellie!

ROBISH: [*In open door, shouting*] Hey, out there! You hear me out there, coppers? [*As* DAN *moves cautiously toward* ROBISH's *back*] I got one of yuh! Who wants it next?

[DAN *moves fast now, driving his shoulder into* ROBISH's *back, sending him catapulting out the front door.* DAN *slams, locks door, as* ELEANOR *comes plunging down the stairs, heedless*]

ELEANOR: Dan, Dan . . .

[DAN *grabs* ELEANOR, *swings her across the room, out of line of the front door. Above,* RALPHIE *starts out of master bedroom just as* GLENN *lifts himself to his feet in* RALPHIE's *bedroom, regaining consciousness.* GLENN *and* RALPHIE *meet at door of master bedroom.* GLENN, *rubbing his head, turns the gun on* RALPHIE *and backs him into the bedroom as:*]

BLACKOUT

THE WALLINGS' ATTIC

CARSON *is kneeling in the window with the binoculars, looking out.* BARD *stands behind him with the rifle pointed out, looking through the telescopic sight.*

BARD: It's Robish . . .

CARSON: Get him, Jesse. I'll give the signal to close in.

BARD: [*Lowering the rifle*] Somebody pushed him out that door.

CARSON: He's heading for the car. Get him, Jesse!

BARD: Five minutes, Carson. Give Hilliard five more minutes!

CARSON: Hilliard might be dead!

BARD: Harry, I'm pleading with you. *Somebody shoved that big guy out the door. Five minutes!*

[*Slight pause.* CARSON *turns, still kneeling, switches on radio, picks up mike*]

CARSON: All right, Jess. [*Into mike*] Fredericks . . . Robish is in the Hilliard car. He's armed. Stop him.

[BARD *picks up the PA mike and speaks into it*]

BARD: [*His voice sounding in distance over PA*] Hilliard. Do you need us? *Hilliard.*

BLACKOUT

HILLIARD HOME

Outside, the floodlights remain on. There is light in living room and in master bedroom. GLENN, *still groggy from the blow, is in bedroom, gun on* RALPHIE, *who is against the wall. In the living room,* DAN *and* ELEANOR *are helping* CHUCK *toward front door; he cannot stand without support.*

BARD'S VOICE: [*The hollow sound of PA system*] Hilliard, can you hear me?

DAN: Get him out of here!

[DAN *unlocks and opens front door*]

CHUCK: I flubbed it, didn't I?

DAN: [*Stepping out, waves off*] Hold fire out there!

RALPHIE: [*In bedroom above—as* GLENN *grabs him and holds him in front of himself as a shield*] Dad! Dad!

DAN: [*As he and* ELEANOR *get* CHUCK *to door*] Get this boy some help.

CHUCK: [*Faintly*] I . . . I couldn't do anything else, I . . .

DAN: [*Taking the pistol from his hand*] You won't need this, son.

ELEANOR: [*Urgently, as she goes out with* CHUCK] Ralphie!

DAN: [*Firmly*] Ralphie's all right!

[ELEANOR *and* CHUCK *go out door.* DAN *turns, looking at pistol he has taken from* CHUCK. *He leaves the front door open wide*]

GLENN: [*Calling*] I'm with him, Hilliard.

RALPHIE: Dad . . . are you coming?

DAN: [*Puts pistol in his pocket, turns to stairs; speaks with grim determination*] I'm coming, son!

GLENN: In here, Hilliard. [*As* DAN *enters bedroom*] I'm still gonna make it . . . still gonna pull it off. [*As* DAN *stops*] You're gonna get me outta this.

DAN: [*Firmly, tonelessly*] Let go of the boy, Griffin.

GLENN: Fat chance, them coppers out there!

BARD'S VOICE: [*Over PA*] Griffin . . . Come out with your hands up . . . No gun!

[DAN *steps to window, opens it, calls out*]

DAN: Stay out of here. Turn off the light! [*The floodlights go out.* DAN *turns to* GLENN] Now. Take your hands off him.

[GLENN *does so, but places the gun at back of* RALPHIE'S *neck*]

GLENN: You move, kid, I'll blow your head off.

DAN: [*Gently, urgently*] Ralph . . . listen to me. That man is not going to hurt you.

GLENN: Try budgin', kid, you'll find out.

DAN: He's not going to hurt you at all because . . .

GLENN: Lay off, my head's bustin', Hank's waitin', lay off . . .

DAN: Ralph . . . have I ever lied to you?

[RALPHIE *shakes his head*]

GLENN: [*Gun against* RALPHIE'S *neck*] Feel that? . . .

DAN: [*To* RALPHIE] Now—I want you to do exactly as I tell you. Because that gun is not loaded.

GLENN: Stop bluffin', Hilliard, and let's get . . .

DAN: It has no bullets in it, Ralph. Do you understand that?

[RALPHIE *nods*]

GLENN: You're lyin'! You wouldn't've brung it in here if . . .

DAN: [*Stepping slightly, to clear the way; shouts*] Run!

[*Without hesitation,* RALPHIE *obeys. He runs . . . fast. He goes out of the bedroom, down the stairs and out the front door. As he starts,* GLENN *pulls the trigger of the revolver. There is a click.* GLENN *is astonished. Then, he tries again and again. A dazed bleak horror mounts* GLENN's *face. He starts for* DAN, *raising the gun to strike him. The sound of an ambulance siren is heard starting up and fading in the distance.* DAN *brings out* CHUCK's *pistol and holds it pointed at* GLENN]

GLENN: [*As he starts to strike* DAN] You goddam . . .

[*He breaks off, staring at the pistol in* DAN's *hand, incredulous. Long pause*]

DAN: Why don't you say something, Griffin? Clickety-clickety-click. [*Steps closer*] You're not talking. Where's your voice now? *Call me pop. Say* something, *damn you!*

GLENN: It ain't gonna be like this . . . Hank's waitin' . . .

DAN: [*Almost brutally*] Griffin . . . your brother's not waiting any-where. He's dead! [GLENN *is glassy-eyed, stunned*] Full of police bullets. *Dead!*

GLENN: [*Suddenly wild*] You're lyin', I don't believe . . . you're lyin'!!

DAN: You did that, too, damn you. . . . *Damn you!*

> [*The life goes out of* GLENN. *He swings full circle now; back to the stunned, depressed, lifeless phase of earlier in the evening. Despair . . . and worse. From now on he has no desire to survive. What follows is the death-wish all the way, finally erupting in his attempt to goad* DAN *into kill-ing*]

DAN: It's your turn, Griffin . . . how do you like it?

GLENN: [*Bleakly*] Go ahead . . . [*Lifelessly*] Get it over with. . . .

DAN: You don't like waiting? I've waited for hours . . . all of us . . . like years . . . all night . . . two days . . .

GLENN: Get it over with! [*He senses the hesitation in* DAN, *changes his tactics shrewdly*] You ain't got it in you!

DAN: [*Low, hard*] I've got it in me. *You* put it there!

GLENN: [*Goading*] Then go ahead!

BARD'S VOICE: [*On the PA*] Hilliard, can you hear me? . . . Your wife's here. And the boy. They're both safe!

> [*Pause.* GLENN *and* DAN *are both staring*]

GLENN: You ain't got it in you!

> [DAN *tenses with the revolver pointed at* GLENN. *Then, suddenly realizing what he has almost done, he lowers the gun, relieved*]

DAN: [*Quietly*] You're right. [*Low—with disgust*] Thank God, you're right! [*Quietly—with great dignity*] Get out of my house. [*Then he steps to* GLENN *and slaps him a resounding, violent blow across the face*] Get out of my house!

> [GLENN *is staggered by the blow. He recoils. There is a*

pause while GLENN *cowers, rubbing his jaw. Then,* GLENN *begins muttering, dazed*]

GLENN: [*His voice whining . . . self-pity . . . a boy again*] I'm gettin' out, pop . . . I'm goin'. Only I'm takin' Hank along. You hit me for the last goddam time . . . You ain't ever gonna hit Hank or me again. [*He moves toward the bedroom door as* DAN *steps out of his way*] I'm takin' Hank along and you ain't gonna see either one of us ever again! [*He turns in the upstairs hall and shouts back at* DAN *in the bedroom*] You can sit here'n rot in your stinkin' house, Mister God! I hated this crummy joint the day I was born!

[GLENN *turns and starts down the stairs as* DAN *follows him to the bedroom door*]

DAN: [*In amazement; weary disgust*] Get out.

GLENN: [*On his way downstairs*] You ain't gonna beat it into Hank'n me! Hank'n me's gonna be right on top! [GLENN, *now at the foot of the stairs, pauses, looks around, still dazed.* DAN *follows him down the stairs, pauses on lower step.* GLENN *turns toward the open door, beckoning to an imaginary* HANK] C'mon, Hank . . . we'll show 'em! [*The floodlights come on outside as* GLENN *steps in the doorway brandishing the gun. He goes out of sight, shouting*] We'll show 'em, Hank, we'll show 'em, Hank, we'll . . .

[*A rifle shot is heard, echoing down the quiet street.* DAN *stands quietly on the stairs. Lights remain on in Hilliard home*]

THE WALLINGS' ATTIC

Lights rise on the attic. BARD *is lowering the rifle. He looks at* CARSON *a moment, a strange expression on his face.*

CARSON: [*Almost reassuringly*] He asked for it, Jess. He . . . he acted like he was begging for it.

[BARD *looks at the rifle, then places it against the wall; slowly sits on the box*]

CARSON: You going over there?

BARD: [*Softly*] In a little while.

CARSON: You feel all right, Jess?

BARD: Just . . . maybe a little disgusted with the human race.

CARSON: Mmmm. Including Hilliard?

BARD: [*Looks up at him, smiles wanly*] Thanks, Harry . . . No, *not* including Hilliard.

CARSON: World's full of Hilliards.

[CARSON *turns and goes down the attic stairs.* BARD *sits quietly, thinking . . . as the lights fade slowly on the attic scene.*

In the Hilliard home, DAN *still stands unmoving on the stairs.* ELEANOR *appears at front door; she looks stunned, worn. She gazes at the havoc that was her home. She moves slowly to the sofa, almost helplessly rearranges a pillow.* RALPHIE *enters behind her; he crosses to* DAN, *whose head is down;* RALPHIE *stands gazing at his father. Outside,* CINDY *appears and enters the pantry, disappears into kitchen a moment. As* CINDY *enters the living room from dining room,* DAN *lifts his head, looks at her; then, slowly, he turns his gaze on* ELEANOR. *Their eyes meet, hold. They stand looking at each other as though cognizant of the miracle . . . as though seeing in each other, and perhaps in the world, more than words could convey*]

DIMOUT

SLOW CURTAIN

Hostile Witness

JACK ROFFEY

Jack Roffey

A taut thriller, with its centerpiece the trial at the Old Bailey of a leading barrister, accused of the murder of a distinguished judge and compelled to conduct his own defense, *Hostile Witness* originally opened in London in 1964 to an exceedingly favorable critical verdict and instant audience popularity.

The reviewer for *The Sunday Times* reported that "it is one of the great merits of this murder mystery, which excites interest from the start and sustains it to the end, that the people matter as well as the plot," a view generally shared by others, including R. B. Marriott of *The Stage* who pronounced it "among the best murder stories I have seen played out in a theatre."

"You might think that no new variations could possibly be rung on courtroom dramas," wrote Felix Barker in the London *Evening News.* "But, draw close and give ear—Jack Roffey has succeeded in *Hostile Witness* which was tried before an enthusiastic jury at the Haymarket Theatre last night. The sentence of this court: a year at least." The sentence was dutifully carried out by appreciative West End theatregoers.

It has long been the general contention of American theatrical managements that most British courtroom dramas (with their robed and bewigged participants, formal court panoply, and ceremonial minutiae) simply could not survive a sea change. Happily, *Hostile Witness* (as did Agatha Christie's *Witness for the Prosecution* in 1954) refuted this theory. Opening in New York in 1966, Jack Roffey's courtroom "whodunit" (with Ray Milland portraying Simon Crawford) took immediate hold and enjoyed a critical reception similar to that received in London. It was judged a "consistently fascinating play" that proved "steadily intriguing" and provided "an entertaining evening of suspense and misleading clues" where "plot, character and suspense are grippingly twisted together."

Although *Hostile Witness* was a substantial success, comparatively little was known about its author. Mr. Roffey himself, however, has provided the following biographical and professional data.

"Born in 1916 in Yokohama, Japan. Came back to England in 1920, speaking fluent Japanese and no English.

"Educated at various schools in southern England, finishing up as a King's Scholar at Canterbury, singing solos in the Cathedral choir, until voice broke to mutual satisfaction all round.

"Failed scholarship to Oxford for reason stated to be that 'views expressed in English essay displayed too marked a socialistic tendency.' Since the subject set was 'Tradition is the means whereby the romance of the past is interested in the prosaism of the present,' this reason taken to be a euphemism for the sad fact that he just wasn't bloody good enough!

"Gravitated to the Sorbonne, Paris, whereby grinding poverty detracted in no way from the most enjoyable and stimulating student days a young man could wish for.

"Joined staff of the Central Criminal Court, Old Bailey, in 1938, leaving it for war service in 1939. Spent an uneventful and smelly war guarding oil refineries in the West Indies, and without firing a shot in anger. Returned to the Old Bailey in 1945, and has been one of the 'back room boys' of the Court ever since.

"Married, with three children. Hobbies include writing (with varying success), horses, gardening, fishing, resurrecting an old house and reading any travel book that exists.

"At present, lives in Lewes, Sussex, and is toying with the idea of learning pottery."

Jack Roffey's earlier West End suspense play, *No Other Verdict*, opened at The Duchess Theatre in January, 1954, but had to curtail a promising run because of a spell of Arctic weather that hit Britain severely and forced many theatres to close.

Hostile Witness was first produced by Peter Saunders at the Haymarket Theatre, London, on November 4, 1964. The cast was as follows:

CHARLES MILBURN	*Charles Leno*
PERCY	*Peter Furnell*
SHEILA LARKIN	*Miranda Connell*
SIMON CRAWFORD	*Michael Denison*
SIR PETER CROSSMAN	*Richard Hurndall*
HAMISH GILLESPIE	*Trevor Reid*
HUGH MAITLAND	*Geoffrey Lumsden*
COURT USHER	*Edward Waddy*
MR. NAYLOR	*Brian Oulton*
CLERK OF THE COURT	*Lionel Gadsden*
SHORTHAND WRITER	*Peter Rose*
MR. SAXBY	*Douglas Malcolm*
POLICEMAN	*Ronald Mansell*
TREASURY SOLICITOR	*Billy John*
BARRISTER	*John Ruck Keene*
BARRISTER	*Gordon Craig*
LADY BARRISTER	*Margaret Ives*
SUPERINTENDENT ELEY	*Hugh Cross*
DR. WIMBORNE	*Malcolm Russell*
MR. JUSTICE OSBORNE	*Ronald Adam*
ALDERMAN	*Leslie Pitt*
PRISON OFFICER	*Philip Lennard*
LADY GREGORY	*Dulcie Bowman*
LADY BARRISTER	*Olive Simpson*

Directed by	Anthony Sharp
Designed by	Anthony Holland
Lighting by	Joe Davis

Hostile Witness had its New York première on February 17, 1966, at the Music Box Theatre, under the auspices of Jay Julien and André Goulston, by arrangement with Peter Saunders. The cast was as follows:

CHARLES MILBURN	*Norman Barrs*
PERCY	*Harvey Jason*
SHEILA LARKIN	*Angela Thornton*
SIMON CRAWFORD	*Ray Milland*
SIR PETER CROSSMAN	*Michael Allinson*
HAMISH GILLESPIE	*Edgar Daniels*
MAJOR HUGH MAITLAND	*Geoffrey Lumsden*
COURT USHER	*Stafford Dickens*
MR. NAYLOR	*Anthony Kemble Cooper*
CLERK OF THE COURT	*Walter Thomson*
POLICEMAN	*Arthur Marlowe*
SUPERINTENDENT ELEY	*Gerald Peters*
DR. WIMBORNE	*Peter Pagan*
MR. JUSTICE OSBORNE	*Melville Cooper*
PRISON OFFICER	*John Clark*
LADY GREGORY	*Margot Stevenson*
SPECTATORS AND COURT PERSONNEL	*Katherine Hynes, Dorothy James, Robert Murch, Alex Reed, Tom McDermott, Jim Oyster*

Directed by	Reginald Denham
Scenery and Lighting by	Ralph Alswang

The action of the play takes place in the Chambers of Simon Crawford, Q.C., in the Central Criminal Court of the Old Bailey and in a Consultation Cell in the Old Bailey, London.

ACT ONE

ACT TWO

ACT ONE

SCENE 1

The chambers of SIMON CRAWFORD, Q.C.—*his private room.
It is a typical room of a leading Q.C., gracefully furnished,
with a large desk and a number of comfortable chairs.
Books line the walls and there is an ordered clutter of
briefs, folders, etc., awaiting attention. A door leads to the
general office beyond, and a wide window looks on to a
quiet courtyard. Prominent on the desk is a studio portrait of a beautiful young girl of nineteen or twenty in a
silver frame. Surprisingly, also on the desk is a bowl of
flowers.*

*When the curtain rises it is early evening—about 4:30 p.m.
on the 29th April, 1964.* CHARLES MILBURN *is discovered at
the desk reading some letters.* PERCY, *a junior clerk, enters.
He is a pleasant lad of about seventeen, but a bit cocky.
He is wearing his mackintosh and carries* CRAWFORD'S *red
barrister's bag. He is singing a pop song as he enters.*

PERCY: Ooops! Sorry. [*He stops singing*]

CHARLES: So Mr. Crawford didn't return from Court with you then, Percy?

PERCY: He'll be along. He just went behind to see the Judge.

CHARLES: [*Sighs*] "He just went behind to see the Judge"—

PERCY: He just went behind to see the Judge—*sir.*

CHARLES: Or "Mr. Milburn."

PERCY: Yes, Mr. Milburn.

CHARLES: That's better. Remember, politeness costs nothing, but you'll get nowhere without it in the Temple. Counsel expect to be addressed as "sir" by a young man of your age, and deservedly so.

PERCY: Yes, sir.

CHARLES: So do senior clerks—sometimes not so deservedly, but they still expect it.

PERCY: [*Laughs*] Yes, sir.

CHARLES: So the jury were not out as long as you feared?

PERCY: Twenty minutes, that's all. They'd just finished arraigning the next job, when in comes the Jury Bailiff. "Agreed in Kelly, my Lord." So the old man interposed them.

CHARLES: And what did the "old man" give Kelly?

PERCY: Give Kelly nothing! We got her off.

CHARLES: On that evidence?

PERCY: They acquitted her, yeah—sir!

CHARLES: Well, well, well, well.

[PERCY *has unpacked the brief bag and* CHARLES *has taken the wastepaper basket and is sharpening a pencil into it*]

PERCY: I've brought the brief back, sir. What d'you want done with it?

CHARLES: Think, boy, think!

PERCY: I have thought, I don't know.

CHARLES: [*Sighs*] Get a fee note made out, and put it on my desk.

PERCY: Oh—yeah—sorry. Proper turn-up for the book, old Kelly getting off, eh? The old Judge was wild!

CHARLES: Who was that—Osborne?

PERCY: Old Ozzy—yeah. When the jury said "Not Guilty" he didn't half look at them old-fashioned. And then the boss gets up grinning and asks if she can be discharged, he wouldn't let her go straight off! "Well, Kelly," he says—you know with that old toad face of his—"Well, Kelly—you have had the benefit of an exceptionally able defense, as a result of which, the jury, in their wisdom, have found you not guilty. When you have recovered from your surprise, you may go."

CHARLES: That's typical.

PERCY: It's been like a circus up there all week. Yesterday he was hearing this little case of rape. It wasn't much of a case—by all accounts the girl raped pretty easy. But she was under sixteen and in the family way, so the jury found the bloke guilty. Anyway, the old man was tearing him off a strip before passing sentence, see—"and as a result of your lust this girl is now pregnant. Well, as ye sow, so shall ye reap—nine months." He's a proper old basket and no mistake. But he's funny with it though.

CHARLES: Yes. Off with you, Percy.

PERCY: Yes, sir. Duty calls. [PERCY *opens door and finds* SHEILA LARKIN *coming in carrying some foolscap.* SHEILA *is a pretty girl in her mid-twenties, a junior counsel in* CRAWFORD's *Chambers*] Ah, Miss Larkin. *Après vous, mamselle.*

SHEILA: Thank you, Percy.

PERCY: My pleasure, miss. [*He goes out, closing the door*]

SHEILA: So much courtesy all of a sudden. Have you been bullying him, Charles?

CHARLES: One cannot bully a lump of granite, Miss Larkin. Only by constant abrasion can one hope to achieve a dull polish. Is there anything I can do for you? Mr. Crawford is not back from Court yet.

SHEILA: He is, actually. He was parking his car as I came in. It's the opinion he asked me to do. I'll leave it on his desk and go home, I think. He'll find fault with it in any case.

CHARLES: Why should he do that?

CRAWFORD: [*Off*] That'll be for three, Percy, in five minutes.

PERCY: [*Off*] Yes, sir.

SHEILA: Want to bet?

[SIMON CRAWFORD, Q.C., *enters, calling over his shoulder. He is a handsome man of late middle age, with a brisk hard manner*]

CRAWFORD: And see it's hot for a change. [CHARLES *takes his coat and hat*] Charles, I'm expecting Sir Peter Crossman and Mr. Gillespie any moment now. I shall need you, so don't get involved.

CHARLES: Very good, sir.

CRAWFORD: What's the time? [*Looks at his watch*] Four-thirty—that doesn't give us long. Don't go, Miss Larkin, I want a word with you. I'm also expecting Superintendent Eley at five.

CHARLES: Superintendent Eley, sir?

CRAWFORD: Yes. After that I anticipate that Sir Peter and Mr. Gilles-

pie will stay on for a while, and I may or may not be leaving. If I
do leave, I want you to see they have everything they require.

CHARLES: I'll attend to them, sir.

[CRAWFORD *gives* CHARLES *a bundle of briefs from desk*]

CRAWFORD: And you can take those with you. I shan't look at them
tonight.

CHARLES: Thank you, sir. And congratulations on the Kelly acquittal.
Percy described it to me as a "turn up for the book."

CRAWFORD: Kelly? Oh, yes, we had quite a—grand finale.

CHARLES: There's one thing I should mention, sir. You'll see from
your desk diary that I have provisionally agreed a consultation for
you in Tyson at Brixton the day after tomorrow.

CRAWFORD: Cancel it and return the brief.

CHARLES: But sir, with respect, you yourself—

CRAWFORD: Damn you, Charles, don't argue.

CHARLES: Very good, sir. [*He goes out*]

CRAWFORD: Sit down, Miss Larkin. [MISS LARKIN *sits*]

CRAWFORD: [*Takes out the opinion*] Is this the opinion?

SHEILA: Yes.

CRAWFORD: I understand you defended a woman named Shaw under the Poor Prisoner's Defense Act last week?

SHEILA: Yes.

CRAWFORD: For which you were paid a brief fee of eighteen guineas,
and two refreshers of twelve guineas each.

SHEILA: Yes.

CRAWFORD: Which you regarded as inadequate.

SHEILA: Yes.

CRAWFORD: Why?

SHEILA: It wasn't a simple case.

CRAWFORD: I see. Have you paused to consider how you came to be
briefed in the first place?

SHEILA: No. But I assumed—

CRAWFORD: Then I will tell you. Your brief was originally accepted by
Charles for a member of these Chambers before it became apparent that neither Mr. Painter nor Mr. Bond would be able to appear. When it did, Charles rightly or wrongly considered the mat-

ter straightforward enough to be handled by Counsel of your length of call, and accordingly gave it to you.

SHEILA: I had Treasury Counsel against me, and his brief was marked at thirty guineas.

CRAWFORD: Indeed—and how do you know that?

SHEILA: I asked him.

CRAWFORD: Ye-es. Miss Larkin, I am head of these Chambers, and any indiscretion by one of its members reflects adversely, not only on Chambers, but also on myself.

SHEILA: I appreciate that, of course, but—

CRAWFORD: It is no part of Counsel's duty to concern himself with what fees should, or should not be paid—least of all by visiting other Chambers and questioning members of the Bar in order to compare their fees with your own.

SHEILA: But I only did so this time, because—

CRAWFORD: I am not concerned with your reasons. You have committed a breach of etiquette which I am not prepared to tolerate in a member of these Chambers. If you wish to remain here, such a thing must not occur again. Is that clear?

SHEILA: Perfectly.

CRAWFORD: That is all. [SHEILA *makes to leave*] One moment. You can take this with you. [*He gives her the opinion*]

SHEILA: What's wrong with it?

CRAWFORD: Nothing, it's very good—apart from the punctuation. It can be typed and sent off. And Miss Larkin—I'd be grateful if you would remain available in Chambers for the next few minutes. I may need to call on you.

SHEILA: Very well. [SHEILA *goes out.* CRAWFORD *sits wearily at desk— then dials a number on the telephone at his side*]

CRAWFORD: Is Major Maitland in the club, please? Mr. Simon Crawford, thank you. Hello, Hugh. It looks as if the time has come. Can you come over to Chambers? Right away, for God's sake! My solicitor and Crossman, Q.C., are due now. I want you to have a word with him. Simply tell him the facts as we discussed them. [*There is a knock at the door*] Hold on a moment. Come in.

[CHARLES *enters*]

CHARLES: Sir Peter Crossman and Mr. Gillespie are here, sir.

CRAWFORD: Good. Ask them to come in. Charles?

CHARLES: Yes, sir?

CRAWFORD: And then come back yourself, and bring Miss Larkin with you.

CHARLES: Very good. This way, gentlemen.

CRAWFORD: [*Into telephone*] Hold on a minute, they've just come. [SIR PETER CROSSMAN *and* HAMISH GILLESPIE *enter.* SIR PETER *is thin, austere and precise—the accepted image of the successful barrister.* GILLESPIE, *on the other hand, is unconventional—happy and untidy and Scottish, facts which tend to obscure his cleverness as a lawyer for those who don't know him*] Peter, Hamish, sit down, will you? [*Into phone*] Can you manage that? I'm most grateful. No. If I feel any emotion it's one of perverted exhilaration. See you later—good-bye. [*He hangs up and crosses to meet his guests*] Peter—Hamish. This is very good of you. [*He offers cigarettes to* SIR PETER] Cigarette?

SIR PETER: Thank you.

CRAWFORD: How's the family, Peter?

SIR PETER: Beset by alarm and despondency. Monica has just failed her driving test, and Jane starts her A levels tomorrow.

CRAWFORD: Too bad. [*He turns to* GILLESPIE] No need to ask you, you miserable old bachelor.

GILLESPIE: A solitary life still has its compensations.

CRAWFORD: Has it? I must confess that, so far, I have failed to rediscover a single one of any importance. [*He glances at the photo on the desk*]

GILLESPIE: No. I'm sorry.

[CHARLES *and* SHEILA *enter.* SIR PETER *and* HAMISH *rise*]

CRAWFORD: Come in. Ah, Miss Larkin, this is Sir Peter Crossman.

SIR PETER: How do you do?

SHEILA: How do you do?

CRAWFORD: And I think you know Mr. Gillespie.

SHEILA: Yes, indeed. Good afternoon.

GILLESPIE: Good afternoon, Miss Larkin.

CRAWFORD: Sit down, Miss Larkin.

GILLESPIE: Will you sit here?

SHEILA: Don't worry. I'll sit there.

CRAWFORD: Charles, ask Percy to make it five cups.

CHARLES: Yes, sir. [*He goes out*]

SIR PETER: They tell me you got the Kelly girl off, Simon, in the face of Osborne J.

CRAWFORD: Yes, I'm glad to say.

SIR PETER: I don't know how the devil you do it.

CRAWFORD: Simply by telling the truth. You should try it sometime.

[CHARLES *reenters*]

GILLESPIE: It's an accepted fact among the criminal classes that juries like his face. I've heard so time and again.

SIR PETER: Have you now?

CRAWFORD: I wonder if they'd care for it as much without a wig?

GILLESPIE: I wouldn't count on that.

CRAWFORD: I may have to.

SIR PETER: Why?

CRAWFORD: For the same reason I have asked you all here this evening. I am about to be arrested.

SIR PETER: Arrested?

CRAWFORD: [*Looking at watch*] Yes. In about twenty minutes. I have an appointment with Superintendent Eley at five.

GILLESPIE: Arrested on what charge?

CRAWFORD: Murder. [*There is a knock at the door*] Come in.

[PERCY *enters with tea tray*]

PERCY: Your tea, sir, five cups.

CRAWFORD: Thank you, Percy. Put it there.

PERCY: Shall I pour it out, sir?

CRAWFORD: No. Thank you, Percy.

PERCY: Thank you, sir.

[PERCY *goes out and* CRAWFORD *starts to pour tea*]

CRAWFORD: How do you like your tea, Peter? Milk and sugar?

SIR PETER: To hell with the tea. Simon, are you serious about this?

CRAWFORD: Perfectly.

SHEILA: Let me do that for you, Mr. Crawford.

CRAWFORD: Thank you, Miss Larkin. [SHEILA *takes over tea-pouring*]

GILLESPIE: Who do they say you murdered, for heaven's sake?

CRAWFORD: Mr. Justice Gregory.

SIR PETER: Good God!

GILLESPIE: But he was your—

CRAWFORD: Yes. Let me assure you, here and now, that I did not kill him.

GILLESPIE: Then what? I mean—how do you come to be involved?

CRAWFORD: You may well ask. Peter, I'm being damned rude in assuming that you're willing to act for me in this. But I'd be grateful for your help.

SIR PETER: Do stop talking nonsense, man.

CRAWFORD: Thank you.

SIR PETER: Why are you involved? What made the police question you in the first place?

CRAWFORD: It's a good deal worse than that. They were rattling handcuffs in my ear the day following the murder, before ever questioning me at all.

GILLESPIE: But why? What explanation?

CRAWFORD: They were "acting on information received."

GILLESPIE: In heaven's name, who from?

CRAWFORD: A man called Armitage.

CHARLES: Armitage?

CRAWFORD: Yes, Armitage. Did you check your desk diary as I asked, Charles? That chap who came here that time, was his name Armitage?

CHARLES: It was, yes, sir.

SIR PETER: What man is this?

CHARLES: It was in January, sir. This man came, said his name was Armitage, and that he had a private appointment with Mr. Crawford for three o'clock.

GILLESPIE: And what was his business?

CHARLES: He wouldn't tell me, sir—said it was strictly private.

SIR PETER: So?

CRAWFORD: I never saw him. By the time I got back from Court, he'd gone.

CHARLES: That's right, sir. He waited for about half an hour; said he couldn't wait any longer and then left. He said he'd phone Mr. Crawford later at his home and fix another time.

SIR PETER: Did you know this man?

CRAWFORD: Until that day I'd never even heard of him.

SIR PETER: So you hadn't made this private appointment?

CRAWFORD: No.

SIR PETER: Did he phone you later at home?

CRAWFORD: No.

GILLESPIE: Charles, what was he like, this man?

CHARLES: Well, I can't remember much about him, sir. He was getting on a bit—sixty—sixty-five. Rather shabby, down-at-heel. I remember his eyes were bad. He had those thick glasses.

SIR PETER: Anyhow, be it the same man or not—what information did he give the police?

CRAWFORD: My motive for killing the Judge.

SIR PETER: I see. What was this alleged motive?

CRAWFORD: How much do you know of the circumstances surrounding my daughter's death?

SIR PETER: I heard something.

CRAWFORD: Jill was knocked down in Gordon Place by a car that didn't stop. Two days later she died of a fractured skull.

SIR PETER: Yes. That much I knew.

CRAWFORD: The police never found the man responsible.

SIR PETER: It *was* a man?

CRAWFORD: Yes. There were two witnesses. Each of them said it was an elderly man—traveling very fast.

GILLESPIE: So what did this Armitage tell the police?

CRAWFORD: First that I'd engaged him as a private investigator to find the man responsible.

GILLESPIE: Had you?

CRAWFORD: No. I'd engaged other investigators.

SIR PETER: Why?

CRAWFORD: The police were getting nowhere.

SIR PETER: But they must have been doing everything possible. What object was there in your proceeding on your own?

CRAWFORD: Logically, none.

SIR PETER: Illogically, then? Did you want to punish him personally in some way?

CRAWFORD: The thought had occurred to me.

SIR PETER: How did you want to punish him?

CRAWFORD: I never got round to that. I became ill, as you know. When my health returned, so did my sense of proportion.

SIR PETER: Did you ever find out who the driver was?

CRAWFORD: No.

GILLESPIE: What has any of that got to do with Gregory?

CRAWFORD: Armitage alleges that on the Friday before the murder, he sent me a letter telling me that Gregory was the man I was looking for.

GILLESPIE: Gregory a hit-and-run driver?

CRAWFORD: Yes.

SIR PETER: Did you ever receive such a letter?

CRAWFORD: No. Although the police found it later, in my desk at home. It was rather badly typed in red, and was signed "James Armitage."

SIR PETER: And you had no knowledge of its existence?

CRAWFORD: None. All I can imagine is that it was connected in some way with a rather dog-eared envelope marked "Private and Confidential" that was delivered to me here in Chambers that same Friday; and that also was typed in red.

SHEILA: Yes, I remember. I signed for that. It came recorded delivery.

CRAWFORD: That envelope contained blank paper.

SIR PETER: I see. Have you still got the envelope and paper?

CRAWFORD: No. I thought it was the work of some crank and threw it away.

SIR PETER: Did you tell Charles, or anyone else in Chambers, that you'd had this crank letter?

CRAWFORD: I certainly intended to. But I can't remember ever doing so.

CHARLES: No, sir. You never mentioned it to me.

SHEILA: Nor me.

SIR PETER: That's a pity.

GILLESPIE: What other evidence have the police got?

CRAWFORD: They haven't seen fit to confide in me as yet, Hamish. Whatever it is, it must be false.

SIR PETER: Nevertheless, it's strong enough for them to charge you with murder.

CRAWFORD: Wrongly.

SIR PETER: I accept that. But the charge still has to be answered.

CRAWFORD: Of course.

SIR PETER: Well then, what is your answer?

CRAWFORD: I was never in the Judge's house that night.

SIR PETER: Then how do you account for any evidence against you?

CRAWFORD: In theory—or in fact?

SIR PETER: Either.

CRAWFORD: In fact—I can't account for it.

SIR PETER: And in theory?

CRAWFORD: Someone is gunning for me, Peter.

GILLESPIE: Gunning for you—or gunning for the Judge?

CRAWFORD: Either, or both. Whichever it was—I was deliberately framed.

SIR PETER: Are you able to support that theory?

CRAWFORD: No. Not yet.

SIR PETER: It's presupposing rather a lot that somewhere in your life there's an unknown madman who hates you enough to do such a thing.

CRAWFORD: I agree—but it's the only possible explanation.

SIR PETER: But Simon, for heaven's sake, have you no suspicion as to who it might be?

CRAWFORD: Not one. By the way, Charles, did you have any luck with the shorthand writers?

CHARLES: Not yet, sir, I'm afraid. So many of the older writers have retired.

CRAWFORD: Well, keep trying. It's very important.

CHARLES: Yes, sir.

CRAWFORD: You see I've been trying to find someone—somewhere— who might remember a threat from the dock against me, or against the Judge, or indeed against both of us.

SIR PETER: Oh, really!

GILLESPIE: Simon, I take it you can support your claim you were never in Gregory's house that night?

CRAWFORD: Within the limits of the medical evidence, yes.

SIR PETER: But only within those limits?

CRAWFORD: That's the only time that matters, isn't it?

SIR PETER: Quite possibly you're right—I really wouldn't know. What are the limits?

CRAWFORD: The pathologist says he died between one and two A.M.

SIR PETER: And where were you at that time?

CRAWFORD: I was lying unconscious on a settee in Hugh Maitland's house.

SIR PETER: Who is Hugh Maitland?

CRAWFORD: He's a friend of mine and of the Judge, and Lady Gregory. You've all been to my house, haven't you? No, Miss Larkin, I don't think you have.

SHEILA: No.

CRAWFORD: Well, let me describe the layout. When you turn into Gordon Mews, where I live, you come first of all to the Judge's house on the right, before you come to mine. Together, our two houses take up the whole of the right-hand side of the mews with garages at the end. The whole of the left-hand side is Maitland's.

SIR PETER: How did you come to be lying unconscious on his settee between one and two A.M. on a Sunday morning?

CRAWFORD: I'd been attacked earlier, outside my own house. Maitland found me there when he was walking his dog. I had been coshed on the back of the head.

GILLESPIE: Simon, you never told me about this.

CRAWFORD: Quite frankly, since then I've had other things to think about.

GILLESPIE: Did you see who coshed you?

CRAWFORD: No, I went out like a light.

GILLESPIE: You say you were attacked outside. Had you opened the door to someone?

CRAWFORD: No. I was on my way home.

GILLESPIE: Where from?

CRAWFORD: Here—Chambers.

GILLESPIE: At midnight—on a Saturday?

[CRAWFORD *glances at photo on desk*]

CRAWFORD: Since—Jill's death I've been working pretty hard. I had a lot to do.

SIR PETER: Can anyone confirm that?

CHARLES: Yes, sir, I can. Mr. Crawford has worked late every weekend for the past three months.

SIR PETER: What time did you reach the mews?

CRAWFORD: Let's see. I left here at eleven-thirty. I was on foot, so I suppose about twelve—twelve-fifteen.

SIR PETER: And what time were you found by Maitland?

CRAWFORD: Wouldn't the answer to that come better from him? He's on his way here now.

SIR PETER: Just as you like. Were you seen by a doctor?

CRAWFORD: Not at the time, no. Maitland tried to get hold of his G.P. but he was out. While he was wondering what to do next I came round.

SIR PETER: Then you went straight home?

CRAWFORD: I tried to, yes, then I found I'd lost my keys.

SIR PETER: Well anyway, you remained with Maitland, or in his house, from the time he found you until the following morning.

CRAWFORD: Yes.

SIR PETER: And he'll testify to that?

CRAWFORD: Of course.

SIR PETER: That's all right then. Naturally, you got in touch with the police.

CRAWFORD: Not that night.

SIR PETER: But Simon, why on earth not?

CRAWFORD: Damn it, I wasn't in a fit state to get in touch with anybody. They had a full report the following day. [*There is a knock at the door*] Come in. [PERCY *enters*] Yes, Percy, what is it?

PERCY: I'm sorry, sir. There's a telephone call for Miss Larkin. It's through to your room, miss.

SHEILA: Will you excuse me, please?

CRAWFORD: Yes, of course.

[SHEILA *follows* PERCY *out, closing door behind her*]

GILLESPIE: Simon, I suppose there's no—

CRAWFORD: Just a moment, Hamish. Peter, will you do me one more favor?

SIR PETER: Yes, certainly, if I'm able.

CRAWFORD: Sheila Larkin—you may have wondered why I had her in here. She's young, but I think she's going to be good. She's never yet been led by a silk of your status, but—

SIR PETER: —but you'd like her to appear with me?

CRAWFORD: Yes.

SIR PETER: I don't want to take any chances.

CRAWFORD: Neither do I, Peter. But this is not taking any chances. She's not just a pretty girl. She's been with me a long time, she's quite ready for this.

SIR PETER: What do you say, Hamish?

GILLESPIE: It's all the same to me—she'll be your junior.

SIR PETER: Would it embarrass you at all if I had a word with the girl first—before saying yes or no?

CRAWFORD: No, of course not. In any case I've got to get changed and I've a lot of things to discuss with Charles. [*He moves to door.* CHARLES *opens it*] I'll send her in to you. Let me know what you decide. Come on, Charles. [CRAWFORD *and* CHARLES *go out*]

SIR PETER: Evidently I said the wrong thing. Do you know the girl?

GILLESPIE: I've seen her in Court a couple of times. Anyway, I back Simon's judgment.

SIR PETER: [*Pouring tea*] Hamish, what the devil do you make of this?

GILLESPIE: He's certainly taking it calmly enough.

SIR PETER: Yes.

GILLESPIE: Is it confidence—or conceit?

SIR PETER: Whatever it is, I wish I had half of it. I mean, damn it all, the police aren't fools. They're not going to charge a man of his standing without being sure of their ground.

GILLESPIE: So can we believe him or can't we?

SIR PETER: If the alibi holds water.

GILLESPIE: That doesn't answer my question.

SIR PETER: The question doesn't really concern us.

GILLESPIE: It concerns me, he's a friend of mine.

SIR PETER: All right, let's say he's a friend of mine, too. Suppose we can't believe him—suppose everything he's told us is a pack of lies—that really he's guilty as hell, and we know it; because he's our friend does that lessen our duty towards him as a client?

GILLESPIE: No.

SIR PETER: Then whether we believe him or not is beside the point, surely. What extraordinary tea this boy makes. No, if when we know the facts, we're able to believe him, well and good. If we can't, well then, we simply defy the Crown to prove their case—or run diminished responsibility.

GILLESPIE: Now, wait a minute!

SIR PETER: Why is he kidding himself, Hamish? What's he frightened of? Why this euphemism that, after Jill's death, he—"became ill"? What he had was a complete mental breakdown. Why not admit it?

GILLESPIE: All right—so he's a bit sensitive. Does it necessarily follow that—?

SIR PETER: Nothing *necessarily* follows! It's an aspect we can't afford to ignore, that's all. Why do you suppose he asked *me*, Hamish?

GILLESPIE: You've crossed swords often enough for him to have a healthy respect for your ability.

SIR PETER: So in times of crisis also, the lion will lie down with the lamb?

GILLESPIE: That's hardly the analogy I'd have chosen myself. Let's say that serpent will coil with serpent? [*They laugh. There is a knock at the door*] Come in.

[SHEILA *opens door and comes in*]

SHEILA: Mr. Crawford said you wanted to see me.

SIR PETER: Ah—yes. Do please sit down, Miss Larkin.

SHEILA: Thank you.

SIR PETER: How long have you been a member of Mr. Crawford's Chambers, Miss Larkin?

SHEILA: Four years.

SIR PETER: Long enough to know some of the answers?

SHEILA: Only—very few, it seems.

SIR PETER: Oh, why do you say that?

SHEILA: I'm afraid Mr. Crawford hasn't a very high opinion of me.

SIR PETER: And what is your opinion of Mr. Crawford? [*She looks from one to the other, nonplused*] No, no, I'm not asking you to be disloyal, Miss Larkin. It's in his interest that I should know. So please be frank.

SHEILA: Well—as an advocate I don't think there's anyone in the Temple to touch him.

SIR PETER: I agree. And as a lawyer?

SHEILA: I think he—tends to be a bit impulsive. To be at his best, he needs a good solicitor behind him.

SIR PETER: Again I agree. And as a man?

SHEILA: You really want me to be frank?

SIR PETER: Please.

SHEILA: I think he's intolerant, and a bully. He has an immense conceit and—because of this he is supremely self-sufficient. I think he's ambitious, and as far as his ambition is concerned, quite ruthless.

SIR PETER: Ruthless enough to commit murder?

SHEILA: Capable of murder, yes.

SIR PETER: Yes? You were about to qualify that?

SHEILA: I—I think he *could* commit murder, but he never would.

SIR PETER: And why not?

SHEILA: Murder is an unconventional crime. He—he would be the last to admit it, but Mr. Crawford is a very conventional person. It's an accepted convention that the Law must be obeyed—especially by those who practice it. He would no more commit murder than he'd steal a box of matches.

SIR PETER: Not even with a powerful motive and the necessary compulsion to do so?

SHEILA: No.

SIR PETER: Then let's hope your faith is not too rudely shaken.

SHEILA: But surely you're not suggesting—

[*The door opens and* CRAWFORD *enters with* MAJOR MAIT-

LAND, *fifty to fifty-five, good-looking with an erect military bearing—well-dressed in a casual but expensive way*]

CRAWFORD: I'm sorry, but it's later than I thought. This is Major Maitland—Sir Peter Crossman—Mr. Gillespie—and Miss Sheila Larkin.

MAITLAND: How do you do?

SHEILA: How do you do?

[*The others greet him and* SIR PETER *gives* CRAWFORD *a nod*]

CRAWFORD: Who, I hope, will be Sir Peter's junior at the trial.

SHEILA: I?

SIR PETER: She will—yes.

CRAWFORD: Good.

SHEILA: But Mr. Crawford, I had no idea—

CRAWFORD: Just do as you're told. See that you don't let me down. Sit down, Hugh.

MAITLAND: Thank you so much.

CRAWFORD: Peter, this is your show.

SIR PETER: Major Maitland, you realize, do you not, the extreme seriousness of Mr. Crawford's position?

MAITLAND: Yes, of course.

SIR PETER: And your own responsibility?

MAITLAND: *My* responsibility?

SIR PETER: As yet we are not in possession of the full facts. But at the moment it would seem his only answer is an alibi, based on the fact that at the time of the Judge's death he was with you.

MAITLAND: That's perfectly true. He was.

SIR PETER: Good. Between what times?

MAITLAND: He spent the night in my house. He had been attacked. I found him and brought him in.

SIR PETER: Yes. But at what time?

MAITLAND: About half past twelve—quarter to one.

SIR PETER: You're quite sure about that?

MAITLAND: Oh, yes, quite sure.

SIR PETER: Why did you make a special note of the time?

MAITLAND: I didn't.

SIR PETER: Well then, how can you be so sure what time it was?

MAITLAND: It—it must have been about then.

SIR PETER: Why?

MAITLAND: Why?

SIR PETER: Yes—why?

MAITLAND: Oh, I see what you mean. I'd given a small dinner party that evening. I'd cleared up after my guests. I took my dog out for a walk, and found him lying there. I really don't know why you are adopting this tone with me, sir. All I want to do is help him and—

SIR PETER: I am adopting this tone, Major Maitland, because it is precisely this tone that will be adopted by the other side when they come to test the strength of an alibi which is supported by only one man—who happens also to be a close friend.

MAITLAND: Yes, yes. I beg your pardon—I—I do quite see that, of course.

SIR PETER: Then, please, try to remember. Did you look at your watch or a clock when you took Crawford into your house?

MAITLAND: No, I'm afraid I didn't—not then.

SIR PETER: Did you look at your watch or a clock at all?

MAITLAND: Crawford remarked on the time later, yes.

SIR PETER: When?

MAITLAND: When he'd recovered, and went to go home. He made some remark like "Good God, is it one-thirty already?"—something like that—"Time I was going"—and I went with him to his door. Then he discovered he had lost his keys, so he came back home with me again, and he spent the night in my spare room.

SIR PETER: And he had already been with you an hour before you accompanied him home?

MAITLAND: About an hour, yes.

SIR PETER: When he made that remark about its being one-thirty already—did you look at the clock?

MAITLAND: Yes, I must have done.

SIR PETER: But do you actually remember doing so?

MAITLAND: Well—yes, it—it's human nature, isn't it? I mean—when somebody makes a remark like that it's automatic, isn't it, to look— a reflex action almost.

SIR PETER: Reflex action or not, Major Maitland, can you definitely say that you looked at that clock and saw the hands pointing to half past one?

[MAITLAND *looks worried and perplexed.* SIR PETER *and* GILLESPIE *exchange a glance, doubtful of* MAITLAND'S *strength as a vital witness—this is not lost on* CRAWFORD]

SIR PETER: Please, Major Maitland, yes or no?

MAITLAND: Yes—yes, I'm sure I did.

SIR PETER: When did you first recall the time?

MAITLAND: I—I'm afraid I don't quite follow you.

SIR PETER: Presumably you discussed the matter with Mr. Crawford— after he was seen by the police, I mean.

MAITLAND: Yes, certainly.

SIR PETER: Well then, in the course of that discussion, was it yourself who established the time as one-thirty—or was it Mr. Crawford who recalled it to you?

MAITLAND: Does it make any difference? It just came out in the course of conversation. We were talking, and he—no, that's right— now I come to think of it, it was I who reminded him.

SIR PETER: You are quite sure of that?

MAITLAND: Isn't that what you want me to say?

SIR PETER: I don't want you to say anything, except the absolute truth.

MAITLAND: That is the truth. I remember. He was anxious about recalling the time, and I was able to reassure him—

SIR PETER: I see. Thank you very much, Major Maitland. Mr. Gillespie will be getting in touch with you.

[MAITLAND *hesitates a moment*]

MAITLAND: Yes—yes, of course. Naturally, I'll do anything I can. Shall I see you later, Simon?

CRAWFORD: Keep Charles company for a bit. I'll join you.

MAITLAND: Right. By all means, of course. Well, good night then.

[*He makes for the door*]

SIR PETER: Good night.

GILLESPIE: Good-bye, sir.

MAITLAND: I hope you think I'll be able to help. [*He goes out*]

SIR PETER: I'm very sorry—I'm hanged if I think so.

CRAWFORD: Don't you believe him?

SIR PETER: It doesn't really matter what I believe, Simon, does it?

CRAWFORD: Only in so far as, if you don't believe him, you don't believe me. He's telling the truth, Peter.

SIR PETER: Yes, quite possibly.

SHEILA: But he was nervous, Sir Peter. If I may say so, you went at him pretty hard.

SIR PETER: Yes, perhaps I did. But let's face it—in any other circumstances, you wouldn't trust that man as a potential key witness any further than you could kick him.

CRAWFORD: If I were persuaded of his truthfulness, I'd trust him.

SIR PETER: What? And risk a letdown? Simon, admit it, on the strength of this afternoon's showing any competent junior could break that man in the box like an egg. Isn't that so, Hamish?

GILLESPIE: Aye.

SIR PETER: How's he going to react to Treasury Counsel? What do you suppose a man like Naylor would do with him in cross-examination?

CRAWFORD: Even Naylor can't cross-examine his own witness.

SIR PETER: What the devil are you talking about? Maitland will be our witness.

CRAWFORD: Oh, no, he won't. Maitland has already made a statement to the police. I haven't, nor am I going to. Therefore the Crown are bound to call Maitland as the only person who saw me in the mews that night. In which case, they call him as a witness of truth, and are bound by what he says—they can't cross-examine. Any cross-examination will be yours—not Naylor's.

SIR PETER: But Naylor still has the last word.

CRAWFORD: In reexamination only.

SIR PETER: Yes, and reexamination can be as deadly as cross if you put your mind to it—you know that just as well as I do.

SHEILA: So we can't trust the alibi as a main line of defense.

SIR PETER: Good heavens, no. We daren't chance it.

CRAWFORD: We've got to chance it—it's all we have.

SIR PETER: At the moment, I grant you. But we don't yet know the full extent of the police case. If we accept that it's based on a false premise, there must be a flaw in it somewhere. It's up to us to find it, and crack it.

CRAWFORD: And if we don't find it?

SIR PETER: Very well—then we're in trouble—but not so much trouble as we'd be in trying to salvage an alibi that's been torpedoed by Treasury Counsel. Don't you agree, Hamish?

GILLESPIE: I agree.

CRAWFORD: And I most certainly do not. [*There is a knock at the door*] Come in. [CHARLES *enters*] Yes, Charles, what is it?

CHARLES: Excuse me, sir, Superintendent Eley is here now.

CRAWFORD: Ah. Thank you, Charles. Tell him I'm just coming.

CHARLES: Very good, sir. [*He goes out.* CRAWFORD *rises and goes for his coat and hat.*]

CRAWFORD: Miss Larkin, there may be one or two things I want from home. If so perhaps either you or Charles could being them along some time?

SHEILA: Yes, of course.

CRAWFORD: Thank you very much. [*He moves to door.*] No more argument, Peter. The alibi goes in. I'll see you all later—at Brixton. [*He goes out*]

CURTAIN

SCENE 2

Court One of the Central Criminal Court, Old Bailey. Some time later. The court is seen from the point of view of the jury—so that when Judge or Counsel addresses the jury he is in fact addressing the audience. Stage right is the Bench, angling slightly to center, with large chairs for the Judge and City dignitaries. Counsel's benches are center back facing front, but angled slightly left. The dock is stage left but it again is angled so that it partly faces front. The witness box is down right facing dock. In front of Counsel's benches is a long table for solicitors and police officers. Below the Judge's bench sit the CLERK OF COURT *and the* SHORTHAND WRITER, *and below and to the right of witness box is a seat for the* COURT USHER.

When the curtain rises the Court is reassembling after the luncheon adjournment. The Bench is empty. Below, however, the Court officials are all in their places. Leading Counsel for the Prosecution, MR. NAYLOR, *is seated at the right with his Junior,* MR. SAXBY, *to his left. At the left end of the front row is* SHEILA LARKIN, *now in wig and gown, sitting alone. There is no sign of* SIR PETER CROSSMAN. GILLESPIE *is seated at the solicitor's table immediately below* SHEILA, *and* SUPERINTENDENT ELEY *sits below* NAYLOR *with a member of the Director of Public Prosecutions staff. For the moment the dock is empty save for a uniformed* PRISON OFFICER. *A few barristers of assorted age and sex occupy the benches behind* NAYLOR *and* SHEILA LARKIN, *and behind them again stands a* POLICE OFFICER. SHEILA *and* GILLESPIE *look vaguely worried as they talk quietly together. They keep glancing toward the door. There is a general relaxed buzz of subdued conversation as the Court waits for the entry of the Judge. This is interrupted by three sharp raps on the Bench door and the* USHER *shouts.*

USHER: Be upstanding in Court.

[*Everyone rises as the* JUDGE, MR. JUSTICE OSBORNE, *takes his place on Bench, ushered in by an Alderman with the customary bowing ceremony. When the* JUDGE *sits, so does everyone else. The* CLERK OF THE COURT *turns from facing the bench to off left and* CRAWFORD *comes into dock accompanied by* PRISON OFFICER. MR. NAYLOR *remains on his feet and waits for* JUDGE *to settle himself*]

JUDGE: Yes, Mr. Naylor?
NAYLOR: If your Lordship pleases— Your Lordship will recall that be-

fore we rose for lunch I was engaged in examining Superintendent Eley. Superintendent, will you go back to the witness box.
[ELEY *rises from table and goes into box*] You have already been
sworn?

ELEY: Yes, sir.

NAYLOR: Superintendent, you have just told us that following a telephone call from Lady Gregory in the early morning of Sunday,
April nineteenth, you at once went to her house at Number One
Gordon Mews, and there saw her husband lying dead in his study
with a knife in his chest.

ELEY: Yes, sir.

NAYLOR: Continue then.

ELEY: I arranged immediately for the attendance of the pathologist
and for the usual photographs and fingerprint tests to be taken.

NAYLOR: Were you able to identify the knife?

ELEY: It was the Judge's own knife. It had been taken from his
writing desk, where it was used as a paper knife.

NAYLOR: Had anything been stolen?

ELEY: No, sir.

NAYLOR: Were there any signs of a struggle?

ELEY: Yes, sir. There were injuries to the palms of both the deceased's hands, as from warding off a knife attack. An occasional
table had been overturned, and some trinkets and some glasses
broken. Also a pair of firedogs in the grate had been knocked over,
and on the boss of one of them were traces of blood and hair.

NAYLOR: Anything else?

ELEY: Yes, sir. Two fingernails on the deceased's right hand were
torn and had bled—and scrapings taken from under the fingernails
of both hands showed a quantity of wool fibres and threads.

NAYLOR: You mentioned broken glasses. How many?

ELEY: Only two—a tumbler and a liqueur glass.

NAYLOR: You fingerprinted the glasses of course?

ELEY: Yes, sir. And analyzed the contents. The tumbler had contained a Scotch and soda—the other an obscure French liqueur.

NAYLOR: Named?

ELEY: *Verveine du Velay*, sir—green—it's not unlike chartreuse.

NAYLOR: Ye-es. Tell me, how was the deceased dressed?

ELEY: In pajamas and dressing gown, sir.

NAYLOR: Then we can assume he wasn't expecting anyone?

SHEILA: [*Rising*] My Lord, that is a quite unwarranted assumption. I would ask my learned friend to confine himself to the facts and to assume nothing.

JUDGE: You stand corrected, Mr. Naylor.

[SHEILA *sits down*]

NAYLOR: If your Lordship pleases. On the following day, Monday, did you have occasion to visit the prisoner at his home?

ELEY: Yes, sir.

NAYLOR: Did you at that time ask to be supplied with sets of his fingerprints and samples of his blood and hair—and did he give these to you?

ELEY: He did, sir.

NAYLOR: At the same time did he draw attention to himself in any way?

ELEY: He showed me an injury to the back of his head, and asked that it be examined by the police doctor.

NAYLOR: Did you take possession of any clothing?

ELEY: A light overcoat, belonging to the prisoner, which was hanging in the hall.

NAYLOR: And was this later taken by you to the Metropolitan Police Laboratory for examination, together with the samples and fingerprints and the objects from the Judge's room?

ELEY: Yes, sir.

NAYLOR: What were the results of the examination?

ELEY: [*Refers to notebook*] Thumb and fingerprints of the prisoner's right hand were found on the knife and the liqueur glass, overlying prints of the deceased—that is to say, the prisoner was the last to handle them.

NAYLOR: May the witness now see the knife, please. Exhibit Two. [*It is handed to* ELEY *by* USHER] Was there anything noteworthy about the prints on the knife?

ELEY: Yes, sir. Whereas the Judge's prints were all with the thumb pointing down the blade—from holding a knife like this [*He demonstrates*] as though for opening letters—the prints of the prisoner were with the thumb pointing up the handle—from holding the knife like this. [*He demonstrates again, holding it as one would for stabbing downwards with a dagger*]

NAYLOR: Would you just show that a little more clearly to the jury? Thank you.

[ELEY *does it once more.* SHEILA *rises*]

SHEILA: My Lord, I'm sure neither my friend nor the Superintendent would wish to mislead the jury on this. The Superintendent has just showed a stabbing motion. In my submission the fact that my client's fingerprints happened to be on the knife in such a position is not evidence that he ever stabbed with it.

ELEY: If I showed a stabbing motion, madam, it was quite involuntary. I'm sorry.

SHEILA: I'm obliged. [*She sits*]

NAYLOR: My Lord, the only point I seek to make at this stage is that fingerprints of the prisoner were on that knife, in what I can only call the generally accepted position for stabbing.

SHEILA: [*Jumping up*] I'm sorry, my Lord. I cannot let that pass. How can it possibly be said there is a generally accepted way of holding a knife for stabbing? Any more than for peeling potatoes.

NAYLOR: Really, my Lord, isn't my friend splitting hairs? The jury are quite capable of—

JUDGE: In a trial for murder, Mr. Naylor, the splitting of hairs is an occupational hazard.

NAYLOR: If your Lordship pleases.

JUDGE: Not always justified, I agree. In this case, Miss Larkin, you were quite right.

SHEILA: My Lord. [*She sits*]

NAYLOR: What about the overturned firedog, Exhibit Three?

[*It is handed to* ELEY *by* USHER]

ELEY: The blood and hair on the boss were identical with the samples taken from the prisoner.

NAYLOR: And the scrapings from under the dead man's nails which showed the wool fibres and threads?

ELEY: The wool fibres and threads were identical with those of the overcoat I removed from the prisoner's house.

NAYLOR: May the witness now see the overcoat, Exhibit Five? [*It is handed to* ELEY *by* USHER] Is that the coat?

ELEY: Yes, sir. It was found to have spots and smears of blood down the front of it.

NAYLOR: What can you tell us about that blood?

ELEY: It was of the blood group of the dead man, sir, Group A.

NAYLOR: What is the blood group of the prisoner?

ELEY: Group A.B., sir.

NAYLOR: Thank you. [*The* USHER *returns the coat to table*] Why did you visit the prisoner at his home that evening?

ELEY: I was acting on information received. I had reason to believe he would be able to help me with my enquiries.

NAYLOR: Apart from the matter of the overcoat and the samples of blood and hair which have already been dealt with, what other conversation took place between you?

ELEY: [*Referring again to notebook*] I asked him if he knew a Mr. James Armitage. He replied that he did not, and he asked me who James Armitage was. I told him I had reason to believe he was a private investigator employed by him to trace the person who killed his daughter, and who had recently sent him a letter telling him who that person was. This he denied, sir. I then asked him if I might search the premises, and to this he agreed. In a locked drawer of the prisoner's own writing desk, I found the letter, Exhibit Six, sir.

NAYLOR: May the witness now see the letter please, Exhibit Six? [*The* USHER *hands it to* ELEY] Is that the letter?

ELEY: Yes, sir.

NAYLOR: Describe it to the Court, and then read it.

ELEY: It is dated April fifteenth and is typed in red—not very well. There is no address. The letter reads: "Dear Mr. Crawford, Thank you for the money—very welcome; the man responsible for your daughter's death was Sir Anthony Gregory. If you don't believe me, put it to him, and see what he says. Yours truly, James Armitage." The signature is written, sir.

NAYLOR: Did you later ask the prisoner if he wished to make a statement?

ELEY: Yes, sir, but he refused.

NAYLOR: And when he was arrested and cautioned?

ELEY: He made no reply, sir.

NAYLOR: Thank you, Superintendent. [NAYLOR *sits.* SHEILA *breaks off an anxious conversation with* GILLESPIE, *rises and addresses the Judge*]

SHEILA: May it please you, my Lord.

JUDGE: What is it, Miss Larkin?

SHEILA: My Lord, my learned leader is in the building, and I can't understand why he isn't here. My Lord, I know he is particularly anxious to cross-examine Superintendent Eley himself, and if, in the circumstances, this could be delayed a few moments until he is found, I—

JUDGE: This Court doesn't sit at the convenience of Counsel, Miss Larkin—nor am I disposed to direct it to do so. If leading Counsel isn't present, it is the duty of Junior Counsel to do the best he can, and tell his leader later what sort of a mess he made of it. Or what sort of mess she made of it. That is what a Junior is for.

SHEILA: Yes, my Lord.

JUDGE: Then do so, and let us waste no more time.

SHEILA: [*Bows*] If your Lordship pleases. Superintendent Eley, this coat belonging to Mr. Crawford—

[SIR PETER *has hurried in and taps* SHEILA *on shoulder.*]

SIR PETER: I hope your Lordship will excuse my seeming discourtesy. I was unavoidably detained.

JUDGE: It's of no consequence, Sir Peter. Miss Larkin was most steadfast in your defense.

SIR PETER: My Lord, I'm most grateful. [*Turns to* SHEILA] Was anything said we didn't anticipate?

SHEILA: No. Only they down-pedaled Armitage more than I thought they would.

SIR PETER: Oh, Naylor's no fool. Never mind, we'll soon put that right. [*He turns and addresses* SUPERINTENDENT ELEY] Superintendent, who is James Armitage?

ELEY: As I have already said, sir, before you came into Court, I understand he is a private investigator.

SIR PETER: Although he's not registered as such?

ELEY: He's not registered as such, no, sir.

SIR PETER: Nor does his name appear at all in the telephone directory?

ELEY: No.

SIR PETER: Nor, since he lodged such detailed information with you concerning Mr. Crawford, have you set eyes on him from that day to this? Although extensive enquiries have been made?

ELEY: No.

SIR PETER: Hardly a reliable informant, would you say?

ELEY: On the face of it perhaps.

SIR PETER: And yet his information is accepted without question?

ELEY: That's not so, sir. It's the duty of the police to check up on all information received. On checking his, it proved to be right, so we acted on it.

SIR PETER: But how do you know it was right?

ELEY: Because I checked it.

SIR PETER: But that's not strictly true, is it? Just let me put an imaginary case to you—

ELEY: I don't understand your implication—

SIR PETER: [Interrupting] Sh. Sh. Sh. Suppose Bill Bloggins has a grudge against Farmer Giles, and decides to burn down his barn. But in doing so, he's clever enough to make it look as if Farmer Giles did it himself. What happens when Bloggins phones you and tells you that Farmer Giles has set fire to his own barn?

ELEY: I investigate.

SIR PETER: And because Bloggins told you so, the unfortunate Giles is automatically arrested and charged with arson?

ELEY: No, sir.

SIR PETER: Why not?

ELEY: Because the odds are my enquiries will show that Bloggins is lying.

SIR PETER: But how would that become apparent unless you questioned him again?

ELEY: It wouldn't. I would question him again.

SIR PETER: Precisely. But you never again questioned Armitage, did you?

ELEY: I didn't have the opportunity.

SIR PETER: So how can you be sure he wasn't lying? How can you be sure that, as with Farmer Giles, the whole thing wasn't specially laid on to throw the blame onto Crawford, when, in fact, the real culprit was Armitage, or someone connected with him?

NAYLOR: [*Rising*] My Lord, Sir Peter knows better than that. If he has a suggestion to make, let him make it. And not ask questions that it is no part of the Superintendent's duty to answer.

SIR PETER: My Lord, I suggest that if my learned friend were to call Armitage here for me to cross-examine, there would be no need for such questions to be asked.

NAYLOR: My Lord, I must object. Your Lordship is well aware—

JUDGE: Let's just get on with the case, Sir Peter.

[NAYLOR *sits*]

SIR PETER: Superintendent, will you please look at the firedog with the blood and hair—Exhibit Three. Oh, you have it there before you.

ELEY: Yes, sir.

SIR PETER: It takes apart, does it not? One bit screws into another?

ELEY: Yes, sir.

SIR PETER: Then take it apart, please. [ELEY *does so*] And now take in your hand the bit showing the blood and hair. That forms a conveniently portable offensive weapon, does it not?

ELEY: Yes, it does.

SIR PETER: Just show it to the jury. Thank you. Put it down. [ELEY *wipes oil off hands onto a handkerchief*] Oh, just remove those things out of the Superintendent's way, will you please? [USHER *moves them*] Now, Superintendent, drawing on your long experience as a police officer, just tell me whether what I am about to suggest to you is at all *possible*. I put it no higher than that for the moment. Suppose—just suppose—that someone with that weapon was waiting in the shadows that night for Crawford to return home, and hit him on the back of the head with it as he was about to open his front door. Possible so far?

ELEY: Yes, sir.

SIR PETER: Suppose that this someone then carried or dragged him into the Judge's house where the Judge was already lying dead, or alternatively brought the necessary objects out into the mews—pressed Crawford's hands round the knife with which the old man had been killed, and round the glass of *Verveine du Velay* it is alleged Crawford drank—still possible?

ELEY: Possible, yes, sir, but—

SIR PETER: Oh, bear with me just a moment longer, Superintendent, that's all I ask. Suppose that this someone then scraped the dead man's hands down the coat Crawford was carrying, so that fibres and threads from it lodged beneath the torn nails, and so that blood was transferred on to the coat itself for all to see. Would not the scientific evidence available to you in those circumstances be identical with the scientific evidence now being produced by the Crown to say that Crawford killed the Judge?

ELEY: Yes, it would.

SIR PETER: Oh, I'm much obliged. Then let me take supposition a step further. Are you aware that Mr. Crawford's keys were stolen that night, which was his reason for spending the night in Major Maitland's house?

ELEY: Major Maitland made a statement to that effect, yes, sir.

SIR PETER: Is there anything to have prevented whoever stole those keys that night—?

ELEY: If they were actually stolen.

SIR PETER: Is there anything to have prevented whoever stole those keys that night from entering his house in his absence and planting that letter, signed James Armitage, in his drawer?

ELEY: I suppose not.

SIR PETER: No. So we are left with this, are we not: that the evidence adduced by the Crown in support of the supposition that Crawford killed the Judge, supports equally the supposition that he was killed by someone else, who saw to it that Crawford should be blamed?

ELEY: With respect, sir, you are forgetting the evidence of his own clerk, that such a letter was delivered to Chambers two days before, and that Armitage himself had called to see Mr. Crawford, by appointment, some time earlier.

SIR PETER: I am forgetting nothing, Superintendent. Now, will you please answer my question. Is there anything in the evidence I specifically put to you that rules out the possibility that Crawford was framed?

ELEY: No, sir.

SIR PETER: Thank you. [*He sits*]

NAYLOR: [*Rising*] Conversely, Superintendent, is there anything in *any* of the evidence that rules out the probability that he was not?

ELEY: No, sir.

NAYLOR: Thank you, Superintendent. Dr. Wimborne now, please. [ELEY *leaves the box and resumes his place at the table. The* USHER *goes for the knife lying on dock*] Would you mind leaving the knife where it is, please.

USHER: Sir. [DR. WIMBORNE *goes to witness box and* USHER *goes and gets Bible and swearing card. A* LAWYER *enters at back*] Silence. [*The* LAWYER *who has come in makes for a seat*] Be still, please. [*To* DR. WIMBORNE] Take the book in your right hand and read from the card.

DOCTOR: I swear by Almighty God that the evidence which I shall give shall be the truth, the whole truth and nothing but the truth.

[USHER *returns to his seat*]

NAYLOR: Doctor, is your full name Charles Wimborne, and are you a registered medical practitioner and Lecturer in Forensic Medicine at St. Paul's Hospital?

DOCTOR: Yes.

NAYLOR: On the nineteenth day of April last, did you perform a postmortem examination upon the body of a man identified to you as Anthony Gregory?

DOCTOR: Yes, I did.

NAYLOR: What did you find?

DOCTOR: He was a well-preserved man of about sixty-five. No organic disease. There was a single entry stab wound, angled downwards, an inch above the left nipple. Exploration of this wound revealed that the heart had been penetrated in two places.

NAYLOR: Two places?

DOCTOR: Yes. The passage of the wound divided into two below the level of the ribs.

NAYLOR: Indicating what—that the deceased had been stabbed twice?

DOCTOR: Possibly.

NAYLOR: Are you able to establish the time of death?

DOCTOR: I first examined the body in the study at seven-thirty A.M. and estimated he had been dead about six hours—taking us back approximately to one-thirty AM. Allowing half an hour each way for fluctuation in temperature—that would establish the time of death within the time bracket of one and two A.M.

NAYLOR: Outside limits?

DOCTOR: Outside limits.

NAYLOR: Will you please look at the knife, Exhibit Two. Could the injury you describe have been inflicted by a weapon of that sort?

DOCTOR: This was the actual weapon. I removed it from the body myself.

NAYLOR: I'm much obliged. At the prisoner's own request, Doctor, did you also examine an injury to the back of his head?

DOCTOR: Yes, I did.

NAYLOR: How much force would have been required to inflict that injury?

DOCTOR: Oh, quite considerable.

NAYLOR: Oh. Will you now please look at the firedog—Exhibit Three. [*To the* USHER] No, no thank you very much. [*The* USHER *has half-risen.* NAYLOR *turns to* ELEY] Superintendent, would you stand it up on the table, please, as if it were in a grate? Thank you. Can you see that quite clearly, Doctor?

DOCTOR: Yes.

NAYLOR: In your expert opinion, would the injury to the prisoner's head be consistent with his falling and hitting the back of his head on this boss on the top? Was it the sort of injury you would expect from such a fall?

DOCTOR: Yes, it was.

NAYLOR: Would a period of unconsciousness neccessarily have resulted?

DOCTOR: That's impossible to say. People react in different ways to head injuries of this sort. Some would be knocked straight out—others wouldn't. You can't generalize.

NAYLOR: Nevertheless, are you able to help me this far: that it would not be impossible for someone suffering such an injury to pick themselves up and walk, say, twenty or thirty yards before passing out?

DOCTOR: There is no set pattern. Anything is possible.

NAYLOR: Thank you, Doctor. [*He sits*]

SIR PETER: [*Rising*] Since anything is possible, Doctor, would it not be equally consistent with such an injury that anyone who suffered it should go out like a light, and remain out for the best part of an hour?

DOCTOR: Certainly.

SIR PETER: Thank you, then we need waste no further time over that. You were present in Court, were you not, when I asked the Superintendent to dismantle the firedog—and you heard the suggestion I put to him?

DOCTOR: Yes, I did.

SIR PETER: Was there anything in the nature of the injury to Crawford's head to show that it must have been caused by his falling on to the firedog—instead of, as I suggested, being coshed with part of it?

DOCTOR: Nothing—no.

SIR PETER: Thank you. Have you a ruler on you, by any chance?

DOCTOR: No, I'm afraid I haven't.

SIR PETER: Hamish—perhaps you—?

CLERK: Sir Peter. [*He passes one to* DOCTOR]

SIR PETER: Thank you very much. Now, Doctor, you have the knife there before you. Will you now measure across the blade at its widest point?

DOCTOR: Exactly one inch.

SIR PETER: In the course of your post-mortem, did you have reason to measure the width of the entry wound you have described?

DOCTOR: Yes. That also was exactly one inch.

SIR PETER: That being so, my learned friend's suggestion that Gregory was stabbed twice with that knife makes nonsense, doesn't it?

DOCTOR: It would call for an amazing degree of accuracy, I agree.

SIR PETER: An impossible degree, wouldn't you say? That knife is extremely sharp; it has a point like a needle. Even one sixteenth of an inch deviation from the path of the original wound would have been measurable on the surface of the skin, wouldn't it?

DOCTOR: Yes.

SIR PETER: So for all practical purposes we can rule out the second stab, actually as a stab?

DOCTOR: I agree.

SIR PETER: From your experience then, are you able to offer any explanation for the division of the wound into two below rib level, and the piercing of the heart in two places?

DOCTOR: If the knife had been partly withdrawn, very carefully, and then pressed home again—that would explain it.

SIR PETER: That's what I thought. But can I take you a step further? The first stab would certainly have killed him, wouldn't it?

DOCTOR: Yes.

SIR PETER: Suppose later it became necessary, for some reason, to remove the knife completely, and then to replace it to look as if it had never been removed—do you follow me?

DOCTOR: Yes.

SIR PETER: In those circumstances, because the knife was so very sharp and pointed, could it not have happened that whoever re-placed it failed to realize they were deviating from the path of the original wound below the rib level?

DOCTOR: That could have happened.

SIR PETER: Thank you very much, Doctor—that is all. [*He sits*]

NAYLOR: [*Rising*] But did it?

DOCTOR: Did it what?

NAYLOR: Happen?

DOCTOR: I have no idea.

NAYLOR: Precisely. Thank you, Doctor. [DOCTOR *returns to seat at table*] My Lord, may I now refer you to page twenty-one of the deposition, the evidence of Major Maitland?

JUDGE: Yes, Mr. Naylor?

NAYLOR: My Lord, some difficulty was foreseen in adducing the ev-idence of Major Maitland by reason of the fact that he is a close friend of the prisoner. He has attended Court under his recognizance, my Lord, but I am instructed that he now refuses to give evidence for the Crown.

JUDGE: Are you applying to treat him as a hostile witness then?

NAYLOR: My Lord, such was my intention. But, as his evidence is merely corroborative, and the facts have been adequately covered by other witnesses, subject to anything your Lordship may say, I was proposing not to call him at all.

JUDGE: Sir Peter?

SIR PETER: [*Half-rising*] I respectfully agree, my Lord.

CRAWFORD: [*Unable to contain himself*] No!

[GILLESPIE *starts to rise.* SIR PETER *stops him*]

GILLESPIE: Simon!

SIR PETER: All right. Leave this to me. My Lord, have I your permission to confer shortly with my client?

JUDGE: Certainly, Sir Peter.

SIR PETER: My Lord, I'm much obliged [*He leaves benches and comes down to dock. He and* CRAWFORD *talk quietly*]

CRAWFORD: Why the hell aren't you calling him?

SIR PETER: It won't help us enough to justify the risk. Can't you see he's done enough damage as it is with his antics? Naylor's already spiked our guns by making him hostile.

CRAWFORD: That doesn't affect his evidence.

SIR PETER: But Simon, that man's evidence—

CRAWFORD: Peter, you've already done damn well with the doctor and the police. There's already considerable doubt, there. Clinch it with this alibi and in ten minutes' time you'll be submitting there's no case to answer.

SIR PETER: I'm very sorry—I'm not prepared to chance the alibi.

CRAWFORD: Is this part of your plan to get me to change my plea?

SIR PETER: No. I'm simply advising you, as urgently as I possibly can—

CRAWFORD: Then are you going to call him or not?

SIR PETER: No, I am not. I must do what I think is right. To call him now would be utterly wrong. If you still insist on calling him, in spite of what I say, I shall be forced to withdraw from the case.

CRAWFORD: Very well, then.

SIR PETER: I'm very sorry, Simon. [*He returns to his place*]

JUDGE: Yes, Sir Peter?

SIR PETER: Unfortunately, my Lord, it would seem that I am no longer able to act in the best interests of my client, and instructions have been withdrawn from me. In the circumstances, I have no option but to express my apologies, and ask leave of the Court to withdraw from the case.

[*There are murmurs of surprise as* SIR PETER *steps out, bows to* JUDGE, *looks at* CRAWFORD *and then goes out*]

JUDGE: Perhaps, Mr. Crawford, you will be good enough to tell me what you propose to do now?

CRAWFORD: My Lord, I am quite content to be represented by Miss Larkin only.

SHEILA: Oh, no!

JUDGE: Miss Larkin, that puts you in some difficulty?

SHEILA: It does indeed, my Lord.

JUDGE: Well, you had better have a word with those instructing you and let me know what you decide. Should you wish to apply for an adjournment, I don't suppose the Clerk of the Court will have any difficulty in finding something else for me to do.

[GILLESPIE *and* SHEILA *go to* CRAWFORD *at the dock. The* CLERK OF THE COURT *confers with the* JUDGE]

GILLESPIE: Simon!

CRAWFORD: I'm not having an adjournment.

GILLESPIE: But it's all we can do.

CRAWFORD: I'm sorry. I can't face any more delay. We go ahead as we stand.

GILLESPIE: Choose any leader you like.

CRAWFORD: No.

GILLESPIE: I'll get him somehow.

SHEILA: But, Mr. Crawford, I can't appear for you on my own, without a leader. I haven't the experience.

CRAWFORD: Let me be the judge of that.

SHEILA: I'm sorry, I—it's too great a responsibility. I must refuse.

GILLESPIE: She's right, Simon.

CRAWFORD: May it please you, my Lord—

JUDGE: Yes?

CRAWFORD: My Lord, I ask the Court's leave to defend myself, and to retain Miss Larkin and Mr. Gillespie to advise me.

JUDGE: Miss Larkin, are you content so to do?

SHEILA: If—that is what Mr. Crawford wants, yes, my Lord.

JUDGE: Mr. Gillespie?

GILLESPIE: Yes, my Lord.

JUDGE: Have you any objection, Mr. Naylor?

NAYLOR: [Half-rising] My Lord, none.

JUDGE: You are quite sure, Mr. Crawford, that this is the course you wish to adopt?

CRAWFORD: Quite sure, my Lord.

JUDGE: Then let it be so.

CRAWFORD: I'm much obliged, my Lord.

JUDGE: Are you quite ready—or would you like time to confer with your advisers?

CRAWFORD: I am quite ready, my Lord.

JUDGE: So be it. [He turns to JURY] Members of the jury, you must, of course, know that personalities in this case have already formed the matter of public comment. Quite certainly, after what has just occurred, there will be a great deal more. With that, you have nothing to do at all. The fact that the prisoner is himself a distinguished member of the Bar, now defending himself—and that the dead man was one of Her Majesty's Judges, has no bearing on the case, and I would ask you to ignore it. Now, Mr. Crawford?

CRAWFORD: If your Lordship pleases, now perhaps my learned friend will be good enough to call Major Maitland?

NAYLOR: [Rising] I hope the prisoner will not refer to me again as his learned friend. I would remind him that our position here today is somewhat different.

CRAWFORD: Friend or not, I nevertheless ask that Major Maitland should be called.

JUDGE: So be it. Call him, Mr. Naylor.

NAYLOR: If your Lordship pleases. May I, then, reserve the right to treat him as a hostile witness should the need arise?

JUDGE: Yes—very well.

NAYLOR: I'm much obliged, my Lord. Major Maitland, please.

POLICE OFFICER: Major Maitland, please!

[MAJOR MAITLAND *enters and is shown where to go by* POLICE OFFICER *and then by* USHER]

USHER: This way, sir, please. Silence! Take the book in your right hand and read from the card.

MAITLAND: I refuse to take the oath. I refuse to give evidence against an innocent man.

JUDGE: Major Maitland, am I right in assuming that your only desire is to help your friend?

MAITLAND: Yes, sir—my Lord.

JUDGE: Then be advised by me that you are not doing so by adopting this attitude. If you do not take the oath, he cannot question you—and if he cannot question you, you are powerless to help him.

MAITLAND: I beg your pardon, my Lord. I didn't understand.

JUDGE: Very well. Then do as you are asked.

USHER: Take the book in your right—[MAITLAND *has it in his left hand*] —right hand, sir, and read from the card.

MAITLAND: I swear by Almighty God that the evidence which I shall give shall be the truth, the whole truth and nothing but the truth.

JUDGE: One more thing. Prosecuting Counsel has indicated that he has no questions to put to you in chief. However, should he wish to do so later by way of reexamination, you will answer. If you do not do so, you will be in contempt of Court and liable to be punished. Now is that clear?

MAITLAND: Quite clear, my Lord, yes—thank you.

JUDGE: Hm! Yes, Mr. Naylor?

NAYLOR: My Lord. Is your name Hugh Beresford Maitland, are you of independent means, do you live at three Gordon Mews, S.W.1?

MAITLAND: Yes.

NAYLOR: I have no further questions. [*He sits*]

CRAWFORD: Major Maitland, do you recall the night of the eighteenth April last?

MAITLAND: What? Yes—most certainly. I say, are you—?

CRAWFORD: Yes.

MAITLAND: I see.

CRAWFORD: Then will you please describe to my Lord and the jury the events of that night, as they affected yourself?

MAITLAND: Yes, of course. I gave a small dinner party that evening. I invited you, and you were unable to come.

CRAWFORD: Was Mr. Justice Gregory a guest at that party?

MAITLAND: Yes, he was.

CRAWFORD: What time did the party break up?

MAITLAND: Quite early. I suppose my last guest must have left around eleven-thirty.

CRAWFORD: What were your movements after that?

MAITLAND: I cleared up a little after my guests had gone. I—I have no resident staff—only a daily woman who comes in. I stacked things in the kitchen for her to wash up next day.

CRAWFORD: And then?

MAITLAND: And then I had a last drink and a smoke before taking my dog out for his walk.

CRAWFORD: What time did you take your dog out?

MAITLAND: That would be about half past twelve.

CRAWFORD: Which way did you walk your dog?

MAITLAND: The way I always go—out into Gordon Place, down to the corner of Clarendon Street, and back home past the post office.

CRAWFORD: A distance of a little over half a mile?

MAITLAND: Yes.

CRAWFORD: So what time did you get back into Gordon Mews?

MAITLAND: About a quarter to one, twenty—quarter to one, yes.

NAYLOR: [Leaning forward—to ELEY, very sotto voce] Have you got a diary—have you?

CRAWFORD: [Over] What happened when you got back into the mews?

MAITLAND: Well, Ben, my dog, he was sniffing about—you know how dogs do—and then suddenly, in the angle just beyond your front steps, he started to bark excitedly and seemed upset. I thought he'd cornered a cat or something. I called him off, but he wouldn't come. And I went over to see what the matter was, and found you lying there.

CRAWFORD: Unconscious?

MAITLAND: Yes.

CRAWFORD: So what did you do?

MAITLAND: I was able to get you over into my house, and telephoned my doctor. I couldn't get hold of him. I was about to phone the hospital and the police when you came round.

JUDGE: Major, just take your hands out of your pockets while you're in the witness box.

MAITLAND: I beg your pardon, my Lord. [*He does so*]

CRAWFORD: And then did I remain with you in your house?

MAITLAND: Yes, until one-thirty when I went with you to your house, when you discovered you had lost your keys, so you came back home with me and I fixed a bed for you in my spare room.

CRAWFORD: What time was that?

MAITLAND: By the time I—left you for the night, it must have been well after two—well after.

CRAWFORD: Well after two. Now, Major Maitland, we have been told that the time bracket within which Mr. Justice Gregory was killed was between one and two A.M. At any time within that bracket was I not in your house—or not in your company?

MAITLAND: No, no—you were with me all the time. You couldn't possibly have killed him. I told them so.

CRAWFORD: Thank you, Major Maitland.

[MAITLAND *makes to leave the box*]

NAYLOR: [*Rising*] Just a moment, Major Maitland, please. You are quite sure about these times?

MAITLAND: Yes.

NAYLOR: With no possibility of error?

MAITLAND: No.

NAYLOR: Presumably you recall consulting your watch—or a clock?

MAITLAND: Yes.

NAYLOR: Ye-es. Do you carry a pocket diary?

MAITLAND: Yes.

NAYLOR: Perhaps you'll be kind enough to turn to the page for Sunday, April the nineteenth.

MAITLAND: Certainly. Yes.

NAYLOR: Read to us what it says at the top.

MAITLAND: It says Sunday, April the nineteenth.

NAYLOR: Go on, please.

MAITLAND: It says "Seven-thirty A.M.—very grave news."

NAYLOR: What else is *printed* there?

MAITLAND: At two A.M. British Summer Time begins.

NAYLOR: You understand what that means?

MAITLAND: Yes.

NAYLOR: It means, does it not, that on the Saturday night before going to bed everyone in the British Isles are supposed to put their clocks on one hour? Doesn't it?

MAITLAND: Yes.

NAYLOR: Did you put your clocks on that night? Did you?

MAITLAND: No.

NAYLOR: Thank you, Major Maitland. [*He sits*]

CRAWFORD: When did you put them on? When?

MAITLAND: I—I didn't. I'm terribly sorry—I must have forgotten. I suppose Mrs. Rice, my daily woman, must have done so on the Sunday.

JUDGE: Mr. Crawford, it's not the usual practice to recross-examine.

CRAWFORD: I beg your pardon, my Lord.

[CRAWFORD *sits, his mind in a turmoil.* SHEILA *rises, but* GILLESPIE *stops her*]

GILLESPIE: Wait—later.

NAYLOR: Thank you, Major Maitland. That is all. My Lord, in view of what has been said, I ask leave to recall Dr. Wimborne.

[MAITLAND *has crossed to dock and is stopped by* POLICE OFFICER]

MAITLAND: [*To* CRAWFORD] I really am most awfully sorry. I didn't think—

POLICE OFFICER: This way, sir. [*He leads* MAITLAND *back to his seat*]

JUDGE: Mr. Crawford. [*Pause*] Mr. Crawford.

CRAWFORD: My Lord.

JUDGE: Have you any objection to Dr. Wimborne being recalled?

CRAWFORD: None, my Lord.

JUDGE: Doctor Wimborne, will you please return to the witness box.

[CRAWFORD *sits.* DR. WIMBORNE *returns to witness box*]

NAYLOR: Doctor, you are already on oath?

DOCTOR: Yes.

NAYLOR: You have told us that you first examined the body at seven-thirty A.M.

DOCTOR: Yes.

NAYLOR: Did you take the time from your own watch?

DOCTOR: Yes.

NAYLOR: And had you put that watch on one hour to comply with the commencement of British Summer Time?

DOCTOR: Yes.

NAYLOR: Ye-es. You have also told us that the body had been dead six hours.

DOCTOR: Yes.

NAYLOR: Establishing the time of death between one and two A.M. British Summer Time?

DOCTOR: Yes.

NAYLOR: But suppose, like Major Maitland, you had not put your watch on that night—what then would you have given as the outside limits of death?

DOCTOR: Between midnight and one o'clock.

NAYLOR: And, by Maitland's time, Crawford was not found by him until twelve-forty-five. Thank you, Doctor.

CURTAIN

ACT TWO

A consultation cell at the Old Bailey. Small dull business-like room, with very small wooden chairs and a small table. The window is barred.

GILLESPIE *and* SHEILA *enter.* SHEILA *is still robed but has taken off her wig.* GILLESPIE *is depressed and angry;* SHEILA *very much on edge. During the ensuing conversation she takes cigarettes and lighter out of her bag and starts to smoke.*

SHEILA: But what can we do?

GILLESPIE: Nothing now. It's too late. He knew best. He was prepared to rely on Maitland and his alibi, in spite of what we felt. Now the whole thing has come unstuck, and that's an end of it.

SHEILA: Unless they can find Armitage.

GILLESPIE: Fat chance of that. If they haven't found him in three weeks, they're not likely to in twelve hours. They haven't just been sitting on their bottoms all this time—I've seen to that.

SHEILA: Sir Peter never trusted that alibi, did he?

GILLESPIE: Did you, after talking to Maitland?

SHEILA: I thought they might muddle him.

GILLESPIE: Muddle him! My God! Not that we did any better. We should have spotted the time discrepancy before ever coming to trial. Then there'd have been no question of alibi in the first place. It was clever of Naylor in court to take that point—damned clever. [*He rises impatiently and opens door*] What the hell are they doing with him? Do they think we've got all night? [*He closes door*] I suppose they'll be on time and a half now—that's the answer. Did you know that Sir Peter had been down to the cells to see Crawford during the lunch adjournment?

SHEILA: He said nothing to me.

GILLESPIE: Nor me. But he went, which was probably half the reason for that bust-up in Court. He wanted to have one last shot at getting him to change his plea.

SHEILA: He wasn't still plugging diminished responsibility?

GILLESPIE: Aye, he was. And rightly so.

SHEILA: Do you believe he did it?

GILLESPIE: Under the stress of the Armitage letter—don't you—now?

SHEILA: No, I don't. He didn't kill him. I know he didn't.

GILLESPIE: How do you know? Does he know, even? He'd been a very sick man, remember. [SHEILA *stares at him, horrified*] Oh—don't look at me like that. D'you think this is any easier for me?

SHEILA: Do you really think he'll go down?

GILLESPIE: He hasn't the ghost of a chance.

SHEILA: Why, oh why can't he ever trust people? We—we all wanted to help him. Why wouldn't he listen to us?

GILLESPIE: Because he's Simon Crawford.

SHEILA: Is that any reason? Do you know how long I've been in his Chambers, Mr. Gillespie? Four years. Can you imagine what it's been like? Have you any idea what it means always to be told things; to have facts and figures—and orders, just stuffed into you all the time like a computer? And little notes just put on your desk, when he's only in the next room? All he had to do was call out, and you could have been in there. Can you believe that? Wouldn't you have thought that, just once, he could have said "Look, I'm in a jam—get me out of this, will you?" or "There's something here I don't quite understand—see what you can make of it, will you?" Wouldn't you have thought, just once—in four years—even if he wasn't in a jam, or he did understand—he could have said it, just to make you feel needed? And now, because of his bloody self-sufficiency, he's in—oh!

[CRAWFORD *is shown in by* PRISON OFFICER. GILLESPIE *crosses to him and helps him sit down*]

GILLESPIE: And about time, too; now come and sit down. I know you've had a hell of a day, but it's not done with yet. I don't want to rush things but we've got some serious thinking to do.

CRAWFORD: Later, Hamish. Just clear out for a moment, will you?

GILLESPIE: Eh?

CRAWFORD: There's something I want to say to Miss Larkin.

GILLESPIE: Aye—very well. Officer? Could you possibly—?

PRISON OFFICER: I think we might stretch a point.

GILLESPIE: Thank you.

[PRISON OFFICER *nods and he and* GILLESPIE *go out*]

CRAWFORD: Sit down. Can I have one of those? [*Indicating packet of cigarettes on table*]

SHEILA: Yes—of course. They're French—do you mind?

CRAWFORD: Not a bit—they probably smoke Players in the Bastille.

SHEILA: Yes. [*She lights a cigarette for him*]

CRAWFORD: I was brought up to admit when I was in the wrong—and to say that I was sorry. I expect you were the same.

SHEILA: Yes.

CRAWFORD: My trouble was I was never in the wrong, so I never admitted it. They'd tell me I was, but I didn't believe them. I had to have proof, and they never succeeded in proving it to my satisfaction.

SHEILA: Aren't all children the same?

CRAWFORD: To begin with, perhaps. Most of them seem to grow out of it pretty quickly. But there are exceptions and I was one of them.

SHEILA: Please, Mr. Crawford, I—

CRAWFORD: At forty-seven, Miss Larkin, I dislike being wrong as much as when I was a child—more perhaps, because one has now lost the child's ability to live only for the present. It's a sign of age when the cares of the day no longer vanish with the setting sun. In short, I'm too old to be proved wrong twice in one day without resenting it.

SHEILA: I don't understand.

CRAWFORD: You were angry when I came in—about me.

SHEILA: Yes.

CRAWFORD: Because I am about to be convicted of murder—or because you have felt unwanted for the past four years? [SHEILA *looks at him in surprise—he points to open grille above door*] You can hear everything out there.

SHEILA: I—I didn't mean that. It was childish of me.

CRAWFORD: If you didn't mean it, why did you say it?

SHEILA: Well, I—I did mean it, I suppose, when I said it. But I only said it because—

CRAWFORD: —because you were upset at the thought of me being sentenced to life imprisonment through mishandling my own case?

SHEILA: It wasn't only—only that. It was everything. The—the evidence being rigged, and not being able to prove it, and then Major Maitland letting you down, and not finding this man, and you telling the truth and no one believing you. It's all so unfair.

CRAWFORD: That's still no excuse for an emotional outburst. Counsel are paid to think, advise, and to act. You can't do any of these things if you fill your head with sentimental rubbish like what's fair or unfair.

SHEILA: Good God, Mr. Crawford, I know that, but . . .

CRAWFORD: Then, if you know it, act on it. Otherwise you'll have suffered your four years' frustration for nothing. And if that doesn't mean anything to you, it does to me, because I resent a waste of time.

SHEILA: I'm sorry.

CRAWFORD: I'm sorry, too. Well, having got to that point, let's see what we can do to put things right. First, because I went for you just now for being emotional doesn't mean that I don't appreciate your—concern for me. I'm very grateful.

SHEILA: Mr. Crawford, I—

CRAWFORD: Secondly, regarding these four years you've spent in my Chambers. I understand your resentment, and the fault was mine. But you see, young counsel with natural ability are few and far between and if you're lucky enough to come across one, you handle him like blown glass.

SHEILA: Blown glass?

CRAWFORD: What I mean is that if young counsel is given his head, nine times out of ten he loses it, and what could have been a shining talent becomes instead a conceited mediocrity. I didn't want that to happen to you.

SHEILA: I didn't know.

CRAWFORD: I took damn good care you shouldn't. Perhaps that's where

I went wrong. There's no good in trying not to fall on your face, if by so doing you land flat on your back. I should have told you before. I'm sorry I didn't. So let me tell you now. Yours is a shining talent. See that you keep it so. Now go and give yourself a drink in the mess and send Hamish in. [SHEILA *stubs out her cigarette, goes to door, finds it locked and rings bell*] And Sheila—this time I do need help. [PRISON OFFICER *opens door,* SHEILA *goes out and door is closed.* CRAWFORD *stubs out cigarette, and sits. Door opens and* GILLESPIE *is let in—door is locked again*] Come in, Hamish.

GILLESPIE: Sheila seemed a bit tensed up. What have you been saying to her?

CRAWFORD: Nothing that shouldn't have been said long ago. Sit down. Help yourself to a delicious glass of water. I made a proper mess of it, didn't I?

GILLESPIE: Aye, you did. So now perhaps at last you'll listen to reason.

CRAWFORD: My dear chap, I'll listen to anything. Make my apologies to Peter.

GILLESPIE: There's time enough for that.

CRAWFORD: Have you seen him?

GILLESPIE: Aye, for a wee while.

CRAWFORD: So he knows?

GILLESPIE: He knows.

CRAWFORD: Uh.

GILLESPIE: Simon, why did you not tell me he'd been to see you in the cells?

CRAWFORD: There didn't seem much point.

GILLESPIE: Had I known, I'd never have let you do what you did. You know that?

CRAWFORD: That's why I didn't tell you.

GILLESPIE: You're an obstinate devil.

CRAWFORD: I'm not arguing.

GILLESPIE: All the same, do you still not think there's something in what he suggested?

CRAWFORD: You mean—to run diminished responsibility?

GILLESPIE: Aye.

CRAWFORD: I think it's a monstrous suggestion. I told him so.

GILLESPIE: So he said. But did you know he was preparing to back it this afternoon, in spite of that?

CRAWFORD: Back it? Back it how?

GILLESPIE: He was going to stop Maitland being called until tomorrow. That way hc'd have had the night to argue with you—persuade you, maybe.

CRAWFORD: He was that sure?

GILLESPIE: Aye—he was. And so am I.

CRAWFORD: I won't listen to you.

GILLESPIE: Look, we both want to do our best for you.

CRAWFORD: But the whole concept of the idea is wrong. I didn't kill the man. I swear to you that is the truth.

GILLESPIE: As you have all along. I accept that, but—

CRAWFORD: Then what are your grounds for telling me now to turn round and say "Yes, I did kill him—but I was ill and wasn't responsible"? I didn't kill him, I wasn't ill. I'd be lying if I said so.

GILLESPIE: But can you be sure?

[Pause]

CRAWFORD: Yes, of course I'm sure.

GILLESPIE: Yet you hesitated—why?

CRAWFORD: I was hoping I hadn't properly understood your implication.

GILLESPIE: But you did understand it, didn't you? Look, you had been sick—

CRAWFORD: I had a bit of a breakdown. We've been into all that.

GILLESPIE: But maybe not deep enough.

CRAWFORD: Hamish, will you stop it?

GILLESPIE: No, I won't. I've got to say this, and you're damned well going to listen. Now you know as well as I do the tricks the mind can play—that the subconscious mind can sometimes reject of its own accord a thing too horrible to remember. Suppose you had been taken sick again?

CRAWFORD: I wasn't. I was discharged as cured. Completely cured.

GILLESPIE: All right, all right. So you were. Six months before. But sickness can return. Suppose something happened in those six months that brought it back again—

CRAWFORD: But what? I've told you all I know. There was nothing else.

GILLESPIE: Except maybe—something your subconscious mind won't allow you to remember.

CRAWFORD: Which is?

GILLESPIE: That you really did see Armitage.

CRAWFORD: No.

GILLESPIE: And as a result of what he told you, your sick mind drove you to this thing which your subconscious now rejects, so that you no longer remember what you did—or how you came to do it.

CRAWFORD: That's not true.

GILLESPIE: But it's possible.

CRAWFORD: No—no.

GILLESPIE: Simon, listen to me for God's sake. Admit to yourself you could have killed him.

CRAWFORD: You don't know what you're saying—I loved him.

GILLESPIE: I know, I know—but put yourself in Peter's position—or in Sheila's, or in mine. Forget you're in the center of this and try to take a detached view. If you were advising someone else in your position, with the facts we know before you—either life imprisonment for a convicted murderer or a possible two years for a sick man in need of help—what would be your advice?

CRAWFORD: Damn you, Hamish, I won't let you do this to me.

GILLESPIE: I have to. Answer me, man, what would you say?

CRAWFORD: I'd say the same as you.

GILLESPIE: Then will you do it?

CRAWFORD: I don't know.

GILLESPIE: Then will you at least see Doctor Hillary?

CRAWFORD: All right, I'll see him. Arrange it with the Governor.

GILLESPIE: Aye, aye. Well, now it may be necessary to have a second opinion. Shall I see Dr. Hillary and ask him to bring a man down at the same time?

CRAWFORD: Do what you like, Hamish.

[*There is a knock at the door*]

GILLESPIE: Yes, what is it?

[*Door opens and* PRISON OFFICER *comes in*]

PRISON OFFICER: Clerk from Mr. Crawford's Chambers to see you, sir; and the Chief asks, will you be much longer.

GILLESPIE: I don't expect so, no. Right, show him in, will you?

PRISON OFFICER: Very good, sir. In here. [*He lets* PERCY *in and then goes out, locking door*]

GILLESPIE: Yes, Percy, what is it?

PERCY: Sorry, sir—message come through to the office for Charles— Mr. Milburn, sir. Something about threats against Mr. Crawford, sir.

CRAWFORD: Well?

PERCY: Well, sir, I took it, because Mr. Milburn is down at Winchester this afternoon. And I thought you'd better have it as soon as possible, sir.

CRAWFORD: Who sent the message, and what is it?

PERCY: One of the old shorthand blokes, sir—name of Cannon or Gannon or something. He phoned to say had we thought of Logan, sir—John Logan. He's pretty sure he made some song and dance against you and the judge in Court, back in 1943, after he was sentenced. He can't remember the details, but he's pretty sure of the name and the date. During the war it was and all the lights in Court went out, and that's what made him remember, sir.

CRAWFORD: Which Court was it?

PERCY: Here, sir—at the Bailey.

[CRAWFORD *crosses and rings bell*]

GILLESPIE: Can you remember any John Logan?

CRAWFORD: Only vaguely. [OFFICER *unlocks and opens door*] Officer, would you do something for me? Ask the Chief to ring through to Miss Larkin—she's in the Bar Mess—and get her to borrow the transcript of the trial of John Logan from the— [*Turning to* PERCY] 1943?

PERCY: Yes, sir.

CRAWFORD: 1943 Court records, and let us have it down here on Mr. Gillespie's undertaking to return it.

PRISON OFFICER: John Logan, 1943?

CRAWFORD: Yes, and hurry, please.

PRISON OFFICER: I'll do my best, sir. [*He goes out*]

CRAWFORD: Was there anything else, Percy?

PERCY: No, sir, only—well, except Mr. Painter and the girls asked me to wish you all the best and good luck—and that goes for me too, sir.

CRAWFORD: Thank you, Percy.

PERCY: Thank you, sir.

CRAWFORD: Hadn't you better get back, and keep them all in order?

PERCY: Yes, sir, right, sir. Good night, sir.

CRAWFORD: Good night, Percy.

GILLESPIE: Ring the bell, boy.

PERCY: It's all right, sir, he hasn't locked it. [*He goes out*]

CRAWFORD: Logan—Logan—

GILLESPIE: That lad of yours seems a likable boy.

CRAWFORD: What? Oh, yes.

GILLESPIE: You know, Charles must be working round the clock collecting this stuff. Where the hell does he get it all?

CRAWFORD: With a man of his loyalty, you don't ask questions. He has some very odd sources.

GILLESPIE: Let's hope this one has more substance than the rest.

CRAWFORD: It's got to have, Hamish.

GILLESPIE: Now who was the judge? Can you remember that?

CRAWFORD: No, I can't.

GILLESPIE: Well, it couldn't have been Gregory, he wasn't on the Bench then.

CRAWFORD: Yes, he was. He was elevated in '43. I remember I was before him a couple of times down at Lewes, just after I came out of hospital.

GILLESPIE: It must have been one of his first cases, then.

CRAWFORD: Yes, it was.

GILLESPIE: Can't you possibly remember what was said?

CRAWFORD: No, but obviously it was a threat of some sort.

GILLESPIE: All right—so it was a threat. How many so-called threats have we followed up over the past ten days?

[SHEILA *enters, carrying a thick bundle of yellow mimeographed sheets and a buff folder with papers, etc.*]

SHEILA: I came as quickly as I could. You wanted these?

CRAWFORD: Transcripts on Logan?

SHEILA: And the original depositions—yes.

CRAWFORD: Thank you.

SHEILA: What's happened?

GILLESPIE: Another tip-off—Percy came along with it.

CRAWFORD: I was right, Hamish, it was Gregory. After sentence—didn't Percy say? [*He finds last pages*] "Mr. Justice Gregory: John Logan, you have been found guilty on the clearest possible evidence of robbery with violence of a most brutal character, as a result of which three men were seriously injured—indeed one may well be crippled for life—men who were simply doing their daily work, as was their right in peace and without fear. Consider yourself lucky that no one has died as a result of your activities, or you would inevitably have gone to the gallows. From your actions then, and from your demeanor throughout this long trial, it is abundantly clear to me that you are a ruthless and dangerous criminal, from whom the public has every right to be protected. And protected it shall be. John Logan, the sentence of this court upon you is that you be imprisoned for life." At this point Logan pointed at Mr. Justice Gregory and at prosecuting Counsel, Mr. Crawford. Logan: "I shall kill you—both of you." [*He throws typescript down*] It looks as if we're in business.

GILLESPIE: Aye, possibly. Possibly. But let's take it step by step. Can you picture the man at all?

CRAWFORD: After twenty-one years? Hamish, you know as well as I do, no counsel can picture the man in the dock five minutes after the trial is over.

GILLESPIE: No, I suppose not.

CRAWFORD: One thing I do recall though—he was color blind.

GILLESPIE: Why that, for heaven's sake?

CRAWFORD: Because that's what led to his arrest. His driver had been injured in the raid and he drove one of the getaway cars himself. Jerry had been over the night before, and the escape route was all churned up and the salvage people were operating single lane traffic with a red and green light. Being color blind, he drove slap through the red and was stopped by the police. It was only a routine stop, but they saw the injured driver in the back—and that was that.

SHEILA: Can you remember, was he an educated man, or—?

CRAWFORD: That's a point. Yes—he had been the brains behind a whole series of similar robberies. The police had been after him for years.

GILLESPIE: Now wait, wait. This man was sentenced in 1943.

CRAWFORD: You mean—is it conceivable that anybody would harbor revenge for so long?

SHEILA: I don't see why not. If you're unbalanced enough to make a threat like that in the first place and mean it—

GILLESPIE: How do we know he meant it?

SHEILA: We don't. But if we're going to follow this line at all, we must assume he did. Well, then. Is fifteen years in prison going to change him? Isn't he more likely to nurse the idea all the time— plan it, replan it—turn it over and over in his mind—until—until it becomes part of him?

GILLESPIE: And then wait a further five years after coming out before doing anything about it?

CRAWFORD: But did he just wait? No, I think Sheila's right.

SHEILA: He's brooded over it all this time and he comes out still with this terrible obsession. The two men responsible for putting him away must be destroyed.

CRAWFORD: And must be implicated in each other's destruction.

GILLESPIE: It's insane.

CRAWFORD: So he's mentally ill. Is that so unusual? Five minutes ago you had no hesitation in suggesting I was. So he comes out of prison with this obsession on his mind and what does he do about it?

GILLESPIE: It's your theory—you tell me.

CRAWFORD: But damn it, man—

SHEILA: [Over] But Mr. Gillespie—I'm sorry—it's pretty obvious surely. Whoever he is this man's a perfectionist. Mr. Crawford was framed impeccably—there wasn't a loophole anywhere.

GILLESPIE: Agreed.

SHEILA: How long do you suppose it took him to be in a position to do that? Would five years be too long? Think what he had to do. He had to get to know every little detail of Mr. Crawford's life and of Gregory's—to find out where they crossed—where they ran together. He had to get to know them—really know them.

GILLESPIE: Are you suggesting this was done by a friend?

SHEILA: Yes. No—I mean by someone who got himself accepted as a friend. No outsider could possibly have known what he knew. He had to be established there already, just waiting—judging his moment.

[*A knock at the door and* PRISON OFFICER *comes in*]

GILLESPIE: Judging his moment?

PRISON OFFICER: Excuse me, sir—Mr. Gillespie.

GILLESPIE: Just a moment, officer. And if that moment hadn't come?

SHEILA: He'd have gone on waiting, or if it had come sooner he wouldn't have waited so long. It didn't matter to him. Don't you see?

GILLESPIE: No, I don't. I'm afraid you're letting your imagination run away with you.

SHEILA: But I'm sure I'm right. It's a line we've got to follow. It's his last chance. Let's at least try it. For God's sake.

GILLESPIE: And because it's his last chance, let's for God's sake try to base ourselves on fact and not on fancy. Yes, officer, what is it?

PRISON OFFICER: The telephone, sir—a young lady from your office. She insists it's very important, sir.

GILLESPIE: Hmm? Oh yes, very well. I'll be back in a moment. [*He goes out with* POLICE OFFICER. CRAWFORD *has meanwhile found photos in folder*]

SHEILA: Mr. Crawford, you're not going to let him put you off, are you? What's wrong?

CRAWFORD: These were in the envelope.

SHEILA: What are they?

CRAWFORD: Pictures of Logan—taken after his arrest.

[*She takes them from him, stares at them intently, and reacts*]

SHEILA: But—it can't be—

CRAWFORD: Add twenty years, and look at the eyes. They don't change. Where have you seen those eyes?

CURTAIN

SCENE 2

Court One of the Central Criminal Court, Old Bailey. The following morning. The JUDGE *has not yet come in. Counsel and others are moving about.* MAITLAND *comes in and goes down to* CRAWFORD *at the Dock.*

LAWYER: Good morning, Mr. Milburn.

CHARLES: Good morning, sir.

LAWYER: Pleasant day again. [*Sees another* LAWYER] Don't you ever find anything else to do?

MAITLAND: I say, Simon—I'm so very sorry about yesterday.

CRAWFORD: Forget it.

MAITLAND: Good luck.

POLICE OFFICER: Will you take your seat, sir.

CHARLES: [*Seeing* NAYLOR *arrive*] Morning, sir.

[MAITLAND *returns to back seat.* CHARLES *crosses to dock*]

CRAWFORD: Charles—

CHARLES: Sir?

CRAWFORD: Where the devil are they?

CHARLES: I don't know, sir. I didn't see them last night and when I got to Chambers this morning they had left and taken Percy with them. There was a note on my desk from Miss Larkin saying they would be here as soon as they could— [*He is interrupted by the three knocks and the* USHER'*s voice*]

USHER: Be upstanding in Court. [*Everyone rises.* CHARLES *moves away from dock, returns to seat.* JUDGE *enters with* ALDERMAN] All persons who have anything to do before my Lords the Queen's Justices of Oyer and Terminer and General Gaol Delivery for the Jurisdiction of the Central Criminal Court, draw near and give your attendance. God Save the Queen.

[*The* JUDGE *bows to* ALDERMAN, *Counsel and jury, then sits.* ALDERMAN *retires.* NAYLOR *remains standing*]

JUDGE: Yes, Mr. Naylor?

NAYLOR: May it please you, my Lord—your Lordship will recall that I was unable to conclude my case yesterday owing to the indisposition of Lady Gregory. Lady Gregory, I am happy to say, has now recovered and is with us. Lady Gregory, please.

POLICE OFFICER: Lady Gregory, please.

[LADY GREGORY *enters, pale and dressed in black. The* USHER *comes forward*]

USHER: This way please, madam. Silence! Take the book in your right hand and read from the card.

LADY G.: I swear by Almighty God that the evidence which I shall give shall be the truth, the whole truth and nothing but the truth.

[*The* USHER *resumes his seat*]

NAYLOR: Lady Gregory, is your full name Phyllis Charmian Gregory; are you the widow of the late Anthony Gregory?

LADY G.: Yes.

NAYLOR: I realize what an ordeal this must be for you. I shall be as brief as possible.

LADY G.: Thank you.

NAYLOR: At approximately seven o'clock on the morning of Sunday, April the nineteenth, did you return to your home from Ottery St. Mary and find your husband lying dead on the floor of his study?

LADY G.: He—had been stabbed—yes.

NAYLOR: Did you at once contact your opposite neighbor, Major Maitland, and did he and Mr. Crawford come over to your house?

LADY G.: Yes.

NAYLOR: And later, when the police arrived, did you identify the body to Superintendent Eley?

LADY G.: Yes.

NAYLOR: Lady Gregory, how well do you know the prisoner?

LADY G.: Intimately. My—my husband and I were closely associated with him for a great many years.

NAYLOR: How so?

LADY G.: He—first entered my husband's Chambers as a pupil in 1937. In 1941, when he was on leave from the Navy, his—his wife was killed in an air raid, and he himself was terribly injured. Jill, his daughter, was only two at the time, and he turned to us for help. We took her in with us and looked after her. Later, when he at last got out of hospital, Anthony—my husband—was able to get him settled in the house next door to us in Gordon Mews, which was then empty.

NAYLOR: And then?

LADY G.: Well, he took up his career again and did very well.

NAYLOR: Still in your husband's Chambers?

LADY G.: Yes.

NAYLOR: And all this time—until your husband's death—you were next door neighbors of his in Gordon Mews?

LADY G.: Yes.

NAYLOR: You've told us that in 1941 he was left alone with his baby daughter, and that you and your husband helped him. Had he no family of his own?

LADY G.: No.

NAYLOR: Would it be going too far then to say that he looked upon you and your husband both as his family, and that his relationship with you was a family one—rather than one based on close friendship?

LADY G.: That would be quite right.

NAYLOR: Thank you. Your husband drove a car, did he not?

LADY G.: Yes.

NAYLOR: Was he a good driver? [*Pause*] Please answer my question, Lady Gregory—was he?

LADY G.: No, he was not.

NAYLOR: Did Crawford ever express his views to you about your husband's driving?

LADY G.: Yes. He—he always hated being driven anywhere by my husband.

NAYLOR: Why?

LADY G.: Because he didn't consider him safe.

NAYLOR: He didn't consider him safe. Because of his—intimate family relationship with you, did Crawford confide in you?

LADY G.: Certainly.

NAYLOR: Do you recall his doing so early in the spring of last year?

LADY G.: Yes, I do.

NAYLOR: What did he tell you?

LADY G.: He was—terribly upset. Jill—his daughter—had died very suddenly, after being knocked down by a car.

NAYLOR: You say he was "terribly upset." What do you mean by that?

LADY G.: I mean he was more upset than—he was almost out of his mind.

NAYLOR: Go on, please.

LADY G.: He—he told my husband and me that if ever he found the man responsible, he—he'd kill him.

NAYLOR: Thank you. One small point. Who in your household drank *Verveine du Velay?*

LADY G.: Only Mr. Crawford.

NAYLOR: Why did you keep it then?

LADY G.: Specially for him. It was more of a joke, really. He loved it, but no one else we knew would touch it.

NAYLOR: Thank you, Lady Gregory. [*He sits*]

CRAWFORD: [*Rising*] Lady Gregory—you and I know each other very well?

LADY G.: Yes.

CRAWFORD: Are you suggesting that I could have believed for one moment that your husband knocked Jill down in the street, and drove on without stopping? You don't really think that, do you?

LADY G.: No.

CRAWFORD: You said just now that, over the years, ours had been a family relationship, and that I had confided in you?

LADY G.: I did—yes.

CRAWFORD: You also confided in me?

LADY G.: Yes.

CRAWFORD: Do you remember my visiting you in your mother's house in Ottery in February of last year?

LADY G.: Yes.

CRAWFORD: Why had I come to see you?

LADY G.: I had quarreled with my husband. You persuaded me to return to him.

CRAWFORD: Do you remember something you said to me in the car on the way home concerning your love for your husband?

LADY G.: It—it's so long ago. I—probably said a good many things, I—

CRAWFORD: Do you remember asking me how it was when a woman loved a man so much, there could come a time when her only wish was to see him dead? Do you?

LADY G.: I didn't mean it. I was angry—upset. You say a lot of things you don't mean.

CRAWFORD: Yes, I know. Are you then suggesting that when I said I could kill this man I was any less angry or upset—or that I meant what I said any more than you did?

LADY G.: No—no. No.

CRAWFORD: Thank you.

NAYLOR: Thank you, Lady Gregory.

USHER: This way, please.

NAYLOR: My Lord, that is the case for the Crown. [*He sits*]

JUDGE: Thank you, Mr. Naylor.

[LADY GREGORY *is accompanied to her seat by the* USHER. CRAWFORD *calls* CHARLES *to dock*]

CRAWFORD: Charles.

CHARLES: Yes, sir.

CRAWFORD: Get them here, quick.

[CHARLES *goes out*]

JUDGE: Mr. Crawford.

CRAWFORD: My Lord?

JUDGE: What I am about to tell you, you know as well as I do. Nevertheless it's my duty to say it. You are not obliged to say anything in reply to the charge against you, but if you wish to do so, there are two courses open to you. Either you can give evidence on your own behalf—on oath—in the witness box, in which case you can be cross-examined by Prosecuting Counsel. Or you can make a statement to the Court from the dock in which case you cannot be cross-examined. In either case, it is open to you to call witnesses. Now will you please tell me what you wish to do.

CRAWFORD: My Lord, before doing either, I wish to make a submission to your Lordship.

JUDGE: On what ground?

CRAWFORD: My Lord, on the ground that I have been denied the opportunity of cross-examining the man Armitage. I ask your Lordship to order his presence here and to adjourn this trial part-heard until he be found. The Crown say they have closed their case. In my submission, they cannot close it without first making this man available to me.

JUDGE: Mr. Naylor?

NAYLOR: [Rising] My Lord, I have given this matter considerable thought.

JUDGE: With what result? Headache?

NAYLOR: Not more than usual when appearing before your Lordship. No, my Lord, I cannot agree with the submission. This point was raised at the lower court also, and the learned magistrate then ruled that on the evidence already adduced, there was a prima facie case against the prisoner. Accordingly he was committed for trial. That same evidence is now before this Court, and must therefore be a matter for the jury. If the prisoner elects to base his defense upon the supposed actions of an unknown man, let him do so.

CRAWFORD: My Lord, with the greatest respect to my learned friend— I beg his pardon—learned Treasury Counsel, I have been forced to take this action by the weight which the Crown has attached to the information laid by this same unknown man. Is the Crown alone to derive benefit from the absence of a key witness, my Lord?

NAYLOR: My Lord, that is a most unwarranted implication—

JUDGE: Yes, yes, Mr. Naylor. Superintendent Eley, will you please return to the witness box? [As ELEY moves across, SIR PETER reenters the Court] I need hardly remind you—Sir Peter, I assume your reentry into the arena is that of an interested spectator and not of an active participant? Otherwise I must—

SIR PETER: Merely as a spectator, my Lord, I assure you.

JUDGE: Very well.

NAYLOR: Where the carrion is—there will the vultures be gathered together.

SIR PETER: In that case I'm in very good company. [*He sits*]

JUDGE: As I was about to say earlier, Superintendent, I need hardly remind you that you are already on oath.

ELEY: No, my Lord.

JUDGE: When this man Armitage first contacted the police, was he seen by you personally?

ELEY: Yes, my Lord.

JUDGE: Were you satisfied as to his integrity?

ELEY: I had no reason to doubt it, my Lord.

JUDGE: Did he furnish you with an address at that time?

ELEY: Yes, my Lord. I went to that address but he'd gone away.

JUDGE: What was it he had, a room—or a flat—or what?

ELEY: No, my Lord, it was a lodging house. Residents had their own rooms, but they ate communally.

JUDGE: Did you speak to the landlord?

ELEY: Yes, I did indeed, my Lord. Armitage had lived there on and off for twelve months. The landlord understood he kept it as a *pied-à-terre* for when he was in London.

JUDGE: And how often was that?

ELEY: The longest he was ever there at a stretch was ten days, my Lord.

JUDGE: Well, when he went away the last time, didn't he indicate to the landlord where he was going—or when he would be back?

ELEY: No, my Lord.

JUDGE: What steps have been taken by you to find him elsewhere?

ELEY: His full description was circulated to all police stations three weeks ago, my Lord. Two detective constables from my division have been following up every lead, however unlikely, for the whole of that period, but without success.

JUDGE: Yes. Well, I really don't see that you could have done any more.

ELEY: Thank you, my Lord.

JUDGE: However, you would be well advised to go on looking. In the event of the prisoner being found guilty, the presence or absence of this man Armitage may assume an even greater importance in another place.

ELEY: Quite so, my Lord.

JUDGE: Mr. Crawford, have you any questions to put to the Superintendent?

CRAWFORD: No, my Lord.

JUDGE: Thank you, Superintendent. [ELEY *returns to his seat*] Mr. Crawford, your submission is not without merit and that fact is reflected in my decision. I do not propose to adjourn your trial until Armitage is found.

CRAWFORD: If your Lordship pleases.

JUDGE: However, should the police be successful in finding him at any stage before I direct the jury to consider their verdict, he shall be interposed and you will have the opportunity of cross-examining him.

CRAWFORD: I'm much obliged, my Lord.

JUDGE: Now perhaps you will answer my earlier question. Do you wish to give evidence on oath or to make a statement from the dock?

CRAWFORD: I will give evidence on oath, my Lord.

JUDGE: Very well.

[CRAWFORD, *with* PRISON OFFICER, *crosses from dock. As he gets there,* SHEILA *and* GILLESPIE *enter*]

CRAWFORD: My Lord, may I first be permitted to have a brief word with those advising me?

JUDGE: Yes, yes.

CRAWFORD: I am much obliged, my Lord.

[SHEILA *and* GILLESPIE *cross to witness box*]

GILLESPIE: We came as soon as we—

CRAWFORD: Never mind that. Did you find anything?

GILLESPIE: We're barking up the wrong tree. Logan is dead.

CRAWFORD: Dead?

GILLESPIE: He's been dead for years.

CRAWFORD: Oh, my God!

GILLESPIE: We've done all we can. You've no choice now, Simon!

[CRAWFORD *ignores him, staring in front of him with un-seeing eyes. With a little hopeless gesture* GILLESPIE *turns, and he and* SHEILA *take their places. After a pause,* CRAWFORD *turns and moves slowly into the witness box where he stands, ignoring the* USHER *who hands him the oath card and New Testament.* CHARLES *reenters and sits*]

USHER: Will you take the oath, sir, please.

CRAWFORD: I swear by Almighty God that the evidence which I shall give shall be the truth, the whole truth and nothing but the truth. [*He pauses a moment to collect his thoughts before addressing the Court*] My Lord, members of the jury. The case against me is based on three things: scientific evidence, a theory of motive, and proof, with the breakdown of my alibi, proof that I had opportunity. I concede now that I had opportunity, but I concede nothing else. I did not kill Mr. Justice Gregory. I had no reason to kill him. Never for one moment did it cross my mind that he'd been responsible for my daughter's death. And I still don't believe it. But because this man Armitage alleges it was so, the police believe it. And accuse me of believing it too. Gregory did not kill my daughter, any more than I killed him. The police have shown you fingerprints, blood and hair—my overcoat even, which, may I remind you, they found hanging up in my hall, not concealed in any way. I don't know how this evidence against me came into being. My former Counsel, Sir Peter Crossman, suggested one possibility as you will remember when he was challenging the police evidence. He may have been right, I don't know; but one thing I do know, someone had reason to kill the Judge, and to see that I should be blamed for it. Somewhere there is a man, or a woman, who has lied and distorted the truth, so that I should stand before you today accused of a murder I did not commit. Members of the jury, what I have told you about myself is the truth, what you have heard of my part in the Judge's death is untruth. But only when this monstrous web of lies and deceit has been blown away, only then can justice be served. My Lord, that is all I have to say.

NAYLOR: [*Rising*] The only web of lies and deceit in this business is of your own making, isn't it?

CRAWFORD: No.

NAYLOR: Let us examine the position a little more closely. You loved your daughter very dearly?

CRAWFORD: Yes.

NAYLOR: So much so that after her death you determined to kill the man responsible for it?

CRAWFORD: Certainly not.

NAYLOR: Nevertheless you told Lady Gregory and her husband that if ever you found that man you'd kill him.

CRAWFORD: That was said in grief and anger, half an hour after my daughter died.

NAYLOR: Are you suggesting then that a threat to kill is any less of a threat because it is uttered in anger?

CRAWFORD: In these circumstances, yes.

NAYLOR: These circumstances being that it now suits your purpose to minimize that threat.

CRAWFORD: Not at all.

NAYLOR: I see. Why did you employ private detectives when the police were doing everything possible?

CRAWFORD: The police were getting nowhere.

NAYLOR: You don't seem to have much of an opinion of the police, do you?

CRAWFORD: On the contrary, I have the highest possible opinion of the police—

NAYLOR: Really? When you didn't trust them to find the man who ran down your daughter? Any more than you trusted them to find the man who coshed you on the head that night and stole your keys.

CRAWFORD: That question never arose.

NAYLOR: But that is precisely the point I am making, Mr. Crawford. It should have done, shouldn't it?

CRAWFORD: The police had a full report the following day.

NAYLOR: But not that night.

CRAWFORD: No.

NAYLOR: No-o. Nor would they have had one the following day. Unless you had been forced to invent some cock-and-bull story on the spur of the moment to explain away that injury to your head.

CRAWFORD: That's not true.

NAYLOR: No doubt the jury hear what you say. But let me return to the question of your daughter's death. Why did you see fit to employ private investigators to find this man? So that you could help the police, or so that you could punish him yourself? In fact you formed an intent to punish him yourself, didn't you?

CRAWFORD: Some such thought crossed my mind. But I never formed an intent.

NAYLOR: I suggest that you did. I suggest that you employed private detectives to find this man—so that you could kill him.

CRAWFORD: I did not. Nor did anyone I ever employed succeed in finding him.

NAYLOR: Oh, come now—one succeeded, didn't he? The one who wrote you that letter.

CRAWFORD: No.

NAYLOR: James Armitage found him for you.

CRAWFORD: No.

NAYLOR: And having found him, you killed him.

CRAWFORD: No.

NAYLOR: Mr. Crawford, you are a man experienced in the law with a successful practice extending over many years.

CRAWFORD: Yes.

NAYLOR: Does not your experience tell you that the case for the Crown is a very strong one?

CRAWFORD: But with one essential weakness—it is based on untruth.

NAYLOR: Is it? Let us examine what you say. You would agree, would you not, that in general we can look to the police to tell the truth?

CRAWFORD: Of course. The point I was trying to make—

NAYLOR: One moment. Let me develop my argument. The police say, with perfect truth, that Gregory was killed—by someone. They also say, again with perfect truth, that, acting on certain information received, they felt it their duty to check up on you.

CRAWFORD: That information was entirely false.

NAYLOR: Grant me they were not to know that until they checked. And, having checked, what do they find? An overt threat to kill the man who killed your daughter, a letter dated two days before

Gregory's death, telling you that he was, in fact, the man; and enough scientific evidence against you on the scene of the crime to convict an archbishop. In all this the police are telling the truth.

CRAWFORD: But based on a false premise. The evidence was rigged.

NAYLOR: So you say. But what truth of your own have you to lay before a jury to offset the truth of the police—however falsely based it may be?

CRAWFORD: I did not kill the Judge.

NAYLOR: Go on.

CRAWFORD: As I seem to have said a thousand times, the information given by Armitage to the police was false. I never employed him as a private investigator. I never received any letter from him. I don't even know who he is.

NAYLOR: How, if the information was false, does it come about that everything found out later by the police confirms it as being true?

CRAWFORD: Because he knew in advance what they would find. The trap was set—and sprung. And I was inside it.

NAYLOR: And this trap was set by Armitage? A man you'd never heard of?

CRAWFORD: Or someone connected with him—yes.

NAYLOR: And that is your only explanation?

CRAWFORD: Yes.

NAYLOR: Then let me put it to you, which interpretation of the facts is the more believable? That you found and killed the man you had threatened to kill, or that from somewhere out of your past has emerged an unknown enemy who hates you enough to kill an innocent man and, in so doing, has succeeded, God knows how, in laying a trail of scientific and factual evidence that can only lead to you. With all your experience do you seriously expect the jury to believe that?

CRAWFORD: Whether they believe it or not is a matter for their judgment, not your comment. It is the truth.

NAYLOR: I suggest to you that it is not. The truth is that you knew the contents of that letter to be a hideous fact, and there was murder in your heart.

CRAWFORD: No.

NAYLOR: You were never attacked that night. Instead you called on

the Judge—you knew he was alone in the house—and he confessed
to you what you knew already—that he was your daughter's killer.

CRAWFORD: No.

NAYLOR: And you killed him.

CRAWFORD: That's not true.

[NAYLOR *sits*]

JUDGE: Mr. Crawford, do you wish to add anything to your previous
statement?

CRAWFORD: No, my Lord.

JUDGE: Then return to the dock.

[CRAWFORD *returns to dock accompanied by* PRISON
OFFICER]

CRAWFORD: My Lord, may I once more ask the Court's indulgence
while I consult with those advising me?

JUDGE: Very well. But don't take too long about it.

CRAWFORD: I'm much obliged, my Lord. [GILLESPIE *and* SHEILA
come over to dock] You say Logan's dead. When did he die?
How?

SHEILA: He was killed in a train blow-up in 1944.

CRAWFORD: But he was in prison then.

SHEILA: They were transferring him from Maidstone to Dartmoor.
The train was shot up by a German night fighter. He and his
escort and two other prisoners were in the last coach which caught
fire. They all died.

CRAWFORD: Was his body identified?

GILLESPIE: So they say.

CRAWFORD: Who say?

GILLESPIE: The prison.

CRAWFORD: Was his death reported?

SHEILA: Not in the papers. I suppose because it was wartime. I
covered the lot.

CRAWFORD: He must have fooled them somehow and got away. It's
the only possible explanation. He must be alive.

GILLESPIE: Even if you're right, how can we prove it?

CRAWFORD: What about fingerprints? Did you get on to Records?

GILLESPIE: I did. All Logan's records have been destroyed.

CRAWFORD: Destroyed?

SHEILA: It's normal procedure—ten years after a criminal's death.

CRAWFORD: I see. Have you got that copy?

GILLESPIE: Aye.

CRAWFORD: Well, let me have it—and the other stuff we got last night as well.

GILLESPIE: You're going ahead then?

CRAWFORD: I've no option. It's my only hope.

GILLESPIE: But, Simon—

CRAWFORD: If nothing comes of it, I'll do as you say.

SHEILA: How can you prove anything now?

CRAWFORD: I can't. I shall have to bluff it out.

SHEILA: But how? You can't go ahead with the plan now.

CRAWFORD: Not all of it, no. I'll have to play it by ear. Did you get on to the War Office?

SHEILA: Yes, there is no record.

GILLESPIE: [*Giving him documents*] Here.

CRAWFORD: Well, that'll do for a start.

JUDGE: Are you quite ready, Mr. Crawford, or would you rather I adjourned the Court?

CRAWFORD: I'm quite ready, my Lord.

SHEILA: Good luck.

[SHEILA *and* GILLESPIE *return to seats*]

JUDGE: Are you proposing to call witnesses on your behalf?

CRAWFORD: My Lord, no. However, since the Court rose last night certain information has come into my possession, as a result of which I now ask the Court's leave to recall certain Crown witnesses, my Lord.

NAYLOR: [*Rising*] My Lord, I must object. The case for the defense is closed, and—

JUDGE: I am well aware of that, Mr. Naylor. However, in the somewhat unusual circumstances, I am prepared to extend every facility to the defense.

CRAWFORD: I'm much obliged, my Lord.

JUDGE: Which of the Crown witnesses do you wish to recall?

CRAWFORD: My Lord, first my clerk, Mr. Milburn.

JUDGE: Very well. Mr. Milburn, will you please return to the witness box?

[CHARLES *rises and goes to box*]

CRAWFORD: Mr. Milburn, you are still on oath.

CHARLES: Yes, sir.

CRAWFORD: I want you to help me if you can, about this man Armitage.

CHARLES: Yes, sir.

CRAWFORD: Yesterday, in reply to Prosecuting Counsel, you told the Court that you had actually spoken to Armitage in January when he came to Chambers to see me, allegedly by appointment.

CHARLES: Yes, sir.

CRAWFORD: Will you give me that exact date again?

CHARLES: January eighteenth, sir.

CRAWFORD: January eighteenth, and the time?

CHARLES: Three o'clock in the afternoon, sir.

CRAWFORD: Three P.M. Thank you. You also told us that on Friday, April seventeenth, you put a personal recorded delivery letter on my desk, the envelope of which was typed in red, and which had been signed for by Miss Larkin?

CHARLES: Yes, sir.

CRAWFORD: Now, although Sir Peter Crossman did not put this to you in cross-examination, would you agree now with my suggestion that both the visit of Armitage and this letter were nothing more than links in a chain of false evidence—deliberately manufactured to frame me?

CHARLES: I would, sir, yes.

CRAWFORD: Do you agree with me from a knowledge of the facts, or simply because you know me?

CHARLES: Because I know you, sir. You are not a man to commit murder.

CRAWFORD: Thank you. How long have you known me, Mr. Milburn?

CHARLES: I've been your clerk for nearly fifteen years, sir. Since 1950.

CRAWFORD: And before that what were you?

CHARLES: I was Junior Clerk in Mr. Robson's Chambers for four years.

CRAWFORD: And before that?

CHARLES: I was in the army, sir. I joined Mr. Robson's soon after I was demobbed.

CRAWFORD: And you served through the war, did you not? From 1939?

CHARLES: Yes, sir.

CRAWFORD: In the Royal Corps of Signals, I think you told me.

CHARLES: Yes, sir.

CRAWFORD: Rising to the rank of Sergeant Major?

CHARLES: Sir.

CRAWFORD: How well would you say we got to know each other in fifteen years, Mr. Milburn?

CHARLES: I would say very well indeed, sir.

CRAWFORD: So if anything were to worry or upset me in Chambers, the most natural thing in the world would have been for me to confide in you, wouldn't it?

CHARLES: Of course.

CRAWFORD: Do you ever remember my so much as mentioning the name James Armitage to you—before you saw him that day in January?

CHARLES: No, sir.

CRAWFORD: Or later telling you I had had a letter from him concerning Mr. Justice Gregory?

CHARLES: Certainly not, sir.

CRAWFORD: Would you then agree with my suggestion that Armitage, as a man, never existed; that he's no more than a character assumed by someone with the sole purpose of destroying me?

CHARLES: I think that must be the truth, sir.

CRAWFORD: And you actually saw him?

CHARLES: In Chambers, yes, sir.

CRAWFORD: Then can't you possibly help me? Are you quite unable to identify him?

CHARLES: Sir—I wish I could help. But you see—it was the clothes and—the hair and the thick glasses, sir, it could have been anyone.

CRAWFORD: A close friend of mine, even? Someone you know quite well by sight?

CHARLES: Well, yes, sir.

CRAWFORD: Perhaps even someone in this court now? Well?

CHARLES: Well, sir, if it was a disguise, and me not expecting it—it —it could have been, sir. But as I say, sir, it—it could have been anyone.

CRAWFORD: Thank you, Mr. Milburn. My Lord, may I now recall Major Maitland, please? [CHARLES *leaves witness box and gives hard look at* MAITLAND *whom he meets in front of dock*] Thank you, Charles.

CHARLES: Thank you, sir. [CHARLES *resumes his seat*]

CRAWFORD: Major, you are still on oath.

MAITLAND: Yes, I am.

CRAWFORD: Will you, then, take out that pocket diary and turn to the page for January eighteenth.

MAITLAND: January the eighteenth? Yes, certainly.

CRAWFORD: You are an assiduous diary keeper, are you not? It is your practice to make a daily entry of some sort?

MAITLAND: It is—yes.

CRAWFORD: Then will you read to us what you had to say for the afternoon of January eighteenth?

MAITLAND: Certainly. Here we are then—"Lunched at club, sole overcooked, complained to Steward." Here we are—P.M.—"bought pair of gloves, and went to—"

CRAWFORD: Went to—what, Major Maitland?

MAITLAND: "—went to Windmill."

JUDGE: Windmill?

MAITLAND: The Windmill Theatre, my Lord.

CRAWFORD: My Lord, it provides a nonstop revue, specializing in female chorus work and tableaux in the nude—

JUDGE: Thank you, Mr. Crawford. I am not so old that memories have already faded beyond recall. I merely wished to clarify the location of the windmill referred to.

CRAWFORD: If your Lordship pleases. What time did you go to the Windmill Theatre and when did you leave?

MAITLAND: I suppose I got there about two-thirty and left about six.

CRAWFORD: You sat the program through twice, then?

MAITLAND: Well—not intentionally, no. I—I remember now, it was the last time I went there. I—I'm afraid I fell asleep.

JUDGE: How old are you, Major Maitland?

MAITLAND: Fifty-eight, my Lord.

JUDGE: Yes—I suppose that's understandable.

CRAWFORD: Were you accompanied on this theatre visit?

MAITLAND: No.

CRAWFORD: No. So there is no one who can confirm that you went there at two-thirty and stayed till six?

MAITLAND: No, there isn't. But why should anyone doubt my word?

CRAWFORD: Why indeed. On the other hand, isn't it equally possible that you did not stay there all that time or even go to the theatre at all?

MAITLAND: I was there. I just don't understand. I—

CRAWFORD: Isn't it equally possible that, instead, you visited my Chambers, wearing pebble lenses and a shabby suit—

MAITLAND: Wearing what?

CRAWFORD: —and passed yourself off to my clerk, who had never then met you, as a private detective called Armitage?

MAITLAND: No, look, Simon—!

CRAWFORD: But it all fits, doesn't it? Your dinner party on the night of the murder to which you knew I couldn't come. The old man fuddled with wine; an easy and unsuspecting victim—my own late return home, with you waiting for me in the shadows?

MAITLAND: Look, Simon, what are you saying?

CRAWFORD: The *Verveine du Velay* you knew only I drank. The police you failed to notify while I was lying injured in your house. The clocks you so carelessly forgot to put on. My missing keys. The letter in my drawer. Opportunity was there for the taking, wasn't it?

MAITLAND: Simon, for God's sake stop! You're saying I killed him. I didn't. I didn't do any of these things. Why on earth should I? What possible motive could I have?

CRAWFORD: I am coming to that, Major Maitland, just be patient. My Lord, may I now have sight of the Armitage letter, Exhibit Six, please? [*It is passed over to him and he looks at it*] Thank you. My Lord, I have been extremely remiss. I find I am unable to proceed with my cross-examination of this witness, unless I once more recall Mr. Milburn. I omitted to put one point to him, my Lord, which is vital to my present line of questioning.

NAYLOR: [*Rising*] My Lord, your Lordship has rightly expressed your willingness to give every assistance to the prisoner, but does your indulgence extend to his reducing the witness box to the level of a bedroom door in a French farce?

CRAWFORD: I forgot to ask one single question. In similar circumstances I think you might have done the same.

JUDGE: That will do, Mr. Crawford.

CRAWFORD: I beg your pardon, my Lord.

JUDGE: Major Maitland, stand down for a moment, but you will not leave the court. Mr. Milburn, go back to the witness box, please.

CRAWFORD: I'm much obliged, my Lord. [NAYLOR *sits*. MAITLAND *goes back to seat, stops to look at* CRAWFORD. CHARLES *returns to box*] I'm sorry to bother you again, Mr. Milburn, but there is just this one point I forgot to put to you regarding the possible relationship between the envelope typed in red which was delivered to Chambers, and the corresponding letter which was found in my desk at home. You've never actually seen that letter, have you?

CHARLES: No, sir.

CRAWFORD: Then will you look at it now, please. [*It is passed over via* GILLESPIE *and* USHER] Do you notice anything unusual about it—apart from the fact that it's typed in red, I mean?

CHARLES: No, I don't think so, sir. The signature doesn't look much like that of an educated person—but that's about all.

CRAWFORD: Nevertheless you would agree that the fact it is typed in red is, in itself, odd?

CHARLES: Very odd indeed, sir—yes.

CRAWFORD: But it's not typed in red, is it?

CHARLES: But you just said—

CRAWFORD: Mr. Milburn, the original letter sent by Armitage was typed in red. What you're holding in your hands is a copy of it, prepared last night in my solicitor's office—but typed in green. Are you color blind, Mr. Milburn?

CHARLES: Well—as a matter of fact I am, sir.

CRAWFORD: Why did you never say so before?

CHARLES: It never occurred to me.

CRAWFORD: Or did you deliberately conceal it?

CHARLES: No, sir, to me it's of no importance. One learns to live with it—a minor disability like that.

CRAWFORD: Wasn't it a great handicap to you in your army career?

CHARLES: Not particularly, sir.

CRAWFORD: Not in the Royal Corps of Signals with all those colored lights and things?

CHARLES: No, sir.

CRAWFORD: Would it surprise you to know that no branch of the Royal Signals has any knowledge of you, and that the War Office has no record that you ever served in the army at all? [Pause]

CHARLES: I'm sorry, sir. I'm afraid I haven't been quite frank with you.

CRAWFORD: It wouldn't seem so—no.

CHARLES: To be honest, I was hoping I wouldn't have had to tell you this, sir. Since—starting work in the Temple, I've—I've practiced an innocent deception, that's all.

CRAWFORD: Perhaps the Court may be allowed to judge the nature of this deception and its innocence.

CHARLES: Forgive me, sir, I—I was never in the Signals. I was never in the army at all.

CRAWFORD: Then why did you pretend you were?

CHARLES: Because I—wanted to work in the Temple, sir. I thought by saying I was in the army I'd stand a better chance than by straightway admitting the truth—that's all.

CRAWFORD: And what was the truth?

CHARLES: That when the war broke out, I—was in prison, sir. And on my discharge, I worked in a munitions factory.

CRAWFORD: So you have lied to me and to the Court?

CHARLES: In that respect, sir, yes.

CRAWFORD: Is the rest of your evidence to be interpreted in the light of that admission?

CHARLES: That is the only matter about which I have not told the whole truth.

CRAWFORD: How is the jury to know that?

CHARLES: I hope they will take my word for it. Look, sir, if I've offended you, I apologize—sincerely. Please forgive me. It was a stupid thing to do. But why do you keep attacking me, sir? What are you trying to get at?

CRAWFORD: I am trying to get at the truth, Mr. Milburn! Yesterday in the Court, Major Maitland was accused of being a hostile witness—not to me, but to the Crown. Today I accuse you of being hostile, not to the Crown but to me.

CHARLES: That—that's not true, sir.

CRAWFORD: What's your name?

CHARLES: My name, sir?

CRAWFORD: Isn't it John Logan?

CHARLES: No, sir.

CRAWFORD: John Logan was a man who was convicted of a serious robbery with violence in this Court twenty years ago.

NAYLOR: [Rising] My Lord, I must object most strongly to this line of questioning.

JUDGE: Please sit down, Mr. Naylor.

[NAYLOR sits]

CRAWFORD: He was sentenced to life imprisonment.

CHARLES: I just don't understand, sir. What's that to do with me?

CRAWFORD: I suggest a great deal, because on that occasion, after sentence, John Logan threatened to kill the presiding Judge and Prosecuting Counsel. The Presiding Judge was Sir Anthony Gregory, the Prosecuting Counsel was myself. You've succeeded with one, haven't you, Logan?

NAYLOR: [Rising] My Lord, I cannot agree to this.

JUDGE: Sit down, Mr. Naylor.

[NAYLOR sits]

CHARLES: My Lord, may I speak? Mr. Crawford keeps attacking me—

JUDGE: Just answer the questions, Mr. Milburn. If there is anything improper in any of them, I shall not allow them to be put.

CRAWFORD: Will you look at these photographs, please. [He produces

two photos—they are passed via GILLESPIE *and* USHER *to* CHARLES]
You remember these pictures being taken?

CHARLES: No. Why should I?

CRAWFORD: Because they are pictures of you.

CHARLES: No.

CRAWFORD: But your name is on them. Look at the back.

CHARLES: The name Logan is written here.

CRAWFORD: That's what I said. Your name was written on them at the prison when they were taken in 1943.

CHARLES: My name is not Logan—and these are not pictures of me.

CRAWFORD: You can't prove that, though, can you?

CHARLES: I don't have to.

CRAWFORD: You may have to. Look at the eyes, Logan. A man's eyes don't change. Other features, maybe—but not his eyes. Your eyes have given you away, Logan. His Lordship will see those pictures in a moment—so will Mr. Naylor—so will the jury. What are you going to say if they decide they are pictures of you? Tell me, what will you say then, Logan?

CHARLES: Stop calling me Logan.

CRAWFORD: Tell me, Logan, what will you say?

CHARLES: I shall say my name is not Logan.

CRAWFORD: It was Logan when you went to prison, though, wasn't it? It wasn't until you escaped that you changed it to Milburn—when you set out to destroy the Judge and me.

CHARLES: That's absurd. I—

CRAWFORD: You became a clerk in my Chambers, didn't you, Logan? For years you studied the Judge and me until there wasn't a thing about us that you didn't know. And then, Logan, you waited until you saw your opportunity in the tragedy of my daughter's death.

CHARLES: No!

CRAWFORD: It was you, Logan, who posed as Armitage, to frame me for a murder that I did not commit. You, Logan, who, in your insane desire for revenge, picked up that knife and with it stabbed to death an innocent old man with no more conscience than when you shot that bank clerk twenty years ago.

CHARLES: That's not true.

CRAWFORD: You murdered Gregory, Logan!

CHARLES: No!

CRAWFORD: Just as you said you would—all those years ago, standing where I am now. That's true, isn't it, Logan?

CHARLES: It's lies, all lies. Why do you keep calling me Logan?

CRAWFORD: Because that's your name! Because you *are* Logan!

CHARLES: How can I be Logan? Logan is dead.

[*Pause*]

CRAWFORD: What did you say? How do you know that Logan is dead?

CHARLES: I read it somewhere in the papers.

CRAWFORD: You did not. It was never reported in any paper. How do you know that Logan is dead? The truth is—he isn't dead, is he, Logan? He's alive and you are he.

CHARLES: No! No!

CRAWFORD: Then I ask you again—how do you know that Logan is dead? *Answer* me.

[*Pause*]

CHARLES: You clever bastard!

[*The court reacts*]

USHER: Silence!

JUDGE: Mr. Crawford, have you any further questions to put to Mr. Logan?

CRAWFORD: No, my Lord. That is the case for the defense.

CURTAIN

Kind Lady

EDWARD CHODOROV

Adapted from a story by Hugh Walpole

Edward Chodorov

In the course of theatre history there have been many
players who made a role indisputably their own, and one
such actress was Grace George, who created the part of
Mary Herries in the original New York production of Edward Chodorov's *Kind Lady* and for years thereafter frequently performed it
in revival, on tour and in summer theatres. Miss George, of course,
had no monopoly on the play—a spate of actresses eventually tried
their hands at it—but to all of those who witnessed her performance
she was indelibly *the* Mary Herries.

Her performance was described as "a triumph of mettlesome
subtlety," and the play itself was hailed as "one of the best melo-
dramas of the modern theatre" and "a deftly frightening play" that
was "an admirable study in terror." Yet, Miss Herries and the de-
tachment of sinister characters who imprison her in her own home
found the road to success an especially arduous one. Adapted by Mr.
Chodorov from Hugh Walpole's story, *The Silver Mask*, the play
had gone the rounds of all the prominent producers in New York
before it ultimately caught the attention of two summer theatre
managers, H. C. Potter and George Haight. After a trial engagement
at Southampton during the summer of 1934 there was another hiatus
for the play. Finally, it arrived in New York on April 23, 1935, and
the next day's press reported that "a first night audience received it
with chills, thrills and bravos." To Brooks Atkinson, then drama
spokesman for *The New York Times*, Chodorov had recreated the
story for the stage "with considerable skill and with no words wasted.
The mood alters from ordinary friendliness to ominous villainy before you realize it. . . . The callousness of the characters develops
slyly. Scene by scene the pressure of these vultures against the help-

less lady becomes so agonizing that the theatregoers are more relieved than she when at length she contrives her deliverance."

Kind Lady was filmed twice. The first version was made in 1935 with Aline MacMahon and Basil Rathbone; the second in 1951 with Ethel Barrymore, Maurice Evans, and Angela Lansbury among its principals.

Edward Chodorov was born on April 17, 1904, in New York City. Enamored of the theatre since childhood, he persuaded his parents to allow him to cross the river to Brooklyn to attend Erasmus Hall High School, which had a rich theatrical tradition and was the spawning ground for such stars as Barbara Stanwyck, Jane Cowl, and Edward Everett Horton. Following his graduation, he went to Brown University, but soon left to find a job in the theatre.

He spent many hours in Broadway automats discussing the drama with another theatrical aspirant, Moss Hart. When Hart eventually procured a position as secretary to a booking office executive, he managed to get Chodorov a job as a stage manager for *Abie's Irish Rose*. In spite of his inexperience, he handled the backstage details so efficiently that he was next dispatched to South Africa to work in a similar capacity for the comedy *Is Zat So?*

When he returned to the United States, the country was in the midst of the depression, and employment in the theatre was scarce, so he took a job writing motion picture publicity. The experience proved fruitful, for it inspired his first play, *Wonder Boy*, a raucous satire on movie-making. The play was produced by Jed Harris in 1931, and although it was something less than a success, it brought him to the attention of Hollywood and he received offers of contracts. Still intent on his career in the theatre, he resisted the offers at first but soon capitulated and spent the next several years working on screenplays for Warner Brothers and First National.

Firmly established after the success of *Kind Lady*, Mr. Chodorov went back to Hollywood in 1935. He was to remain there, with time out for plays, for almost a decade as a writer and producer for several major studios.

Mr. Chodorov's other works for the theatre include: *Cue for Passion* (in collaboration with H. S. Kraft); *Those Endearing Young*

Charms; Decision; Common Ground; Signor Chicago; Oh, Men! Oh, Women!; Monsieur Lautrec; and *Listen to the Mocking Bird.*

Hugh Walpole (1884–1941) was one of the century's most prolific and popular writers. His first novel, *The Wooden Horse*, was issued in 1909, and thereafter, with the exception of 1917, he published at least one a year. His writings also encompassed other literary areas ranging from short stories to playwriting, children's tales to belles-lettres. His sales were enormous and he was much in demand as a lecturer, especially in the United States. In 1918 he was appointed Commander of the Order of the British Empire and in 1937 he was knighted by King George VI.

Kind Lady was first produced at the Booth Theatre, New York, on April 23, 1935, by H. C. Potter and George Haight. The cast was as follows:

MR. FOSTER	*Francis Compton*
MARY HERRIES	*Grace George*
LUCY WESTON	*Irby Marshal*
ROSE	*Marie Paxton*
PHYLLIS GLENNING	*Florence Britton*
PETER SANTARD	*Alan Bunce*
HENRY ABBOTT	*Henry Daniell*
ADA	*Justine Chase*
DOCTOR	*Alfred Rowe*
MR. EDWARDS	*Thomas Chalmers*
MRS. EDWARDS	*Elfrida Derwent*
AGGIE EDWARDS	*Barbara Shields*
GUSTAV ROSENBERG	*Jules Epailly*

Directed by	H. C. Potter
Setting by	Jo Mielziner

Kind Lady was first presented in London by Gilbert Miller and Milton Shubert on June 11, 1936, at the Lyric Theatre. The cast was as follows:

MR. FOSTER	*Edward Irwin*
MARY HERRIES	*Sybil Thorndike*
LUCY WESTON	*Mabel Terry-Lewis*
ROSE	*Marie Paxton*
PHYLLIS GLENNING	*Agatha Carroll*
PETER SANTARD	*Alexander Clark*
HENRY ABBOTT	*Robert Douglas*
ADA	*Jean Shepeard*
DOCTOR	*David Hawthorne*
MR. EDWARDS	*Charles Mortimer*
MRS. EDWARDS	*Elfrida Derwent*
AGGIE EDWARDS	*Viola Merrett*
GUSTAV ROSENBERG	*Clarence Derwent*

General Stage Director: Lewis Allen

The action of the play takes place in the living room of Mary Herries' home in Montague Square, London.

PROLOGUE

An afternoon in spring.

ACT ONE

SCENE 1: *Late Christmas Eve, several years before.*
SCENE 2: *After dinner, the following January.*

ACT TWO

An afternoon later in January.

ACT THREE

An afternoon the following summer.

EPILOGUE

SCENE

The downstairs living room in Mary Herries' house in Montague Square, London.

The room proper is a large, comfortably furnished living room reflecting the excellent taste and character of Mary Herries. Many of its furnishings, the pictures in particular, are objets d'art. In the right wall are two large casement windows with fine lace curtains and heavy drapes. In the left wall is a large fireplace (downstage) and a door (upstage) leading to the dining room. Above the mantel is a large oil painting, a Whistler.

Up center is a large arch. Going upstage through the arch one rises two steps to a platform that extends off right to the front hall and door, and off left to the rear of the house. Upstage of the platform two more steps lead to a bay window, and stair landing. Leading left from this bay window landing is a flight of stairs to the upper part of the house.

Between the windows at right is a desk and chair. A sofa with a coffee table in front of it is at right. Against the right section of the back wall is a chest and in the corner there is a table with a lamp.

In front of the fireplace is a low upholstered fire seat. Two large overstuffed chairs with a drum table between them occupy the left side of the stage.

Against the left side of the back wall is a chest and at its right there is a low table with a lamp. On the wall above these are an El Greco, and a Whistler. Above the furniture at up right on the back wall are two more Whistlers.

Between the windows in the bay window there is a large chest. The windows have drapes and curtains.

A chandelier hangs in the hall and there are wall brackets at right and left on the pilasters framing the big center arch.

PROLOGUE

*There is a slight rearrangement of furniture on stage right.
The sofa is between the windows right with the coffee
table below it. The desk is right with a side chair behind
it and another side chair at its left.*

*On the right and left back walls and over the fireplace the
"old masters" have been replaced by "moderns."*

*At Rise: Empty stage. It is raining outside. It is late
afternoon.*

*After the curtain rises, the doorbell is heard ringing. After
a moment it rings again. A* SERVANT *is seen crossing from
the rear of the house toward the front door. The doorbell
rings again.*

MR. FOSTER: [*Off*] Mr. Abbott, please.

SERVANT: [*Off*] Mr. Abbott's out.

FOSTER: [*Entering. He is a small man. He carries an umbrella, hat,
and brown paper envelope, and wears a coat*] I'm from the bank,
Foster's the name. I had an appointment for four o'clock. [SERVANT
gestures him to sit down and wait] Then, if you don't mind, I'll
take off my coat—it's damp.

[FOSTER *removes his coat, gives it, his hat and umbrella to*
SERVANT *who exits right and after leaving them crosses out
left.* FOSTER *in the meantime has come down into the room
proper, gone to the desk, and left his envelope there. He
then glances out the window and then at the pictures. His
attention is drawn to someone coming down the stairs. It is*
MARY HERRIES. *She comes down from upstairs uncertainly
and rather furtively. She looks off left, turns, and starts off
right*]

FOSTER: [*Stopping her*] How do you do? [MARY *stops but doesn't answer*] I am waiting for Mr. Abbott, if you please, madam. I'm from the bank. I have an appointment for four o'clock, but since he's not here, perhaps—

MARY: Mr. Abbott—is—not here?

FOSTER: No. Servant said he was out. Perhaps I should come back later.

MARY: They—don't usually keep people waiting.

FOSTER: That's all right. I don't mind waiting. Only I hope I'm not in the way.

MARY: No. You're not in the way. Of course not— From the bank?

FOSTER: Blakely's, madam.

MARY: Oh, yes. I know that bank very well. I used to do business with Blakely's Bank.

FOSTER: Excuse me, madam. But is there any possibility that Mr. Abbott may not be here shortly? I'm to see another gentleman at five.

MARY: You've never been here before?

FOSTER: No, madam.

MARY: Then you've never seen me before. I don't see many people —from outside.

FOSTER: Oh.

MARY: Don't you think it odd that I never see anyone?

FOSTER: Why—I don't know, Mrs.—

MARY: Miss—Mary Herries.

FOSTER: Oh. [*Then, suddenly*] Herries? It seems to me I remember the name, madam. It's been on our books for years.

MARY: Yes— It has been. For years.

FOSTER: But I thought—I mean I took it for granted—that you were away. Abroad, or some place. For several years, I think?

MARY: No, I've been here—always. [*She crosses to dining room door and closes it. Then comes back to* FOSTER] Don't you want to know why I never see anyone?

FOSTER: Uh—what is that, madam?

MARY: It's a very interesting reason. Very interesting. I think you might be very interested. You might be the very one.

[*During this last speech the lights have been slowly fading —and at the end of the speech the stage is in total darkness*]

ACT ONE

SCENE 1

The lights fade up very shortly and we find the stage is set as first described.

LUCY WESTON is discovered sitting in the chair in front of the fireplace. In another chair there is an open suitcase with wrapped Christmas packages in it. There are also some packages on the table and an envelope.

It is late Christmas Eve, several years before the Prologue. A small Christmas tree is on the chest in the bay window.

ROSE: [*Entering with a piece of red ribbon and a tray containing a whiskey decanter, syphon, and glasses*] This is all I could find, Mrs. Weston.

[ROSE *puts tray on chest and crosses to table and ties up a Christmas package*]

LUCY: Fine! That will do nicely. Now let me see. Cynthia, Peter, John, Harold, Kitten and Sybil. That's seven. Seven nieces and nephews. Rose, think of it. And I didn't have to go through a thing to have them! It is quite different when I have my own chickabiddies.

ROSE: Oh—Mrs. Weston!

LUCY: What's this? [*She notices a package which hasn't been put in suitcase*] "Rose." Now who in heaven's name! Has my brother had another child? I mean his wife? Dear me, it's hard to keep track, Rose— [*Looks at* ROSE] Oh, my heavens! It's *you!* I nearly packed it with the others. Well, now the cat's out of the bag. [*Hands package to* ROSE] Merry Christmas, Rose.

ROSE: Oh, thank you, Mrs. Weston. The same to you and many more.

LUCY: Well—we won't count how many more. And— [*Takes en-velope*] —this. For looking after me so nicely this visit.

ROSE: [*Takes envelope*] Oh, Mrs. Weston. This is too much!

LUCY: When you open it you won't say that. Well, things are going to get better some day. Those go in the bag to take with me to-morrow. Don't let me forget. Am I all packed?

ROSE: [*Putting packages in suitcase*] Yes, madam. Except for the blouse at the cleaner's. I'll send that on to you the moment it comes.

LUCY: That's fine. What time is it?

ROSE: [*Puts suitcase on floor*] After eleven o'clock, madam.

LUCY: What time are these operas usually over, Rose?

ROSE: It's hard to say, Mrs. Weston. But Miss Herries always leaves early when the weather's bad.

LUCY: There's one place I will not be found on Christmas Eve—and that is an opera house. Well—I have to leave in half an hour. Miss Herries is sure to be back by then, isn't she?

ROSE: [*Going upstairs*] That's hard to say, Mrs. Weston.

> [*Front doorbell rings.* ROSE *puts suitcase on landing and goes to answer it*]

PHYLLIS: [*Off*] Is Miss Herries in?

ROSE: [*Off*] No, miss, she's not back from the opera.

> [PHYLLIS *enters*]

PHYLLIS: Oh, dear, I was sure she'd be here. [*Sees* LUCY] Mrs. Weston! Merry Christmas.

LUCY: Hello, Phyllis, Merry Christmas!

PHYLLIS: I'm doing the rounds of the relatives, bearing gifts. [ROSE *picks up suitcase and is crossing toward stairs.* PHYLLIS *turns toward hall*] Peter! Come in—don't stand out there in the hall. [*To* ROSE] Don't go, please. [ROSE *stops at foot of stairs*] Peter!

PETER: [*Off*] Huh?

LUCY: [*Confidentially*] Is this—

PHYLLIS: I don't know yet, but I think so. [PETER *enters, carrying small package*] Peter, this is Mrs. Weston. Mrs. Weston, Mr. Santard. [*Takes package*]

PETER: How do you do?

LUCY: How do you do?

PHYLLIS: Please put this—by the tree tomorrow morning. [*Gives* ROSE *package*]

ROSE: Yes, miss. [*Exits upstairs*]

PHYLLIS: Peter's an American.

PETER: You know—

[*Acknowledging this,* PETER *gives slight Indian war cry*]

PHYLLIS: No, Peter, not *that* American!

PETER: Sorry.

PHYLLIS: Say something nice, Peter.

PETER: [*To* MRS. WESTON] Are you Aunt Mary?

LUCY: No, I'm just—visiting—Phyllis's Aunt Mary.

PETER: I've heard a great deal about Aunt Mary and— [*Brightly, for* PHYLLIS's *benefit*]—I've wanted to meet her! [*Nods to* PHYLLIS *with a "How's that?" expression*]

PHYLLIS: You see—Peter and I—thought it would be a good idea to *bring* Aunt Mary her present—and now she isn't here! Peter!

PETER: [*Who has been looking around the room*] Oh! How do you like London, Mrs. Weston?

LUCY: Why—I should be asking that of you!

PETER: I know—that's why I asked you first.

PHYLLIS: Don't mind Peter, Mrs. Weston. No one in New York would dream of giving him a job so his father sent him over here!

LUCY: I think he's very charming. Sit down, and tell me about— [*Sees decanter*] Oh, would you like a drink?

PETER: Yes, please—and *no* ice.

PHYLLIS: No, Peter. No time.

PETER: [*Bowing politely to* LUCY] Merry Christmas.

PHYLLIS: Sorry, Mrs. Weston. We have miles and miles of driving to do. [*Telephone*] Good night.

LUCY: Good night. [*Crossing toward telephone on desk*]

PETER: [*Going off*] Good-bye.

[ROSE *enters down the stairs*]

PHYLLIS: Don't tell Aunt Mary we were here. Present—secret. Merry Christmas. [*Exits, followed by* ROSE]

LUCY: Merry Christmas, Phyllis. [*At telephone*] Hello? Hello, Bunny! I'm on my way! Really I am—I thought I might induce Mary Herries to "step out" this once— What do you mean she's "no fun"?— Of course you don't know her— The car?— Oh, lovely — Yes—half an hour. Right you are. [*Hangs up*]

PHYLLIS: [*Off*] Merry Christmas.

ROSE: [*Off*] Merry Christmas, miss.

> [ROSE *enters, crosses to dining room and returns with a plate of sandwiches on a tray*]

LUCY: Oh, those look good! [ROSE, *about to put sandwiches on table, comes to* LUCY *and offers them*] Er—no. Not until I'm down ten more pounds. [*Turns away but looks back at sandwiches*] Oh, well. Christmas comes but once a year. [*Takes a sandwich*] Thank you. [*She sits on sofa*]

ROSE: [*Putting sandwiches on table*] Is there anything else, madam?

LUCY: No—except my trunk. I'm sure I'll be in no mood tomorrow to worry about that.

ROSE: [*Takes whiskey and syphon from chest and puts them on table*] The baggage people promised to be here at seven sharp they said.

LUCY: Well, if they're pretty and have curly hair you wake me up, Rose. Otherwise I'll leave their money on the dressing table.

ROSE: [*Laughs*] Yes, madam. [*Exits to dining room*]

> [*The door is heard to open and* MARY HERRIES *enters*]

MARY: Hello! Head better, dear? [*Rings bell for* ROSE]

LUCY: Much.

MARY: Good! [*Turns to hall*] Come in. [HENRY ABBOTT *appears. He is tall, handsome, emanates strength and charm immediately. Shabbily, miserably dressed*] Here's a hungry young man we've got to feed, Lucy.

HENRY: [*Very quietly, half smiling*] Just a cup of tea, thanks.

MARY: Oh, nonsense. You've made me take you in here at this time of night. You'll have to justify it.

HENRY: I'm afraid I couldn't manage much more.

[ROSE *enters from dining room*]

MARY: Rose, would you make some tea, and let this gentleman have anything else he wants. [*To* HENRY] If you feel better.

HENRY: Just some tea.

[*There is a moment's pause*]

ROSE: [*Who has been eyeing him*] This way, please. [*He turns and follows* ROSE *out without any further sign*]

MARY: [*Puts purse on table*] Poor chap.

LUCY: Where did you find him?

MARY: Just outside—I've never done this before! I never even give to beggars on the street. Anyway, all I had was a one pound note. [*Reflects*] There's something about him. Don't you think? [*Puts wrap on desk chair*]

LUCY: Mmm.

MARY: Matter of fact. Made me feel awfully sorry for him. I just couldn't leave him standing there. But I'd never have brought him in if you weren't here. [*Laughs*] Haven't I been trying to convince you that I'm getting sillier all the time! I really should apologize!

LUCY: [*Taking a cigarette*] What for?

MARY: After all, heaven knows *what* he is.

LUCY: What he looks like probably—a rather charming, hungry young man.

MARY: Isn't he? Striking, I mean.

LUCY: Very.

MARY: So unusual.

LUCY: Very. How was Covent Garden?

MARY: [*Taking off gloves*] Horrible, I thought. The place reeked of mackintoshes and galoshes. I could see the strings resenting it bitterly. I hate London at this time of year.

LUCY: In a few weeks I'll be home—in my garden—with an armful of the loveliest azaleas *you* ever saw.

MARY: What a persistent woman! Oh, I feel so stupid refusing.

LUCY: Well now, why refuse? Now look here! Why shouldn't you give yourself a month of Riviera sun and warmth? What's keeping you here?

MARY: I don't know. It's simply—

LUCY: Simply rot.

MARY: Lucy, I'd love to go back with you.

LUCY: Then why not?

MARY: But I'm just comfortable here, I suppose—

LUCY: Why do you avoid everyone?

MARY: [*Not listening*] You know, Lucy, he didn't ask me for money.

LUCY: What??? Ohh.

MARY: He simply stood there with the most disarming smile and said: "I wonder if I might have a cup of tea on Christmas Eve."

LUCY: Very touching. I asked you why you avoid everyone.

MARY: [*Sits*] I? I don't do anything of the sort. I've just been busy— that's all.

LUCY: Don't tell me, Mary Herries. Won't you come with me tonight, just this once? Bunny would love to have you.

MARY: No, thank you, Lucy.

LUCY: Oh, ho! You're going to have a nice little chat with Tiny Tim.

MARY: Who?

LUCY: The striking young beggar you met in the fog—or snow—on Christmas Eve.

MARY: I am not! When he's had something to eat, Rose can let him out through the basement.

LUCY: Aren't you going to give him some money or something?

MARY: No, I am not.

LUCY: At least you must let him thank you.

MARY: Not necessarily.

LUCY: Well—if you want to sit all alone on Christmas Eve—I'll stay with you. I'll ring up Bunny. [*Starts*]

MARY: [*Rises and crosses to* LUCY] No, Lucy. I won't let you. Please go and have a good time.

[ROSE *enters*]

ROSE: He's finished, madam.

MARY: [*Turns to* ROSE] What?

ROSE: He's had his tea.

MARY: Very well, Rose. You can show him out downstairs.

ROSE: But— [*She pauses*]

MARY: Yes—?

ROSE: He says he wants to thank you.

LUCY: There!

MARY: That's very nice of him. Tell him he's quite welcome.

LUCY: Mary!

ROSE: Yes, Miss Herries.

[*She turns to go, but* HENRY *enters*]

HENRY: [*Half smiling; a peculiar somber smile*] I've had my tea. You're very kind.

MARY: I was happy to help you.

HENRY: I wanted to thank you, that's all.

MARY: Of course.

[*There is a pause*]

HENRY: [*Sees sandwiches on table*] I—I wonder if I might take a few of those sandwiches.

LUCY: [*Ill-at-ease*] Please do!

MARY: Of course.

HENRY: [*Crosses to table*] I'll eat them outside.

[*Doorbell.* ROSE *goes*]

LUCY: [*Mischievously*] Eat them here!

[MARY *looks uncomfortably at* LUCY]

HENRY: Thank you. I'm able to now, I think. [*Looks at whiskey*]

MARY: [*Weakly*] Have some whiskey if you like.

HENRY: I will.

[ROSE *enters.* HENRY *mixes a whiskey and soda*]

ROSE: The car's at the door for Mrs. Weston. [*Exits*]

LUCY: Oh, dear! Well— [*Mischievously*] Good night, Mary, and—a Merry Christmas.

MARY: Merry Christmas, Lucy. I'll see you in the morning.

LUCY: I hope so. [*She goes*]

HENRY: [*Looking at paintings*] You've a few nice things here. [MARY *smiles nervously, looking covertly back over her shoulder for* ROSE] That's a good El Greco. [*Points*]

MARY: [*Indicates immediately she is quite astonished*] It's not bad.

HENRY: One of his early ones; they're not common.

MARY: No. There aren't two hundred people in London who'd know that! Are you an artist?

HENRY: Not really. One of many confused talents.

MARY: You talk as if you knew something about painting.

HENRY: I suppose I do. [*He starts toward sandwiches*]

MARY: Look here—if you really want something to eat now—those stale sandwiches—

HENRY: They're exactly right. Again, thanks. And again forgive me for disturbing you like this.

[ROSE *enters and gets* MARY's *wrap at desk*]

MARY: You haven't. It isn't every day one bumps into an El Greco lover on the street.

[ROSE *exits, a bit uneasy*]

HENRY: [*Looking around again*] You collect seriously.—

MARY: [*Amused*] How do you tell? Is this room that bad?

HENRY: [*Quickly*] It's lovely of course. But it takes a collector to jam a Whistler, an El Greco, and a Ming horse all together, doesn't it?

MARY: [*After a moment*] Well, whatever you are, you have an educated eye—no question about that! And you're right about the jam. [*Carries horse from left chest and puts it on right chest*] There seems to be a difference between my maid and myself as to just where this bronze belongs!

HENRY: Your maid is a strong-minded woman.

MARY: [*Laughs*] You've found that out? Rose is a good soul—and devoted to me. She won't go to bed now until she's quite sure you don't mean to murder me. [*Sits.* HENRY *laughs and drinks*] What do you do?

HENRY: Nothing. Everything. The last year I've had odd jobs I shouldn't like to mention in this house. [*Puts glass on table*]

MARY: But you certainly have a good eye—and knowledge. Collecting *is* my one interest.

HENRY: Mine, too, once—and not wasted. [*Sits*] I find it very comforting to remember, standing in the line on the embankment.

MARY: The line?

HENRY: The bread line.

MARY: Oh.

HENRY: As a connoisseur of lines—I should say it was the best in London—and wonderfully philanthropic. I bothered you tonight because the two odd miles to the embankment seemed to stretch like eternity in the snow.

MARY: I'm glad you did.

HENRY: I, too.

MARY: [*Pause*] Are you alone?

HENRY: Alone, as they say, in the world?

MARY: Yes.

HENRY: Practically. I have a wife—and a child.

MARY: Oh—really?

HENRY: A nursing child.

MARY: [*Very sympathetically*] What do you do?

HENRY: We do rather nicely comparatively. Ada—my wife—is a delicate creature who scrubs floors occasionally, when she's lucky, in an office building in the city—a Fragonard charwoman.

MARY: A nursing child. That's dreadful.

HENRY: Not at all. What Ada makes pays the rent of our hovel in South Wharf Road—and buys approximately enough food for herself and the little brute, of course.

MARY: South Wharf Road. You live—

HENRY: In the neighborhood. I've admired the outside of your house many times—from the drinking trough opposite.

MARY: [*Rises*] And I'm going to send you back to your house right now.

HENRY: [*Rises*] Of course—I'm keeping you up.

MARY: That's an unkind remark, young man. I could sit here and tell

you how I got that El Greco until you beg for mercy. But I won't
—for a very good reason. [*Starts*]

HENRY: [*Stopping her*] I should like to hear.

MARY: Oh, no. [*Turns back to* HENRY] All my life the mistakes
that I've made—and there have been plenty—have all arisen from
the same thing—my heart swamping my good sense. [*She looks at
him*] I'm telling you this because you're obviously a very unusual
and intelligent young man—and you've just told me a terribly
pathetic story.

HENRY: [*Smiling*] Thank you. I'm sorry.

MARY: I'm afraid of it—and you. I had a birthday a short time ago,
and I thought at last I'm too old to be foolish any more. But here
I am—helping an entirely unknown man into my house in the
middle of the night and listening to a tale that's going to make me
see white-faced babies in my dreams for a week.

HENRY: He's red as a herring—and looks like one.

MARY: Believe me—I don't care. Everything about you conspires to
make me help you. Why—you even live around the corner! Well,
I'm not going to help you. I'm a selfish old maid—and I never
want to see you again—or hear anything more about that young
girl you've presented with a baby. You're probably the worst sort
of criminal. [*Turns and moves away as she finishes speech, then
turns back quickly*] Wait a minute. [*She goes upstairs and off*]

> [HENRY *looks after her quietly. Finishes whiskey and
> puts glass on table. Then slowly crosses and easily picks
> up a white jade cigarette case from table, examines it,
> takes out cigarette, taps it against the case, looks at case
> again, then puts it in his pocket in the most natural manner
> in the world—as if it had come from there. He lights his
> cigarette. As* MARY *comes down carrying a heavy cloth coat
> with a fur collar, over her arm,* HENRY *puts out cigarette*]

MARY: [*Hands him coat*] Give this to your wife.

HENRY: That's good of you.

MARY: [*Going on as she gets her purse from table*] She'd better
let a tailor do the alterations. Here. [HENRY *crosses to her*] And
you'd better get some shoes.

HENRY: [*Without the slightest emotion*] You're saving our lives.

MARY: Nonsense. [*He looks at the money in his hand*] It's all I have in the house—so you needn't bother holding me up now, you see?

HENRY: It *was* foolish of you to let a tramp in here at this time of night.

MARY: So I've been told. But an old woman like me—what's the difference?

HENRY: I could have cut your throat.

MARY: You might have—but you'd have been sorry.

HENRY: Oh, no. The police never catch anybody any more.

MARY: [*Going to arch*] Don't let's worry about that.

HENRY: Not tonight. It would be ungrateful.

MARY: Good-bye.

[HENRY *crosses to her*]

HENRY: Good night. [*Exits*]

MARY: [*Calling off*] Good luck. And—Merry Christmas!

[MARY *comes in. Hesitates in arch. Goes to look for cigarette case on table, then on chest, then on mantel*]

ROSE: [*Enters*] Is there anything you want, madam?

MARY: [*Looks for cigarette case*] No, Rose. You can go to bed.

ROSE: Yes, madam. Good night. [*Starts to go*]

MARY: Rose. Have you seen my cigarette case?

ROSE: [*Comes to table*] The white jade, madam? [MARY *nods*] It was layin' right there this evening.

MARY: I thought so. [*Pause as they both reflect about* HENRY] Oh, well—never mind.

ROSE: I'd say he took it, madam.

MARY: Oh, no, Rose.

ROSE: Do you know where to find him, madam?

MARY: Mmmmm. It doesn't matter.

ROSE: Oh, dear—that's too bad. [*Puts stopper in decanter on table*]

MARY: No, Rose—he didn't take it—I remember now—I had it with me in the taxi.

ROSE: I didn't like him at all, madam. Too good-lookin'.

MARY: [*Sits*] He was good-looking, wasn't he?

ROSE: Too much so— I don't believe he was hungry at all. The way he sat in the kitchen! "You're not hungry," I said to myself— "you're too good-looking. And you're up to something." And sure enough. [*Picks up sandwich plate*]

MARY: No, Rose. [ROSE *stops and turns to* MARY] I left it in the taxi, I'm sure.

ROSE: [*Shaking her head*] Yes, madam. [*Picks up glass from coffee table and goes to dining room door*] Good night. [*Exits*]

> [*Christmas chimes from a church ring out.* MARY *doesn't answer. Looks toward arch right. Turns front—shrugs shoulders*]

CURTAIN

ACT ONE

Night. Two weeks later, January.

PHYLLIS *is sitting on couch reading.* PETER *is standing in front of Troubetzkoi on table with glass.* PETER *looks at Troubetzkoi for a pause. He walks away, half-looking at Troubetzkoi, then stops, returns to statue, looks at it again. He puts glass down deliberately on table. Takes out match, strikes it and holds it to statue.*

PHYLLIS: Peter! Peter, put those matches away and sit down.

[PETER *hastily shakes out match and picks up brandy glass*]

PETER: [*Indicates Troubetzkoi*] That—is a woman. Phyllis! We must get one of those.

PHYLLIS: Yes, dear.

[*Looking at her,* PETER *walks imitating a tightrope walker. He stops in front of picture, looks at it—then suddenly—with extreme deliberation, he puts his glass down on chest*]

PHYLLIS: Peter, *please* don't set off any more matches!

[PETER *picks up glass*]

PETER: Phyllis—who's that tall thin girl last night with the— [*Makes series of adenoidal noises saying:*] "So pleased to meet you so very nice"—can't understand a word she says—who *is* that?

PHYLLIS: That, my dear—will be your cousin Elizabeth.

[PETER *looks at her for a moment*]

PETER: That'll be nice. And *who*—was the fat gentleman with the— [*Indicates fat stomach*] and—the— [*Indicates pompous look and monocle*]

PHYLLIS: [*Cuts in*] If you're attempting to describe Sir Arthur Verne—he's a *very* dear friend of mother's—and happens to be a *very* distinguished man.

PETER: [*Agreeing quickly*] Yes—yes, indeed—I could see that. [*Suddenly gets a glint in his eyes and goes into the next speech as though he were tremendously puzzled*] But who—who—was the little feller! [*He extends his hand about chest high*]

PHYLLIS: Who?

PETER: You know— [*Drops his hand about a foot*] The *little* feller.

PHYLLIS: What are you talking about?

PETER: [*Drops his hand to about a foot from the floor—bending way over—and holding this stance. Speaks patiently*] The *little* feller!—with the— [*Lifts his hand to pull at his chin*]

PHYLLIS: With the *what*—

PETER: The goatee!

PHYLLIS: Peter—get *up!*

PETER: [*Straightens*] But who *is* he? Really!

PHYLLIS: There's no one like that in our family.

PETER: No? [*He shudders*]

PHYLLIS: No.

PETER: Funny. I keep seeing him everywhere.

PHYLLIS: Peter, you simply mustn't drink brandy.

PETER: There's only *one* of your family that I really like.

PHYLLIS: Really?

PETER: [*Pointing wisely upstairs*] Aunt Mary.

PHYLLIS: [*Rises*] We are rude, Peter, but we simply must dash off!

PETER: [*Sitting*] Well, let's not! Let's stay here instead.

PHYLLIS: [*With mock weariness, but real annoyance*] Darling—how can we?

PETER: I feel mellow and witty and dignified all at once for the first time in my life! I don't want to go out in the cold world!

PHYLLIS: [*Patronizingly*] It has been awfully nice—but you have no sense of responsibility.

PETER: I like it here! This is what I call gracious living and it's the first dinner party I've enjoyed in a long while.

PHYLLIS: Much as you hate doing the rounds, you've simply *got* to. I don't like these continual introductions either. But do you make it any easier for me? No! You act as though I were whipping you through hoops or something!

PETER: Can't stand being introduced—wholesale.

PHYLLIS: You spend most of the time standing around and grinning foolishly at everyone.

PETER: I'm not grinning foolishly now. I like Miss Herries—and I'm crazy about this house—and I hope that— [*Closes his eyes*]—the solidification—of our relationship will permit me to run in and out of here at frequent intervals. [*Both laugh*] Furthermore, she has the best wine I ever tasted. [*He reaches for brandy decanter*]

PHYLLIS: [*Taking his glass out of his hand and putting it on table*] Don't imagine you can pop in and out of here whenever you please!

PETER: [*Lighting cigarette*] Why not?

PHYLLIS: Aunt Mary isn't a very sociably inclined lady.

PETER: She's damn nice.

PHYLLIS: I know. We must see her more often, really. Most of the family don't, you know.

PETER: I'll see her without the family any time.

PHYLLIS: We've all neglected her shamefully.

PETER: Your dear mother.

PHYLLIS: Oh, no—it's not mother. She couldn't keep me away. I don't know why—I'm so horribly busy.

PETER: Trotting me around to meet cousins and uncles.

PHYLLIS: I hope she doesn't think this was that kind of a duty call. Wonder what she's doing?

PETER: You hinted strongly enough that a wedding present would be acceptable.

PHYLLIS: Now, Peter, that's not done.

PETER: Maybe she's gone to get us a present right now.

PHYLLIS: How many times must I tell you that I'm not showing you off to my relations just to get presents from them?

PETER: Then why visit the Howards tonight? Why not stay here awhile?

PHYLLIS: George Howard's not a relative. He's your best client. Or will be now that he knows you're going to marry me.

PETER: I feel as if I were getting married for business reasons.

PHYLLIS: Marriage *is* a business.

PETER: Yeah!

PHYLLIS: Yes!

PETER: I suppose I'll go to the Howards whether I want to or not. And all the other places. [*Rises and turns to* PHYLLIS] "How do you do? Yes—I'm the lucky fellow! When? Oh, about the first of June. Yes! The first of June. What? Oh, I'm an American bond salesman. Do you want any nice bonds so I can get married?"

PHYLLIS: Oh! "I want you to meet Peter. I met him in New York, but he's over here now. [*Looks around*] Oh, where has he gone. Peter, Peter, here Peter! Oh, there you are! This is Aunt Evelyn. Oh, he's only joking, Aunt Evelyn. He's making believe he's shy. Say something to Aunt Evelyn, Peter."

PETER: "Hello, Aunt Evelyn."

PHYLLIS: There! [*Sits on sofa*]

PETER: I wish your grandfather hadn't been so prolific.

[MARY *enters from stairs*]

MARY: I waited until the last second with this—because I just want to give it to you—and let that be the end of it. [*Hands* PHYLLIS *a small box*] Don't open it now—your grandfather gave it to me— long time ago—to wear at *my* wedding. [*Smiles brightly*] It's very old—but you'll love it.

[PETER *drifts left looking at statue, puts out cigarette on table*]

PHYLLIS: I know I shall, Aunt Mary. But why so soon?

MARY: Oh—I don't know—I never know where I'm liable to be when people get married.

PHYLLIS: Oh— [*Very sweetly*] Thank you, Aunt Mary. I hope you don't think we came here tonight just to—

MARY: No, no. Even if it were I wouldn't mind. And I know the next time it will be because you want to come.

PETER: Miss Herries, may I ask who did that?

MARY: Which?

PETER: This one—the statue.

MARY: Troubetzkoi, Mr. Santard.

PETER: Troubetzkoi, eh? What's it supposed to be?

MARY: I really don't know who she is. I think it's listed in the catalogue as "Figure" or something equally enlightening.

PETER: I think it's grand. Phyllis, we must get one of this fellow's things sometime.

PHYLLIS: Yes, yes—all right, darling. That's the fourth time tonight you've said that.

PETER: Is it? I must like it.

MARY: Do you like it very much, Mr. Santard?

PETER: [With mock sadness] Please call me "Peter."

MARY: All right, Peter. I'll tell you what I'll do. I'll give it to you for a wedding present.

PETER: What—really?

PHYLLIS: Oh, no, Aunt Mary. I won't dream of it. You simply mustn't!

MARY: [Sits] No—no. It's all settled.

PHYLLIS: But you must be awfully fond of it yourself.

MARY: I am. But I want you to have it—if you like it too, Phyllis.

PHYLLIS: Oh—I like it.— [Gives a look of disgust to PETER]

MARY: It's the best present I can think of for me to give you.

PHYLLIS: Honestly, Aunt Mary—after one drink of cold water, Peter wouldn't know if Troubetzkoi or Madame Tussaud did it.

PETER: What's the difference? And anyway I know very well who did it—Troubetzkoi. [Snaps fingers and returns to contemplating it]

MARY: Then that's that. [She imitates his finger snap]

PETER: Have you any more Troubetzkoi's in the house?

MARY: Oh, yes. Didn't you notice the one in the dining room?

PETER: Whereabouts?

MARY: On the sideboard.

PETER: [Picking up brandy glass from table] I'll have another look at it.

MARY: Do.

PETER: [As he passes into dining room, he salutes PHYLLIS with the glass] Troubetzkoi!!

PHYLLIS: [Silent for a moment, then very formal] Look, Aunt Mary. We really must go. The Howards will be terribly offended and we can't afford that.

MARY: No, indeed!

PHYLLIS: I didn't mean it that way. Really, Aunt Mary—

MARY: That's all right.

PHYLLIS: *I* want to be friends with you—even if mother insists on being an idiot!

MARY: [*With a laugh*] The Howards are expecting you!

PHYLLIS: [*Looks for a moment at* MARY. *Shakes her head and goes to door*] Peter!

PETER: [*Off*] Huh!

PHYLLIS: Say good-bye to Aunt Mary.

PETER: [*Off*] Good-bye, Aunt Mary.

[MARY *laughs*]

PHYLLIS: Peter!

PETER: [*Enters*] Yes?

PHYLLIS: We're leaving!

PETER: Oh! Sorry! [*To* MARY] What did you say the name of that fellow was?

MARY: Troubetzkoi.

PETER: Oh, yes.

PHYLLIS: [*Quietly, shaking her head*] Oh, you *are* a fool!

PETER: What's the matter?

PHYLLIS: [*Pointing at* MARY] Here's someone with banks full of lovely money—and nothing to do with it except buy statues—and you go and get us a statue for a wedding present!

[*Doorbell rings*]

PETER: [*To* MARY] Don't you think she's a little commercial?

MARY: [*Rises*] No, Peter. Just frank. All our family is addicted to frankness.

PETER: Thanks for the tip. You must tell me all about the family.

PHYLLIS: Come on, Peter.

[ROSE *crosses to hall door*]

MARY: Come and see me in a few months and pick up the Troubetzkoi.

PETER: May I come sooner than that and look at it—and look at you?

MARY: Do that! And I'll see if I need any bonds.

PETER: Did she tell you you had to buy bonds, too?

PHYLLIS: Why not? She's always buying them from *somebody*.

PETER: My God!

[MARY *laughs.* ROSE *enters*]

ROSE: Madam!

MARY: What is it, Rose?

ROSE: It's—!

HENRY: [*Enters*] I beg your pardon. I'll wait outside. [*He goes off*]

MARY: [PETER *and* PHYLLIS *look at each other. A little embarrassed*] That's a young man whom I—never mind—you're in a hurry. It's all right, Rose. Get Miss Glenning's and Mr. Santard's things. [ROSE *exits.* PHYLLIS *looks at* PETER *with a "What do you know?"*] And now—run along, you two. Keep your "appointments." I hope I haven't made you too late.

PETER: Of course not. Please forget about it.

MARY: [*As she reaches entrance to hall, speaks to* HENRY] Will you come in here?

HENRY: [*As he passes*] I'm very sorry.

MARY: Please sit down.

[MARY *goes off.* HENRY *sits*]

PHYLLIS: [*Handing* PETER *box*] Put the box in your pocket, darling, and be very careful.

[PHYLLIS *and* PETER *exit, glancing back at* HENRY]

MARY: [*Off*] That's a lovely wrap, Phyllis.

PETER: [*Off*] I'll remember that hopping in and out business!

[ROSE *crosses and goes off*]

MARY: [*Off. Laughs*] Please do!

PHYLLIS: [*Off*] Good night, Aunt Mary. I'll ring you up. Honestly!

PETER: [*Off*] Good night—and permit an old man to bless you.

MARY: [*Off—laughing*] Good night.

[*Door slams.* MARY *returns*]

HENRY: [*Rises, takes cigarette case from his pocket and holds it out*] I pawned it.

MARY: [*Takes it*] What a disgraceful thing to do.— And what are you going to steal next?

HENRY: My wife made some money last week. That will see us through for a while.

MARY: Don't you ever do any work?

HENRY: I paint—but no one will touch my pictures. They're not modern enough.

MARY: You must show me some of your pictures sometime.

HENRY: I have some here. They're in the hall. You probably didn't notice. [*He goes out and returns immediately from the hall with two canvases, face to face—crosses to desk*]

[MARY *puts cigarette case on table*]

MARY: Let's see what you have. [HENRY *places one picture on desk. He holds up another picture showing a cowherd playing his pipes to a group of cows. There is a pause while she looks at them*] Oh, those are very bad.

HENRY: I know they are. You must understand that my esthetic taste is very fine. I appreciate only the best things—like your cigarette case. But I can paint nothing but these. It's very exasperating.

MARY: It must be.

HENRY: [*Crosses to her a bit*] Won't you buy one?

MARY: You don't mean it?

HENRY: Why not?

MARY: But what should I do with it? I'd have to hide it!

HENRY: Not necessarily. Bad as they are, they have something, I think. [*Puts cow picture on floor against sofa*]

MARY: I don't see it—whatever it is. I really don't want one.

HENRY: Please buy one, anyway.

MARY: [*Retreating a pace*] No—but of course not.

HENRY: [*Comes closer to her*] Yes, please. [*She looks at him, disturbed by his peculiar insistence. At any rate there is something of the rabbit and the snake in this passing tableau*] My wife is waiting in the street just opposite—waiting for me to call her.

MARY: [*Recovering herself*] What on earth for?

HENRY: She wanted to thank you. And I wanted her to see some of your lovely things.

MARY: How can you let her wait out in that deathly cold?

HENRY: I didn't like to bring her without your permission. And I don't like her to see me begging.

MARY: Well, you go straight out and take her home.

HENRY: [*Not moving*] Can't I possibly persuade you— This one with the cows isn't so bad.

MARY: [*Shaking her head as she looks at it*] It's peculiar enough. What is it supposed to be?

HENRY: It's a Swiss scene. In Switzerland the cowherd pipes his cows from the pasture! He plays a traditional melody. *Ranz des Vaches* they call it. I read about it and I thought it was a rather nice macabre idea.

MARY: You've achieved a sinister quality in it, at any rate. How much is it?

HENRY: Five guineas. The other one is seven.

MARY: [*Laughing*] You're really amusing. And quite absurd. They're not worth anything at all.

HENRY: They may be one day. You never know with modern pictures.

MARY: I'm quite sure about those.

HENRY: [*Crosses to picture of cow, takes it to* MARY] But I must sell one tonight—whatever you think of them. [*Holds out cow picture*] Please buy it. [*But he is not pleading*]

MARY: [*After a pause*] I'm a perfect fool. [*She is crossing toward desk.* HENRY *puts picture behind chair then crosses to desk for check*] What's your name? [*Writing check at desk*]

HENRY: Henry—Abbott. The baby's Henry, too.

MARY: [*Rises, hands him check*] Here—and please understand that I never want to see you again. Never. You will not be admitted. It's no use speaking to me in the street. If you bother me, I shall tell the police.

HENRY: [*In spite of this he has not let go of her hand which he took when he reached for the check. He does so now, folding the check and putting it in pocket*] Hang that in the right light and it won't be bad. [*He moves away a bit*]

MARY: You didn't get those shoes. Those are terrible.

HENRY: I'll be able to now.

MARY: The first thing you do is rescue that poor girl. You're a thorough brute, young man.

HENRY: She's used to it.

MARY: More shame to you!

HENRY: You can see her from here. [*He crosses to window*] There she is.

MARY: [*Goes to window*] With the baby! Oh!! [*Gasps*]

HENRY: Ada!!! My God!! [*He runs out*]

MARY: [*Running to arch*] Rose! Rose!

ROSE: [*Rushing in*] Yes, madam!

MARY: Run out and help him—the baby!!! [*As* ROSE *half turns*] Never mind! Take my coat! Run! [*Almost pushing her.* ROSE *runs out.* MARY *goes to window, thrusts shade aside. Watches*] Oh! [*Suddenly goes quickly out to hall again. After a second* HENRY *enters, carrying* ADA. MARY *follows*] On the sofa!

> [ROSE *enters with the baby.* HENRY *carries* ADA *to sofa and places her on it. He has taken* ADA's *head in his hands, shaking it, drops it, grabs her hands, almost immediately lets go, pours drink of brandy from decanter on coffee table, puts it to her lips, it dribbles back*]

HENRY: Ada! Ada! [*Again tries unsuccessfully to give her whiskey. To* MARY] What shall we do?

MARY: [*Quietly holding her heart*] Isn't there any doctor near here —somewhere, Rose?

ROSE: Yes, madam. In the block of flats at the top of the street.

MARY: Get him! Get someone—the nurse—if there's no one there, call an ambulance.

ROSE: Yes, madam. [*Gives baby to* MARY. *Starts to go*]

HENRY: [*Rises and meets* ROSE. *Holding her with one hand*] I'll go. [*Rushes out*]

ROSE: [*Looks after* HENRY, *turns to* MARY] Miss Herries—

MARY: [*Almost simultaneously*] Get that bottle of smelling salts . . .

ROSE: Yes, madam.

> [ROSE *runs upstairs.* MARY *tries to rub* ADA *and hold baby.*

She looks helplessly from ADA *to the baby, puts baby in chair, returns to* ADA, *crosses to window, then to baby. Takes baby.* ROSE *rushes in with smelling salts which she puts in front of* ADA'S *nose.* ADA *stiffens but does not come to*]

MARY: It's all my fault—all my fault for letting him—

ROSE: What's the matter with her, madam?

MARY: Go on, go on!

[ROSE *administers smelling salts, rubs* ADA *in a very inexperienced manner.* HENRY *and* DOCTOR *enter*]

HENRY: Here! [*He does not take baby from* MARY, *but crosses to sofa.* DOCTOR *crosses to sofa and looks at* ADA] Ada! Ada!

ROSE: I'll take it, madam.

[MARY *gives baby to* ROSE]

DOCTOR: [*To* HENRY] Exposure. [*Picks up* ADA] You'd better put her to bed at once.

MARY: Bed? She—

HENRY: You see, Doctor—

DOCTOR: [*To* ROSE] Where's a bedroom?

MARY: [*Looks at* ROSE] Why—

DOCTOR: Upstairs? [*This to* ROSE *with the baby. He carries* ADA *out; as he goes*] Don't worry. Nothing serious. Needs rest and nourishment. [*To* ROSE] Some hot soup. Chicken broth.

[DOCTOR *exits upstairs, followed by* ROSE. MARY *starts to go, turns back to* HENRY *who is moving about unconcernedly, lighting a cigarette.* MARY, *greatly agitated, hurries upstairs.* HENRY *is calmly looking at room. Sees his painting of the cows. Picks it up. Looks about the room. Selects the mantel. Puts his picture there. Stands back looking at it. Sits, admiring his picture. He is totally unconcerned about what has just happened*]

CURTAIN

ACT TWO

Two weeks later. January.

The scene is the same. However, the desk is now behind the sofa at right center. The coffee table is to the right of the sofa. A side chair is behind the desk and another is between the windows.

HENRY *is at the desk. The doorbell rings.* HENRY *looks up from a paper he has been writing on—then resumes.* ROSE *comes in and crosses the room. She is dressed in street clothes. She walks, looks straight ahead, her hands folded before her.*

HENRY: [*Not looking up*] Rose. [ROSE *stops, facing him but not looking at him. He looks up now*] You're all dressed up, Rose. Why?

ROSE: I think you *know* why, Mr. Abbott.

HENRY: Leaving us?

ROSE: I think you know I *am*, Mr. Abbott.

[*She stands there as if anxious to continue the conversation—to get something off her chest. But after a moment, he looks down at his paper*]

HENRY: Answer the bell.

[*She hesitates for a moment, then pressing her lips, walks off*]

MR. EDWARDS: [*Off*] Mr. Henry Abbott here?

ROSE: [*She comes into room, and, not looking at* HENRY, *starts to cross toward dining room*] People outside.

HENRY: Who are they?

ROSE: [*Not stopping*] I don't know.

HENRY: [*Gently, as if admonishing a child*] Rose! Ask them to come in.

[*She stops, hesitates as though she were inwardly under-going a struggle. Then turns and goes to arch*]

ROSE: Come in. [*She exits*]

[MR. EDWARDS *appears, followed by "his wife and daughter,* AGGIE." MR. EDWARDS *is a thick-set, reddish and bulbous-faced man with a hearty hoarse voice.* MRS. EDWARDS *is short, black-clad and eminently respectable looking.* AGGIE *is a thin, sharp-faced girl whose eyes and hands are rarely still.* MR. EDWARDS *is carrying a portable gramophone*]

MR. EDWARDS: Hello, Henry.

[HENRY *gets up*]

MRS. EDWARDS: How's Ada, Henry?
HENRY: Much better.
AGGIE: Hello, Henry.

[HENRY *nods*]

MRS. EDWARDS: We brought Aggie with us.
MR. EDWARDS: We thought we'd better—
MRS. EDWARDS: How's the baby, Henry?
MR. EDWARDS: Doing well, Henry?
HENRY: [*Nods*] Ada will be glad to see you all.
MRS. EDWARDS: And we'll be awfully glad to see her—poor Ada.
MR. EDWARDS: I brought the gramophone. Thought she might like to hear some music.
MRS. EDWARDS: Layin' up in bed, you know.
HENRY: Sit down, and I'll call Miss Herries.
MRS. EDWARDS: Oh, Henry—the way I look. [*Sits*]
HENRY: I shall have to ask permission to bring you upstairs.
MR. EDWARDS: Sure, Henry—that's only right!
HENRY: Sit down. [*He goes upstairs*]
MR. EDWARDS: [*Looking over the room.* AGGIE *goes and picks up*

bronze on table] Very nice layout. [*Puts gramophone on coffee table and hat on end of desk*]

MRS. EDWARDS: I should say it is. My—isn't it pretty!

MR. EDWARDS: Looks like a house I stayed in once—in Melbourne in Australia.

MRS. EDWARDS: Put that down, Aggie!

MR. EDWARDS: Same layout. I'd be able to tell better if I saw the whole house. [*To* AGGIE, *who is touching things on mantel*] Aggie! I wish you would talk to her, mother. Nice thing if somebody saw her. [*Sits*]

MRS. EDWARDS: Father's right, Aggie. You ought to learn to behave yourself in a decent place.

[AGGIE *walks to arch. They watch her, she looks out and returns to room, crossing to desk*]

MR. EDWARDS: [*After another moment*] You notice how nobody has pianos any more?

MRS. EDWARDS: [*Nodding*] If you lived in a house with a court you'd hear the children practicing, all day long.

MR. EDWARDS: It's the wireless that's spoiled it for pianos.

MRS. EDWARDS: [*Not looking at her*] Sit down, Aggie. Didn't you hear Henry say to sit down?

[AGGIE *crosses to fool with gramophone on coffee table*]

MR. EDWARDS: Yep—now it's the wireless. But anything that's pushed out of a wire—sounds like it.

[AGGIE *is opening gramophone*]

MRS. EDWARDS: Ts, ts. Oh, leave it be!

MR. EDWARDS: [*Has risen with surprising swiftness to* AGGIE *and stands over her*] Don't you realize there's somebody sick around here?

[AGGIE *looks frightened, stops playing with gramophone and examines other objects on coffee table. After a moment* MR. EDWARDS *starts to arch*]

MRS. EDWARDS: I'll warrant we'll have to take you off your job, Aggie, and put you back in school, to learn some manners.

MR. EDWARDS: [*Looking upstairs*] That staircase—just like this house in Melbourne—in Australia. A very good sign.

MRS. EDWARDS: I never *knew* you were in Australia, father.

MR. EDWARDS: Sure—I must have told you. Been everywhere.

MRS. EDWARDS: [*Shaking her head, puzzled*] Perhaps you did.

MR. EDWARDS: Didn't I ever mention about staying in this house that used to belong to Lord—Greville? Something like that.

MRS. EDWARDS: [*Thinking*] I don't remember the name.

MR. EDWARDS: Fine feller—black sheep. Came to Australia and made a pile of money.

MRS. EDWARDS: Never got married!

MR. EDWARDS: No—real black sheep. Lived all alone. Got peculiar in his old age with all that money. Used to keep it around the house, they said.

MRS. EDWARDS: Must have been a tough customer.

MR. EDWARDS: [*Nodding, lips pursed*] That's what they said.

MRS. EDWARDS: All that money around the house, ts, ts.

MR. EDWARDS: In gold—gold bars. Some of 'em as long as your arm.

MRS. EDWARDS: Ts, ts. I suppose they found it all after he died?

MR. EDWARDS: No. I can't say they did. No. [*Laughs*] Stop worryin' about it, mother!

MRS. EDWARDS: Well, it's interesting! My goodness!

MR. EDWARDS: I hope Ada ain't too sick to see us.

[AGGIE *crosses to painting*]

MRS. EDWARDS: Henry said she was all right—she was much better, he said.

MR. EDWARDS: Yep—but you know Ada ain't a strong girl. If she's been layin' in bed for two weeks—there's something wrong with her.

MRS. EDWARDS: Very nice of this lady, isn't it, father?

MR. EDWARDS: I should say. She sounds like a real fine woman.

MRS. EDWARDS: [AGGIE *is touching the things on table*] Keep your hands off, Aggie!

[HENRY *comes down stairs*]

HENRY: [*Speaking from landing*] Miss Herries begs to be excused. She hopes to meet you all some other time.

MRS. EDWARDS: [*Rises*] I hope she ain't sick, Henry?

HENRY: No. [*Gestures them to go up*]

MR. EDWARDS: Should I bring up the gramophone, Henry?

HENRY: I don't think so—no.

MR. EDWARDS: [*Setting it at back of sofa*] I'll just set it here out of the way then.

MRS. EDWARDS: [*Crosses toward stairs.* AGGIE *drifts behind her*] Oh —this is certainly a *beautiful* house, Henry!

MR. EDWARDS: [*Propelling* AGGIE] Go on, Aggie.

[*Doorbell rings when* MRS. EDWARDS *is at foot of stairs,* AGGIE *behind her on bay window landing,* MR. EDWARDS *and* HENRY *on hall platform. Bell rings second time. For some reason the four of them stop dead still. There is a pause*]

HENRY: [*Indicates*] Two flights up—the little room at the head of the stairs.

[*Slowly they move up again*]

MR. EDWARDS: [*The last*] Lots of visitors today, Henry.

[*He is off.* HENRY *waits on the landing.* ROSE *enters and crosses. He watches her. She goes off. A moment later*]

LUCY: [*Off*] Hello, Rose. Is Miss Herries in?

ROSE: [*Off*] Yes, madam.

[LUCY *enters room, followed by* ROSE. *She stops on seeing* HENRY]

HENRY: How do you do? [LUCY *nods in surprise*] I'll tell Miss Herries, Rose. [*To* LUCY] Excuse me. [*He goes upstairs*]

LUCY: [*Stopping* ROSE] Rose! Isn't that the young man Miss Herries brought in here one night?

ROSE: Yes, madam—it is.

LUCY: [*As if she knew something now*] Oh.

[ROSE *goes off.* LUCY *crosses to desk to remove her gloves*]

MARY: [*Coming down*] Lucy!

LUCY: Mary, dear.

MARY: Not even a picture postcard! [*Kisses her*]

LUCY: Didn't you get my letter?

MARY: No.

LUCY: [*Disturbed*] Oh, that's too bad!

MARY: Forget about it. Have a good time?

LUCY: That letter worries me.

MARY: [*Laughs*] Really? You probably addressed it wrong. [*Sits*]

LUCY: No. Oh, well. How are you, Mary?

MARY: Oh, fairly well. *You* look splendid.

LUCY: Thanks. I feel as though I'd never get warm again!

MARY: Just an excuse to get back to the Riviera, isn't it?

LUCY: I'm leaving this afternoon. I'm flying to Paris.

MARY: Oh, I'm sorry!

LUCY: That's what I wrote. I didn't think I'd have a chance to see you. Then I decided to come around for a minute anyway.

MARY: I'm glad you did!

LUCY: I just couldn't write you as I did and let it go at that. And when you didn't answer—I knew something was wrong.

MARY: What are you talking about?

LUCY: I'll tell you simply and to the point—if you'll tell me what's been going on here.

MARY: Going on? [*After a moment she sits back*] Please say what you have to say, Lucy, before I go completely out of my mind.

LUCY: All right. Some days after we got to St. Moritz, a lady joined us. She had just arrived—and she had it on *excellent authority*—steady on—that you had taken a man to live with you—

MARY: [*After a moment, as though this were the last straw, murmurs*] What?

LUCY: I laughed her down of course—told her she was a silly woman, I insulted her frightfully. [*Slowly*] It didn't do much good.

MARY: But who would say a thing like that?

LUCY: She from whom all such blessings flow—your sister Emily.

MARY: Emily! It's incredible! How would she know?

LUCY: She didn't say.

MARY: [*Very puzzled—thinking*] Emily.

LUCY: Women like that make mountains out of blades of grass—you know that.

MARY: Oh! Ho!

LUCY: You've traced it!

MARY: No. My niece Phyllis—and her fiancé—were here one night. They saw him—but why would they— Oh, no!

LUCY: Saw who?

MARY: Lucy—it's true.

LUCY: What!?

MARY: I have taken a man in to live with me—and his wife and child.

LUCY: That one—you brought in here on Christmas Eve?

MARY: Hmmm. He came back with his wife. She fainted and I put her up for the night. She's been here ever since.

LUCY: [*Sits. After a pause*] Oh, Mary, Mary. My poor Mary!

MARY: That's only part of it. My cook left me last week—and Rose gave me notice. I've been on my knees to her in the kitchen. She insists on going.

LUCY: Who are those people?

MARY: I don't know. It's become nightmarish. What will I do without Rose? I'll never replace her.

LUCY: [*Dismissing this*] Rose! Throw those people out! How ill is she?

MARY: I don't know—I can't tell. I know *I've* been feeling badly the past few days. My heart has been raising red hell.

LUCY: Oh, Mary! [*Pause, then decisively*] It's insane! You're being used in the most ridiculous and criminal manner.

MARY: Well, goodness knows, I begged for it!

LUCY: I know you! Throw them out! You've simply *got* to!

MARY: I suddenly feel very old and helpless.

[*Doorbell*]

LUCY: [*Quietly*] You fool, Mary—I haven't the heart to scream at you.

MARY: Now they've got friends upstairs—visiting. I don't know why that should bother me. But it does—intensely.

LUCY: Will you please get rid of them—and take a plane tomorrow with me? I'll wait on.

MARY: A plane?

LUCY: A train then.

[ROSE *crosses to door*]

MARY: I never felt more like it. I really want to.

LUCY: Fine!

MARY: Not tomorrow of course. I've got to clean up this mess. And if I go I'll close the house.

LUCY: Next week then—

MARY: Perhaps, in a week or so.

DOCTOR: [*Off*] Good afternoon.

ROSE: [*Off*] Good afternoon.

MARY: Now who? [*Rises*]

LUCY: You certainly have a busy house.

ROSE: [*Entering*] It's the doctor, madam.

MARY: Oh! Go straight up, Doctor.

[ROSE *starts to lead way*]

DOCTOR: [*To* MARY] Thank you. [*To* ROSE] That's quite all right. I know the way.

[DOCTOR *goes upstairs.* ROSE *goes off*]

LUCY: I should go—but I'm not going to—until you promise to close this house and get out of here.

MARY: All right, I promise.

LUCY: Good. [*She rises*] I must rush. [*Crosses to desk and gets gloves*] I expressed everything through the St. Moritz. But there's a coat I want—and some shoes.

MARY: Go on, then. [*Smiles wanly. Speaks simply*] And thank you.

LUCY: Now remember—you've *promised!*

MARY: All right!

LUCY: Well—good-bye—and God bless you. [*Starts*] Get rid of those strange leeches!

MARY: I will. [*As they go through the arch*] Give my love to Phil and the children.

LUCY: Thank you, dear. When will I hear from you?

[ROSE *enters*]

MARY: I'll write.

LUCY: The minute you've decided—I wish you could come and tell me what you think of this coat. I'm spending far too much. Good-bye—

MARY: Have a nice trip, Lucy. [*Door slams*]

ROSE: [*As* MARY *comes in*] Miss Herries—

MARY: [*Surprised as she looks at* ROSE's *clothes*] Going already, Rose?

ROSE: Yes, madam. I was just waiting to say good-bye.

MARY: [*After a moment, as if tired of the whole thing. Crosses to desk*] Well—I suppose if you've made up your mind to leave, you'd better.

ROSE: Yes, madam. I'm sorry. I'd like to come back in a while.

MARY: Let me have your address?

ROSE: It's on the bill hook—in the pantry.

MARY: [*Sees* EDWARDS' *hat on desk and distastefully puts it on chair between windows*] All right.

ROSE: Good-bye, Miss Herries.

MARY: Rose, I wish I really knew why you were leaving. Is it the work, Rose?

ROSE: I told you, madam.

MARY: What's the matter?

ROSE: Nothing, madam, I told you—I want to visit my sister in New-castle.

MARY: I don't believe that. You've never *mentioned* a sister all the time you've been with me. Now look here, Rose, I didn't intend to plead with you to stay on. But I've decided to close the house. If you'll wait a week you can go where you like and I'll be glad to take you back in about three months.

ROSE: [*With a trace of eagerness*] You're closing the house, Miss Herries?

MARY: This week.

ROSE: But excuse me, madam— What's happening to them?

MARY: The Abbotts? They're leaving, of course.

ROSE: They are?

MARY: Oh. So it *is* the Abbotts. Why didn't you say so?

ROSE: Miss Herries—! [*She cannot speak*]

MARY: What is it? What are you crying for?

ROSE: Miss Herries. I don't want to go!

MARY: Then why?

ROSE: It isn't the work, madam, I don't mind that.—

MARY: What's wrong then? You must tell me!

ROSE: Are you sure they're leaving, madam?

MARY: Quite sure.

MARY: Him, too?

MARY: Yes! What *is* it, Rose? [*Taking* ROSE's *arm.* ROSE *pauses uncertainly*] Has Mr. Abbott said anything to you?

ROSE: No, madam. [*Bursts out*] It ain't what he says! I can't explain what I mean, Miss Herries! There's something about him! I'm afraid!

MARY: Afraid of what—?

ROSE: I don't know. I'm afraid to stay here.

MARY: What is it, Rose? Try to tell me.

ROSE: That Mrs. Abbott—

MARY: Yes.

ROSE: She's not ill, madam. She lays up there in that bed—lookin' like she's dyin'. But she ain't ill—and never was!

MARY: Never was?

ROSE: No, madam! There's some people always look that way—an' she's one of 'em. But I know she's not ill!

MARY: *How* do you know?

ROSE: I just do, madam. She's been putting it on all the time!

MARY: Putting it on?

ROSE: Yes. And the baby! Did you notice something funny about it?

MARY: No.

ROSE: Did you ever hear it cry?

MARY: [*After quite a pause, as if she just realized*] No.

ROSE: Neither did I! Never! I never heard it make a sound. I think it *can't*, Miss Herries. It wants to—but it can't.

MARY: [A *quick involuntary phrase*] Oh, no.

ROSE: Yes, madam—that's what I think. And something else—it don't look like her. It looks foreign—like an Italian baby. But it's not hers.

MARY: How can you tell—it's just an infant?

ROSE: No, it's not. Not as young as he said! Oh, I don't know, Miss Herries! I'm just scared to death—! [*She cries again. There is a pause*]

MARY: Rose, please stop crying.

ROSE: I'm sorry, madam.

MARY: I want you to pack up whatever belongs to the baby—at once.

ROSE: Yes, madam.

MARY: Then take a directory and see if you can find some private hospital which has an ambulance we can hire to call for Mrs. Abbott.

ROSE: Yes, madam?

MARY: Wait a minute. [ROSE *turns*] Tell them we don't want anyone taken to the hospital. We just want to hire the ambulance and an attendant for about an hour.

ROSE: I will, Miss Herries.

MARY: Tell them we'll ring up again—and let them know—will you, Rose?

ROSE: Yes, madam.

MARY: Straightaway. Now go on and don't be afraid of anything.

ROSE: [*Turning to* MARY] I don't want to be foolish, madam. As long as they're goin'—

MARY: It's all right. I'm sorry you didn't tell me all this before.

ROSE: I didn't want to interfere, Miss Herries. I thought perhaps you had some special reason.

MARY: I've just been very stupid, Rose. Now please go and do as I asked.

ROSE: Yes, madam.

[*She goes.* MARY *watches her off—then suddenly goes to stairs, reaches landing and is about to go up when she pauses as the sound of voices reaches her. She hesitates for a*

moment then returns to room, standing by fireplace. Lights
dim from here to end of the act]

MRS. EDWARDS: [*Off*] Good-bye. Aggie, say good-bye to Ada.

AGGIE: [*Off*] Good-bye, Ada.

MR. EDWARDS: [*Off*] That's a good girl.

MRS. EDWARDS: [*Off*] Mind your manners and you'll keep your
friends. Ha! Ha!

MR. EDWARDS: [*Off*] Good-bye, Ada.

[*Door slams. Pause*]

MRS. EDWARDS: [*Off*] We shouldn't have come, father.

MR. EDWARDS: [*Off*] She's a pretty sick girl.

MRS. EDWARDS: [*Off*] Ts, ts. I hope we haven't done any harm.

MR. EDWARDS: [*Off*] Country air—that's what she needs.

MRS. EDWARDS: [*Off*] Leave that alone, Aggie!

MR. EDWARDS: [*Off*] There ain't an ounce of flesh on her. [*As he
finishes he comes into view*]

MRS. EDWARDS: You'd hardly know what was whiter—her or the
sheets. I—

[*She, too, has come into view and stops at seeing* MARY.
Behind MRS. EDWARDS *is* AGGIE; *from dining room comes*
HENRY]

HENRY: Miss Herries, these are Ada's friends; Mr. and Mrs. Edwards and their daughter, Aggie.

[MARY *nods*]

MR. EDWARDS: How do you do, ma'am?

MRS. EDWARDS: We've just been up to *see* Ada. My—she's a sight,
isn't she?

HENRY: I'm afraid the excitement was too much.

[AGGIE *drifts to desk*]

MRS. EDWARDS: I hope we haven't done any harm.—

MR. EDWARDS: She's just all in! Not an ounce of flesh on her, ma'am.

HENRY: It occurred to me upstairs. We're looking for a cook. If I
may take the liberty of recommending Mrs. Edwards—

MRS. EDWARDS: Now, Henry.

HENRY: I know she's worked in the very best homes.

MRS. EDWARDS: As a cook only, ma'am.

HENRY: And with Aggie to help—if Rose insists on going—I thought we could struggle along for a while.

MARY: Thank you. I won't need anyone. I'm closing the house.

HENRY: [Moves toward MARY] Really, Miss Herries?

MARY: I'm not well, either. I need a rest.

HENRY: That's too bad.

MARY: I'm glad your friends are here. They can help move Ada. I'm hiring a private ambulance.

HENRY: You mean move her today?

MARY: Oh, yes!

HENRY: Where shall I take her?

MARY: Take her home!

HENRY: I would—willingly—but, we have no home. [MARY starts to speak] We were so far behind on the rent—we were dispossessed a week ago, I thought I told you.

MARY: I'm afraid your troubles can't concern me any longer. Take Ada any place you please.

MRS. EDWARDS: That's a pretty hard way to talk, Miss Herries.

MARY: You must understand, I don't want to seem brutal—but I think Mrs. Abbott is well enough to go now—and I wish you all good day.

MRS. EDWARDS: I'm sure you've been kindness itself, Miss Herries. Ada knows that, I'm sure. But to move her now would be to kill her, that's all. Any movement and she'll drop at your feet.

HENRY: Besides we have no place to go—as I've told you.

MARY: [Controlling herself] But this lady—

MRS. EDWARDS: Oh, Lord, Miss Herries—we only have two rooms—

MR. EDWARDS: That's a good idea, ma'am! There ain't space now to swing a cat in!

AGGIE: Popper coughs all night, anyway.

MRS. EDWARDS: Keep still, Aggie!

MR. EDWARDS: And there's the kid, mind you!

MARY: [To HENRY] I don't care to discuss it! You will get Ada out of here today!

[HENRY *looks at her steadily*]

MRS. EDWARDS: It might be life and death, you know. Do you think she ought—?

MARY: I told you I didn't care to discuss it! [*To* HENRY] I believed your bad luck stories—and I've done everything in my power to help you! I think it's pretty obvious that you've imposed on me in the crudest way!

HENRY: I'm sorry you think that.

MARY: You will please oblige me by getting out of here as quickly as possible.

HENRY: That's more easily said than done.

MARY: Why you—! Leave at once, all of you!

[*They do not move.* MRS. EDWARDS *looks about her*]

MRS. EDWARDS: [*After pause*] Such a fine big house, ma'am. It's wonderful how clean it is with only one help.

MR. EDWARDS: Yep. I was telling mother—that's my wife, Mrs. Edwards over here, how much it looks like a house I stayed in once in Melbourne, in Australia.

MARY: [*To* HENRY] Will you please—!

MR. EDWARDS: [*Makes a small movement toward* MARY] It's the staircase made me think of it—same layout. Used to be a private house. Turned into a lodging house later—when I stayed there.

MARY: [*To* EDWARDS] Leave immediately, or I shall call the police!

MR. EDWARDS: Lady who ran it—she was a leftover from the old days. A real character, ma'am. I stayed on the top floor. [MARY *crosses to ring bell. He follows*] That was the cheapest in those times.

[MARY *goes to the bell. Just before she reaches it,* HENRY *puts his hand out gently and covers it. They have somehow formed a semi-circle about her*]

MARY: [*To* HENRY] How dare you!

[DOCTOR *comes down stairs and stands with the rest.* MARY *sees him and reacts*]

MRS. EDWARDS: Would you believe it, Miss Herries—he's never told me a word of this!

MR. EDWARDS: Well, the old lady used to start from the bottom floor in the morning. [MARY *turns to see* MR. EDWARDS *coming toward her*] Knock, knock, knock—how do you like your ham and eggs this morning, sir? Thank you, sir. [MARY *starts backing away*] Second floor. Knock, knock, knock. How do you like your ham and eggs this morning, sir. [*As* MARY *has backed away,* HENRY, MRS. EDWARDS *and* DOCTOR *have joined* MR. EDWARDS *in their slow walk forcing* MARY *downstage. They have her surrounded*] Thank you, sir. Third floor—

MARY: [*To* HENRY] This is monstrous! What do you want of me?

MR. EDWARDS: Well, ma'am, by the time she reached me—I was mightly glad to get myself a cup of tea! [*Laughs*]

MRS. EDWARDS: He was a one when I married him, Miss Herries!

MARY: What do you want?

HENRY: What about my pay for all these weeks?

MARY: Pay—?

HENRY: My pay.

MRS. EDWARDS: His pay.

MR. EDWARDS: [*Sings*]

> "When the time comes to pay—
> You must pay."

[MARY *staggers slightly. She looks around at them*]

MARY: [*Starts to speak, but doesn't. She puts her hand to her heart —then looks around at the others. They are all watching her, quietly, starts to speak again—then bends over slightly as if in pain. Stands gasping*] Oh! [*Then groans and staggers to couch, moves toward desk with arms outstretched but suddenly sinks to couch—half lying*] Oh, please! In the drawer—the green bottle—! [*Tries to point to the desk drawer*] Oh, quickly, please! [*She is choking. Suddenly with a deep groan she collapses on the couch. They look at her*]

MRS. EDWARDS: Ts, ts, ts—poor woman.

MR. EDWARDS: Luck—! The minute I laid eyes on that staircase I knew it!

[HENRY *snaps fingers to* DOCTOR, *who bends and touches her heart, who straightens and:*]

DOCTOR: Still going.

HENRY: Take her upstairs. [*He gives* EDWARDS *the key*]

MR. EDWARDS: Sure, Henry—you bet.

[MR. EDWARDS *bends to pick her up.* DOCTOR *helps.* AGGIE, *who has been standing over her, now kneels and claws at* MARY's *bracelet*]

AGGIE: Gimme that!

MR. EDWARDS: [*Pushes her away*] Why don't you behave yourself?

MRS. EDWARDS: You're just like a little *animal*, Aggie!

MR. EDWARDS: [*Takes bracelet, looks at it, starts to pocket it*] It's a cheap one.

HENRY: Let me see. [*Looks and throws it to* AGGIE] There now, be quiet.

MR. EDWARDS: [*Pulls* MARY *to sitting position.* DOCTOR *takes her under arm,* EDWARDS *by feet*] Upsa-daisy!

MRS. EDWARDS: Don't hurt yourself, father.

MR. EDWARDS: [*As he goes up to landing carrying* MARY] Oh, you're not such a heavy old lady. Say good-bye to everybody. [*As he goes up sings under his breath*]

"Where are the friends that—that we used to know
long, long ago—long, long ago?
Where are—"

HENRY: [*Crosses to bell*] Sh, sh, sh, sh, sh.

[DOCTOR *and* EDWARDS *go up carrying* MARY]

MRS. EDWARDS: Came awful sudden, didn't it, Henry? Very unexpected. Saved a *lot* of trouble, I should say.

HENRY: [*Rings bell. To* AGGIE, *who is examining bracelet*] Put that away, please!

MRS. EDWARDS: [*Settling herself on the couch properly*] Sit down, Aggie.

> [AGGIE *sits.* HENRY *takes bills from pocket and counts some off. Holds bills in his hand.* ROSE *enters, stops and looks around*]

HENRY: Miss Herries asked me to give you this, Rose. Unless you changed your mind and stayed.

ROSE: Why—Miss Herries wanted me to stay on a week—she asked me to.

HENRY: I know—we thought of taking Mrs. Abbott home today—but that's impossible. [*Watches her face*] I know you complained about us, Rose. Miss Herries told me, I convinced her that you were wrong. Well, which is it? Will you stay? If not—this lady is ready to take your place.

ROSE: [*After a pause*] I'll go.

HENRY: [*Hands her money*] Here, then.

ROSE: I've *been* paid.

HENRY: I persuaded Miss Herries to give you this—in place of the extra week. [ROSE *takes the money*] I'm not as bad as you think, Rose. But as long as you can't bear the sight of us—you'd *better* go. [ROSE *turns uncertainly and starts*] Did you order the ambulance?

ROSE: [*Stopping*] No.

HENRY: Whom did you call?

ROSE: St. Mary's Hospital—

HENRY: As long as you've spoken to them—would you call again before you leave and ask them not to come on— Never mind, I'll call them myself. St. Mary's Hospital. Thank you, Rose.

> [ROSE *does not leave immediately*]

HENRY: Good-bye.

> [HENRY *watches* ROSE *off.* AGGIE *follows her to arch, stands looking after her*]

MRS. EDWARDS: Very nicely done, Henry. Come away from there, Aggie!

[AGGIE *crosses to window.* DOCTOR *comes in from stairs*]

HENRY: [*Taking money out—to* DOCTOR] The maid, Rose. [*To* MRS. EDWARDS] Call St. Mary's Hospital, Paddington.

MRS. EDWARDS: Yes, Henry. [*Crosses to desk as she speaks to* DOCTOR] The maid will be coming out of the basement.

HENRY: [*Gives* DOCTOR *money*] Here.

DOCTOR: 'k you.

HENRY: Don't lose her.

[DOCTOR *goes off*]

MRS. EDWARDS: [*Looking in phone book*] Aggie, come away from that window.

HENRY: Sit down!

[AGGIE *sits, scared.* HENRY *crosses to fireplace. Downstairs comes a strange figure. It is* ADA *in a nightgown. She comes into the room, doing almost a little dance. A sharp laugh from* ADA *draws* MRS. EDWARDS' *attention to her*]

MRS. EDWARDS: [*At phone*] Ada—you're going to catch your death of cold walking around here barefoot! Paddington 7831, please. Thank you. [ADA *really begins to dance, around center of room. She takes a little springing side step around the room, holding the sides of her nightgown*] Now that's enough, Ada—the floor is awfully draughty! [ADA *suddenly begins to laugh—a strange animalic laugh*] Ada!

[ADA *dances toward* HENRY]

HENRY: Keep still!!

[HENRY *almost simultaneously has hit her across the mouth with the back of his hand. She gives a low cry, clasping both her hands to her mouth, and almost doubled up,* ADA *crosses to console, whimpering. She looks very much like an animal looking for a place to hide. Down the stairs comes* MR. EDWARDS *heralding his approach by whistling "Long, Long Ago."* HENRY *crosses to foot of stairs, takes key from* EDWARDS]

MR. EDWARDS: [*Goes to window and looks out*] Oh, that's fine! There goes Rose and there goes Doc. [*He leaves the window and crosses to gramophone*]

HENRY: [*To* MRS. EDWARDS] What's the matter, don't they answer?

MRS. EDWARDS: Ringing. Hello? St. Mary's Hospital? This is the maid who called you a little while ago about an ambulance for an invalid. Montague Square? Yes.

HENRY: Never mind, they took her in a taxi.

MRS. EDWARDS: Well, please never mind—they took her in a taxi—

HENRY: To her own doctor.

> [EDWARDS *puts gramophone on table. Takes crank out of pocket and winds it*]

MRS. EDWARDS: To her own doctor.

HENRY: Make sure the ambulance hasn't left.

MRS. EDWARDS: The ambulance hasn't left, has it? Thank you. [*Hangs up. To* HENRY] No. They take their time.

MR. EDWARDS: What's the matter, Ada?

HENRY: [*Going to* ADA] Never mind. [*Puts his arm around her. She responds but he quickly turns to business. To* MRS. EDWARDS] Get the baby out of here. [*He crosses to window*]

MR. EDWARDS: [*Unlocking clasps on gramophone*] That's the trouble, Henry. Can't you just forget about it?

MRS. EDWARDS: [*Rises*] No. Henry's right, father. It's just a nuisance here, poor little thing.

MR. EDWARDS: What about Ada, Henry?

HENRY: Ada stays.

MRS. EDWARDS: What for, Henry? She's done her job.

MR. EDWARDS: Henry's right, mother. You wouldn't want Ada roaming around the streets.

> [MRS. EDWARDS *exits upstairs*]

HENRY: [*To* MR. EDWARDS] See that the Italian woman gets the baby back tonight.

MR. EDWARDS: Whatever you say, Henry.

HENRY: Shutters nailed in her room?

MR. EDWARDS: Coming up, Henry. [*Lifting lid of gramophone as*

if it were covering a big surprise. And that's the way he talks]
There you are, Henry! Ain't that nice?

> [*Without replying,* HENRY *takes a hammer and some nails out of record compartment in gramophone and exits upstairs*]

MR. EDWARDS: [*Taking a record from cover slot, puts it on the disc. Calls up the stairs*] I'm going to board over the window tomorrow anyway, Henry—! [*Returns to gramophone, starts it going. It is an orchestra playing. He leans over, listening.* ADA *listens*] I'm crazy about that record— Ain't it nice, Ada? [ADA, *who has been listening and moving her head to the rhythm, now starts to dance again.* MRS. EDWARDS *is heard coming down the stairs*]

MRS. EDWARDS: Oh, he's a sweet little feller— Oh, he's a sweet little feller. [AGGIE *meets* MRS. EDWARDS, *trying to see baby*] Go away, Aggie! Frightening the poor little chap. [MRS. EDWARDS *goes to sofa, sits, talking to baby*]

MR. EDWARDS: [*Whistling, he goes to* MRS. EDWARDS] Cootchie— cootchie—coo. [*Tickles baby*]

MRS. EDWARDS: [*Slapping* MR. EDWARDS' *hand*] Now, now, now! [AGGIE *stands listening to the music.* ADA *is swaying to the music.* MR. EDWARDS *goes to* ADA. MRS. EDWARDS *continues her baby talk throughout*] Oh, isn't he a sweet little baby. Whoooo. *Sweet* little feller. Whoooo—(Et cetera, et cetera).

> [ADA *and* MR. EDWARDS *start dancing.* ADA *breaks out into an exultant laugh*]

CURTAIN

ACT THREE

*The same room. The arrangement of the furniture is the
same as in the Prologue. The only exception is that there
are no "moderns" on the back right wall. There is a
solitary "old master" there.*

It is an afternoon during the following summer.

MRS. EDWARDS *is seated in chair, peeling potatoes.* MR.
EDWARDS *is seated, reading a newspaper.* MARY HERRIES *sits
in the overstuffed chair. She is in a half-daze, an un-
believing dream. The other two pay no attention to her as
long as she keeps quiet. Finally, she attempts, slowly, to
rise.* MR. EDWARDS *notices this, pays no attention, lets her
struggle and rise.* MRS. EDWARDS *rises.* MARY *looks at* MRS.
EDWARDS *and sits. Then* MR. EDWARDS *resumes his reading.*

*The doorbell rings, followed by two knocks on the door
knocker. A trace of a glance passes between the* EDWARDS,
a ray of hope is visible in MARY. MRS. EDWARDS *goes to the
window and then goes to the door. There is a pause, then
she returns with the mail.* MR. EDWARDS *has risen to meet*
MRS. EDWARDS. MARY's *eyes follow the letters as they pass
from* MRS. EDWARDS *to* MR. EDWARDS *and then back to the
desk, in a neat pile.* MR. EDWARDS *returns to his newspaper
at chair. She looks for a time at the letters on the desk
and finally at* MR. EDWARDS *who nods a solemn "No, no."*
MRS. EDWARDS *takes her potatoes out. That closes the
incident and there is inaction until the door is heard to
open.* MRS. EDWARDS *goes to door and meets* HENRY, *who
enters.* HENRY *pays no attention to* MARY, *but questions*
MRS. EDWARDS. *What they say is as much for* MARY's
benefit as for anyone else's. HENRY *carries a portfolio.*

HENRY: Is Miss Herries in?

MRS. EDWARDS: [A pause, during which MR. EDWARDS slowly rises and looks at MARY] Oh, no, sir—Miss Herries is traveling.

HENRY: Is that so? I had no idea.

MRS. EDWARDS: [ADA enters slowly and sits in front of fireplace] Yes, sir. She left for America three weeks ago. From there she was going to South America—and from there to Australia.

HENRY: [Looking about the room] Really! Strange she didn't let us know.

MRS. EDWARDS: [Very quietly and for MARY's ears] Miss Herries had a bad nervous breakdown, sir. She wouldn't see anyone. She left very suddenly.

HENRY: Well! I'm sorry to hear it.

MRS. EDWARDS: Yes, sir. We're closing the house for the time being.

HENRY: You are the—?

MRS. EDWARDS: Housekeeper, sir.

HENRY: Thank you. Very good! [Puts portfolio on desk, looks at mail, never looking at MARY. MARY looks at HENRY in the manner of a paralytic almost—an unwavering, dull stare, her head moving very slightly from side to side. HENRY crosses and addresses MARY as if she had just appeared, very much as if he were dealing with a child] Well! How do you feel, Miss Herries? [She gives no sign she has heard] How do you feel?

MARY: [After a long time, very low] Let me go!

HENRY: Let you go where, Miss Herries?

MARY: [After another long time] What do you want?

HENRY: We want you to get well as soon as possible, Miss Herries. You know that. [A slight pause, after which he looks up at MRS. EDWARDS] I'm afraid she's not much better, Mrs. Edwards.

MRS. EDWARDS: No, sir, I'm afraid not.

HENRY: [To MARY] The nurse tells me you haven't been eating well. [MARY slowly looks at MRS. EDWARDS, then back to HENRY] You should, you know. It's very important.

MARY: What do you want?

MRS. EDWARDS: I do think she seems to be more herself, sir.

HENRY: [Nods] Do you understand what we are saying, Miss Herries?

[*After a pause,* MARY *slowly nods grimly. There is an immediate reaction on all of them*]

MR. EDWARDS: Well, that's fine!

MRS. EDWARDS: I knew it!

HENRY: I'm so glad. You're pulling through at last, Miss Herries. You'll be up and about in no time now.

MARY: Let me go! Let me go!! Let me go!!!

[HENRY *looks at* MRS. EDWARDS *and shakes his head*]

HENRY: [*Takes pen and paper from pocket*] Will you sign this paper, Miss Herries? [*She looks at them, uncomprehendingly.* MR. EDWARDS *crosses with his newspaper. He places newspaper on* MARY's *lap*] Will you sign it now so your affairs can be taken care of? Here, please. [*Points out place*]

MRS. EDWARDS: [*Crosses to* MARY, *takes pen from* HENRY] I'll help, dear. [*Puts pen in her hand, and holds the back of her fist*] Go on!

[MARY *remains motionless, only her heavy breathing can be heard*]

HENRY: Sign, Miss Herries. It's best.

MARY: Will you let me—go? I won't tell.

HENRY: Go on, Miss Herries.

MRS. EDWARDS: Here we go. "Mary," a nice "M" now.

MARY: No. No.

HENRY: You must, Miss Herries—do you hear?

MRS. EDWARDS: "Mary." [*Trying to guide pen*]

MARY: No. No. [*Suddenly she gets up—screaming, spilling pen, paper and newspaper on floor*] No—!

[MRS. EDWARDS *grabs* MARY's *shoulders and forces her to sit again*]

MRS. EDWARDS: Stop it, you old—

[HENRY *almost hits* MRS. EDWARDS *for being so rough with* MARY. MRS. EDWARDS *moves away a bit*]

MR. EDWARDS: Here we are now. [*Picking up pen, paper, newspaper from floor. He places them on* MARY's *lap. Puts pen in her hand. Prompts*] "Mary—"

MARY: [*With every bit of resolution and finality but still in a dull, weak voice*] No. No.

[*There is a pause. All look at* HENRY *except* MARY]

HENRY: [*Quietly*] Tomorrow, then. Or the day after. [*He takes pen, paper and newspaper from* MARY. *To the others*] Take her out. [*He goes to desk, puts pen and paper there*]

MRS. EDWARDS: Don't be afraid, Miss Herries, I'll take care of you. I'm here.

[*They help her to rise and help her toward the stairs*]

MR. EDWARDS: That's a good girl.

MRS. EDWARDS: We'll have a nice little walk.

[MRS. EDWARDS *and* MARY *go upstairs.* MR. EDWARDS *stops on landing.* HENRY *returns to papers at desk.* ADA *lingers.* HENRY *looks up and talks to her in somewhat the same way he has talked to* MARY]

HENRY: Hello, Ada. Everything all right?

ADA: Yes, Henry!

HENRY: You like it here?

ADA: Yes, Henry!

HENRY: So do I. [*Pause*] Ada.

ADA: Yes, Henry?

HENRY: [*As if he were suggesting a game*] Go upstairs and watch— and listen!

ADA: Yes, Henry! [*She goes, eager to do what he asks*]

[HENRY *crosses and gets the Whistler and places it in front of fireplace—then goes to desk and sits.* EDWARDS *looks back up the stairs—turns to* HENRY—*shakes his head*]

HENRY: Don't be impatient, Edwards.

MR. EDWARDS: Whatever you say, Henry.

HENRY: Miss Herries is a very fine woman. She has character. She has *strength—*

MR. EDWARDS: That's true—but—

[HENRY *is reading the mail*]

HENRY: Imagination—hope. She still has hope, Edwards.

MR. EDWARDS: Stubborn.

HENRY: *Time,* Edwards.

MR. EDWARDS: Perhaps.

HENRY: There is a dealer from Paris coming this afternoon to look at the Whistler. [*Gestures to the picture propped against the fireplace*]

MR. EDWARDS: Here?

HENRY: He will also see Miss Herries—talk to her.

MR. EDWARDS: *Talk* to her, Henry!

HENRY: It would be comforting to have Miss Herries realize that if she ever should be in a position to appeal to anyone—no one would believe her.

MR. EDWARDS: Don't like it.

HENRY: Well, I'm going to try it, Edwards. [*Looks through letter*] Ah! Lucy Weston is returning to London. [*This announcement worries* EDWARDS, *who moves away a bit and turns back to* HENRY] Dear Lucy. I shall look forward to seeing her again. [*He notices* EDWARDS' *worry*] What is it, Edwards?

EDWARDS: It's about leaving this place.

HENRY: *You* may, if you want to.

EDWARDS: I didn't mean that. [*Pause*] How was Paris?

HENRY: Very nice.

EDWARDS: Buy any pictures?

HENRY: Sold a few.

EDWARDS: Mind if I see the list?

HENRY: All right. [*Gives list to* EDWARDS]

MR. EDWARDS: [*He is impressed by list*] Quite right, Henry. There's a time to— After a while the odds keep stretching.

HENRY: [*Quietly and patiently*] We *live* here, Edwards. We are Miss Herries' best friends—her only friends—in London. The only ones who have cared for her since her—illness. I should think that idea would appeal to *you*. *Steady* employment. [*Doorbell*] That should be the man from Bernstein et Fils.

MR. EDWARDS: [*Calling upstairs*] Mother!

HENRY: [*Who has crossed to the window*] Wait! It isn't. It's Peter.

MR. EDWARDS: Peter!

[MRS. EDWARDS *comes down the stairs*]

HENRY: [*Picks up portfolio and papers*] Show him in. [HENRY *exits to dining room*. MR. EDWARDS *goes upstairs*. MRS. EDWARDS *waits until* MR. EDWARDS *is on the way then goes to the hall. All this is done casually*]

MRS. EDWARDS: [*Off*] Yes, sir?

PETER: [*Off*] I'm Mr. Santard.

MRS. EDWARDS: [*Off*] Oh, yes, sir. You rang up several weeks ago.

PETER: [*Off*] That's right.

MRS. EDWARDS: [*Off*] Will you come in, sir?

PETER: [*Off*] Thank you. [*He enters*. MRS. EDWARDS *follows*] You are the—

MRS. EDWARDS: The housekeeper, sir. Mrs. Edwards.

PETER: I told *Mrs*. Santard, Miss Herries' niece, what you said and we all thought it would be a good idea for one of us to hop around sometime and get the details.

MRS. EDWARDS: Yes, sir.

PETER: America, you said?

MRS. EDWARDS: Yes, sir. I believe she had a friend there—in California.

PETER: You don't know who—or where? We're going to America ourselves—

MRS. EDWARDS: She didn't say.

PETER: She left no forwarding address of any kind?

MRS. EDWARDS: Only Thomas Cook in Melbourne, sir—in April.

PETER: Australia?

MRS. EDWARDS: Yes, sir. She's going around the world.

PETER: And nothing until then?

MRS. EDWARDS: Not that I know, sir. I mean not with me.

PETER: Do you know why Miss Herries left so suddenly?

MRS. EDWARDS: No, sir. Her heart was bothering her, I think—and the maid told me she was awful nervous.

PETER: Do you know where that maid is?

MRS. EDWARDS: With Miss Herries, I believe, sir.

PETER: Was Miss Herries being treated by a doctor?

MRS. EDWARDS: Not that I know, sir. I came just before she left—and all I was told was to close the house and wait till Mr. Henry Abbott dismissed me.

PETER: Mr. Henry Abbott? Who's that?

MRS. EDWARDS: He's the agent, sir, in charge of the pictures.

PETER: What do you mean—in charge of them?

MRS. EDWARDS: I believe he's selling them, sir.

PETER: [*After a pause*] Is he here now?

MRS. EDWARDS: Yes, sir. Would you like to see him?

PETER: Please.

[*She goes out.* PETER *takes a cigarette from a case in his pocket, lights it.* HENRY *comes in*]

HENRY: Mr. Santard?

PETER: How do you do? I believe I saw you here one night—some time ago.

HENRY: Oh, yes. I brought some of my pictures to show Miss Herries—

PETER: Can you throw light on her mysterious disappearance?

HENRY: [*Laughs*] I think so. Please sit down. [*Indicates chair*]

PETER: Thank you. [*Sits*]

HENRY: I'm sorry I wasn't here when you rang up this morning.

PETER: You see, my wife sent her aunt an invitation to our wedding and received a letter from the housekeeper!

HENRY: [*Makes notations on paper on desk*] I'm awfully sorry. I must have been away—on the Continent. Had I been here when your invitation came, I—

PETER: That's all right. What's the old lady up to—sneaking away like that?

HENRY: She did, didn't she? [*Laughs*] But I can't say I blame her.

PETER: What happened?

HENRY: Well—nothing particularly. She had been fed up for a long time, I think, and she had been planning this trip.

PETER: I understand you are selling her pictures?

HENRY: Just a few—I am also buying others. But I want you to believe that financially I have no interest in the matter.

PETER: Of course.

HENRY: I mean, I am doing this for nothing.

PETER: [*Slight pause*] Do you know why she didn't come to the wedding?

HENRY: Yes. [*Smiles*] It isn't difficult. I feel greatly responsible, to an extent. [*Pause*] I'm afraid we'll have to turn psychological for a beginning.

PETER: Whatever you say.

HENRY: Well, then—you know something about Miss Herries—

PETER: I met her only once. I liked her immensely.

HENRY: A very fine, gentle, sweet woman.

PETER: That's what I thought—

HENRY: But a lonely woman. I seem to be delivering a lecture on—

PETER: No—go ahead.

HENRY: An old maid, afraid of being a polite nuisance to her friends. A sensitive middle-aged woman— No relative but a sister— Emily—

PETER: [*Nods*] My mother-in-law.

HENRY: Whom she hasn't seen for years.

PETER: I wish I could say the same. I can understand that.

HENRY: Well, Miss Herries had a great fondness for my wife—

PETER: Oh—

HENRY: I should explain my position here—Miss Herries is a very generous woman. You probably know that she befriended both my wife and myself—

PETER: No, I didn't.

HENRY: She lent us money—enabled me to make a few commissions —and when my wife was ill kept her here. [PETER *nods*] I stayed too, of course, and here's where I come in, and why I say I feel great responsibility.

PETER: [*Leans forward*] I think I understand!

HENRY: [*Sparring*] Really?

PETER: Please go on.

HENRY: In some way I was seen here, casually by someone, who immediately spread the most damnable silly rumor, that Miss Herries had taken a man to live with her.

PETER: I know. That was Phyllis—my then fiancée. My now wife.

HENRY: I'm sorry.

PETER: You're right. *She's* damned sorry about it now. Her mother knew she had been here and kept pumping her until Phyllis happened to mention it—just gossip, I thought.

HENRY: I'm afraid so. One of Miss Herries' friends told her and that hurt her so, I believe, that it was the real reason for her "mysterious disappearance," as you say.

PETER: Yes, yes, I see.

HENRY: [*Crosses to desk, gets list*] So—she went, leaving me certain items in her collection to dispose of. I'm to deposit the money in Blakely's Bank and send a report to Australia in April. It's quite a responsibility.

PETER: Sounds like it.

HENRY: [PETER *rises and crosses to meet him*] Here's her list. You can see she's stipulated the minimum amounts to be obtained on each—and quite a few of these prices are pre-war.

PETER: I wouldn't know a thing about it—except that she has some pretty fine stuff.

HENRY: [*Nods*] Most of it is extremely desirable. But art collectors don't pay as much as they used to.

PETER: I guess you art collectors were the first to feel the pinch of hard times.

HENRY: Both as artist and agent I can tell you, Mr. Santard. You're most emphatically right.

[*They both laugh*]

PETER: Great stuff, anyway. [*Giving list back to* HENRY] I had a fine time here, picking out things I'd like to own.

HENRY: I know! If ever temptation worried me, it did in this house.

[*Puts list back on desk*]

PETER: [*Pointing to wall*] There was a swell looking painting on that wall—

HENRY: An El Greco. That unfortunately was sold to a museum in Brussels.

PETER: Oh, yes. And a Ming horse.

HENRY: Alas, that too is gone.

PETER: There were a few other things that hit me. I remember those two particularly.

HENRY: [*Smiling*] Well— [*Getting list from desk*] There are a few things, if you feel inclined—

PETER: Not a chance—but let's see anyway. [*Takes list from* HENRY, *looks at it and whistles*] Whew— I'm just a poor bond salesman—

HENRY: [*Laughs*] I think Miss Herries might consider a reduction— for a relative.

PETER: [*Laughs*] Yes, I suppose she might. Oh, say—there's one thing I could be interested in. There was a statue on this table. [*Points to table*] I forget who did it.

HENRY: A statue?

PETER: I remember—Troubetzkoi!

HENRY: Oh, yes.

PETER: Does that happen to be in stock?

HENRY: Oh, yes. There it is. [*Points*]

PETER: Oh, there. Yes. Isn't it funny I thought it was—no, you're right. I was a little—you know, the night I was here. [HENRY *smiles*] In fact, I thought I remembered Miss Herries promising to give it to us for a wedding present. But—I suppose she changed her mind after Phyllis spilled that gossip.

HENRY: I'll be glad to remind Miss Herries if you could suggest some tactful method.

PETER: [*Laughs*] Never mind. Anyway it doesn't look as nice as it did the night I first saw it. The hell with it.

> [*Doorbell rings.* MRS. EDWARDS *crosses toward the front door*]

HENRY: I shall tell Miss Herries in my next letter that you called.

PETER: Do that. [*Reflects*] No—you'd better not. The other half of the family have all decided not to—bother her—until she asks them to.

HENRY: I'm extremely sorry. [MRS. EDWARDS *brings in a cablegram, hands it to* HENRY, *who opens it*] Excuse me.

> [MRS. EDWARDS *leaves.* HENRY *reads cable without any sign of emotion, and puts it in his pocket*]

PETER: Well, I'm off. My—wife and I are going to live in America, you know.

HENRY: Indeed.

PETER: I'm going to take charge of a branch out in Kansas City. Ever hear of it?

HENRY: Oh, yes.

PETER: God help me!

HENRY: Good luck, sir!

PETER: Thank you, sir! [*Starts*] Well, I'll tell the—family about Miss Herries—not that it matters much, I suppose.

HENRY: [*Follows* PETER] I shall be here until Miss Herries returns and I'll be glad to do anything I can—

PETER: [*Laughs*] That's all right. Good-bye.

> [HENRY *sees* PETER *out.* MR. *and* MRS EDWARDS *come on and wait until* HENRY *returns. They enter from dining room.* HENRY *reenters, still fingering the cablegram. He looks at them a bit triumphantly*]

MR. EDWARDS: Nicely done, Henry.

HENRY: [*Crossing to window to watch* PETER *leave*] Yes, I think so. [*Then, handing cable to* EDWARDS] This is interesting.

> [EDWARDS *reads.* HENRY *sits at desk*]

MRS. EDWARDS: What is it, father?

MR. EDWARDS: Feller named Weston cables that his wife, Lucy, was killed in an airplane crash near Marseilles.

MRS. EDWARDS: My goodness—

> [MR. EDWARDS *hands cable back to* HENRY]

HENRY: That settles it. I think that when Miss Herries hears of *this*, things will be much simpler. [*Pause*] It also adds a note of permanency to the whole venture. For now, Miss Herries has no one but me. [*Doorbell*] That should be Rosenberg. [*Crosses to window and looks out. Then to* EDWARDS] Let her come down. I want her to meet this chap.

MRS. EDWARDS: Oh, Henry—

HENRY: I'll go out through the basement and come around and let myself in—in a few minutes. Show the man in here. Then you let Miss Herries into this room. Listen carefully. Don't let the man get away if she starts anything. [HENRY *rearranges things on desk*]

MRS. EDWARDS: [*A little fearfully*] Who is it, Henry?

MR. EDWARDS: It's a dealer from Paris. [*Nodding that it's all right. Doorbell*]

HENRY: [*Crossing to dining room door*] Go on. [MR. EDWARDS *goes upstairs*. MRS. EDWARDS *again waits until he has gone up. She looks back at* HENRY *as if a little afraid of this step.*] All right.

[*Reassuringly,* MRS. EDWARDS *goes to the door.* HENRY *lingers until he hears* ROSENBERG'S *voice, then goes out*]

MRS. EDWARDS [*Off*] Yes, sir?

MR. ROSENBERG: [*Off*] Monsieur Henry Abbott.

MRS. EDWARDS: [*Off*] Yes, sir.

MR. ROSENBERG: [*Off*] Monsieur Gustav Rosenberg, Bernstein et Fils. My card.

MRS. EDWARDS: [*Off*] Come in, sir. [*Shows in* MR. ROSENBERG, *a Frenchman*] Mr. Abbott is expected. Will you wait here, sir.

MR. ROSENBERG: Thank you.

[MR. ROSENBERG *looks around the room, spots the Whistler and comes down to it, putting his hat on table.* MRS. EDWARDS *backs out. He glances at the windows and sees the shutters and realizes that he cannot get more natural light— examines the canvas—front and back. He takes out his handkerchief, spits on it, and rubs the lower right, then the lower left corner of the canvas. He does not find any trace of a signature—which doesn't bother him particularly, how- ever. What does disturb him is the fact that his handkerchief is black with dirt. He is putting his handkerchief back in his pocket, and sitting in a chair as* MARY HERRIES *comes down the stairs*]

MARY: [*Stops on platform, sees* MRS. EDWARDS *off right, then comes into room*] Who—who are you?

[*She knows that the* EDWARDSES *are listening and that*

she must play the part she is expected to play. This man,
however, is a perfect stranger—he may be one of HENRY'S
satellites—this may be another trap]

MR. ROSENBERG: [*Rising*] Good afternoon, madame. I am M.
Gustav Rosenberg, Bernstein et Fils.

MARY: What are you doing here?

MR. ROSENBERG: [*A little puzzled*] I—I am M. Gustav Rosenberg.
M. Abbott has invited me to look at this painting.

MARY: Painting?

MR. ROSENBERG: Yes—this painting—this Whistler.

MARY: [*Hurt*] No! Oh.

MR. ROSENBERG: What is it, madame; are you ill?

MARY: Oh, no. I'm quite all right. Only sometimes—I forget. [*She
must make sure who he is*] I've even forgotten who you said
you were.

MR. ROSENBERG: [*Now beginning to worry*] M. Rosenberg, madame.
Bernstein et Fils, Paris.

MARY: Oh, yes. But are you *really*? [*Suddenly, with more intensity*]
How do I know you are M. Rosenberg, from Paris?

MR. ROSENBERG: [*Presenting business card*] My card, madame.

MARY: [*This is not enough identification*] No!

MR. ROSENBERG: My passport. [*Shows it to her*]

MARY: [*Looks at it quickly, realizes that here may be a friend.
Then she senses that the others are listening and speaks for their
benefit*] Oh. Well, it doesn't make any difference. You'll forget
me. *Everybody's forgotten me. I'm supposed to be away.* Henry
writes all my letters.

ROSENBERG: [*A bit puzzled*] Pardon, madame?

MARY: *No one else sees me.* [*She takes a letter from her dress*]
How do you like that picture? [*Points to* HENRY's *painting of the
"Ranz des Vaches" on wall*]

MR. ROSENBERG: That? Oh, yes—yes—yes.

MARY: [*Points at letter which she has taken out of her dress*] Please
look at this! [*Then, for the benefit of the others*] It's Henry's
picture. [*Puts the letter in his pocket*] Henry Abbott did it all.
Do you see?

MR. ROSENBERG: I—I don't know— [*Reaches into his pocket*] Madame—what is *this*?

MARY: [*Pulls his hand away from his pocket*] The cowherd is playing the flute. And the cows are listening. [*Points to the arch*] They're listening very carefully, do you see?

MR. ROSENBERG: Yes—to be sure—

MARY: [*Points to his pocket*] You must look at it.

MR. ROSENBERG: Oh—yes—yes, of course—

MARY: Henry isn't a very good painter. [*Low and pleading for* ROSENBERG *to believe her*] He's the very worst sort— [*Her voice rises so the others may hear*] of a painter.

MR. ROSENBERG: Yes—yes, indeed! [*He looks around, hoping someone will enter*]

MARY: [*Pointing to letter*] I'd tell that to anyone—even to *Lucy Weston*—who lives in *Mentone—Mentone—*[*Then, for the benefit of the others*] But she's too far away. Do you agree with me?

MR. ROSENBERG: Yes, madame—yes. [*Anything to quiet her*] Please sit down.

MARY: [*Sits quietly*] Are you going to wait for Mr. Abbott? Or— [*Rises*] Will you go *away now* and come back later?

MR. ROSENBERG: I was told to wait here, madame.

MARY: You could come back later.

MR. ROSENBERG: I am sorry, madame. I have other appointments. I am in London for a few hours only. Please sit down, madame.

[MARY *sits in chair*]

MARY: But you will remember what I've said about— [*Pointing to letter in his pocket*] —the picture?

ROSENBERG: Yes, madame.

[*The front door is heard closing*]

MARY: Please—help me—*do something!*

[HENRY ABBOTT *enters the room*]

HENRY: Mr. Rosenberg! [*Shaking hands*]

MR. ROSENBERG: Ah! Mr. Abbott!

HENRY: You've had a look at the Whistler, I suppose?

MR. ROSENBERG: Yes—I—I have. I am glad you are here.

HENRY: [*Sees that everything has gone as planned*] Yes. [*Crosses to the Whistler*] Well—what do you think of it?

MR. ROSENBERG: [MARY *gives him a look of pleading*] Oh, yes—yes.

HENRY: Do you think Bernstein et Fils will be interested?

> [*All through this,* MARY *is sitting quietly without making a move, watching* MR. ROSENBERG *with desperate hope*]

MR. ROSENBERG: [*A bit distracted by* MARY, *forces himself to discuss the picture*] As I have told you, M. Abbott, Bernstein et Fils are not interested in Whistler—except for this one client.

HENRY: Yes, of course.

MR. ROSENBERG: Like so many Whistlers, it has sunken in and darkened to an extraordinary degree.

HENRY: Undoubtedly a good cleaning and one coat of mastic will bring out any details—

MR. ROSENBERG: Of course—this light—[*He shrugs, turns, sees* MARY, *turns back to* HENRY, *picks up hat*] Might I suggest that you have it sent to our London correspondent—Leicester Galleries, Leicester Square for further examination.

HENRY: Oh, it's genuine, all right.

MR. ROSENBERG: Of course. You will also accompany the painting with the history and the letter of authenticity.

HENRY: Oh, yes.

> [MARY *looks pleadingly at* ROSENBERG]

ROSENBERG: Au 'voir, M'sieur. [*He starts*]

HENRY: Good day, Mr. Rosenberg.

MR. ROSENBERG: [*Stops, turns back*] Ah—uh—Mr. Abbott—

HENRY: [*Goes to him*] Yes?

MR. ROSENBERG: The lady gave me this. [*Produces letter*] Perhaps it would be better—

HENRY: Oh, yes. Thank you for understanding.

MR. ROSENBERG: Au 'voir, M'sieur Abbott.

HENRY: Au 'voir.

> [MR. ROSENBERG *goes.* HENRY *follows him off.* MR. EDWARDS *enters, followed by* MRS. EDWARDS *and* ADA]

MR. EDWARDS: Well!

HENRY: [*Reenters—nods—a close call—then gives letter to* MARY] Here's your letter.

MARY: [*Low—with despair, still sitting*] God!

MR. EDWARDS: From listening, I'd have sworn she was—

HENRY: You are to be complimented, Miss Herries. [*Then to* MRS. EDWARDS] Take her upstairs.

MARY: [*Gets up and faces* HENRY, *firmly, resolutely, and with as much strength as she can muster. She speaks evenly and quietly*] Don't be too sure, Henry Abbott. Things end somehow—sometime— Someone— It's been too easy for you. How you must despise yourselves! [*Almost a whisper*] You wretched people—!

> [*There is a pause.* MARY *starts upstairs.* MRS. EDWARDS *offers to help, but* MARY *draws away. Then, as* MARY *goes up the stairs:*]

FADE OUT

EPILOGUE

The lights dim up and we find the scene as it was at the end of the Prologue. MARY *and* MR. FOSTER *are seated.*

MR. FOSTER: [*Greatly agitated*] Good God—I beg your pardon, Miss Herries—but I mean—

MARY: You do believe me, don't you?

FOSTER: Miss Herries! Really, I—I—I—

MARY: The rain has stopped. Henry will soon be here.

FOSTER: [*Rising and pacing*] This is dreadful—dreadful. What's to be done?

MARY: [*Hands him note*] Please take this. Take it.

> [FOSTER *looks at the note. Then door slams.* FOSTER *hurriedly puts away note.* HENRY *enters and sees* FOSTER]

HENRY: Hello, Foster. You waited, thank you. I'm sorry to be late. [*He turns on lights and then notices* MARY] Oh, Aunt Mary! [*He crosses to her*] Down for your tea, dear?

MARY: Yes.

HENRY: Where is it?

MARY: No one was here.

HENRY: No one here? I don't understand. [*Rings bell, then crosses to desk*] Now, Mr. Foster. You want me to sign these papers, don't you?

FOSTER: The signature required by the Inland Revenue.

HENRY: Fine. Where do I sign, Mr. Foster?

FOSTER: Here, sir. This will clear your income tax through June of this year.

HENRY: Till June. [*He starts signing*]

MR. EDWARDS: [*Who has entered and put coffee table in front of* MARY. *He is in the uniform of the traditional butler*] You rang, sir?

HENRY: [*Crosses to* MARY *with a protective air*] Yes, Edwards. I will not have you all away from the house at the same time. Miss

Herries should never be without someone at her call. I've told
you that before.

MR. EDWARDS: We are very sorry, sir, but the rain held us up. I had
to take Mrs. Edwards to the doctor. She's not feeling well, sir.
And we thought—

HENRY: I want it definitely understood that Miss Herries is not to
be left alone at any time. You were engaged to attend to Miss
Herries' wants at all hours. If that isn't plain I shall have to get
someone who will. Make it clear to Mrs. Edwards. And we'll have
tea now.

MR. EDWARDS: Yes, sir. Mrs. Edwards is preparing it.

[*He goes toward dining room, stands aside so* MRS. ED-
WARDS *can come in with tea tray, which she places on coffee
table before* MARY. MR. EDWARDS *exits.* HENRY *has gone
back to desk, immediately*]

HENRY: Now, then, Mr. Foster. Sorry. [*Resumes signing income
tax blanks*]

FOSTER: That's all right, sir.

MRS. EDWARDS: [*After she has placed tea in front of* MARY] I'm
sorry about being out, Mr. Abbott.

HENRY: All right, Mrs. Edwards. [*He finishes signing.* MRS. EDWARDS
exits] Thank you, Mr. Foster.

FOSTER: [*Picks up papers and puts them in his envelope*] Not at
all. [*Crosses to* MARY] Good day, madam.

MARY: Oh, you're leaving? Good day, then.

FOSTER: [*Turns to* HENRY *who has risen*] Good day, Mr. Abbott.

HENRY: Good day, Mr. Foster. [MR. FOSTER *starts out.* HENRY *lets
him go almost out, then stops him*] Mr. Foster. [FOSTER *stops,
looks at* HENRY, *then slowly comes back into room*] You've never
been here before, have you?

FOSTER: No, sir.

HENRY: I'm sorry there was no one here.

FOSTER: [*After a moment*] Oh—I understand, Mr. Abbott.

[ADA, *in the costume of a trained nurse comes downstairs*]

HENRY: I thought you might not know.

FOSTER: That's quite all right, sir. [*He sees* ADA *arranging* MARY'S *shawl, then* ADA *exits*] She had me going for a few moments, Mr. Abbott.

[MARY *registers despair*]

HENRY: Ah, yes. [FOSTER *starts out once again. He stops him*] Mr. Foster, my aunt is sometimes left alone—as she was today. Carelessness on the part of the servants. [*Then a deliberate statement—not a question*] She gave you something—a note. [*He holds out his hand*]

FOSTER: Oh! [*This is an ambiguous "oh"—and there is life and death in the balance. A look passes between* FOSTER *and* MARY] No, sir! Good day, Mr. Abbott.

[*He exits. The door slams.* HENRY *slowly turns and crosses to* MARY *and stands looking at her. After a moment,* MR. EDWARDS *enters from dining room. He, too, is puzzled and nervous. With his head he beckons* MRS. EDWARDS *on. She joins* MR. EDWARDS *and both look at* MARY. ADA *is heard running down the stairs. She stops, frightened. Then* MR. EDWARDS *comes down behind* MARY. *He looks at* MARY, *then at* HENRY]

MR. EDWARDS: What do you think, Henry?

[HENRY *does not answer. He is still watching* MARY. MR. EDWARDS *starts toward the upper window. Just before he reaches it—doorbell.* MR. EDWARDS *hurries to upper window, followed by* ADA *and* MRS. EDWARDS. HENRY *hurries to downstage window. They all look out. The doorbell rings, and knocking. Slowly the* EDWARDSES *and* HENRY *straighten up and look at each other—then at* MARY. *Doorbell and knocking again.* MARY *slowly rises from her chair. She seems to grow in stature. She throws off her shawl*]

MARY: *I'll* answer!

[*The doorbell is ringing and the knocking is louder and more commanding as* MARY *is crossing to go out*]

CURTAIN

The Innocents

WILLIAM ARCHIBALD

Based on "The Turn of the Screw" by
Henry James

William Archibald

Probably the outstanding theatrical *succès d'estime* of the early 1950s, *The Innocents* still ignites fervent enthusiasm, even impassioned ardor, among its votaries, and with the progression of time the William Archibald stage adaptation of Henry James's *The Turn of the Screw* has evolved into a classic horror play.

The opening of *The Innocents* brought forth encomiums from the first-night jurors who found the play to be "an achievement of a high order" and "a fine and delicate tale of indefinable horror" that was "truly spellbinding." The critical verdict was almost unanimous and perhaps might best be summarized by Brooks Atkinson's review in the *New York Times:* "At last we have a horror play that adults can admire and enjoy. Henry James's classic ghost story has become a perfectly wrought drama in a style he could thoroughly approve."

In spite of the superb production directed by Peter Glenville (with Beatrice Straight giving a memorable performance as Miss Giddens) and the lavish welcome accorded the presentation, *The Innocents* ran for only 141 performances which, by Broadway's commercial yardstick, was something less than a rousing success. Yet, the play engendered much discussion, admiration, and even controversy. The latter was prompted by a chorus of Jamesians who loudly pointed up the fact that in the original story the ghosts were ambiguous, in Archibald's treatment they weren't. In his rebuttal, the dramatist declared that he was guided by what is inherent in the original and what James himself had said in the preface to his published story; it is the reader's own intensified imagination that supplies the particulars in abundance.

Although the New York engagement of *The Innocents* lasted just a little over four months, the play, ironically, was one of the biggest successes of the year (1952) in London, a fact that would have pleased expatriate Henry James, who became a British subject in 1915. The play also was made into a successful movie, starring Deborah Kerr as the harassed governess, and won for Mr. Archibald and Truman Capote, who collaborated on the script, the Mystery Writers of America award for best screenplay in 1961.

The son of a British diplomat, William Archibald was born on March 7, 1917, in Trinidad, British West Indies. He earned a degree in botany at St. Mary's College in Trinidad, then came to New York in 1937 to study dancing with Charles Weidman and Doris Humphrey. He first appeared on Broadway in 1938 as a principal in John Murray Anderson's revue, *One for the Money*, and later was seen in *Two for the Show*; *All in Fun*; Olsen and Johnson's *Laffing Room Only*; and Billy Rose's *Concert Varieties*, wherein he and Imogene Coca performed a comic variation of Nijinsky's ballet, *The Afternoon of a Faun*, that became a highlight of the show.

During his nonperforming hours, he wrote several short stories that subsequently were published, and, in 1945, he collaborated with composer Baldwin Bergersen on *Carib Song*, a West Indian musical with Katherine Dunham and Avon Long as its stars. In 1948, he and Bergersen were commissioned to do a lyric drama for the Ballet Society, the result of which was *Far Harbour* and gave Mr. Archibald his first directing stint.

After *The Innocents*, he turned to films and was coauthor with George Tabori of the screenplay for Alfred Hitchcock's *I Confess*, which starred Montgomery Clift and Anne Baxter. This was followed by a dramatization of another Henry James story, *Portrait of a Lady*, produced on Broadway in 1954 with Jennifer Jones.

Several years later, Mr. Archibald once again joined forces with Baldwin Bergersen on a musical, *The Crystal Heart*, and it had its premiere in London (1957) with Gladys Cooper in a rare singing role; and in 1962, he directed the New York production of his drama, *The Cantilevered Terrace*, with Mildred Dunnock as star.

William Archibald died in 1970, and one sadly realized that the theatre had lost an adventurous writer and a man of many theatrical gifts.

The Innocents was first produced at The Playhouse, New York, on February 1, 1950, by Peter Cookson. The cast was as follows:

FLORA	*Iris Mann*
MRS. GROSE	*Isobel Elsom*
MISS GIDDENS	*Beatrice Straight*
MILES	*David Cole*

Also: *Andrew Duggan and Ella Playwin*

Directed by	Peter Glenville
Setting and Lighting by	Jo Mielziner
Costumes by	Motley
Music by	Alex North

The Innocents was first presented in London on July 3, 1952, at Her Majesty's Theatre. The cast was as follows:

FLORA	*Carol Wolveridge*
MRS. GROSE	*Barbara Everest*
MISS GIDDENS	*Flora Robson*
MILES	*Jeremy Spenser*

Directed by	Peter Glenville
Setting and Lighting by	Jo Mielziner
Costumes by	Motley
Music by	Alex North

SCENE: *The drawing room of a country house in England,*
1880.

ACT ONE

ACT TWO

ACT ONE

SCENE 1

The drawing room of an old country house in Essex, England.

The room is large, high-ceilinged. Directly center of rear wall, a French window opens onto a garden. It is a window that rises up and up until its summit is half lost in the shadows of the ceiling; heavy, dark curtains hang framing it—these can be drawn by pulling at the cord that hangs to right of window. Lighter silk curtains hang across window—these, too, can be drawn together.

To the left of center is a plush-covered love seat; back of love seat is a graceful desk on which are accessories for letterwriting and a lamp. Back of desk is a chair; a table right of desk; an ottoman at center; an armchair right; a spinet and stool up right; a cabinet in alcove up left. There is a door down right and another up left.

A staircase rises from down right, to up right. On landing at head of staircase is an unseen door to two rooms; beside this door stands a grandfather clock. From the landing, a passage is suggested, leading off, right. Above landing, right, and unseen, is a small skylight which, depending on the time of day, allows some light to fall onto top chair.

This setting, the only one used throughout, should be secondary to the light within it. The walls should be free of decoration, and of shades of one color. All exits should be undecorated and of the same color as the walls, so that they are not apparent until opened. The French window should seem to be the only entrance and exit to the room.

A carpet, of a color that supports that of the walls, covers the entire floor space and the stairs and landing.

The curtains at the French window are open. It is four-thirty o'clock in the afternoon. Sunlight floods the room.

FLORA *sits at the spinet. She is a little girl, eight years old, with long hair tied with a neat bow. She sits with straight back, her feet barely touching the floor.*

FLORA: [*Singing as she plays the piano*]
> O, bring me a bonnet,
> O, bring me a bonnet,
> O, bring me a bonnet of bright rosy red—
> With white roses on it,
> With white roses on it,
> O, bring me a bonnet to wear on my head—

[*The melody seems to be repeated far away.* FLORA *turns quickly as* MRS. GROSE *enters from door down right.* MRS. GROSE *is in her sixties and wears the starched apron and frilly cap of a housekeeper of the period*]

MRS. GROSE: Have you been sitting quietly, Miss Flora?

FLORA: I haven't been doing anything else for hours. Where have you been, Mrs. Grose?

MRS. GROSE: [*An excitement apparent in her every movement*] You've rumpled your dress— Now, Miss Flora—

FLORA: [*Smiling, teasing as* MRS. GROSE *pulls at her sash*] Oh, no! That's a tuck that was always there—

MRS. GROSE: It wasn't this morning. Now, do sit down and don't muss yourself.

FLORA: There'd be less chance of that if I remain standing, don't you think? When will she get here, Mrs. Grose?

MRS. GROSE: [*Dusting things already spotless*] At any moment—the carriage'll bring her soon— Did *you* put those leaves in her room?

FLORA: They are pretty, aren't they?

MRS. GROSE: Leaves! With a whole garden of flowers!

FLORA: [*Following* MRS. GROSE *about the room*] Is my uncle coming with her?

MRS. GROSE: [*Paying little attention to her*] Your uncle?

FLORA: I expect he's too busy— [*Pause*] Is she very pretty?

MRS. GROSE: [*Preoccupied*] I'm sure she is.

FLORA: She might be ugly. Do I need another governess?

MRS. GROSE: Why, yes. You'll like her—won't you?

FLORA: Oh, yes— Will Miles like her?

MRS. GROSE: Master Miles? Of course.

FLORA: He'll be home from school soon—

MRS. GROSE: For the holidays. Not before.

FLORA: He might be. Mightn't he, Mrs. Grose? Before that?

MRS. GROSE: There'd be no reason. [*Turns; her face puckering up*] Oh, Miss Flora, lamb! You miss him, don't you?

FLORA: I'm not lonely—though I'd like to see Miles. I'd like it if he were *always* here.

MRS. GROSE: Of course you would, precious. But Miss Giddens will think of things to do—and won't she be amazed at how clever you are—!

FLORA: Am I? [*As* MRS. GROSE *nods*] Then—do I need another governess? And—are all governess' alike?

MRS. GROSE: [*Continuing to dust and rearrange furniture*] They're different as one person is from another.

FLORA: [*Thoughtfully*] It'd be an interesting thing if she'd let me get all dirty then put me to bed without a bath—

MRS. GROSE: [*Hardly listening as she dusts*] Ha!

FLORA: Perhaps I won't have to study my books—perhaps we'll spend the time with conversations or, if we feel like it on a particular day, we might just sit and stare at each other—lots of people do—

MRS. GROSE: Only when they have nothing to say. There's no chance of *that* with *you* around.

FLORA: When I don't talk you think I'm ill—

MRS. GROSE: Ha! Is that why you have so much to say? [*Fondly*] I don't believe it!

FLORA: Things pop into my head. There doesn't seem much sense in leaving them there—

MRS. GROSE: [*Paying little attention to her*] Don't you get all hot and mussy, now, Miss Flora.

FLORA: How could I? I'm standing still—and, do you know? [*Looks slowly up at the ceiling*] I feel quite small when I'm not moving—

MRS. GROSE: You'll grow soon enough.

FLORA: Oh, it's not *that*, Mrs. Grose? Why do people run past tall trees?

MRS. GROSE: I haven't got time for riddles, Miss Flora.

FLORA: It isn't a *riddle*. [*Wandering over to the window*] I feel terribly small— I feel as though I could crawl under the carpet and be completely flat—

MRS. GROSE: If you go on feeling you'll make yourself ill.

FLORA: [*Singing*] "O, Bring Me A Bonnet." [*Looking out to garden*] Oh, it's lovely watching a person come at you from a long way off!

MRS. GROSE: You'll be sick.

FLORA: [*Still looking out*] Of course she may not like it here. Then she'll pack her things and leave—

MRS. GROSE: [*On her knees, peering under spinet*] Do you put leaves under here just to tease me, Miss Flora? If you must bring leaves into the house, couldn't you put them in a box?

FLORA: [*Not turning*] They'd stifle. She's coming up the drive—and she isn't in a carriage at all— [*Turns from the window; wide-eyed*] She's walking—

MRS. GROSE: [*All nervous excitement now, crumbling the leaves in her hand, letting them drop as she gets to her feet*] Is it Miss Giddens, Miss Flora? Or are you teasing? And why would she be walking? The carriage went to fetch her— [*Bending down to pick up leaves*]

FLORA: She has just a *little* bag in her hand—wouldn't she have a trunk if she's going to stay?

MRS. GROSE: Oh, dear! She couldn't carry her trunk— Everything was so neat— What will she think?

FLORA: There, there. Everything is neat. I'll close the piano—then *everything* will be tidy. [*Closes the spinet with all the seriousness of a well-behaved child*] Now. Shall I go to the window and go to meet her?

MRS. GROSE: No, no. It's not in your place as a little lady. Sit quietly, Miss Flora— [*She pushes the window open, then waits on the threshold, patting at the creases in her apron, straightening her cap, looking off. As* MRS. GROSE *opens window,* FLORA *sits on love seat. To the person who comes walking up the drive*] Miss Giddens?

[FLORA *turns her head to French window*]

MISS GIDDENS: [*From garden. Her voice is youthful and breathless*] It's beautiful! It's all so beautiful! The gardens, I mean— I had to walk from the gate— I had to see it all! The carriage took my trunk around to the back— I hope you don't mind?

MRS. GROSE: [*Stepping backwards into the room*] Dear, no— I thought the carriage had missed you— [*Turning*] Miss Flora— here is Miss Giddens—

[MISS GIDDENS *steps into the room. She is young, pretty, dressed for traveling. She carries a small bag*]

MISS GIDDENS: [*As* FLORA *curtsies to her*] How do you do, Flora? [FLORA *curtsies again, smiling*] And you—you are Mrs. Grose— the housekeeper, of course?

MRS. GROSE: [*Curtseying*] Yes, miss—and you must forgive me. I meant to have tea ready for you—but, now—I'll have it here if you don't mind waiting a moment— [*She goes, in confusion, to door, then turns, flushed and beaming*] I'm *glad* you've come— [*Exits*]

MISS GIDDENS: [*To* MRS. GROSE] Thank you. Well, Flora—?

[MISS GIDDENS *and* FLORA *stand, silently for a moment, smiling at each other*]

FLORA: Would you like to take off your hat?

MISS GIDDENS: [*Sitting on love seat, taking off hat*] Thank you—

FLORA: [*Taking hat from her*] I shall put it here— Won't you sit down? [*Puts hat on desk*]

MISS GIDDENS: Thank you. Come sit by me— [FLORA *goes to sit on love seat*] We must get to know each other, you know—

FLORA: Oh, I'm sure we will. You're staying, aren't you? You told Mrs. Grose your trunk was here—

MISS GIDDENS: [*Laughing*] Why, of course I'm staying! I wouldn't be much of a governess if I didn't—now would I? So, I *shall*— [*Wooing her*] —if you'd like me to?

FLORA: Oh, yes— [*Pauses*] I hope you'll like your room—

MISS GIDDENS: I'm sure it's lovely—

FLORA: If you don't—you may choose another— There are thirty-five—most of them closed—and think of it! One hundred and forty windows! Shall we go into the garden and count them?

MISS GIDDENS: [*Charmed by the politeness*] I *would* like to—but poor Mrs. Grose would be alone with her tea—and I did say I'd like some.

FLORA: *You* didn't. *She* said she'd get it.

MISS GIDDENS: [*Taken aback; laughing*] Oh— It wouldn't be polite, now would it? To go walking in the garden?

FLORA: *I* often do. There are several ways you can walk, you know, if you don't walk on the drive—

MISS GIDDENS: [*Nonplussed, but trying*] Several ways? You mean hopping and skipping?

FLORA: [*In amazement*] Do *you* hop and skip?

MISS GIDDENS: I do—on occasion—

FLORA: I've never had a governess who did *that*—

MISS GIDDENS: Well, we're each a little different.

FLORA: [*Her smile disappears*] "Different"?

MISS GIDDENS: [*Puzzled, laughs after a pause that, because of its suddenness, seems much longer than it actually is*] Just as you are different from—from, well say, Mrs. Grose— [FLORA *does not move, nor does she seem to be listening.* MISS GIDDENS *makes another try*] You're eight years old, aren't you, dear?

[*Chimes*]

FLORA: Yes—

MISS GIDDENS: And Miles? He's twelve, isn't he?

FLORA: Yes—

MISS GIDDENS: And as good as you are, I'm sure!

FLORA: [*In a very small voice*] I expect we're both a little naughty sometimes—

MISS GIDDENS: [*Drawing* FLORA *to her, kissing her on her cheek*] Of course you are! And I shall love you for it!

MRS. GROSE: [*Entering, carrying a tray of tea things*] You're famished for a cup, I'm sure—after your long journey—so I'll set it down and leave you and the little lady to talk— [*Sets tray on desk*]

MISS GIDDENS: Mrs. Grose? Won't you sit with me a while? There're things I'd like to ask you—

MRS. GROSE: Things, miss?

MISS GIDDENS: Yes— I don't know the habits of the house—it would make it easier if you told me—

MRS. GROSE: Why, yes, if you'd like, miss. [*Remains standing*]

MISS GIDDENS: [*Rising*] Will you have some tea, Flora?

FLORA: No, thank you.

MISS GIDDENS: [*Going to desk*] Do sit down, Mrs. Grose.

MRS. GROSE: [*Sitting on chair at desk*] Thank you, miss—

MISS GIDDENS: [*Pours tea into cups; as she does this she starts to laugh softly, looking at* MRS. GROSE, *then* FLORA, *who sits quietly*] And I was so afraid!

FLORA: [*Wonderingly*] Afraid?

MISS GIDDENS: Timid, Flora—couldn't make up my mind for days— Should I accept this post—should I? Shouldn't I? None of my brothers or sisters could help me! I wouldn't ask advice! [*Laughs*]

FLORA: [*Laughing*] I never take advice!

MRS. GROSE: [*Seriously*] Now, Miss Flora—

MISS GIDDENS: [*As she takes a cup of tea to* MRS. GROSE, *who rises embarrassedly*] But why should one take advice, Mrs. Grose? Or give it? [*As* MRS. GROSE *remains standing—cup in hand—slightly ill-at-ease*] Do sit down, Mrs. Grose— [*As she returns to love seat, sits*] Of course, advice is forced upon you, in as large a family as mine was—

FLORA: [*Fascinated*] How large?

MISS GIDDENS: Very large. In a very small house. Secrets were difficult.

FLORA: But "possible"?

MISS GIDDENS: Not for long.

FLORA: That *must* have been annoying.

MISS GIDDENS: Well— [*Laughing*] Of course we shared our secrets when we were your age—but grownups never knew—

FLORA: [*Laughing with her*] They never do—do they?

MRS. GROSE: Now, Miss Flora—

MISS GIDDENS: [*To* MRS. GROSE, *smiling*] Oh, they found out after a

while! My family believed in open doors and after-dinner con-
ferences—

MRS. GROSE: And a very *sensible* thing, too, miss—

FLORA: [*To* MISS GIDDENS] Is it?

MRS. GROSE: [V*exedly*] Miss *Flora*—

MISS GIDDENS: [R*ealizing that perhaps she has been a little too free
with* FLORA] Yes, Flora. A *very* sensible thing— [*Smiling*] Now,
wouldn't you like to walk in the garden while I speak to Mrs.
Grose? [*She goes with* FLORA *to window*]

FLORA: [*The perfect "obedient" child*] Why, yes, if you'd like me
to, Miss Giddens.

MISS GIDDENS: And I'll come out when I've had a cup of tea— [FLORA
curtsies to her, goes through French window and out into garden]
Poor little thing. She looks so lonely out there—

MRS. GROSE: Lonely, miss? Most independent. Just as soon wander off
by herself—though as easy with company as any—

MISS GIDDENS: [*Looking out*] She *is* lonely, though. Perhaps it's because I grew up in a large family— Well, at least she has a beautiful
garden to walk in— [*Softly*] It *is* a beautiful garden—so quiet,
so peaceful— The thickness of the trees seem to form a wall between one path and another. As I walked under them I had a feeling of solitude—and yet, I also felt that I was not completely
alone— [*Turning to* MRS. GROSE] When you walked in the garden
—your first day here—what did you think, Mrs. Grose?

MRS. GROSE: [*Softly*] I was young, miss— I thought it was all very
beautiful—

MISS GIDDENS: [*Moving away from window; looking about room,
taking in each detail of it*] How awful if it were an ugly one!
[*She laughs softly*] How awful if this room were cold and ugly!
I was almost afraid it might be! [*Returns to love seat. Sits down;
takes her cup*]

MRS. GROSE: [*Puzzled*] Might be, miss?

MISS GIDDENS: [*Seriously*] No. I didn't think that. I suppose I knew
it would be beautiful—because his house on Harley Street was—
[*Pause*] Mrs. Grose—perhaps it isn't any of my business—but he,
their uncle, when I spoke to him—when he engaged me—he was
so brief with me. He said he didn't want to be bothered by letters

from me about the children— He said that, you know—he made it seem *the* important part of his terms. He said—under no condition was I to *bother him.* Doesn't he love them?

MRS. GROSE: [*Uncomfortably*] I'm sure he does—in his fashion, miss, if you'll excuse me—

MISS GIDDENS: I don't understand how he could choose to ignore them. But I know so little— Only that their parents died soon after Miss Flora's birth and that *he* is their sole guardian—

MRS. GROSE: Yes, miss— But you must understand, miss— He's not a young man and he's never enjoyed good health— He was always a studious man—wrapped up in his work— He's never had any family responsibilities before— [*Gently*] But he does keep this house on—espccially for them. He *is* doing all that can be expected—

MISS GIDDENS: Yes, after all, Miles and Flora aren't his children— And, he certainly *was* absorbed in his work— He could scarcely spare the time to interview me and spent most of it talking about his collection of Chinese paintings— [*Looks about the room*] I see he's got some of them here— I must admit they're rather beautiful—but I couldn't help being angry when he spoke to mc about not bothering him about the children. [*Gently*] You see, I have been in the midst of my family, first as a child, then as a guardian to my younger brothers and sisters— [*Rising, moving about the room, taking in the details of it*] It isn't enough to give a child a house and garden as beautiful as these— [*Wryly*] I'm afraid I showed him how angry I was. I'm afraid *that* is why he engaged me—because I "stood up" to him. I was caught. I showed how much I loved children—and that I would do *anything* to make them happy. That was all he wanted, apparently— Someone to take the responsibility off *his* shoulders. Well, here I am. [*Gently*] And I'm embarrassing you— I don't mean to. [*Laughs*] And what an easy task it will be! An affectionate task! And all within a large roomy house surrounded by a lovely garden! [*Determinedly*] And—when he pays us a visit—

MRS. GROSE: I don't expect he will, miss. He's been here only once or twice that I can bring to mind. Though there were times in the months just passed when—

MISS GIDDENS: [*Taken aback*] When *what*, Mrs. Grose?

MRS. GROSE: When *he* should have been the one to shoulder the—

MISS GIDDENS: The what, Mrs. Grose?

MRS. GROSE: Bygones is bygones.

MISS GIDDENS: Not if I'm to do my work satisfactorily—

MRS. GROSE: Pardon me, miss. It isn't to do with you—you'd best forget I spoke—so—so out of place. [*She rises*]

MISS GIDDENS: [*Stubbornly*] Mrs. Grose. What was she like?

MRS. GROSE: [*Uncomfortably*] Who, miss?

MISS GIDDENS: The lady who was here before.

MRS. GROSE: The last governess? She was also young and pretty, miss, even as you—

MISS GIDDENS: [*Smiling with embarrassment*] He doesn't mind them being young and pretty!

MRS. GROSE: [*Turning to her, vehemently*] Oh, no—it was the way he liked everyone! [*Flushing*] I mean—why should the Master mind?

MISS GIDDENS: But of whom did you speak *first*?

MRS. GROSE: [*Blankly*] Why, of *him*.

MISS GIDDENS: Of the Master?

MRS. GROSE: Of who else?

[*They search each other's faces*]

MISS GIDDENS: [*Casually*] Mrs. Grose—was she—my predecessor—careful, particular—in her work?

MRS. GROSE: [*Against her will*] About some things—yes—

MISS GIDDENS: But not about all?

MRS. GROSE: Well, miss, she's passed on. I won't tell tales.

MISS GIDDENS: [*Quickly*] I understand your feeling—but— Did she die here?

MRS. GROSE: No—she went away.

[FLORA *appears at window*]

MISS GIDDENS: Went *away*? To die? She was taken ill you mean—and went home?

MRS. GROSE: She was not taken ill so far as *appeared* in this house. She—she left it to go home, she said, for a short holiday. At the very moment I was expecting her back I heard from the Master that she was dead.

MISS GIDDENS: But of what?

> [*The* TWO WOMEN *stare at each other. Through scene, lights dim. Only from the French window comes a last ray of sunlight*]

FLORA: [*In a small, clear voice*] Miss Giddens—aren't you coming for a walk?

THE LIGHTS FADE

SCENE 2

Three hours later.

This scene begins in semi-darkness. MISS GIDDENS'S *voice overlaps transition music.*

Lights come up slowly. A pale moonlight comes through the French window.

MISS GIDDENS *sits on the love seat.* FLORA *sits beside her, sleepily; she is wearing a long white nightgown.*

Candle, lighted, on desk. FLORA *leans against* MISS GIDDENS'S *shoulder.*

MISS GIDDENS: [*Softly, reading from book*] "In the winter time, when deep snow lay on the ground, a poor boy was forced to go out on a sledge to fetch wood. When he had gathered it together, and packed it, he wished, as he was frozen with cold, not to go home at once but to light a fire and warm himself a little—"

FLORA: How would he light it?

MISS GIDDENS: Well—I suppose he had a flint on which to strike—

FLORA: Oh—

MISS GIDDENS: [*Reading*] "So—he scraped away the snow, and as he was thus cleaning the ground, he found—a tiny, golden key! Hereupon he thought that where the key was, the lock must be also—so he dug in the ground and found—an iron chest! 'If the key does but fit it!' thought he; 'no doubt there are precious things in that little box!' He searched, but no keyhole was there. At last—he discovered one! But so small that it was hardly visible. He tried it, and the key fitted it exactly. Then he turned it once round—and now we must wait until he has quite unlocked it and opened the lid—and then we shall learn what wonderful things were lying in that box."

FLORA: Was he a little boy like Miles?

MISS GIDDENS: He might even have *been* Miles.

FLORA: Oh— What was in the box?

MISS GIDDENS: Why, we shall have to wait until it's opened.

FLORA: *When* will it be?

MISS GIDDENS: It doesn't say—but it's fun guessing. What do *you* think is in the box?

FLORA: I think I'd rather wait until it's opened—

MISS GIDDENS: And if it isn't?

FLORA: Then I'll just *imagine* things.

MISS GIDDENS: [*More to herself than to* FLORA] Yes— [*Closes book. Shivering as though a sudden draught has entered the room*] It's cold— Aren't you cold, dear?

FLORA: No. [*Snuggling closer to* MISS GIDDENS] I'm half-asleep, I think. Shall I stay in your room tonight?

MISS GIDDENS: [*Looking about the room. Absentmindedly*] If you'd like to—

FLORA: Mrs. Grose wanted to give you a larger room—but I said: She'll only be there when she's asleep and big rooms have a way of growing bigger at night. Mrs. Grose says they *don't*, but that's because *she* doesn't like the dark and won't open her eyes.

[*The* SHADOW *of a man appears against the silk curtains of the window. As though a man had approached the window, the* SHADOW *looms until it fills the window.* FLORA *yawns, then she giggles*]

FLORA: I wish there was some way to sleep in several rooms at once— Mrs. Grose was quite startled by the thought—

MISS GIDDENS: [*Laughing, a little nervously*] I don't wonder!

[*The* SHADOW *recedes as though the man steps away*]

FLORA: [*Laughing*] She gets so upset about things like that! Do you know what she did about the rooms in the attic? [MISS GIDDENS *rises from the love seat, a puzzled frown on her face. She looks toward window*] Why—what's the matter, Miss Giddens, dear?

MISS GIDDENS: [*Smiling quickly*] Nothing. What about the attic rooms?

FLORA: They are empty, but you can see everything that once was in them!

MISS GIDDENS: [*Looking toward window again*] Can you—?

FLORA: Yes. The chairs—*everything*—has left a mark. It looks as though the pictures are still hanging and, if you look closely, you can see the carpet, though it's been rolled up and put away! [*She watches* MISS GIDDENS *and waits for a moment; then:*] Mrs. Grose doesn't like the idea. She has locked up all those rooms and several more— [*She yawns, watching* MISS GIDDENS, *who is looking about the room as though she senses something amiss*] But I— Oh, I wish my room was like that!

MISS GIDDENS: [*Looking at her—smiling—trying to appear unconcerned*] It'd—it'd be uncomfortable. Nothing to sit on—and how would you go to bed?

FLORA: I wouldn't. I'd much rather not, anyway.

MISS GIDDENS: [*Sitting down beside her again*] I'm afraid you'll have to—now.

FLORA: Must I? Then, first, tell me a story out of your head.

MISS GIDDENS: [*Once more preoccupied*] Out of my head?

FLORA: With *me* in it. And Mrs. Grose and Miles—and you.

MISS GIDDENS: [*Rising, taking* FLORA *by the hand*] Come along, then. [*They start toward the stairs*] Once upon a time—once upon a time there was a ship called Bly—

FLORA: [*Sleepily*] That's the name of this house—I know—

MISS GIDDENS: [*Pausing at foot of staircase, looking up to ceiling as though she hears something there*] It was also—it was also the name of a very old ship— [*As they go upstairs*] This ship had long corridors and empty rooms and an old square tower—just like this house. It had a crew. Their names were— Do you know what their names were?

FLORA: [*Sleepily*] What were they?

MISS GIDDENS: [*As they reach the landing*] Why, their names were Flora and Mrs. Grose and Miss Giddens—and, yes, still another— and *his* name was Miles.

[*They enter room off landing. Immediately, as* MISS GIDDENS *says "Miles," a thin vibration comes from far away— more of trembling of all inanimate things than of sound itself—and with this vibration, the* SHADOW *again appears at the window, filling the window, blocking out the moonlight, almost as though about to enter the room as:*]

THE LIGHTS FADE

SCENE 3

The following morning.

It is a clear, beautiful day. The French door is wide open. The garden is apparent by its reflected light, green and cool, that fills the room.

MRS. GROSE *is polishing the furniture. After a moment, she reaches into one of the pockets of her apron, pulls out two letters, places them on desk, looks out into the garden, then continues with her polishing.*

FLORA *comes through door on landing, and, unnoticed by* MRS. GROSE, *comes down, halfway, to sit on a stair. Her chin in her hands, she watches* MRS. GROSE *quietly.*

FLORA: [*Softly*] Where is Miss Giddens?

MRS. GROSE: Ah! Miss Flora! You startled me! Aren't you supposed to be in the schoolroom, now? Miss Giddens won't like it—and on her second day here, too—

FLORA: [*Undisturbed*] I finished my writing. Where is she?

MRS. GROSE: Picking some flowers—though I'm sure she'd stop if she knew you weren't doing what she told you to do. You get back now, there's a lamb.

FLORA: [*Patiently*] But I've finished my writing—then I copied out a rhyme I knew by heart:

> In sleep she seemed to walk forlorn,
> Till cold winds woke the gray-eyed morn
> about the lonely moated grange.
> She only said, "The day is dreary,
> He cometh not," she said;
> She said, "I am aweary, aweary,
> I would that I were dead."

MRS. GROSE: [*Appalled*] What was she thinking of to have you learn that!

FLORA: She gave me O's to copy—but *they* were so easy—

MRS. GROSE: [*Beneath her breath*] Then it's clear from whom you learned *that*, missy! [*Flicks angrily at her desk*] And there's no telling what else!

FLORA: Are you dusting the ship, Mrs. Grose, dear?

MRS. GROSE: [*Grimly*] I'm dusting a desk—a ship, indeed!

FLORA: Miss Giddens says Bly is a ship—

MRS. GROSE: Then *you'll* get seasick, no doubt!

FLORA: Oh, no. But Miss Giddens was.

MRS. GROSE: [*Across room, dusting spinet*] Ah, Miss Flora—

FLORA: Well, I thought she was, for she came upstairs and I wasn't asleep, though I kept my eyes shut—and I heard her say: "Flora? Flora, dear?" And she could hardly get her voice out, so I expect she *was* sick, for she was very restless all night. I heard her.

MRS. GROSE: [*Laughing in spite of herself*] Miss Flora!

FLORA: [*Laughing with her as she comes down stairs, goes to French door*] So I should find her—for she may have fallen down—[*Goes out into garden*]

MRS. GROSE: [*Laughing with amazement*] Fallen down, indeed! "Are you dusting a ship!" [*A moment passes, then, as* MISS GIDDENS' *approach is heralded by her shadow at the window*] What a lovely day, miss!

MISS GIDDENS: [*Entering from garden*] Yes, it is.

MRS. GROSE: Didn't you get the flowers, miss? The vases are filled for them—

MISS GIDDENS: No—I forgot them— [*Crosses to staircase. Stops. Turning back to* MRS. GROSE] Mrs. Grose—?

MRS. GROSE: Yes, miss?

MISS GIDDENS: Mrs. Grose—you know where the path ends in a clump of elms, beyond the lawn, close to the woods?

MRS. GROSE: Yes, miss—

MISS GIDDENS: [*Lost in what she describes*] I was standing there— I was about to pick the flowers—but, suddenly, I felt that I was being stared at. I turned, expecting to find that it was you or Miss Flora who had come to call me— Instead, I saw a man, a stranger —who stared at me, Mrs. Grose—who stood there, casually, as though he belonged here—

MRS. GROSE: You're sure, miss, it wasn't the gardener or his boy?

MISS GIDDENS: No one I knew. [*Trying to laugh*] I stood there waiting for him to approach me. I was sure of a reason for his being there and so I waited—and he—he waited with me—not coming closer—standing there, fifty yards away, though it seemed that he was as near to me as you are— [*She shakes her head as though to rid herself of the thought*] And then, even though there was that distance between us, I could feel his eyes on me—bold, insolent— He stared at me as though *I* were being *indecent*— I felt as though I was looking into someone's room— He stared at me, Mrs. Grose, as though *I* were the intruder! [*She laughs weakly*]

MRS. GROSE: And he is gone, miss—?

MISS GIDDENS: Oh, yes! He went away—as casually as he had come— though, for all I know, he might be still in the garden, somewhere, or in the woods— And the ridiculous thing, Mrs. Grose, is that only now am I angry! Not when I was *there*, mind you, when I might have questioned him—but now, when I am *here*—quite safe from him—I feel angry—and—a trifle ill— [*She shakes her head again and moves toward the desk*]

MRS. GROSE: [*Staring at her*] But, miss—

MISS GIDDENS: [*Disturbed, not wanting to go on with it*] Don't be concerned for me—I didn't sleep well. Let us forget it.— I see there are letters for me.

MRS. GROSE: Wouldn't you like some tea, miss—?

MISS GIDDENS: [*Who has quickly, nervously opened the first of two letters*] It's from my youngest sister—and here— [*Turning to* MRS. GROSE, *a picture in her hand*] —here—she has sent a picture that I forgot to bring with me—of my family. I've never been without it—and yet I forgot it—and so she sent it— [*Gives* MRS. GROSE *the picture, starts opening the second letter*]

MRS. GROSE: [*Looking at the picture*] How you must miss them—! Is this your first time away from them, miss?

MISS GIDDENS: [*Frowning at letter in her hand*] Yes. How like their uncle. He's forwarded this letter without even opening it. It's from Master Miles' school. Their uncle has written on the back— "whatever it is, deal with it. Don't bother me with it. Not a word."

MRS. GROSE: Oh, that's his way, miss. He never did like being bothered. What a pretty picture this is. A big family is what I like. Let them muss the furniture up a bit, I say. A scratch won't hurt here and there if there's happiness in a house—

MISS GIDDENS: [*All her uncertainty returning*] What am I to do? How am I to deal with this?

MRS. GROSE: With what, miss?

MISS GIDDENS: Master Miles. He's been dismissed from school.

MRS. GROSE: [*After a long pause*] Dismissed—?

MISS GIDDENS: Sent home.

MRS. GROSE: [*Blankness*] But aren't they all—?

MISS GIDDENS: Only for the holidays. Miles can't go back—at all.

MRS. GROSE: What has he done—? [*As* MISS GIDDENS *hesitates*] Is he really *bad*? Do the gentlemen say so?

MISS GIDDENS: They go into no details—they simply express their regret. They say it is impossible to keep him—

MRS. GROSE: Why?

MISS GIDDENS: That he is an injury to the others.

MRS. GROSE: It's too dreadful to say such cruel things! See him first, miss, *then* believe it if you can! You might as well think ill of Miss Flora, bless her!

MISS GIDDENS: Oh, I know that, Mrs. Grose—but what am I to do? Am I to question him when I meet him at the coach this afternoon?

MRS. GROSE: This afternoon—?

MISS GIDDENS: Yes— Shall I put it to him?— Boldly?

MRS. GROSE: See him first, miss, before you think badly of him—
It's cruel—too cruel—to write things like that about him!

MISS GIDDENS: You've never known him to be bad?

MRS. GROSE: Never known him— Oh, I don't pretend *that!*

MISS GIDDENS: You like them with the spirit to be naughty? So do I.
But not to the degree to contaminate.

MRS. GROSE: To—?

MISS GIDDENS: To corrupt.

MRS. GROSE: [*Laughing oddly—with a bold humor*] Are you afraid
he'll corrupt *you?*

MISS GIDDENS: [*Wryly*] What a comfort you are—If I'd had a good
night's sleep I'd be able to think this out and not be silly about
it— But I didn't sleep—

MRS. GROSE: Miss Flora said that.

MISS GIDDENS: Did she? I hardly thought—

MRS. GROSE: And that you bent over her and spoke her name.

MISS GIDDENS: Yes—because [*Checks herself*] I wondered if she were
thirsty—

MRS. GROSE: [*Gently*] Why didn't you call me—if you were taken
ill?

MISS GIDDENS: Ill? Why, no. It was my first night here—that was all.
After my home, small, crowded, this house with so many rooms
empty—all shut up—so quiet and— [*There is a deadly stillness before she speaks again*] And—I seemed to hear someone walking beneath my window— [*Covers her eyes with her hand*] I mustn't
think about it— It's odd, though— I can't get it out of my mind—
He stared at me so boldly— I could feel an intense silence into
which all the sounds of the garden dropped—leaving me, as he
walked away, with nothing to stare at but emptiness— Then—the
smell of flowers—overpowering— [*She sways as though about to
fall. Chimes*] I—I must go to Flora, now— [*Starts to climb
stairs*]

MRS. GROSE: [*With a sudden realization*] She's not up there—miss—

MISS GIDDENS: [*Turning to her*] Where—then? [*As MRS. GROSE,
frightened, looks toward window*] In the garden—?! [*She runs*

across the room, to the window. MRS. GROSE *follows her, quickly]*
Flora! [Exits out window] Flora!

MRS. GROSE: Miss Flora! Miss Flora! Miss Flora!

[FLORA *enters door left and goes to window]*

MISS GIDDENS: [*Off*] Flora! Flora!

THE LIGHTS FADE

SCENE 4

Twilight. The same day.

The window is open. The lamps are not lighted, for the day has not quite passed, though the golden afterglow that fills the room will soon fade.

This moment of twilight is silent but anticipates the break that soon comes from the garden.

FLORA'S VOICE: [*From the garden*] We're here, Mrs. Grose! Mrs. Grose! [*Entering. Running across to door*] Miles! Miles is back!

MRS. GROSE: [*Off*] Here I am, lamb!

FLORA: [*Turning again to window*] Hurry! He's grown—he's so tall! You won't recognize him! [*Running to window*] The darling boy! Oh, hurry! Please hurry, Mrs. Grose!

MRS. GROSE: [*Off*] I am—I'm doing the best I can—bless you!

FLORA: [*Running out to garden*] Miles! Where are you, Miles? Don't hide from me, now! Where are you! [*Her voice dies away in the distance*]

MRS. GROSE: [*Off*] Oh, dear! I'll be out directly! [*As she enters,* MISS GIDDENS *appears at the window. She stops as she sees* MISS GIDDENS] Well, miss? Master Miles?— Where is he?

MISS GIDDENS: [*Flatly*] Somewhere in the garden. He ran off amongst the trees.

MRS. GROSE: [*Sensing the tension in* MISS GIDDENS] It *is* all right, isn't it, miss? I mean—what did he say to you?

MISS GIDDENS: [*Coming into room*] About the reason for his being sent home? Nothing. Nothing seems to bother him.

MRS. GROSE: You see? I told you there would be no trouble about it— [*Starts toward window*]

MISS GIDDENS: I *don't* see. [*As* MRS. GROSE *stops*] We sat across from each other in the carriage and he was all smiles and not in the least concerned, if that's what you mean. Other than that—

MRS. GROSE: But you *do* like him?

MISS GIDDENS: Oh, he's charming. I expected, at least, that he'd be uneasy—that he'd say something about his school—

MRS. GROSE: [*Pleading*] But he's just come home, miss. It'll come out. He'll tell you. I know he will—

MISS GIDDENS: Oh, no. I'll have to get it out of him.

MRS. GROSE: And it'll be nothing at all!

MISS GIDDENS: Then why hasn't he said something?

[*At this moment,* MILES *appears at window. He is twelve years old; a handsome child whose face reflects a remarkable innocence, whose bearing is gentlemanly and proud. He looks at* MISS GIDDENS, *then with a great smile of welcome, goes to* MRS. GROSE]

MRS. GROSE: [*Embracing him*] Master Miles—dear Master Miles—

FLORA: [*Running in from garden. Sits on ottoman*] Oh, there you are! I looked all over the garden for you! [*Fondly*] Why do you tease me so!

MILES: [*Looking at* MRS. GROSE *as she releases him*] You look as though you'd like to cry. Aren't you glad to see me?

MRS. GROSE: I'm that happy—I—

FLORA: She means she's so happy she could weep! But *I* was sick when I heard you were coming! My stomach turned over.

MISS GIDDENS: [*Sharply*] Is supper ready, Mrs. Grose?

MRS. GROSE: [*Startled*] Why—yes, miss.

MISS GIDDENS: [*Coldly*] You must be hungry, Miles.

MILES: [*Sits on ottoman*] Yes, thank you, Miss Giddens.

FLORA: Just think, Mrs. Grose—Miles ate four little cakes on the coach! And a wheel came off!

MRS. GROSE: [*Softly*] Did it now?

MILES: [*Looking about the room. Completely at ease*] No. It almost did. A man fixed it and then we went along beautifully.

MRS. GROSE: Four cakes—and *I* made a pudding for you—

MILES: I actually ate only two. A little girl ate the others and her mother became quite angry. So I fibbed.

MISS GIDDENS: [*Sharply*] Why, Miles?

MILES: Oh, because the lady wouldn't scold *me*. So, of course, I *said* I'd eaten *four*. So you see, Mrs. Grose, I shall be able to enjoy your pudding.

[*The light from the sky dies away with* MILES'S *last words. The room is in darkness*]

FLORA: Hello!

MILES: Hello!

MISS GIDDENS: [*Takes off her hat*] Flora, wouldn't you like to go with Mrs. Grose—and have her give you a taper—then you could light the lamps?

FLORA: May I?

MISS GIDDENS: And Mrs. Grose, would you see to supper?

FLORA: [*Still plaintively*] And may I have supper with you and Miles?

MISS GIDDENS: I don't see why not.

FLORA: [*Following* MRS. GROSE, *who goes silently to door*] And may Mrs. Grose have supper with us?

MRS. GROSE: Dear me, that wouldn't—

MISS GIDDENS: That *would* be nice.

FLORA: [*Taking* MRS. GROSE *by the hand*] She *shall*. Won't you?

MRS. GROSE: [*Hardly audible—as they exit*] If you'd like it, Miss Flora—

MISS GIDDENS: [*Now that she is alone with* MILES, *she seems filled with indecision. She turns to desk, places her hat upon it, opens the drawer, shuts it, then turns to him. Too casually*] Well, Miles? Don't you want to tell me something?

MILES: [*Returns her look with a charming smile*] Something?

FLORA: [*Entering, with a lighted taper in her hand*] Do I look like an evening star? [*She doesn't seem to notice the silence between* MILES *and* MISS GIDDENS] We'll all have stomach aches, I'm sure. I saw the pudding and it's beautiful.

MILES: [*Going over to her, his hands in his pockets*] I shan't.

FLORA: [*Beaming at him*] No. You *never* do. I don't see how you

manage not to—what with third helpings and all. [*A close intimate companionship exists between them. As though they deliberately ignore her,* MISS GIDDENS *is left on her own; she is aware
of this—she involuntarily moves out of their way as they approach the desk,* MILES *steps forward and lifts the globe from the
desk lamp, gallantly.*] Thank you. If I have *even* a second helping
I almost *die.*

MILES: [*Smiling at her*] Silly. You dislike second helpings?

FLORA: [*Beaming at him as he replaces globe on lamp*] Oh, no. I
love them.

MISS GIDDENS: Miles.

FLORA: [*As though* MISS GIDDENS *weren't in the room*] I shall die of
them one day, of course. But I do think it'll be worth it— [*Lighting lamp, then blowing out flame of taper*] Especially if it's *pudding.* Not the soggy kind, you know— [*Places taper on desk, takes
MILES by the hand. Together they go to staircase*] The chewy
kind—with raisins in it—

MISS GIDDENS: [*Firmly*] Miles!

MILES: [*Turning, all smiles*] I should wash my hands for supper,
shouldn't I?

> [MILES *and* FLORA *run, silently, up the stairs and through
> door on landing.* MISS GIDDENS *looks up at landing as a
> burst of laughter comes from the room behind the door.
> Then she angrily sits down, opens desk drawers, takes the
> letter out, rapidly reads through it. With sudden decision,
> she begins to write. A few moments pass. She rises, goes to
> French window, closes it but does not draw the curtains;
> she returns to desk, continues writing.* MILES *comes through
> door on landing and down the staircase*]

MILES: Am I disturbing you, Miss Giddens?

MISS GIDDENS: [*Pretending disinterestedness*] Not at all.

MILES: Flora's hiding.— When she's hidden, I'm to find her.

MISS GIDDENS: [*Writing*] Well, don't be too noisy.

MILES: [*Goes to French window. Looks out into garden over which
complete darkness has fallen. After a moment*] It must be nice
out in the garden, now—

MISS GIDDENS: [*Not looking up*] Too dark to be pleasant.

MILES: I'm not afraid of the dark. Are you?

MISS GIDDENS: [*Taken aback; looking at him*] Sometimes—

MILES: Why?

MISS GIDDENS: There's nothing to be afraid of, really—

MILES: I know that. Why are you afraid?

MISS GIDDENS: I suppose—I suppose I'm timid.

MILES: [*Seriously*] You shouldn't be. Everything's the same at night as it is by day. You're in a room and it's dark—so you light a lamp and—there's nothing but chairs and tables! Just as there always were!

> [*He gives a delightful laugh.* MISS GIDDENS *is finding it difficult to retain her anger against him*]

MISS GIDDENS: [*Looking up at him*] If everything were as simple as that—

MILES: But it is! Though grownups don't see it—usually. On the coach, the little girl's mother was nervous about the wheel—not while it was about to fall off—but after it was fixed. She said she was going to faint!— All because the wheel might have come off— which it *didn't!* You see? It's all in what you *think* might happen. Most of the time it doesn't.

MISS GIDDENS: [*Touches him on the arm*] Miles—

FLORA'S VOICE: Miles!

MISS GIDDENS: Sometime—we must talk about— [*She smiles at him —then she shakes her head*] Not now, though.

FLORA'S VOICE: I'm hid, Miles!

MILES: You don't suppose I might stretch my legs a bit out there, do you?

MISS GIDDENS: And disappoint Flora who's hidden and waiting?

MILES: No—I couldn't do that, could I? [*He goes across to stairs*]

FLORA'S VOICE: Miles!

MILES: I'm coming. [*As he starts to climb stairs, smiling at* MISS GIDDENS] I'm glad you're here, Miss Giddens. I'm sure we'll get along splendidly together— I'll catch you! [*Goes off, into room on landing*]

[MISS GIDDENS *picks up the letter she has started, looks at it, begins to tear it up*]

MRS. GROSE: [*Entering. She is carrying a small bag and some books*] Here are Master Miles's books, miss—

MISS GIDDENS: [*Rising quickly from the desk*] I've been stupid, Mrs. Grose—how could I have been so stupid? You were right—I should have given him a chance— Well, I shall!

MRS. GROSE: You've spoken to him, miss?

MISS GIDDENS: Not about his school—not yet. How could I have made up my mind so quickly about him—I who have brothers? When I think of the rage I felt toward him fifteen minutes ago! Oh, a fine governess I make, Mrs. Grose!

MRS. GROSE: What will you say, then?

MISS GIDDENS: In answer to the letter? Nothing until I've spoken to Master Miles.

MRS. GROSE: And to his uncle?

MISS GIDDENS: Oh, I shan't bother *him*—I'll handle it myself. Master Miles will help me— He's an intelligent boy— I've been so unfair to him! Meeting him at the coach with what amounted to a stony silence— Well— [*Laughs*] He'll have his chance to tell *his* side of the story— Then, we'll see—

MRS. GROSE: [*Close to tears, but smiling*] Miss— Would you mind, miss—?

[*They embrace, then* MRS. GROSE *exits*]

FLORA'S VOICE: [*From room off landing; shrieking with laughter*] Oh, Miles! How did you find me?

MISS GIDDENS: [*Smiling. Going to staircase*] Flora—

FLORA: [*Coming onto landing*] Yes, Miss Giddens?

MISS GIDDENS: Don't get so excited, dear.

FLORA: How can I help it? Miles is so clever at finding me out. Now he's hiding— [*She listens; then in a whisper*] I hear him rustling—which means he's pretending he's getting under the bed. But he won't. He'll be somewhere else—and I'll *never* find him— It's quite frightening!

MISS GIDDENS: [*Laughing*] To know someone's there, in the room with you, and yet you can't see them? But that's the fun of it!

FLORA: You hear them breathing *right* behind you—but you don't dare turn around to look—!

MISS GIDDENS: And when you do they're not there at all!

FLORA: You find them when you least expect to!

MISS GIDDENS: They jump out at you!

FLORA: A terrible thing! But such fun! [*As* MISS GIDDENS, *laughing, goes to draw curtains at window*] Poor Miss Giddens— Do you feel better now?

MISS GIDDENS: [*Taken aback; not drawing the curtains*] Better—?

FLORA: You know—about everything.

MILES'S VOICE: [*Calling*] Flora!

FLORA: [*Running off, into room off landing*] Oh, I'll never find you! [MISS GIDDENS *stares after her, frowning*] I've found you! I've found you!

> [MISS GIDDENS *crosses room as though to go upstairs. But as she reaches stairs she comes to a sudden stop. She does not turn, but she is fully aware of the* MAN *who has appeared, framed in the window, staring in from the garden. His face is close to the glass of the window. Slowly,* MISS GIDDENS *turns to face him across the room. Music up. She does not cry out, nor does she move until the* MAN *steps backwards into the darkness of the garden. For a moment after he has gone,* MISS GIDDENS *remains still, then she runs to window, opens it and goes out into the garden after him. Music fades. There is an absolute silence for a long moment.* MRS. GROSE *enters. She comes to an abrupt stop, her hand covers her mouth to stifle a scream—for* MISS GIDDENS *has reappeared in the window, framed there, blank terror apparent in her face*]

MRS. GROSE: What—what in the name of goodness is the matter?

MISS GIDDENS: He was here—again.

MRS. GROSE: Who, miss—?

MISS GIDDENS: He stared in at the window—just as he did in the garden this afternoon— He stared—only, this time, he looked right past me as though he were looking for someone else—

> [*Shrill, excitable laughter comes from* MILES *and* FLORA *as*

they play in their room beyond the landing. MISS GIDDENS *looks up at the landing]*

MRS. GROSE: Do you fear for them?

MISS GIDDENS: Don't *you?*

MRS. GROSE: [*After a long moment*] But—what is he like?

MISS GIDDENS: No one I've seen around here— [*Sits on ottoman*] He has red hair—very red, close and curling. A long pale face. His eyebrows are dark—dark and arched. His eyes seemed sharp—strange—awfully. I only know clearly that they are small and—very fixed. [MRS. GROSE *stares at her with a horror that grows as she continues*] His mouth is wide, his lips thin. He's tall—erect—well dressed, but certainly not—a gentleman—

MRS. GROSE: [*Gasping*] A gentleman? Not he!

MISS GIDDENS: You *know* him?

MRS. GROSE: [*Almost a whisper*] Quint.

MISS GIDDENS: Quint?

MRS. GROSE: Peter Quint. His own man, his valet, when the Master was here. When the Master left— Quint was alone—

MISS GIDDENS: Alone?

MRS. GROSE: Alone with us— In charge.

MISS GIDDENS: And then—?

MRS. GROSE: He went.

MISS GIDDENS: Went where?

MRS. GROSE: God knows where. He died.

THE LIGHTS FADE

SCENE 5

The following morning.

It is a bleak and rainy morning. A cold, gray light comes from the garden in which, no doubt, every twig on every tree is dripping.

MILES *and* FLORA *are seated at desk. They are hard at work at some task set them by* MISS GIDDENS.

MISS GIDDENS *is seated on ottoman. She is working on some embroidery which is stretched before her on a frame. On the ottoman, beside her, lies a small box of pencils, school-books and a large pincushion. Every now and then she looks up to stare at one corner or another of the room. Every stab of her needle shows the tension under which she now lives.*

The only sound is the high, thin scratching of slate pencils on slates as MILES *and* FLORA *do their task—a nerve-racking sound—a sound that is heard before the lights come up and that continues with nail-biting insistency.*

MISS GIDDENS *presses her hand onto her forehead.*

FLORA: [*Looking at* MISS GIDDENS] Why are you doing this—? [*She repeats* MISS GIDDENS*'s gesture*] You looked as though you were pushing something away— [*She goes to window, wipes a pane vigorously*]

MISS GIDDENS: Flora. Sit down.

FLORA: [*Looking out into garden*] Oh, look! There's a bird with an enormous worm! Mayn't we go out?

MISS GIDDENS: [*Sharply*] Certainly not! It's raining.

FLORA: Oh, no, it isn't. It's dripping from every twig and leaf and branch—but—

MISS GIDDENS: Will you sit *down?*

FLORA: Why, of course— [*Returns to desk immediately and absorbs herself in her task. After a moment:*] Oh, Miles! Your pencil *does* have a terrible squeak!

MILES: I can't help it, you know—

FLORA: Can't you? I thought you were doing it on purpose.— I wish I could— [*She tries. Her slate pencil snaps in two*] Oh, dear—

MISS GIDDENS: *Now*, what's the matter?

FLORA: It's my pencil—

MISS GIDDENS: You shouldn't bear down on it so. [*Reaching into box beside her*] Here's another.

FLORA: [*Going to her*] Does the squeak of Miles's pencil send shivers through you? It does through *me*—

MISS GIDDENS: [*Shortly*] No. [*Repenting*] I know it's a horrible day—but could you try and do your task—quietly, dear?

FLORA: Does your head hurt, Miss Giddens? [*To* MILES] Oh, Miles —poor Miss Giddens.

MISS GIDDENS: [*Trying to laugh, failing miserably*] Flora—Flora, dear—my head doesn't hurt—

FLORA: [*Sitting on ottoman*] Doesn't it? [*Taking* MISS GIDDENS's *hand*] You're warm— Miles? I do believe Miss Giddens has a fever!

MILES: Has she? May I get you a cup of tea, Miss Giddens? Or a plaster?

MISS GIDDENS: [*Laughing, though nearer tears*] A plaster? Whatever for? I'm not ill—you dear things! It's the rain—and not being able to go out into the garden—and tiring my eyes with—with *this*— [*She sticks her needle into the pincushion*]

FLORA: Then, why do you bother about it if you don't like it?

MISS GIDDENS: [*Trying to laugh*] It's my task for the day—like your spelling and geography—though nothing seems to be getting finished while we go on about nothing—

MILES: It's the rain that does it. *I* know—because I'm all turned about when I wake up and find the sun isn't out—

FLORA: [*Excitedly*] I know! I know! *I* get a funny feeling that *something's* going to happen! I wait all day—but nothing *ever* does— It's so disappointing—what with having to stay in—

MISS GIDDENS: Well, you're *not* going out.

FLORA: Not even with a hat?

MISS GIDDENS: Not even with a hat.

MILES: Don't keep on at Miss Giddens like that, Flora. We must do what she wishes, you know—

MISS GIDDENS: [*Almost breaking down. Her hand going to her eyes —then quickly away*] I—

FLORA: Of course we must. [*Putting her arm around* MISS GIDDENS's *shoulder*] I'm being naughty, aren't I?

MISS GIDDENS: No— It is I who am behaving wickedly— What a grumpy old governess you have!

FLORA: [*Kissing her—with charming affection*] You're not grumpy at all! Is she, Miles?

MILES: Of course she isn't. Though I wouldn't wonder if she were—

FLORA: Nor would I—with *everything* so horrible.

MISS GIDDENS: [*Hardly able to breathe*] Horrible—?

FLORA: [*Softly*] Why, yes—you know. [*Smiling up at her*] The rain—Miles's squeaky pencil—and my naughtiness— Why, I wasn't even trying to be good!

MISS GIDDENS: [*Almost crying with relief*] But you *are* good! You both are!

FLORA: Well, I *might* try a little harder, don't you think? [*Disengages herself gently from* MISS GIDDENS's *arms. Goes to desk*]

MISS GIDDENS: [*Rising quickly*] Why—no! Why should you? If it's gloomy outside—that's no reason why we should be gloomy here! Let's play!

FLORA: [*Delightedly*] Play?

MISS GIDDENS: Yes! Why not? We've worked—haven't we? Well, then— [*To* FLORA] You can choose the game!

FLORA: Hide-and-seek!

MISS GIDDENS: No!

> [*So sharp is* MISS GIDDENS's *voice that* FLORA's *hand goes to her own mouth as though she has screamed*]

FLORA: [*In tears; looking down at floor, whispering*] I'm—sorry— I thought you said I could choose the game—

MISS GIDDENS: [*Going swiftly to her. Kneeling before her, taking her in her arms*] I did—I did say that—and you may. But let's not hide from each other— Mrs. Grose has dusted and tidied all morning and it wouldn't be kind of us to—to untidy the room all over again—would it? And what's the fun of hide-and-seek if you can't pull the beds apart and hide in cupboards?

FLORA: [*Without spirit*] Then—*you* choose a game.

MILES: *I* shall.

MISS GIDDENS: You see, dear? Miles has an idea!

MILES: [*Rising from desk*] Dressing-up.

MISS GIDDENS: That's a wonderful game! I can remember "dressing-up" with my brothers and sisters on rainy days—why didn't I think of it! It's ever so much more fun than—well, than anything else I can think of! We used to pretend— Oh, a hundred things! Here—

use my handkerchief, dear— [Gives FLORA a handkerchief] Kings and queens—beggars and thieves!

FLORA: [Still crestfallen] May we?

MISS GIDDENS: [Rising to her feet] Of course you may.

MILES: Come along, then, Flora— [Takes her hand]

[They cross to staircase]

MISS GIDDENS: Why—where are you going—?

MILES: [At foot of staircase as FLORA continues up] To dress up— Didn't you say we may?

MISS GIDDENS: [Starting to follow them] I'll—I'll go with you.

MILES: But then you'd know what we were—there'd be no surprise—

[He turns and goes up the staircase to FLORA, who waits on landing. Together, they go into room, closing the door behind them. MISS GIDDENS remains at center, unable to move. She keeps her eyes on landing. Not the slightest sound is heard; it is as though the trees in the garden have stopped dripping, as though the earth itself has stopped turning]

MRS. GROSE: [Enters. Staring at MISS GIDDENS, then up at landing. Softly] Miss?

MISS GIDDENS: [Not turning. Almost inaudibly] I let them go— Mrs. Grose, I let them go—

MRS. GROSE: Where, miss—?

MISS GIDDENS: Up there— [All the bleakness of the garden seems to come indoors. She covers her face with her hands. Her voice comes wearily] I let them go— All morning I kept them with me. Now— I've let them go—

MRS. GROSE: Couldn't you stop them—?

MISS GIDDENS: [Her hands dropping from her face] How? What reason could I give them? I see a man at the window—I ask you who it is—you tell me who it was—that he is dead— [Violently] Last night it was as though a nightmare possessed me! It was a nightmare, I told myself—it would pass, it must pass! All the things I would have asked you had I been able—I couldn't come to you even when the children were in bed—I couldn't allow myself to think further—it was a nightmare! I told myself it would pass! But it is no longer dark—it is daylight. And I *know* it— A man, something that was a man, looked in at me *from its grave!* [*Her voice never rises above a harsh whisper*] Should I call them now? What shall I say to them?

MRS. GROSE: Miss—I—

MISS GIDDENS: [*Without interruption*] I can't go up after them! I made Flora cry because I wouldn't let her play hide-and-seek! Because I thought of them hiding—and of how I would go through the rooms and find each one empty! I would call to them—they wouldn't answer— They would be up there alone— What would come at them—first from one room and then—from another—? [*Terror*] *Why* has he come *back!* Do you think? [*Her words die away. She stares through the dimness at* MRS. GROSE. *Little but their faces can be seen—so feeble is the light from the garden—so strange at morning—so much more, this dimness, than that loss of light that comes from a cloud passing over the sun.* MISS GIDDENS *moves, slowly, across to* MRS. GROSE *until she is but a step from her*] Mrs. Grose— How did he die—?

MRS. GROSE: Quint? Quint died early one morning—on the road from the village. They said at the inquest that he had slipped on the icy slope. He had been drinking. There was a wound on his head—from falling, they said. But I saw him. It was I who found him. The wound was terrible. He had died in pain!—Such pain, miss!— It was there in his face. His eyes were still opened— It wasn't an accident. I knew it couldn't be—for there were things in his life that would have accounted for violence done him—

MISS GIDDENS: What things?

MRS. GROSE: [*Numbly, as though beaten*] Disorders— Secret disorders—vices I don't guess at—

[*Again, the silence crowds the room*]

MISS GIDDENS: [*As though a great weight presses on her*] They have never mentioned the time they were with him—his name—

MRS. GROSE: Don't try them—don't try them, miss—

MISS GIDDENS: Were they together—often—? Quint and Miles?

MRS. GROSE: [*Tremendous disgust bursting from her*] It wasn't *him*! It was Quint's own fancy! To spoil him! Quint was much too free!

MISS GIDDENS: [*As though struck in the face*] Too free with *him*? With that *child*?

MRS. GROSE: Too free with everyone!

MISS GIDDENS: Mrs. Grose!

MRS. GROSE: *I* knew it! But the Master didn't!

MISS GIDDENS: And you never told him?

MRS. GROSE: He hated complaints!

MISS GIDDENS: *I* would have told!

MRS. GROSE: I was wrong— I was wrong—but I was afraid—

MISS GIDDENS: Afraid? Afraid of what?

MRS. GROSE: Of Quint. No one could go against him. He fancied himself master. He used his position here to do what he wanted. Oh, he was handsome enough!—but evil—such power he had over people!— He was a devil—!

MISS GIDDENS: You were afraid of him! Not of his effect on the children? They were in your charge!

MRS. GROSE: No! They were not in mine! The Master hated complaints! If people were all right to *him*—he wouldn't be bothered with more! So Quint gave all the orders, even about them.

MISS GIDDENS: And you could bear it!

MRS. GROSE: No! I couldn't—and I can't now!

MISS GIDDENS: [*The thought striking her with tremendous power*] Why has he come back?— Not—not—

[*She turns, looks up at landing as the door opens slowly. Through doorway steps* FLORA. *She has dressed herself in what might have been a curtain once—heavily brocaded cloth that gleams about her shoulders, is caught at her waist by a ribbon to fall behind her in a long train. She wears a pincushion on her head. She steps, daintily, to the top stair. As she reaches halfway down the staircase,* MILES *appears on landing. He has wound a sheet about his head to form a turban. He bends down, gathers* FLORA's *train to him and so, moving slowly as though part of an outlandishly costumed*

*masque, they continue down the staircase. Not a sound
comes from* MISS GIDDENS]

FLORA: [*At foot of staircase*] I have borrowed your pincushion, if
you don't mind— [*Then she and* MILES *bow low to each other
and cross the room to the spinet. Thunder.* FLORA *stops, listens,
smiles*] Thunder— [MILES *bows to her and, taking a taper from
a box on the spinet, lights it and applies the flame to the candelabra*] Miss Giddens, dear? Would you sit there? [*She makes an
airy gesture toward the love seat.* MISS GIDDENS *and* MRS. GROSE
*obey silently. They sit, stiffly, hardly visible in the light from the
candelabra on the spinet.* MILES *arranges* FLORA'S *train about her
feet. They again bow to each other*] Now, I shall sing a song and
Miles shall play for me. [MILES *seats himself at the spinet, strikes
a chord.* FLORA, *very grandly, clasps her hands together and sings*]

> Once there was a merry king,
> Who had a face of blue—
> He lived in a room
> At the top of the stair
> With his handsome daughters two-oo,
> With his handsome daughters two.
>
> The older girl was tall and broad,
> The tallest girl was she.
> She combed her hair
> Each early morn
> With the top of a chestnut tree-ee,
> With the top of a chestnut tree.
>
> The younger girl was small and thin,
> The smallest girl was she—
> She washed her face
> In a walnut shell
> And galloped away on a flea-ee,
> And galloped away on a flea.

Now. Miles shall sing for you and I shall play.

[MILES *rises, bows to* FLORA, *dusts the spinet stool,*

helps her to it, and when she is seated, arranges her train.
He takes candelabra and holds it before him. Thunder. He
then bows to MISS GIDDENS *and* MRS. GROSE. FLORA *strikes a*
chord]

MILES: [*Candelabra in his hand*]

What shall I sing?
To my Lord from my window?
What shall I sing?
For my Lord will not stay—
What shall I sing?
For my Lord will not listen—
Where shall I go?
For my Lord is away—

Whom shall I love
When the moon is arisen?
Gone is my Lord
And the grave is His prison—

[*He begins to move upstage.* MISS GIDDENS *and* MRS. GROSE
watch him without moving. A strange, low vibration begins;
a discord of sound as though something is trying to enter
the room—soft but persistent]

What shall I say
When my Lord comes a-calling?
What shall I say
When He knocks on my door?
What shall I say
When His feet enter softly,
Leaving the marks
Of His grave on my floor?

[*He reaches window*]

Enter! My Lord! Come from your prison!
Come from your grave!
For the moon is arisen!

[*Thunder*]

[*As he sings the last line, he throws the window open. The silk curtains blow into the room. Stepping beyond the threshold, he remains there, framed in the window, looking off; the candles he holds flutter in the wind; the vibration rises with the wind. He remains motionless there*]

MISS GIDDENS: [*Rising from love seat, staring at him*] Mrs. Grose—! He knows! He *knows!*

[*The vibration stops abruptly*]

FLORA: [*Turning from spinet. A puzzled frown mixed with a strange half-smile on her face. Softly*] Knows what, Miss Giddens?

[*Thunder*]

SLOW CURTAIN

ACT TWO

That night.

FLORA *is heard singing as curtain rises.*

FLORA'S VOICE: [*From room beyond landing, singing*]
        O, bring me a bonnet,
        O, bring me a bonnet,
        O, bring me a bonnet of bright rosy red—
        With white roses on it,
        With white roses on it,
        O, bring me a bonnet to wear on my head—

> [*Halfway through song, lights come up. One lamp is lit. The curtains are drawn across window.* MRS. GROSE *stands by spinet, looking up at landing, listening to* FLORA'S *song*]

FLORA'S VOICE: [*She laughs as she stops singing*] Isn't that a lovely song, Miss Giddens?

MISS GIDDENS'S VOICE: It is— Now go to sleep—and don't pull the covers off. [MISS GIDDENS *appears on landing*]

FLORA'S VOICE: There's something dripping outside my window— Do come and see what it is?

MISS GIDDENS: It's just the rain.

FLORA'S VOICE: Is it *still* raining? I don't suppose we'll be able to go to church—shall we?

MISS GIDDENS: I'm sure it'll have stopped by morning—

FLORA'S VOICE: There's a beetle crawling on my neck!

MISS GIDDENS: Good night, Flora.

FLORA: [*Coming on to landing*] Is the box with the golden key opened yet?

MISS GIDDENS: [*Starting down staircase*] I'm afraid not.

FLORA: I know what's in it.

MISS GIDDENS: [*Continuing down staircase*] You can tell me in the morning. Go to sleep.

FLORA: [*Leaning on banister*] I *am* asleep. I'm having a lovely dream. I'm on a ship called Bly. We're going through a terrible storm. The waves are washing over the decks and—

MISS GIDDENS: [*At foot of staircase*] Flora! Go—to—bed this instant—

[FLORA *goes into her room immediately, closes door*]

MRS. GROSE: [*Softly*] Well, miss—? [*As* MISS GIDDENS *looks at her*] Forgive me, miss—but I thought, perhaps—whatever I may have said before—perhaps their uncle should be told—now— [*She falters*]

MISS GIDDENS: What should he be told, Mrs. Grose?

MRS. GROSE: I don't know for certain—but you would know what to say, miss—

MISS GIDDENS: How—how would I say it?

MRS. GROSE: You could write him—

MISS GIDDENS: And what would *you* say?— In a letter?

MRS. GROSE: But it isn't my place, miss—to write—

MISS GIDDENS: [*Intensely, but in a whisper*] Then put yourself in my place—understand what stops me. What would their uncle think if he should receive a tale of— After all—you haven't seen anything— What if *I* have been imagining things? Is there anything I could write that would make sense to him?

MRS. GROSE: Write, miss. Ask him to come—

MISS GIDDENS: And have him laugh at me? [*Desperately*] I've taken it on—whatever it is—

MRS. GROSE: There's only one thing that matters—the children mustn't be frightened—if you won't write—then, take them away!

MISS GIDDENS: [*A small panic*] Where?

MRS. GROSE: Anywhere—away from here—

MISS GIDDENS: If I took them away what good would that do? I should have to bring them back—this is their home— What reason would I give their uncle for keeping them away—?

MRS. GROSE: He won't ask, miss—

MISS GIDDENS: He would want to know *why,* if I kept them away!

MRS. GROSE: But we must protect them—

MISS GIDDENS: From what? From my imagination? What if I have been imagining things? Wouldn't it be better if *I* left?

MRS. GROSE: [*With horror*] You can't leave, miss!

MISS GIDDENS: I'm not trying to run from it!

MRS. GROSE: You *can't* leave unless you take them with you—away from here—

MISS GIDDENS: What if they see him—and pretend they don't—

MRS. GROSE: You mustn't think that— They wouldn't—

MISS GIDDENS: This morning—

MRS. GROSE: That—it was a childish game—!

MISS GIDDENS: It seemed a *game* to you! Was it more than that? Am *I* wrong in believing it *more than that?*

MRS. GROSE: [*Bewildered, despairing*] More?

MISS GIDDENS: You saw—and *heard* Miles!

MRS. GROSE: Playing a game!

MISS GIDDENS: You said Quint spoiled him—was too free with him—

MRS. GROSE: You can't blame Master Miles for that! No one could go against Quint!

MISS GIDDENS: What *effect* did it have on him!?

MRS. GROSE: [*She does not understand—but what she senses makes her protect* MILES—*always she believes him innocent*] On Master Miles? I saw nothing, nothing wicked in him— I've never said to you that I saw anything *bad*— I saw the restlessness in him, yes, to be with Quint—to talk to him—to ask him questions. [*Before* MISS GIDDENS *can speak*] But could you *blame* him for that? It was what *any* boy would feel having no father, needing a man's companionship—*Quint* encouraged him—

MISS GIDDENS: How!

MRS. GROSE: [*Unable to pull back*] How—? I— Taking him away from his lessons—continually— Taking him away for hours— [*Try ing to clarify it to herself, excuse it*] Miss Jessel—*she* was the governess—*she* didn't forbid it— What could *I* do? I could only watch and yet do nothing—to see—as I saw, from early morning, the restlessness in Master Miles to—go out across the garden—with *him*—holding on to *his* hand and asking questions in a voice that

came to me—clear as I stood at the window— I heard his questions
—but Quint's answers?—I never heard *them*.— *His* voice kept low
until it brought the child's down to a whisper—both figures moving
away— And I unable to go after them— [*For a moment, her
sobbing is the only sound.* MISS GIDDENS *seems held by the picture
created*] Miss Jessel—she didn't forbid it—and I—I was told—to
mind my business—

MISS GIDDENS: Then—you *were* aware of—

MRS. GROSE: Nothing wicked in Master Miles!

MISS GIDDENS: [*The picture is complete for her, suddenly—it needs
great control for her to be able to speak*] But you knew Quint for
what he was! Couldn't Quint have corrupted Miles? And couldn't
Miles have deceived you with pretended innocence!?

MRS. GROSE: Fooled me—?

MISS GIDDENS: Would he have wanted you to know?

MRS. GROSE: Know *what*, Miss—!?

MISS GIDDENS: Whatever they were—the things that Quint told him—
[*She stops in horror at what she suggested. She remains staring
into space as though the thought holds her—as though she elab-
orates upon it within herself—until, whatever conclusion she has
reached, it overpowers her. Weakly, spent with emotion*] I don't
know— Am I wrong—? I don't know—I don't know—let me sit in
your room for a while— [*She moves, slowly;* MRS. GROSE *follows
her—not looking at her*] I must be careful— [*Reaches desk, picks
up the lamp on desk*] I must be careful in what I think—

[*They exit. As room remains dark but for a faint gray
moonlight from the garden, a soft music enters—a suave
atonality—then a diminuendo until nothing but the loud
ticking of the clock is heard to sharpen each second that
passes—then, clearly, the clock chimes two—and a silence
follows—sudden and appalling.* MILES *closes door. From the
landing a small whiteness passes onto the stairs and down
to the room and across the faint light from the garden—it
disappears in the shadows down right—another whiteness
descends the stairs. From the spinet comes a run of notes—
then a quick brightness as a match is struck. In this light,*

FLORA *becomes visible as she lights a candle on the cande-*
labra and takes it with her to center. She wears a long white
nightgown. MILES *comes from staircase. He wears long white*
nightshirt. He stops and sits on floor, center. He is intent on
something that he creates on the floor before him—some-
thing that is soon recognizable as being the beginning of a
house-of-cards. FLORA, *standing at his side, watches silently*
as the miniature paper walls rise—then she bends down,
blows at them and they collapse. She and MILES *laugh softly,*
and the building of the house starts again. They are playing
a game, as children will, during forbidden hours, and their
movements are unhurried and self-assured. In the small light
of the candle, they seem self-contained, though, against the
high walls and along the wide floor, their shadows are dis-
torted and enormous as though other beings within the
same room]

MILES: [*Softly*] There is some cake in the pantry—

[FLORA *smiles and nods.* MILES *moves, quickly and silently,*
to door and off. FLORA *kneels before the cards strewn on the*
carpet—her left hand holds the candle above her head—her
right hand shifts the cards. She brings one close to her,
peering at it. As she does this, the FIGURE OF A WOMAN
appears on the landing—a woman dressed in deepest black
—tall and rigid. FLORA *carefully returns the card to its pack,*
slowly rises to her feet and, turning to landing, faces the
FIGURE *on the landing—stretching out her hand toward it.*
Music fades. As though in answer, a deep moan comes from
the FIGURE *on the landing—a wretched sound without pity*
for any—a sound which continues for a long moment. As
this moan dies away MISS GIDDENS *takes a single step into*
room. She carries a lighted candle. She stares directly at the
FIGURE *on the landing, then at* FLORA. *She sways as though*
about to fall. The FIGURE *moves away into the shadows of*
the landing and is no longer seen]

FLORA: [*Turns slowly and kneels again before the cards, her candle held high—fully aware of* MISS GIDDENS. *Singing softly, in a mono-tone, as she picks up one card and then another*]

     The queen of hearts
     She made some tarts
     All on a summer's day—

MISS GIDDENS: [*Her voice thin and like the scratch of a nail*] Who is it—!

FLORA: [*As though startled; dropping the candle*] Oh—! I've burnt my finger! How you startled me, Miss Giddens, dear!

MISS GIDDENS: [*As if she wakes from a nightmare*] Who is it!

FLORA: It is I, Miss Giddens—and— [*She giggles*] —won't Miles be surprised— He's in the pantry—

MISS GIDDENS: Who is it!

FLORA: [*Gently*] It is I—Flora— We've been naughty, Miles and I—

MISS GIDDENS: Who was that!

FLORA: Where—?

MISS GIDDENS: On the staircase!

FLORA: [*Turning to landing; as though bewildered*] There? There's no one there— [*Looking at* MISS GIDDENS; *as though about to cry*] You're frightening me—

MISS GIDDENS: You're *not* frightened!

FLORA: [*Laughs delightedly*] Oh, you're teasing me—! [*Turning to* MILES *as he enters, a plate of cake in his hand*] We're caught, Miles! Miss Giddens has caught us being naughty!

MILES: [*Smiling*] Is she very angry—?

FLORA: [*To* MISS GIDDENS, *who is standing rigidly*] You're not, are you? [*To* MILES, *who joins her*] I don't think she is—she's still half-asleep, I expect—and she'd like to get—to bed—and—so should we—and— [*She looks longingly at the plate in his hands*] —we'd better not have any cake— [*Her voice dropping to a whisper*] I don't think she'd like it if we did— [FLORA *places plate on spinet*] *I've* been punished—I burnt my finger—

  [*They cross to staircase and begin to go up to landing.* MISS GIDDENS *stares at them as though she does not see them. She seems self-contained in her terror and unbelief of what she has witnessed. They smile at her as they reach the top*]

FLORA: Good night, Miss Giddens—dear—

MILES: Good night, Miss Giddens—

[*They exit upstairs—closing the door softly behind them— like the miniature figures of an old clock*]

MISS GIDDENS: [*For a moment, she does not move. Then her head cranes forward. Numbly*] Who was it—? [*She goes to foot of staircase. At the foot of the stairs she stops. She looks toward the window. There is nothing there but the pale moonlight, the far, nebulous distances of the garden. She moves to the scattered cards, places the candlestick on the floor and kneels, slowly, beside it. Her hand moves against the cards. Whispers*] Who was it—? [*She rises slowly, goes to window—stands there, looking out to garden. Her hand goes up to curtain cord. Soundlessly, she draws the curtains together, cutting off the pale light from the garden, shutting herself in with the candlelight and the deep shadows of the room. Whispers*] Was it—? [*She shakes her head—a quick movement, as though something has caught itself in her hair. Now, as she speaks, her voice is thin, questioning—her words are directed toward herself—starting in a low monotone. Her voice is that of a woman talking in her sleep, the broken sentences meaning little in themselves—but together, fragmentary yet composing a whole, filling the room with the completeness of a nightmare. Her body passes through all the extremes of terror—from utmost rigidity to spasmodic tremblings*] I—I—I must sleep—I must sleep—I can't sleep— [*Her movements take her to the desk*] I must write—I must write— What shall I write—? What shall I say—? I must sleep— I can't think— I must write— [*Suddenly—running to foot of stairs—staring up at landing*] Who was it—? [*She becomes rigid*] Was it she—? [*She moves, stepping backwards—her eyes never leaving the landing which, untouched by light, is an emptiness beyond the stairs. She suddenly collapses to her knees, her hands saving the rest of her body from reaching the floor. She picks up a card as though seeing it for the first time. She drops it as if it were on fire. Her body crouches down until her arms cover her head, her hair touches the floor. No sound comes from her*]

[FLORA *appears on the landing. Silently, swiftly she moves down the stairs and to the window—almost without disturbing the curtains; she gets behind them. All at once, a high giggle is heard from the window.* MISS GIDDENS *lifts her head as though listening. She lifts herself from the floor. Her movements are uncertain as she goes to the window. Then, sharply, she pulls at the curtain cord. The curtains part.* FLORA *is standing quietly, facing into the garden*]

FLORA: [*Smiling at* MISS GIDDENS] Why, I thought I saw you walking in the garden—

[*She slips past* MISS GIDDENS, *who makes no move to stop her, and goes running across the room and up the staircase. No sound from her as she goes into her room, closing the door behind her.* MISS GIDDENS *pushes at the window. It swings open. The moonlight is brilliant, white but cold. It floods the room, throwing* MISS GIDDENS'S *shadow far behind her. She steps backwards into the room as the shadow of someone in the garden follows her. She stops.* MILES *appears at window. He is wearing his nightshirt—his feet are bare— he remains on the threshold*]

MISS GIDDENS: [*Her voice barely audible—unemotional—with the personality—her words are merely spoken*] How did you get into the garden—

MILES: [*Smiling, waiting a moment*] Through my window.

MISS GIDDENS: And why did you go out—? What were you doing there—

MILES: If I tell you—will you understand? [*Smiles*] I did it to have you do this—

MISS GIDDENS: Do what—

MILES: Think me, for a change, bad—when I'm bad I *am* bad— [*Laughs softly*]

MISS GIDDENS: [*Still in an unemotional monotone*] And—how did you know I would find out—

MILES: Oh—I planned that with Flora. She was to get up and look out—and you were to find her—and you did, didn't you?

MISS GIDDENS: You didn't think that I might be displeased.

MILES: Oh, yes. How otherwise should I have been bad enough? Are you angry?

MISS GIDDENS: Your feet are wet—you might catch cold—you must go to bed—

[*She does not move, but still faces the window as* MILES *comes from window and starts toward staircase*]

MILES: [*Stopping at stairs, turning to her slowly; speaking in a voice that is low and seemingly gentle*] Why don't you stop it?

MISS GIDDENS: [*Not turning; her voice still flat and unemotional*] Stop what, Miles—

MILES: [*After a long pause*] What you are doing—

MISS GIDDENS: [*Not turning*] What am I doing, Miles—

MILES: [*Although he does not raise his voice there is a new sharpness in it*] For one thing, you're meddling— You can't stop me going out if I choose to— You're just a governess— Wouldn't it be better if you remembered that? [*Starts to move across to staircase, his voice now charming and casual. He laughs softly, charmingly*] It is difficult, isn't it? This whole situation? [*Reaches staircase, starts up it. Speaking over his shoulder*] Couldn't you write to my uncle? [*As* MISS GIDDENS *neither answers nor moves*] You can't, can you? He so *hates* being bothered— [*Stops and looks at her for a moment*] Oh, it isn't that I mind being with you and Mrs. Grose and Flora— [*Smiling*] I rather like it—and I do like you— [*Turns and continues up to landing; on landing, he looks down at her and she, as though against her will, turns and looks up at him. He stares down at her smiling*] But is it the best thing? Being with a governess *all* the time? [*Pause. Then, very softly, casually*] A boy wants other things, you know— [*He turns away, enters his room and closes the door softly behind him*]

[MISS GIDDENS *remains in the strained, staring position she has taken. Her shadow curves and flickers in the candlelight —then, as though her body imitates the quivering of her shadow, she begins to tremble. Her mouth opens—no sound comes from her. She remains thus, caught within a palpita-*

*tion of terror. Then, as though awakening from a nightmare,
she screams:*]

MISS GIDDENS: Mrs. Grose—! [*As she screams, the clock chimes the
quarter-hour and, with this sudden sound, she moves—running to
door. She leans into the darkness, off*] Mrs. Grose—! [*As her
screams die away, a silence falls for a moment—then the sound of
the clock's ticking seems to swell. She turns from the door. Her
movements are mechanical, as though she feels the need of movement without reason. In the candlelight, she is a figure dwarfed by
shadow without substance.* MRS. GROSE *enters. She carries a candle;
her hair is in two braids, a shawl is about her shoulders, she wears a
nightgown. As* MRS. GROSE *enters,* MISS GIDDENS'S *words come pouring from her—her voice rising and falling—questioning—not waiting for an answer.* MRS. GROSE *stands in stunned silence. She looks
rapidly into every corner of the room*] Why have you kept it
from me!

MRS. GROSE: Miss—*miss*—I—

MISS GIDDENS: *What* have you kept from me? [*Twisting to look up at
landing*] You must tell me— Miss Jessel—why did she leave!
[*Turning again, to* MRS. GROSE] And—Miles— [*Going to* MRS.
GROSE—*close to her*] I'll make you tell me!

MRS. GROSE: [*A deep emotion beneath the bewilderment*] What has
she to do with Master Miles—?

MISS GIDDENS: *What* have you kept from me?

MRS. GROSE: Nothing— I promise you—nothing that could concern
you—

MISS GIDDENS: Why did she leave!

MRS. GROSE: [*Against her will*] I thanked heaven she left—

MISS GIDDENS: Why! Why?

MRS. GROSE: [*Not understanding—against her will*] She couldn't
have stayed— [*Returning* MISS GIDDENS'S *stare*] You ask why I
held back what I know? About *her*? Because I couldn't bring myself
to think about her! When she left— [*Without interruption*] —
when she left I wouldn't see her— Here—with two children! Not
caring, you see! Thinking only of herself and of *him*! (*Disgust dis-
torts her voice*] Using this house, every room—*any* room— I came

upon them once in this very room, sitting together, laughing together loudly. And then at night the dreadful silence that toward morning was broken by her weeping. I would hear her walking through the halls calling his name. He did what he wished with her. She left to go home, she said. And then we heard she had killed herself.

MISS GIDDENS: [*Harshness and repulsion*] And yet you let the children be with them? You should have taken them away!

MRS. GROSE: [*Sobbing*] They were not in my charge— I was in no position—

MISS GIDDENS: [*Harshly*] What if the children were aware of the relationship?

MRS. GROSE: No—!

MISS GIDDENS: What if they used the children to hide what went on between them?

MRS. GROSE: No—miss—

MISS GIDDENS: They made the children *lie* to you! How did they use them? What did they tell them, show them, *make* them do—!

MRS. GROSE: No, miss—no—it's not possible—

MISS GIDDENS: [*It is as though she speaks in her sleep; she speaks not only to* MRS. GROSE, *but also to herself—questioning and answering. And* MRS. GROSE *listens as though she is caught by the same dream*] She was here— [*Looking at the floor, then slowly looks up at landing*] —up there—a woman—Miss Jessel—her eyes fixed on Flora— fixed with a fury of intention—as though to get hold of her—to share with the child the torments she suffers. She's come back! [*Pause*] You don't believe me— Then ask Flora! [*Her hands over her face*] No—! She'll lie!

MRS. GROSE: [*With difficulty*] Miss—how *can* you!

MISS GIDDENS: [*Her hands drop to her sides*] And Miles— You should have heard him! Reminding me to keep my place!—not to *meddle*—in *what*? [*Looking up at landing*] The look he gave me as he reached the top of the stairs— [*Her head jerks away in revulsion*] It is difficult—even as one woman to another—to tell you what I felt as he stared down at me— He was not a child! I felt obscene.

MRS. GROSE: [*Going quickly to her*] Stop it, miss—! Stop it—! [*Takes* MISS GIDDENS *by the shoulders*]

MISS GIDDENS: [*Pauses as though for breath. A long drawn-out sigh comes from her; her voice is now piteous and pleading*] I am so tired— [*As* MRS. GROSE *again goes to her, takes her arm; gently, but with an emotion that is akin to fear*] Dear God, help me— I am so tired—!

THE LIGHTS FADE

SCENE 2

The following afternoon. Sunday.

Though it has not rained for hours, it is a grey day. The curtains are pulled open, the French window is open. Now and again, through the scene, the light brightens and fades as clouds move away from or crowd over the sun. The clock chimes half-past one. A few moments pass.

MISS GIDDENS *appears on landing.*

As MISS GIDDENS *reaches last stair,* MRS. GROSE *appears in garden, at window. She wears a bonnet; a shawl is about her shoulders.*

MRS. GROSE: [*Enters room*] Good afternoon, miss— [*She remains at window. She is obviously uneasy—uncertain as to what should be her next move*] I didn't wake you, miss. I hope I did right.

MISS GIDDENS: [*Her voice is flat, unemotional*] I heard you leave— I was not sleeping—I was writing a letter.

MRS. GROSE: [*Waits a moment. Then, softly; sighing*] I am glad, miss—

MISS GIDDENS: I have written to their uncle— I am resigning from this post—

MRS. GROSE: [*Coming toward her; anxiously*] Ah, miss—

MISS GIDDENS: [*Flatly*] You suggested I should write—

MRS. GROSE: Only to have him come here—to have him help—

MISS GIDDENS: He could only ask me to leave— I am saving him that trouble— [*With tremendous control to keep herself from screaming*] The responsibility is too great—

MRS. GROSE: No, miss, please—you can't—

MISS GIDDENS: [*Her voice under control*] —It is not an hysterical letter, Mrs. Grose— I shall wait for his answer— Then I shall leave— [*Desperately, though controlled*] I cannot stay here— [MRS. GROSE *is at a loss for words, but is obviously near to tears*] Until I leave, I shall do my best—after that— Where are the children—?

MRS. GROSE: In the garden, miss— I—

MISS GIDDENS: You *left* them—?

MRS. GROSE: [*Taken aback*] It isn't too damp, miss.— They promised to keep near the house—and—

MISS GIDDENS: [*Harshly*] Tell them to come in—

MRS. GROSE: [*She stares for a moment at* MISS GIDDENS] Yes, miss— [*To* FLORA, *outside window*] Oh, there you are. Miss Giddens wants you to come in. [*She turns abruptly away, goes to window and into garden*]

FLORA: [*Appears at window. She wears a bonnet, gloves, a neat Sunday-coat. She carries a hymnal in her hand. As she enters through window*] Very well. Miles and I were talking about the soloist. She had such a *squeaky* voice! Tra-la, she sang—but I thought she was choking. *I* wouldn't sing in a choir if I had a voice like that. Good afternoon, Miss Giddens—

MISS GIDDENS: Good afternoon—Flora— [*They remain where they are—as though each sizes up the other*] Flora—

FLORA: [*Looking down at the floor. Quickly*] Oh, look—a dead beetle! [*Kneeling down to look*] You'd never know it was dead except that it's on its back and isn't kicking— Miss Giddens? Can you hear a beetle's heart beating?

MISS GIDDENS: No.

FLORA: Can't you? *I* can. This one is quite dead—it isn't trampled on or anything. It's just dead. Decidedly dead. Do you suppose it smells? [*She bends down until her nose touches the floor*] It doesn't.

MISS GIDDENS: Throw it outside—Flora—

FLORA: [*Picking up the beetle*] Oh, no! Mayn't I keep it? [*Rising *quickly before* MISS GIDDENS *has a chance to speak*] I shall put it with my handkerchiefs and ribbons— [*Running to staircase*] Beetles don't decay, you know— [*Running up staircase*] They get drier and drier like a twig— [*Suddenly singing as she runs up to landing*]

> Beetles don't decay—
> Beetles don't decay—
> Beetles don't decay, my love,
> Beetles don't decay—

[*She runs into room, off landing, leaving the door open*]

MISS GIDDENS: [*Again a strange panic begins to possess her*] Flora—!

FLORA: [*From her room*] I won't be long. [*Singing*]

> Choose a ribbon-blue—
> Choose a ribbon-red—
> Better choose a ribbon-black,
> For the beetle's dead—

Oh! Miss Giddens!

MISS GIDDENS: [*Unable to move; staring up to landing*] What is it!

FLORA: [*Her head appearing through door of her room*] Another one! Another beetle! He was on my bed! Imagine finding beetles on Sunday! [*Her head disappears back into room. Singing*]

> Beetles on Sunday!
> Beetles on Sunday!
> What a lovely thing to find
> Two beetles on Sunday!

[*Coming out to landing*] There— They're tucked away in my ribbons. [*Running down stairs*] Mrs. Grose *hates* beetles. [*She stops, staring at* MISS GIDDENS *for a long moment. Then in an excited whisper*] Do you know what happened once?

MISS GIDDENS: [*Going to meet her; almost inaudibly*] Here—let me take off your hat—

FLORA: [*As* MISS GIDDENS *unties ribbons*] Once Mrs. Grose gave me some porridge and I ate all of it. And the last spoonful had a beetle in it! I chewed on it and I chewed on it and it tasted like twigs.

MISS GIDDENS: Let me take off your gloves—

FLORA: [*Stretching out her hand*] I said to Mrs. Grose: "Oh, look! I'm eating a beetle!" And she said: "Spit out the nasty thing, Miss Flora!" But I couldn't because I had swallowed it—and Mrs. Grose wouldn't believe it *was* a beetle—so I said: "Shouldn't *I* know how beetles taste?" And she got quite angry. [*As* MISS GIDDENS *suddenly kneels to pull her close and hold her tightly*] Why—you're crying— Miss Giddens, you're crying— Why are you crying? Are you ill, Miss Giddens, dear? You mustn't cry— It's not going to church that makes you feel that way, I expect— [*Pulling at* MISS GIDDENS *to make her rise; very gently*] We'll sit—over there— [*Nodding at love seat*] And you may help me cut out pictures for my paste-book— [*She leads* MISS GIDDENS *over to love seat—and* MISS GIDDENS, *sobbing with a low, dry sound, allows her, as though she has no will of her own*] Now—sit here and don't worry about a thing— [MISS GIDDENS *sits, her eyes tightly closed*] When Miles and Mrs. Grose come in we'll sing a song or two or maybe play a game—quietly, as it's Sunday— [*Going to French window, looking out*] I can see them—at the end of the garden. Miles has lost his hat, I think—the careless boy— [*Pause*] He's running away from Mrs. Grose and she's having difficulty chasing him.—He's throwing leaves at her, now— [*A strange, subtle sadness creeps into her voice*] They're having fun—but so are we—I don't wish I were out there. I'd rather be here with you— [*Her hands are clasped behind her back—she looks forlorn. Going to desk, pulling open a drawer, taking a sheaf of pages and scissors*] I haven't cut out pictures since last summer— Now you can tell me what they mean— Here's a picture of a porcupine—but it says it's a "Hysterix Cristata"— And here's a lizard—but underneath is written "Lacerta Calotes"— Why? Miss Giddens, why? [*She sits on love seat; frowning*]

MISS GIDDENS: [*In a low voice, not opening her eyes*] Those are Latin names—

FLORA: But *isn't* this a porcupine?

MISS GIDDENS: [*Opening her eyes to stare at page—blankly—her mind filled with other thoughts*] Yes.

FLORA: Then I shall paste it in my book and write "Porcupine" under it— [*She busies herself with the scissors*]

MRS. GROSE'S VOICE: [*Distantly, from the garden*] Master Miles! Master Miles!

FLORA: Miles is being naughty. [*Continues to cut*] I can't get all the bristles. They're too little. But they're so many that I don't think one or two will matter. [*She places cut-out beside her, carefully, and starts to cut another*] If it's clear tomorrow may we go out on the pond? It's pretty, though it's full of leaves and twigs— There's a little boat tied under the willows. Miles used to go there before he went away to school—

MISS GIDDENS: [*In a small, tight voice*] Alone?

FLORA: [*Intent on her cutting*] Oh, no. And he told me he saw a hand waving on the bottom but Mrs. Grose said: "Stuff and nonsense!" "Stuff and nonsense," she said!

MRS. GROSE'S VOICE: Master Miles! Master Miles!

MISS GIDDENS: [*Suddenly sitting up—her back rigid—her hands clenched in her lap—her voice sharp and cold*] With whom did Miles go?

[FLORA *stares at her. The light seeps away. Everything in the room seems to lose its solidity and to undulate as though under water*]

FLORA: [*Sharply*] Oh, dear! I know it's going to rain again! How dark everything's getting— I can hardly see—and it isn't even two o'clock. [*The excitement that possesses a child when a thunderstorm is imminent seems to take hold of her. She scatters the pictures as she jumps up from love seat*] I must cover my beetles, poor things! [*So quickly does she move that* MISS GIDDENS *has no time to stop her. She runs up staircase—singing as she runs*]

> Beetles don't decay!
> Beetles don't decay!
> Beetles don't decay, my love!
> Beetles don't decay!

MRS. GROSE'S VOICE: [*Nearer now*] Master Miles! Master Miles!

FLORA'S VOICE: [*From her room off landing*]

> Choose a ribbon—blue!
> Choose a ribbon—red!

Better choose a ribbon—black!
For the beetle's dead!

[MISS GIDDENS *does not call again—instead her eyes turn to look down right, where, a part of the shadows, stands the* FIGURE OF A WOMAN *as though just entering. Rigidly, this silhouetted* FIGURE *remains facing upstage, its head tilted toward the landing on which* FLORA *now reappears—her eyes downcast as she steps slowly from one stair to another. Her voice is low, as though she speaks to herself*]

FLORA: [*Softly*] The poor, poor things—thought I'd forgotten them —thought I'd leave them there—getting colder and colder—of course I wouldn't— [*Singing softly, eyes still on her feet as she descends staircase*]

Put him in a box—
Put him in a box—
Put the beetle in a box—

MRS. GROSE: [*Appearing at French window. Breathlessly, as she enters room*] Master Miles has hidden himself. Miss! I've called and I've called—and—

MISS GIDDENS: [*Rising from love seat in one movement. Forcing herself not to scream*] She's there—she's there! [MRS. GROSE *stops short. She stares at* MISS GIDDENS] Flora!

FLORA: [*On last stair; staring at* MISS GIDDENS] Yes—?

MISS GIDDENS: [*Rigid*] Look, Flora!

FLORA: [*Her eyes fixed on* MISS GIDDENS] I—I don't see anything—

MISS GIDDENS: There! There! There! You *see* her! You see her as well as you see me!

FLORA: I don't—I don't see anyone—*really*—truly—I don't— I don't see anyone— [*Screaming, as she runs across room to* MRS. GROSE, *who is staring, her hands over her mouth, at the* FIGURE] I'm frightened!

MRS. GROSE: [*Swiftly taking* FLORA *in her arms*] She isn't there! Nobody's there! How can she be? She's dead and buried! [*She faces* MISS GIDDENS; *all her protective instincts toward* FLORA *blotting out her terror*]

FLORA: [*Her face distorted with hatred—her voice choked and ugly—*

spitting the words at MISS GIDDENS] I see nothing! I never have!
You're cruel! Wicked! I hate you! I hate you! I hate you! [*Burying her head against* MRS. GROSE] Take me away—take me away
from her— She's cruel— Take me away from her— Take me
away— Take me away— She's cruel—wicked— I don't want to see
her again— I hate her— I hate her!

[FLORA'S *sobs rise as:*]

THE LIGHTS FADE

SCENE 3

Twilight. The same afternoon.

*The rain has passed, but through the window comes a
sulphurous light, coming directly into the room, which
seems to deepen the shadows of the far corners, to stress
them so that the room is divided into shadow and substance. A strong wind circles the house.*

MISS GIDDENS *is on the love seat.* MRS. GROSE *comes in.
She has a coat over her arm. She is dressed for traveling.
She is caught by the agitation of departure. Every moment
she remains in the house is one of added terror. She
comes, quickly, to the stairs. She speaks in a hushed voice.*

MRS. GROSE: Miss? Miss Giddens? [*Up to window, looking out to
garden*] Miss Giddens?
MISS GIDDENS: [*From love seat*] I am here.
MRS. GROSE: [*Startled; turning to her*] The carriage is waiting,
miss— Everything we'll need is packed: we must leave, now—
MISS GIDDENS: And Miss Flora?— Where is she?
MRS. GROSE: In my room— [*Embarrassed, but the importance of
departure uppermost in her mind*] She is dressed and waiting—
MISS GIDDENS: But she won't come down?
MRS. GROSE: [*Near to tears; fumbling*] She will—when we are
about to leave— I tried to get her to come to you—
MISS GIDDENS: [*Quietly*] But she wouldn't. I didn't expect her to.

MRS. GROSE: She will, miss— It's only that she is afraid— She's frightened as long as she is in this house—

MISS GIDDENS: Frightened? That is anger, Mrs. Grose.

MRS. GROSE: Ah, miss— If you could have heard her—

MISS GIDDENS: Crying? I did. And I heard you comforting her. I know all the tricks she must have played to get your sympathy.

MRS. GROSE: [Tears] It isn't that—it isn't. It's fear—so much fear in that child— She even made me promise—made me lock her in my room—

MISS GIDDENS: [Quietly] So that I could not get to her.

MRS. GROSE: But only because—because you might ask, again—

MISS GIDDENS: And because I wouldn't question her once we were in the carriage? I couldn't, could I?— With you there to stop me?

MRS. GROSE: I would have to. [Desperation] You are wrong about it—you couldn't be right— Thinking that—about her— [With tremendous agitation] Please, miss— You will see—once out of this house—how wrong you have been— [Looking down at the coat she is holding] Here is Master Miles's coat— Where is he? He must put his coat on— We must leave, quickly—

MISS GIDDENS: He is in the garden.

MRS. GROSE: [Turning to window] He must put his coat on— The carriage is waiting—

MISS GIDDENS: He knows that.

MRS. GROSE: I shall call him— We must all leave, now—

MISS GIDDENS: He is hiding. He's been hiding ever since he came back from church. He won't come to you.

MRS. GROSE: [Turning back; bewildered] Then—you call him, miss— The carriage is waiting—

MISS GIDDENS: He is not going.

MRS. GROSE: [Not grasping it] We all are—

MISS GIDDENS: He is staying here. With me.

MRS. GROSE: [Unable to move] Why—?

MISS GIDDENS: I think it best.

MRS. GROSE: [Horror] To keep him here? In this house?

MISS GIDDENS: You must take Miss Flora to her uncle.

MRS. GROSE: And not—Master Miles?

MISS GIDDENS: No. Not Master Miles.

MRS. GROSE: [*Desperation, horrified bewilderment*] Why? Why? You'd keep him here? Instead of taking him away? Why?

MISS GIDDENS: To face him with it.

MRS. GROSE: What you imagine? You'd face him with that?

MISS GIDDENS: [*Her control is wearing thin*] What I imagine? After what you saw this morning?

MRS. GROSE: Because of it—because of what I saw—we must take them away— [*Running to window*] Master Miles! Come in, Master Miles!

MISS GIDDENS: [*Raising her voice, but still with a tremendous control*] He won't come to you!

MRS. GROSE: [*Standing at window, her head bent, her whole body forced against her tears*] Make him!

MISS GIDDENS: He is hiding— I went looking for him— I called to him— Once, I thought I saw him, amongst the trees—spoke to him as if he *might* be there—telling him that I wanted to help him— asking him to come to me— There was no answer. Then I saw clearly—what I *must* do.

MRS. GROSE: And if he doesn't come—back?

MISS GIDDENS: The carriage will leave. He will think we've all gone. Then he will come to the house.

MRS. GROSE: If he does—how will you bring yourself to ask him— Can *you* face it? Not caring what you make a child meet with?

MISS GIDDENS: Not *caring*? You have seen—

MRS. GROSE: [*Violently; as credo*] Whatever I have seen—I cannot believe them part of it! That this house is filled with evil, yes, I believe that— But that the children are—? I cannot believe it! I cannot believe it!

MISS GIDDENS: They are.

MRS. GROSE: Take them away—let us take them away!

MISS GIDDENS: You can take Flora—she is young—she can be made to forget away from here— But Miles? Must end it here. It isn't easy for me—Mrs. Grose. I almost ran from it— I sat there and had my thoughts take hold of me so that I would have screamed had my breath obeyed me— All that was base in Quint lives in Miles. He lives with the memory, the longing for all that Quint taught him. I must free him of it. Even if I must hurt him.

MRS. GROSE: You'll drive him too far—! No child could survive such terrors—!

MISS GIDDENS: You will take Flora to her uncle. And you must give him my letter! I have written what I believe to be true. [*Searching desk drawer*] It isn't here—

MRS. GROSE: Think of the danger— Come away—

MISS GIDDENS: [*Blankly*] I put it here—in this drawer—

MRS. GROSE: Then where is it? No! He wouldn't do that—

MISS GIDDENS: [*Coldly, without emotion*] You shall have to tell their uncle— I know you will tell him the truth. As much of it as you understand. And, now, you must go. [*As though holding herself in readiness*]

MRS. GROSE: [*As she goes, slowly*] God help you. God help you both— [*Exits*]

> [MISS GIDDENS *does not move for a moment. Then she turns from the desk mechanically and goes to love seat and sits there. Her face is expressionless. She is rigid, waiting. A low music is heard: A sonorous, slow-moving, passing-of-time. With this music the twilight fades—seeps away—until she can be barely seen. The strong clatter of carriage wheels passes through the garden and is gone. The high sound of insects toward night can be heard—and, always, the harmonies cross each other, until, as though* MISS GIDDENS'S *thoughts merge into a single one, the clock is heard, alone: a climax of whirring works before chiming— As the chimes die away,* MILES *appears at the window, dimly seen—enters room. He comes into the room—crosses—starts to climb stairs—stops*]

MILES: Why are you sitting in the dark, Miss Giddens? I knew you'd still be here. [*She lights lamp*] You know—I might have stayed out there, in the garden, quite a bit longer.— Only I thought of you sitting here. I thought: "How dull for Miss Giddens!" I thought: "Why, I'm not doing anything to amuse her!" Rude of me, wasn't it?—leaving you alone? But I won't anymore. [*Sits*] Well, here we are. The two of us alone. I hope you don't mind?

MISS GIDDENS: Being alone with you? Not at all. What else should I stay on for? Miles, I want to talk to you. [*She is afraid but does not show it*] Miles— You know—or perhaps you don't—but, this is the first position I have ever held—

MILES: [*Lightly*] It's been too much for you? But Flora's gone and you were her governess— So it's sort of a holiday for you, isn't it?—not having her here?

MISS GIDDENS: You—are still in my charge.

MILES: [*Laughing for a moment*] Actually, I'm not your responsibility, you know.

MISS GIDDENS: You might as well accept me as being in charge of you.

MILES: Does it make you happier to think that you are? [*With a little bow*] Very well, then, whatever you wish.

MISS GIDDENS: What were you doing in the garden?

MILES: Haven't you ever been in a garden?

MISS GIDDENS: Yes.

MILES: Well? [*Laughs lightly*]

MISS GIDDENS: [*Pause*] Miles— You could help me by being honest.

MILES: I haven't lied—you haven't asked me anything I don't want to answer.

MISS GIDDENS: Are there such things?

MILES: You ask such funny questions! What was I doing in the garden. As though there were other things to do besides looking at or picking flowers or wading in the pond or climbing trees—

MISS GIDDENS: Then why didn't you come to me when I called you?

MILES: [*Amazement*] *Did* you? I *saw* you, you know. You were walking around, almost in a circle, looking from side to side as though you expected to meet someone—

MISS GIDDENS: Then why didn't you come to me!

MILES: I thought you wanted to be alone. I was quite close to you. I said: "Miss Giddens!"—in quite a loud voice—

MISS GIDDENS: That is not true! You never called to me! I should have heard you!

MILES: [*As though hurt*] Why on earth do you ask me questions if every time I answer you, you say it isn't true?

MISS GIDDENS: Because you are not answering me! Why don't you tell me the truth!

MILES: I do. But you pay no attention to it. [*Smiling*] Would you like it if I started asking *you* questions?

MISS GIDDENS: I'd answer them—

MILES: [*With terrible directness*] Why, then, aren't we with Mrs. Grose and Flora?

MISS GIDDENS: Because— [*Almost crying*] Ah, Miles, you won't come out with it yourself— How, then, can I?

MILES: [*With delight*] You see? You won't answer my question!

MISS GIDDENS: [*Pleading—no longer trying to control her tears—her tenderness*] Miles, I'm not a cruel person— However unfair I may seem to you—I am not cruel. Sometimes I am foolish— I make mistakes, and, at the moment, I am very tired. But I am not cruel. I was taught to love people and to help them— I was taught to help them even if, sometimes, they didn't want to be helped. Even if, sometimes, it should hurt them. Whatever you may have done, whatever you may have done—I am not against you. I have stayed here to help you— I don't think it's your fault. It *isn't* your fault— Won't you let me help you, won't you?

MILES: [*His whole body rigid. A sneering smile on his face. He stares at her for a full moment*] Why don't you stop pretending?

[*They do not move, nor do they take their eyes from each other for a long moment. An absolute silence fastens itself onto the room. Then* MISS GIDDENS *rises slowly. Her body is as rigid as* MILES's—*her back as though held by steel. She is stunned, emotionally, but she has not been swayed in her decision. She moves stiffly and with deliberate steps*]

MILES: What are you doing?

MISS GIDDENS: [*As she goes to desk, picks up tray of food and crosses to table*] You must be hungry— You—had—no—tea. I kept something for you. Sit down.

MILES: I'm not hungry.

MISS GIDDENS: Sit down.

MILES: [*Sitting down at table*] I've never eaten in here. It isn't a dining room. What would Mrs. Grose think? [*As* MISS GIDDENS *goes to love seat*] I'll get crumbs on the carpet— [*As* MISS GIDDENS *pays no attention to him*] Is Flora really ill?

MISS GIDDENS: [*Not looking at him*] She might have become so had she remained.

MILES: *Why* did Mrs. Grose lock her in her room today?

MISS GIDDENS: [*Looking at him as he apparently concentrates on eating*] Don't you know?

MILES: I can guess.

MISS GIDDENS: What?

MILES: [*Slight smile*] She had a fever.

MISS GIDDENS: [*Looking down at her embroidery*] She—did not have a fever. You know that.

> [*As* MISS GIDDENS *continues to sew, the figure of* QUINT *appears at the window, outlined against the darkness of the garden, his eyes on* MILES's *back. A high vibration is heard, rising as* MILES *stiffens in his chair, fully aware of* QUINT. *He begins to turn his head slowly. As he begins to turn his head,* MISS GIDDENS *raises hers to look at him. She is not aware of* QUINT. MILES *realizes this. With a sudden sweep of his hand he knocks his plate onto the floor. As the plate hits the floor, the vibration stops.* QUINT *disappears from window*]

MISS GIDDENS: Why did you do that!

MILES: [*Visibly trembling*] Because—because I wanted to! Now— I've made you angry.

MISS GIDDENS: I'm not angry, Miles.

MILES: [*His face strangely drawn*] Yes. You are. You're angry. We're alone and there isn't anyone to talk to and you're angry.

MISS GIDDENS: [*She kneels to pick up tray*] If I am—you've given me reason to be.

MILES: [*Tight-lipped. After a moment*] Weren't your brothers ever naughty?

MISS GIDDENS: Sometimes they were—when they were young.

MILES: And now? Are they wicked in a grown-up way?

MISS GIDDENS: I don't know.

MILES: [*His voice dying away; almost peevishly*] I—I wish I could go away—

MISS GIDDENS: [*After a long moment*] To another school—?

MILES: I don't think I should suit *any* school—

MISS GIDDENS: Why do you say that—?

MILES: [*Looking away from her*] Do you think I would?

> [*The light of the candles barely light* MISS GIDDENS *and* MILES]

MISS GIDDENS: I don't see any reason why you wouldn't— [*Pause*] You're like any boy—

MILES: [*Almost a whisper*] Am I? It would be easier, wouldn't it, if we were all alike? There would be no need for these conversations, and you wouldn't be upset and I—I'd be left alone. It's odd, though, but I don't think I'd like it much, and yet I am alone, even now, quite alone.

MISS GIDDENS: Miles!

MILES: [*Does not look at her*] And everything you do makes it worse. Because you don't think I'm like any boy, and you're so certain. [*Turning his head to look at her, slowly*] But *you* may be wrong, you know. [*Slow smile*] And if you are—what on earth shall you do? [*As* MISS GIDDENS *continues to look at him*] Is that why you're afraid? [*Softly, but with terrible directness*] You *are* afraid, you know— [*Looking at her. Then a sudden burst, and a strange temper*] Why is it so bad—my throwing things on the floor! Why! Other people can do—

MISS GIDDENS: But there's so much more—isn't there!

MILES: [*Looking down quickly, fumbling with his napkin, taking his time. Then in a small, careful voice*] Is there—? [*Softly*] Other kinds of—naughtiness—? —Or what?

MISS GIDDENS: The real reason why you were out in the garden when you were supposed to be in bed!

MILES: [*Quickly, trying to force a smile*] I *told* you it was to show you that I—

MISS GIDDENS: And you took a letter from the desk.

MILES: [*Looking from one spot on the floor to another. Finally staring down at his feet*] Yes. I took it.

[A long moment passes]

MISS GIDDENS: [A sharp whisper that has the quality of a scream] Why did you take it!

MILES: [Looking down] To see what you said about me—

MISS GIDDENS: You opened the letter?

MILES: I opened it—

MISS GIDDENS: [With a tremendous effort] And—what did you find—?

MILES: You said you were leaving—you said you had to leave— [Slowly looking up at her. He speaks the words with a careful directness—straight at her] You said: "Dear Sir, I think that I am ill—"

[Neither moves for a long moment. MILES never takes his eyes off MISS GIDDENS]

MISS GIDDENS: [Staring at him; her voice is low and unemotional] What did you do with the letter—?

MILES: I burnt it—

MISS GIDDENS: Did you take other things?— Is that what you did at school—?

MILES: Did I steal—?

MISS GIDDENS: Was it for that that you won't be allowed to go back—?

MILES: [He waits—as she does not answer] No. I didn't steal.

MISS GIDDENS: Then—Miles. What did you do—?

[A low vibration, beginning as an almost inaudible hum, fills the pause—ceasing with MILES's next words]

MILES: [Looking, as though in vague pain, all around the room—drawing his breath with difficulty] I—well—I said things—

MISS GIDDENS: To whom did you say them—

MILES: [He gives a sick little headshake] I don't remember their names—

MISS GIDDENS: Were there so many—?

MILES: No—only a few— [A sickly shame] Those I liked—

MISS GIDDENS: And they—repeated them—

MILES: To—those they liked. The Masters heard—I didn't know they'd tell.

MISS GIDDENS: The Masters never told— That's why I ask you—

MILES: [*In a low voice*] I suppose they were too bad—the things I said—to write home—

MISS GIDDENS: Miles—

MILES: [*Almost a whisper as he looks down at his feet*] Yes—?

MISS GIDDENS: Where did you first hear these things—?

[*Again the vibration is heard.* MILES *and* MISS GIDDENS *seem to freeze on* MISS GIDDENS's *last question*]

MILES: Why—I—I made them up—

MISS GIDDENS: Miles!

[*An answering throb, deep and vibrating, is heard*]

MILES: [*Whisper*] Yes—?

MISS GIDDENS: Who told you to say them?!

MILES: I made them up— I just told you that— [*Edging away from table*] They came into my head— [*He moves away, with small pauses, and a seemingly casual manner*] I would like to go to bed now. I am tired— May I?

MISS GIDDENS: What were they?! These things you said—?!

MILES: [*At spinet. Looking down at keys, a strange smile on his face*] You wouldn't like them.

MISS GIDDENS: What were they, Miles—?!

MILES: [*Not turning; still smiling*] You know so much—can't you guess, then?

MISS GIDDENS: Shall I tell you who it was that said them?

MILES: [*Looking at her; quickly*] It was a boy—a boy at school— that's all— I won't say them again— I promise—

MISS GIDDENS: Shall I tell you his name?!

MILES: [*Moving toward stairs; looking at the floor as he walks slowly*] What does it matter? It wasn't anything—

MISS GIDDENS: It wasn't a boy at school—!

MILES: [*Looking at her sharply*] You can't get away with this, you know! I know why you're doing this!

MISS GIDDENS: What did *he* say to you when you went walking by the pond?

MILES: [*Desperately*] This afternoon? Why, no one was there— Who would be there?

MISS GIDDENS: Not this afternoon!

MILES: When then? Yesterday?

MISS GIDDENS: [*Strongly*] *Not* yesterday. Before I came here—to live in this house.

[*Powerful vibration, sharp, ringing*]

MILES: I was at school!

MISS GIDDENS: And before that?!

[*Stronger, sharper vibration*]

MILES: [*His head thrust out toward her*] I know why you're asking me all these questions! You're afraid! That's why!

MISS GIDDENS: [*Cutting in sharply*] And not only the things you said—things you've done!—and what you *might* do—!

MILES: [*Ugly*] Oh, yes, I *might!* You're afraid—that's why you try to make me admit something— [*Swiftly looking at the window, then at MISS GIDDENS, then back to window, then again at MISS GIDDENS*]

MISS GIDDENS: Miles!

MILES: You're in it and you won't stop at anything, will you?

MISS GIDDENS: Miles! I want to help you! Let me help you!

MILES: You keep saying that! But there's nothing you can do, is there?! Because I know Flora isn't ill— You frightened her because you didn't know what else to do!

MISS GIDDENS: [*Moving toward him*] Miles!

MILES: [*Stepping backwards to staircase*] But *I'm* not a baby! What *are* you going to do! What will you say to my uncle! He'll laugh at you! [*The vibration grows all the while: strange tonalities pass above it. A desperation grows in MILES*] I'll tell him! I'll tell him what you're like! He'll believe me! He'll see what you are! Flora will tell him! *I'll* tell him! I'll tell him that you're vile— He won't believe what *you* say! Because you're dirty! Dirty! Dirty!

MISS GIDDENS: You've never stopped seeing him, have you, Miles!

MILES: Don't ask me, Miss Giddens!

MISS GIDDENS: You still want to be with him, don't you, Miles?

MILES: [*Before he can stop himself—a terrible scream*] He's dead!

> [As MILES *screams, the figure of* QUINT *appears at the window—standing there, against the darkness of the garden. All the musical vibrations stop. But a low thumping is heard—a sound as that of a heart—low and in a broken rhythm*]

MISS GIDDENS: [*Now with a desperate pleading*] Who, Miles! His *name!* Give me his name!

MILES: He's dead! He's dead!

MISS GIDDENS: Give me his name!

MILES: He'll hurt me! Stop it, Miss Giddens!

MISS GIDDENS: Reject him, for he is here, now, at the window!

MILES: Miss Giddens, you don't know, you don't know!

MISS GIDDENS: Reject him or he'll destroy you! I'm here to help you.

MILES: [*Clinging to her desperately*] You can't! Don't you see? You can't. You don't understand. He'll hurt me! You can't help!

MISS GIDDENS: You will be free! Confess! His name!

MILES: [*Breaking away; then with a tremendous directness*] Quint! Peter Quint!

MISS GIDDENS: Now! Miles, now!

> [*For a moment there is almost absolute silence—the only sound is the now loud thumping, as of a heart quickening its beat. For a second,* MILES *is still at landing, then, with a tremendous shudder, he forces himself to turn to the window*]

MILES: [*Facing the window, his arms flung before him. A scream*] Leave me—! Leave me—! [As he screams, QUINT's *arms rise before him as though to touch* MILES *across the distance.* MILES's *body begins to crumple. He half turns back to* MISS GIDDENS. *His voice comes thinly and piteously*] Miss Giddens—Miss Gidde— [*He spins as though to escape something. He tries to cry out again—but he falls to the ground*]

[*The sound of a heart stops.* QUINT *slowly disappears into the darkness of the garden*]

MISS GIDDENS: [*Moving as though suddenly released, swiftly she goes to* MILES *and kneels beside him, taking him in her arms as if cradling him*] He is gone—he is gone, Miles, dear Miles—and we're alone and nothing can hurt you anymore—nothing can hurt you— I am here and he—he has gone— He can never return. He has lost you and you are free— [*A soft, gentle music is heard— almost a lullaby*] Nothing can hurt you anymore—nothing can hurt you. There is only good in you now— Miles, dear Miles— [*She strains him to her*] You see? You are safe—you are safe and I am here with you—to hold you—to help you—to love you— [*Her words are a soft, weeping hysteria*] You see—? I have always wanted to help you—never to hurt you— It was almost too late, Miles, dear Miles—but you've won— You won back goodness and kindness— You are free— [*On these last words she looks down at* MILES]

> [*Slowly, her arms release his body, and absolute horror marks her face. As* MILES'S *body falls back, a thin, shrieking sound, a musical sound—but dissonant and piercing, is heard. A sudden wind comes from the garden. The silk curtains at the window blow into the room. Dried leaves swirl across the threshold of the window. Even the moonlight, cold and grey, seems to enter and surround* MISS GIDDENS *as she kneels beside* MILES'S *body*]

MISS GIDDENS: [*Her voice comes sobbingly*] —You are free—you're free. You're free—

> [*Then her sobs distort her words and cover them and hide them as:*]

SLOW CURTAIN

Night Must Fall

EMLYN WILLIAMS

Emlyn Williams

Almost forty years after it initially chilled London audiences, Emlyn Williams's *Night Must Fall* remains a classic of the macabre. A model of construction, it is designed with precise engineering of tension and suspense, "presenting Grand Guignol in the semi-realistic trappings of criminal psychology." Here, as critic Ivor Brown said, was "that scarcity, real horror . . . brilliantly imagined and as brilliantly enacted." It was an extraordinary tour de force and promptly established Emlyn Williams in the top rank of the theatre both as author and actor. It also started a fashion; the character of Dan, with his menacing, sultry charm, was one of the first, if not the first, of a long line of modern psychopathic killers of stage and screen.

Night Must Fall was the first play in which Emlyn Williams the dramatist deliberately wrote a part for Emlyn Williams the actor. "I'd had five plays produced in London, with varying degrees of success; I now badly wanted to write a new one. Just as badly, I wanted to play the leading part in it, for I was beginning to feel sure that there was only one living playwright sufficiently interested in my acting to write a part which only I could play. *Me*."

For years, Williams had been fascinated by real-life murders and accounts of murder trials and he was intrigued with the idea of writing a play in which the audience knew, as the curtain rose, that the murderer had not only "done it," but was to be hanged for his crime, then to proceed from there. The opportunity came to him in the summer of 1934 while riding in a London tube. An evening newspaper happened to be running a series on notorious crimes and on this particular day it recounted a 1929 murder that occurred in Margate. One Sidney Fox, aged twenty-eight, had murdered his invalid mother by setting fire to her for the insurance. In Williams's own words: "'Monster!' screamed the headline in the tube. 'Good gracious,' said the woman opposite me, 'look at his photo, you wouldn't think butter would . . .' Then she stared again. 'Good gr . . . but it's the Sidney somebody brought to tea at my auntie's in Surbiton the week before it happened, and he had a glass of milk instead of tea—but he was so nice and *ordinary* . . .' 'Monster!' screamed the front page. The train stopped, she got out. I did not know it, but I had the play."

Williams started off with Dan and his victim as mother and son, but (as often happens) found that "absolute truth in the theatre can be too shocking." He started notes. "Notes about Fox (and other murderers, one of whom dismembered his victim, another who lost his nerve to the point of keeping the dead body in his room for weeks) and for physical characteristics and idiom, a contemporary I knew who was not a criminal but might have been. For the facial picture of Dan, I did not have to look far: I put a fag-end between my lips and looked in the mirror."

Night Must Fall ran for 435 performances in London. It subsequently was presented in New York and in countless other cities of the world and in 1937 it was made into a film with Robert Montgomery. (A later version was released in 1963 with Albert Finney.) "Since then," Mr. Williams has written, "I am assured, there has not been, anywhere on the face of the globe, any aspiring young character actor, professional or amateur, who has not played the part. I believe it, when I recall the Dans who have since called to see me in every dressing room from Wolverhampton to Woollangong."

Emlyn Williams was born on November 26, 1905, in Mostyn, Flintshire, Wales. After studying at the Holywell County School under a remarkable teacher, Miss Cooke, who later served as the model for the character of Miss Moffat in his play, *The Corn is Green*, he won a scholarship to Christ Church, Oxford. It was there that he developed a passionate interest in the theatre and appeared for the first time on stage. It was there, too, that his first produced play, *Vigil*, was presented by the Oxford University Dramatic Society.

He made his professional acting debut in London in 1927 in *And So To Bed* and ever since, he has been one of the theatre's leading figures, often serving in a threefold capacity as playwright, actor, and director. In addition to *Night Must Fall*, Mr. Williams, as dramatist, has been represented on stage by the following plays, in most of which he also appeared: *A Murder Has Been Arranged; Port Said; Spring 1600; He Was Born Gay; The Corn is Green* (winner of the New York Drama Critics' Circle Award for the best foreign play, 1941); *The Light of Heart; The Morning Star; Pen Don; The Druid's Rest; The Wind of Heaven; Trespass; Accolade; Someone Waiting; Beth;* and three adaptations, *The Late Christopher Bean, The Master Builder,* and *A Month in the Country.*

As an actor in works of other authors, he has performed in dozens of plays including: *The Case of the Frightened Lady* (known here as *Criminal At Large*); *On the Spot; The Man I Killed; The Winslow Boy; Montserrat; Shadow of Heroes; Daughter of Silence; A Man for All Seasons; The Deputy;* and—what may well be his supreme acting triumph to date—his solo performances as Charles Dickens in *Bleak House* and *Mixed Bill,* in which he has toured extensively throughout the world.

He also has been seen frequently on screen, notably in: *The Citadel; They Drive By Night; Jamaica Inn; The Stars Look Down; Major Barbara; Hatter's Castle; The Last Days of Dolwyn; Ivanhoe; The Magic Box; The Deep Blue Sea; I Accuse; The Wreck of the Mary Deare;* and *The L-Shaped Room.*

He has published two books: *George,* an early autobiography, and *Beyond Belief,* a chronicle of the infamous Moors Murders that took place in Britain in the mid-sixties.

A recipient of many honors and awards during his long and successful career, Emlyn Williams won royal recognition in 1962 when he was made a Commander of the Order of the British Empire by Queen Elizabeth II.

Night Must Fall was first produced by J. P. Mitchelhill at the Duchess Theatre, London, on May 31, 1935. The cast was as follows:

THE LORD CHIEF JUSTICE	*Eric Stanley*
MRS. BRAMSON	*Dame May Whitty*
OLIVIA GRAYNE	*Angela Baddeley*
HUBERT LAURIE	*Basil Radford*
NURSE LIBBY	*Dorothy Langley*
MRS. TERENCE	*Kathleen Harrison*
DORA PARKOE	*Betty Jardine*
INSPECTOR BELSIZE	*Matthew Boulton*
DAN	*Emlyn Williams*

Directed by   Miles Malleson

Night Must Fall was first presented in the United States at the Ethel Barrymore Theatre, New York, on September 28, 1936, by Sam H. Harris. The cast was as follows:

THE LORD CHIEF JUSTICE	*Ben Webster*
MRS. BRAMSON	*Dame May Whitty*
OLIVIA GRAYNE	*Angela Baddeley*
HUBERT LAURIE	*Michael Shepley*
NURSE LIBBY	*Shirley Gale*
MRS. TERENCE	*Doris Hare*
DORA PARKOE	*Betty Jardine*
INSPECTOR BELSIZE	*Matthew Boulton*
DAN	*Emlyn Williams*

Directed by	Mr. Williams
(Based on the original London staging by	Miles Malleson)

BEFORE THE PLAY

The orchestra plays light tunes until the house lights are turned down; the curtain rises in darkness, accompanied by solemn music: the opening chords of Holst's "The Perfect Fool." A small light grows in the middle of the stage and shows the LORD CHIEF JUSTICE *sitting in judgment wearing wig and red robes of office, in the Court of Criminal Appeal. His voice, cold and disapproving, gradually swells up with the light as he reaches his peroration.*

LORD CHIEF JUSTICE: . . . and there is no need to recapitulate here the arguments for and against this point of law, which we heard in the long and extremely fair summing up at the trial of the appellant at the Central Criminal Court. The case was clearly put to the jury; and it is against sentence of death for these two murders that the prisoner now appeals. Which means that the last stage of this important and extremely horrible case has now been reached. On a later page in the summing up, the learned judge said this . . . [*Turning over papers*] . . . "This case has, through the demeanour of the prisoner in the witness-box, obtained the most widespread and scandalous publicity, which I would beg you most earnestly, members of the jury, to forget." I cannot help but think that the deplorable atmosphere of sentimental melodrama which has pervaded this trial has made the *theatre* a more fitting background for it than a court of law; but we are in a court of law, nevertheless, and the facts have been placed before the court. A remarkable and in my opinion praiseworthy feature of the case has been that the *sanity* of the prisoner has never been called into question; and, like the learned judge, the Court must dismiss as mischievous pretense the attitude of this young man who stands convicted of two brutal murders in cold blood. This case has, from beginning to end, exhibited no feature calling for sympathy; the evidence has on every point been conclusive, and on this evidence the jury have convicted the appellant. In the opinion of the Court there is no reason to interfere with that conviction, and this appeal must be dismissed.

> [*The chords of solemn music are heard again, and the stage gradually darkens. A few seconds later the music merges into the sound of church bells playing far away, and the lights come up on:*]

ACT ONE

*The sitting room of Forest Corner, Mrs. Bramson's bunga-
low in a forest in Essex. A fine morning in October.*

*Center back, a small hall; in its left side the front door of
the house. Thick plush curtains can be drawn across the
entrance to the hall; they are open at the moment. Windows, one on each side of the hall, with window seats and
net curtains beyond which can be glimpsed the pine trees
of the forest. In the left wall, upstage, a door leading to
the kitchen. In the left wall, downstage, the fireplace;
above it, a cretonne-covered sofa, next to a very solid cupboard built into the wall; below it a cane armchair. In the
right wall, upstage, a door leading to* MRS. BRAMSON's *bedroom. In the right wall downstage, wide-open paned doors
leading to the sunroom. Right downstage, next to the sunroom, a large dining table with four straight chairs round
it. Between the bedroom and the sunroom, a desk with
books on it, a cupboard below it, and a hanging mirror on
the wall above. Above the bedroom, a corner medicine
cupboard. Between the hall and the right window, an occasional table.*

*The bungalow is tawdry but cheerful; it is built entirely
of wood, with an oil lamp fixed in the wall over the occasional table. The room is comfortably furnished, though
in fussy and eccentric Victorian taste: stuffed birds, High-
land cattle in oils, antimacassars, and wax fruit are unobtrusively in evidence. On the mantelpiece, an ornate
chiming clock. The remains of breakfast on a tray on the
table.*

MRS. BRAMSON *is sitting in a wheelchair in the center of the
room. She is a fussy, discontented, common woman of*

fifty-five, old-fashioned both in clothes and coiffure; NURSE
LIBBY, *a kindly, matter-of-fact young north-country
woman in district nurse's uniform, is sitting on the sofa,
massaging one of her hands.* OLIVIA GRAYNE *sits on* MRS.
BRAMSON's *right, holding a book; she is a subdued young
woman of twenty-eight, her hair tied severely in a knot,
wearing horn-rimmed spectacles; there is nothing in any
way remarkable about her at the moment.* HUBERT LAURIE
is sitting in the armchair, scanning the Daily Telegraph.
*He is thirty-five, moustached, hearty and pompous, wear-
ing plus fours and smoking a pipe.*

A pause. The church bells die away.

MRS. BRAMSON: [*Sharply*] Go on.

OLIVIA: [*Reading*] ". . . Lady Isabel humbly crossed her attenuated
hands upon her chest. 'I am on my way to God,' she whispered,
'to answer for all my sins and sorrows.' 'Child,' said Miss Carlyle,
'had I anything to do with sending you from . . . [*Turning over*]
. . . East Lynne?' Lady Isabel shook her head and cast down her
gaze."

MRS. BRAMSON: [*Aggressively*] Now that's what I call a beautiful
character.

NURSE: Very pretty. But the poor thing'd have felt that much better
tucked up in 'ospital instead of lying about her own home, gassing
her 'ead off—

MRS. BRAMSON: Sh!

NURSE: Sorry.

OLIVIA: [*Reading*] "'Thank God,' inwardly breathed Miss Corny
. . . 'Forgive me,' she said loudly and in agitation. 'I want to see
Archibald,' whispered Lady Isabel."

MRS. BRAMSON: You don't see many books like *East Lynne* about
nowadays.

HUBERT: No, you don't.

OLIVIA: [*Reading*] "'I want to see Archibald,' whispered Lady
Isabel. 'I have prayed Joyce to bring him to me, and she will
not——'"

MRS. BRAMSON: [*Sharply*] Olivia!

OLIVIA: Yes, auntie?

MRS. BRAMSON: [*Craftily*] You're not skipping, are you?

OLIVIA: Am I?

MRS. BRAMSON: You've missed out about Lady Isabel taking up her cross and the weight of it killing her. I may be a fool, but I do know *East Lynne*.

OLIVIA: Perhaps there were two pages stuck together.

MRS. BRAMSON: Very convenient when you want your walk, eh? Yes, I *am* a fool, I suppose, as well as an invalid.

OLIVIA: But I thought you were so much better——

NURSE: You'd two helpings of bacon at breakfast, remember——

MRS. BRAMSON: Doctor's orders. You know every mouthful's agony to me.

HUBERT: [*Deep in his paper*] There's a man here in Weston-super-Mare who stood on his head for twenty minutes for a bet and he hasn't come to yet.

MRS. BRAMSON: [*Sharply*] I thought this morning I'd never be able to face the day.

HUBERT: But last night when you opened the port——

MRS. BRAMSON: I've had a relapse since then. My heart's going like anything. Give me a chocolate.

> [OLIVIA *rises and fetches her a chocolate from a large box on the table*]

NURSE: How does it feel?

MRS. BRAMSON: Nasty [*Munching her chocolate*] I *know* it's neuritis.

NURSE: You know, Mrs. Bramson, what you want isn't massage at all, only exercise. Your body——

MRS. BRAMSON: Don't you dictate to me about my body. Nobody here understands my body or anything else about me. As for sympathy, I've forgotten the meaning of the word. [*To* OLIVIA] What's the matter with your face?

OLIVIA: [*Startled*] I—I really don't know.

MRS. BRAMSON: It's as long as my arm.

OLIVIA: [*Dryly*] I'm afraid it's made like that. [*She crosses the room, and comes back again*]

MRS. BRAMSON: What are you walking up and down for? What's the matter with you? Aren't you happy here?

OLIVIA: It's a bit lonely, but I'll get used to it.

MRS. BRAMSON: Lonely? All these lovely woods? What *are* you talking about? Don't you like nature?

NURSE: Will that be all for today?

MRS. BRAMSON: I suppose it'll have to be.

NURSE: [*Rising and taking her bag from the sofa*] Well, I've that confined lady still waiting in Shepperley. [*Going into the hall*] Toodle-oo!

MRS. BRAMSON: Mind you call Wednesday. In case my neuritis sets in again.

NURSE: [*Turning in the hall*] I will that. And if paralysis pops up, let me know. Toodle-oo!

> [*She marches cheerily out of the front door.* MRS. BRAMSON *cannot make up her mind if the last remark is sarcastic or not. She concentrates on* OLIVIA]

MRS. BRAMSON: You know, you mustn't think just because this house is lonely you're going to get a rise in salary. Oh, no . . . I expect you've an idea I'm worth a good bit of money, haven't you? . . . It isn't my money you're after, is it?

OLIVIA: [*Setting chairs to rights round the table*] I'm sorry, but my sense of humour can't stand the strain. I'll have to go.

MRS. BRAMSON: Can you afford to go?

OLIVIA: [*After a pause, controlling herself*] You know I can't.

MRS. BRAMSON: Then don't talk such nonsense. Clear the breakfast things.

> [OLIVIA *hesitates, then crosses to the kitchen door*]

MRS. BRAMSON: [*Muttering*] Sense of humour indeed, never heard of such a thing.

OLIVIA: [*At the door*] Mrs. Terence, will you clear away? [*She goes to the left window, and looks out*]

MRS. BRAMSON: You wait, my girl. Pride comes before a fall. Won't catch a husband with your nose in the air, you know.

OLIVIA: I don't want a husband.

MRS. BRAMSON: Don't like men, I suppose? Never heard of them, I suppose? Don't believe you. See?

OLIVIA: [*Resigned*] I see. It's going to be a fine day.

MRS. BRAMSON: [*Taking up* East Lynne *from the table*] It'll cloud over, I expect.

OLIVIA: I don't think so. The trees look beautiful with the sun on them. Everything looks so clean. [*Lifting up three books from the window seat*] Shall I pack the other half of Mrs. Henry Wood?

MRS. BRAMSON: Mrs. Henry Wood? Who's Mrs. Henry Wood? Pack the other half of Mrs. Henry Wood? What *are* you talking about?

OLIVIA: She wrote your favourite book—*East Lynne*.

MRS. BRAMSON: [*Looking at her book*] Oh . . . [*Picking a paper out of it*] What's this? [*Reading ponderously*] A sonnet. "The flame of passion is not red but white, not quick but slow——"

OLIVIA: [*Going to her and snatching it from her with a cry*] Don't!

MRS. BRAMSON: Writing *poetry!* That's a hobby and a half, I must say! "Flame of passion . . ." *Well!*

OLIVIA: [*Crossing to the fireplace*] It's only a silly poem I amused myself with at college. It's not meant for anybody but me.

MRS. BRAMSON: You're a dark horse, you are.

[MRS. TERENCE *enters from the kitchen. She is the cook, middle-aged, Cockney and fearless. She carries a bunch of roses*]

MRS. TERENCE: [*Grimly*] Would you be wanting anything?

MRS. BRAMSON: Yes. Clear away.

MRS. TERENCE: That's Dora's job. Where's Dora?

OLIVIA: She's gone into the clearing for some firewood.

MRS. BRAMSON: You can't expect the girl to gather firewood with one hand and clear breakfast with the other. Clear away.

MRS. TERENCE: [*Crossing to the table, under her breath*] All right, you sour-faced old hag.

[HUBERT *drops his pipe.* MRS. BRAMSON *winces and looks away.* MRS. TERENCE *clears the table*]

HUBERT: [*To* OLIVIA] What—what was that she said?

MRS. TERENCE: She 'eard. And then she 'as to save 'er face and pretend she 'asn't. She knows nobody but me'd stay with 'er a day if I went.

MRS. BRAMSON: She oughtn't to talk to me like that. I know she steals my sugar.

MRS. TERENCE: That's a living lie. [*Going round to her*] Here are your roses.

MRS. BRAMSON: You've cut them too young. I knew you would.

MRS. TERENCE: [*Taking up her tray and starting for the kitchen*] Then you come out and pick the ones you want, and you'll only 'ave yourself to blame.

MRS. BRAMSON: That's a nice way to talk to an invalid.

MRS. TERENCE: If you're an invalid, I'm the Prince of Wales. [*She goes back into the kitchen*]

OLIVIA: Would you like me to read some more?

MRS. BRAMSON: No. I'm upset for the day now. I'd better see she does pick the right roses. [*Wheeling herself, muttering*] That woman's a menace. Good mind to bring an action against her. She ought to be put away. . . . [*Shouting*] Wait for me, wait for me!

[*Her voice dies away in the kitchen. The kitchen door closes.* HUBERT *and* OLIVIA *are alone*]

OLIVIA: That's the fifth action she threatened to bring this week. [*She crosses to the right window*]

HUBERT: She's a good one to talk about putting away. Crikey! She'll be found murdered one of these days . . . [*Suddenly reading from his paper*] "In India a population of three and a half hundred million is loyal to Britain; now——"

OLIVIA: Oh, Hubert! [*Good-humoredly*] I thought I'd cured you of that.

HUBERT: Sorry.

OLIVIA: You've only had two weeks of her. I've had six. [*A pause. She sighs restlessly*]

HUBERT: Fed up?

OLIVIA: It's such a very inadequate expression, don't you think . . . [*After a pause*] How bright the sun is today . . . [*She is pensive, far-away, smiling*]

HUBERT: A penny for 'em.

OLIVIA: I was just thinking . . . I often wonder on a very fine morning what it'll be like . . . for night to come. And I never can. And yet it's got to . . . [*Looking at his perplexed face*] It *is* silly, isn't it?

[DORA *comes in from the kitchen with a duster and crosses towards the bedroom. She is a pretty, stupid, and rather sluttish country girl of twenty, wearing a maid's uniform. She looks depressed*]

OLIVIA: Who are those men, Dora?

DORA: What men, miss?

OLIVIA: Over there, behind the clearing.

DORA: Oh . . . [*Peering past her*] Oh. 'Adn't seen them. What are they doing poking about in that bush?

OLIVIA: [*Absently*] I don't know. I saw them yesterday, too, further down the woods.

DORA: [*Lamely*] I expect they're looking for something. [*She goes into the kitchen*]

HUBERT: She looks a bit off-colour, doesn't she?

OLIVIA: The atmosphere must be getting her down, too.

HUBERT: I'm wondering if I'm going to be able to stand it myself. Coming over here every day for another week.

OLIVIA: [*Smiling*] There's nothing to prevent you staying at *home* every day for another week . . . is there?

HUBERT: [*Still apparently reading the paper*] Oh, yes, there is. What d'you think I invite myself to lunch every day for? You don't think it's the old geyser, do you?

OLIVIA: [*Smiling*] No. [*She comes down to the table*]

HUBERT: Don't want to sound rude, et cetera, but women don't get men proposing to them every day, you know . . . [*Turning over a page*] Gosh, what a wizard machine——

OLIVIA: [*Sitting at the left of the table*] I can't think why you want to marry me, as a matter of fact. It isn't the same as if I were very pretty, or something.

HUBERT: You do say some jolly rum things, Olivia, upon my soul.

OLIVIA: I'll tell *you* why, then, if it makes you feel any better. You're cautious; and you want to marry me because I'm quiet. I'd make you a steady wife, and run a home for you.

HUBERT: There's nothing to be ashamed of in being steady. I'm steady myself.

OLIVIA: I know you are.

HUBERT: Then why aren't you keen?

OLIVIA: [*After a pause, tolerant but weary*] Because you're an unmitigated bore.

HUBERT: A bore? [*Horrified*] *Me*, a bore? Upon my word, Olivia, I think you're a bit eccentric, I do really. Sorry to be rude, and all that, but that's put the kibosh on it! People could call me a thing or two, but I've never been called a bore!

OLIVIA: Bores never are. People are too bored with them to call them anything.

HUBERT: I suppose you'd be more likely to say "Yes" if I were an unmitigated bounder?

OLIVIA: [*With a laugh*] Oh, don't be silly . . .

HUBERT: [*Going to her*] You're a rum girl, Olivia, upon my soul you are. P'raps that's why I think you're so jolly attractive. Like a mouse one minute, and then this straight-from-the-shoulder business . . . What *is* a sonnet?

OLIVIA: It's a poem of fourteen lines.

HUBERT: Oh, yes, Shakespeare . . . Never knew you did a spot of rhyming, Olivia! Now that's what I mean about you . . . We'll have to start calling you Elizabeth Brontë! [*She turns away. He studies her*] You *are* bored, aren't you?

> [*He walks to the sunroom. She rouses herself and turns to him impetuously*]

OLIVIA: I'm being silly, I know—of course I *ought* to get married, and *of course* this is a wonderful chance, and——

HUBERT: [*Moving to her*] Good egg! Then you will?

OLIVIA: [*Stalling*] Give me a—another week or two—will you?

HUBERT: Oh. My holiday's up on the twenty-seventh.

OLIVIA: I know I'm being tiresome, but——

MRS. BRAMSON: [*In the kitchen*] The most disgraceful thing I've ever heard——

HUBERT: She's coming back . . .

[OLIVIA *rises and goes to the right window.* HUBERT *hurries into the sunroom.* MRS. BRAMSON *is wheeled back from the kitchen by* MRS. TERENCE, *to the center of the room.* MRS. BRAMSON *has found the pretext for the scene she has been longing to make since she got up this morning*]

MRS. BRAMSON: Fetch that girl here. This minute.

MRS. TERENCE: Oh, leave the child alone.

MRS. BRAMSON: Leave her alone, the little sneak thief? Fetch her here.

MRS. TERENCE: [*At the top of her voice*] Dora! [*Opening the front door and calling into the trees*] Dora!

OLIVIA: What's Dora done now?

MRS. BRAMSON: Broken three of my Crown Derby, that's all. Thought if she planted them in the rose-bed I wouldn't be well enough to see them, I suppose. Well, I *have* seen.

MRS. TERENCE: [*Crossing and calling to the bedroom*] You're wanted.

DORA'S VOICE: What for?

MRS. TERENCE: She wants to kiss you good morning, what d'you think . . .

[*She collects the table cloth, fetches a vase from the mantelpiece, and goes into the kitchen.* DORA *enters gingerly from the bedroom carrying a cup and saucer on a tray*]

DORA: Did you want me, mum?

MRS. BRAMSON: Crown Derby to you, my girl.

DORA: [*Uncertain*] Beg pardon, mum?

MRS. BRAMSON: I suppose you think that china came from Marks and Spencer?

DORA: Oh . . . [*Snivelling*] Oh . . . oh . . .

OLIVIA: [*Coming between* DORA *and* MRS. BRAMSON] Come along, Dora, it's not as bad as all that.

DORA: Oh yes, it is . . . Oh . . .

MRS. BRAMSON: You can leave, that's all. You can leave. [*Appalled,* DORA *drops the tray and breaks the saucer*] That settles it. Now you'll *have* to leave.

DORA: [*With a cry*] Oh, please I . . . [*Kneeling and collecting broken china*] Oh, ma'am—I'm not meself, you see . . . [*Snivelling*] I'm in—terrible trouble . . .

MRS. BRAMSON: Have you been stealing?

DORA: [*Shocked*] Oh, no!

OLIVIA: [*After a pause*] Are you going to have a baby?

[*After a pause*, DORA *nods*]

DORA: [*Putting the china in her apron*] The idea of me stealing . . . I do go to Sunday School anyways. . . .

MRS. BRAMSON: So that's the game. Wouldn't think butter would melt in her mouth . . . You'll have to go, of course; I can't have that sort of thing in this house—and stop squeaking! You'll bring my heart on again. It's all this modern life. I've always said so. All these films and rubbish.

OLIVIA: My dear auntie, you can't have a baby by just sitting in the pictures.

MRS. BRAMSON: Go away, and don't interfere.

[OLIVIA *goes to the left window.* DORA *rises*]

MRS. BRAMSON: [*Triumphantly*] So you're going to have a child. When?

DORA: [*Sniffling*] Last August Bank Holiday . . .

MRS. BRAMSON: What? . . . Oh!

DORA: I 'aven't got a penny only what I earn—and if I lose my job 'ere——

MRS. BRAMSON: He'll have to marry you.

DORA: Oh, I don't think he's keen . . .

MRS. BRAMSON: I'll *make* him keen. Who is the gentleman?

DORA: A boy I know; Dan his name is—leas' 'e's not a gentleman. He's a pageboy at the Tallboys.

MRS. BRAMSON: The Tallboys? D'you mean that new-fangled place all awnings and loudspeakers and things?

DORA: That's right. On the by-pass.

MRS. BRAMSON: Just the nice ripe sort of place for mischief, it always looked to me. All those lanterns . . . What's his character, the good-for-nothing scoundrel?

DORA: Oh, he's nice, really. He done the wrong thing by me, but he's all right, if you know what I mean . . .

MRS. BRAMSON: No, I don't. Where does he come from?

DORA: He's sort of Welsh, I think. 'E's been to sea, too. He's funny of course. Ever so open. Baby-face, they call him. Though I never seem to get 'old of what 'e's thinking somehow——

MRS. BRAMSON: I'll get hold of what he's thinking, all right. I've had my knife into that sort ever since I was a girl.

DORA: Oh, mum, if I got him to let you speak to him—d'you think, I could stay on?

MRS. BRAMSON: [*After a pause*] If he marries you at once.

DORA: Shall I—— [*Eagerly*] As a matter of fact, ma'am, he's gone on a message on his bicycle to Payley Hill this morning, and he said he might pop in to see me on the way back——

MRS. BRAMSON: That's right; nothing like visitors to brighten your mornings, eh? I'll deal with him.

DORA: Yes . . . [*Going, and turning at the kitchen door in impulsive relief*] Oh, ma'am——

MRS. BRAMSON: And I'll stop the Crown Derby out of your wages.

DORA: [*Crestfallen*] Oh!

MRS. BRAMSON: What were you going to say?

DORA: Well, ma'am, I *was* going to say I don't know how to thank you for your generosity . . .

[*She goes into the kitchen. The clock chimes*]

MRS. BRAMSON: Olivia!

OLIVIA: Yes, auntie?

MRS. BRAMSON: You've forgotten again. Medicine's overdue. Most important.

[OLIVIA *crosses to the medicine cupboard and fetches the medicine.* MRS. TERENCE *comes in from the kitchen with a vase of flowers and barges between the sofa and the wheelchair*]

MRS. TERENCE: [*Muttering*] All this furniture . . .

MRS. BRAMSON: [*To her*] Did *you* know she's having a baby?

MRS. TERENCE: [*Coldly*] She did mention it in conversation.

MRS. BRAMSON: Playing with fire, that's the game nowadays.

MRS. TERENCE: [*Arranging flowers as* OLIVIA *gives* MRS. BRAMSON *her medicine*] Playing with fiddlesticks. We're only young once; that 'ot summer too. She's been a fool, but she's no criminal. And, talking of criminals, there's a p'liceman at the kitchen door.

MRS. BRAMSON: A what?

MRS. TERENCE: A p'liceman. A bobby.

MRS. BRAMSON: What does he want?

MRS. TERENCE: Better ask 'im. I know *my* conscience is clear; I don't know about other people's.

MRS. BRAMSON: But I've never had a policeman coming to see me before!

[DORA *runs in from the kitchen*]

DORA: [*Terrified*] There's a man there! From the p'lice! 'E said something about the Tallboys! 'E—'e 'asn't come about me, 'as 'e?

MRS. TERENCE: Of course, he 'asn't——

MRS. BRAMSON: He may have.

MRS. TERENCE: Don't frighten the girl; she's simple enough now.

MRS. BRAMSON: [*Sharply*] It's against the law, what she's done, isn't it? [*To* DORA] Go back in there till he sends for you.

[DORA *creeps back into the kitchen*]

OLIVIA: [*At the left window*] He isn't a policeman, as a matter of fact. He must be a plainclothesman.

MRS. TERENCE: [*Sardonically*] Scotland Yard, I should think.

[BELSIZE *is seen outside, crossing the left window to the front door*]

MRS. BRAMSON: That place in those detective books? Don't be so silly.

MRS. TERENCE: He says he wants to see you very particular—— [*A sharp rat-tat at the front door. Going to the hall*] On a very particular matter . . . [*Turning on* MRS. BRAMSON] And don't you start callin' *me* silly! [*Going to the front door, and opening it*] This way, sir . . .

[BELSIZE *enters, followed by* MRS. TERENCE. *He is an en-*

tirely inconspicuous man of fifty, dressed in tweeds; his suavity hides an amount of strength]

BELSIZE: Mrs. Bramson? I'm sorry to break in on you like this. My card . . .

MRS. BRAMSON: [*Taking it, sarcastically*] I suppose you're going to tell me you're from Scotland Ya—— [*She sees the name on the card*]

BELSIZE: I see you've all your wits about you!

MRS. BRAMSON: Oh. [*Reading incredulously*] Criminal Investigation Department!

BELSIZE: [*Smiling*] A purely informal visit, I assure you.

MRS. BRAMSON: I don't like having people in my house that I don't know.

BELSIZE: [*The velvet glove*] I'm afraid the law sometimes makes it necessary.

[MRS. TERENCE *gives him a chair next to the table. He sits.* MRS. TERENCE *stands behind the table*]

MRS. BRAMSON: [*To her*] You can go.

MRS. TERENCE: I don't want to go. I might 'ave to be arrested for stealing sugar.

BELSIZE: Sugar? . . . As a matter of fact you might be useful. Any of you may be useful. Mind my pipe?

[MRS. BRAMSON *blows in disgust and waves her hand before her face*]

MRS. BRAMSON: Is it about my maid having an illegitimate child?

BELSIZE: I beg your pardon? . . . Oh, no! That sort of thing's hardly in my line, thank God . . . Lonely spot . . . [*To* MRS. TERENCE] Long way for you to walk every day, isn't it?

MRS. TERENCE: I don't walk. I cycle.

BELSIZE: Oh.

MRS. BRAMSON: What's the matter?

BELSIZE: I just thought if she walked she might use some of the paths, and have seen—something.

MRS. BRAMSON: Something of what?

MRS. TERENCE: Something?

BELSIZE: I'll tell you. I——

[*A piano is heard in the sunroom, playing "The Merry Widow" waltz*]

BELSIZE: [*Casually*] Other people in the house?

MRS. BRAMSON: [*Calling sharply*] Mr. Laurie!

[*The piano stops*]

HUBERT'S VOICE: [*As the piano stops in the sunroom*] Yes?

MRS. BRAMSON: [*To* OLIVIA, *sourly*] Did *you* ask him to play the piano?

[HUBERT *comes back from the sunroom*]

HUBERT: [*Breezily*] Hello, house on fire or something?

MRS. BRAMSON: Very nearly. This is Mr.-er-Bel——

BELSIZE: Belsize.

MRS. BRAMSON: [*Dryly*] Of Scotland Yard.

HUBERT: Oh . . . [*Apprehensive*] It isn't about my car, is it?

BELSIZE: No.

HUBERT: Oh. [*Shaking hands affably*] How do you do?

BELSIZE: How do you do, sir . . .

MRS. BRAMSON: He's a friend of Miss Grayne's here. Keeps calling.

BELSIZE: Been calling long?

MRS. BRAMSON: Every day for two weeks. Just before lunch.

HUBERT: Well——

OLIVIA: [*Sitting on the sofa*] Perhaps I'd better introduce myself. I'm Olivia Grayne, Mrs. Bramson's niece. I work for her.

BELSIZE: Oh, I see. Thanks. Well now . . .

HUBERT: [*Sitting at the table, effusively*] I know a chap on the Stock Exchange who was taken last year and shown over the Black Museum at Scotland Yard.

BELSIZE: [*Politely*] Really——

MRS. BRAMSON: And what d'you expect the policeman to do about it?

HUBERT: Well, it was very interesting, he said. Bit ghoulish, of course——

BELSIZE: I expect so . . . [*Getting down to business*] Now I wonder if any of you've seen anything in the least out of the ordinary round here lately? Anybody called—anybody strange wandering about in the woods—overheard anything?

[*They look at one another*]

MRS. BRAMSON: The only visitor's been the doctor—and the district nurse.

MRS. TERENCE: Been ever so gay.

HUBERT: As a matter of fact, funny thing did happen to me. Tuesday afternoon it was, I remember now.

BELSIZE: Oh?

HUBERT: [*Graphically*] I was walking back to my cottage from golf, and I heard something moving stealthily behind a tree, or a bush, or something.

BELSIZE: [*Interested*] Oh, yes?

HUBERT: Turned out to be a squirrel.

MRS. BRAMSON: [*In disgust*] Oh! . . .

HUBERT: No bigger than my hand! Funny thing to happen, I thought.

BELSIZE: Very funny. Anything else?

HUBERT: Not a thing. By Jove, fancy walking in the woods and stumbling over a dead body! Most embarrassing!

MRS. TERENCE: I've stumbled over bodies in them woods afore now. But they wasn't dead. Oh, no.

MRS. BRAMSON: Say what you know, and don't talk so much.

MRS. TERENCE: Well, I've told 'im all I've seen. A bit o' love now and again. Though 'ow they make do with all them pine needles beats me.

BELSIZE: Anything else?

MRS. BRAMSON: Miss Grayne's always moping round the woods. Perhaps *she* can tell you something.

OLIVIA: I haven't seen anything, I'm afraid . . . Oh—I saw some men beating the undergrowth—

BELSIZE: Yes, I'm coming to that. But no tramps, for instance?

OLIVIA: N-No. I don't think so.

HUBERT: Always carry a stick's my motto, I'd like to see a tramp try anything on with me. A-ha! Swish!

MRS. BRAMSON: What's all the fuss about? Has there been a robbery, or something?

BELSIZE: There's a lady missing.

MRS. TERENCE: Where from?

BELSIZE: The Tallboys.

MRS. BRAMSON: That Tallboys again——

BELSIZE: A Mrs. Chalfont.

MRS. TERENCE: Chalfont? Oh yes! Dyed platinum blonde—widow of a colonel, so she says, livin' alone, so she says, always wearing them faldalaldy openwork stockings. Fond of a drop, too. That's 'er.

HUBERT: Why, d'you know her?

MRS. TERENCE: Never set eyes on 'er. But you know how people talk. Partial to that there, too, I'm told.

MRS. BRAMSON: What's that there?

MRS. TERENCE: Ask no questions, I'll tell no lies.

BELSIZE: [*Quickly*] Well, anyway . . . Mrs. Chalfont left the Tallboys last Friday afternoon without a hat, went for a walk through the woods in this direction, and has never been seen since. [*He makes his effect*]

MRS. BRAMSON: I expect she was so drunk she fell flat and never came to.

BELSIZE: We've had the woods pretty well thrashed. [*To* OLIVIA] Those would be the men you saw. Now she was . . .

HUBERT: [*Taking the floor*] She may have had a brainstorm, you know, and taken a train somewhere. That's not uncommon, you know, among people of her sort. [*Airing knowledge*] And if what we gather from our friend here's true—and she's both a dipso-maniac *and* a nymphomaniac——

MRS. BRAMSON: Hark at the walking dictionary!

BELSIZE: We found her bag in her room; and maniacs can't get far without cash . . . however dipso or nympho they may be . . .

HUBERT: Oh.

BELSIZE: She was a very flashy type of wo—she *is* a flashy type, I should say. At least I hope I should say. . . .

MRS. BRAMSON: What d'you mean? Why d'you hope?

BELSIZE: Well . . .

OLIVIA: You don't mean she may be . . . she mayn't be alive?

BELSIZE: It's possible.

MRS. BRAMSON: You'll be saying she's been murdered next!

BELSIZE: That's been known.

MRS. BRAMSON: Lot of stuff and nonsense. From a policeman, too. Anybody'd think you'd been brought up on penny dreadfuls.

[OLIVIA *turns and goes to the window*]

BELSIZE: [*To* MRS. BRAMSON] Did you see about the fellow being hanged for the Ipswich murder? In last night's papers?

MRS. BRAMSON: I've lived long enough not to believe the papers.

BELSIZE: They occasionally print facts. And murder's occasionally a fact.

HUBERT: Everybody likes a good murder, as the saying goes! Remember those trials in the *Evening Standard* last year! Jolly interesting. I followed——

BELSIZE: [*Rising*] I'd be very grateful if you'd all keep your eyes and ears open, just in case . . . [*Shaking hands*] Good morning . . . good morning . . . good morning, Mrs. Bramson. I must apologize again for intruding——[*He turns to* OLIVIA *who is still looking out the window*] Good morning, Miss . . . er . . .

[*A pause*]

OLIVIA: [*Starting*] I'm so sorry.

BELSIZE: Had you remembered something?

OLIVIA: Oh, no . . .

MRS. BRAMSON: What were you thinking, then?

OLIVIA: Only how . . . strange it is.

BELSIZE: What?

OLIVIA: Well, here we all are, perfectly ordinary English people. We woke up . . . no, it's silly.

MRS. BRAMSON: Of course it's silly.

BELSIZE: [*Giving* MRS. BRAMSON *an impatient look*] No, go on.

OLIVIA: Well, we woke up this morning, thinking, "Here's another day." We got up, looked at the weather, and talked; and here we all are, still talking. . . . And all that time——

MRS. BRAMSON: My dear girl, who are you to expect a policeman——

BELSIZE: [*Quelling her sternly*] If you please! I want to hear what she's got to say. [*To* OLIVIA] Well?

OLIVIA: All that time . . . there may be something . . . lying in the woods. Hidden under a bush, with two feet just showing. Perhaps one high heel catching the sunlight, with a bird perched on the end of it; and the other—a stockinged foot, with blood . . . that's dried into the openwork stocking. And there's a man walking about somewhere, and talking, like us; and he woke up this morning, and looked at the weather . . . And he killed her. . . . [*Smiling, looking out the window*] The cat doesn't believe a word of it anyway. It's just walking away.

MRS. BRAMSON: Well!

MRS. TERENCE: Ooh, Miss Grayne, you give me the creeps! I'm glad it *is* nothing, that's all I can say . . .

BELSIZE: I don't think the lady can quite describe *herself* as ordinary, after that little flight of fancy!

MRS. BRAMSON: Oh, that's nothing; she writes poetry. Jingle jingle——

BELSIZE: I can only hope she's wrong, or it'll mean a nice job of work for us! . . . Well, if anything funny happens, nip along to Shepperley police station. Pity you're not on the phone. Good morning . . . Good morning.

MRS. TERENCE: This way . . . [*She follows* BELSIZE *into the hall*]

BELSIZE: No, don't bother . . . Good morning. . . .

[*He goes out.* MRS. TERENCE *shuts the door after him*]

MRS. BRAMSON: [*To* HUBERT] What are *you* staring at?

HUBERT: [*Crossing to the fireplace*] Funny, I can't get out of my mind what Olivia said about the man being somewhere who's done it.

MRS. TERENCE: [*Coming into the room*] Why, Mr. Laurie, it might be you! After all, there's nothing in your face that *proves* it isn't!

HUBERT: Oh, come, come! You're being a bit hard on the old countenance, aren't you?

MRS. TERENCE: Well, 'e's not going to walk about with bloodshot eyes and a snarl all over his face, is he? [*She goes into the kitchen*]

HUBERT: That's true enough.

MRS. BRAMSON: Missing woman indeed! She's more likely than not at this very moment sitting in some saloon bar. Or the films, I shouldn't wonder. [*To* OLIVIA] Pass me my wool, will you . . .

> [OLIVIA *crosses to the desk. A knock at the kitchen door.* DORA *appears, cautiously*]

DORA: *Was* it about me?

OLIVIA: Of course it wasn't.

DORA: [*Relieved*] Oh . . . please, mum, 'e's 'ere.

MRS. BRAMSON: Who?

DORA: My boy fr—my gentleman friend, ma'am, from the Tallboys.

MRS. BRAMSON: I'm ready for him. [*Waving aside the wool which* OLIVIA *brings to her*] The sooner he's made to realize what his duty is, the better. I'll give him Baby-face!

DORA: Thank you, ma'am. [*She goes out through the front door*]

HUBERT: What gentleman? What duty?

OLIVIA: The maid's going to have a baby. [*She crosses and puts the wool in the cupboard of the desk*]

HUBERT: Is she, by Jove! . . . Don't look at me like that, Mrs. Bramson! I've only been in the country two weeks. . . . But is *he* from the Tallboys?

MRS. BRAMSON: A pageboy or something of the sort.

> [DORA *comes back to the front door, looks back and beckons. She is followed by* DAN, *who saunters past her into the room. He is a young fellow wearing a blue pillbox hat, uniform trousers, a jacket too small for him, and bicycle-clips: the stub of a cigarette dangles between his lips. He speaks with a rough accent, indeterminate, but more Welsh than anything else. His personality varies considerably as the play proceeds: the impression he gives at the moment is one of totally disarming good humour and childlike unself-consciousness. It would need a very close observer to suspect that there is something wrong somewhere—that this personality is completely assumed.* DORA *shuts the front door and comes to the back of the sofa*]

MRS. BRAMSON: [*Sternly*] Well?

DAN [*Saluting*] Mornin', all!

MRS. BRAMSON: So you're Baby-face?

DAN: That's me. [*Grinning*] Silly name, isn't it? [*After a pause*] I must apologize to all and sundry for this fancy dress, but it's my working togs. I been on duty this mornin', and my hands isn't very clean. You see, I didn't know as it was going to be a party.

MRS. BRAMSON: Party?

DAN: [*Looking at* OLIVIA] Well, it's ladies, isn't it?"

HUBERT: Are you shy with ladies?

DAN: [*Smiling at* OLIVIA] Oh, yes.

[OLIVIA *moves away coldly.* DAN *turns to* MRS. BRAMSON]

MRS. BRAMSON: [*Cutting*] You smoke, I see.

DAN: Yes. [*Taking the stub out of his mouth with alacrity and taking off his hat*] Oh, I'm sorry. I always forget my manners with a cigarette when I'm in company. . . . [*Pushing the stub behind his ear, as* OLIVIA *crosses to the armchair*] I always been clumsy in people's houses. I am sorry.

MRS. BRAMSON: You know my maid, Dora Parkoe, I believe?

DAN: Well, we have met, yes . . . [*With a grin at* DORA]

MRS. BRAMSON: [*To* DORA] Go away! [DORA *creeps back into the kitchen*] You walked out with her last August Bank Holiday?

DAN: Yes. . . . Excuse me smiling, but it sounds funny when you put it like that, doesn't it?

MRS. BRAMSON: You ought to be ashamed of yourself.

DAN: [*Soberly*] Oh, I am.

MRS. BRAMSON: How did it happen?

DAN: [*Embarrassed*] Well . . . we went . . . did *you* have a nice Bank Holiday?

MRS. BRAMSON: Answer my question!

HUBERT: Were you in love with the wench?

DAN: Oh, yes!

MRS. BRAMSON: [*Triumphantly*] When did you first meet her?

DAN: Er-Bank Holiday morning.

MRS. BRAMSON: Picked her up, I suppose?

DAN: Oh, no, I didn't pick her up! I asked her for a match, and then I took her for a bit of a walk, to take her mind off her work——

HUBERT: You seem to have succeeded.

DAN: [*Smiling at him, then catching* MRS. BRAMSON's *eye*] I've thought about it a good bit since, I can tell you. Though it's a bit awkward talking about it in front of strangers; though you all look very nice people; but it is a *bit* awkward——

HUBERT: I should jolly well think it is awkward for a chap! Though of course, never having been in the same jam myself——

MRS. BRAMSON: I haven't finished with him yet.

HUBERT: In that case I'm going for my stroll. . . . [*He makes for the door to the hall*]

OLIVIA: You work at the Tallboys, don't you?

DAN: Yes, miss. [*Grinning*] Twenty-four hours a day, miss.

HUBERT: [*Coming to* DAN's *left*] Then perhaps you can tell us something about the female who's been murdered. [*An unaccountable pause.* DAN *looks slowly from* OLIVIA *to* HUBERT *and back again*] Well, *can* you tell us? You know there was a Mrs. Chalfont staying at the Tallboys who went off one day?

DAN: Yes.

HUBERT: And nobody's seen her since?

DAN: I know.

MRS. BRAMSON: What's she like?

DAN: [*To* MRS. BRAMSON] But I thought you said—or somebody said—something about—a murder?

HUBERT: Oh, we don't *know*, of course, but there *might* have been, mightn't there?

DAN: [*Suddenly effusive*] Yes, there might have been, yes!

HUBERT: Ever seen her?

DAN: Oh, yes. I used to take cigarettes an' drinks for her.

MRS. BRAMSON: [*Impatiently*] What's she *like*?

DAN: What's she like? . . . [*To* MRS. BRAMSON] She's . . . on the tall side. Thin ankles, with one o' them bracelets on one of 'em. [*Looking at* OLIVIA] Fair hair—— [*A sudden thought seems to arrest him. He goes on looking at* OLIVIA]

MRS. BRAMSON: Well? Go on!

DAN: [*After a pause, in a level voice*] Thin eyebrows, with white marks, where they was pulled out . . . to be in the fashion, you know. . . . Her mouth . . . a bit thin as well, with red stuff painted round it, to make it look more; you can rub it off . . . I suppose. Her neck . . . rather thick. Laughs a bit loud; and then it stops. [*After a pause*] She's . . . very lively. [*With a quick smile that dispels the atmosphere he has unaccountably created*] You can't say I don't keep my eyes skinned, can you?

HUBERT: I should say you do! A living portrait, if ever there was one, what? Now——

MRS. BRAMSON: [*Pointedly*] Weren't you going for a walk?

HUBERT: So I was, by Jove! Well, I'll charge off. Bye-bye. [*He goes out the front door*]

OLIVIA: [*Her manner faintly hostile*] You're very observant.

DAN: Well, the ladies, you know . . .

MRS. BRAMSON: If he weren't so observant, that Dora mightn't be in the flummox she is now.

DAN: [*Cheerfully*] That's true, ma'am.

OLIVIA: [*Rising*] You don't sound very repentant.

DAN: [*As she crosses, stiffly*] Well, what's done's done's my motto, isn't it?

[*She goes into the sunroom. He makes a grimace after her and holds his left hand out, the thumb pointing downward*]

MRS. BRAMSON: And what does that mean?

DAN: She's a nice bit of ice for next summer, isn't she?

MRS. BRAMSON: You're a proper one to talk about next summer when Dora there'll be up hill and down dale with a perambulator. Now look here, young man, immorality——

[MRS. TERENCE *comes in from the kitchen*]

MRS. TERENCE: The butcher wants paying. And 'e says there's men ferreting at the bottom of the garden looking for that Mrs. Chalfont and do you know about it.

MRS. BRAMSON: [*Furious*] Well, they won't ferret long, not among my pampas grass! . . . [*Calling*] Olivia! . . . Oh, that girl's never there. [*Wheeling herself furiously towards the kitchen as* MRS. TERENCE *makes a move to help her*] Leave me alone. I don't want to be pushed into the nettles today, thank you. . . . [*Shouting loudly as she disappears into the kitchen*] Come out of my garden, you! Come out!

MRS. TERENCE: [*Looking towards the kitchen as* DAN *takes the stub from behind his ear and lights it*] Won't let me pay the butcher, so I won't know where she keeps 'er purse; but I do know, so put that in your pipe and smoke it!

DAN: [*Going to her and jabbing her playfully in the arm*] They say down at the Tallboys she got enough inside of 'er purse, too.

MRS. TERENCE: Well, nobody's seen it open. If *you* 'ave a peep inside, young fellow, you'll go down in 'istory, that's what you'll do. [DAN *salutes her. She sniffs*] Something's boiling over.

> [*She rushes back into the kitchen as* OLIVIA *comes back from the sunroom*]

OLIVIA: Did Mrs. Bramson call me, do you know?

> [*A pause. He surveys her from under drooping lids, rolling his cigarette on his lower lip*]

DAN: I'm sorry. I don't know your name.

OLIVIA: Oh. [*She senses his insolence, goes self-consciously to the desk and takes out the wool*]

DAN: Not much doin' round here for a girl, is there? [*No answer*] It is not a very entertaining quarter of the world for a young lady, is it?

> [*He gives it up as a bad job.* DORA *comes in from the kitchen*]

DORA: [*Eagerly*] What did she . . . [*Confused, seeing* OLIVIA] Oh, beg pardon, miss. . . .

> [*She hurries back into the kitchen.* DAN *jerks his head after her with a laugh and looks at* OLIVIA]

OLIVIA: [*Arranging wool at the table*] I'm not a snob, but in case you ever call here again, I'd like to point out that though I'm employed by my aunt, I'm not quite in Dora's position.

DAN: Oh, I hope not. . . . [*She turns away, confused. He moves to her*] Though I'll be putting it all right for Dora. I'm going to marry her. And I——

OLIVIA: [*Coldly*] I don't believe you.

DAN: [*After a pause*] You don't like me, do you?

OLIVIA: No.

DAN: [*With a smile*] Well, everybody else does!

OLIVIA: [*Absorbed in her wool-sorting*] Your eyes are set quite wide apart, your hands are quite good . . . I don't really know what's wrong with you.

> [DAN *looks at his outspread hands. A pause. He breaks it and goes nearer to her*]

DAN: [*Persuasively*] You know, I've been looking at you, too. You're lonely, aren't you? I could see——

OLIVIA: I'm sorry, it's a waste of time doing your stuff with me. I'm not the type. [*Crossing to the desk and turning suddenly to him*] Are you playing up to Mrs. Bramson?

DAN: Playin' up?

OLIVIA: It crossed my mind for a minute. You stand a pretty poor chance there, you know.

DAN: [*After a pause, smiling*] What d'you bet me?

> [OLIVIA *turns from him, annoyed, and puts the wool away.* MRS. BRAMSON *careers in from the kitchen in her chair*]

MRS. BRAMSON: They say they've got permits to look for that silly woman—who are *they*, I'd like to know? If there's anything I hate, it's these men who think they've got authority.

OLIVIA: I don't think they're quite as bad as men who think they've got charm. [*She goes back into the sunroom.* DAN *whistles*]

MRS. BRAMSON: What did she mean by that?

DAN: Well, it's no good her thinkin' *she's* got any, is it?

MRS. BRAMSON: [*Sternly*] Now, young man, what about Dora? I——

DAN: Wait a minute . . . [*Putting his hat on the table and going to her*] Are you sure you're comfortable like that? Don't you think, Mrs. Bramson, you ought to be facin' . . . a wee bit more this side, towards the sun more, eh? [*He moves her chair round till she is in the center of the room, facing the sunroom*] You're looking pale, you know. [*As she stares at him, putting the stub in an ashtray on the table*] I am sorry. Excuse rudeness. . . . Another thing, Mrs.

Bramson—you don't mind me sayin' it, do you?—but you ought to have a rug, you know. This October weather's very treacherous.

MRS. BRAMSON: [*Blinking*] Pale? Did you say pale?

DAN: Washed out. [*His wiles fully turned on, but not overdone in the slightest*] The minute I saw you just now, I said to myself—now there's a lady that's got a lot to contend with.

MRS. BRAMSON: Oh . . . Well, I have. Nobody knows it better than me.

DAN: No, I'm sure. . . . Oh, it must be terrible to watch everybody else striding up and down enjoying everything, and to see everybody tasting the fruit——[*As she looks at him, appreciation of what he is saying grows visibly in her face*] I'm sorry . . . [*Diffidently*] I didn't ha' ought to say that.

MRS. BRAMSON: But it's true! As true as you are my witness, and nobody else—— [*Pulling herself together*] Now look here, about that girl——

DAN: Excuse me a minute . . . [*Examining her throat, like a doctor*] Would you mind sayin' something?

MRS. BRAMSON: [*Taken aback*] What d'you want me to say?

DAN: Yes . . .

MRS. BRAMSON: Yes. What?

DAN: There's a funny twitching in your neck when you talk—very slight, of course—nerves, I expect——But I hope your doctor knows all about it. . . . D'you mind if I ask what your ailments are?

MRS. BRAMSON: . . . Hadn't you better sit down?

DAN: [*Sitting*] Thank you.

MRS. BRAMSON: Well, I have the most terrible palpitations. I——

DAN: Palpitations? [*Whistling*] But the way you get about!

MRS. BRAMSON: Oh?

DAN: It's a pretty bad thing to have, you know. D'you know that nine women out of ten in your position'd be just sittin' down giving way?

MRS. BRAMSON: Would they?

DAN: Yes, they would! I do know, as a matter of fact. I've known people with palpitations. Somebody very close to me . . . [*After a pause, soberly*] They're dead now . . .

MRS. BRAMSON: [*Startled*] Oh!

DAN: My mother, as a matter of fact . . . [*With finely controlled emotion, practically indistinguishable from the real thing*] I can just remember her.

MRS. BRAMSON: Oh?

DAN: She died when I was six. I know that, because my dad died two years before that.

MRS. BRAMSON: [*Vaguely*] Oh.

DAN: [*Studying her*] As a matter o' fact——

MRS. BRAMSON: Yes?

DAN: Oh, no, it's a daft thing——

MRS. BRAMSON: [*The old tart note creeping back*] Come along now! Out with it!

DAN: It's only fancy, I suppose . . . but . . . you remind me a bit of her.

MRS. BRAMSON: Of your mother? [*As he nods simply, her sentimentality stirring*] Oh . . .

DAN: Have *you* got a son?

MRS. BRAMSON: [*Self-pityingly*] I haven't anybody at all.

DAN: Oh . . . But I don't like to talk too much about my mother. [*Putting a finger unobtrusively to his eye*] Makes me feel . . . sort of sad. . . . [*With a sudden thought*] She had the same eyes very wide apart as you, and—and the same very good hands.

MRS. BRAMSON: [*Looking interestedly at her fingers*] Oh? . . . And the same palpitations?

DAN: And the same palpitations. You don't mind me talking about your health, do you?

MRS. BRAMSON: No.

DAN: Well, d'you know you ought to get used to letting *other* people do things for you.

MRS. BRAMSON: [*A great truth dawning on her*] Yes!

DAN: You ought to be *very* careful.

MRS. BRAMSON: Yes! [*After a pause, eyeing him as he smiles at her*] You're a funny boy to be a pageboy.

DAN: [*Shyly*] D'you think so?

MRS. BRAMSON: Well, now I come to talk to you, you seem so much better class—I mean, you know so much of the world.

DAN: I've knocked about a good bit, you know. Never had any advantages, but I always tried to do the right thing.

MRS. BRAMSON: [*Patronizingly*] I think you deserve better—— [*Sharply again*] Talking of the right thing, what about Dora?

DAN: [*Disarming*] Oh, I know I'm to blame; I'm not much of a chap, but I'd put things straight like a shot if I had any money. . . . But, you see, I work at the Tallboys, get thirty bob a week, with tips—but listen to me botherin' you with my worries and rubbish the state you're in . . . well!

MRS. BRAMSON: No! I can stand it.

[OLIVIA *comes back from the sunroom*]

MRS. BRAMSON: [*Pursing her lips, reflectively*] I've taken a liking to you.

DAN: Well . . . [*Looking round at* OLIVIA] That's very kind of you, Mrs. Bramson.

MRS. BRAMSON: It's the way you talked about your mother. That's what it was.

DAN: Was it?

OLIVIA: [*At the left window*] Shall I pack these books?

DAN: [*Going to her with alacrity, taking the parcel from her*] I'll post them for you.

OLIVIA: Oh . . .

DAN: I'm passing Shepperley post office on the bike before post time tomorrow morning. With pleasure!

MRS. BRAMSON: Have you got to go back?

DAN: Now? Well no, not really . . . I've finished my duty now I done that errand, and this is my half-day.

MRS. BRAMSON: [*Imperiously*] Stay to lunch.

DAN: [*Apparently taken aback, after a look at* OLIVIA] Well—I don't like to impose myself——

MRS. BRAMSON: In the kitchen, of course.

DAN: Oh, I know——

MRS. BRAMSON: There's plenty of food! Stay to lunch!

DAN: Well—I don't know . . . all right, so long as you let me help a bit this morning. . . . Don't you want some string for this? Where's it kep'?

MRS. BRAMSON: That woman knows. In the kitchen somewhere.

DAN: Through here?

> [*He tosses the books on the sofa and hurries into the kitchen.* MRS. BRAMSON *holds out her hands and studies them with a new interest*]

MRS. BRAMSON: That boy's got understanding.

OLIVIA: Enough to marry Dora?

MRS. BRAMSON: You ought to learn to be a little less bitter, my dear. Never hook a man if you don't. With him and that Dora, I'm not so sure it wasn't six of one and half a dozen of the other. I know human nature, and mark my words, that boy's going to do big things.

> [*A scurry in the garden.* MRS. TERENCE *rushes in from the front door, madly excited*]

MRS. TERENCE: The paper boy's at the back gate, and says there's a placard in Shepperley, and it's got "News of the World—Shepperley Mystery" on it!

MRS. BRAMSON: What!

OLIVIA: They've got it in the papers!

MRS. TERENCE: They've got it in the papers! D'ye want any? [*Beside herself*]

MRS. BRAMSON: Catch him quick!

MRS. TERENCE: First time I ever 'eard of Shepperley being in print before—hi! [*She races out the front door*]

MRS. BRAMSON: Running around the house shouting like a lunatic! Sensation mad! Silly woman!

> [DORA *runs in from kitchen*]

DORA: They've got it in the papers!

MRS. BRAMSON: Go away!

MRS. TERENCE: [*Off*] I've bought three!

MRS. BRAMSON: [*Shouting*] Be QUIET!

> [MRS. TERENCE *runs back with three Sunday newspapers and gives one to* OLIVIA *and one to* MRS. BRAMSON]

OLIVIA: [*Sitting left of the table*] I expect it is a bit of an event.

MRS. TERENCE: [*Leaning over the table, searching in her paper*] 'E says they're selling like ninepins——

MRS. BRAMSON: [*Turning pages over, impatiently*] Where *is* it? . . .

MRS. TERENCE: Oh, I expect it's nothing after all. . . .

OLIVIA: Here it is . . . [*Reading*] "Disappeared mysteriously . . . woods round the village being searched" . . . then her description . . . tall . . . blonde . . .

MRS. TERENCE: Blonde? I should think she is . . . I can't find it!

OLIVIA: Here's something . . . "A keeper in the Shepperley woods was closely questioned late last night, but he has heard nothing, beyond a woman's voice in the woods on the afternoon in question, and a man's voice, probably with her, singing 'Mighty Lak a Rose.' Inquiries are being pursued . . ."

MRS. BRAMSON: "Mighty Lak a Rose." What rubbish! . . .

MRS. TERENCE: Oh, yes . . . It's the 'eadline in this one. [*Humming the tune absently as she reads*] "Don't know what to call you, but you're mighty lak a rose" . . . Those men have done rummaging in the garden, anyway.

MRS. BRAMSON: I must go this minute and have a look at my pampas grass. And if they've damaged it I'll bring an action.

MRS. TERENCE: Fancy Shepperley bein' in print——

MRS. BRAMSON: Wheel me out, and don't talk so much.

MRS. TERENCE: [*Manoeuvring her through the front door*] I could talk me 'ead off and not talk as much as some people I could mention.

> [OLIVIA *is alone. A pause. She spreads her paper on the table and finds* DAN's *hat under it. She picks it up and looks at it;* DAN *comes in from the kitchen with a ball of tangled string, a cigarette between his lips. He is about to take the books into the kitchen, when he sees her. He crosses to her*]

DAN: Excuse me . . . [*Taking the hat from her, cheerfully*] I think I'll hang it in the hall, same as if I was a visitor. . . . [*He does so, then takes up the books, sits on the sofa, and begins to unravel the string. A pause*] You don't mind me stayin' and havin' a bit o' lunch . . . in the kitchen, do you?

OLIVIA: It's not for me to say. As I told you before, I'm really a servant here.

DAN: [*After a pause*] You're not a very ordinary servant, though, are you?

OLIVIA: [*Turning over a page*] N-no. . . .

DAN: Neither am I. [*He unpicks a knot, and begins to hum absent-mindedly. The humming gradually resolves itself into faint singing*] "I'm a pretty little feller . . . everybody knows . . ." [OLIVIA *looks up; a thought crosses her mind. She turns her head and looks at him. The curtain begins to fall slowly. Singing, as he intently unravels the string*] "Don't know what to call me—but I'm mighty lak a rose . . ."

THE CURTAIN IS DOWN

ACT TWO

SCENE 1

An afternoon twelve days later. The weather is a little duller. MRS. BRAMSON is sitting on the right of the table in her invalid chair, puzzling out a game of patience. She has smartened up her appearance in the interval and is wearing purple, and earrings. OLIVIA is sitting opposite her, smoking a cigarette, a pencil and pad on the table in front of her; and is pondering and writing. A portable gramophone on a small table next to the desk is playing the H.M.V. dance record of "Dames", or any jaunty tune with suitable words. A pause. MRS. BRAMSON coughs. She coughs again, and looks at OLIVIA, waving her hand before her, clearing away billows of imaginary smoke.

OLIVIA: I'm sorry. Is my cigarette worrying you?

MRS. BRAMSON: [*Temper*] Not at all. I like it!

[OLIVIA *stubs out her cigarette with a resigned look and goes on making notes.* DAN *enters from the kitchen, keeping time to the music, carrying a bunch of roses, wearing overalls over flannel trousers and a brown golf jacket, and smoking. He goes to the fireplace and clumps the roses into a vase on the mantelpiece, humming the tune. He crosses to the gramophone, still in rhythm,* MRS. BRAMSON *keeping time skittishly with her hands. He turns off the gramophone and looks over* OLIVIA's *shoulder at what she is writing*]

DAN: [*Singing*] "Their home addresses . . . and their caresses . . . linger in my memory of . . . those beautiful dames" . . . [*His hand to his forehead*] That's me!

[OLIVIA *looks at him coldly and continues her notes*]

MRS. BRAMSON: It won't come out . . .

> [DAN *shrugs his shoulders, stands behind* MRS. BRAMSON'S *chair, and studies her play.* OLIVIA *follows his example from her side*]

OLIVIA: [*Pointing to two cards*] Look.

MRS. BRAMSON: [*Infuriated*] I saw that! Leave me alone, and don't interfere. [*A pause,* DAN *makes a quick movement and puts one card on another. Pleased and interested, quite unconscious of the difference in her attitude*] Oh, yes, dear, of course.

OLIVIA: [*As* MRS. BRAMSON *makes a move*] No, that's a spade.

MRS. BRAMSON: [*Sharply*] No such thing; it's a club. It's got a wiggle on it.

DAN: They both got wiggles on 'em. [*Pointing to another card*] This is a club.

MRS. BRAMSON: Oh, yes, dear, so it is!

OLIVIA: [*Writing*] The ironmonger says there *were* two extra gallons of paraffin not paid for.

MRS. BRAMSON: And they *won't* be paid for either—not if I have to go to law about it. [*A pause. She coughs absently*]

DAN: I'm sorry. Is my cigarette worrying you!

MRS. BRAMSON: Oh, no, dear.

> [*This has its effect on* OLIVIA. DAN *sits on the left of the table, where* East Lynne *is open on the table*]

MRS. BRAMSON: I'm sick of patience.

DAN: [*Reading laboriously*] "You old-fashioned child——"

MRS. BRAMSON: What?

DAN: *East Lynne.*

MRS. BRAMSON: Oh . . .

DAN: [*Reading*] "'You old-fashioned child!' retorted Mrs. Vane, 'Why did you not put on your diamonds?' 'I—did—put on my diamonds,' stay-mered Lady Isabel. 'But I—took them off again.' 'What on earth for?'" That's the other lady speaking there——

MRS. BRAMSON: Yes, dear . . .

DAN: "'What on earth for?' . . . 'I did not like to be too fine,' answered Lady Isabel, with a laugh"— [*Turning over*]—"and a blush. 'They glittered so! I feared it might be thought I had put them on to look fine.'"

MRS. BRAMSON: [*Absently*] Good, isn't it?

DAN: [*Flicking ash*] Oh, yes, realistic. . . . [*Reading*] "'I see you mean to set up among that class of people who pree-tend to dee-spise ornyment,' scornfully ree-marked Mrs. Vane. 'It is the ree-finement of aff-affectation, Lady Isabel——'"

[*An excited knock at the kitchen door.* DORA *enters.* DAN *turns back the page and surveys what he has been reading, scratching his head*]

MRS. BRAMSON: [*The old edge to her voice*] What is it?

DORA: Them men's in the wood again.

MRS. BRAMSON: What men?

DORA: The men lookin' for that Mrs. Chalfont.

[*A pause.* DAN *hums under his breath*]

MRS. BRAMSON: You don't mean to tell me they're still at it? But they've been pottering about since . . . when was that day Mr. Dan left the Tallboys?

DORA: [*Stressing a little bitterly*] Mister Dan?

DAN: [*Smiling*] Ahem! . . .

DORA: Mister Dan first came to work for you, mum, a week last Monday. . . .

MRS. BRAMSON: Well, I think it's a disgrace——

DORA: I've found something!

[DAN's *humming stops abruptly; he swivels round and looks at* DORA, *his face unseen by the audience.* OLIVIA *and* MRS. BRAMSON *stare at* DORA; *a pause*]

MRS. BRAMSON: You've found something?

OLIVIA: What?

DORA: [*Excitedly*] This!

[*She holds out her left arm and lets fall from her fist the length of a soiled belt. A pause.* OLIVIA *puts down her pencil and pad, goes to her, and looks at the belt*]

OLIVIA: Yes, of course, it's mine! I missed it last week. . . .

MRS. BRAMSON: [*Baulked of excitement*] Oh, yes, I thought I recognized it . . . What nonsense! . . .

[DAN *looks at her chuckling*]

DORA: [*Going, dolefully*] I'm ever so disappointed. . . .

[*She goes into the kitchen.* OLIVIA *goes to the armchair by the fireplace*]

MRS. BRAMSON: She'll be joining Scotland Yard next . . . Go on, dear.

DAN: [*Reading*] "'It is the ree-finememt of affectation, Lady Isabel—'" [*The clock chimes. Clapping his hands, to* MRS. BRAMSON] Ah!

MRS. BRAMSON: [*Pleased*] Oh, Danny . . .

[*He hurries to the medicine cupboard and pours medicine into a spoon.* HUBERT *comes in from the front door*]

HUBERT: [*Eagerly*] Have you heard?

MRS. BRAMSON: [*Eagerly*] What?

HUBERT: Dora's found a belt!

MRS. BRAMSON: [*Disappointed again*] Oh . . . It was Olivia's.

HUBERT: I say, what a shame! . . .

MRS. BRAMSON: Tch, tch! . . . All this sensation-mong—— [DAN *drowns her speech by deftly pouring the spoonful of medicine down her throat. He pushes her chocolate box towards her, and strides briskly into the hall*] Horrid. . . .

DAN: [*Taking a soft hat from the rack and putting it on*] Good for you, though, the way you are . . .

MRS. BRAMSON: Yes, dear.

DAN: [*Coming into the room, and beginning to take off his overalls*] And now it's time for your walk . . . [*Smiling at* OLIVIA] It's all right, I got trousers on . . . [*Peeling the overalls over his feet and tossing them on to the left window seat*] Listen to me talking about your walk, when you'll be in a chair all the time . . . [*Chuckling, to* HUBERT] That's funny, isn't it! . . . [*Going to*

MRS. BRAMSON] Come on, I got your shawl and your rug in the hall. . . .

MRS. BRAMSON: [*As he wheels her into the hall*] Have you got my pills?

DAN: I got them in my pocket.

MRS. BRAMSON: And my chocolates?

DAN: I got them in my pocket, too. Here's your hat—better put it on yourself.

MRS. BRAMSON: Yes, dear.

DAN: And here's your shawl.

MRS. BRAMSON: It isn't a shawl, it's a cape.

DAN: Well, I don't know, do I? And I carry your rug on my shoulder . . . [*To the others*] See you later! Be good! [*Shutting the front door, his voice dying, as the chair passes the left window*] Down this way today. . . .

[*A pause.* HUBERT *and* OLIVIA *look at each other*]

OLIVIA: [*Suddenly*] What do *you* think of him?

HUBERT: [*A little taken aback*] Him? Grannie's white-headed boy, you mean? Oh, he's all right. [*Heavily*] A bit slow in the uptake, of course. I wish he'd occasionally take that fag-end out of his mouth.

OLIVIA: He does. For *her*.

HUBERT: That's true. That's why he's made such a hit with her. Funny, I haven't been able to manage it. In two weeks too . . . it's uncanny.

OLIVIA: Uncanny? . . . I think it's clever.

HUBERT: You don't think he's a wrong 'un, do you?

OLIVIA: What do we know about him?

HUBERT: Why . . . his Christian name——

OLIVIA: And that's all.

HUBERT: He looks pretty honest.

OLIVIA: Looks? [*After a pause*] It's rather frightening to think what a face can hide . . . I sometimes catch sight of one looking at me. Careful lips, and blank eyes . . . And then I find I'm staring at myself in the glass . . . and I realize how successfully I'm hiding the thoughts I know so well . . . and then I know we're all . . .

strangers. What's behind *his* eyes? [*After a pause, with a smile*] You're quite right, it *is* morbid.

HUBERT: D'you think he's a thief or something? By Jove, I left my links on the washstand before lunch——

OLIVIA: He's acting . . . every minute of the time. I know he is! But he's acting pretty well, because I don't know *how* I know. . . . He's walking about here all day, and talking a little, and smiling, and smoking cigarettes. . . . Impenetrable . . . that's what it is! What's going on—in his mind? What's he thinking of? [*Vehemently*] He *is* thinking of something! All the time. What is it?

> [DAN *enters from the front door and smiles broadly at them*]

DAN: Anybody seen my lady's pills? It's a matter of life and death . . . I thought I had 'em.

> [*Hubert chuckles*]

OLIVIA: [*After a pause, in a level voice*] Oh, yes. They're in the top drawer of the desk. I'm so sorry.

DAN: Thank you.

> [*He salutes her, goes to the desk, and takes out the pills. They watch him*]

MRS. BRAMSON: [*Off*] Danny!

HUBERT: [*To say something*] Is she feeling off colour again?

DAN: [*On his way to the front door*] Off colour? She'd never been on it, man! To hear her go on you'd think the only thing left is artificial respiration. And chocolates. . . . [*Laughing and calling*] Coming! [*He goes, shutting the front door behind him*]

HUBERT: No, really, you have to laugh!

OLIVIA: But what you've just seen . . . that's exactly what I mean! It's acting! He's not being himself for a minute—it's all put on for our benefit . . . don't you see?

HUBERT: [*Banteringly*] D'you know, I think you're in love with him.

OLIVIA: [*With rather more impatience than is necessary*] Don't be ridiculous.

HUBERT: I was only joking.

OLIVIA: He's common and insolent, and I dislike him intensely.

[MRS. TERENCE *comes in from the kitchen*]

MRS. TERENCE: What'll you 'ave for tea, scones or crumpets? Can't make both.

OLIVIA: What *d'you* think of Dan?

MRS. TERENCE: Dan? Oh, 'e's all right. Bit of a mystery.

HUBERT: Oh.

MRS. TERENCE: [*Shutting the kitchen door and coming into the middle of the room*] Terrible liar, o' course. But then a lot of us are. Told me he used to 'unt to 'ounds and 'ave 'is own pack. Before 'e went up in the world and went as a pageboy I suppose.

OLIVIA: [*To* HUBERT] You see? He wouldn't try that on with us, but couldn't resist it with her.

HUBERT: I wonder how soon the old girl'll get his number? . . . Oh, but fair play, we're talking about the chap as if he were the most terrible——

MRS. TERENCE: Why, what's 'e done?

HUBERT: Exactly.

OLIVIA: I don't know, but I feel so strongly . . . Is Dora there? . . . [*Calling cautiously*] Dora!

MRS. TERENCE: Oh, she won't know anything. She's as 'alf-witted as she's lazy, and that's sayin' a lot. She'd cut 'er nose off to stop the dust bin smelling sooner than empty it, she would.

[DORA *comes in from the kitchen, wiping her hands on her apron*]

DORA: Did somebody say Dora?

OLIVIA: Has Dan said any more about marrying you?

DORA: No. *She* 'asn't brought it up again, either.

OLIVIA: Does he talk to you at all?

DORA: [*Perplexed*] Oh . . . only how-do-you-do and beg-your-pardon. I've never really spent any time in 'is company, you see. Except, o' course——

HUBERT: Quite. What's your idea of him?

DORA: Oh . . . [*Moving to the center of the room*] 'E's all right.

Takes 'is fun where 'e finds it. And leaves it. . . . Cracks 'imself up, you know. Pretends 'e doesn't care a twopenny, but always got 'is eye on what you're thinking of 'im . . . if you know what I mean.

OLIVIA: Yes, I do. That incredible vanity . . . they always have it. Always.

HUBERT: Who?

[A pause]

OLIVIA: Murderers.

[A pause. They stare at her]

HUBERT: Good God! . . .

MRS. TERENCE: D'you mean . . . this woman they're looking for?

OLIVIA: I'm sure of it.

MRS. TERENCE: But 'e's such a—such a ordinary boy——

OLIVIA: That's just it—and then he's suddenly so . . . extraordinary. I've felt it ever since I heard him sing that song—I told you——

HUBERT: That "Mighty Lak a Rose" thing, you mean? Oh, but it's a pretty well-known one——

OLIVIA: It's more than that. I've kept on saying to myself: No, murder's a thing we read about in the papers; it isn't real life, it can't touch us . . . but it can. And it's here. All round us. In the forest . . . in this house. We're . . . living with it [After a pause, rising decisively] Bring his luggage in here, will you, Mrs. Terence?

MRS. TERENCE: [Staggered] 'Is luggage? [Recovering, to DORA] Give me a 'and. [Wide-eyed, she goes into the kitchen, followed by DORA]

HUBERT: I say, this is a bit thick, you know—spying——

OLIVIA: [Urgently] We may never have the house to ourselves again.

[She runs to each window and looks across the forest. MRS. TERENCE returns carrying luggage; one large and one small suitcase. DORA follows, lugging an old-fashioned thick leather hatbox. MRS. TERENCE places the suitcase on the table; DORA plants the hatbox in the middle of the floor]

MRS. TERENCE: [*In a conspiratorial tone*] This is all.

HUBERT: But look here, we can't do this——

> [OLIVIA *snaps open the lid of the larger suitcase with a jerk. A pause. They look, almost afraid.* DORA *moves to the back of the table*]

MRS. TERENCE: [*As* OLIVIA *lifts it gingerly*] A dirty shirt . . .

HUBERT: That's all right.

OLIVIA: A clean pair of socks . . . packet of razor blades . . .

HUBERT: We shouldn't be doing this—I feel as if I were at school again.

MRS. TERENCE: Singlet . . .

OLIVIA: Half ticket to Shepperley Palais de Danse . . .

MRS. TERENCE: Oh, it's a proper 'aunt!

DORA: Oh, 'ere's a pocketbook. With a letter. [*She gives the letter to* MRS. TERENCE *and the pocketbook to* OLIVIA]

HUBERT: Look here, this is going a bit too far—you can't do this to a chap——

MRS TERENCE: [*Taking the letter from the envelope*] Don't be silly, dear, your wife'll do it to you 'undreds of times. . . . [*Sniffing the notepaper*] Pooh . . . [*Reading, as they crane over her shoulder*] "Dear Baby-face my own . . ." Signed Lil . . .

OLIVIA: What awful writing . . .

MRS. TERENCE: [*Reading heavily*] ". . . Next time you strike Newcastle, O.K. by me, baby . . ." Ooh!

HUBERT: Just another servant-girl . . . Sorry, Dora . . .

DORA: [*Lugubriously*] O.K.

OLIVIA: [*Rummaging in the pocketbook*] Bus ticket to Thorburton, some snaps . . .

MRS. TERENCE: Look at 'er *bust!*

OLIVIA: Here's a group . . . Look, Hubert. . . .

> [HUBERT *joins her in front of the table*]

HUBERT: This wench is rather fetching.

MRS. TERENCE: [*Coming between them*] Look at 'er! . . . The impudence, 'er being taken in a bathing suit! . . .

DORA: He's not in this one, is 'e?

HUBERT: [*Impressed*] Oh, I say . . . there *she* is!

MRS. TERENCE: ⎫
⎬ Who?
DORA: ⎭

HUBERT: The missing female! In front of the tall man. . . . You remember the photograph of her in the *Mirror?*

DORA: It's awful to think she may be dead. Awful . . .

MRS. TERENCE: Looks ever so sexy, doesn't she?

DORA: 'Ere's one of a little boy——

OLIVIA: How extraordinary . . .

HUBERT: What?

OLIVIA: It's himself.

DORA: The little Eton collar . . . Oh, dear . . . ever so sweet, isn't it?

MRS. TERENCE: Now that's what I call a real innocent face . . .

HUBERT: [*Going to the center of the room*] Well, that's that . . .

OLIVIA: Wait a minute, wasn't there another one? [*Seeing the hat-box*] Oh, yes . . .

HUBERT: [*Lifting it on to the chair*] Oh, this; yes . . .

DORA: Old-fashioned, isn't it?

MRS. TERENCE: I should think he got it from a boxroom at the Tallboys——

OLIVIA: [*Puzzled*] But it looks extraordinary——

[*She gives a sudden gasp. They look at her. She is staring at the box. A pause*]

HUBERT: What is it?

OLIVIA: I don't know . . . Suppose there is something . . . inside it?

[*A pause. They stare at her, fascinated by her thought. The front door bangs. They are electrified into action; but it is too late. It is* DAN. *He goes briskly to the table*]

DAN: She wants to sit in the sun now and have a bit of *East Lynne.* Talk about changin' her mind——[*He sees the suitcase on the table before him, and is motionless and silent. A pause. The others dare not move. He finally breaks the situation, takes up* East Lynne *from the table, and walks slowly back to the front door. He stops, looks at* HUBERT, *smiles and comes down to him. His manner is normal—too normal*] Could I have it back, please? It's the only one I got. . . .

HUBERT: Oh . . . yes, of course . . . [*Handing him the pocket-book*]

DAN: [*Taking it*] Thank you very much.

HUBERT: Not at all . . . I . . . [*To* OLIVIA] Here, you deal with this. It's beyond me.

DAN: [*To him*] Did you see the picture of me when I was a little fellow?

HUBERT: Yes . . . Very jolly.

DAN: [*Turning to* MRS. TERENCE] Did *you?* It was in the inside of my wallet.

MRS. TERENCE: Oh . . . was it?

DAN: Yes. Where I should be keeping my money, only any bit of money I have I always keep *on* me. [*Turning to* HUBERT] Safer, don't you think?

HUBERT: [*Smiling weakly*] Ye'es . . .

DAN: I only keep one ten-bob note in this wallet, for emergencies . . . [*Looking*] That's funny, it's gone. [*He looks at* HUBERT. *The others look blankly at one another*] . . . I expect I dropped it somewhere . . . what did you think of the letter?

HUBERT: Letter?

DAN: You got it in your hand.

HUBERT: Well, I didn't—er——

DAN: Means well, does Lil; but we had a row. [*Taking back the letter*] She would spy on me. And if there's anything I hate, it's spyin'. Don't you agree?

HUBERT: Ye'es.

DAN: I'd sooner have anything than a spy. [*To* MRS. TERENCE] Bar a murderer, o' course. [*A pause. He is arranging his property in his wallet*]

HUBERT: [*Incredulous*] What—what did you say?

DAN: [*Turning to him, casually*] Bar a murderer, o' course.

[OLIVIA *steps forward.* MRS. TERENCE *steps back from the chair on which the hatbox has been placed*]

OLIVIA: [*Incisively*] Talking of murder, do you know anything about Mrs. Chalfont's whereabouts at the moment?

> [DAN *turns to her, and for the first time sees the hatbox. He stands motionless. A pause*]

DAN: Mrs. Who?

OLIVIA: You can't pretend you've never heard of her.

DAN: [*Turning to* HUBERT, *recovering himself*] Oh, Mrs. Chalfont's whereabouts! I thought she said her name was Mrs. Chalfontswear. [*Profusely*] Silly . . . Swear—about—couldn't think——

OLIVIA: Well?

DAN: [*Still looking at* HUBERT, *brightly after a pause*] I've nothin' to go on, but I think she's been . . . murdered.

HUBERT: Oh, you do?

DAN: Yes, I do.

MRS. TERENCE: Who by?

DAN: They say she had several chaps on a string, and——[*Suddenly*] There was one fellow, a London chap, a bachelor, very citified—with a fair moust——[*He stares at* HUBERT]

HUBERT: [*Touching his moustache, unconsciously*] What are you looking at me for?

DAN: Well . . . you wasn't round these parts the day she bunked, was you?

HUBERT: Yes, I was, as a matter of fact.

DAN: [*Significantly*] Oh . . .

MRS. BRAMSON'S VOICE: [*Calling in the garden*] Danny!

HUBERT: [*Flustered*] What in God's name are you getting at?

> [DAN *smiles, shrugs his shoulders regretfully at him, and goes out through the front door.* OLIVIA *sits at the table*]

MRS. TERENCE: [*To* HUBERT, *perplexed*] Are you *sure* you didn't do it, sir?

HUBERT: I'm going out for a breath of air. [*He takes his hat and stick as he goes through the hall, and goes out through the front door*]

MRS. TERENCE: [*To* OLIVIA] You don't still think——

OLIVIA: I won't say any more. I know how silly it sounds.

[DORA *runs into the kitchen, snivelling*]

MRS. TERENCE: [*To* OLIVIA] The way you worked us all up. Doesn't it all go to show——

> [*She hears* DAN *return, and looks round apprehensively. He goes to the table slowly and looks at the two suitcases*]

DAN: [*Smiling to* MRS. TERENCE] Would you mind, please, givin' me a hand with the tidyin' up . . . [*Taking up the suitcases*] And carryin' the other one? . . . [*Going into the kitchen, followed by* MRS. TERENCE *carrying the hatbox*] Looks as if we're goin' on our holidays, doesn't it? . . .

> [OLIVIA *is alone for a moment. She stares before her, perplexed.* DAN *returns. She looks away. He looks at her, his eyes narrowed. A pause. Studying her, he takes from the pocket of his jacket a formidable-looking clasp-knife, unclasps it, and tests the blade casually with his fingers. He glances at the mantelpiece, crosses to it, takes down a stick and begins to sharpen the end of it.* OLIVIA *watches him. A pause*]

OLIVIA: Did you do it?

> [*He whittles at the stick*]

DAN: You wouldn't be bad lookin' without them glasses.

OLIVIA: It doesn't interest me very much what I look like.

DAN: Don't you believe it. . . . [*Surveying the shavings in the hearth*] Tch! . . . Clumsy . . . [*Looking round and seeing a newspaper lying on the table*] Ah . . . [*Crossing to the table, then smiling, with the suspicion of a mock bow*] Excuse me . . . [*He unfolds the newspaper on the table and begins to whittle the stick over it*]

OLIVIA: You're very conceited, aren't you?

DAN: [*Reassuringly*] Yes. . . .

OLIVIA: And you *are* acting all the time, aren't you?

DAN: [*Staring at her, as if astonished*] Actin'? Actin' what? [*Leaning over the table, on both arms*] Look at the way I can look you in the eyes. I'll stare you out. . . .

OLIVIA: [*Staring into his eyes*] I have a theory it's the criminals who *can* look you in the eyes, and the honest people who blush and look away.

DAN: [*Smiling*] Oh . . .

OLIVIA: [*After a pause, challenging*] It's a very blank look, though, isn't it?

DAN: [*Smiling*] Is it?

OLIVIA: You *are* acting, aren't you?

DAN: [*After a pause, in a whisper, almost joyfully*] Yes!

OLIVIA: [*Fascinated*]: And what are you like when you stop acting?

DAN: I dunno, it's so long since I stopped.

OLIVIA: But when you're alone?

DAN: Then I act more than ever I do.

OLIVIA: Why?

DAN: I dunno; 'cause I like it . . . [*Breaking the scene, pulling a chair round to the table*] Now what d'ye say if *I* ask a question or two for a change? [*Sitting in the chair, facing her*] Just for a change . . . Why can't you take a bit of an interest in some other body but me?

OLIVIA: [*Taken aback*] I'm not interested in you. Only you don't talk. That's bound to make people wonder.

DAN: I can talk a lot sometimes. A drop o' drink makes a power o' difference to me. [*Chuckling*] You'd be surprised. . . . Ah . . . [*He returns to his work*]

OLIVIA: I wonder if I would. . . .

DAN: I know you would. . . .

OLIVIA: I think I can diagnose you all right.

DAN: Carry on.

OLIVIA: You haven't any feelings . . . at all . . . [*He looks slowly up at her. She has struck home*] But you live in a world of your own . . . A world of your own imagination.

DAN: I don't understand so very well, not bein' so very liter-er-airy.

OLIVIA: You follow me perfectly well.

[*He shrugs his shoulders, laughs, and goes on whittling*]

DAN: D'you still think there's been a bit o' dirty work?

OLIVIA: I don't know what to think now. I suppose not.

DAN: [*Intent on his work, his back to the audience*] Disappointed?

OLIVIA: What on earth do you mean?

DAN: Disappointed?

OLIVIA: [*Laughing, in spite of herself*] Yes, I suppose I am.

DAN: Why?

OLIVIA: [*The tension at last relaxed*] Oh, I don't know . . . Because nothing much has ever happened to me, and it's a dull day, and it's the depths of the country . . . I don't know . . .

> [A *piercing scream from the bottom of the garden. A pause*]

MRS. BRAMSON: [*Shrieking, from the other side of the house*] Danny! . . . Danny!

> [*The clatter of footsteps in the garden.* DORA *runs in from the hall, breathless and terrified*]

DORA: They're diggin' . . . in the rubbish pit . . .

OLIVIA: Well?

DORA: There's something sticking out . . .

OLIVIA: What?

DORA: A hand . . . Somebody's hand! . . . Oh, Miss Grayne . . . somebody's hand . . . [*She runs whimpering into the kitchen, and* OLIVIA *rises and runs to the left window and looks out*]

MRS. BRAMSON'S VOICE: [*Calling off*] Danny!

> [DAN *rises slowly, his back to the audience.* OLIVIA *turns and suddenly sees him. Horror grows in her face. The blare of music. The lights dim out*]

SCENE 2

> The music plays in darkness for a few bars, then the curtain rises again. The music fades away.

> Late afternoon, two days later. OLIVIA *is seated above the table snipping long cuttings from newspapers and pasting them into a ledger. A knock at the front door. She starts*

nervously. Another knock. MRS. TERENCE *comes in from the kitchen carrying a smoothing-iron.*

MRS. TERENCE: If it's the police again, I'll bash their helmets in with this. If it lands me three months, I will.

OLIVIA: They're from Scotland Yard, and they don't wear helmets.

MRS. TERENCE: Then they're going to get 'urt. . . . [*Going into the hall*] I can tell by their looks what they think. And they better not think it, neither.

OLIVIA: And what do they think?

MRS. TERENCE: [*Over her shoulder*] They think it's me. I *know* they think it's me. [*She goes into the hall and opens the front door*]

HUBERT: [*Outside*] Good afternoon, Mrs. Terence.

MRS. TERENCE: Oh . . . come in, sir. [*Coming back into the room*] It's a civilian for a change. [*She is followed by* HUBERT]

HUBERT: [*To* OLIVIA] I say, this is all getting pretty terrible, isn't it?

OLIVIA: Yes, terrible.

MRS. TERENCE: Oh, terrible, terrible. There's one word for it; it's terrible. Forty-eight hours since they found 'er. They'll never get 'im now.

HUBERT: Terrible.

MRS. TERENCE: There was another charabanc load just after two o'clock. All standing round the rubbish 'eap eating sandwiches. Sensation, that's what it is.

OLIVIA: Would you like some food, Hubert?

HUBERT: Well, I——

MRS. TERENCE: They're still looking for the 'ead.

HUBERT: [*To* OLIVIA, *with a slight grimace*] No, thanks. I had lunch.

MRS. TERENCE: Mangled, she was, mangled. . . . Did you see your name in the paper, sir?

HUBERT: I—er—did catch a glimpse of it, yes.

MRS. TERENCE: Little did you think, sir, when you was digging that pit for my rubbish, eh? 'E may 'ave been watching you digging it . . . ooh! I have to sit in my kitchen and think about it.

HUBERT: Then why don't you leave?

MRS. TERENCE: [*Indignantly*] How can I leave with the whole village waitin' on me to tell 'em the latest? [*Going towards the kitchen*] I 'eard 'er 'ead must have been off at one stroke. One stroke. . . .

HUBERT: Really . . .

MRS. TERENCE: [*Turning at the door*] She wasn't interfered with, though. [*She goes into the kitchen*]

HUBERT: How they all love it. . . . How's the old lady bearing up in the invalid chair, eh?

OLIVIA: She's bursting out of it with health. And loving it more than anybody. This is my latest job—a press-cutting book. There was a picture of her in the *Chronicle* yesterday; she bought twenty-six copies.

HUBERT: [*Taking his pipe out*] She'll get to believe she did it herself in the end. . . . Is she in?

OLIVIA: She's gone over to Breakerly to interview a local paper.

HUBERT: The lad pushing the go-cart? . . . He's the devoted son all right, isn't he?

OLIVIA: [*After a pause*] I don't talk to him much.

HUBERT: Nice fellow. I've thought a lot about that prying into his things—pretty bad show, you know. [*Going to the left window*] I wonder if they'll ever nab him?

OLIVIA: [*With a start*] What do you mean?

HUBERT: The fellow who did it . . . Wonder what he's doing now.

OLIVIA: I wonder.

HUBERT: Damn clever job, you know, quietly . . . That was a rum touch, finding that broken lipstick in the rubbish heap . . . You know, the fact they still have no idea where this woman's head is——

OLIVIA: [*Convulsively*] Don't . . .

HUBERT: Sorry.

OLIVIA: [*After a pause*] It's a bit of a strain.

HUBERT: [*Earnestly*] Then why don't you leave?

OLIVIA: I—I couldn't afford it.

HUBERT: But you *could* if you married me! Now, look here—— [*Going to her*] You said you'd tell me today. So here I am—er—popping the question again. There's nothing much to add, except to go over the old ground again, and say that I'm not what you'd call a terrible brainy chap, but I am straight.

OLIVIA: Yes, I know.

HUBERT: Though, again, I'm not the sort that gets into corners with a pipe, and never opens his mouth from one blessed year's end to the other. I can talk.

OLIVIA: Yes, you can.

HUBERT: An all-round chap, really—that's me.

OLIVIA: Yes.

HUBERT: Well?

OLIVIA: I'm sorry, Hubert, but I can't.

HUBERT: You can't? But you told me that day we might make a go of it, or words to that effect——

OLIVIA: I've thought it over since then, and I'm afraid I can't.

[A pause]

HUBERT: What's changed you?

OLIVIA: Nothing's changed me, Hubert. I've just thought the matter over that's all.

[A pause. He crosses towards the fireplace]

HUBERT: Is it another man?

OLIVIA: [Startled] Don't be silly. [Collecting herself] What man could I possibly meet cooped up here?

HUBERT: Sorry. Can't be helped. Sorry.

DAN: [In the garden] There we are. Nice outing, eh——

OLIVIA: So am I.

[The front door opens and DAN wheels in MRS. BRAMSON. He is as serene as ever, but more animated than before. He is dressed the same as in the previous scene, and is smoking his usual cigarette. HUBERT sits at the table]

DAN: [Hanging up her rug in the hall] Back home again—I put your gloves away——

MRS. BRAMSON: [As he wheels her in] I feel dead. [To HUBERT] Oh, it's you . . . I feel dead.

DAN: [Sitting beside her on the sofa, full of high spirits] Don't you

be a silly old 'oman, you look as pretty as a picture—strawberries
and cream in your face, and not a day over forty; and when I've
made you a nice cup of tea you'll be twenty-five in the sun and
eighteen with your back to the light, so you think yourself lucky!

MRS. BRAMSON: [*As he digs her in the side*] Oh, Danny, you are a
terror! [*To the others*] He's been at me like this all the way. I
must say it keeps me alive.

DAN: [*As she hands him her hat and cape*] But you feel dead. I
get you.

MRS. BRAMSON: [*Kittenish*] Oh, you caution! You'll be the death of
me.

DAN: [*Wagging his finger at her*] Ah-ha! [*Hanging up her things
in the hall*] Now what'd you like a drop of in your tea—gin,
whisky, liqueur brandy, or a nice dollop of sailor's rum, eh?

MRS. BRAMSON: Just listen to him! Now don't make me laugh, dear,
because there's always my heart.

DAN: [*Sitting beside her again*] You've lost your heart, you know
you have, to the little feller that pushes your pram—you know you
have!

MRS. BRAMSON: [*Laughing shrilly*] Pram! Well! [*Her laugh cut
short*] It's wicked to laugh, with this—this thing all round us.

DAN: [*Sobering portentously*] I forgot. [*As she shivers*] Not in a
draught, are you? [*Shutting the front door and coming down to
HUBERT*] D'you remember, Mr. Laurie, me, pulling your leg about
you havin' done it? Funniest thing out! . . . Talk about laugh!

MRS. BRAMSON: [*Fondly*] Tttt! . . .

DAN: [*A glint of mischief in his eyes*] I think I better get the tea
before I get into hot water. [*He goes towards the kitchen*]

OLIVIA: Mrs. Terence is getting the tea.

DAN: [*At the door*] She don't make tea like me. I'm an old sailor,
Miss Grayne. Don't you forget that. [*He goes into the kitchen*]

OLIVIA: I'm not interested, I'm afraid.

MRS. BRAMSON: [*Wheeling herself to the front of the table*] Look
here, Olivia, you're downright rude to that boy, and if there's one
thing that never gets a woman anywhere, it's rudeness. What have
you got against him?

HUBERT: Surely he's got more to say for himself today than when I met him before.

MRS. BRAMSON: Oh, he's been in rare spirits all day.

HUBERT: Johnny Walker, judging by the whiff of breath I got just now.

MRS. BRAMSON: Meaning whisky?

HUBERT: Yes.

OLIVIA: I've never heard you make a joke before, Hubert.

HUBERT: Didn't realize it was one till I'd said it. Sorry.

MRS. BRAMSON: It's not a joke; it's a libel. [*A knock at the front door*] Come in. The boy's a teetotaller.

[NURSE LIBBY *enters from the front door*]

HUBERT: Sorry, my mistake.

NURSE: Good afternoon. Shall I wait for you in your bedroom?

MRS. BRAMSON: Yes. I feel absolutely dead.

NURSE: [*Turning at the bedroom, eagerly*] Anything new *re* the murder?

HUBERT: I believe her head was cut off at one stroke.

NURSE: [*Brightly*] Oh, poor thing . . .

[*She goes into the bedroom.* DAN *returns from the kitchen, carrying a tray of tea and cakes*]

DAN: There you are, fresh as a daisy. Three lumps, as per usual, and some of the cakes you like——

MRS. BRAMSON: [*As he pours out her tea*] Thank you, dear. . . . Let me smell your breath. [*After smelling it*] Clean as a whistle. Smells of peppermints.

OLIVIA: Yes. There were some in the kitchen.

HUBERT: Oh.

MRS. BRAMSON: [*To* HUBERT, *as* DAN *pours out two more cups*] So you won't stay to tea, Mr.—er——

HUBERT: Er—[*Rising*]—no, thank you . . . [DAN *sits in* HUBERT'S *chair*] I think I'll get off before it's dark. Good-bye, Mrs. Bramson. Good-bye, Mr.—er——

DAN: [*Grinning and saluting*] Dan. Just Dan. [*He opens the press-cutting ledger*]

HUBERT: [*To* OLIVIA] Good-bye.

OLIVIA: [*Rises*] Good-bye, Hubert. I'm sorry.

> [DAN *raises his cup as if drinking a toast to* MRS. BRAMSON.
> *She follows suit*]

HUBERT: Can't be helped. . . . It'll get dark early today, I think.
Funny how the evenings draw in this time of year. Good night.

DAN: Good night.

HUBERT: [*To* OLIVIA] Good-bye.

OLIVIA: Good-bye. [*She goes to the right window seat*]

> [HUBERT *leaves*]

MRS. BRAMSON: Johnny Walker, indeed! Impertinence!

DAN: [*Drinking tea and scanning press-cuttings*] Johnny Walker?

MRS. BRAMSON: Never you mind, dear . . . Any more of those terrible
people called? Reporters? Police?

DAN: [*Gaily*] There's a definite fallin' off in attendance today.
Sunday, I expect.

MRS. BRAMSON: Hush, don't talk like that, dear.

DAN: Sorry, mum.

MRS. BRAMSON: And don't call me "mum"!

DAN: Well, if I can't call you Mrs. Bramson, what can I call you?

MRS. BRAMSON: If you were very good, I might let you call me . . .
mother!

DAN: [*Mischievously, his hand to his forehead*] O.K., mother.

MRS. BRAMSON: [*Joining in his laughter*] Oh, you are in a mood
today! [*Suddenly, imperiously*] I want to be read to, now.

DAN: [*Crossing to the desk in mock resignation*] Your servant,
mother o' mine . . . What'll you have? *The Channings? The Red
Court Farm?*

MRS. BRAMSON: I'm tired of them.

DAN: Well . . . oh! [*Taking a large Bible from the top of the desk*]
What about the Bible?

MRS. BRAMSON: The Bible?

DAN: It's Sunday, you know. I was brought up to it!

MRS. BRAMSON: So was I . . . *East Lynne*'s nice, though.

DAN: Not so nice as the Bible.

MRS. BRAMSON: [*Doubtfully*] All right, dear; makes a nice change. . . . Not that I don't often dip into it.

DAN: I'm sure you do. [*Blowing the dust off the book*] Now where'll I read?

MRS. BRAMSON: [*Unenthusiastic*] At random's nice, don't you think, dear?

DAN: At random . . . Yes . . .

MRS. BRAMSON: The Old Testament.

DAN: [*Turning over leaves thoughtfully*] At random in the Old Testament's a bit risky, don't you think so?

[MRS. TERENCE *comes in from the kitchen*]

MRS. TERENCE: [*To* MRS. BRAMSON] The paper boy's at the door again and says you're in the *News of the World* again.

MRS. BRAMSON: [*Interested*] Oh! . . . [*Simulating indifference*] That horrible boy again, when the one thing I want is to blot the whole thing out of my mind.

MRS. TERENCE: 'Ow many copies d'you want?

MRS. BRAMSON: Get three.

MRS. TERENCE: And 'e says there's a placard in Shepperley with your name on it.

MRS. BRAMSON: What does it say?

MRS. TERENCE: "Mrs. Bramson Talks". [*She goes back towards the kitchen.*

MRS. BRAMSON: Oh. [*As* MRS. TERENCE *reaches the kitchen door*] Go at once into Shepperley and order some. At once!

MRS. TERENCE: Can't be done.

MRS. BRAMSON: Can't be done? What d'you mean, can't be done? It's a scandal. What are you paid for?

MRS. TERENCE: [*Coming back, furious*] I'm not paid! And 'aven't been for two weeks! And I'm not coming tomorrow unless I am. Put that in your copybook and blot it. [*She goes into the kitchen, banging the door*]

MRS. BRAMSON: Isn't paid? Is she mad? [*To* OLIVIA] Are you mad? Why don't you pay her?

OLIVIA: [*Coming down*] Because you don't give me the money to do it with.

MRS. BRAMSON: I—[*Fumbling at her bodice*]—wheel me over to that cupboard.

[OLIVIA *is about to do so, when she catches* DAN'S *eye*]

OLIVIA: [*To* DAN *pointedly*] Perhaps *you'd* go into the kitchen and get the paper from Mrs. Terence?

DAN: [*After a second's pause, with a laugh*] Of course I will, madam! Anythin' you say! Anythin' you say!

[*He careers into the kitchen, still carrying the Bible.* MRS. BRAMSON *has fished up two keys on the end of a long black tape.* OLIVIA *wheels her over to the cupboard above the fireplace*]

OLIVIA: If you give me the keys, I'll get it for you.

MRS. BRAMSON: No fear! [*She unlocks the cupboard; it turns out to be a small but very substantial safe. Unlocking the safe, muttering to herself*] Won't go into Shepperley, indeed . . . never heard of such impertinence . . . [*She takes out a cash box from among some deeds, unlocks it with the smaller key, and takes out a mass of five-pound and pound notes*] The way these servants— what are you staring at?

OLIVIA: Isn't it rather a lot of money to have in the house?

MRS. BRAMSON: "Put not your trust in banks" is my motto, and always will be.

OLIVIA: But that's hundreds of pounds! It——

MRS. BRAMSON: [*Handing her two notes*] D'you wonder I wouldn't let you have the key?

OLIVIA: Has . . . anybody else asked you for it?

MRS. BRAMSON: [*Locking the cash box and putting it back in the safe*] I wouldn't let a soul touch it. Not a soul. Not even Danny. [*She snaps the safe, locks it, and slips the keys back into her bosom*]

OLIVIA: Has *he* asked you for it?

MRS. BRAMSON: It's enough to have these policemen prying, you forward girl, without——

OLIVIA: [*Urgently*] Please! Has he?

MRS. BRAMSON: Well, he did offer to fetch some money yesterday for the dairy. But I wouldn't give him the key. Oh, no!

OLIVIA: Why?

MRS. BRAMSON: Do I want to see him waylaid and attacked, and my key stolen? Oh, no, I told him, that key stays on me——

OLIVIA: Did he—know how much money there is in there?

MRS. BRAMSON: I told him. Do you wonder I stick to the key, I said— what *is* the matter with you, all these questions?

OLIVIA: Oh, it's no use——

[*She goes to the armchair below the fireplace and sits in it.* DAN *returns from the kitchen, with a copy of the* News of the World; *the Bible tucked under his arm, a cigarette stub between his lips*]

DAN: He says they're sellin' like hot cakes! [*Handing the paper to* MRS. BRAMSON] There you are, I've found the place for you— whole page, headlines an' all . . .

MRS. BRAMSON: Oh, yes. . . .

[DAN *stands with one knee on the sofa, and turns over the pages of his Bible*]

MRS. BRAMSON: [*Reading breathlessly, her back to the fireplace*] ". . . The Victim's Past" . . . with another picture of me underneath! [*Looking closer, dashed*] Oh, taken at Tonbridge the year before the war; really it isn't right . . . [*To* OLIVIA, *savouring it*] "The Bungalow of Death! . . . Gruesome finds . . . Fiendish murderer still at large . . . The enigma of the missing head . . . where is it buried? . . ." Oh yes! [*She goes on reading silently to herself*]

DAN: [*Suddenly in a clear voice*] ". . . Blessed is the man . . . that walketh not in the counsel of the ungodly . . . nor standeth in the way of sinners . . . nor sitteth in the seat of the scornful . . ."

MRS. BRAMSON: [*Impatiently*] Oh, the print's too small . . .

DAN: [*Firmly*] Shall I read it to you?

MRS. BRAMSON: Yes, dear, do. . . .

[*He shuts the Bible with a bang, throws it on the sofa,*

and takes the paper from her. OLIVIA *watches him intently;*
he smiles at her slowly and brazenly as he shakes out the
paper]

DAN: [*Reading laboriously*] ". . . The murderer committed the
crime in the forest most—in the forest, most likely strippin' be-
forehand——" [DORA *comes in from the kitchen, and stands at*
the door, arrested by his reading. She is dressed in Sunday best]
". . . and cleansin' himself afterwards in the forest lake——"

MRS. BRAMSON: Tch! tch!

DAN: [*Reading*] ". . . He buried the body shallow in the open pit,
cunnin'ly chancin' it bein' filled, which it was next day, the
eleventh——" [*Nodding to* OLIVIA] That was the day 'fore I
come here. . . .

MRS. BRAMSON: So it was. . . .

DAN: [*Reading*] "The body was nude. Attempts had been made
to . . . turn to foot of next column . . ." [*Doing so*] "Attempts
had been made to . . . era-eradicate fingerprints with a knife . . ."
[*Far away, the tolling of village bells*] ". . . The head was
severed by a skilled person, possibly a butcher. The murderer——"
[*He stops suddenly, raises his head, smiles, takes the cigarette*
stub, puts it behind his ear, and listens]

OLIVIA: What's the matter?

MRS. BRAMSON: Can you hear something? Oh, I'm scared.

DAN: I forgot it was Sunday. . . . They're goin' to church in the
villages. All got up in their Sunday best, with prayer books, and
the organ playin', and the windows shinin'. Shinin' on holy things,
because holy things isn't afraid of the daylight.

MRS. BRAMSON: But Danny, what on earth are you——

DAN: [*Quelling her*] But all the time, the daylight's movin' over
the floor, and by the end of the sermon the air in the church is
turning grey . . . And people isn't able to think of holy things
so much no more, only of the terrible things that's goin' on
outside, that everybody's readin' about in the papers! [*Looking at*
OLIVIA] Because they know that though it's still daylight, and
everythin's or'nary and quiet . . . today will be the same as all
the other days, and come to an end, and it'll be night. . . . [*After*

a pause, coming to earth again with a laugh at the others, throwing the newspaper on the sofa] I forgot it was Sunday!

MRS. BRAMSON: [*Overawed*] Good gracious . . . what's come over you, Danny?

DAN: [*With exaggerated animation*] Oh, I speechify like anything when I'm roused! I used to go to Sunday School, see, and the thoughts sort of come into my head. Like as if I was reading off a book! [*Slapping the Bible*]

MRS. BRAMSON: Dear, dear . . . You should have been a preacher. You should!

[DAN *laughs loudly and opens the Bible*]

DORA: [*Going to the table and collecting the tea tray*] I never knew 'e 'ad so many words in 'is 'ead. . . .

MRS. BRAMSON: [*Suddenly*] I want to lie down now, and be examined.

DAN: [*Rising*] Anything you say, mother o' mine . . . Will you have your medicine in your room as well, eh?

MRS. BRAMSON: Yes, dear . . . Olivia, you *never* got a new bottle yesterday!

DAN: [*As he wheels her into her bedroom*] I got it today while you were with the chap. . . . Popped in at the chemist's.

MRS. BRAMSON: Oh, thank you, dear. The one by the mortuary? . . . Oh, my back . . . Nurse!

[*Her voice is lost in the bedroom. The daylight begins to fade. The church bells die away*]

DORA: My sister says all this is wearin' me to a shadow.

OLIVIA: It is trying, isn't it?

DORA: You look that worried, too, Miss Grayne.

OLIVIA: Do I?

DORA: As if you was waiting for something to 'appen.

OLIVIA: Oh?

DORA: Like an explosion. A bomb, or something.

OLIVIA: [*Smiling*] I don't think that's very likely. . . . [*Lowering her voice*] Have you talked to Dan at all this week?

DORA: Never get the chance. 'E's too busy dancin' attendance on Madam Crocodile . . .

[DAN *comes back from the bedroom, his cigarette stub between his lips*]

DORA: [*Going towards the kitchen*] I'm off. You don't catch me 'ere after dark.

DAN: Why, will ye be late for courting?

DORA: If I was, they'd wait for me. Good afternoon, Miss Grayne. Good afternoon . . . *sir*.

DAN: [*Winking at* OLIVIA] Are you sure they'd wait?

DORA: You ought to know.

[*She goes into the kitchen.* DAN *and* OLIVIA *are alone.* DAN *crosses to the sofa with a laugh, humming gaily*]

DAN: "Their home addresses . . . and their caresses . . ." [*He sits on the end of the sofa*]

OLIVIA: You've been drinking, haven't you?

DAN: [*After a pause, quizzically*] You don't miss much, do you?

OLIVIA: [*Significantly*] No.

DAN: [*Rubbing his hands*] I've been drinking, and I feel fine! . . . [*Brandishing the Bible*] You wouldn't like another dose of reading?

OLIVIA: I prefer talking.

DAN: [*Putting down the Bible*] Carry on.

OLIVIA: Asking questions.

DAN: [*Catching her eye*] Carry on! [*He studies his outspread hands*]

OLIVIA: [*Crisply*] Are you sure you were ever a sailor! Are you sure you weren't a butcher?

[*A pause. He looks at her, slowly, then breaks the look abruptly*]

DAN: [*Rising with a smile and standing against the mantelpiece*] Aw, talkin's daft! *Doin's* the thing!

OLIVIA: You can talk, too.

DAN: Aw, yes! D'you hear me just now? She's right, you know, I should ha' been a preacher. I remember, when I was a kid, sittin' in Sunday school—catching my mother's eye where she was sitting by the pulpit, with the sea behind her; and she pointed to the pulpit, and then to me, as if to say, that's the place for you. . . . [*Far away, pensive*] I never forgot that.

[*A pause*]

OLIVIA: I don't believe a word of it.

DAN: Neither do I, but it sounds wonderful. [*Leaning over confidentially*] I never saw my mam, and I never had a dad, and the first thing I remember is . . . Cardiff Docks. And you're the first 'oman I ever told that, so you can compliment yourself. Or the drink. [*Laughing*] I think it's the drink.

OLIVIA: You *do* live in your imagination, don't you?

DAN: [*Reassuringly*] Yes . . . It's the only way to bear with the awful things you have to do.

OLIVIA: What awful things?

DAN: Well . . . [*Grinning like a child and going back to the sofa*] Ah-ha! . . . I haven't had as much to drink as all that! [*Sitting on the sofa*] Ah-ha! . . .

OLIVIA: You haven't a very high opinion of women, have you?

[DAN *makes a gesture with his hands, pointing the thumbs downwards with a decisive movement*]

DAN: Women don't have to be drunk to talk. . . . You don't talk that much though, fair play. [*Looking her up and down, insolently*] You're a dark horse, you are. [*A pause. She rises abruptly and stands at the fireplace, her back to him. She takes off her spectacles*] Ye know, this isn't the life for you. What is there to it? Tell me that.

OLIVIA: [*Somberly*] What is there to it . . . ?

DAN: Yes . . .

OLIVIA: Getting up at seven, mending my stockings or washing them, having breakfast with a vixenish old woman and spending the rest of the day with her, in a dreary house in the middle of a wood and going to bed at eleven . . . I'm plain, I haven't got any money, I'm shy, and I haven't got any friends.

DAN: [*Teasing*] Don't you *like* the old lady?

OLIVIA: I could kill her. [*A pause. She realizes what she has said*]

DAN: [*With a laugh*] Oh, no, you couldn't! . . . Not many people have it in them to kill people. . . . Oh, no!

> [*She looks at him. A pause. He studies the palms of his hands, chuckling to himself*]

OLIVIA: And what was there to *your* life at the Tallboys?

DAN: My life? Well . . . The day don't start so good, with a lot of stuck-up boots to clean, and a lot of silly high heels all along the passage waitin' for a polish, and a lot of spoons to clean that's been in the mouths of gapin' fools that looks through me as if I was a dirty window hadn't been cleaned for years. . . . [*Throwing his stub into the fire in a sudden crescendo of fury*] Orders, orders, orders; go here, do this, don't do that you idiot, open the door for me, get a move on—I was never meant to take orders, never! . . . Down in the tea-place there's an old white beard wigglin'. "Waiter, my tea's stone cold." [*Furiously*] I'm not a waiter, I'm a millionaire, and everybody's under me! . . . And just when I think I got a bit o' peace . . . [*His head in his hands*] . . . there's somebody . . . lockin' the the bedroom door . . . [*Raising his head*] . . . won't let me get out; talk, talk, talk, won't fork out with no more money, at me, at me, at me, won't put no clothes on, calls me everythin', lie on the floor and screams and screams, so nothin' keeps that mouth shut only . . . [*A pause*] It's raining out of the window, and the leaves is off the trees . . . oh, Lord . . . I wish I could hear a bit o' music . . . [*Smiling, slowly*] . . . And I do, inside o' myself! And I have a drop of drink . . . and everything's fine! [*Excited*] And when it's the night . . .

OLIVIA: [*With a cry*] Go on!

> [*A pause. He realizes she is there, and turns slowly and looks at her*]

DAN: [*Wagging his finger with a sly smile*] Aha! I'm too fly for you! You'd like to know, wouldn't you? Aha! *Why* would you like to know? [*Insistently, mischievously*] Why d'you lie awake . . . all night?

OLIVIA: Don't! . . . I'm frightened of you! . . .

DAN: [*Triumphantly, rising and facing her, his back half to the audience*] Why?

OLIVIA: [*Desperate*] How do you know I lie awake at night? Shall I tell you why? Because you're awake yourself. You *can't sleep!* There's one thing that keeps you awake . . . isn't there? One thing you've pushed into the back of your mind and you can't do any more about it, and you never will . . . And do you know what it is? . . . It's a little thing. A box. Only a box. But it's . . . rather heavy. . . .

[*DAN looks at her. A long pause. He jerks away with a laugh and sits at the sofa again*]

DAN: [*Quietly, prosaically*] The way you was going through my letters the other day—that had to make me smile. . . . [*His voice dies away. Without warning, as if seeing something in his mind which makes him lose control, he shrieks loudly, clapping his hands over his eyes: then is silent. He recovers slowly and stares at her. After a pause, in a measured voice*] It's the only thing that keeps me awake, mind you! The only thing! [*Earnestly*] But I don't know what to do. . . . You see, nothing worries me, nothing in the world, only . . . I don't like a pair of eyes staring at me . . . [*His voice trailing away*] . . . with no look in them. I don't know what to do . . . I don't know . . . [*Without warning he bursts into tears. She sits beside him and seems almost about to put her arms about him. He feels she is there, looks into her eyes, grasps her arm, then pulls himself together, abruptly. Rising*] But it's the only thing! I live by myself . . . [*Slapping his chest*] . . . inside here—and all the rest of you can go to hang. After I've made a use of you, though! Nothing's going to stop me! I feel fine! I—— [BELSIZE *crosses outside. A sharp knock at the front door. She half rises. He motions her to sit again. With his old swagger*] All right! Anybody's there, I'll deal with 'em—— I'll manage myself all right! You watch me! [*He goes to the front door and opens it*]

BELSIZE: [*At the door, jovially*] Hello, Dan! How's things?

DAN: [*Letting him in and shutting the door*] Not so bad. . . .

[*He brings* BELSIZE *into the room*]

BELSIZE: [*As* OLIVIA *goes*] Afternoon, Miss Grayne!

OLIVIA: [*Putting on her spectacles*] How do you do. . . . [*She makes an effort to compose herself and hurries across to the sunroom*]

[BELSIZE's *attitude is one of slightly exaggerated breeziness:* DAN's *is one of cheerful naïveté almost as limpid as on his first appearance*]

BELSIZE: Bearing up, eh?

DAN: Yes, sir, bearin' up, you know. . . .

BELSIZE: We haven't scared you all out of the house, yet, I see!

DAN: No chance!

BELSIZE: All these bloodcurdlers, eh?

DAN: I should say so!

BELSIZE: No more news for me, I suppose?

DAN: No chance!

BELSIZE: Ah . . . too bad. Mind if I sit down?

DAN: [*Pointing to the sofa*] Well, this is the nearest you get to comfort in this house, sir.

BELSIZE: No, thanks, this'll do. . . . [*Sitting on a chair at the table, and indicating the cuttings*] I see you keep apace of the news.

DAN: I should say so! They can't hardly wait for the latest on the case in this house, sir.

BELSIZE: Ah, well, it's only natural . . . I got a bit of a funny feeling bottom of my spine myself crossing by the rubbish heap.

DAN: Well, will you have a cigarette, sir? . . . [*His hand to his jacket pocket*] Only a Woodbine——

BELSIZE: No, thanks.

DAN: [*After a pause*] Would you like to see Mrs. Bramson, sir?

BELSIZE: Oh, plenty of time. How's she bearing up?

DAN: Well, it's been a bit of a shock for her, them finding the remains of the lady at the bottom of her garden, you know.

BELSIZE: The remains of the lady! I wish you wouldn't talk like that. I've seen 'em.

DAN: [*Looking over his shoulder at the cuttings*] Well, you see, I haven't.

BELSIZE: You know, I don't mind telling you, they reckon the fellow that did this job was a bloodstained clever chap.

DAN: [*Smiling*] You don't say?

BELSIZE: [*Casually*] He was blackmailing her, you know.

DAN: Tch! tch! Was he?

BELSIZE: Whoever he was.

DAN: She had a lot of fellows on a string, though, didn't she?

BELSIZE: [*Guardedly*] That's true.

DAN: Though this one seems to have made a bit more stir than any of the others, don't he?

BELSIZE: Yes. [*Indicating the cuttings*] Regular film star. Made his name.

DAN: [*Abstractedly*] If you *can* make your name without nobody knowin' what it is, o' course.

BELSIZE: [*Slightly piqued*] Yes, of course. . . . But I don't reckon he's been as bright as all that.

DAN: [*After a pause*] Oh, you don't?

BELSIZE: No! They'll nab him in no time.

DAN: Oh . . . Mrs. Bramson'll be that relieved. And the whole country besides. . . .

BELSIZE: Look here, Dan, any self-respecting murderer would have taken care to mutilate the body to such a degree that nobody could recognize it—and here we come and identify it first go! [DAN *folds his arms and looks thoughtful*] Call that clever? . . . What d'you think?

[DAN *catches his eye and crosses to the sofa*]

DAN: Well sir, I'm a slow thinker, I am, but though it might be clever to leave the lady unide—unide——

BELSIZE: Unidentified.

DAN: [*Sitting on the edge of the sofa*] Thank you, sir. . . . [*Laboriously*] Well, though it be clever to leave the lady unidentified and not be caught . . . hasn't he been more clever to leave her identified . . . and still not be caught?

BELSIZE: Why didn't you sleep in your bed on the night of the tenth?

[*A pause.* DAN *stiffens almost imperceptibly*]

DAN: What you say?

BELSIZE: Why didn't you sleep in your bed on the night of the murder?

DAN: I did.

BELSIZE: [*Lighting his pipe*] You didn't.

DAN: Yes, I did. Oh—except for about half an hour—that's right. I couldn't sleep for toffee and I went up the fire escape—I remember thinkin' about it next day when the woman was missing, and trying to remember if I could think of anything funny——

BELSIZE: What time was that? [*He rises, crosses to the fireplace, and throws his match into it*]

DAN: Oh, about . . . oh, you know how you wake up in the night and don't know what time it is. . . .

BELSIZE: [*Staring at him doubtfully*] Mmm . . .

DAN: I could never sleep when I was at sea, neither, sir.

BELSIZE: Mmm. [*Suddenly*] Are you feeling hot?

DAN: No.

BELSIZE: Your shirt's wet through.

DAN: [*After a pause*] I've been sawin' some wood.

BELSIZE: Why didn't you tell us you were having an affair with the deceased woman?

DAN: Affair? What's that?

BELSIZE: Come along, old chap, I'll use a straighter word if it'll help you. But you're stalling. She was seen by two of the maids talking to you in the shrubbery. Well?

[*A pause.* DAN *bursts into tears, but with a difference. His breakdown a few minutes ago was genuine; this is a good performance, very slightly exaggerated.* BELSIZE *watches him dispassionately, his brows knit*]

DAN: Oh, sir . . . it's been on my conscience . . . ever since . . .

BELSIZE: So you did have an affair with her?

DAN: Oh, no, sir, not that! I avoided her ever after that day she stopped me, sir! . . . You see, sir, a lady stayin' where I was workin', an' for all I knew married, an' all the other fellers she'd been after, and the brazen way she went on to me. . . . You're only human, aren't you, sir, and when they asked me about her, I got frightened to tell about her stopping me. . . . But now you know about it, sir, it's a weight off my mind, you wouldn't believe. . . . [*Rising, after seeming to pull himself together*] As a matter of fact, it was the disgust-like of nearly gettin' mixed up with her that was keepin' me awake at nights.

BELSIZE: I see . . . You're a bit of a milksop, aren't you?

DAN: [*Apparently puzzled*] Am I, sir?

BELSIZE: Yes . . . That'll be all for today. I'll let you off this once.

DAN: I'm that relieved, sir!

BELSIZE: [*Crossing to the table for his hat*] But don't try and keep things from the police another time.

DAN: No chance!

BELSIZE: They always find out, you know.

DAN: Yes, sir. Would you like a cup o' tea, sir?

BELSIZE: No, thanks. I've got another inquiry in the village. . . . [*Turning back, with an afterthought*] Oh, just one thing—might as well just do it, we're supposed to with all the chaps we're questioning, matter of form—if you don't mind, I'll have a quick look through your luggage. Matter of form. . . .

DAN: Oh, yes.

BELSIZE: Where d'you hang out?

DAN: [*Tonelessly*] Through the kitchen . . . here, sir . . . First door facin' . . .

BELSIZE: First door, facing——

DAN: You can't miss it.

BELSIZE: I'll find it.

DAN: It's open, I think. [BELSIZE *goes into the kitchen. A pause.* DAN *looks slowly round the room. Turning mechanically to the kitchen door*] You can't miss it . . .

[*A pause. The noise of something being moved, beyond the kitchen.* DAN *sits on the sofa with a jerk, looking before him. His fingers beat a rapid tattoo on the sides of the sofa. He looks at them, rises convulsively and walks round the room, grasping chairs and furniture as he goes. He returns to the sofa, sits, and begins the tattoo again. With a sudden wild automatic movement he beats his closed fists in rapid succession against the sides of his head.* BELSIZE *returns carrying the hatbox*]

BELSIZE: [*Crossing and placing the hatbox on the table*] This one's locked. Have you got the key?

[DAN *rises, and takes a step into the middle of the room. He looks at the hatbox at last*]

DAN: [*In a dead voice*] It isn't mine.
BELSIZE: Not yours?
DAN: No.
BELSIZE: Oh? . . . Whose is it, then?
DAN: I dunno. It isn't mine.

[OLIVIA *stands at the sunroom door*]

OLIVIA: I'm sorry, I thought . . . Why, Inspector, what are you doing with my box?
BELSIZE: Yours?
OLIVIA: It's got all my letters in it!
BELSIZE: But it was in . . .
OLIVIA: Oh, Dan's room used to be the boxroom.
BELSIZE: Oh, I see . . .
OLIVIA: I'll keep it in my wardrobe; it'll be safer there . . .

[*With sudden feverish resolution, she picks up the box and carries it into the kitchen.* DAN *looks the other way as she passes him*]

BELSIZE: I'm very sorry, miss. [*Scratching his head*] I'm afraid I've offended her . . .
DAN: [*Smiling*] She'll be all right, sir . . .
BELSIZE: Well, young feller, I'll be off. You might tell the old lady I popped in, and hope she's better.

DAN: [*Smiling and nodding*] Thank you, sir. . . . Good day, sir.

BELSIZE: Good day.

> [*He goes out through the front door into the twilight, closing it behind him*]

DAN: Good day, sir . . .

> [*A pause.* DAN *crumples to the floor in a dead faint*]

QUICK CURTAIN

ACT THREE

SCENE 1

Half an hour later. The light has waned; the fire is lit and throws a red reflection into the room. DAN *is lying on the sofa, eyes closed.* NURSE LIBBY *sits at the end of the sofa holding his pulse.* MRS. TERENCE *stands behind the sofa with a toby jug of water.*

NURSE: There, lovey, you won't be long now. . . . Ever so much steadier already. . . . What a bit o' luck me blowin' in today! . . . Tt! tt! Pouring with sweat, the lad is. Whatever's he been up to?

MRS. TERENCE: When I walked in that door and saw 'im lyin' full stretch on that floor everything went topsy-wopsy. [*Pressing the jug to* DAN's *lips*] It did! The room went round and round. . . .

NURSE: [*As* DAN *splutters*] Don't choke 'im, there's a love. . . .

MRS. TERENCE: D'you know what I said to meself when I saw 'im lyin' there?

NURSE: What?

MRS. TERENCE: I said, "That murderer's been at 'im," I said, "and it's the next victim." I did!

NURSE: So you would! Just like the pictures. . . . 'Old your 'ead up, love. . . .

MRS. TERENCE: [*As* NURSE LIBBY *supports* DAN's *head*] Got a *nice* face, 'asn't he?

NURSE: Oh *yes!* . . . [*As* DAN's *eyes flicker*] Shh, he's coming to . . . [DAN *opens his eyes and looks at her*] Welcome back to the land of the living!

MRS. TERENCE: Thought the murderer'd got you!

[*A pause.* DAN *stares, then sits up abruptly*]

DAN: How long I been like that?

NURSE: We picked you up ten minutes ago, and I'd say it was twenty minutes before that, roughly-like, that you passed away.

MRS. TERENCE: Passed away, don't frighten the boy! . . . Whatever come over you, dear!

DAN: I dunno. Felt sick, I think. [*Recovering himself*] Say no more about it, eh? Don't like swinging the lead. . . . [*His head in his hand*]

MRS. TERENCE: Waiting 'and and foot on Madam Crocodile, enough to wear King Kong out . . .

NURSE: That's better, eh?

DAN: It is really getting dark?

MRS. TERENCE: It's a scandal the way the days are drawin' in. . . . 'Ave another sip——

DAN: [*As she makes to give him more water, to* NURSE LIBBY] You haven't such a thing as a nip of brandy?

NURSE: [*Opening her bag*] Yes, lovey, I nearly gave you a drop just now——

> [DAN *takes a flask from her and gulps; he takes a second mouthful. He gives it back, shakes himself, and looks before him*]

MRS. TERENCE: Better?

DAN: Yes. . . . Clears the brain no end. . . . Makes you understand better. . . . [*His voice growing in vehemence*] Makes you see what a damn silly thing it is to get the wind up about anything. *Do* things! Get a move on! Show 'em what you're made of! Get a move on! . . . Fainting indeed . . . Proper girl's trick, I'm ashamed o' meself . . . [*Looking round, quietly*] The light's going . . . the daytime's as if it's never been; it's dead. . . . [*Seeing the others stare, with a laugh*] Daft, isn't it?

> [DORA *brings in an oil lamp from the kitchen; she is wearing her outdoor clothes. She crosses to the table, strikes a match with her back to the audience and lights the lamp, then the wall light. The twilight is dispelled*]

NURSE: [*Shutting her bag, rising*] You'll be all right; a bit light-headed after the fall I expect. [*Going to the hall*] Well, got an

abscess the other side of Turneyfield, *and* a slow puncture. So
long, lovey.

DAN: [*Sitting up*] So long!

NURSE: Be good, all!

[*She bustles out of the front door. A pause.* DAN *sits
looking before him, drumming his fingers on the sofa*]

DORA: [*Closing the right window curtains*] What's the matter with
him?

MRS. TERENCE: Conked out.

DORA: Conked out? Oh, dear. . . . D'you think 'e see'd something?
I'll tell you what it is!

MRS. TERENCE [*Closing the left window curtains*] What?

DORA: The monster's lurking again.

[*Mechanically* DAN *takes a box of matches and a cigarette
from his pocket*]

MRS. TERENCE: I'll give you lurk, my girl, look at the egg on my toby!
Why don't you learn to wash up, instead of walkin' about talking
like three-halfpennyworth of trash?

DORA: I can't wash up properly in that kitchen; with that light. Them
little oil lamps isn't any good except to set the place on fire.
[*She goes into the kitchen*]

[DAN *drums his fingers on the sofa.* MRS. BRAMSON *wheels
herself in from the bedroom*]

MRS. BRAMSON: I dropped off. Why didn't somebody wake me?
Have I been missing something?

MRS. TERENCE: That Inspector Belsize called.

MRS. BRAMSON: [*Testily*] Then why didn't somebody wake me?
Dan, what did he want?

DAN: Just a friendly call.

MRS. BRAMSON: You seem very far away, dear. What's the matter
with you? . . . Dan!

DAN: Bit of an 'eadache, that's all.

MRS. BRAMSON: Doesn't make you deaf, though, dear, does it?

MRS. TERENCE: Now, now, turnin' against the apple of your eye; can't 'ave that goin' on——

[*A sharp knock at the front door.* DAN *starts up and goes towards the hall*]

MRS. BRAMSON: [*To* MRS. TERENCE] See who it is.

MRS. TERENCE: [*At the front door, as* DAN *is about to push past her*] Oh . . . it's only the paraffin boy . . . [*To the boy outside, taking a can from him*] And you bring stuff on a Saturday night another time.

[DAN *is standing behind* MRS. BRAMSON's *chair*]

MRS. BRAMSON: I should think so——

[MRS. TERENCE *comes into the room.* DAN *strikes a match for his cigarette*]

MRS. TERENCE: [*With a cry*] Oh! Can't you see this is paraffin? [*She puts the can on the floor outside the hall*]

MRS. BRAMSON: You went through my side like a knife——

MRS. TERENCE: If people knew what to do with their money, they'd put electric light in their 'omes 'stead of dangerin' people's lives.

[*She goes into the kitchen.* DAN *stares before him, the match flickering*]

MRS. BRAMSON: [*Blowing out the match*] You'll burn your fingers! Set yourself on fire! Absent-minded! . . . I woke up all of a cold shiver. Had a terrible dream.

DAN: [*Mechanically*] What about?

MRS. BRAMSON: Horrors . . . I'm freezing. Get me my shawl off my bed, will you, dear? . . . [*As he does not move*] My shawl, dear!

[DAN *starts, collects himself, and smiles his most ingratiating smile*]

DAN: I *am* sorry, mum. In the Land of Nod, I was! Let me see, what was it your highness was after? A shawl? No sooner said than done. . . . You watch me! One, two, three! [*He runs into the bedroom*]

MRS. BRAMSON: Silly boy . . . silly boy . . . [OLIVIA *comes in quickly from the kitchen. She is dressed to go out and carries a suitcase*] Where are you off to?

OLIVIA: I've had a telegram. A friend of mine in London's very ill.

MRS. BRAMSON: What's the matter with her?

OLIVIA: Pneumonia.

MRS. BRAMSON: Where's the telegram?

OLIVIA: I—I threw it away.

MRS. BRAMSON: Where'd you throw it?

OLIVIA: I—I threw it away.

MRS. BRAMSON: You haven't had any telegram.

OLIVIA: [*Impatiently*] No, I haven't!

MRS. BRAMSON: What's the matter with you?

OLIVIA: I can't stay in this house tonight.

MRS. BRAMSON: Why not?

OLIVIA: I'm frightened.

MRS. BRAMSON: Oh, don't be——

OLIVIA: Listen to me. I've never known before what it was to be terrified. But when I saw today beginning to end, and tonight getting nearer and nearer . . . I felt my fingertips getting cold. And I knew it was fright . . . stark fright. I'm not a fool, and I'm not hysterical . . . but I've been sitting in my room looking at myself in the glass, trying to control myself, telling myself what are real things . . . and what aren't. I don't know any longer. The day's over. The forest's all round us. Anything may happen. . . . You shouldn't stay in this house tonight. That's all.

MRS. BRAMSON: [*Blustering*] It's very silly of you, trying to scare an old woman with a weak heart. What have you to be frightened of?

OLIVIA: There's been a murder, you know.

MRS. BRAMSON: Nobody's going to murder *you!* Besides, we've got Danny to look after us. He's as strong as an ox, and no silly nerves about him . . . what *is* it you're afraid of?

OLIVIA: I——

MRS. BRAMSON: Shy, aren't you? . . . Where are you staying to-night?

OLIVIA: In Langbury, with Hubert Laurie and his sister.

MRS. BRAMSON: Not too frightened to make arrangements with *him*, eh.

OLIVIA: Arrangements?

MRS. BRAMSON: Well, some people would call it something else.

OLIVIA: [*Losing her temper*] Oh, won't you see . . .

MRS. BRAMSON: I'm very annoyed with you. How are you going to get there?

OLIVIA: Walking.

MRS. BRAMSON: Through the forest? Not too frightened for that, I see.

OLIVIA: I'd rather spend tonight in the forest than in this house.

MRS. BRAMSON: That sounds convincing, I must say. Well, you can go, but when you come back, I'm not so sure I shall answer the door. Think that over in the morning.

OLIVIA: The morning? . . .

DAN'S VOICE: [*In the bedroom, singing*] ". . . their home addresses . . . and their caresses . . . linger in my memory of those beautiful dames . . ."

> [OLIVIA *listens, holding her breath; she tries to say some-thing to* MRS. BRAMSON, *and fails. She makes an effort, and runs out of the front door. It bangs behind her.* DAN *comes back from the bedroom, carrying the shawl*]

DAN: [*Overcasual*] What was that at the door?

MRS. BRAMSON: My niece. Gone for the night, if you please.

DAN: Gone . . . for the night? [*He stares before him*]

MRS. BRAMSON: Would you believe it? Says she's frightened. . . . [*A pause*] Come along with the shawl, dear, I'm freezing. . . .

DAN: [*With a laugh, putting the shawl round her*] Don't know what's up with me——

> [*He goes to the table and looks at a newspaper.* MRS. TER-ENCE *comes in from the kitchen, her coat on*]

MRS. TERENCE: Well, I must go on my way rejoicin'.

MRS. BRAMSON: Everybody seems to be going. What *is* all this?

MRS. TERENCE: What d'you want for lunch tomorrow?

MRS. BRAMSON: Lunch tomorrow? . . . Let me see . . .

DAN: Lunch? Tomorrow? . . . [*After a pause*] What about a nice little steak?

MRS. BRAMSON: A steak, let me see . . . Yes, with baked potatoes——

DAN: And a nice roly-poly puddin', the kind you like?

MRS. BRAMSON: I think so.

MRS. TERENCE: Something light. O.K. Good night.

> [*She goes back into the kitchen.* DAN *scans the newspaper casually*]

MRS. BRAMSON: [*Inquisitive*] What are you reading, dear?

DAN: [*Breezily*] Only the murder again. About the clues that wasn't any good.

MRS. BRAMSON: [*Suddenly*] Danny, d'you think Olivia's a thief?

DAN: Shouldn't be surprised.

MRS. BRAMSON: What!

DAN: Her eyes wasn't very wide apart.

MRS. BRAMSON: [*Working herself up*] Goodness me . . . my jewel box . . . what a fool I was to let her go—my earrings . . . the double-faced——

> [*She wheels herself furiously into her bedroom.* DORA, *her hat and coat on, comes in from the kitchen in time to see her go*]

DORA: What's up with her?

DAN: [*Still at his paper*] Think's she been robbed.

DORA: Oh, is that all . . . That's the fourth time this month she's thought that. One of these days something *will* 'appen to her and will I be pleased? Oh, baby! . . . Where's Mrs. Terence?

DAN: Gone, I think.

DORA: [*Frightened*] Oh, law, no! [*Calling*] Mrs. Terence!

MRS. TERENCE: [*Calling in the kitchen*] Ye'es!

DORA: You 'aven't gone without me, 'ave you?

MRS. TERENCE: [*Appearing at the kitchen door, spearing a hatpin into her hat*] Yes, I'm 'alf-way there, what d'you think?

DORA: You did give me a turn! [*Going to the table and taking the box*] I think I'll 'ave a choc. [*Walking towards the hall*] I couldn't 'ave walked a step in those trees all by myself. Coming?

DAN: [*Suddenly*] I'd have come with you with pleasure, only I'm going the other direction. Payley Hill way.

MRS. TERENCE: [*Surprised*] You going out?

DORA: Oh?

DAN: [*In the hall, putting on hat and mackintosh*] Yes, I still feel a bit funny.

MRS. TERENCE: But you can't leave 'er 'ere by herself!

DORA: She'll scream the place down!

DAN: [*Overexplanatory*] I asked her, this very minute, and she don't seem to mind. You know what she is. Said it'll do me good, and won't hear of my stayin'. It's no good arguin' with her.

> [DORA *puts the chocolates down on the occasional table. She and* MRS. TERENCE *follow* DAN *into the hall*]

DORA: No good arguin' with her—don't I know it!

MRS. TERENCE: You 'ave a nice walk while you get the chance; you wait on 'er too much. . . . [*Closing the plush curtains so that they are all out of sight*] Ooh, ain't it dark. . . . Got the torch, Dora?

DORA: O.K., honey.

MRS. TERENCE: Laws, I'd be frightened goin' off by meself. . . . Well, we'd best 'urry, Dora. . . . Good night, Dan. Pity you aren't coming our way——

DAN'S VOICE: See you in the morning! Good night!

DORA'S VOICE: O.K.! . . . Toodle-oo!

> [*The door bangs. A pause*]

DAN'S VOICE: [*Outside the left window*] Good night!

MRS. TERENCE'S VOICE: [*Outside the right window*] Good night!

DORA: [*Same*] Good night!

> [*Silence*]

MRS. TERENCE: [*Farther away*] Good night!

DORA: [*Same*] Good night!

> [MRS. BRAMSON *comes trundling back from the bedroom in her chair*]

MRS. BRAMSON: Good night here, good night there; anybody'd think

it was the night before Judgment Day. What's the matter with
. . . [*Seeing the room is empty*] Talking to myself. Wish people
wouldn't walk out of rooms and leave me high and dry. Don't
like it. [*She wheels herself round to the table. A pause. She looks
round impatiently*] Where's my chocolates? . . . [*She looks
round again, gets up out of her chair for the first time in the
play, walks quite normally across the room to the mantelpiece,
sees her chocolates are not there, walks up to the occasional table,
and takes up the box*] That girl's been at them again . . . [*She
walks back to her chair, carrying the chocolates, and sits in it again.
She begins to munch. She suddenly stops, as if she has heard something*] What's that? . . . [*She listens again. A cry is heard far
away*] Oh, God . . . Danny! [*The cry is repeated*] Danny!
[*The cry is heard a third time*] It's an owl . . . Oh, Lord! [*She
falls back in relief, and eats another chocolate. The clock strikes
the half-hour. Silence. The silence gets on her nerves. After a
pause, calling softly*] Danny! . . . [*As there is no answer*]
What's the boy doing in that kitchen? [*She takes up the newspaper, sees a headline, and puts it down hastily. She sees the Bible
on the table, opens it, and turns over pages. After a pause, suddenly*] I've got the jitters. I've got the jitters. I've got the jitters.
. . . [*Calling loudly*] Danny! [*She waits; there is complete
silence. She rises, walks over to the kitchen door, and flings it wide
open. Shouting*] Danny! [*No reply*] He's gone. . . . They've
all gone. . . . They've left me. . . . [*Losing control, beating her
hands wildly on her Bible*] Oh, Lord, help a poor woman. . . .
They've left me! [*Tottering to the sunroom*] Danny . . . where
are you? . . . Danny. . . . I'm going to be murdered. . . . I'm
going to be murdered! . . . Danny . . . [*Her voice rising, until
she is shrieking hysterically*] Danny! Danny! Danny! [*She stops
suddenly. Footsteps on the gravel outside the front door. In a
strangled whisper*] There's something outside . . . something
outside. . . . Oh, heavens . . . [*Staggering across to the sofa*]
Danny, where are you? Where are you? There's something outs—
[*The front door bangs. She collapses on the sofa, terrified, her
enormous Bible clasped to her breast*] Oh, Lord, help me . . .
help me . . . Oh, Lord, help . . . [*Muttering, her eyes closed*]

. . . Forgive us our trespasses . . . [*The curtains are suddenly parted. It is* DAN, *a cigarette between his lips. He stands motionless, his feet planted apart, holding the curtains. There is murder in his face. She is afraid to look, but is forced to at last*] Danny . . . Oh . . . Oh . . .

DAN: [*Smiling, suddenly normal and reassuring*] That's all right. . . . It's only Danny. . . .

MRS. BRAMSON: Thank God. . . . [*Going off into laughing hysteria*] Ah . . . ah . . . ah. . . .

> [DAN *throws his cigarette away, lays his hat on the occasional table, throws his mackintosh on the left window seat, and sits beside her, patting her, looking round to see no one has heard her cries*]

MRS. BRAMSON: I'll never forgive you, never. Oh, my heart . . . Oh, oh—oh——

> [*He runs across to the medicine cupboard and brings back a brandy bottle and two glasses*]

DAN: Now have a drop of this . . . [*As she winces at the taste*] Go on, do you good . . . [*As she drinks*] I am sorry, I am really . . . You see, they wanted me to see them to the main path, past the rubbish heap, see, in case they were frightened. . . . Now, that's better, isn't it?

> [*They are seated side by side on the sofa*]

MRS. BRAMSON: I don't know yet. . . . Give me some more. . . . [*He pours one out for her, and one for himself. They drink*] All alone, I was . . . [*Her face puckering with self-pity*] Just an old woman calling for help . . . [*Her voice breaking*] . . . and no answer.

DAN: [*Putting the bottle on the floor beside him*] Poor old mum, runnin' about lookin' for Danny——

MRS. BRAMSON: [*Sharply*] I wasn't running about as much as all that. . . . Oh, the relief when I saw your face——

DAN: I bet you wasn't half glad, eh?

MRS. BRAMSON: You're the only one that understands me, Danny, that's what you are——

DAN: [*Patting her*] That's right——

MRS. BRAMSON: I don't have to tell you everything I've been through. I don't have to tell you about my husband, how unkind and ungodly he was—I wouldn't have minded so much him being ungodly, but oh, he *was* unkind . . . [*Sipping*] And I don't have to tell *you* how unkind he was. You know. You just know . . . whatever else I've not been, I was *always* a great one on psychology.

DAN: You was. [*He takes her glass and fills it again, and his own*]

MRS. BRAMSON: I'm glad those other people have gone. Awful screeching common women. Answer back, answer back, answer back . . . Isn't it time for my medicine? [*He hands her glass back. They both drink. He sits smiling and nodding at her*] That day you said to me about me reminding you of your mother . . . [*As he slowly begins to roll up his sleeves a little way*] These poets and rubbishy people can think all they like about their verses and sonnets and such—that girl Olivia writes sonnets—would you believe it——

DAN: Fancy.

MRS. BRAMSON: They can think all they like, that was a beautiful thought. [*Her arm on his shoulder*] And when you think you're just an ignorant boy, it's . . . it's startling.

DAN: [*With a laugh*] That's right.

MRS. BRAMSON: I'll never forget that. Not as long as I live . . . [*Trying to stem the tears*] I want a chocolate now.

DAN: Right you are! . . . [*Placing her glass and his own on the floor and walking briskly to the table*] A nice one with a soft center, the kind you like . . . Why, here's one straight away . . . [*He walks slowly to the back of the sofa. In a level voice*] Now shut your eyes . . . open your mouth. . . .

MRS. BRAMSON: [*Purring*] Oh, Danny . . . You're the only one . . . [*She shuts her eyes. He stands behind her, and puts the chocolate into her mouth. His fingers close slowly and involuntarily, over her neck; she feels his touch, and draws both his hands down, giggling, so that his face almost touches hers. Maudlin*] What strong hands they are. . . . You're a pet, my little chubby-face, my baby-face, my Danny. . . . Am I in a draught? [*A pause.* DAN *draws his hands slowly away, walks to the back, and shuts the plush curtains*] I've got to take care of myself, haven't I?

DAN: [*Turning slowly and looking at her*] You have. [*He picks up the paraffin can briskly and goes towards the kitchen*]

MRS. BRAMSON: What are you——

DAN: Only takin' the paraffin tin in the kitchen.

[*He goes into the kitchen*]

MRS. BRAMSON: [*Half to herself*] That girl should have carried it in. Anything to annoy me. Tomorrow—— [*Turning and seeing that he is gone*] Danny! [*Shrieking suddenly*] Danny!

[DAN *runs back from the kitchen*]

DAN: What's the matter?

[*He looks hastily towards the hall to see no one has heard*]

MRS. BRAMSON: Oh dear, I thought——

DAN: [*Sitting on the back of the sofa*] I was only putting the paraffin away. Now—— [*He leans over the sofa, and raises his arms slowly*]

MRS. BRAMSON: [*Putting her hand on his arm*] I think I'll go to bed now.

DAN: [*After a pause, dropping his arm*] O.K.

MRS. BRAMSON: And I'll have my supper tray in my room. [*Petulantly*] Get me back into my chair, dear, will you?

DAN: [*Jerkily*] O.K. [*He crosses to the invalid chair*]

MRS. BRAMSON: Has she put the glass by the bed for my teeth?

DAN: [*Bringing over the chair*] I put it there myself. [*He helps her into the chair and pulls it over towards the bedroom*]

MRS. BRAMSON: [*Suddenly, in the middle of the room*] I want to be read to now.

DAN: [*After a pause of indecision*] O.K. [*Clapping his hands, effusively*] What'll you have? The old *East Lynne*?

MRS. BRAMSON: No. I don't feel like anything sentimental tonight . . .

DAN: [*Looking towards the desk*] What'll you have then?

MRS. BRAMSON: I think I'd like the Bible.

[*A pause. He looks at her*]

DAN: O.K.

MRS. BRAMSON: [*As he goes smartly to the sofa, fetches the Bible, pulls up a chair to the right of her, sits and looks for the place*] That piece you were reading . . . It's Sunday. . . . Isn't that nice . . . all the aches and pains quiet for once . . . pretty peaceful . . .

DAN: [*Reading*] "Blessed is the man that walketh not in the counsel of the ungodly, nor standeth in the way of sinners, nor sitteth in the seat of the scornful. . . ."

MRS. BRAMSON: [*Drowsily*] You read so nicely, Danny.

DAN: Very kind of you, my lady. [*Reading a little breathlessly*] "But his delight is in the law of the Lord; and in His law doth he meditate day and night——"

MRS. BRAMSON: Sh!

DAN: What? Can you hear something?

MRS. BRAMSON: Yes! A sort of—thumping noise . . . [*She looks at him suddenly, leans forward, and puts her right hand inside his jacket*] Why, Danny, it's you! It's your heart . . . beating! [*He laughs*] Are you all right, dear?

DAN: Fine. I been running along the path, see . . . [*Garrulously*] I been out of training, I suppose; when I was at sea I never missed a day running round the decks, o' course. . . .

MRS. BRAMSON: [*Sleepily*] Of course . . .

DAN: [*Speaking quickly, as if eager to conjure up a vision*] I remember those mornings—on some sea—very misty—pale it is, with the sun like breathing silver where he's coming' up across the water, but not blowin' on the sea at all . . . and the sea gulls standing on the deck rail looking at themselves in the water on the deck, and only me about and nothing else. . . .

MRS. BRAMSON: [*Nodding sleepily*] Yes . . .

DAN: And the sun. Just me and the sun.

MRS. BRAMSON: [*Nodding*] There's no sun now, dear; it's night!

[*A pause. He drums his fingers on the Bible*]

DAN: Yes . . . it's night now. [*Reading, feverishly*] "The ungodly are not so, but are like the chaff which the wind driveth away——"

MRS. BRAMSON: I think I'll go to bye-byes. . . . We'll have the rest tomorrow, shall we? [*Testily*] Help me, dear, help me, you know what I am——

DAN: [*Drumming his fingers: suddenly, urgently*] Wait a minute. . . . I—I've only got two more verses——

MRS. BRAMSON: Hurry it up, dear. I don't want to wake up in the morning with a nasty cold.

DAN: [*Reading slowly*] ". . . Therefore the ungodly shall not stand in the judgment, nor sinners in the congregation of the righteous . . . For the Lord knoweth the way of the righteous . . . but the way of the ungodly . . . shall perish. . . ." [*A pause. He shuts the Bible loudly, and lays it on the table.* MRS. BRAMSON *can hardly keep awake*] That's the end.

MRS. BRAMSON: Is it? . . . Ah, well, it's been a long day——

DAN: Are you quite comfortable?

MRS. BRAMSON: A bit achy. Glad to go to bed. Hope that woman's put my bottle in all right. Bet she hasn't——

DAN: Sure you're comfortable? Wouldn't you like a cushion back of your head?

MRS. BRAMSON: No, dear, just wheel me——

DAN: I think you'll be more comfortable with a cushion. [*Rising, humming*] "I'm a pretty little feller, everybody knows . . . dunno what to call me . . ."

[*He goes deliberately across, humming, and picks up a large black cushion from the sofa. His hands close on the cushion and he stands silent a moment. He moves slowly back to the other side of her; he stands looking at her, his back three-quarters to the audience and his face hidden: he is holding the cushion in both hands.* MRS. BRAMSON *shakes herself out of sleep and looks at him*]

MRS. BRAMSON: What a funny look on your face, dear. Smiling like that . . . [*Foolishly*] You look so kind . . . [*He begins to raise the cushion slowly*] So kind . . . [*Absently*] What are you going to do with that cushion? . . .

[*The lights dim gradually into complete darkness, and the music grows into a thunderous crescendo*]

SCENE 2

The music plays a few bars, then dies down proportionately as the lights come up again.

Half an hour later. The scene is the same, with the same lighting; the room is empty and the wheelchair has been removed.

DAN *comes in from the sunroom, smoking the stub of a cigarette. He crosses smartly, takes the bottle and glasses from the floor by the sofa and places them on the table, pours himeslf a quick drink, places the bottle on the floor next to the desk, throws away his stub, takes another cigarette from his pocket, puts it in his mouth, takes out a box of matches, and lights a match. The clock chimes. He looks at it, seems to make a decision, blows out the match, throws the matchbox on the table, takes* MRS. BRAMSON'S *tape and keys from his trouser pocket, crosses quietly to the safe by the fireplace, opens it, takes out the cash box, sits on the sofa, unlocks the cash box, stuffs the keys back into his trousers, opens the cash box, takes out the notes, looks at them, delighted, stuffs them into his pockets, hurries into the sunroom, returns a second later with the empty invalid chair, plants it in the middle of the room, picks up the cushion from the floor above the table, looks at it a moment, arrested, throws it callously on the invalid chair, hurries into the kitchen, returns immediately with the paraffin, sprinkles it freely over the invalid chair, places the can under the table, lifts the paraffin lamp from the table, and is just about to smash it over the invalid chair when there is a sound of a chair falling over in the sunroom. His face inscrutable, he looks towards it. He carries the lamp stealthily to the desk, puts it down, looks round, picks a chair from near the table, and stands at the sun-room door with the chair held high above his head.*

The stagger of footsteps; OLIVIA *stands in the doorway to the sunroom. She has been running through the forest; her clothes are wild, her hair has fallen about her shoulders, and she is no longer wearing spectacles. She looks nearly beautiful. Her manner is quiet, almost dazed.* DAN *lowers the chair slowly and sits on the other side of the table. A pause.*

OLIVIA: I've never seen a dead body before . . . I climbed through the window and nearly fell over it. Like a sack of potatoes or something. I thought it was, at first. . . . And that's murder. [*As he looks up at her*] But it's so ordinary . . . I came back . . . [*As he lights his cigarette*] . . . expecting . . . ha [*Laughing hysterically*] . . . I don't know . . . and here I find you, smoking a cigarette . . . you might have been tidying the room for the night. It's so . . . ordinary . . . [*After a pause, with a cry*] Why don't you *say* something!

DAN: I thought you were goin' to stay the night at that feller's.

OLIVIA: I was.

DAN: What d'you come back for?

OLIVIA: [*The words pouring out*] To find you out. You've kept me guessing for a fortnight. Guessing hard. I very nearly knew, all the time. But not quite. And now I do know.

DAN: Why was you so keen on finding me out?

OLIVIA: [*Vehemently, coming to the table*] In the same way any sane, decent-minded human would want—would want to have you arrested for the monster you are!

DAN: [*Quietly*] What d'you come back for?

OLIVIA: I . . . I've told you . . . [*He smiles at her slowly and shakes his head. She sits at the table and closes her eyes*] I got as far as the edge of the wood. I could see the lights in the village . . . I came back.

[*She buries her head in her arms.* DAN *rises, looks at her a moment regretfully, puts away his cigarette, and stands with both hands over the invalid chair*]

DAN: [*Casually*] She didn't keep any money anywhere else, did she?

OLIVIA: I've read a lot about evil——

> [DAN *realizes his hands are wet with paraffin and wipes them on his trousers*]

DAN: Clumsy . . .

OLIVIA: I never expected to come across it in real life.

DAN: [*Lightly*] You didn't ought to read so much. I never got through a book yet. . . . But I'll read you all right. . . . [*Crossing to her, leaning over the table, and smiling at her intently*] You haven't had a drop of drink, and yet you feel as if you had. You never knew there was such a secret part inside of you. All that book-learnin' and moral-me-eye here and social-me-eye there—you took that off on the edge of the wood same as if it was an overcoat . . . and you left it there!

OLIVIA: I hate you. I . . . hate you!

DAN: [*Urgently*] And same as anybody out for the first time without their overcoat, you feel as light as air! Same as I feel, sometimes—only I never had no overcoat—— [*Excited*] Why—this is my big chance! You're the one I can tell about meself! Oh, I'm sick o' hearin' how clever everybody else is—I want to tell 'em how clever *I* am for a change! . . . Money I'm going to have, and people doin' what they're told, and *me* tellin' them to do it! There was a 'oman at the Tallboys, wasn't there? She wouldn't be told, would she? She thought she was up 'gainst a soft fellow in a uniform, didn't she? She never knew it was *me* she was dealin' with— [*Striking his chest in a paroxysm of elation*]—Me! And this old girl treatin' me like a son 'cause I made her think she was a chronic invalid—ha! She's been more use to me tonight [*Tapping the notes in his jacket pocket, smartly*] than she has to any other body all her life. Stupid, that's what people are . . . stupid. If those two hadn't been stupid they might be breathin' now; you're not stupid; that's why I'm talkin' to you. [*With exaggerated self-possession*] You said just now murder's ordinary. . . . Well, it isn't ordinary at all, see? And I'm not an ordinary chap. There's one big difference 'tween me and other fellows that try this game. I'll *never be found out*. 'Cause I don't care a—— [*Snapping his fingers, grandly*]

The world's goin' to hear from me. That's me. [*Chuckling*] You wait. . . . [*After a pause*] But you can't wait, can you?

OLIVIA: What do you mean?

DAN: Well, when I say I'll never be found out, what I mean is, no living soul will be able to tell any other living soul about me. [*Beginning to roll up a sleeve, nonchalantly*] Can you think of anybody . . . who can go tomorrow . . . and tell the police the fire at Forest Corner . . . wasn't an accident at all?

OLIVIA: I—I can.

DAN: Oh, no, you can't.

OLIVIA: Why can't I?

DAN: Well, I'm up against a very serious problem, I am. But the answer to it is as simple as pie, to a fellow like me, simple as pie . . . [*Rolling up the other sleeve a little way*] She isn't going to be the only one . . . found tomorrow . . . in the fire at Forest Corner. . . . [*After a pause*] Aren't you frightened? You ought to be! [*Smiling*] Don't you think I'll do it?

OLIVIA: I know you will. I just can't realize it.

DAN: You know, when I told you all that about meself just now, I'd made up my mind then about you. [*Moving slowly after her, round the table, as she steps back towards the window*] That's what I am, see? I make up me mind to do a thing, and I do it . . . You remember that first day when I come in here? I said to meself then, "There's a girl that's got her wits about her; she knows a thing or two; different from the others." I was right, wasn't I? You —— [*Stopping abruptly, and looking round the room*] What's that light in here?

OLIVIA: What light?

DAN: There's somebody in this room's holdin' a flashlight.

OLIVIA: It can't be in this room. . . . It must be a light in the wood.

DAN: It can't be.

[*A flashlight crosses the window curtain.* OLIVIA *turns and stares at it*]

OLIVIA: Somebody's watching the bungalow. . . .

[*He looks at her, as if he did not understand*]

DAN: [*Fiercely*] Nobody's watching! . . . [*He runs to the window. She backs into the corner of the room*] I'm the one that watches! They've got no call to watch me! I'll go out and tell them that, an' all! [*Opening the curtains in a frenzy*] I'm the one that watches! [*The light crosses the window again. He stares, then claps his hands over his eyes. Backing to the sofa*] Behind them trees. [*Clutching the invalid chair*] Hundreds back of each tree . . . Thousands of eyes. The whole damn world's on my track! . . . [*Sitting on the edge of the sofa, and listening*] What's that? . . . Like a big wall fallin' over into the sea. . . . [*Closing his hands over his ears convulsively*]

OLIVIA: [*Coming down to him*] They mustn't come in. . . .

DAN: [*Turning to her*] Yes, but . . . [*Staring*] You're lookin' at me as if you never seen *me* before. . . .

OLIVIA: I never have. Nobody has. You've stopped acting at last. You're real. Frightened. Like a child. [*Putting her arm about his shoulders*] They mustn't come in. . . .

DAN: But everything's slippin' away. From underneath our feet . . . Can't you feel it? Starting slow . . . and then hundreds of miles an hour . . . I'm goin' backwards! . . . And there's a wind in my ears, terrible blowin' wind. . . . Everything's going past me like the telegraph poles. . . . All the things I've never seen . . . faster and faster . . . backwards—back to the day I was born. [*Shrieking*] I can see it coming . . . the day I was born! . . . [*Turning to her, simply*] I'm goin' to die. [*A pause. A knock at the front door*] It's getting cold.

[*Another knock; louder. She presses his head to her*]

OLIVIA: It's all right. You won't die. I'll tell them I *made* you do it. I'll tell lies—I'll tell——

[*A third and louder knock at the front door. She realizes that she must answer, goes into the hall, opens the front door, and comes back, hiding DAN from view*]

BELSIZE: [*In the hall*] Good evening. . . . Sorry to pop back like this . . . [*He comes into the room, followed by DORA and MRS.*

TERENCE, *both terrified. Looking round*] Everything looks all right here.

MRS. TERENCE: I tell you we *did* 'ear her! Plain as plain! And we'd gone near a quarter of a mile——

DORA: Plain as plain——

MRS. TERENCE: Made my blood run cold. "Danny!" she screamed, "Danny, where are you?" she said. She wanted 'im back, she did, to save 'er——

DORA: Because she was bein' murdered. I know it! I'd never a' run like that if I 'adn't 'eard——

BELSIZE: We'll soon find out who's right. . . . Now then—— [*As* OLIVIA *steps aside behind the sofa*] Hello, Dan!

DAN: [*Quietly, rising and standing by the fireplace*] Hello.

BELSIZE: [*Standing behind the invalid chair*] Second time today, eh? . . .

DAN: That's right.

BELSIZE: How's the old lady?

DAN: [*After a pause*] Not so bad, thanks, inspector! Gone to bed and says she didn't want to be disturbed——

BELSIZE: Smell of paraffin . . .

DAN: [*With a last desperate attempt at bluster*] You know what she's like, inspector, a bit nervy these days—— [*As* BELSIZE *goes to the bedroom and flashes a light into it*] I'd no sooner got round the corner she screamed for me—"Danny, Danny, Danny!" she was screaming—Danny she calls me, a pet name for Dan, that is——

[BELSIZE *goes into the sunroom*]

DAN: [*Rambling on mechanically*] I told her so then. I said "It's dangerous, that's what it is, havin' so much paraffin in the house." That paraffin—she shouldn't ha' had so much paraffin in the house——

[*His voice trails away. Silence.* BELSIZE *comes back, his face intent, one hand in a coat pocket. A pause*]

BELSIZE: [*To* OLIVIA] What are you doing here?

OLIVIA: I'm concerned in——

DAN: [*Loudly, decisively, silencing her*] It's all right. [*Crossing to* BELSIZE *and swaggering desperately, in front of the women*] I'm the fellow. Anything I'm concerned in, I run all my myself. If there's going to be any putting me on a public platform to answer any questions, I'm going to do it by myself . . . [*Looking at* OLIVIA] . . . or not at all. I'll manage meself all right——

BELSIZE: I get you. Like a bit of limelight, eh?

DAN: [*Smiling*] Well . . .

BELSIZE: [*As if humouring him*] Let's have a look at your hands, old boy, will you?

> [*With an amused look at* OLIVIA, DAN *holds out his hands. Without warning,* BELSIZE *claps a pair of handcuffs over his wrists.* DAN *stares at them a moment, then sits on the sofa, and starts to pull at them furiously over his knee. He beats at them wildly, moaning and crying like an animal. He subsides gradually, looks at the others and rises*]

DAN: [*Muttering, holding his knee*] Hurt meself . . .

BELSIZE: That's better. . . . Better come along quietly. . . .

> [*He goes up towards the hall.* DAN *follows him, and takes his hat from the occasional table. As he puts it on he catches sight of his face in the mirror*]

BELSIZE: [*To the others, crisply, during this*] I've a couple of men outside. I'll send 'em in. See that nothing's disturbed. . . . Coming, old chap?

DORA: What's 'e doin'?

MRS. TERENCE: He's lookin' at himself in the glass. . . .

> [*A pause*]

DAN: [*Speaking to the mirror*] This is the real thing, old boy. Actin'. . . . That's what she said, wasn't it? She was right, you know . . . I've been playing up to you, haven't I? I showed you a trick or two, didn't I? . . . But this is the real thing. [*Swaying*] Got a cigarette? . . . [*Seeing* OLIVIA] You're not goin' to believe what she said? About helpin' me?

BELSIZE: [*Humouring him*] No. [*Putting a cigarette between*

DAN's *lips and lighting it*] Plenty of women get a bit hysterical about a lad in your position. You'll find 'em queuing up all right when the time comes. Proposals of marriage by the score.

DAN: [*Pleased*] Will they?

BELSIZE: Come along——

[DAN *turns to follow him.* DORA *is in the way*]

DAN: Oh, yes . . . I forgot about you. . . . [*Smiling, with a curious detached sadness*] Poor little fellow. Poor little chap . . . [*Looking round*] You know, I'd like somethin' now I never wanted before. A long walk, all by meself. And just when I can't have it. [*Laughing*] That's contrary, isn't it?

BELSIZE: [*Sternly*] Coming?

DAN: [*Looking at* OLIVIA] Just comin'.

[*He goes to* OLIVIA, *takes out his cigarette, puts his manacled arms round her, and kisses her suddenly and violently on the mouth. He releases her with an air of bravado, puts back his cigarette, and looks at her*]

DAN: Well, I'm goin' to be hanged in the end. . . . But they'll get their money's worth at the trial. You wait!

[*He smiles, and raises his hand to his hat brim with the old familiar jaunty gesture of farewell. He walks past* BELSIZE *and out through the front door.* BELSIZE *follows him. The bang of the front door.* OLIVIA *falls to the sofa. The sound of* DORA's *sobbing*]

CURTAIN

An Inspector Calls

J. B. PRIESTLEY

J. B. Priestley

The opening of *An Inspector Calls* was a major event of the 1946 London theatre season. Produced by the Old Vic Theatre Company with a superb cast headed by Ralph Richardson, Margaret Leighton and Alec Guinness, and directed by Basil Dean, the play also restored J. B. Priestley to a theatrical area that he successfully invaded in 1932 with *Dangerous Corner*: the suspense play with a pronounced social conscience. Like its predecessor, *An Inspector Calls* finds the author gathering together a group of people, seemingly wrapped in respectability, then by remorseless cross-examination leaves them a self-convicted assemblage of guilty persons. Yet, while reality pervades in *An Inspector Calls*, there also is a singular undercurrent of mysticism flowing through the play, particularly in the enigmatic character of Inspector Goole. Who precisely is this mysterious caller, the man-from-the-street with the polite urgency and the sudden frost in his voice? Is he indeed a police inspector, and if not who (in this world or the next) can he be? Does he, in short, speak with the tongue of man or of angel?

One of Britain's foremost men of letters, John Boynton Priestley, who prefers to be known as J. B. Priestley, was born at Bradford, England, on September 13, 1894. He was educated there and at Trinity Hall, Cambridge, where he began his illustrious career as a writer, though it actually wasn't until 1929 that he reached his peak with his picaresque novel *The Good Companions*. In 1931, he collaborated with Edward Knoblock on a dramatization and any doubts of Priestley's innate theatrical capacity were soon at rest. The play ran for 331 performances, and for some time thereafter, Priestley, the dramatist, tended to overshadow the other Priestleys: novelist, journalist, and essayist. Encouraged by its reception, he decided to persevere as a playwright and in 1932 turned out *Dangerous Corner*, written in a week, "chiefly to prove that a man might produce long novels and yet be able to write effectively, using the strictest economy, for the stage."

Dangerous Corner also foreshadowed a later development in Priestley's career: his "time" plays that started in 1937 with *Time and the Conways*, bringing to the theatre his dramatic demonstration of J. W. Dunne's theory of Serialism, "the curious feeling which almost everyone has now and then experienced—that sudden, fleeting, disturbing conviction that something which is happening at the moment happened before."

Since 1931, Mr. Priestley has contributed over thirty plays to the theatre. In addition to the aforementioned, they include: *Eden End; I Have Been Here Before; Johnson Over Jordan; The Linden Tree; Laburnum Grove; When We Are Married; They Came to a City; Mr. Kettle and Mrs. Moon; Music at Night; Bees on the Boat Deck;* and *A Severed Head*, adapted with Iris Murdoch from her novel of the same name and which ran for well over 1,000 performances in London. He also has collaborated on two plays, *Dragon's Mouth* and *The White Countess*, with his present wife, Jacquetta Hawkes, a well-known archaeologist and writer.

His novels, stories, essays, criticisms, histories, and autobiographical writings fill more than fifty published volumes, indisputably making him one of the century's most prolific and widely read authors.

Throughout his career, Priestley's professionalism, both in drawing substantial characters and in deftly spinning the plot fabrics of his plays, has been impressive. He can enrich a play with touches of shrewd, humorous and sentimental observation and when called for there also is a pertinacious reformer at work. A man who will not bow to compromise in his plays, he has been championed by some of the world's foremost drama assessors. Alan Dent said of Priestley: "We urgently need his fine, uncommon, questing mind in the theatre. He is a true dramatist—always an interesting one, and sometimes a first-rate one." To J. C. Trewin he is "one of the first of our dramatists: an exasperating, obstinate fellow, no doubt, but a dramatist with a love of life, a love of the theatre, a great capacity for work, and a gift for exploration and inquiry."

Priestley's passion for the theatre has not been confined to play-writing: for two eventful years he was actively associated in the management of the Duchess Theatre (London) and he also served as the first president of the worldwide International Theatre Institute.

An Inspector Calls was first produced by the Old Vic Theatre Company at the New Theatre, London, on October 1, 1946. The cast was as follows:

ARTHUR BIRLING	*Julien Mitchell*
GERALD CROFT	*Harry Andrews*
SHEILA BIRLING	*Margaret Leighton*
SYBIL BIRLING	*Marian Spencer*
EDNA	*Marjorie Dunkels*
ERIC BIRLING	*Alec Guinness*
INSPECTOR GOOLE	*Ralph Richardson*

Directed by   Basil Dean

An Inspector Calls was first presented in the United States at the Booth Theatre, New York, on October 21, 1947, by Courtney Burr and Lassor H. Grosberg. The cast was as follows:

ARTHUR BIRLING	*Melville Cooper*
GERALD CROFT	*John Buckmaster*
SHEILA BIRLING	*Rene Ray*
SYBIL BIRLING	*Doris Lloyd*
EDNA	*Patricia Marmont*
ERIC BIRLING	*John Merivale*
INSPECTOR GOOLE	*Thomas Mitchell*

Directed by	Sir Cedric Hardwicke
Setting, Lighting, and Costumes by	Stewart Chaney

SCENE: *The dining room of the Birlings' house in Brumley, an industrial city in the North Midlands.*

TIME: *An evening in spring, 1912.*

ACT ONE

Dining room of a fairly large suburban house, belonging to a fairly prosperous manufacturer. It is a solidly built room, with good solid furniture of the period. Upstage right there is an alcove with a heavy sideboard. A door from the alcove leads to the kitchen. Upstage left is a large double door used almost exclusively. A fireplace is along the right wall with a curtained window on either side. There are two leather armchairs on either side of the fireplace and downstage from it an ornate floor lamp and a small table with telephone. A little upstage of center is a solid but not too large dining room table with solid set of dining room chairs around it. A few imposing but tasteless pictures and engravings. The general effect is substantial and comfortable and old-fashioned but not cozy and homelike.

The four BIRLINGS *and* GERALD *are seated at table, with* ARTHUR BIRLING *at one end, his wife at the other,* ERIC BIRLING *downstage, and* SHEILA *and* GERALD CROFT *seated upstage.* EDNA, *a neatly dressed parlormaid, in her late twenties, is just clearing table, which has no cloth, of dessert plates, champagne glasses and champagne bottle, taking them to sideboard, then going back to table with decanter of port. Port glasses are already on table. All five are in evening dress of the period, the men in tails and white ties.* ARTHUR BIRLING *is a heavy-looking, rather portentous man in his middle fifties, with fairly easy manners but rather provincial in his speech. His wife is about fifty, a rather cold woman and her husband's social superior.* SHEILA *is a pretty girl in her early twenties, very pleased with life and rather excited.* GERALD CROFT *is an attractive chap about thirty, rather too manly to be a dandy, but very much the easy well-bred young-man-about-town.* ERIC *is in his middle twenties, not quite at ease, half shy, half assertive. At the moment they have all had a good dinner, are celebrating a special occasion, and are pleased with themselves.*

BIRLING: Thank you, Edna. That's right. [*Pushes port toward* GERALD. EDNA *crosses to sideboard*] You ought to like this port, Gerald. As a matter of fact, Finchley assured me it's exactly the same port your father gets from him.

GERALD: Then it'll be all right. The governor prides himself on being a good judge of port. I don't pretend to know much about it.

[EDNA *crosses down to table*]

SHEILA: [*Gaily, possessively*] I should jolly well think so, Gerald. I'd hate you to know all about port—like one of these purple-faced old men.

[EDNA *crosses to sideboard*]

BIRLING: Here, I'm not a purple-faced old man.

SHEILA: No, not yet. But then you don't know all about port—do you?

BIRLING: [*Noticing that his wife,* SYBIL, *has not taken any*] Now then, Sybil, you must take a little tonight. Special occasion, y'know, eh?

SHEILA: Yes, go on, mummy. You must drink our health.

[EDNA *goes to table*]

MRS. BIRLING: [*Smiling*] Very well, then. Just a little, thank you. [*To* EDNA, *who is about to go with tray*] All right, Edna. I'll ring from the drawing room when we want coffee. Probably in about half an hour.

[EDNA *crosses to kitchen door*]

EDNA: [*Going*] Yes, ma'am.

[EDNA *goes out. They now have all the glasses filled.* BIRLING *beams at them and clearly relaxes*]

BIRLING: Well, well—this is very nice. Very nice. Good dinner, too, Sybil. Tell Cook from me.

GERALD: [*Politely*] Absolutely first class.

MRS. BIRLING: [*Reproachfully*] Arthur, you're not supposed to say such things——

BIRLING: Oh—come, come—I'm treating Gerald like one of the family. And I'm sure he won't object.

SHEILA: [*With mock aggressiveness*] Go on, Gerald—just you object!

GERALD: [*Smiling*] Wouldn't dream of it. In fact, I insist upon being one of the family now. I've been trying long enough, haven't I? [*As* SHEILA *does not reply, with more insistence*] Haven't I? You know I have.

MRS. BIRLING: [*Smiling*] Of course she does.

SHEILA: [*Half serious, half playful*] Yes—except for all last summer when you never came near me, and I wondered what had happened to you.

GERALD: And I've told you—I was awfully busy at the works all that time.

SHEILA: [*Same tone as before*] Yes, that's what *you* say.

MRS. BIRLING: Now, Sheila, don't tease him. When you're married you'll realize that men with important work to do sometimes have to spend nearly all their time and energy on their business. You'll have to get used to that, just as I had. Isn't that so, Arthur?

BIRLING: Quite, quite.

SHEILA: I don't believe *I* will. [*Half playful, half serious. To* GERALD] So you be careful.

GERALD: Oh—I will, I will.

[ERIC *suddenly guffaws. Rises, crosses to fender. His parents look at him*]

SHEILA: [*Severely*] Now—what's the joke?

ERIC: I don't know—I just suddenly felt I had to laugh.

SHEILA: You're squiffy.

ERIC: I'm not.

MRS. BIRLING: What an expression, Sheila! Really, the things you girls pick up these days!

ERIC: [*Sits on fender*] If you think that's the best she can do——

SHEILA: Don't be an ass, Eric.

MRS. BIRLING: Now stop it, you two. Arthur, what about this famous toast of yours?

BIRLING: [*Rising*] Yes, of course. [*Clears his throat*] Well, Gerald, I know you agreed that we should only have this quiet little family party. It's a pity Sir George and—er—Lady Croft can't be with us, but they're abroad and so it can't be helped. As I told you, they sent me a very nice cable—couldn't be nicer. I'm not sorry that we're celebrating quietly like this——

MRS. BIRLING: Much nicer, really.

GERALD: I quite agree.

BIRLING: So do I, but it makes speechmaking more difficult.

ERIC: [*Not too rudely*] Well, don't do any.

BIRLING: What?

ERIC: Don't do any.

BIRLING: Oh, yes, I will. This is one of the happiest nights of my life. And one day, I hope, Eric, when you've a daughter of your own, you'll understand why. Gerald, I'm going to tell you frankly, without any pretenses, that your engagement to Sheila means a tremendous lot to me. She'll make you happy. I'm sure you'll make her happy. You're just the kind of son-in-law I've always wanted. Your father and I have been friendly rivals in business for some time now—though Crofts Limited are both older and bigger than Birling and Company—and now you've brought us together, and perhaps we may look forward to the time when Crofts and Birlings are no longer competing but are working together—for lower costs and higher prices.

GERALD: Hear, hear! And I think my father would agree to that, too.

MRS. BIRLING: Now, Arthur, I don't think you ought to talk business on an occasion like this.

SHEILA: Neither do I. All wrong.

BIRLING: Quite so, I agree with you. I only mentioned it in passing. What I did want to say was—that Sheila's a lucky girl—and, Gerald, I think you're a pretty fortunate young man, too.

GERALD: I know I am—just this once anyhow.

BIRLING: [*Rises, raising his glass*] So here's wishing the pair of you —the very best that life can bring. Gerald and Sheila!

ERIC: All the best.

MRS. BIRLING: [*Raising her glass, smiling*] Yes, Gerald.

ERIC: [*Rather noisily*] All the best! She's got a nasty temper sometimes—but she's not bad really. Good old Sheila!

MRS. BIRLING: Yes, Sheila, darling. [*Rises, as does* ERIC] Our congratulations and very best wishes!

GERALD: Thank you.

[ALL *sit*]

SHEILA: Chump! I can't drink to this, can I? When do *I* drink?

GERALD: You can drink to me.

SHEILA: [*Quiet and serious now*] All right, then. I drink to you.

[*Rises. For a moment they look at each other*]

GERALD: [*Quietly. Rising*] Thank you. And I drink to you—and hope I can make you as happy as you deserve to be.

SHEILA: [*Pause. Trying to be light and easy. Sits*] You be careful— or I'll start weeping.

GERALD: [*Smiling. Sitting*] Well, perhaps this will help to stop it.

[*Produces a ring case*]

SHEILA: [*Excited*] Oh—Gerald—you've got it—is it the one you wanted me to have?

GERALD: [*Giving case to her*] Yes—the very one.

SHEILA: [*Taking out ring*] Oh—it's wonderful! Look—mummy—— [*To* MRS. BIRLING] Isn't it a beauty? Oh—darling——

[*Kisses* GERALD *hastily*]

ERIC: Steady, old girl! The buffs.

SHEILA: [*Who has put ring on, admiringly*] I think it's perfect. Now I really feel engaged.

MRS. BIRLING: So you ought, darling. It's a lovely ring. Be careful with it.

SHEILA: Careful! I'll never let it go out of my sight for an instant. Look, Eric.

MRS. BIRLING: [*Smiling*] Well, it came just at the right moment. That was clever of you, Gerald. Now, Arthur, if you've no more to say, I think Sheila and I had better go into the drawing room and leave you men——

[*She and* GERALD *rise*]

BIRLING: [*Rather heavily*] I just want to say this. [GERALD *and* MRS. BIRLING *sit.* BIRLING, *noticing that* SHEILA *is still admiring her ring*] Are you listening, Sheila? This concerns you, too.

SHEILA: I'm sorry, daddy. Actually, I was listening.

[*She looks attentive, as they all do*]

BIRLING: [*Holding them a moment before continuing. Tries to cross legs through speech*] I'm delighted about this engagement and I hope it won't be too long before you're married. And I want to say this. There's a good deal of silly talk about these days—*but*—and I speak as a hardheaded business man, who has to take risks and know what he's about—I say, you can ignore all this silly pessimistic talk. When you marry, you'll be marrying at a very good time. Yes, a very good time—and soon it'll be an even better time.

GERALD: I believe you're right, sir.

ERIC: What about war?

BIRLING: What? Don't interrupt, Eric. I was coming to that. Just because the Kaiser makes a speech or two, or a few German officers have too much to drink and begin talking nonsense, you'll hear some people say that war's inevitable. And to that I say—fiddlesticks! The Germans don't want war. Nobody wants war, except some half-civilized folks in the Balkans. And why? There's too much at stake these days. Everything to lose and nothing to gain by war.

ERIC: Yes, I know—but still—

BIRLING: Just let me finish, Eric. You've a lot to learn yet. And I'm talking as a hardheaded, practical man of business. And I say there isn't a chance of war. The world's developing so fast that it'll make war impossible. Look at the progress we're making. In a year or two we'll have aeroplanes that will be able to go anywhere. And look at the way the automobile's making headway—bigger and faster all the time. And then ships. Why, a friend of mine went over this new liner last week—forty-six thousand eight hundred tons —forty-six thousand eight hundred tons—New York in five days— and every luxury—and unsinkable, absolutely unsinkable. That's what you've got to keep your eye on, facts like that, progress like that—and not a few German officers talking nonsense and a few scaremongers here making a fuss about nothing. Now you three young people, listen to this—and remember what I'm telling you now. In twenty or thirty years' time—let's say, in the forties—you may be giving a little party like this—your son or daughter might be getting engaged—and I tell you, by that time you'll be living in a world that'll have forgotten all these Capital versus Labor agitations and all these silly little war scares. There'll be peace and prosperity and rapid progress everywhere—except of course in Russia, which will always be behind-hand, naturally.

[MRS. BIRLING *shows signs of interrupting*]

MRS. BIRLING: Yes, dear—I know.

BIRLING: Yes, my dear, I know—I'm talking too much. But we can't let these Bernard Shaws and H. G. Wellses do all the talking. We hardheaded practical businessmen must say something sometime. And we don't guess—we've had experience—and we *know*.

MRS. BIRLING: [*Rising. Others rise.* BIRLING *to fireplace for cigars*] Yes, of course, dear. Well—don't keep Gerald in here too long. Eric— [*To door*] —I want you a minute.

[*She and* SHEILA *and* ERIC, *whistling "Rule Britannia," go out.* GERALD *opens door for them*]

BIRLING: Cigar?

GERALD: No, thanks. I can't really enjoy them.

BIRLING: [*Taking one himself*] Ah, you don't know what you're missing. I like a good cigar. [*Indicating decanter*] Help yourself to the port.

[BIRLING *lights his cigar and* GERALD, *who has lit a cigarette, helps himself to port, then sits*]

GERALD: Thanks.

BIRLING: [*Confidentially*] By the way, there's something I'd like to mention—in strict confidence—while we're by ourselves. I have an idea that your mother—Lady Croft—while she doesn't object to my girl—feels you might have done better for yourself socially—— [GERALD, *rather embarrassed, begins to murmur some dissent, but* BIRLING *checks him*] No, Gerald, that's all right. Don't blame her. She comes from an old county family—landed people and so forth —and so it's only natural. But what I wanted to say is—there's a fair chance that I might find my way into the next Honors List. Just a knighthood, of course.

GERALD: Oh—I say—congratulations!

BIRLING: [*At fireplace*] Thanks. But it's a bit too early for that. So don't say anything. But I've had a hint or two. You see, I was Lord Mayor here two years ago when Royalty visited us. And I've always been regarded as a sound, useful party man. So—well—I gather there's a very good chance of a knighthood—so long as we behave ourselves, don't get into the police court or start a scandal— eh? [*Laughs complacently*]

GERALD: [*Laughs*] You seem to be a very well-behaved family to me——

BIRLING: We think we are——

GERALD: So if that's the only obstacle, sir, I think you might as well accept my congratulations now.

BIRLING: Thank you. No, no, I couldn't do that. And don't say anything yet.

GERALD: I say, could I say something to my mother about this? I know she'd be delighted.

BIRLING: Well, when she comes back, you might drop a hint to her.

[*They both laugh.* ERIC *enters*]

ERIC: What's up? Started telling your stories yet?

BIRLING: No. Want another glass of port? [*Sits*]

ERIC: [*Sitting down*] Yes, please. [*Takes decanter and helps himself*] Mother says we mustn't stay too long. But I don't think it matters. I left 'em talking about clothes again. You'd think a girl had never had any clothes before she gets married. Women are potty about 'em.

BIRLING: Yes, but you've got to remember, my boy, that clothes mean something quite different to a woman. Not just something to wear—and not only something to make 'em look prettier—but —well, a sort of sign or token of their self-respect.

GERALD: That's true.

ERIC: [*Eagerly*] Yes, I remember—— [*But he checks himself*]

BIRLING: Well, what do you remember?

ERIC: [*Confused*] Nothing.

BIRLING: Nothing?

GERALD: [*Amused*] Sounds a bit fishy to me.

BIRLING: [*Taking it in same manner*] Yes, you don't know what some of these boys get up to nowadays. More money to spend and time to spare than I had when I was Eric's age. They worked us hard in those days and kept us short of cash. Though even then— we broke out and had a bit of fun sometimes.

GERALD: I'll bet you did.

BIRLING: [*Solemnly*] But this is the point. I don't want to lecture you two young fellows again. But what so many of you don't seem to understand now, when things are so much easier, is that a man has to make his own way—has to look after himself—and his family, too, of course, when he has one—and so long as he does that he won't come to much harm. But the way some of these cranks talk and write now, you'd think everybody has to look after everybody else, as if we were all mixed up together like bees in a hive—a man has to mind his own business and look after himself and his own— and——

[*We hear sharp ring of a front doorbell.* BIRLING *stops to listen*]

ERIC: Somebody at the front door.

BIRLING: All right, Eric. Edna'll answer it. Well, have another glass of port, Gerald—and then we'll join the ladies. That'll stop me giving you good advice.

ERIC: Yes, you've piled it on a bit tonight, father.

BIRLING: Special occasion. And feeling contented, for once, I wanted you to have the benefit of my experience.

[EDNA *enters*]

EDNA: Please, sir.

BIRLING: Yes?

EDNA: An inspector's called.

BIRLING: An inspector? What kind of inspector?

EDNA: A police inspector. He says his name's Inspector Goole.

BIRLING: Don't know him. Does he want to see me?

EDNA: Yes, sir. He says it's important.

BIRLING: All right, Edna. Show him in here. [EDNA goes out] It may be something about a warrant. I'm still on the Bench.

GERALD: [Lightly] Eric's probably been up to something. [Nodding confidentially to BIRLING] And that would be awkward, wouldn't it?

BIRLING: [Humorously] Very.

ERIC: [Who is uneasy, sharply] Here, what do you mean?

GERALD: [Lightly] Only something we were talking about before you came in. A joke really.

ERIC: [Still uneasy] Well, I don't think it's very funny.

BIRLING: [Sharply, staring at him] What's the matter with you?

ERIC: [Defiantly] Nothing.

[EDNA opens door and announces]

EDNA: Inspector Goole.

[The INSPECTOR enters, and EDNA goes out, closing door. The INSPECTOR need not be a big man, but he creates at once an impression of massiveness, solidity, and purposefulness. He is a man in his fifties, dressed in a plain darkish suit of the period. He speaks carefully, weightily, and has a disconcerting habit of looking hard at the person he addresses before actually speaking]

INSPECTOR: Mr. Birling?

BIRLING: [Rises] Good evening, Inspector. You're new, aren't you?

INSPECTOR: [Crosses to him] Yes, sir. Only recently transferred.

BIRLING: I thought you must be. I was an alderman for years—and Lord Mayor two years ago—and I'm still on the Bench—so I know the Brumley police officers pretty well—and I thought I'd never seen you before.

INSPECTOR: Quite so.

BIRLING: Yes. Sit down, Inspector.

INSPECTOR: [*Sitting*] Thank you, sir.

BIRLING: Have a glass of port—or a little whiskey.

INSPECTOR: No, thank you, Mr. Birling. I'm on duty.

BIRLING: [*Shifting chair*] Well, what can I do for you? Some trouble about a warrant?

INSPECTOR: No, Mr. Birling.

BIRLING: [*After a pause, with a touch of impatience*] Well, what is it then?

INSPECTOR: I'd like some information, if you don't mind, Mr. Birling. Two hours ago a young woman died in the Infirmary. She'd been taken there this afternoon because she'd swallowed a lot of strong disinfectant. Burnt her inside out, of course.

ERIC: [*Involuntarily*] My God!

INSPECTOR: Yes, she was in great agony. They did everything they could for her at the Infirmary, but she died. Suicide, of course.

BIRLING: [*Rather impatiently*] Yes, yes. Horrible business. [*Drinks*] But I don't understand why you should come here, Inspector——?

INSPECTOR: [*Cutting through, massively*] I've been round to the room she had, and she'd left a letter there and a sort of diary. Like a lot of these young women who get into various kinds of trouble, she'd used more than one name. But her original name— her real name—was Eva Smith.

BIRLING: [*Thoughtfully*] Eva Smith?

INSPECTOR: Do you remember her, Mr. Birling?

BIRLING: [*Slowly*] No—I seem to remember hearing that name— Eva Smith—somewhere. But it doesn't convey anything to me. And I don't see where I come into this.

INSPECTOR: She was employed in your works at one time.

BIRLING: [*Crossing over toward fireplace*] Oh—that's it, is it? Well, we've several hundred young women there, y'know, and they keep changing.

INSPECTOR: This young woman, Eva Smith, was a bit out of the ordinary. I found a photograph of her in her lodgings. Perhaps you'd remember her from that?

[INSPECTOR *takes photograph, about post card size, out of pocket and goes to* BIRLING. *Both* GERALD *and* ERIC *rise to have a look at photograph, but* INSPECTOR *interposes himself between them and photograph. They are surprised and rather annoyed.* BIRLING *stares hard, and with recognition, at photograph, which* INSPECTOR *then replaces in his pocket*]

GERALD: [*Showing annoyance*] Any particular reason why I shouldn't see this girl's photograph, Inspector?

INSPECTOR: [*Coolly, looking hard at him*] There might be.

ERIC: And the same applies to me, I suppose?

INSPECTOR: Yes.

GERALD: I can't imagine what it could be. [*Crosses to his chair*]

ERIC: Neither can I. [*Sits*]

BIRLING: And I must say I agree with them, Inspector.

INSPECTOR: It's the way I like to go to work. One person and one line of inquiry at a time. Otherwise, there's a muddle.

BIRLING: I see. [*Moves restlessly, then turns*] I think you've had enough of that port, Eric!

[ERIC *turns a chair or two to face downstage. This, with the two armchairs, now gives the place almost the appearance of a sitting room.* INSPECTOR *is watching* BIRLING, *and now* BIRLING *notices him*]

INSPECTOR: I think you remember Eva Smith now, don't you, Mr. Birling?

BIRLING: Yes, I do. She was one of my employees, and then I discharged her.

ERIC: Is that why she committed suicide? When was this, Father?

BIRLING: Just keep quiet, Eric, and don't get excited. This girl left us nearly two years ago. Let me see—it must have been in the early autumn of 1910.

INSPECTOR: Yes. End of September, 1910.

BIRLING: That's right.

GERALD: Look here, sir. Wouldn't you rather I was out of this? [*Rises*]

BIRLING: I don't mind your being here, Gerald. And I'm sure you've no objection, have you, Inspector? Perhaps I ought to explain first that this is Mr. Gerald Croft—son of Sir George Croft—you know, Crofts Limited.

INSPECTOR: Mr. Gerald Croft?

BIRLING: [*Sits*] Yes. Incidentally, we've been modestly celebrating his engagement to my daughter Sheila.

INSPECTOR: I see. Mr. Croft is going to marry Miss Sheila Birling?

GERALD: [*Smiling*] I hope so.

INSPECTOR: [*Gravely*] Then I'd prefer you to stay.

GERALD: [*Surprised*] Oh—all right.

BIRLING: [*Somewhat impatiently*] Look—there's nothing mysterious —about this business—at least not so far as I'm concerned. It's a perfectly straightforward case, and as it happened more than eighteen months ago—nearly two years ago—obviously it has nothing whatever to do with the wretched girl's suicide. Eh, Inspector?

INSPECTOR: No, sir. I can't agree with you there.

BIRLING: Why not?

INSPECTOR: Because what happened to her then may have determined what happened to her afterwards, and what happened to her afterwards may have driven her to suicide. A chain of events.

BIRLING: Oh, well—put like that, there's something in what you say. Still, I can't accept any responsibility. If we are all responsible for everything that happened to everybody we'd had anything to do with, it would be very awkward, wouldn't it?

INSPECTOR: Very awkward.

BIRLING: We'd all be in an impossible position, wouldn't we?

ERIC: By Jove, yes. And as you were saying, dad, a man has to look after himself——

BIRLING: Yes, well, we needn't go into all that.

INSPECTOR: Go into what?

BIRLING: Oh—just before you came—I'd been giving [*Pours port*] these young men a little good advice. Now—about this girl, Eva Smith. I remember her quite well now. She was a lively, good-looking girl—country-bred, I fancy—and she'd been working in one of our machine shops for over a year. A good worker, too. In fact, the foreman there told me he was ready to promote her into what we called a leading operator—head of a small group of girls. But after they came back from their holidays that August, they were all rather restless, and they suddenly decided to ask for more money. They were averaging about twenty-two shillings, which was neither more nor less than is paid generally in our industry. They wanted the rates raised so that they could average about twenty-five shillings a week. I refused, of course.

INSPECTOR: Why?

BIRLING: [Surprised] What! Did you say "Why"?

INSPECTOR: Yes. Why did you refuse?

BIRLING: Well, Inspector, I don't see that it's any concern of yours how I choose to run my business. Is it now?

INSPECTOR: It might be, you know.

BIRLING: I don't like that tone.

INSPECTOR: I'm sorry. But you asked me a question.

BIRLING: And you asked me a question, too, before that, a quite unnecessary question, too.

INSPECTOR: It's my duty to ask questions.

BIRLING: Well, it's my duty to keep labor costs down, and if I'd agreed to this demand for a new rate we'd have added about twelve per cent to our labor costs. Does that satisfy you? So I refused. Said I couldn't consider it. We were paying the usual rates and if they didn't like those rates, they could go and work somewhere else. It's a free country, I told them.

ERIC: It isn't if you can't go and work somewhere else.

INSPECTOR: Quite so.

BIRLING: [To ERIC] Look—just you keep out of this. You hadn't even started in the works when this happened. So they went on strike. That didn't last long, of course.

GERALD: Not if it was just after the summer holidays. They'd be all broke—if I know them.

BIRLING: Right, Gerald. They mostly were. And so was the strike, after a week or two. Pitiful affair. Well, we forgave them, we let them all come back—at the old rates—except the four or five ringleaders, who'd started the trouble. I went down myself and told them to clear out. And this girl, Eva Smith, was one of them.

She'd had a lot to say, I remember—far too much—so she had to go.

GERALD: You couldn't really have done anything else.

ERIC: He could. He could have kept her on instead of throwing her out. I call it tough luck.

BIRLING: Rubbish! If you don't come down sharply on some of these people, they'd soon be asking for the earth.

GERALD: I should say so!

INSPECTOR: They might. But after all it's better to ask for the earth than to take it.

BIRLING: [*Staring at* INSPECTOR] What did you say your name was, Inspector?

INSPECTOR: Goole.

BIRLING: [*Rises, crosses to him*] Goole, how do you get on with our Chief Constable? Colonel Roberts?

INSPECTOR: I don't see much of him.

BIRLING: Perhaps I ought to warn you that he's an old friend of mine, and that I see him fairly frequently. We play golf together sometimes up at the West Brumley.

INSPECTOR: [*Drily*] I don't play golf.

BIRLING: I didn't suppose you did.

ERIC: [*Bursting out*] Well, I think it's a dam' shame!

INSPECTOR: [*Sits*] No, I've never wanted to play.

ERIC: No, I mean about this girl—Eva Smith. Why shouldn't they try for higher wages? We try for the highest possible prices. And I don't see why she should have been sacked just because she'd a bit more spirit than the others. You said yourself she was a good worker. I'd have let her stay.

BIRLING: [*Rather angrily. Steps toward* ERIC] Unless you brighten your ideas, you'll never be in a position to let anybody stay or to tell anybody to go. It's about time you learnt to face a few responsibilities. That's something this public school and varsity life you've had doesn't seem to have taught.

ERIC: [*Sulkily*] Well, we don't need to tell the Inspector all about that, do we?

BIRLING: I don't see we need to tell the Inspector anything more. In fact, there's nothing I can tell him. I told the girl to clear out, and she went. That's the last I heard of her. [*To Inspector*] Have you any idea what happened to her after that? Get into trouble? Go on the streets?

INSPECTOR: [*Rather slowly*] No, she didn't exactly go on the streets. [SHEILA *has now entered, and crosses to* BIRLING. IN-SPECTOR *and* GERALD *rise*]

SHEILA: [*Gaily*] What's this about streets? [*Noticing* INSPECTOR] Oh—sorry. I didn't know. Mummy sent me in to ask you why you didn't come along to the drawing room?

BIRLING: We shall be along in a minute now. Just finishing.

INSPECTOR: I'm afraid not.

BIRLING: [*Abruptly*] There's nothing else, y'know. I've just told you that.

SHEILA: What's all this about?

BIRLING: Nothing to do with you, Sheila. Run along.

[*She starts to go*]

INSPECTOR: No, wait a minute, Miss Birling. [SHEILA *drifts back*]

BIRLING: [*Angrily, crossing to him*] Look here, Inspector, I con-sider this uncalled for and officious. I've half a mind to report you. I've told you all I know—and it doesn't seem to me very important—and now there isn't the slightest reason why my daughter should be dragged into this unpleasant business.

SHEILA: [*Coming further in*] What business? What's happening?

INSPECTOR: [*Impressively*] I'm a police inspector, Miss Birling. This afternoon a young woman drank some disinfectant, and died, after several hours of agony, tonight in the Infirmary.

SHEILA: Oh—how horrible! Was it an accident?

INSPECTOR: No. She wanted to end her life. She felt she couldn't go on any longer.

BIRLING: Well, don't tell me that's because I discharged her from my employment nearly two years ago!

ERIC: That might have started it.

SHEILA: Did you, dad? [*Sits*]

BIRLING: Yes. The girl had been causing trouble in the works. I was quite justified.

GERALD: Yes, I think you were. I know we'd have done the same thing. Don't look like that, Sheila.

SHEILA: [*Rather distressed*] Sorry! It's just that I can't help thinking about this girl—destroying herself so horribly—and I've been so happy tonight. Oh, I wish he hadn't told me. What was she like? Quite young?

INSPECTOR: Yes. Twenty-four.

SHEILA: Pretty?

INSPECTOR: She wasn't pretty when I saw her today, but she had been pretty—very pretty.

BIRLING: That's enough of that.

GERALD: And I don't really see that this inquiry gets you anywhere, Inspector. It's what happened to her since she left Mr. Birling's works that is important.

BIRLING: Obviously. I suggested that some time ago.

GERALD: And we can't help you there, because we don't know.

[*Sits*]

INSPECTOR: [*Slowly*] Are you sure you don't know? [*He looks at* GERALD, *then at* ERIC, *then at* SHEILA]

BIRLING: And are you suggesting now that one of them knows something about this girl?

[ERIC *and* GERALD *rise*]

INSPECTOR: Yes.

BIRLING: You didn't come here just to see *me* then?

INSPECTOR: No. [*Other four exchange bewildered and perturbed glances. Pause*]

BIRLING: [*Looking at* ERIC, *then back to* INSPECTOR—*pats shoulder. With marked change of tone*] Well, of course, if I'd known that earlier, I wouldn't have called you officious and talked about reporting you. You understand that, don't you, Inspector? I thought that—for some reason best known to yourself—you were making the most of this tiny bit of information I could give you. I'm sorry. This makes a difference. [*To fireplace*] You sure of your facts?

INSPECTOR: Some of them—yes.

BIRLING: They don't seem to amount to very much, though. Do they?

INSPECTOR: The girl's dead, though.

SHEILA: What do you mean by saying that? You talk as if we were responsible—

BIRLING: Just a minute, Sheila. Now, Inspector, perhaps you and I had better go and talk this over quietly in a corner—

SHEILA: Why should you? He's finished with you. He says it's one of us now.

BIRLING: Yes, and I'm trying to settle it sensibly for you.

GERALD: [Sits] Well, there's nothing to settle as far as I'm concerned. I've never known an Eva Smith.

ERIC: [Sits] Neither have I.

SHEILA: Was that her name? Eva Smith?

GERALD: Yes.

SHEILA: Never heard it before.

GERALD: So where are you now, Inspector?

INSPECTOR: Where I was before, Mr. Croft. I told you—that like a lot of these young women, she'd used more than one name. She was still Eva Smith when Mr. Birling sacked her—for wanting twenty-five shillings a week instead of twenty-two. But after that she stopped being Eva Smith. Perhaps she'd had enough of it.

ERIC: Can't blame her.

SHEILA: [To BIRLING] I think it was a mean thing to do. Perhaps that spoilt everything for her.

BIRLING: Rubbish! [To INSPECTOR] Do you happen to know what became of her after she left my employment?

INSPECTOR: Yes. She was out of work for the next two months. Both her parents were dead so that she'd no home to go back to. And she hadn't been able to save much out of what Birling and Company had paid her. So after two months, with no work, no money coming in, and living in lodgings, with no relatives to help her, few friends, lonely, half-starved, she was feeling desperate.

SHEILA: [Warmly] I should think so. It's a shame.

INSPECTOR: [Crossing to her] There are a lot of young women

living that sort of existence, Miss Birling, in every city and big town in this country. If there weren't, the factories and warehouses wouldn't know where to look for cheap labor. Ask your father.

[BIRLING *sits by fireplace*]

SHEILA: But these girls aren't cheap labor. They're *people*.

INSPECTOR: [*Drily*] I've had that notion myself from time to time. In fact, I've thought that it would do us all a bit of good if sometimes we tried to put ourselves in the place of these young women counting their pennies in their dingy little back bedrooms.

SHEILA: Yes, I expect it would. But what happened to her then?

INSPECTOR: She had what seemed to her a wonderful stroke of luck. She was taken on in a shop—and a good shop, too—Milward's.

SHEILA: Milward's! We go there—in fact, I was there this afternoon. [*Archly to* GERALD]—for *your* benefit.

GERALD: [*Smiling*] Good!

SHEILA: Yes, she was lucky to get taken on at Milward's.

INSPECTOR: That's what she thought. [*Moves few steps toward* SHEILA] And it happened that at the beginning of December that year—1910—there was a good deal of influenza about, and Milward's suddenly found themselves shorthanded. So that gave her her chance. And from what I can gather, she liked working there. It was a nice change from a factory. She enjoyed being among pretty clothes, I've no doubt. And now she felt she was making a good fresh start. You can imagine how she felt.

SHEILA: Yes, of course.

BIRLING: And then she got herself into trouble there, I suppose?

INSPECTOR: After about a couple of months, just when she felt she was settling down nicely, they told her she'd have to go.

BIRLING: Not doing her work properly?

INSPECTOR: There was nothing wrong with the way she was doing her work. They admitted that.

BIRLING: There must have been something wrong?

INSPECTOR: [*Looks at* SHEILA] All she knew was—that a customer complained about her—and so she had to go.

SHEILA: [*Staring at him, agitated*] When was this?

INSPECTOR: [*Impressively*] At the end of January—last year.

SHEILA: What did this girl look like? [*Rises*]

INSPECTOR: If you'll come over here, I'll show you. [*He moves down to floor-lamp.* SHEILA *crosses to him. He produces photograph. She looks at it closely, recognizes it with a little cry, gives half-stifled sob, and then runs out.* INSPECTOR *puts photograph back into his pocket and stares speculatively after her. The other three stare in amazement for a moment and rise*]

BIRLING: What's the matter with her? [*Angrily*] Why the devil do you want to go upsetting the child like that?

INSPECTOR: I didn't do it. She's upsetting herself.

BIRLING: Well—why—why?

INSPECTOR: I don't know—yet. That's something I have to find out.

BIRLING: [*Still angrily*] Well—if you don't mind—I'll find out first.

GERALD: Shall I go to her?

BIRLING: [*Crossing to door*] No, leave this to me. I must also have a word with my wife—tell her what's happening. [*Turns at door, staring at* INSPECTOR *angrily*] We were having a nice family celebration tonight. And a nasty mess you've made of it now, haven't you?

INSPECTOR: [*Steadily, crossing to fireplace*] That's more or less what I was thinking earlier tonight.

BIRLING: What?

INSPECTOR: When I was in the Infirmary looking at what was left of Eva Smith. A nice little promising life there, I thought, and a nasty mess somebody's made of it.

> [ERIC *sits.* BIRLING *looks as if about to make some retort, then thinks better of it, and goes out, closing door sharply behind him.* GERALD *and* ERIC *exchange uneasy glances.* INSPECTOR *ignores them*]

GERALD: [*Crossing to him*] I'd like to have a look at that photograph now, Inspector.

INSPECTOR: All in good time.

GERALD: I don't see why——

INSPECTOR: [*Cutting in, massively*] You heard what I said before, Mr. Croft. One line of inquiry at a time. Otherwise we'll all be talking at once and won't know where we are. If you've anything to tell me, you'll have an opportunity of doing it soon.

GERALD: [*Rather uneasily*] Well, I don't suppose I have——

ERIC: [*Suddenly bursting out. Rises*] Look here, I've had enough of this.

INSPECTOR: [*Drily*] I daresay.

ERIC: [*Uneasily*] I'm sorry—but you see—we were having a little party—and I've had a few drinks, including rather a lot of champagne—and I've got a headache—and as I'm only in the way here— I think I'd better turn in. [*Starts to door*]

INSPECTOR: And I think you'd better stay here.

ERIC: Why should I? [*By doorway*]

INSPECTOR: It might be less trouble. If you turn in, you might have to turn out again soon.

GERALD: Getting a bit heavy-handed, aren't you, Inspector?

[ERIC *crosses to chair*]

INSPECTOR: Possibly. But if you're easy with me, I'm easy with you.

GERALD: After all, y'know, we're respectable citizens and not dangerous criminals.

INSPECTOR: Sometimes there isn't as much difference as you think. Often, if it was left to me, I wouldn't know where to draw the line.

GERALD: Fortunately, it isn't left to you, is it?

INSPECTOR: No, it isn't. But some things *are* left to me. Inquiries of this sort, for instance. [*Enter* SHEILA, *who looks as if she's been crying*] Well, Miss Birling?

SHEILA: [*Coming in, closing door*] You knew it was me all the time, didn't you?

INSPECTOR: I had an idea it might be—[GERALD *crosses to* SHEILA]— from something the girl herself wrote.

SHEILA: I've told my father—he didn't seem to think it amounted to much—but I felt rotten about it at the time, and now I feel a lot worse. Did it make much difference to her?

INSPECTOR: Yes, I'm afraid it did. It was the last real steady job she had. When she lost it—for no reason that she could discover—she decided she might as well try another kind of life.

SHEILA: [*Miserably*] So I'm really responsible?

INSPECTOR: No, not entirely. A good deal happened to her after that. But you're partly to blame. Just as your father is.

ERIC: But what did Sheila do?

SHEILA: [*Distressed, as* GERALD *sits*] I went to the manager at Milward's and I told him that if they didn't get rid of that girl, I'd never go near the place again and I'd persuade mother to close our account with them.

INSPECTOR: And why did you do that?

SHEILA: Because I was in a furious temper.

INSPECTOR: And what had the girl done to make you lose your temper?

SHEILA: When I was looking at myself in the mirror I caught sight of her smiling at the salesgirl, and I was furious with her. I'd been in a bad temper anyhow.

INSPECTOR: And was it the girl's fault?

SHEILA: No, not really. It was my own fault. [*Suddenly, to* GERALD] All right, Gerald, you needn't look at me like that. At least, I'm trying to tell the truth. I expect you've done things you're ashamed of.

GERALD: [*Surprised*] Well, I never said I hadn't. I don't see why——

INSPECTOR: Never mind about that. You can settle that between you afterwards. [*To* SHEILA] What happened?

SHEILA: I'd gone in to try something on. It was an idea of my own— —mother had been against it, and so had the salesgirl—but I insisted. As soon as I tried it on, I knew they'd been right. It just didn't suit me at all. I looked silly in the thing. Well, this girl had brought the dress up from the workroom, and when the salesgirl— Miss Francis—had asked her something about it, this girl, to show us what she meant, had held the dress up, as if she was wearing it. And it just suited her. She was the right type for it, just as I was the wrong type. She was a very pretty girl, too—with soft fine hair and big gray eyes—and that didn't make it any better. Well, when I tried the thing on and looked at myself and knew that it was all wrong, I caught sight of this girl smiling at Miss Francis—as if to say, "Doesn't she look awful?"—and I was absolutely furious. I lost my temper. I was very rude to both of them, and then I went to the manager and told him that this girl had been very impertinent—and—and—— [*She almost breaks down, but just controls herself. Crosses to chair, sits.* GERALD *rises*] How could I know what would happen afterwards? If she'd been some miserable plain little creature, I don't suppose I'd have done it. But she looked as if she could take care of herself. I couldn't be sorry for her.

INSPECTOR: In fact, in a kind of way, you might be said to have been jealous of her?

SHEILA: Yes, I suppose so.

INSPECTOR: And so you used the power you had, as a daughter of a good customer and also of a man well known in the town, to punish the girl just because she made you feel like that.

SHEILA: Yes, but it didn't seem to be anything very terrible at the time. Don't you understand? And if I could help her now, I would——

INSPECTOR: [*Harshly*] Yes, but you can't! It's too late. She's dead.

ERIC: My God, it's a bit thick, when you come to think of it——

SHEILA: [*Stormily. Rises*] Oh, shut up, Eric! I know, I know. It's the only time I've ever done anything like that, and I'll never do it again to anybody. I've noticed them giving me a sort of look sometimes at Milward's—I noticed it even this afternoon—and I suppose some of them remember. I feel now I can never go there again. Oh—why had this to happen?

INSPECTOR: [*Sternly*] That's what I asked myself tonight when I was looking at that dead girl. And then I said to myself, "Well, we'll try to understand why it had to happen." And that's why I'm here, and why I'm not going until I know *all* that happened. Eva Smith lost her job with Birling and Company because the strike failed and they were determined not to have another one. At last she found another job—under what name I don't know—in a big shop, and had to leave there because you were annoyed with yourself and passed the annoyance on to her. Now she had to try something else. So first she changed her name to Daisy Renton——

GERALD: [*Startled. Pulling himself together*] Can I get myself a drink, Sheila?

[SHEILA *merely nods, still staring at him, and he goes across to tantalus on sideboard for a whiskey*]

INSPECTOR: Where is your father, Miss Birling?

SHEILA: He went into the drawing room. Eric, will you take the Inspector along there, please? [*As* ERIC *moves,* INSPECTOR *looks from* SHEILA *to* GERALD, *then goes out, with* ERIC, *who opens door*] Well, Gerald?

GERALD: [*Trying to smile*] Well what, Sheila?

SHEILA: How did you come to know this girl—Eva Smith?

GERALD: I didn't.

SHEILA: Daisy Renton, then—it's the same thing?

GERALD: Why should I have known her?

SHEILA: Oh, don't be stupid! We haven't much time. You gave yourself away as soon as he mentioned her other name.

GERALD: All right. I knew her. Let's leave it at that.

SHEILA: We can't leave it at that!

GERALD: Now listen, darling——

SHEILA: No, that's no use. You not only knew her but you knew her very well. Otherwise, you wouldn't look so guilty about it. When did you first get to know her? [*He does not reply*] Was it after she left Milward's? When she changed her name, as he said, and began to lead a different sort of life? Were you seeing her last spring and summer, during that time when you hardly came near me and said you were so busy? Were you? [*He does not reply, but looks at her*] Yes, of course you were!

GERALD: I'm sorry, Sheila. But it was all over and done with, last summer. I haven't set eyes on the girl for at least six months. I don't come into this suicide business.

SHEILA: I thought *I* didn't, half an hour ago.

GERALD: You don't. Neither of us does. [*Crosses to her*] So—for God's sake—don't say anything to the Inspector!

SHEILA: About you and this girl?

GERALD: Yes. We can keep it from him.

SHEILA: [*Laughs rather hysterically*] Why—you fool—*he knows!* Of course he knows. And I hate to think how much he knows that we don't know yet. You'll see. You'll see.

[*She looks at him almost in triumph. He looks crushed. Door slowly opens and* INSPECTOR *appears, looking steadily and searchingly at them as:*]

THE CURTAIN FALLS SLOWLY

ACT TWO

At rise, scene and situation are exactly as they were at end of Act One. INSPECTOR *remains at door for a few moments looking at* SHEILA *and* GERALD. *Then comes forward, leaving door open behind him.*

INSPECTOR: [*To* GERALD] Well?

SHEILA: [*With hysterical laugh, to* GERALD] You see? What did I tell you?

INSPECTOR: What did you tell him?

GERALD: [*With an effort*] Inspector, I think Miss Birling ought to be excused from any more of this questioning. She's told you all she knows. She's had a long exciting and tiring day—we were celebrating our engagement, you know—and now she's obviously had about as much as she can stand. You heard her.

SHEILA: He means that I'm getting hysterical now.

INSPECTOR: And are you?

SHEILA: Probably.

INSPECTOR: Well, I don't want to keep you here. I've no more questions to ask you.

SHEILA: No, but you haven't finished asking questions—have you?

INSPECTOR: No.

SHEILA: [*To* GERALD] You see? [*To* INSPECTOR] Then I'm staying.

GERALD: Why should you? It's bound to be unpleasant and disturbing.

INSPECTOR: And you think young women ought to be protected against unpleasant things?

GERALD: If possible—yes.

INSPECTOR: Well, we know one young woman who wasn't, don't we?

GERALD: I suppose I asked for that.

SHEILA: Be careful you don't ask for any more, Gerald.

GERALD: I only meant to say to you—why stay when you'll obviously hate it?

SHEILA: It can't be any worse for me than it has been. And it might be better.

GERALD: I see——

SHEILA: What do you see?

GERALD: You've been through it and now you want to see someone else go through it.

SHEILA: [*Bitterly*] So that's what you think I'm really like! I'm glad I realized it in time, Gerald.

GERALD: No, no, I didn't mean——

SHEILA: Yes, you did! And if you'd really loved me, you couldn't have said that. You listened to that nice story about me. I got that girl sacked from Milward's. And now you've made up your mind I must obviously be a selfish, vindictive creature.

GERALD: I neither said that, nor even suggested it.

SHEILA: Then why say I want to see somebody else put through it? That's not what I meant at all.

GERALD: All right then, I'm sorry.

SHEILA: Yes, but you don't believe me. And this is just the wrong time not to believe me.

INSPECTOR: [*Massively, taking charge*] Allow me, Miss Birling. [*To* GERALD] I can tell you why Miss Birling wants to stay on, and why she says it might be better for her if she did. A girl died tonight. A pretty lively sort of girl, who never did anybody any harm. But she died in misery and agony—hating life——

SHEILA: [*Distressed. Sits*] Don't, please—I know, I know—and I can't stop thinking about it——

INSPECTOR: [*Ignoring this*] Now, Miss Birling has just been made to understand what she did to this girl. She feels responsible. And if she leaves us now, and doesn't hear any more, then she'll feel she's entirely to blame, she'll be alone with her responsibility, the rest of tonight, all tomorrow, all the next night——

SHEILA: [*Eagerly*] Yes, that's it. And I know I'm to blame—and I'm desperately sorry—but I can't believe—I won't believe—it's simply my fault that in the end she—she committed suicide. That would be too horrible——

INSPECTOR: [*Sternly, to them both*] You see, we have to share something. If there's nothing else, we'll have to share our guilt.

SHEILA: [*Staring at him*] Yes. That's true. [*Wonderingly*] I don't understand about you?

INSPECTOR: [*Calmly*] There's no reason why you should.

SHEILA: [*Rises, goes to him*] I don't know much about police inspectors—but the ones I have met weren't a bit like you.

MRS. BIRLING: [*Enters, smiling, "social"*] Good evening, Inspector.

INSPECTOR: Good evening, madam.

MRS. BIRLING: [*Same easy tone*] I'm Mrs. Birling, y'know. My husband has just explained why you're here, and while we'll be glad to tell you anything you want to know, I don't think we can help you much.

SHEILA: No, mother—please!

MRS. BIRLING: [*Affecting great surprise*] What's the matter, Sheila?

SHEILA: [*Hesitantly*] I know it sounds silly——

MRS. BIRLING: What does?

SHEILA: [*Sits*] You see, I feel you're beginning all wrong. And I'm afraid you'll say something or do something that you'll be sorry for afterwards.

MRS. BIRLING: I don't understand you!

SHEILA: We all started like that—so confident, so pleased with ourselves, until he began asking us questions.

[MRS. BIRLING *looks from* SHEILA *to* INSPECTOR]

MRS. BIRLING: [*Steps to him*] You seem to have made a great impression on this child, Inspector.

INSPECTOR: [*Coolly*] We often do on the young ones. They're more impressionable.

[*He and* MRS. BIRLING *look at each other for a moment. Then* MRS. BIRLING *turns to* SHEILA *again*]

MRS. BIRLING: You're looking tired, dear. I think you ought to go to bed—and forget about this absurd business. You'll feel better in the morning.

SHEILA: Mother, I couldn't possibly go. Nothing could be worse for me. We've settled all that. I'm staying here until I know why that girl killed herself.

MRS. BIRLING: Nothing but morbid curiosity!

SHEILA: No, it isn't.

MRS. BIRLING: Please don't contradict me like that. And in any case, I don't suppose for a moment that we can understand why the girl committed suicide. Girls of that class—

SHEILA: [*Urgently*] Mother, don't—please don't! For your own sake, as well as ours, you mustn't—

MRS. BIRLING: [*Annoyed*] Mustn't—what? Really, Sheila!

SHEILA: [*Slowly, carefully now. Rises, crosses to her*] You mustn't try to build up a kind of wall between us and that girl. If you do, then the Inspector will just break it down. And it'll be all the worse when he does.

MRS. BIRLING: I don't understand you. [*To* INSPECTOR] Do you?

INSPECTOR: Yes. And she's right.

MRS. BIRLING: [*Haughtily*] I beg your pardon!

INSPECTOR: [*Very plainly*] I said yes—I do understand her. And she's right.

MRS. BIRLING: That—I consider—is a trifle impertinent, Inspector. [SHEILA *gives a short, hysterical laugh*] Now, what is it, Sheila?

SHEILA: I don't know. Perhaps it's because *impertinent* is such a silly word. But, mother, do stop before it's too late.

MRS. BIRLING: If you mean that the Inspector will take offense——?

INSPECTOR: [*Calmly*] No, no. I never take offense.

MRS. BIRLING: I'm glad to hear it. Though I must add that it seems to me that *we* have more reason for taking offense.

INSPECTOR: Let's leave *offense* out of it, shall we?

GERALD: I think we'd better, Mrs. Birling.

SHEILA: So do I.

MRS. BIRLING: [*Rebuking them*] *I'm* talking to the Inspector now, if you don't mind. [*To* INSPECTOR, *rather grandly. Crosses and sits in armchair above fireplace*] I realize that you may have to conduct some sort of inquiry, but I must say that so far you seem to be conducting it in a rather peculiar and offensive manner. You know, of course, that my husband was Lord Mayor only two years ago and that he's still a magistrate?

GERALD: [*Rather impatiently*] Mrs. Birling, the Inspector knows all that. And I don't think it's a very good idea to remind him.

SHEILA: It's crazy. Stop it, please. Mother!

INSPECTOR: They're right, y'know.

MRS. BIRLING: [*Trying to crush him*] Really!

INSPECTOR: [*Imperturbable*] Yes. Now what about Mr. Birling?

MRS. BIRLING: He's coming back in a moment. He's just talking to my son, Eric, who seems to be in an excitable silly mood.

INSPECTOR: What's the matter with him?

MRS. BIRLING: Eric? Oh—I'm afraid he may have had rather too much to drink tonight. We were having a little celebration here——

INSPECTOR: Isn't he used to drinking?

MRS. BIRLING: No, of course not. He's only a boy.

INSPECTOR: No, he's a young man.

SHEILA: And he drinks far too much.

MRS. BIRLING: [*Very sharply*] Sheila!

SHEILA: [*Urgently*] I don't want to get poor Eric into trouble. He's probably in enough trouble already. But we really must stop these silly pretenses. This isn't the time to pretend that Eric isn't used to drink. He's been steadily drinking too much for the last two years.

MRS. BIRLING: [*Staggered. Rises*] It isn't true! You know him, Gerald—and you're a man—you must know it isn't true.

INSPECTOR: [*As* GERALD *hesitates. Turning to him*] Well, Mr. Croft?

GERALD: [*Apologetically, to* MRS. BIRLING] I'm afraid it is, y'know. Actually I've never seen much of him outside this house—but, well, I have gathered that he does drink pretty hard.

MRS. BIRLING: [*Bitterly*] And this is the time you choose to tell me!

SHEILA: [*Crossing to her*] Yes, of course it is. That's what I meant when I talked about building up a wall that's sure to be knocked flat. It makes it all the harder to bear.

MRS. BIRLING: But it's you—and not the Inspector here—who's doing it——

SHEILA: Yes, but don't you see? *He hasn't started on you yet!*

MRS. BIRLING: [*After pause, recovering herself*] If necessary I shall be glad to answer any questions the Inspector wishes to ask me. Though naturally I don't know anything about this girl.

INSPECTOR: [*Gravely*] We'll see, Mrs. Birling.

[Enter BIRLING, *who closes door behind him]*

BIRLING: *[Rather hot, bothered]* I've been trying to persuade Eric to go to bed, but he won't. Now he says you told him to stay up. Did you?

INSPECTOR: Yes, I did.

BIRLING: Why?

INSPECTOR: Because I shall want to talk to him, Mr. Birling.

BIRLING: I can't see why you should, but if you must, then I suggest you do it now. Have him in and get it over, then let the lad go.

INSPECTOR: No, I can't do that yet. I'm sorry, but he'll have to wait.

BIRLING: Now look here, Inspector——

INSPECTOR: *[With authority]* He must wait his turn.

SHEILA: *[To* MRS. BIRLING*]* You see?

MRS. BIRLING: No, I don't. And please be quiet, Sheila.

BIRLING: *[Angrily]* Inspector, I've told you before, I don't like your tone nor the way you're handling this inquiry. And I don't propose to give you much more rope.

INSPECTOR: You needn't give me any rope.

SHEILA: *[Rather wildly, with laugh]* No, he's giving *us* rope—so that we'll hang ourselves!

BIRLING: *[To* MRS. BIRLING*]* What's the matter with that child?

MRS. BIRLING: Overexcited. And she refuses to go. *[With sudden anger, to* INSPECTOR*]* Well, come along—what is it you want to know?

INSPECTOR: *[Coolly]* At the end of January, last year, this girl Eva Smith had to leave Milward's, because Miss Birling compelled them to discharge her, and then she stopped being Eva Smith, looking for a job, and became Daisy Renton, with other ideas. *[Sharply, turning on* GERALD*]* Mr. Croft, when did you first get to know her?

[An exclamation of surprise from BIRLING *and* MRS. BIRLING*]*

GERALD: Where did you get the idea that I did know her?

SHEILA: *[Sits on arm of chair]* It's no use, Gerald. You're wasting time.

INSPECTOR: As soon as I mentioned the name Daisy Renton, it was obvious you'd known her. You gave yourself away at once.

SHEILA: [Bitterly,] Of course he did!

INSPECTOR: And anyhow, I knew already. When and where did you first meet her?

GERALD: All right, if you must have it. I met her first some time in March last year, in the bar at the Palace. I mean the Palace Music Hall here in Brumley——

SHEILA: Well, we didn't think you meant Buckingham Palace.

GERALD: [To SHEILA] Thanks. You're going to be a great help, I can see. You've said your piece, and you're obviously going to hate this, so why on earth don't you leave us to it?

SHEILA: Nothing would induce me. I want to understand what happens when a man says he's so busy at the works that he can hardly ever find time to come and see the girl he's supposed to be in love with. I wouldn't miss it for——

INSPECTOR: [With authority] Be quiet, please. Yes, Mr. Croft—in the bar at the Palace Variety Theatre . . . ?

GERALD: [Sits] I happened to go down there one night, after a rather long dull day, and as the show wasn't very bright, I went down into the bar for a drink. It's a favorite haunt of women of the town——

MRS. BIRLING: Women of the town?

INSPECTOR: Prostitutes.

MRS. BIRLING: Yes—but here—in Brumley——

INSPECTOR: One of the worst cities in the country for prostitution.

BIRLING: Quite true. But I see no point in mentioning the subject—especially—— [Indicating SHEILA]

MRS. BIRLING: It would be much better if Sheila didn't listen to this story at all.

SHEILA: But you're forgetting I'm supposed to be engaged to the hero of it! Go on, Gerald. You went down into the bar, which is a favorite haunt of women of the town.

GERALD: I'm glad I amuse you——

INSPECTOR: [Sits, sharply] Come along, Mr. Croft! What happened?

GERALD: I didn't intend to stay down there long. I hate those hard-eyed dough-faced women. But then I noticed a girl who looked quite different. [SHEILA *crosses to chair, sits*] She was very pretty —soft brown hair and big dark eyes— [*He breaks off*] My God [*Rises*]

INSPECTOR: What's the matter?

GERALD: [*Distressed*] Sorry—I—well, I've suddenly realized—taken it in properly—that she's dead——

INSPECTOR: [*Harshly*] Yes, she's dead. Go on!

GERALD: This girl was charmingly dressed, too—in a simple inexpensive sort of way—and altogether she looked young and fresh and charming—and—what shall I say?—the opposite of hard and tough, and able to look after herself—— She was quite out of place down there. And obviously she wasn't enjoying herself. Old Joe Meggarty, half-drunk and goggle-eyed, had wedged her into a corner with that obscene fat carcass of his——

MRS. BIRLING: There's no need to be disgusting. And surely you don't mean Alderman Meggarty?

GERALD: Of course I do! He's a notorious womaniser and one of the worst sots and rogues in Brumley——

MRS. BIRLING: [*Staggered*] Well, really! Alderman Meggarty! Well, we *are* learning something tonight!

SHEILA: [*Coolly*] Of course we are! But everybody knows about that horrible old Meggarty. A girl I know had to see him at the Town Hall one afternoon and she only escaped with a torn blouse——

BIRLING: [*Sharply shocked*] Sheila!

INSPECTOR: [*To* GERALD] Go on.

GERALD: This girl saw me looking at her and then gave me a glance, obviously an S.O.S. So I went across and told Joe Meggarty some nonsense—that the manager had a message for him or something— got him out of the way—and then told the girl that if she didn't want any more of that sort of thing, she'd better let me take her out of there. She agreed at once.

INSPECTOR: Where did you go?

GERALD: We went to the County Hotel, which I knew would be quiet at that time of night, and we had a drink or two and talked.

INSPECTOR: Did she drink much at that time?

GERALD: No. She only had a port and lemonade—or some such concoction. All she wanted was to talk—a little friendliness—and I gathered that Joe Meggarty's advances had left her rather shaken—as well they might.

INSPECTOR: She talked about herself?

GERALD: Yes. I asked her questions about herself. She told me her name was Daisy Renton, that she'd lost both parents, that she came originally from somewhere outside Brumley. [Sits] She also told me she'd had a job in one of the works here and had had to leave after a strike. She said something about the shop, too, but wouldn't say which it was, and she was deliberately vague about what happened. I couldn't get any exact details from her about her past life. She wanted to talk about herself—just because she felt I was interested and friendly—but at the same time she wanted to be Daisy Renton—and not Eva Smith. In fact, I heard that name for the first time tonight. What she did let slip—though she didn't mean to—was that she was desperately hard up and at that moment was actually hungry. I made the people at the County find some food for her.

INSPECTOR: And then you decided to keep her—as your mistress?

MRS. BIRLING: [Rising] What?

SHEILA: Of course, mother. It was obvious from the start. Go on, Gerald. Don't mind mother.

GERALD: [Steadily] I discovered, not that night but two nights later, when we met again—not accidentally this time, of course—that in fact she hadn't a penny, and was going to be turned out of the miserable back room she had. It happened that a friend of mine, Charlie Brunswick, had gone off to Canada for six months and let me have the key of a nice little set of rooms he had—in Morgan Terrace—and had asked me to keep an eye on them for him and use them if I wanted to. [MRS. BIRLING sits] So I insisted on Daisy moving into those rooms of Charlie's, and I made her take some money to keep her going there. [Carefully, to INSPECTOR] I want you to understand that I didn't install her there so that I could make love to her. That came afterwards. I made her go to Morgan Terrace because I was sorry for her, and

didn't like the idea of her going back to the Palace bar. I didn't
ask for anything in return.

INSPECTOR: I see.

SHEILA: Yes, but why are you saying that to *him?* You ought to be
saying it to *me.*

GERALD: [*Rises*] I suppose I ought, really. I'm sorry, Sheila. Somehow I——

SHEILA: [*Cutting in, as he hesitates*] I know. Somehow he makes
you. [*To* MRS. BIRLING] He does, y'know.

INSPECTOR: But she became your mistress?

GERALD: Yes. I suppose it was inevitable. She was young and pretty
and warm-hearted—and intensely grateful. I became at once the
most important person in her life—you understand?

INSPECTOR: Yes. She was a woman. She was lonely. [*To* GERALD]
Were you in love with her?

SHEILA: [*Rises*] Just what I was going to ask!

BIRLING: [*Angrily*] I really must object—

INSPECTOR: [*Turning on him, sharply*] Why should *you* do any protesting? It was you who turned the girl out in the first place.

BIRLING: [*Rather taken aback*] Well, I only did what any employer
might have done. And what I was going to say was that I protest against the way in which my daughter, a young unmarried
girl is being dragged into this—

INSPECTOR: [*Sharply*] Your daughter isn't living on the moon. She's
here in Brumley, too.

SHEILA: [*To* BIRLING, *who sits*] Yes, and it was I who had the girl
turned out of her job at Milward's. *And* I'm supposed to be engaged to Gerald. And I'm not a child, don't forget. I've a right to
know. *Were* you in love with her, Gerald?

GERALD: [*Hesitatingly*] It's hard to say. I didn't feel about her the
way she felt about me.

SHEILA: [*With sharp sarcasm*] Of course not! You were the wonderful fairy prince. You must have adored it, Gerald.

GERALD: All right—I did. Nearly any man would have done.

SHEILA: That's probably about the best thing you've said tonight. At
least it's honest. Did you see her every night?

GERALD: No. I wasn't telling you a complete lie when I said I'd been very busy at the works all that time. We *were* very busy. But of course I did see a good deal of her.

MRS. BIRLING: [*Rising*] I don't think we want any further details of this disgusting affair——

SHEILA: I do! And anyhow, we haven't had any details yet.

GERALD: And you're not going to have any. [*To* MRS. BIRLING] You know, Mrs. Birling, it wasn't disgusting.

MRS. BIRLING: It's disgusting to me!

SHEILA: Yes, but you didn't come into this, did you, mother?

GERALD: [*To Inspector*] Is there anything else you'd like to know—that you ought to know?

INSPECTOR: Yes. When did this affair end?

GERALD: I can tell you exactly. In the first week of September. I had to go away for several weeks then—on business—and by that time Daisy knew it was coming to an end. So I broke it off definitely before I went.

INSPECTOR: How did she take it?

GERALD: Better than I'd hoped. She was—very gallant—about it.

SHEILA: [*With irony*] That was nice for you.

GERALD: No, it wasn't. [*He waits for a moment, then in a low troubled tone*] She told me she'd been happier than she'd ever been before—but that she knew it couldn't last—hadn't expected it to last. She didn't blame me at all. I wish to God she had now. Perhaps I'd feel better about it.

INSPECTOR: She had to leave those rooms?

GERALD: Yes, we'd agreed about that. She'd saved a little money during the summer—she'd lived very economically on what I'd allowed her—and didn't want to take any more from me, but I insisted on a parting gift of enough money—though it wasn't so very much—to see her through to the end of the year.

INSPECTOR: Did she tell you what she proposed to do after you'd left her?

GERALD: No. She refused to talk about that. I got the idea, once or twice from what she said, that she thought of leaving Brumley. Whether she did or not—I don't know. Did she?

INSPECTOR: Yes. She went away for about two months. To some seaside place.

GERALD: By herself?

INSPECTOR: Yes. I think she went away—to be alone, to remember all that had happened between you.

GERALD: How do you know that?

INSPECTOR: She kept a rough sort of diary. And she said there that she had to go away and be quiet and remember "just to make it last longer." She felt that there'd never be anything as good for her again—so she had to make it last longer.

GERALD: [GRAVELY] I see. Well, I never saw her again, and that's all I can tell you.

INSPECTOR: [Rising] It's all I want to know from you.

GERALD: In that case—as I'm rather more—upset—by this business than I probably appear to be—and—well, I'd like to be alone for a little while—I'd be glad if you'd let me go.

INSPECTOR: Go? Where? Home?

GERALD: No. I'll just walk out—somewhere by myself. I'll come back.

INSPECTOR: All right, Mr. Croft. [GERALD starts to go]

SHEILA: But just in case you forget—or decide not to come back, Gerald, I think you'd better take this with you. [Hands him ring. BIRLING rises, takes step to MRS. BIRLING]

GERALD: I see. Well, I was expecting this.

SHEILA: I don't dislike you as I did half an hour ago, Gerald. In fact, in some odd way, I rather respect you more than I've ever done before. I knew anyhow you were lying about those months last year when you hardly came near me. I knew there was something fishy about that time. And now at least you've been honest. And I believe what you told us about the way you helped her at first. Just out of pity. And it was my fault really that she was so desperate when you first met her. But this *has* made a difference. You and I aren't the same people who sat down to dinner here. We'd have to start all over again, getting to know each other——

BIRLING: Now, Sheila, I'm not defending him. But you must understand that a lot of young men——

SHEILA: Don't interfere, please, father. Gerald knows what I mean, and you apparently don't.

GERALD: Yes, I know what you mean. [He goes to door] But I'm coming back—if I may.

SHEILA: All right.

MRS. BIRLING: Well, really, I don't know. I think we've just about come to an end of this wretched business——

GERALD: I don't think so. Excuse me. [*Pause. He goes out*]

MRS. BIRLING: Well, really—I don't know. [*They watch him go in silence. We hear front door slam*]

SHEILA: [*To INSPECTOR*] You know, you never showed him that photograph of her.

INSPECTOR: No. It wasn't necessary. And I thought it better not to.

MRS. BIRLING: You have a photograph of this girl?

INSPECTOR: Yes. I think you'd better look at it.

MRS. BIRLING: I don't see any particular reason why I should——

INSPECTOR: Probably not. But you'd better look at it.

MRS. BIRLING: Very well. [*He produces photograph and she looks hard at it*]

INSPECTOR: [*Taking back photograph*] You recognize her?

MRS. BIRLING: No. Why should I?

INSPECTOR: Of course she might have changed lately, but I can't believe she could have changed so much.

MRS. BIRLING: I don't understand you, Inspector?

INSPECTOR: You mean you don't choose to, Mrs. Birling.

MRS. BIRLING: [*Angrily*] I meant what I said!

INSPECTOR: You're not telling me the truth.

MRS. BIRLING: I beg your pardon!

BIRLING: [*Angrily, to INSPECTOR*] Look here, I'm not going to have this, Inspector. You'll apologize at once.

INSPECTOR: Apologize for what—doing my duty?

BIRLING: No, for being so offensive about it. I'm a public man——

INSPECTOR: [*Massively*] Public men, Mr. Birling, have their responsibilities as well as their privileges.

BIRLING: Possibly. But you weren't asked to come here to talk to me about my responsibilities.

SHEILA: Let's hope not. Though I'm beginning to wonder.

MRS. BIRLING: Does that mean anything, Sheila?

SHEILA: It means that we've no excuse now for putting on airs and that if we've any sense we won't try. Now you're pretending you don't recognize her from that photograph. I admit I don't know why you should, but I know jolly well you did in fact recognize her, from the way you looked. And if you're not telling the truth, why should the Inspector apologize? And can't you see, both of you, you're making it worse? [*She turns away. We hear front door slam again*]

MRS. BIRLING: [*Sits*] Gerald must have come back.

INSPECTOR: Unless your son has just gone out.

BIRLING: I'll see. [*He goes out quickly*]

INSPECTOR: [*Crossing to fireplace*] Mrs. Birling, you're a member—a prominent member—of the Brumley Women's Charity Organization, aren't you? [MRS. BIRLING *does not reply*]

SHEILA: [*Pause*] Go on, mother. You might as well admit it. [*To* INSPECTOR] Yes, she is. Why?

INSPECTOR: [*Calmly*] It's an organization to which women in distress can appeal for help in various forms. Isn't that so?

MRS. BIRLING: [*With dignity*] Yes. We've done a great deal of useful work in helping deserving cases.

INSPECTOR: There was a meeting of the interviewing committee two weeks ago?

MRS. BIRLING: I daresay there was.

INSPECTOR: You know very well there was, Mrs. Birling. You were in the chair.

MRS. BIRLING: And if I was, what business is it of yours?

INSPECTOR: [*Severely*] Do you want me to tell you—in plain words? [*Enter* BIRLING, *looking rather agitated*]

BIRLING That must have been Eric.

MRS. BIRLING: [*Alarmed*] Have you been up to his room?

BIRLING: Yes. And I called out on both landings. It must have been Eric we heard go out then.

MRS. BIRLING: Silly boy! Where can he have gone to?

BIRLING: I can't imagine. But he was in one of his excitable queer moods, and even though we don't need him here——

INSPECTOR: [*Sharply*] We do need him here! And if he's not back soon, I shall have to go and find him. [BIRLING *and* MRS. BIRLING *exchange bewildered and rather frightened glances*]

SHEILA: He's probably just gone to cool off. He'll be back soon.

INSPECTOR: I hope so.

MRS. BIRLING: And why should you hope so?

INSPECTOR: I'll explain why when you've answered my questions, Mrs. Birling.

BIRLING: Is there any reason why my wife should answer questions from you, Inspector?

INSPECTOR: Yes, a very good reason. You'll remember that Mr. Croft told us—quite truthfully, I believe—that he hadn't spoken to or seen Eva Smith since last September. But Mrs. Birling spoke to and saw her only two weeks ago.

SHEILA: [Astonished] Mother!

BIRLING: Is this true?

MRS. BIRLING: [After pause] Yes, quite true.

INSPECTOR: She appealed to your organization for help?

MRS. BIRLING: Yes.

INSPECTOR: Not as Eva Smith?

MRS. BIRLING: No. Nor as Daisy Renton.

INSPECTOR: First, she called herself Mrs. Birling——

BIRLING: [Astounded] Mrs. Birling!

MRS. BIRLING: Yes. I think it was simply a piece of gross impertinence —quite deliberate—and naturally that was one of the things that prejudiced me against her case.

BIRLING: [Sits] And I should think so! Damned impudence!

INSPECTOR: You admit being prejudiced against her case?

MRS. BIRLING: Yes.

SHEILA: Mother, she's just died a horrible death—don't forget.

MRS. BIRLING: I'm very sorry. But I think she had only herself to blame.

INSPECTOR: Was it owing to your influence, as the most prominent member of the committee, that help was refused the girl?

MRS. BIRLING: Possibly.

INSPECTOR: Was it or was it not your influence?

MRS. BIRLING: [Stung] Yes, it was. I didn't like her manner. She'd impertinently made use of our name, though she pretended afterwards it just happened to be the first she thought of. She had to admit, after I began questioning her, that she had no claim to the name, that she wasn't married, and that the story she told at first—

about a husband who'd deserted her—was quite false. It didn't take me long to get the truth—or some of the truth—out of her.

INSPECTOR: Why did she want help?

MRS. BIRLING: You know very well why she wanted help.

INSPECTOR: No, I don't. I know why she *needed* help. But as I wasn't there, I don't know what she asked from your committee.

MRS. BIRLING: I don't think we need discuss it.

INSPECTOR: You have no hope of *not* discussing it, Mrs. Birling.

MRS. BIRLING: If you think you can bring any pressure to bear on me, Inspector, you're quite mistaken. [*Rises, crosses to fireplace*] Unlike the other three, I did nothing I'm ashamed of or that won't bear investigation. The girl asked for assistance. We are asked to look carefully into the claims made upon us. I wasn't satisfied with this girl's claim—she seemed to me to be not a good case—and so I used my influence to have it refused. And in spite of what's happened to the girl since, I consider I did my duty. So if I prefer not to discuss it any further, you have no power to make me change my mind. I've done nothing wrong—and you know it.

INSPECTOR: [*Very deliberately*] I think you did something terribly wrong—and that you're going to spend the rest of your life regretting it. I wish you'd been with me tonight at the Infirmary. You'd have seen——

SHEILA: [*Bursting in*] No, no, please! Not that again. I've imagined it enough already.

INSPECTOR: [*Very deliberately*] Then the next time you imagine it, just remember that this girl was going to have a child.

SHEILA: [*Horrified*] No! Oh—horrible—horrible! How could she have wanted to kill herself?

INSPECTOR: Because she'd been turned out and turned down too many times. This was the end.

SHEILA: [*Sits*] Mother, you must have known.

INSPECTOR: It was because she was going to have a child that she went for assistance to your mother's committee.

BIRLING: [*Rises*] Look here, this wasn't Gerald Croft——

INSPECTOR: [*sharply*] No, no! Nothing to do with him. [BIRLING *sits*]

SHEILA: Thank goodness for that, anyhow!

INSPECTOR: [*To* MRS. BIRLING] And you've nothing further to tell me, eh?

MRS. BIRLING: I'll tell you what I told her. Go and look for the father of the child. It's *his* responsibility.

INSPECTOR: That doesn't make it any the less yours. She came to you for help, at a time when no woman could have needed it more. And you not only refused it yourself, but saw to it that the others refused it, too. She was here alone, friendless, almost penniless, desperate. She needed not only money, but advice, sympathy, friendliness. You've had children. You must have known what she was feeling. And you slammed the door in her face.

SHEILA: [*Rises. With feeling*] Mother, I think it was cruel and vile.

BIRLING: [*Dubiously*] I must say, Sybil, that when this comes out at the inquest, it isn't going to do us much good. The press might easily take it up——

MRS. BIRLING: [*Agitated now.*] Oh, stop it, both of you! And please remember before you start accusing me of anything again that it wasn't *I* who had her turned out of her employment—which probably began it all. [*To* INSPECTOR] In the circumstances, I think I was justified. The girl had begun by telling us a pack of lies. Afterwards, when I got at the truth, I discovered that she knew who the father was, she was quite certain about that, and so I told her it was her business to make him responsible. [*Crosses to armchair*] If he refused to marry her—and in my opinion he ought to be compelled to—then he must at least support her.

INSPECTOR: And what did she reply to that?

MRS. BIRLING: Oh—a lot of silly nonsense.

INSPECTOR: What was it?

MRS. BIRLING: [*Sits*] Whatever it was, I know it made me finally lose all patience with her. She was giving herself ridiculous airs. She was claiming elaborate fine feelings and scruples that were simply absurd in a girl in her position.

INSPECTOR: [*Very sternly*] Her position now is that she lies with a burnt-out inside on a slab.

BIRLING: [*Tries to protest*] Now look here.

[INSPECTOR *turns on him*]

INSPECTOR: Don't stammer and yammer at me again, man. [BIRLING sits] *What did she say?*

MRS. BIRLING: [*Rather cowed*] She said that the father was only a youngster—silly, wild, and drinking too much. There couldn't be any question of marrying him—it would be wrong for them both. He had given her money, but she didn't want to take any more money from him.

INSPECTOR: Why didn't she want to take any more money from him?

MRS. BIRLING: All of a lot of nonsense—I didn't believe a word of it.

INSPECTOR: I'm not asking you if you believed it. I want to know what she said. Why didn't she want to take any more money from this boy?

MRS. BIRLING: Oh—she had some fancy reason. As if a girl of that sort would ever refuse money!

INSPECTOR: [*Sternly*] I warn you, you're making it worse for yourself. What reason did she give for not taking any more money?

MRS. BIRLING: Her story was—that he'd said something one night, when he was drunk, that gave her the idea that it wasn't his money.

INSPECTOR: Where had he got it from then?

MRS. BIRLING: He'd stolen it.

INSPECTOR: So she'd come to you for assistance because she didn't want to take stolen money?

MRS. BIRLING: That's the story she finally told, after I'd refused to believe her original story—that she was a married woman who'd been deserted by her husband. I didn't see any reason to believe that one story should be any truer than the other. Therefore you're quite wrong to suppose I shall regret what I did.

INSPECTOR: But if her story was true, if this boy had been giving her stolen money, then she came to you for help because she wanted to keep this youngster out of any more trouble—isn't that so?

MRS. BIRLING: Possibly. But it sounded ridiculous to me. So I was perfectly justified in advising my committee not to allow her claim for assistance.

INSPECTOR: You're not even sorry now, when you know what happened to the girl?

MRS. BIRLING: I'm sorry she should have come to such a horrible end. But I accept no blame for it at all.

INSPECTOR: Who is to blame then?

MRS. BIRLING: First, the girl herself. Secondly, I blame the young man who was the father of the child she was going to have. If, as she said, he didn't belong to her class, and was some drunken young idler, then that's all the more reason why he shouldn't escape.

INSPECTOR: And if her story is true—that he was stealing money——?

MRS. BIRLING: [*Rather agitated now. Rises. Pacing*] There's no point in assuming that . . .

INSPECTOR: But suppose we do, what then?

MRS. BIRLING: Then he'd be entirely responsible——

INSPECTOR: So he's the chief culprit anyhow.

MRS. BIRLING: Certainly! And he ought to be dealt with very severely——

SHEILA: [*With sudden alarm*] Mother—stop—stop!

BIRLING: Be quiet, Sheila!

SHEILA: But don't you see——?

MRS. BIRLING: [*Severely*] You're behaving like a hysterical child tonight! [SHEILA *begins crying quietly.* MRS. BIRLING *turns to* INSPECTOR] And if you'd take some steps to find this young man and then make sure that he's compelled to confess in public his responsibility—instead of staying here asking quite unnecessary questions—then you really would be doing your duty.

INSPECTOR: [*Grimly*] Don't worry, Mrs. Birling. I *shall* do my duty.

[*Looks at his watch*]

MRS. BIRLING: [*Triumphantly*] I'm glad to hear it. [*Turns away from him*] And now, no doubt, you'd like to say good night. [*Crosses to doorway*]

INSPECTOR: Not yet. I'm waiting.

MRS. BIRLING: Waiting for what?

INSPECTOR: To do my duty.

[BIRLING *rises*]

SHEILA: [*Distressed*] Now, mother—don't you see?

MRS. BIRLING: [*Turns to* SHEILA, *then to* INSPECTOR, *as door slams. Understanding now*] But surely . . . I mean . . . It's ridiculous . . . [*Crosses to chair, ready to collapse. She stops and exchanges a frightened glance with* BIRLING]

BIRLING: [*Terrified now*] Look, Inspector, you're not trying to tell us that—that my boy—is mixed up in this——?

INSPECTOR: [*Sternly*] If he is, then we know what to do, don't we? Mrs. Birling has just told us.

BIRLING: [*Thunderstruck*] My God! But—look here——

MRS. BIRLING: [*Agitated*] I don't believe it! I won't *believe* it . . .

SHEILA: [*Crossing to her*] Mother—I begged you and begged you to stop——

[INSPECTOR *holds up a hand. They wait, looking toward door.* ERIC *enters, looking extremely pale and distressed. He meets their inquiring stares as:*]

THE CURTAIN FALLS SLOWLY

ACT THREE

Exactly as at end of Act Two, ERIC is standing just inside the room and the others are staring at him.

ERIC: You know, don't you?

INSPECTOR: [*As before*] Yes, we know.

[ERIC *shuts door and comes further in*]

MRS. BIRLING: [*Distressed*] Eric, I can't believe it. There must be some mistake. You don't know what we've been saying.

SHEILA: It's a good job for him he doesn't, isn't it?

ERIC: Why?

SHEILA: Because mother's been busy blaming everything on the young man who got this girl into trouble, and saying he shouldn't escape and should be made an example of——

BIRLING: That's enough, Sheila.

ERIC: [*Bitterly*] You haven't made it any easier for me, have you, mother?

MRS. BIRLING: But I didn't know it was *you*—I never dreamt. Besides, you're not that type—you don't get drunk——

SHEILA: Of course he does! I told you he did.

ERIC: *You* told her. Why, you little sneak!

SHEILA: No, that's not fair, Eric. I could have told her months ago, but of course I didn't. I only told her tonight because I knew everything was coming out—it was simply bound to come out tonight—so I thought she might as well know in advance.— I've already been through it, don't forget.

MRS. BIRLING: Sheila, I simply don't understand your attitude.

BIRLING: Neither do I. If you'd had any sense of loyalty——

INSPECTOR: [*Cutting in, smoothly*] Just a minute, Mr. Birling. There'll be plenty of time, when I've gone, for you all to adjust your family relationships. But now I must hear what your son has to tell me. [*Sternly, to the three of them*] And I'll be obliged if you'll let us get on without any further interruptions. [*Turning to* ERIC]

ERIC: [*Miserably*] Could I have a drink first?

BIRLING: No!

INSPECTOR: [*Firmly*] Yes. [*As* BIRLING *looks like interrupting explosively*] I know—he's your son and this is your house—but look at him.

BIRLING: [*To* ERIC] All right. Go on. [ERIC *goes for a whiskey. His whole manner of handling the decanter and then the drink shows his familiarity with quick heavy drinking. The others watch him narrowly. Bitterly*] I understand a lot of things now that I didn't understand before.

INSPECTOR: Don't start on that. I want to get on. [*To* ERIC] When did you first meet this girl?

ERIC: One night last November.

INSPECTOR: Where did you meet her?

ERIC: In the Palace bar. I'd been there an hour or so with two or three chaps. I was a bit squiffy.

INSPECTOR: What happened then?

ERIC: I began talking to her, and stood her a few drinks. I was rather far gone by the time we had to go.

INSPECTOR: Was she drunk, too?

ERIC: She told me afterwards that she was a bit, chiefly because she'd not had much to eat that day.

INSPECTOR: Had she gone there—to solicit?

ERIC: No, she hadn't. She wasn't that sort, really. But—well, I suppose she didn't know what to do. There was some woman who wanted her to go there. I never quite understood about that.

INSPECTOR: You went with her to her lodgings that night?

ERIC: Yes, I insisted—it seems. I'm not very clear about it, but afterwards she told me she didn't want me to go in, but that— well, I was in that state when one easily turns nasty—and I threatened to make a row.

INSPECTOR: So she let you in?

ERIC: Yes. And that's when it happened. And I didn't even remember—that's the hellish part. Oh—my God! How stupid it all is!

MRS. BIRLING: [Rises. With a cry] Oh—Eric—how could you?

BIRLING: [Sharply] Sheila, take your mother along to the drawing room——

SHEILA: [Protesting] But—I want to——

BIRLING: [Very sharply] You heard what I said! [Gentler] Go on, Sybil.

[SHEILA takes MRS. BIRLING out. Then BIRLING closes door and comes in. ERIC sits]

INSPECTOR: [Crossing to ERIC] When did you see her again?

ERIC: About a fortnight afterwards.

INSPECTOR: By appointment?

ERIC: No. And I couldn't remember her name or where she lived. It was all very vague. But I happened to see her again in the Palace bar.

INSPECTOR: More drinks?

ERIC: Yes, though this time I wasn't so bad.

INSPECTOR: But you went to her room again?

ERIC: Yes. And this time we talked a bit. She told me something about herself and I talked, too. Told her my name and what I did.

INSPECTOR: And you made love again?

ERIC: Yes. I wasn't in love with her or anything—but I liked her— she was pretty and a good sport——

BIRLING: [Harshly] So you had to go to bed with her?

ERIC: [Rises] Well, I'm old enough to be married, aren't I? And I'm not married, and I hate these fat old tarts round the town— the ones I see some of your respectable friends with——

BIRLING: [Angrily] I don't want any of that talk from you——

INSPECTOR: [Very sharply] I don't want any of it from either of you! Settle it afterwards. Did you arrange to see each other after that?

ERIC: Yes. And the next time—or the time after that—she told me she thought she was going to have a baby. She wasn't quite sure. And then she was.

INSPECTOR: Of course. And of course she was worried?

ERIC: Yes, and so was I. I was in a hell of a state about it.

INSPECTOR: Did she suggest that you ought to marry her?

ERIC: No. She didn't want me to marry her. Said I didn't love her—and all that. In a way, she treated me—as if I were a kid. Though I was nearly as old as she was.

INSPECTOR: So what did you propose to do?

ERIC: Well, she hadn't a job—and didn't feel like trying again for one—and she'd no money left—so I insisted on giving her enough money to keep her going—until she refused to take any more——

INSPECTOR: How much did you give her altogether?

ERIC: I suppose—about fifty pounds all told.

BIRLING: Fifty pounds—on top of drinking and going round the town! Where did you get fifty pounds from?

[ERIC *does not reply*]

INSPECTOR: That's my question, too.

ERIC: [*Miserably*] I got it—from the office——

BIRLING: *My* office?

ERIC: Yes.

INSPECTOR: You mean—you stole the money?

ERIC: Not really.

BIRLING: [*Angrily*] What do you mean—*not really?*

[ERIC *does not reply because now* MRS. BIRLING *and* SHEILA *come back.* ERIC *sits*]

SHEILA: This isn't my fault. [*Sits*]

MRS. BIRLING: [*To* BIRLING, *crossing to him*] I'm sorry, Arthur, but I simply couldn't stay in there. I had to know what's happening.

BIRLING: [*Savagely*] Well, I can tell you what's happening! He's admitted he was responsible for the girl's condition, and now he's telling us he supplied her with money he stole from the office.

MRS. BIRLING: [*Shocked*] Eric! You stole money?

ERIC: No, not really. I intended to pay it back.

BIRLING: We've heard that story before. How could you have paid it back?

ERIC: I'd have managed somehow. I had to have some money——

BIRLING: I don't understand how you could take as much as that out of the office without somebody knowing.

ERIC: There were some small accounts to collect, and I asked for cash——

BIRLING: Gave the firm's receipt and then kept the money, eh?

ERIC: Yes.

BIRLING: You must give me a list of those accounts. I've got to cover this up as soon as I can. You damned fool—why didn't you come to me when you found yourself in this mess?

ERIC: Because you're not the kind of father a chap could go to when he's in trouble—that's why.

[MRS. BIRLING *sits in chair*]

BIRLING: [*Angrily*] Don't talk to me like that! Your trouble is—you've been spoilt.

INSPECTOR: And my trouble is—that I haven't much time. You'll be able to divide the responsibility between you when I'm gone. [*To* ERIC] Just one last question, that's all. The girl discovered that this money you were giving her was stolen, didn't she?

ERIC: [*Miserably*] Yes. That was the worst of all. She wouldn't take any more, and she didn't want to see me again. [*Sudden startled tone. Rises, crosses to* INSPECTOR] Here, but how did you know that? Did she tell you?

INSPECTOR: No. She told me nothing. I never spoke to her.

SHEILA: She told mother.

MRS. BIRLING: [*Alarmed*] Sheila!

SHEILA: Well, Eric has to know.

ERIC: [*To* MRS. BIRLING] She told you? Did she come here—but then she couldn't have done that, she didn't even know I lived here. What happened? [MRS. BIRLING, *distressed, shakes her head, but does not reply*] Come on, don't just look like that. Tell me—tell me—what happened?

INSPECTOR: [*With calm authority*] I'll tell you. She went to your mother's committee for help. Your mother refused that help.

ERIC: [*Nearly at breaking point*] Then—you killed her! She came to you to protect me—and you turned her away—yes, and you killed her—and the child she'd have had, too—my child—your own grandchild—you killed them both—damn you, damn you——

MRS. BIRLING: [*Very distressed now. Rises*] No—Eric—please—I didn't know—I didn't understand——

ERIC: [*Almost threatening her*] You don't understand anything—you never did! You never even tried—you——

SHEILA: [*Rises, frightened*] Eric, don't—don't——

BIRLING: [*Furious, intervening*] Why, you hysterical young fool—get back—or I'll——

INSPECTOR: [*Taking charge, masterfully*] Stop! [BIRLING *crosses to fireplace.* ERIC *sits. They are suddenly quiet, staring at him*] I don't need to know any more. Neither do you. This girl killed herself—and died a horrible death. But each of you helped to kill her. Remember that. Never forget it. [*He looks from one to other, carefully*] But then I don't think you ever will. Remember what you did, Mrs. Birling. You turned her away when she most needed help. You refused her even the pitiable little bit of organized charity you had in your power to grant her. Remember what you did——

ERIC: [*Unhappily*] My God—I'm not likely to forget!

INSPECTOR: Just used her for the end of a stupid drunken evening, as if she was an animal, a thing, not a person. No, you won't forget. [*Looks at* SHEILA]

SHEILA: [*Bitterly*] I know. I had her turned out of a job. I started it.

INSPECTOR: You helped—but didn't start it. [*Rather savagely, to* BIRLING] You started it! She wanted twenty-five shillings a week instead of twenty-two. You made her pay a heavy price for that. And now she'll make you pay a heavier price still.

BIRLING: [*Unhappily*] Look, Inspector—I'd give thousands—yes thousands——

INSPECTOR: You're offering the money at the wrong time, Mr. Birling. [*He makes move as if concluding the session, possibly shutting up notebook, etc. Then surveys them sardonically*] No, I don't think any of you will forget. Nor that young man, Croft, though he had some affection for her at least, and made her happy for a time. Well, Eva Smith's gone. You can't do her any more harm. And you can't do her any good now, either. You can't even say, "I'm sorry, Eva Smith."

SHEILA: [*Who is crying quietly*] That's the worst of it.

INSPECTOR: One Eva Smith has gone—but there are millions and millions of Eva Smiths and John Smiths still left with us, with their lives, their hopes and fears, their suffering and chance of happiness, all intertwined with our lives, with what we think and say and do. We don't live alone. We are members of one body. We are responsible for each other. And I tell you that the time will soon come when if men will not learn that lesson, then they will be taught it in fire and blood and anguish. We don't live alone. Good-night.

[*He walks straight out, leaving them staring, subdued and wondering.* SHEILA *is still crying quietly.* MRS. BIRLING *has collapsed into a chair.* ERIC *is brooding desperately.* BIRLING, *the only active one, hears front door slam, moves hesitatingly toward door, stops, looks gloomily at other three, then pours himself a drink, which he hastily swallows. He then crosses up to window, opens it, and crosses to table*]

BIRLING: [*Angrily, to* ERIC] You're the one I blame for this!

ERIC: I'll bet I am.

BIRLING: [*Angrily*] Yes, and you don't realize yet all you've done! Most of this is bound to come out. There'll be a public scandal.

ERIC: Well, I don't care now.

BIRLING: You! You don't seem to care about anything. But *I* care! I was almost certain for a knighthood in the next honors' list——

ERIC: [*Laughing*] Oh—for God's sake! What does it matter now whether they give you a knighthood or not?

BIRLING: [*Stormily*] It doesn't matter to *you!* Apparently nothing matters to you. But it may interest you to know that until every penny of that money you stole is repaid, you'll work for nothing. And there's going to be no more of this drinking round town—picking up women in the Palace bar——

MRS. BIRLING: [*Coming to life*] I should think not. Eric, I'm absolutely ashamed of you.

ERIC: Well, I don't blame you. But don't forget I'm ashamed of you as well—yes, both of you.

BIRLING: [*Angrily*] Drop that! There's every excuse for what both your mother and I did—it turned out unfortunately, that's all——

SHEILA: [*Scornfully*] *That's all.*

BIRLING: Well, what have you to say?

SHEILA: I don't know where to begin.

BIRLING: Then don't begin! Nobody wants you to.

SHEILA: I behaved badly, too. I know I did. I'm ashamed of it. But now you're beginning all over again to pretend that nothing much has happened——

BIRLING: Nothing much has happened! Haven't I already said there'll be a public scandal—unless we're lucky—and I'm the one who'll suffer.

SHEILA: But that's not what I'm talking about. I don't care about that. The point is, you don't seem to have learnt anything.

BIRLING: Don't I? Well, you're quite wrong there. I've learnt plenty tonight! And you don't want me to tell you what I've learnt, I hope? When I look back on tonight—when I think of what I was feeling when the five of us sat down to dinner at that table—— [*Sits*]

ERIC: Yes, and do you remember what you said to Gerald and me after dinner, when you were feeling so pleased with yourself? You told us that a man has to make his own way, and that we weren't to take any notice of these cranks who tell us that everybody has to look after everybody else, as if we were all mixed up together. Do you remember? Yes—and then one of those cranks walked in— the Inspector. [*Laughs bitterly*] I didn't notice you told *him* that it's every man for himself.

SHEILA: [*Sharply attentive*] Is that when the Inspector came, just after father had said that?

ERIC: Yes. What of it?

MRS. BIRLING: [*With some excitement*] Now what's the matter, Sheila?

SHEILA: It doesn't matter much now, of course—but *was* he really a police inspector?

BIRLING: Well, if he wasn't, it matters a devil of a lot. Makes all the difference.

SHEILA: No, it doesn't.

BIRLING: Don't talk rubbish. Of course it does.

SHEILA: Well, it doesn't to me. And it oughtn't to you, either.

MRS. BIRLING: Don't be childish, Sheila.

SHEILA: [*Flaring up*] I'm not being. If you want to know, it's you two who are being childish—trying not to face the facts.

BIRLING: I won't have that sort of talk! Any more of that and you leave this room.

ERIC: That'll be terrible for her, won't it?

SHEILA: [*Sits*] I'm going anyhow in a minute or two. But don't you see, if all that's come out tonight is true, then it doesn't much matter who it was who made us confess? And it *was* true, wasn't it? That's what's important—and it's what we did that's important—and not whether a man is a police inspector or not.

ERIC: He was *our* police inspector, all right.

SHEILA: That's what I mean, Eric. [*Turning to her parents*] But if it's any comfort to you—and it isn't to me—I have an idea—and I had it all along vaguely—that there was something curious about him. [*To* BIRLING] He never seemed like an ordinary police inspector.

BIRLING: [*Rather excited. Rises*] You're right. I felt it, too. [*To* MRS. BIRLING] Didn't you?

MRS. BIRLING: Well, I must say his manner was quite extraordinary: so—so rude—and assertive——

BIRLING: Then look at the way he talked to me. Telling me to shut up—and so on. He must have known I was an ex-Lord Mayor and a magistrate and so forth. Besides—the way he talked—you remember. I mean, they don't talk like that. I've had dealings with dozens of them.

SHEILA: All right. But it doesn't make any real difference, y'know.

MRS. BIRLING: Of course it does.

ERIC: No, Sheila's right. It doesn't.

BIRLING: [*Angrily*] That's comic, that is, coming from you! You're the one it makes *most* difference to. You've confessed to theft, and now he knows all about it, and he can bring it out at the inquest, and then if necessary carry it to court. He can't do anything to your mother and Sheila and me—except perhaps make us look a bit ashamed of ourselves in public—but as for you, he can ruin you. And then you tell us it doesn't make any real difference. It makes *all* the difference!

SHEILA: [*Slowly*] You know, all *he* did really was to make *us* confess. We hardly ever told him anything he didn't know. Did you notice that?

BIRLING: That's nothing. He had a bit of information, left by the girl, and made a few smart guesses—but the fact remains that if you hadn't talked so much, he'd really have had little to go on. [*Looks angrily at them*] And really, when I come to think of it, why you all had to go letting everything come out like that, beats me.

SHEILA: It's all right talking like that now. But he made us confess.

MRS. BIRLING: He certainly didn't make me *confess*—as you call it. I told him quite plainly that I thought I had done no more than my duty.

SHEILA: Oh—mother!

BIRLING: The fact is, you allowed yourselves to be bluffed. Yes—bluffed.

MRS. BIRLING: [*Protesting*] Now really—Arthur.

BIRLING: No, not you, my dear. But these two. That fellow obviously didn't like us. He was prejudiced from the start. Probably a Socialist or some sort of crank—he talked like one. And then, instead of standing up to him, you let him bluff you into talking about your private affairs. You ought to have stood up to him.

ERIC: [*Sulkily*] Well, I didn't notice *you* standing up to him.

BIRLING: No, because by that time you'd admitted you'd been taking money. What chance had I after that? I was a fool not to have insisted upon seeing him alone.

ERIC: That wouldn't have worked.

SHEILA: Of course it wouldn't.

MRS. BIRLING: Really, from the way you children talk, you might be wanting to help *him*, instead of us. Now just be quiet so that your father can decide what we ought to do. [*Looks expectantly at* BIRLING]

BIRLING: [*Dubiously*] Yes—well. We'll have to do something—and get to work quickly, too. [*Pause. As he now hesitates there is a ring at front door. They look at each other in alarm*] Now who's this? Had I better go?

[ERIC *rises*]

MRS. BIRLING: No. Edna'll go. I asked her to wait up to make us some tea.

SHEILA: It might be Gerald coming back?

BIRLING: [*Relieved*] Yes, of course. I'd forgotten about him.

[EDNA *appears*]

EDNA: It's Mr. Croft.

[GERALD *appears*, EDNA *withdraws*]

GERALD: I hope you don't mind my coming back? I had a special reason for doing so. When did that Inspector go?

SHEILA: Only a few minutes ago. He put us all through it——

MRS. BIRLING: [*Warningly*] Sheila!

SHEILA: Gerald might as well know.

BIRLING: [*Hastily*] Now—now—we needn't bother him with all that stuff.

SHEILA: All right. [*To* GERALD] But we're all in it—up to the neck. It got worse after you left.

GERALD: How did he behave?

SHEILA: He was—frightening.

BIRLING: If you ask me, he behaved in a very peculiar and suspicious manner.

MRS. BIRLING: The rude way he spoke to Mr. Birling and me—it was quite extraordinary! Why?

[*They all look inquiringly at* GERALD]

BIRLING: [*Excitedly*] You know something. What is it?

GERALD: [*Slowly*] That man wasn't a police officer.

BIRLING: [*Astounded*] What?

MRS. BIRLING: Are you certain?

GERALD: I'm almost certain. That's what I came back to tell you.

BIRLING: [*Excitedly*] Good lad! You asked about him, eh?

GERALD: Yes. I met a police sergeant I know down the road. I asked him about this Inspector Goole and described the chap carefully to him. He swore there wasn't any Inspector Goole or anybody like him on the force here.

BIRLING: You didn't tell him——?

GERALD: No, no. I passed it off by saying I'd been having an argument with somebody. But the point is—this sergeant was dead certain they hadn't any inspector at all like the chap who came here.

BIRLING: [*Excitedly*] By jingo! A fake!

MRS. BIRLING: [*Triumphantly*] Didn't I tell you? Didn't I say I couldn't imagine a real police inspector talking like that to us?

GERALD: Well, you were right. There isn't any such inspector. We've been *had*.

BIRLING: [*Beginning to move*] I'm going to make certain of this.

MRS. BIRLING: What are you going to do?

BIRLING: Ring up the Chief Constable—Colonel Roberts.

MRS. BIRLING: Careful what you say, dear.

BIRLING: [*Now at telephone*] Of course. [SHEILA *crosses in a bit*] Brumley 5721. [*To others, as he waits*] I was going to do this anyhow. I've had my suspicions all along. [*Into phone*] Roberts, please. Mr. Arthur Birling here . . . Oh, Roberts—Birling. Sorry to ring you up so late, but can you tell me if an Inspector Goole has joined your staff lately . . . ? Goole. G-O-O-L-E . . . a new man. [*Here he may describe the appearance of actor playing* INSPECTOR] I see . . . yes . . . well, that settles it . . . No, just a little argument we were having here . . . Good night. [*Puts down phone and looks at others*] There's nobody who even looks like the man who came here. That man definitely wasn't a police inspector at all. As Gerald says—we've been had.

MRS. BIRLING: I felt it all the time. He never talked like one. He never even looked like one.

BIRLING: This makes a difference, y'know. In fact, it makes all the difference.

SHEILA: [*Bitterly*] I suppose we're all nice people now!

BIRLING: If you've nothing more sensible than that to say, Sheila, you'd better keep quiet.

ERIC: She's right, though.

BIRLING: [*Angrily*] And *you'd* better keep quiet, anyhow! If that *had* been a police inspector and he'd heard you confess——

MRS. BIRLING: [*Warningly*] Arthur—careful!

BIRLING: [*Hastily*] Yes, yes.

SHEILA: [*Sits*] You see, Gerald, you don't happen to know the rest of our crimes and idiocies.

GERALD: That's all right, I don't want to. [*To* BIRLING] What do you make of this business now? Was it a hoax?

BIRLING: Of course. Somebody put that fellow up to coming here and hoaxing us. Believe it or not, there are people in this town who dislike me enough to do that. We ought to have seen through it from the first. In the ordinary way, I believe I would have done. But coming like that, bang on top of our little celebration, just when we were all feeling so pleased with ourselves, naturally it took me by surprise.

MRS. BIRLING: I wish I'd been here when that man first arrived. I'd have asked *him* a few questions before I allowed him to ask us any.

SHEILA: It's all right saying that now.

MRS. BIRLING: I was the only one of you who didn't give in to him. And now I say we must discuss this business quietly and sensibly and decide if there's anything to be done about it.

BIRLING: [*With hearty approval*] You're absolutely right, my dear. Already we've discovered one important fact—that that fellow was a fraud and we've been hoaxed—and that may not be the end of it by any means.

GERALD: I'm sure it isn't.

BIRLING: [*Keenly interested*] You are, eh? Good! [*To* ERIC, *who is restless*] Eric, sit down.

ERIC: [*Sulkily*] I'm all right.

BIRLING: All right? You're anything but all right. And you needn't stand there—as if—as if——

ERIC: As if—what?

BIRLING: As if you'd nothing to do with us. Just remember your own position, young man. If anybody's up to the neck in this business, you are, so you'd better take some interest in it.

ERIC: I do take some interest in it. I take too much, that's my trouble.

SHEILA: It's mine, too.

BIRLING: Now listen, you two. If you're still feeling on edge, then the least you can do is to keep quiet. Leave this to us. I'll admit that fellow's antics rattled us a bit. But we've found him out—and all we have to do is to keep our heads. Now it's our turn.

SHEILA: Our turn to do—what?

MRS. BIRLING: [*Sharply*] To behave sensibly, Sheila—which is more than you're doing.

ERIC: [*Bursting out*] What's the use of talking about behaving sensibly? You're beginning to pretend now that nothing's really happened at all. And I can't see it like that. This girl's still dead, isn't she? Nobody's brought her to life, have they?

SHEILA: [*Eagerly*] That's just what I feel, Eric. And it's what they don't seem to understand.

ERIC: Whoever that chap was, the fact remains that I did what I did. And mother did what she did. And the rest of you did what you did to her. It's still the same rotten story whether it's been told to a police inspector or to somebody else. According to you, I ought to feel a lot better— [*To* GERALD] I stole some money, Gerald, you might as well know— [*As* BIRLING *tries to interrupt*] I don't care, let him know. The money's not the important thing. It's what happened to the girl and what we all did to her that matters. And I still feel the same about it, and that's why I don't feel like sitting down and having a nice cozy talk.

SHEILA: [*Rising*] And Eric's absolutely right. And it's the best thing any one of us has said tonight and it makes me feel a bit less ashamed of us. You're just beginning to pretend all over again.

BIRLING: Look—for God's sake!

MRS. BIRLING: [*Protesting*] Arthur!

BIRLING: Well, my dear, they're so damned exasperating. They just won't try to understand our position or to see the difference between a lot of stuff like this coming out in private, and a downright public scandal.

ERIC: [*Shouting*] And I say the girl's dead and we all helped to kill her—and that's what matters—

BIRLING: [*Also shouting, threatening* ERIC] And I say—either stop shouting or get out! [*Glaring at him, but in quiet tone*] Some fathers I know would have kicked you out of the house anyhow by this time. So hold your tongue if you want to stay here.

ERIC: [*Quietly, bitterly*] I don't give a damn now whether I stay here or not.

BIRLING: You'll stay here long enough to give me an account of that money you stole—yes, and to pay it back, too.

SHEILA: But that won't bring Eva Smith back to life, will it?

ERIC: And it doesn't alter the fact that we all helped to kill her.

GERALD: But is it a fact?

ERIC: Of course it is. You don't know the whole story yet.

SHEILA: I suppose you're going to prove now you didn't spend last summer keeping this girl instead of seeing me, eh?

GERALD: I did keep a girl last summer. I've admitted it. And I'm sorry, Sheila.

SHEILA: Well, I must admit you came out of it better than the rest of us. The Inspector said that.

BIRLING: [*Angrily*] He wasn't an Inspector!

SHEILA: [*Flaring up*] Well, he inspected us, all right! And don't let's start dodging and pretending now. Between us we drove that girl to suicide.

GERALD: Did we? Who says so? Because I say—there's no more real evidence we did than there was that that chap was a police inspector.

SHEILA: Of course there is.

GERALD: No, there isn't. Look at it. A man comes here pretending to be a police officer. It's a hoax of some kind. Now what does he do? Very artfully working on bits of information he's picked up here and there, he bluffs us into confessing that we've all been mixed up in this girl's life in one way or another.

ERIC: And so we have.

GERALD: *But how do you know it's the same girl?*

BIRLING: [*Eagerly*] Now wait a minute! Let's see how that would work. Now—— [*Hesitates. Crosses to fireplace*] No, it wouldn't.

ERIC: We all admitted it.

GERALD: All right, you all admitted something to do with a girl. But how do you know it's the *same* girl? [*He looks around triumphantly at them. As they puzzle this out, he turns to* BIRLING, *after pause*] Look here, Mr. Birling. You sack a girl called Eva

Smith. You've forgotten, but he shows you a photograph of her and then you remember. Right?

BIRLING: Yes, that part's straightforward enough. But what then?

GERALD: Well, then he happens to know that Sheila once had a girl sacked from Milward's shop. He tells us that it's this same Eva Smith. And he shows her a photograph that she remembers.

SHEILA: [*Sitting*] Yes. The same photograph.

GERALD: How do you know it's the same photograph? Did you see the one your father looked at?

SHEILA: No, I didn't.

GERALD: And did he see the one the Inspector showed you?

SHEILA: No, he didn't. I see what you mean.

GERALD: We've no proof it was the same photograph and therefore no proof it was the same girl. Now take me. I never saw a photograph, remember. He caught me out by suddenly announcing that this girl changed her name to Daisy Renton. I gave myself away at once because I'd known a Daisy Renton.

BIRLING: [*Eagerly*] And there wasn't the slightest proof that this Daisy Renton was really Eva Smith.

GERALD: Exactly.

BIRLING: We've only his word for it, and we'd his word for it that he was a police inspector and we know now he was lying. So he could have been lying all the time.

GERALD: Exactly. He probably was. Now what happened after I left?

MRS. BIRLING: [*Crossing to armchair, sits*] I was upset because Eric had left the house, and this man said that if Eric didn't come back, he'd have to go and find him. [BIRLING *sits before fireplace*] Well, that made me feel worse still. And his manner was so severe and he seemed so confident. Then quite suddenly he said I'd seen Eva Smith only two weeks ago.

BIRLING: Those were his exact words.

MRS. BIRLING: And like a fool, I said, yes, I had.

BIRLING: I don't see now why you did that. She didn't call herself Eva Smith when she came to see you at the committee, did she?

MRS. BIRLING: No, of course she didn't. And I ought to have said so. But, feeling so worried, when he suddenly turned on me with those questions, I answered more or less as he wanted me to answer.

SHEILA: But, mother, don't forget that he showed you a photograph of the girl before that, and you obviously recognized her.

GERALD: Did anybody else see that photograph?

MRS. BIRLING: No, he showed it only to me.

GERALD: Then, don't you see, there's still no proof it was really the same girl. He might have shown you the photograph of any girl who applied to the committee. And how do we know she was either Eva Smith or Daisy Renton?

BIRLING: Gerald's dead right. He could have used a different photograph each time, and we'd be none the wiser. We may all have been recognizing different girls?

GERALD: Exactly. Did he ask you to identify a photograph, Eric?

ERIC: No. He didn't need a photograph by the time he'd got round to me. But obviously it must have been the girl I knew who went round to see mother.

GERALD: Why must it?

ERIC: She said she had to have help because she wouldn't take any more stolen money. And the girl I knew had already told me that.

GERALD: Even then, that may have been all nonsense.

ERIC: [Rising] I don't see much nonsense about it when a girl goes and kills herself. You may be getting yourselves out nicely, but I can't. Nor can mother. We did her in all right.

BIRLING: [Eagerly] Don't be in such a hurry to put yourself into court. That interview with your mother could have been just as much a put-up job, like all this police inspector business. The whole damned thing can have been a piece of bluff.

ERIC: [Angrily] How can it? The girl's dead, isn't she?

GERALD: But what girl? There were probably four or five different girls.

ERIC: That doesn't matter to me. The one I knew is dead.

BIRLING: Is she? *How do we know she is?*

GERALD: That's right. You've got it. How do we know any girl killed herself today?

BIRLING: [Looking at them triumphantly] Now answer that one.

ERIC: But—look here—it all began with that.

BIRLING: That doesn't mean it's true.

GERALD: As a matter of fact, it didn't begin with that. It began with this fellow announcing himself as a police inspector. And we know now that he wasn't—just somebody hoaxing us.

SHEILA: I see what you mean. But for all that I wouldn't be too sure about the hoaxing part. He didn't look like a hoaxer to me. [*Rises*]

BIRLING: Of course he didn't. Otherwise, he'd have been wasting his time. He had to give an impressive performance.

MRS. BIRLING: It didn't deceive me.

BIRLING: Well—perhaps not. But look at it from his point of view. We're having a little celebration here and feeling rather pleased with ourselves. Now he has to work this trick on us. Well, the first thing he has to do is to give us such a shock that after that he can bluff us all the time. So he starts right off. A girl has just died in the Infirmary. She drank some strong disinfectant. Died in agony——

ERIC: All right, don't pile it on.

BIRLING: [*Triumphantly*] There you are, you see. Just repeating it shakes you a bit. And that's what he had to do. Shake us at once—and then start questioning us—until we didn't know where we were. Oh—let's admit that. He took us all right. He had the laugh on us.

ERIC: He could laugh his head off—if I knew it really was all a hoax.

BIRLING: I'm convinced it is. No police inquiry. No one girl that all this happened to. No scandal——

SHEILA: [*Sits*] And no suicide?

GERALD: [*Decisively*] We can settle that at once.

SHEILA: How?

GERALD: By calling up the Infirmary. Either there's a dead girl there or there isn't.

BIRLING: [*Uneasily. Rises*] It 'ud look a bit queer, wouldn't it—ringing up at this time of night——

GERALD: I don't mind doing it. Mind you, they may have a girl there who committed suicide, and that may have given this fellow the idea of coming here and frightening us. But even if there is, we've no way of knowing if it's the one who's been talked about tonight.

MRS. BIRLING: [*Emphatically*] And if there isn't——

GERALD: Then obviously that's the final and definite proof that the whole thing is a sell. And now we'll see. [*He goes to telephone and looks up number. Others watch tensely*] Brumley eight-nine-eight-six . . . Is that the Infirmary? This is Mr. Gerald Croft—of Crofts Limited . . . yes. . . . We're rather worried about one of our employees. Have you had a girl brought in this afternoon who committed suicide by drinking disinfectant—or any suicide? . . . [SHEILA *rises*] Yes, I'll wait. [*As he waits, others show their nervous tension.* BIRLING *wipes his brow.* SHEILA *shivers,* ERIC *clasps and unclasps his hands, etc.*] Yes? . . . You're certain of that . . . I see . . . Well, thank you very much. Good night. [*Puts down receiver and looks at them*] No girl has died in there today. No girl's been brought in after drinking disinfectant. They haven't had a suicide for months.

BIRLING: [*Triumphantly*] There you are! Proof positively. The whole story's just a lot of moonshine. Nothing but an elaborate sell! [*Produces a huge sigh of relief*] Nobody likes to be sold as badly as that—but—for all that—— [*Smiles at them all*] What a relief! Gerald, a drink.

GERALD: [*Smiling*] Thanks, I think I could just do with one now.

BIRLING: [*Going to sideboard*] So could I.

MRS. BIRLING: [*Smiling*] And I must say, Gerald, you've argued this very cleverly, and I'm most grateful.

GERALD: [*Going for his drink*] Well, you see, while I was out for a walk I'd time to cool off and think things out a little.

BIRLING: [*Giving him drink*] Yes, he didn't keep you on the run as he did the rest of us. I'll admit now he gave me a bit of a scare at the time. But I'd a special reason for not wanting any public scandal just now. [*Has his drink now, and raises glass.* GERALD *sits*] Well, here's to us. Come on, Sheila, don't look like that. All over now.

SHEILA: [*Slowly*] The worst part is. But you're forgetting one thing I still can't forget. Everything we said had happened really had happened. If it didn't end tragically, then that's lucky for us. But it might have done.

BIRLING: [*Jovially*] But the whole thing's different now. Come, come, you can see that, can't you? [*Imitating* INSPECTOR *in his final speech*] You all helped to kill her. [*Pointing at* SHEILA *and* ERIC *and laughing*] And I wish you could have seen the look on your faces when he said that. And the artful devil knew all the time nobody had died and the whole story was bunkum. Oh, he was clever. But he who laughs last—whatever it is. [SHEILA *moves toward door*] Going to bed, young woman?

SHEILA: [*Tensely*] I want to get out of this. It frightens me the way you talk.

BIRLING: [*Heartily*] Nonsense! You'll have a good laugh over it yet. Fellow comes here and starts inventing——

SHEILA: He didn't invent what each of us admitted to doing—did he?

BIRLING: Well, what if he didn't? Look, you'd better ask Gerald for that ring you gave back to him, hadn't you? Then you'll feel better.

SHEILA: [*Passionately*] You're pretending everything's just as it was before!

ERIC: I'm not!

SHEILA: No, but these others are.

BIRLING: Well, isn't it? We've been had, that's all.

SHEILA: So nothing really happened! So there's nothing to be sorry for, nothing to learn. We can all go on behaving just as we did.

MRS. BIRLING: Well, why shouldn't we?

SHEILA: I tell you—whoever that Inspector was, it was anything but a joke. You knew it then. You began to learn something. And now you've stopped. You're ready to go on in the same old way.

BIRLING: [*Amused*] And you're not, eh?

SHEILA: No, because I remember what he said, how he looked, and what he made me feel. And it frightens me the way you talk, and I can't listen to any more of it. [GERALD *rises, crosses to her*]

BIRLING: Well, go to bed then, and don't stand there being hysterical.

MRS. BIRLING: She's overtired. In the morning she'll be as amused as we are.

GERALD: Everything's all right now, Sheila. [*Holds up engagement ring*] What about this ring?

SHEILA: No, not yet. It's too soon. I must think.

BIRLING: [*Pointing to* ERIC *and* SHEILA] Now look at the pair of them —the famous younger generation who know it all. And they can't even take a joke—— [*Telephone rings sharply. A moment's complete silence.* BIRLING *goes to answer it*] Yes? . . . Mr. Birling speaking . . . *What?*—Here—— [*But obviously the other person has rung off. He puts telephone down slowly and looks in a panic-stricken fashion at others*] That was the police. A girl has just died —on her way to the Infirmary—after swallowing some disinfectant. And a police inspector is on his way here—to ask some—questions——

[*As they stare guiltily and dumbfounded*]

THE CURTAIN FALLS SLOWLY

Uncle Harry

THOMAS JOB

Thomas Job

The year 1942 was a particularly chilling one for Broadway theatregoers with three of the modern stage's foremost thrillers running concurrently: *Angel Street, Arsenic and Old Lace,* and *Uncle Harry.* There were enough lethal theatrical doings to entertain audiences for years, and *Uncle Harry* chalked up a sturdy run of 430 performances. Termed by *Life* magazine as "a new Broadway hit that makes murder a parlor pastime," it also had the added attraction of revealing two erstwhile romantic stars, Joseph Schildkraut and Eva Le Gallienne (who first played together in *Liliom* in 1921), in noncustomary guises as the quietly sinister poisoner and the wrongly accused avenging sister.

As Emlyn Williams does in *Night Must Fall,* so does Thomas Job reveal his murderer's identity at the beginning of the play. He thereafter proceeds to follow that murderer carefully through the commission of a perfect crime. According to one critic of the period: "The attention of the audience is held taut, not with the suspense that is the major sustaining force of nine out of ten murder mystery plays, but by building the evidence by which the wrong person is convicted of the crime with such circumstantial perfection that the story interest is never dulled."

Thomas Job was born in Carmarthen, South Wales. He took his M.A. at the University of Wales before coming to the United States in 1924. He first became an instructor in the history of the English language at a Midwestern college and later taught playwriting and dramatic literature at Yale University and the Carnegie Institute of Technology.

Although he had been writing plays for almost a decade, *Barchester Towers* was his initial work to be presented on the New York stage.

An adaptation of Anthony Trollope's novel, it opened in 1937 with Ina Claire as star, and while it was respectfully received, it did not survive the season.

In 1940 Sir Barry Jackson produced his drama *Alas, Regardless* at the Birmingham (England) Repertory Theatre; and after *Uncle Harry*, there were New York productions of *Therese* (1945)—based on Emile Zola's *Therese Raquin* and performed by Eva Le Gallienne, Dame May Whitty and Victor Jory—and *Land's End* (1946).

Following the success of *Uncle Harry*, the dramatist spent a good deal of time on the West Coast writing for the films. He died in Santa Monica, California, in 1947, at the age of forty-six.

A movie version of Thomas Job's most successful play was released in 1945 under the Hollywood-ized title of *The Strange Affair of Uncle Harry* and it starred George Sanders, Geraldine Fitzgerald, and Ella Raines.

Uncle Harry was first produced at the Broadhurst Theatre, New York, on May 20, 1942, by Clifford Hayman (in association with Lennie Hatten). The cast was as follows:

MISS PHIPPS	*Wauna Paul*
MR. JENKINS	*Guy Sampsel*
UNCLE HARRY	*Joseph Schildkraut*
HESTER	*Adelaide Klein*
LETTIE	*Eva Le Gallienne*
LUCY	*Beverly Roberts*
NONA	*Leona Roberts*
GEORGE WADDY	*Stephen Chase*
D'ARCY	*John McGovern*
ALBERT	*A. P. Kaye*
BLAKE	*Ralph Theadore*
BEN	*Karl Malden*
THE GOVERNOR	*J. Colville Dunn*
MR. BURTON	*Bruce Adams*
MATRON	*Isabel Arden*

Directed by	Lem Ward
Settings by	Howard Bay
Costumes by	Peggy Clark
Lighting by	Moe Hack

Uncle Harry was first presented in London by H. M. Tennent, Ltd., on March 29, 1944, at the Garrick Theatre. The cast was as follows:

HESTER QUINCEY	*Ena Burrill*
LETTIE QUINCEY	*Beatrix Lehmann*
HARRY QUINCEY	*Michael Redgrave*
NONA	*Susan Richards*
LUCY FORREST	*Rachel Kempson*
GEORGE WADDY	*Ian Colin*
MR. JENKINS	*Keith Campbell*
MISS PHIPPS	*Grace Denbeigh-Russell*
D'ARCY	*Arthur Davis*
ALBERT	*John Garside*
JIMMY	*Robert Young*
MR. BLAKE	*Hugh Stewart*
BEN	*Lee Fox*
GOVERNOR	*Donald Finlay*
MR. BURTON	*John Clevedon*
ECCLES	*Harrop Allin*
ROBERTS	*Margery Bryce*

Directed by   William Armstrong and Michael Redgrave

SCENE: *A small town. 1909–1912.*

ACT ONE

SCENE 1: *The Tavern.*
SCENE 2: *Teatime.*

ACT TWO

SCENE 1: *Musical Interlude.*
SCENE 2: *The Nightcap.*

ACT THREE

SCENE 1: *The Verdict.*
SCENE 2: *Confession.*

ACT ONE

SCENE 1: *The Tavern*

The parlor of the Blue Bell Tavern. It is furnished in typical, stuffy fashion with a table rear center left, fitted into an L-shaped bench. Through a large open arch, right, can be seen the end of the bar, and down right is a small piano. Other chairs down right and up center, windows in left wall. A news rack down left, a hat tree at right. The walls are hung with sporting prints.

A late afternoon in August.

As the curtain rises, MISS PHIPPS, *young, stout and very much the barmaid, enters with a mug of ale, followed by* MR. JENKINS, *a small commercial traveler.*

MISS PHIPPS: I'll bring your beer into the back room, you'll be more comfortable in here than in the bar, Mr.—er— [*Puts mug on the table*]

MR. JENKINS: [*Coming to table*] Jenkins is the name, miss. Known to the firm as Up Jenkins. Little joke we have.

MISS PHIPPS: Because you're up and coming, Mr. Jenkins, eh?

MR. JENKINS: Doesn't take you a minute to catch on, miss. I do consider it quite a compliment though. You've got to be up and coming in these hard times, otherwise where are you? [*He sits on the bench*]

MISS PHIPPS: In the soup. [*She starts, apparently to leave*]

MR. JENKINS: Right. It's the same in everything—politics, business, religion, I don't care what. You've got to act quick and act thoughtful at the same time. Even murder. Not that I hold with murder, but if you do murder you've got to be smart as a whip. Take this Tomkins fellow. [*Taps newspaper*]

MISS PHIPPS: He was a brute. Burying his wife's poor legs in the chicken yard.

MR. JENKINS: You're too human, miss. You've got to look at the job technically. Now burying the legs wasn't a mistake. It was the head—that's where he went wrong—hesitating about the head, finally resorting in despair to the fireplace. What's the result—"Prisoner Pays the Penalty."

MISS PHIPPS: Hung!

MR. JENKINS: Not up and coming!

VOICE FROM THE BAR: Miss Phipps!

MISS PHIPPS: Coming up! Sorry, Mr. Jenkins.

MR. JENKINS: No sorrier than I am, Miss Phipps. But there it is—the customers won't wait for you and Pelham's Perfection Soap won't wait for me. I've got to make out these returns. [*Takes notebook from pocket and opens it on table*]

MISS PHIPPS: Returns? What are they?

MR. JENKINS: Just something to keep us business men out of mischief.

MISS PHIPPS: Dare say you need it, Mr. Jenkins.

MR. JENKINS: Ah!

[MISS PHIPPS *exits to bar.* MR. JENKINS *puts more papers on table, draws a fountain pen from his pocket, takes a sip from the tankard, and settles down to work. From the bar where he has been sitting,* UNCLE HARRY *emerges, apparently absorbed in a newspaper*]

UNCLE HARRY: Hanged, eh?

MR. JENKINS: [*Startled*] What?

UNCLE HARRY: Tomkins must be satisfied.

MR. JENKINS: You gave me quite a start, sir.

UNCLE HARRY: I was referring to the Tomkins case. I was saying that Tomkins must be rather pleased at the way things have turned out.

MR. JENKINS: No doubt, no doubt. I bet he's cavorting round in hell this minute—jolly as a two-year-old.

UNCLE HARRY: [*Crossing to table*] Perhaps. But the end crowns the work, Mr. Jenkins. Murderers, like artists, must be hung to be appreciated.

MR. JENKINS: [*Laughing*] I don't agree with you there, sir. Murderers have to lie low. They owe it to themselves.

UNCLE HARRY: Yes, that's the paradox of murder. It's very sad. Because murder is a beautiful art if you look at it properly. Yes, that's the pathetic part of it. Did you read about the Quincey case, Mr. Jenkins?

MR. JENKINS: Happened a couple of years ago, didn't it? I didn't bother to follow it up. Too plain.

UNCLE HARRY: You do that murder a great injustice, you do really. That, sir, was one of the few perfect murders.

MR. JENKINS: But that case was settled just like that! [*Snaps fingers*]

UNCLE HARRY: So they say. Nevertheless they're wrong. Quite wrong.

MR. JENKINS: [*Writing in notebook*] Fourteen and nine and eighteen and three and—

UNCLE HARRY: You don't believe me?

MR. JENKINS: Er—well— It isn't that I don't believe you—

UNCLE HARRY: [*Takes off his hat and sits*] I'll have to convince you, I see. It'll be a pleasure, since your analysis of the Tomkins' case struck me as shrewd. But Tomkins was too ingenious, and ingenuity always defeats itself. Tomkins tried to create circumstances, not take advantage of them. An artist, Mr. Jenkins, must create from what *is*. He invents nothing, he arranges.

MR. JENKINS: Does he?

UNCLE HARRY: Have you ever read *Murder as One of the Fine Arts* by Thomas de Quincey? [MR. JENKINS *shakes his head*] Ah, you should—you'd find it instructive. De Quincey emphasizes the fact that your true murderer works with a few bold, decisive strokes. Some say that the Quincey family here was descended from him, but the relationship was never established. I'm not disturbing you, am I?

MR. JENKINS: No, but this home work—

UNCLE HARRY: [*Pushing the returns aside*] You'll find the tale very stimulating.

MR. JENKINS: But see here—

UNCLE HARRY: [*Staring at* MR. JENKINS] You don't care to hear it?

MR. JENKINS: Just as you say!

UNCLE HARRY: You'll need some more refreshment. [*Calls*] Miss Phipps.

MISS PHIPPS: [*Off*] Coming up!

UNCLE HARRY: The Quinceys lived in a pleasant little house, on Union Street, here in town. You know, respectable—

MR. JENKINS: Stuffy-like?

UNCLE HARRY: Precisely, Mr. Jenkins. You'll find it's parallel all over —Europe, the States—

MR. JENKINS: My wife's cousin lives in Boston.

UNCLE HARRY: Exactly. Well, Harry Quincey lived here with his two unmarried sisters, Hester and Lettie. The family was not important, but quite beyond reproach. One of these mixed marriages, father English, mother French.

MR. JENKINS: Me, I'm pure English.

UNCLE HARRY: Extraordinary. The parents died, and these three were left a legacy. Not much, but enough to keep them in comfort if they lived together. Note that, Mr. Jenkins, *if* they lived together. You can see at once the situation that a clause like that would create.

MR. JENKINS: Private incomes, huh? I'm against private incomes. I'm a salaried man myself.

UNCLE HARRY: So I should judge from your air of uneasy self-righteousness.

MISS PHIPPS: [*Enters*] What do you want?

UNCLE HARRY: This gentleman could do with another beer. [*She stares at him but does not move*] What's the matter, Miss Phipps? Don't you want to fill the order? [*She goes into bar*] Everyone called Quincey, "Uncle Harry"—

MR. JENKINS: Uncle Harry?

UNCLE HARRY: A term of affection and contempt which the boys of the local grammar school fastened on him. He used to teach drawing there gratuitously since he wasn't a qualified teacher. The name Uncle Harry clung, but he never really liked it.

MR. JENKINS: Why not?

UNCLE HARRY: We all liked to be considered sharp fellows, sir, and the term "Uncle" somehow irritates by its suggestion of ineffectuality.

MR. JENKINS: I say, will this tale take up much time? Because if—

UNCLE HARRY: It will, but it won't bore you. Indeed, it may upset you a little. [*Calls*] Miss Phipps? [*She appears from bar*] Change the gentleman's order to brandy.

MISS PHIPPS: Change the gentleman's order to brandy. [*She exits*]

UNCLE HARRY: It does us good, Mr. Jenkins, to be upset from time to time.

MR. JENKINS: [*Rising*] If you don't mind, I'll turn on the lights—

UNCLE HARRY: Let me persuade you not to. What I have to say best suits the twilight.

MR. JENKINS: [*Sits again*] You're giving me the creeps.

UNCLE HARRY: It isn't creepy—just quiet. Very quiet.

MISS PHIPPS: [*Enters with brandy which she puts on table in front of MR. JENKINS*] Your brandy. [*She stands there looking at UNCLE HARRY*]

[MR. JENKINS *drinks hurriedly*]

UNCLE HARRY: Thank you, Miss Phipps—

[*She goes*]

MR. JENKINS: A bit afraid of you, isn't she?

UNCLE HARRY: Naturally. You see, I'm the murderer. [MR. JENKINS *rises in fright, staring at* UNCLE HARRY] I'm Uncle Harry.

MR. JENKINS: What! [*He sits again*]

UNCLE HARRY: Now take it easy, Mr. Jenkins. I just want you to listen.

MR. JENKINS: Why are you running around loose?

UNCLE HARRY: Because of the cunning ways of God. I'm trying to circumvent them through you and through thoughtful men like you. I tell lots of people.

MR. JENKINS: What are you trying to get out of it?

UNCLE HARRY: I want the world to know me for what I am. Then I won't be Uncle Harry any more. Then perhaps Lettie will let me be.

MR. JENKINS: Lettie?

[*The lights begin to dim*]

UNCLE HARRY: Don't be impatient. I'll explain it all. Ironic, isn't it? Tomkins hangs on the gallows and Uncle Harry walks the streets as free as air—yet he's far from satisfied. Now follow me closely, Mr. Jenkins, and you'll see how success, like a curse, has a curious way of coming home to roost.

THE CURTAIN FALLS

SCENE 2 : *Teatime*

The living room of the QUINCEY'S, *very neat and comfortable and indicating a conservative though not particularly old-fashioned taste. Windows in the right wall. Door up right leads outside, another door rear left leads to kitchen. Up center is a stairway, and just left of that an open fireplace. There is an easy chair in front of the fireplace, with two small sofas right and left of it, a coffee table between the sofas. A large table with four chairs at right center. A kidney-shaped table against the right wall. A whatnot down left. A bookcase between the stairs and mantel. An easel with picture down right. It is a wet afternoon in October.* HESTER *is seated facing* LUCY *on sofa left.* LETTIE *is standing between them.* HESTER *is forty-eight, a large, domineering woman.* LETTIE *is forty-two, smaller and less obviously aggressive, though she has a touch of waspishness that can be effective enough when she chooses to use it. Both women share an indefinable air of self-righteousness.* LUCY *is obviously a visitor, a perfectly nice, healthy young woman of about thirty. Her outstanding characteristic is her extreme normality. She has obviously dressed up for the occasion and is determined not to show how triumphant she feels.*

HESTER: [*She is examining a ring*] Three rubies!
LETTIE: They're small, but there are three of them. [*Gives her the ring*]
HESTER: A lovely setting too.

LETTIE: Makes the stones look so much bigger.

[*Gives the ring to* LUCY]

HESTER: From all I can see, Lucy, you're a lucky girl.

LUCY: Aren't I just! And at thirty. [*Puts on ring*]

LETTIE: No one would think you're a day over twenty-nine.

LUCY: Thirty, Lettie. Thirty. So I've just got in under the wire.

HESTER: And how old is your fiancé?

LUCY: Thirty-eight. He's a widower.

LETTIE: Any children?

LUCY: Not yet.

HESTER: Lucy, you're a caution!

LETTIE: Imagine what a surprise this will be to Harry.

LUCY: A nice one, I hope.

HESTER: Bound to be.

LETTIE: Thinking he'd left you high and dry has bothered him no end.

HESTER: Harry's so sensitive.

LUCY: Glad to take a load off his conscience.

LETTIE: I said to Harry at the time, "If that girl doesn't sue you for breach of promise, Harry, well, she's a saint, that's all."

LUCY: [*Looking at her pointedly*] If I'd sued anyone, it wouldn't have been Harry.

HESTER: [*Covering up*] And I can't tell you how sweet I think you were to call and tell us about Mr.—er—Mr.—

LUCY: Waddy. George Waddy.

HESTER: Oh, yes—Waddy.

LETTIE: Aren't you glad now, Lucy, that you decided to wait?

LUCY: Did *I* decide? I don't remember.

HESTER: Home's the best place for Harry.

LUCY: That's what you said at the time, Hester.

HESTER: Did I? Doesn't that show you now?

LUCY: It does, Hester dear, it shows me.

LETTIE: [*After a brief, uncomfortable pause*] Oughtn't we to start tea?

HESTER: Without Harry?

LUCY: I don't think you should go to the trouble. Besides, I've about a million things to do and—

LETTIE: [*Sits on sofa by* LUCY] I bet you're buying the trousseau.

LUCY: Oh—a little here and there. It's all going to be quite simple.

HESTER: Lettie, what are you grinning at?

[*There is a knock at the door*]

LETTIE: It's Harry. [*Getting up*] I'll let him in.

HESTER: [*Rising*] It's my turn. [*She goes to door*]

LUCY: I wonder what he'll say.

UNCLE HARRY: [*As* HESTER *opens door for him*] Here I am at last. [*He enters and begins removing coat and hat, hangs them on hall tree*]

LETTIE: Oh, you forgot to wear your galoshes, Harry. [*To* LUCY] You'd be amazed how often he forgets them. We have a surprise, Harry, a visitor.

UNCLE HARRY: Who is it?

HESTER: You'll never believe it.

LETTIE: You come in and see.

UNCLE HARRY: Now you've got me all excited. [*He comes in. He is a quiet, unobtrusive man who gives the impression of being little. His features are delicate and fine but marred by a pudginess, the result of being spoilt for about forty years. His hands are small and beautiful, and he has a warm, hesitant way of talking*] Hello, Lucy!

LUCY: Hello, Harry!

UNCLE HARRY: After all these years!

HESTER: Three.

LETTIE: Four in March.

UNCLE HARRY: I've missed you.

LUCY: Catch me believing that.

UNCLE HARRY: Honestly, I did.

LETTIE: Her visit isn't the only surprise.

HESTER: Tell him, Lucy.

LETTIE: Yes, hurry or we will.

LUCY: Well—I hardly know how to start. It—it's like this. [*She fizzles out*]

UNCLE HARRY: Yes?

LETTIE: She's engaged. That's the long and short of it.

HESTER: To Mr. George Waddy, engineer.

LUCY: [*Defiantly*] And doing nicely, too.

LETTIE: Show Harry your ring, dear.

LUCY: [*Extending her left hand*] It isn't much.

UNCLE HARRY: Very lovely.

HESTER: Three rubies, did you notice?

UNCLE HARRY: I noticed, all right. Did you come to tell me this, Lucy?

LUCY: I just wanted you to know.

LETTIE: She knew how interested we'd be.

UNCLE HARRY: [*Turns to* LETTIE] Is tea ready?

HESTER: In two shakes of a lamb's tail. I was baking a cake to celebrate.

LETTIE: And I'm making a pie. This is going to be high tea.

UNCLE HARRY: It's the least we can do for the lady— Excuse me. [*Runs up stairs*]

HESTER: He turned pale. Did you see, Lettie?

LETTIE: I'm sure I didn't. And besides, why should he?

HESTER: White as a sheet. You never keep your eyes open for these little—

LUCY: [*Uneasily*] Really, Hester, I don't feel I should stay to tea. The train leaves at five-thirty and I've got such a lot—

HESTER: Nonsense, Lucy. This is a celebration. You wouldn't let us down?

LETTIE: Harry'd be heartbroken too.

LUCY: Heaven forbid.

[*Sits on sofa.* NONA, *the maid, enters from the kitchen. The solid retainer type and as chatty as you might expect. She is fresh, hearty and about fifty*]

NONA: I ran pins through it, twice.

HESTER: How did they look, Nona?

NONA: Pretty clean, the second go.

HESTER: Then the cake's ready. Excuse me, Lucy, if I fly.

[*She exits to kitchen, leaves door open.* LETTIE *arranges tea things on table*]

NONA: Well, Miss Lucy, this *is* a surprise.

LUCY: Hello, Nona!

NONA: Never expected to see you here again.

LUCY: Sorry?

NONA: Come to kiss and be friends, have you?

LUCY: [*Embarrassed*] Well, just to be friends.

LETTIE: There's someone else in the picture, Nona.

NONA: Oh, I'm sorry. [*She exits to kitchen*]

LETTIE: Nona was always very fond of you, Lucy.

LUCY: Glad somebody is.

LETTIE: [*Turns and crosses to* LUCY] I've never disliked you, Lucy. It was only I didn't think you were the right girl for Harry.

LUCY: Is there a *right* girl for him?

LETTIE: Probably. She'll show up sometime. And if she doesn't, where's the tragedy?

LUCY: Harry will never get married. But you might have given him a chance.

LETTIE: Who's stopping him?—Lucy, you didn't come here to compare the two, did you?

HESTER: [*Reentering from kitchen with sugar bowl*] If you don't want that pie of yours to burn, Lettie, you'd better take it out.

LETTIE: [*Looking at her watch*] It'll be all right for another six minutes.

HESTER: Very well. If you want to rely on the recipe it's on your own head.

LETTIE: I don't rely on anything. I just know. You just *want* it to be soggy, don't you?

HESTER: I was merely trying to help.

LETTIE: Who told *you* to look at it, anyway? [*Goes out to the kitchen*]

[LUCY *rises*]

HESTER: [*Picks up chair and takes it to table*] What she doesn't understand is that in cooking you've got to stand over it. These recipes— [UNCLE HARRY *comes downstairs. He has changed into a youngish tweed suit a bit too tight for him. His tie is quite lively*] Harry, why *did* you go and put on that old suit?

UNCLE HARRY: [*On landing*] Thought I'd like a change.

HESTER: Smells of moth balls, doesn't it, Lucy?

LUCY: Slightly.

LETTIE: [*Off in kitchen*] Hester!

HESTER: Well, I'll leave you two together.

[*Exits to kitchen. They look at each other; giggle self-consciously*]

UNCLE HARRY: Did you come to gloat, Lucy?

LUCY: Only to clear the air.

UNCLE HARRY: Thank you for wanting to do that.

LUCY: Don't thank me. I just wanted to start over with a clean slate, that's all.

UNCLE HARRY: Very sensible of you.

LUCY: I think it is.

NONA: [*Enters with a pitcher of cream for the tea. Laughing*] Bless my soul! Uncle Harry, what are you wearing that old suit for?

UNCLE HARRY: Just wanted a change, Nona.

NONA: [*Crossing to him*] You haven't worn it for years. Look how tight it is.

LUCY: Men either shrink or spread over forty.

NONA: [*Pulling at coat*] He's fair bursting out of it.

UNCLE HARRY: Suppose you continue with tea, Nona.

NONA: [*Puts pitcher on table*] I know. Three's a crowd. 'Scuse me. [*Exits to kitchen*]

LUCY: [*With forced cheerfulness*] Well, Harry, how about it? [*Puts out her hand*]

UNCLE HARRY: [*Ignoring her hand*] All is forgiven, eh?

LUCY: All.

UNCLE HARRY: You don't have anything to forgive me for.

LUCY: Don't I?

UNCLE HARRY: You know I wanted to marry you.

LUCY: Not enough to give up Hester and Lettie, though.

UNCLE HARRY: And all these years I've thought—

LUCY: [*Turns away toward windows*] So have I— And thank God that's over.

UNCLE HARRY: Time's a great healer, isn't it?

LUCY: So is another man.

UNCLE HARRY: So you did come to gloat after all.

LETTIE: [*Enters after a moment's silence carrying a sugar bowl. Crosses to table*] Harry, what on earth have you got that old suit on for?

UNCLE HARRY: I thought I'd like a change.

LETTIE: I was about to give it to the Salvation Army. What have I said now?

LUCY: He just wanted a change.

LETTIE: Well, I must say I'm glad to see you taking an interest in your clothes, Harry. Perhaps this will rouse you into buying a new suit at last. Mr. Ackerman has some first-class autumn suitings in his window and I thought the brown one on the left with a stripe would be most becoming.

UNCLE HARRY: The old one's good enough for me.

LETTIE: That's Harry for you. He collects old things like a magpie. You should see your letters, Lucy.

UNCLE HARRY: Lettie—

LETTIE: Just my fun. He keeps them all tied up, Lucy.

LUCY: In a pink ribbon?

LETTIE: In a shoelace.

UNCLE HARRY: Easier to untie.

LETTIE: Remind me to dust them, Harry, when I clean your top right-hand drawer on Saturday. Shan't be long now. [*Exits to kitchen*]

UNCLE HARRY: Some day I'll throw something at her. Something hard!

LUCY: She wouldn't notice it.

[*A pause*]

UNCLE HARRY: [*Crossing to* LUCY. *Fingering his lapel*] Remember?

LUCY: I do.

UNCLE HARRY: Beacon Hill.

LUCY: I know.

UNCLE HARRY: The evening we climbed up there. [LUCY *turns away*] Did you ever tell George Waddy about that evening?

LUCY: [*Defiantly*] Yes, I did!

UNCLE HARRY: You do believe in cards on the table, don't you? What did he say?

LUCY: He said forget it.

UNCLE HARRY: Modern sort of man, isn't he?

LUCY: Yes.

UNCLE HARRY: [*Takes her left hand. Fingers her ring*] It's not as easy to forget as George seems to think. At least it isn't to me. Look. [*Points to a canvas on easel*] Like it?

LUCY: [*Going toward easel*] Harry—Harry, that's lovely.

UNCLE HARRY: [*Following her*] I did it from memory. I didn't dare go back.

LUCY: Why didn't you?

UNCLE HARRY: [*Sits on edge of armchair*] It wouldn't have looked the same.

LUCY: No—no, it wouldn't, not any more.

UNCLE HARRY: There's the tree, our tree, you notice.

LUCY: Where you cut our names.

UNCLE HARRY: [*Laughing*] I've put them in, hearts and all.

LUCY: [*Laughing*] Like a couple of kids.

UNCLE HARRY: Grand, wasn't it?

LUCY: It was—I like the view of the town in the sunset light. Remember how we picked out your house and I said it was following us around?

UNCLE HARRY: [*Rises and turns away*] It *was* following us around. You had flowers in your hair.

LUCY: And we talked of the life we were going to have and it was all so perfect—and so easy.

UNCLE HARRY: [*Coming to her*] Well—well—you're not crying, Lucy?

LUCY: [*A bit shaky*] It was so long ago.

> [*He is about to kiss her.* HESTER *in doorway sees them, coughs slightly. They break apart*]

HESTER: [*Entering with steaming cake*] There we are.

LUCY: Scrumptious.

HESTER: It'll do. Now as soon as I've helped Lettie with that pie of hers— [*Starts out*]

UNCLE HARRY: Lettie's pies are an inspiration.

HESTER: [*This stops her*] She does pretty well.

LUCY: You always were jealous of Lettie's cooking, weren't you?

HESTER: Jealous! Of her? Rubbish! [*Exits to kitchen. Slams door*]

LUCY: Must be pretty grim for you.

UNCLE HARRY: I hope you'll be happy with this George.

LUCY: Leave it to me.

UNCLE HARRY: You're fond of him?

LUCY: Immensely.

UNCLE HARRY: As fond as you were of me?

LUCY: With you it was— [*Turns to him*]

UNCLE HARRY: What will it be with George?

LUCY: The real thing. A home, a family.

UNCLE HARRY: A family!

LUCY: Yes, babies and all. No lady's complete without babies.

UNCLE HARRY: Is George also eager for babies?

LUCY: He says he can hardly wait to start. The devil!

UNCLE HARRY: Hot blooded fellow! [*Turns and crosses right*]

LUCY: Why shouldn't he be? [*Pause*] What's wrong, Harry?

UNCLE HARRY: Nothing.

LUCY: Jealous?

UNCLE HARRY: What do you think? [*Turns back to her*]

LUCY: You mustn't be a dog in the manger.

UNCLE HARRY: [*Bitterly; crosses to her*] Having a hell of a good time, aren't you?

LUCY: Do you blame me? Harry, *what* are you trying to do?

UNCLE HARRY: [*Kisses her*] Not so easy to forget, is it, Lucy? [*Kisses again*]

[UNCLE HARRY *releases her and moves away*]

HESTER: [*Off*] See, the sugar's coming through brown. Take it out.

LETTIE: [*Off*] No it won't. You must wait till the first bubble.

HESTER: [*Off*] If you do you'll—

LETTIE: [*Off*] Am I making this or are you?

UNCLE HARRY: [*Closes kitchen door with a peculiar bitter expression. Turns to* LUCY] Lucy, if it weren't for those two, would you —would you come back to me?

LUCY: Would there be any "you" to come back to? It would be the same all over again.

UNCLE HARRY: Not this time.

LUCY: No? You've been spoiled so much, that I don't believe you could live as a man ought to. You're too used to being smothered.

UNCLE HARRY: [*Moving toward her*] Lucy—

LUCY: Don't torture yourself. Hester and Lettie are eternal.

UNCLE HARRY: [*Comes to her*] Would you marry me? George or no George?

LUCY: That, Uncle Harry, is a leading question.

UNCLE HARRY: That's all I wanted to know.

[LETTIE *enters with pie.* HESTER *with teapot*]

HESTER: Well, now we can all sit down.

[UNCLE HARRY *crosses up to hall tree and looks in mirror*]

LETTIE: Lucy, you look all hot and bothered. Has Harry been teasing you? He's a dreadful tease.

[HESTER *sits at the table*]

LUCY: Isn't he, though?

UNCLE HARRY: [*Pulls up armchair to table*] Here you are, Lucy. The big chair for the guest of honor.

LUCY: [*Sitting*] A real sit-down tea. You shouldn't have.

LETTIE: No trouble. [*Sits*]

UNCLE HARRY: [*Sitting*] Hot cake, eh? We take this at our own risk but it will be worth it.

LETTIE: Harry, don't you eat it. You know your digestion.

HESTER: It won't hurt him a bit. [*Pours tea and passes cups*]

LETTIE: I'll cut you a tiny piece. It's just that I worry about him— Now, Lucy, let's have all the gossip about George, shall we? She was only just beginning to tell us when you came in, Harry.

LUCY: He was here on construction work—the new bridge at Torrence. I told you he was an engineer, didn't I? Well, it moved like lightning.

LETTIE: What, the bridge?

LUCY: The engagement. He took me home a few times in his auto-mobile—so the next thing I knew I was telling him if that's how he felt he'd better ask Father and that's all there was to it.

UNCLE HARRY: These lightning wooers aren't very imaginative, are they?

LUCY: George doesn't just sit around being nice if that's what you mean. *He* gets things done.

HESTER: That's one on you, Harry.

NONA: [*Entering, carrying a small dog*] He wants to come in he says and say hello to the visitor.

LUCY: Why, it's Weary Willie. Didn't know he was still alive.

UNCLE HARRY: [*Rising, pushes chair back*] Hello, old man. How are the poor ears today?

LUCY: [*Rising. Going to pat dog*] How's the boy?

LETTIE: Don't touch him, Lucy. He's ill.

UNCLE HARRY: Poor Weary Willie—he's getting so old. Waggles his head all the time.

LETTIE: He's a sight. Nona, what did you bring him in for?

NONA: Miss Lucy was always fond of him and so—

LETTIE: The idea! Take him out at once.

HESTER: He's doing no harm.

LETTIE: Oh, isn't he? Dying on his feet and us in the middle of our tea.

UNCLE HARRY: It isn't his fault, is it?

LETTIE: That can't be helped. He smells. Take him along, Nona.

NONA: [*As she goes, speaking to dog*] It isn't her fault you're not dead already. But Mr. Harry stuck up for you.

[UNCLE HARRY *crosses with her*]

HESTER: What about me, Nona?

NONA: You, too.

[*Exits with dog to kitchen.* LUCY *sits again*]

LETTIE: He might be the death of us.

UNCLE HARRY: [*Crossing back to table; sitting*] Isn't it about time for your pie, Lettie?

LETTIE: [*Rising*] Perhaps you're right, Harry. We shouldn't let it get cold.

UNCLE HARRY: Here's the *pièce de résistance*, Lucy. When Lettie makes a pie that's an event.

LETTIE: [*Simpering*] Oh, Harry—it's nothing really!

UNCLE HARRY: [*To* LUCY] Wait till you taste it!

HESTER: It may be a bit soggy. Lettie wasn't sure.

LETTIE: I'm perfectly sure. It was only Nona who had her doubts—and you, Hester. [*Cuts two pieces of pie and passes them to* LUCY *and* UNCLE HARRY]

HESTER: I still have.

LETTIE: I can see why—you just don't understand pastry.

HESTER: Oh, don't I?

LUCY: [*Tastes the pie*] It's just wonderful!

LETTIE: There!

HESTER: [*Puts out hand and takes* UNCLE HARRY'S *plate away from him*] Gooseberries! Canned Gooseberries! Too much acid for Harry!

UNCLE HARRY: [*Laughing*] Now look here—

LETTIE: [*Grabbing plate from* HESTER] How dare you, Hester! [*Rises*] ⎱ [*Together*]

HESTER: You never stop to consider his health—

LETTIE: I suppose you always do! You forced him to eat that awful hot cake.

HESTER: Awful—it was perfect—besides, it couldn't hurt him a bit. Not a bit.

LETTIE: Everything *you* do is perfect—and if other people suffer from your perfection that's their fault. And if Harry—

HESTER: It was just for Harry's good—

LETTIE: I wonder. I wonder if you took it away just because he was enjoying it and I made it.

HESTER: Oh, how childish of you, Lettie!

LETTIE: It's a wonder to me that poor Harry doesn't go mad with your constant bothering him.

HESTER: [*Rising; furiously*] Bothering—you call it bothering and me devoting my whole life to him!

LETTIE: It would be better for everyone if you didn't! I sometimes think one of us would be all that Harry needs to look after him.

HESTER: You, I suppose!

LETTIE: I think—

HESTER: And I think—

UNCLE HARRY: Ladies—ladies. [LETTIE *crosses to table and both sit*] I'll compromise. I'll eat half of it. [UNCLE HARRY *begins to divide his piece in dead silence. There is a ring at the door.* UNCLE HARRY *passes the other piece to* HESTER. NONA *enters from kitchen, crosses to front door*] You take this half, Hester. Go on, I insist.

HESTER: [*Stabbing furiously at pie*] Pièce de résistance!

NONA: [*Crosses to* LUCY] There's a gentleman outside and he's asking for you. Name of Waddy.

LUCY: George!

HESTER: [*Rising*] How wonderful!

LETTIE: And you never told us he was coming.

UNCLE HARRY: [*Rising*] Did you plan that, Lucy, as an extra surprise?

LUCY: No, really, I didn't. I can't think why—

HESTER: [*To* NONA] Well, don't keep the gentleman waiting. Show him in, Nona.

NONA: This *is* exciting! [*She goes to front door and opens it*]

LUCY: Now what can he be up to, coming here?

LETTIE: [*Rising*] What, indeed?

HESTER: Isn't she shy!

[LUCY *rises*]

NONA: Here he is!

[*She moves back and* GEORGE WADDY *comes in. He is a good-looking, practical man about forty, dressed in tweeds, a bit self-conscious and very much the fiancé*]

LUCY: George, what on earth—?

GEORGE: [*Kisses her*] Oh, there you are, darling. Hope I'm not intruding, but I was down on business with the automobile so I thought—

LUCY: Of course you did, darling, and it'll be lovely.

GEORGE: I hate to drag you away—

LUCY: I was on the point of going. Now I'll introduce you to the nice Quincey family. This is George Waddy. Hester, Lettie and— and Uncle Harry.

GEORGE: I've heard so much about you all that an introduction is hardly needed—[*To* UNCLE HARRY]—especially to you.

UNCLE HARRY: I was afraid of that.

GEORGE: I feel that I owe you a lot, sir.

UNCLE HARRY: I—I'm glad to meet the better man.

GEORGE: Not the better—just the luckier.

UNCLE HARRY: It's the same thing.

GEORGE: [*Gives* LUCY *an energetic hug*] If I'm half as good as she deserves I'd be an angel.

LUCY: George—! Do you know that he's really a poet pretending to be an engineer.

[NONA *crosses to kitchen door, exits*]

HESTER: Won't you have some tea, Mr. Waddy?

LUCY: Do, darling. It's a grand spread.

GEORGE: [*Crossing to table*] I'd love to but I had a late lunch.

LETTIE: [*Sitting*] Then just have a cup of tea in your hand.

GEORGE: Well—er—thanks—

HESTER: It'll warm you for the trip.

GEORGE: [*Sitting*] Thanks.

HESTER: And a piece of my cake.

[*Passes cake. He takes a big bite, mumbles,* "Mmm—good cake." HESTER *beams and sits*]

GEORGE: [*With a mouthful*] I'd like to see your drawings some time, Mr. Quincey.

LUCY: You must call him Uncle Harry—everyone does.

GEORGE: Uncle Harry it is.

UNCLE HARRY: I haven't done anything for three years.

LETTIE: Oh, Harry, what a whopper! [*She crosses to easel*]

HESTER: The man's always painting.

LUCY: He's just being modest.

LETTIE: Look at this, Mr. Waddy. [*Shows canvas*]

UNCLE HARRY: Please.

GEORGE: [*Rises and squints at painting*] Plums!

HESTER: [*Rises and brings another painting from below window*] This is my favorite. It's a picture of a tiger. He did it when the circus was in town.

GEORGE: [*Frowning*] That's something fierce.

HESTER: Will you look at the perspective. There it is behind bars.

UNCLE HARRY: Sorry, Mr. Waddy.

GEORGE: Quite all right, Uncle Harry. Most entertaining.

LETTIE: [*Crosses to easel*] Here's my favorite. Beacon Hill.

LUCY: And mine.

[LETTIE *flashes a look at her*]

GEORGE: When I was in town last they dragged me to this Van Gow exhibit. Do you like him? Bit eccentric, mind, but it's amazing how that man can show you the very guts of his soul, if you see what I mean.

[UNCLE HARRY *and* LETTIE *exchange looks*]

UNCLE HARRY: You don't see mine by any chance in that, do you?

GEORGE: [*Studies picture, then* UNCLE HARRY] Can't say I do!

UNCLE HARRY: Just as well. [*Turns away*]

LUCY: You must do us something for a wedding present, Harry. We'll give it the place of honor.

GEORGE: Right over the mantelpiece. [*Goes to fireplace*]

LUCY: And you can boast that you know the artist—personally.

GEORGE: [*Putting down the cup on mantel*] That was grand. Well, darling—

LUCY: [*Starts*] I'll get my coat.

UNCLE HARRY: I'll get it. [*Gets her coat from the hall tree*]

GEORGE: [*Takes coat from* UNCLE HARRY] Thank you! [*Puts coat on* LUCY]

LUCY: [*With a giggle*] He's so possessive.

HESTER: You haven't told us the day.

GEORGE: Can't be soon enough.

LUCY: We're still arguing about it.

GEORGE: It'll be soon. Make no mistake about that, young woman. [*Crosses up to hall tree*]

LUCY: [*To* UNCLE HARRY] It was so nice. Thank you. Goodbye, Uncle Harry.

LETTIE: Hold on a minute, Lucy. I've got something for you. Special. [*She goes upstairs*]

UNCLE HARRY: When shall I see you again, Lucy?

LUCY: At the wedding.

UNCLE HARRY: At the wedding!

[LUCY *crosses up to hall tree for hat which she puts on*]

GEORGE: [*To* UNCLE HARRY] Goodbye, Uncle Harry. It's been a treat to have met you. I used to be mighty jealous of you, I don't mind saying.

UNCLE HARRY: And you're not jealous any more?

GEORGE: Not a scrap. Not any more.

UNCLE HARRY: That's good.

HESTER: Now, don't forget. Whenever you're in town——

GEORGE: [*Crossing to door*] Catch me missing a chance of a tea like this!

LUCY: [*Goes to table for bag*] As soon as we can retaliate, you'll have to come to see *us!*

LETTIE: [*Returns with a package. Mysteriously*] Here it is.

LUCY: [*Conventionally*] How lovely! What is it?

LETTIE: George would be furious.

GEORGE: [*At door*] What would I be furious about?

LETTIE: Not really furious, Mr. Waddy. Furious in a nice sort of way.

[GEORGE *opens front door*]

UNCLE HARRY: Perhaps I'd be. Open it up.

LETTIE: Lucy's through with taking orders from you, you bully. Look at it when you get home, darling.

LUCY: Well, thanks in anticipation. [*Goes to door*] Remember, Uncle Harry, we expect a picture. Anything but Beacon Hill. [*They exit*]

[LETTIE *has seen couple to front door.* HESTER *goes to table,
takes cake, etc., and goes into the kitchen.* UNCLE HARRY
watches from window, GEORGE *slams door.* GEORGE'S *voice is
heard,* "Damn nice little fellow."]

UNCLE HARRY: Thank you very much, Mr. Waddy. Damn you!

LETTIE: [*Reenters*] Temper! Temper!

UNCLE HARRY: What right has that big, blundering—

LETTIE: You ought to be sorry for him. Think what's in store for him.

UNCLE HARRY: The thought has crossed my mind.

LETTIE: Lucy's going to make a man of him. She told me.

UNCLE HARRY: I hope he cracks in the process!

LETTIE: She used to say exactly the same thing about you. The cheek
of her.

UNCLE HARRY: She'd have done it, too.

LETTIE: Lucy's idea of a husband is a man who spends half his time
getting increases in salary and the other half in kissing her and so
forth.

UNCLE HARRY: A nice little program! [*Sits in easy chair*]

LETTIE: She'd never spoil you the way we do.

UNCLE HARRY: Yes. I'm spoiled. Quite.

LETTIE: You've got to be spoiled. I remember Mother used to say,
"Harry's got to have his—"

HESTER: [*From kitchen*] Lettie! How many hands do you think
Nona and I have?

LETTIE: Four.

HESTER: Very well, then. Hurry up and make it six.

LETTIE: I'm talking to Harry. I'll be in presently. [*Closes kitchen
door*] I sometimes think it's a pity about Hester. She means well
but does she understand you? [*Crosses to* UNCLE HARRY]

UNCLE HARRY: Not the way you do.

LETTIE: That's it, Harry. Exactly. You can be as nice as nice. You can
work your fingers to the bone for somebody—not that Hester does
that but she thinks she does. You can do everything but what's the
good if you don't understand? I suppose it's because she's older so
we mustn't blame her. [*Sits on arm of his chair*]

UNCLE HARRY: No, for God's sake. Let's blame nobody.

LETTIE: She doesn't know what it is to be together. Like us.

UNCLE HARRY: Yes, isn't it wonderful?

HESTER: [*From kitchen*] Lettie!

LETTIE: Oh, shut up! I'm coming. We're pretty well off really. Hester or no Hester. Sort of settled. Father knew a thing or two when he left us just enough to stick together. He was a great one for family.

UNCLE HARRY: Yes. His family. [*Pause*] Hadn't you better go and give Hester a hand before she blows the kitchen roof off?

LETTIE: I must, I suppose. [*Rises*] Yes, it's all very comfortable, and to think that that Lucy—well, she's got a nice little surprise waiting for her when she gets home.

UNCLE HARRY: Surprise!

LETTIE: I gave her back her old letters.

UNCLE HARRY: My letters!

LETTIE: Bootlace and all. You won't want them any more. Will you? [*Waits for an answer*] Will you, Harry?

UNCLE HARRY: [*Rises. Very quiet*] No, no. Why should I?

LETTIE: It'll show her we're done with her. For good. [*Pause again. She becomes anxious*] Won't it?

UNCLE HARRY: Unquestionably.

LETTIE: [*Very hurt*] You're cross with me.

UNCLE HARRY: [*Violently*] Cross with you! [*Quiet again*] All you do is make me look like a fool.

LETTIE: Oh, don't be cross with me. I couldn't bear it. It was nasty of me, I know, now I look back on it. Horrid. But I knew you'd understand. I just had to. It's all right, Harry, isn't it?

UNCLE HARRY: [*Turns away from her*] Yes, it's all right. [*Sits*]

LETTIE: Kiss and be friends then. [*Kisses him on cheek*] We've got to put up with each other's little ways, haven't we? It's the only way to get along. Smile at me, sir, or I'll go and drown myself in the teapot. There. [*Kneels beside him*]

UNCLE HARRY: Go and help Hester.

LETTIE: Besides I always hated them.

UNCLE HARRY: What?

LETTIE: Those letters. [*Exits to kitchen, closes door*]

UNCLE HARRY: [*Gets up; crosses rapidly as if to follow. He takes the cup from the mantel and deliberately breaks it. He crosses to painting and looks at it, saying:*] Soon I'll be coming back.

LETTIE: [*Entering from kitchen*] That was lording it over us if you like.

HESTER: [*Entering from kitchen*] Did you ever see anything like it?

NONA: [*Entering with tray*] I saw through her little game like a flash. She came to crow over Uncle Harry.

HESTER: Much good it did her!

LETTIE: You're certainly well out of that. [*Takes chair from table and crosses down left with it*]

HESTER: If it wasn't for us she'd have caught you, too. [*Takes chair from table and puts it up right*]

NONA: At least she can't say we didn't give her a good tea. [*Exits to kitchen with tea things on tray*]

LETTIE: Still, Hester, you shouldn't have argued at the table.

HESTER: I like that! You going on that way about my cake!

LETTIE: I never in my life saw anything as *small* as you taking that piece of pie away from Harry.

HESTER: Oh, you didn't! You asked for it. And besides—

UNCLE HARRY: [*Loudly*] Stop it!—I'm sorry— Please stop it!

HESTER: I won't forget that in a hurry. [*Exits to kitchen*]

LETTIE: [*Seeing broken cup at fireplace*] Upon my soul! [*Picks up pieces*]

UNCLE HARRY: Oh—George Waddy left it on the edge of the mantel-piece and—

LETTIE: Thank heaven it's only the second-best set. [*Crosses with pieces to table*]

UNCLE HARRY: Mr. Waddy spills his food. Look at this. [*Holds up piece of cake*]

LETTIE: Give it to me.

UNCLE HARRY: No. Weary Willie could do with a snack. [*Goes to kitchen*] Here you are, William.

LETTIE: I bet he won't take it.

UNCLE HARRY: [*Off*] Come on, fellow. Just what the doctor ordered. Here.

HESTER: [*Off*] He's off his feed.

NONA: [*Off*] Milk is all he's good for now.

UNCLE HARRY: [*Coming in. Closes door*] The old fellow's sick. Too sick ever to get better, I'm afraid.

LETTIE: He'd be better off out of his misery.

UNCLE HARRY: Nonsense, Lettie, he— Perhaps you're right, perhaps you're right at that. [*Crosses to easy chair*]

LETTIE: Harry, you really agree with me?

UNCLE HARRY: He knows he isn't necessary any more.

LETTIE: It would be for the best all 'round.

UNCLE HARRY: But Hester—

LETTIE: She'd boil, that's all. Simply boil.

UNCLE HARRY: Yes, indeed. We'll have to keep it dark from Hester. [*Sits*]

LETTIE: That'll be fun.

UNCLE HARRY: Hardly fun, Lettie. It's an unpleasant business. I hate to do it.

LETTIE: It's better than letting him suffer. When will we do it?

UNCLE HARRY: The sooner the better. Tonight, perhaps.

LETTIE: How does one go about it?

UNCLE HARRY: Poison, Lettie. Poison will be quickest and Hester will never know.

LETTIE: [*Pause*] Chloroform?

UNCLE HARRY: No, he'll struggle too much. Hydrocyanic acid will do the trick.

LETTIE: What's that?

UNCLE HARRY: Something very quick—same as prussic acid.

LETTIE: Will it hurt?

UNCLE HARRY: It'll be over too soon.

LETTIE: Ugh!

[*Silence*]

UNCLE HARRY: [*Pause*] Lettie! You might get some if you're downtown tonight.

LETTIE: I was going to the Post Office.

UNCLE HARRY: Drop in at the druggist's and get some.

LETTIE: Can you buy it just like that?

UNCLE HARRY: You have to sign for it. Sign my name. Ben's will be the best place. Ben won't make any difficulty.

LETTIE: I'll go right away, then I won't have to help wash up. [*Goes up to hall tree for hat*]

UNCLE HARRY: Sneak out, eh?

LETTIE: It'll serve her right for the way she behaved at tea. [*Puts on hat and scarf*] How much of the stuff shall I get?

UNCLE HARRY: Tell Ben what you want it for. Say you want a good dose.

HESTER: [*From kitchen*] Lettie!

[*Pause*]

UNCLE HARRY: She's calling you. Think how she'll feel when she finds you gone!

LETTIE: [*Gets coat*] That's just what she needs! [*Opens door*]

UNCLE HARRY: Don't forget—Ben's.

LETTIE: I'll remember.

[*Exits. Front door bangs.* HARRY *rises and crosses to table*]

HESTER: [*Entering, hurriedly, from kitchen*] Look here, Lettie, we can't let Nona do *all*— Where is she?

UNCLE HARRY: Out!

HESTER: Well, I *like* that, and all those dishes! [*Sees broken cup*] What's this? [*Crosses to table*]

UNCLE HARRY: It's a cup.

HESTER: Who broke it?

UNCLE HARRY: I did.

HESTER: Nonsense! You never broke anything in your life. So that's why she ran away?

UNCLE HARRY: She's going to say that George broke it.

HESTER: She is, is she? Oh, won't I give it to her for this.

UNCLE HARRY: Please don't.

HESTER: But it's the second-best set.

UNCLE HARRY: Well, leave it until I get back from the Blue Bell. [*Crosses to hall tree and gets coat*]

HESTER: Are you going to that place tonight?

UNCLE HARRY: [*Putting on coat*] It's Wednesday night. Got to. Sorry.

HESTER: I wish you wouldn't. [*Goes up and gets his hat and umbrella*]

UNCLE HARRY: I'm not very keen about going. It's raining, but the boys have to have someone play the piano. I can't let them down.

HESTER: Harry, when are you going to stop being a little martyr?

UNCLE HARRY: Soon, very soon now.

HESTER: No one gives a thank-you for all you do.

UNCLE HARRY: That's right, Hester. You've got to be a devil to make people really esteem you. [*Puts on hat*] Wait till I get back, before hauling poor Lettie over the coals.

HESTER: All right. I want you to be here when I face her with it, anyway. And don't you defend her.

UNCLE HARRY: I won't lift a finger to defend her. Not a little finger! [*He looks at* HESTER *speculatively, almost gleefully. Then he begins to chuckle*]

HESTER: What are you looking at me like that for?

UNCLE HARRY: Just taking a good look at you, Hester. You're such a big, live woman.

HESTER: Don't be a fool, Harry! And what in heaven's name is there to laugh at?

UNCLE HARRY:

> "When the rain rains and the goose winks,
> Little knows the gosling what the goose thinks."

[*He smiles at her enigmatically and turns to go.* HESTER *looks after him and then turns forward as:*]

THE CURTAIN FALLS

ACT TWO

*The scene is immediately after the preceding one. The
Blue Bell Tavern, as before. There is now an old oak chair
standing down center.* UNCLE HARRY *is seated at the piano
playing "A Capital Ship," and his friends,* ALBERT, D'ARCY
and BLAKE, *the proprietor of the Blue Bell, are singing en-
thusiastically but not too well.* ALBERT *is short, a bit on the
portly side and quite the sporting gentleman in his loud
checked suit.* D'ARCY *is the town lawyer, small, precise,
and neat; while* BLAKE *is a typical tavern owner, big,
healthy, and hail-fellow-well-met. They are in the middle
of the chorus as the curtain rises.*

ALL: "Then blow ye winds, heigh ho,
    A-roving I will go—
    I'll stay no more on England's shore,
    So let the music play-ay-ay—
    I'm off for the morning train;
    I'll cross the raging main,
    I'm off to my love with a boxing glove
    Ten thousand miles away."

ALBERT: [*Adding an extra measure with enthusiasm*] "So far
away—"

D'ARCY: [*Very much annoyed at this*] Oh, Albert, Albert, there
you go. Americanizing again.

ALBERT: I can't help it, Mr. D'Arcy. It comes over me like that.

    [D'ARCY *snatches music from his hand*]

BLAKE: You can't expect a man to go against his convictions.

D'ARCY: He's got to if he wants to sing in a quartette.

ALBERT: If you'd only give me a chance at the Swanee one. [*Sings*]

> "I want to see my sister Flo
> Keeping time with Uncle Joe,
> Singing a song of Dixie on the old banjo."

D'ARCY: No, no harmony.

ALBERT: Well, look at the feeling it's got. [*Drops to one knee and sings a few more lines*]

> "I want to see my dear old mother,
> Oh Lordy, Lordy, how I love her."

D'ARCY: [*This is almost too much for him*] No. It would ruin our reputation.

ALBERT: All right then, stick-in-the-mud. Stick-in-the-mud! [*Turns to piano and gets his mug of beer*]

UNCLE HARRY: [*Rising and crossing to table*] What about another round, gentlemen?

D'ARCY: [*Sitting*] We shouldn't, but we will.

BLAKE: Miss Phipps!

MISS PHIPPS: [*Enters with tray*] Yes sir?

ALBERT: The same! [*Puts empty mug on her tray*]

BLAKE: Small scotch.

D'ARCY: The same!

UNCLE HARRY: Another double scotch!

MISS PHIPPS: [*This is unusual for* UNCLE HARRY] Another double?

UNCLE HARRY: Double, double, toil and trouble.

[MISS PHIPPS *exits to bar*]

D'ARCY: Going a bit strong, aren't you, tonight?

UNCLE HARRY: I need to.

BLAKE: He feels happy, that's why. Don't you, Uncle Harry?

UNCLE HARRY: Not happy. I'd merely *like* to be happy, Blake.

BLAKE: Who wouldn't? Though I'm a big, jolly man, I'm not as jolly as I look. Oh, no!

D'ARCY: "Blessed are the meek for they shall inherit the earth!"

BLAKE: Is that so? Look at Uncle Harry here. He's meek all right but where has it got him?

MISS PHIPPS: [*Enters and places drinks*] Here I am again.

ALBERT: [*Draws center chair to below table and sits*] And welcome as the Queen of the May. The talk was getting a bit too deep for me.

MISS PHIPPS: I don't believe it. I heard you. Singing them songs. Pretty naughty!

UNCLE HARRY: They're very old-fashioned, Miss Phipps. Nothing is naughty unless it's new.

MISS PHIPPS: [*She stops to analyze this*] I never thought of that. [*Exits*]

UNCLE HARRY: Gentlemen, our topic is meekness.

ALBERT: [*Bangs mug on table*] That's it—meekness. Hell of a thing, meekness.

BLAKE: That's what I say.

UNCLE HARRY: And where would we be without it?

ALBERT: Where has it got you, my boy?

UNCLE HARRY: I'm not a bit—

ALBERT: Oh, no? If you weren't so meek your sisters— [*Rises*]

UNCLE HARRY: Yes. What have you to say about my sisters?

ALBERT: Oh, nothing, nothing. When did they have their last little tiff?

[HARRY *sits on bench*]

D'ARCY: Shut up, you damn fool!

BLAKE: [*Seated at piano*] Haven't you } [*Together*] any tact?

ALBERT: Well—but everyone knows they do. Just like cats and dogs.

UNCLE HARRY: It is not true!

D'ARCY: [*Rising*] Of course it's not true. The thing to do with Albert is to pay no attention to him. He's a gossip.

ALBERT: Who's a gossip?

D'ARCY: Let's face the facts—you are. [*Sits*]

ALBERT: [*Rising and angrily defending himself*] It isn't a question of gossip. You can see for yourself, whenever he comes in after they've been fighting you've only got to look at him. Like someone who's been kicked in the seat of his trousers and is doing his damnedest to act as if he hadn't been kicked in the seat of his trousers. Oh, you can't miss it. I bet there's been more trouble tonight.

UNCLE HARRY: Just a slight argument.

ALBERT: There you are. I know. [*Pats* UNCLE HARRY *on the shoulder*] I'm sorry, old man. It's too bad. We're all sorry for you. Aren't we, gents?

D'ARCY: [*Rising*] Now you bring the subject up—we are. You're a lesson, Uncle Harry, a great moral lesson. We all ought to be like you. We aren't and we don't want to be, but we ought to want to be like you, make no mistake about that.

BLAKE: That's putting the matter in a nutshell.

UNCLE HARRY: [*Rises*] This is kind of you, gentlemen. But I assure you the reports are grossly exaggerated. If there is some slight bickering, who's to blame for it? I'm to blame. [*Sits*]

ALBERT: You're to blame! He says he's to blame. Anyone would as soon blame Jesus.

D'ARCY: [*Shocked*] Albert!

ALBERT: All right. I wasn't being blasphemous. What's more, he does remind me of Jesus in the small.

UNCLE HARRY: Hester and Lettie are too fond of me.

BLAKE: It's because they're not married.

UNCLE HARRY: That's right. Lettie wants to do all the work and Hester says no—and there you are! Still, Lettie shouldn't have said it.

D'ARCY: Said what, Uncle Harry?

UNCLE HARRY: Oh, it was just nothing, just nothing.

ALBERT: But what was it? Uncle Harry, we're all friends here.

[*They all gather around him*]

D'ARCY: Of course we are.

BLAKE: Sure.

UNCLE HARRY: That's right. Does a man good to get these things off his chest. Lettie said this afternoon that one of them was enough to look after me. That hurt Hester.

BLAKE: H-m. Too bad!

UNCLE HARRY: Just in the heat of the moment, of course. But still—

D'ARCY: We should never let our tempers get the best of us.

UNCLE HARRY: That's right!

ALBERT: [*Rises*] That's damn right. Shake hands on it, Uncle Harry.

[*They do*]

UNCLE HARRY: Albert—

BEN: [*Poking his head inside, entering rapidly*] Have you heard this one?

[BEN *is a young, sociable fellow. Obviously accustomed to being the life and soul of the party*]

D'ARCY: Ben! [*Points to bar*] Miss Phipps.

BLAKE: You got to think of her morals.

BEN: [*Taking off his raincoat and hanging it up*] All drunk again, I see.

D'ARCY: Drunk!

ALBERT: [*Sits*] Us!

BLAKE: Just sociable.

BEN: I'll have to hurry and catch up. [*Calls*] Phippsy.

MISS PHIPPS: [*Off*] Be right with you, Mr. Ben.

BEN: Sorry I'm late, gentlemen, but we druggists— [MISS PHIPPS *enters from bar*] Oh, there you are, sweetness and light!

MISS PHIPPS: [*Obviously fond of* BEN] Oh, go along!

BEN: Another new dress!

MISS PHIPPS: Like it?

BEN: A bit low in the V but who cares? More *joie de* V, as it were. Two beers, Miss Phipps, in a hurry. [*She exits*] I like to have a beer in each hand—gives me a balance. Albert, what's a good substitute for beer?

ALBERT: [*Smart as a whip*] Gin.

BEN: No—another beer. [*He roars at his own joke.* MISS PHIPPS *returns with his drinks*] Thank you, light of my life, farewell. Here's how! [*Crosses to table; sees* UNCLE HARRY] Oh, there you are, old Caesar Borgia.

D'ARCY: That's not his name.

BEN: [*Sits on bench*] Your sister, Lucrezia Borgia, was in tonight.

ALBERT: Sounds like a couple of foreigners to me.

D'ARCY: So they were, Albert, my boy—historical foreigners. They'd poison you at the drop of a hat.

UNCLE HARRY: I'm afraid I don't quite follow you, Ben.

BEN: See, he's trying to cover up his tracks. Sending your sister to get poison!

UNCLE HARRY: [*Quickly*] Was it Lettie?

BEN: Certainly it was and she signed your name.

UNCLE HARRY: Signed my name for what?

BEN: For the poison. Didn't you know you have to sign for it?

UNCLE HARRY: Do you?

BEN: She seemed to know more about this than you do.

UNCLE HARRY: What did she get?

BEN: Hydrocyanic acid.

UNCLE HARRY: Beg your pardon?

BEN: Prussic acid.

UNCLE HARRY: I suppose she wanted it to clean clothes.

BEN: [*This tickles him*] That's a good one. Clean clothes, eh? One whiff of that stuff and that's the last clothes you'll ever clean. So you be careful.

UNCLE HARRY: Is it as deadly as all that?

BEN: It's quick—that's the best you can say for it. Weary Willie won't suffer long but it'll pinch him a bit at first.

UNCLE HARRY: [*Surprised*] My dog?

BEN: She said that something ran out of his poor ears all the time.

UNCLE HARRY: That's all wrong.

BEN: What?

UNCLE HARRY: Nothing—it's all right.

BEN: You're sure, aren't you?

UNCLE HARRY: It's all right—it's quite all right.

BLAKE: That's the sad part about dogs; they die.

ALBERT: This acid stuff, Ben. What does it do to you?

BEN: Plenty. Hydrocyanic acid unites with the haemoglobin in the blood to the exclusion of oxygen.

D'ARCY: [*Shaking his head*] That's bad.

BEN: And that causes chemical suffocation.

ALBERT: Is that worse than just plain suffocation?

BEN: Anything chemical is worse than anything plain. I saw a case once of prussic acid poisoning. It wasn't nice.

BLAKE: A human case?

BEN: Human! It had been human.

ALBERT: Geez!

D'ARCY: Why aren't we singing?

UNCLE HARRY: [*Rising*] Sorry—I really have to be going.

ALBERT: [*Looking at his watch*] So early? It's only nine o'clock!

BLAKE: You always stay till ten-fifteen.

UNCLE HARRY: [*He feels his forehead*] Must be the whiskey. I don't feel very well. [*Takes scarf*] Ben, you'll play for the boys.

BLAKE: Ben, indeed!

BEN: Certainly. [*Gets* UNCLE HARRY's *coat from tree and helps him into it*]

UNCLE HARRY: Good night, gentlemen!

THE GENTLEMEN: Good night! Good night, Uncle Harry!

BEN: Don't do anything I wouldn't do.

UNCLE HARRY: [*Turning*] Ben, what sort of stuff did you say Lettie got?

BEN: Hydrocy—I mean prussic acid.

UNCLE HARRY: And it kills dogs?

BEN: Kills anything.

[UNCLE HARRY *shakes his head, then exits*]

BEN: [*Watching him go*] You know, it's sort of odd, boys. Shouldn't be surprised if she was planning to kill the dog behind the poor chap's back. He didn't seem to know much about it.

BLAKE: Never seems to know much of anything.

ALBERT: Always was absentminded.

BEN: You should have seen Sister Lettie buying the stuff. Sly as if she had murder up her sleeve. Wouldn't talk to my partner either. Nothing would do for her but she had to see me.

ALBERT: Why did he leave so early?

BLAKE: It was the whiskey, he said.

BEN: Whiskey has its faults but it doesn't make a man go home early.

[ALL *drink as:*]

THE CURTAIN FALLS

SCENE 2: *The Nightcap*

Back in the living room.

The time is 9:30. The same night. The wind has risen and rain beats furiously against the window.

The gaslights have been lit and the fire is burning brightly.

LETTIE *is sitting on the sofa below the fire. By the easy chair is a pair of man's slippers carefully placed, also a smoking jacket.*

LETTIE: [*Reading*]
"A slumber did my spirit seal
I had no human fears;
She seem'd a thing that could not feel
The touch of earthly years.

No motion has she now, no force
She neither hears nor sees—"
[*The doorbell rings; she puts the open book on the sofa, rises and crosses to open the door*] Where have you been?

UNCLE HARRY: [*Entering*] Just drinking water with three friends, Lettie.

LETTIE: [*Taking his hat and umbrella*] What three friends? [*Hangs hat on hall tree and puts umbrella in stand*]

UNCLE HARRY: Haig and Haig and Johnny Walker. [*Laughs*] That's supposed to be a joke, Lettie.

LETTIE: Oh, you've been down at that Blue Bell again?

UNCLE HARRY: Certainly. It's Wednesday night. Didn't Hester tell you?

LETTIE: Not a word. She hasn't said a word to me all evening.

UNCLE HARRY: Where's Madam now?

LETTIE: She's in her room.

UNCLE HARRY: In bed?

LETTIE: No, she's sitting there in the dark—all in the cold. Well, if she wants to make a martyr of herself, she's welcome.

UNCLE HARRY: [*Looking at ceiling*] In one of her moods again, is she? [*Taking off his coat*]

LETTIE: [*Crosses to him, helps to take off coat*] I suppose she's furious because I didn't help with the washing up. [*Takes coat to hall tree and hangs it up*]

UNCLE HARRY: [*Crossing to easy chair; puts on smoking jacket*] Lettie, did you get that stuff?

LETTIE: I did, and did I have trouble! Ben just wouldn't give it to me at first, and then I told him you wanted it, and he said he supposed you knew what you were about.

UNCLE HARRY: [*Sits in his chair; takes off shoes and puts on slippers*] That's just like Ben—cautious. Where is it?

LETTIE: [*Taking a small package from the table*] Here it is! Ben said there was enough here to settle the hash of a whole kennel. [*She hands him the package*]

UNCLE HARRY: H'm! [*Handles package*] A little thing to cause so much pain. [*Gives it back to her*] Better put it out of the way!

LETTIE: Are we going to use it tonight?

UNCLE HARRY: I don't know. Anyway, hide it for the time being. I shouldn't like Hester to see it—and Nona might want to use it for her cough. Put it in that jar with the matches. [*Puts on his slippers*] I'm the only one who uses that jar. [LETTIE *is about to put it in*] Perhaps you'd better write something on the wrapper.

LETTIE: It says "Poison" as large as life. That should be enough.

UNCLE HARRY: Nobody notices print. Here— [*Hands her pencil*] write "Danger" or "Don't touch" on it.

LETTIE: I'll put both. [*Crosses to table and writes on package*]

UNCLE HARRY: You can't be too careful in these matters— [LETTIE *puts package in bowl on mantel*] What have you been reading?

LETTIE: Trying to read some poetry. Wordsworth. Terribly childish, isn't it?

UNCLE HARRY: [*Laughs*] Terribly childish! That's rather good for

Wordsworth. Only children and wise old men understand him. [*Reads*]

> "No motion has she now, no force
> She neither hears nor sees
> Roll'd round in earth's diurnal course
> With rocks and stones and trees."

There's simple majesty for you, Lettie!

LETTIE: Isn't it just that the girl is dead?

UNCLE HARRY: Yes, but still part of the living world.

LETTIE: [*Sits on sofa*] What good would that do her? What are you going to read to me tonight?

UNCLE HARRY: We'll see. We must calm Madam Hester down first.

LETTIE: I feel very much like letting her stew in her own juice for a while. She's really cross because Lucy preferred my pie.

UNCLE HARRY: There's the matter of the cup, too.

LETTIE: What cup?

UNCLE HARRY: The broken one. She thinks you've done it.

LETTIE: How dare she? Why I've never in my life—

UNCLE HARRY: I told her that. [*The front door opens and* NONA *enters*] There's Nona. [*Rises*]

LETTIE: [*Rising, furiously*] How dare she! Well, of all the—

UNCLE HARRY: Hello, Nona! How's the fiancé tonight?

NONA: Hubert was depressed.

LETTIE: Isn't he always?

NONA: He was worse than ever tonight. And I don't blame him.

LETTIE: Harry, did Hester really say that I—? Did she?

UNCLE HARRY: She was positive.

NONA: And why wouldn't he be depressed in this rain? He isn't a duck.

LETTIE: Whenever Hester gets the chance to put the blame on me—

NONA: There we stood under the arcade in the pouring rain and then I said, "Hubert, what's the use, kissing or no kissing?" That's why I'm home early.

LETTIE: How many times have I told you, Nona, that you can bring Hubert into the kitchen if it's raining? Raining hard, that is.

NONA: He doesn't like it. He says you come in too often.

UNCLE HARRY: Tell him he should be more charitable. Lettie likes a little excitement too.

LETTIE: [*Crossing to* NONA] Did you see me break a cup, Nona?

NONA: What cup?

LETTIE: The cup that George Waddy used. Did I break it or didn't I?

NONA: Why should you?

LETTIE: There! [*Exits quickly upstairs*]

NONA: What's wrong now, Uncle Harry?

UNCLE HARRY: I don't know, Nona. Some small disturbance.

NONA: Again!

UNCLE HARRY: [*Sternly*] Nona!

NONA: All right. I'm not saying a word.

UNCLE HARRY: [*Filling pipe from humidor on table*] Don't criticize people, Nona.

NONA: I just say what I think.

UNCLE HARRY: [*Sitting*] That's what they all say. Do you mind reaching me a match from the jar? I'm too comfortable to move.

NONA: Here you are. [*Takes a match from the bowl on the mantel, lights it and gives it to* UNCLE HARRY]

UNCLE HARRY: Thanks. [*Waits for a moment and lets the match go out*] Confound it, it's gone out.

NONA: [*Feeling in the bowl*] Plenty more where that came from. [*Rummages*] Here's a whole box. [*Produces package*] These ain't matches. [*Reads*] "Danger." "Don't touch." Gosh!

UNCLE HARRY: What the dickens do you have there?

NONA: I don't know. Something that Miss Lettie's been writing on.

UNCLE HARRY: H'm. Must be a joke.

NONA: Shall I open it?

UNCLE HARRY: You shall not. I think I'd better look after this.

NONA: That'll be best for everyone. I think, Mr. Harry, that even dynamite would be safe with you.

UNCLE HARRY: We'll have to ask Miss Lettie what it is.

NONA: And the sooner I know the better I'll feel. I don't mind "Danger." It's the "Don't touch" part that gets me.

[*There are distinct sounds of angry raised voices upstairs*]

UNCLE HARRY: [*Listening*] What is going on up there?

NONA: Those two girls!

UNCLE HARRY: Excuse me—I think I'd better— [*Rises, crosses to table and puts package on it. Exiting quickly upstairs with* "What's going on up there?"]

NONA: Poor Uncle Harry, you do have a dreadful time. [*Opens package which* UNCLE HARRY *has left on the table*] "Hydrocyanic acid." [*She mispronounces the word*] Well—that's a new one. "Hydrocyanic acid."

> [*Begins to wrap it up, then thinks better and begins to uncork it*]

LETTIE: [*Comes downstairs. On landing*] Put that down!

NONA: I—I found it in the jar and—

LETTIE: Put it down, you fool! If you even smelt it you'd be a sick woman.

NONA: Gosh!

LETTIE: You might even die. It's prussic acid.

NONA: Well, what on earth would you want with prussic acid in a decent house?

LETTIE: That's my own business.

NONA: All right—it's between you and it.

LETTIE: You're always prying and peering. Some day you'll pry once too often.

NONA: I've been here nearly thirty years. You'd think I had some rights.

LETTIE: If you must know, we're going to put the dog out of his misery.

NONA: With that?

LETTIE: Yes. Mr. Harry ordered it. Don't tell Hester.

NONA: [*Incredulous*] Mr. Harry ordered it?

LETTIE: Yes, of course he ordered it.

NONA: H'm. [*Mutters*] Mr. Harry ordered it! [*Exits into kitchen and closes door*]

> [UNCLE HARRY *comes downstairs with* HESTER. LETTIE, *hearing them, quickly sits on sofa and pretends to read*]

UNCLE HARRY: [HESTER *doesn't say a word*] Sit down, Miss Quincey, ma'am, and make yourself comfortable. [HESTER *sits on opposite sofa*] That's it. Now say a kind word to the lady. [*Sits in easy chair*]

HESTER: [*Snapping*] I suppose I should—to the head of the house.

LETTIE: [*Snapping the book shut*] Head of the house!

HESTER: Who clsc is? I'd like to know!

UNCLE HARRY: [*Rising*] Anybody would think you were both about five years old.

HESTER: All I ask for is a little peace.

UNCLE HARRY: That's a good one.

LETTIE: That *is*.

UNCLE HARRY: [*Impatiently*] Quiet, Lettie. We all know you just do it out of high spirits, but other people don't believe that. You're a fine, dignified couple of women but as soon as you start in on each other, bang goes the dignity and you behave—

HESTER: I won't be talked to that way.

UNCLE HARRY: [*Rapping on the table with his pipe*] It's just for your own good. You don't want to be the laughing stock of the town, do you?

HESTER and LETTIE: Who is?

UNCLE HARRY: [*Crossing to them*] I'm afraid you both are rapidly becoming so. You know how they talk. That business this afternoon was most unfortunate. Lucy—

HESTER: That woman!

LETTIE: We all know what she thinks about } [*Together*] us, anyway.

UNCLE HARRY: All the more reason why you should be careful when she's present. She has a tongue.

HESTER: She certainly has.

UNCLE HARRY: [*Pause. He has made his point*] Well!

HESTER: [*She gives in*] Oh, I suppose you are right.

LETTIE: You are, Harry, quite right. I sometimes think, though, that Hester and I will only be at peace in our graves.

UNCLE HARRY: Easy, ladies, easy—nothing like not letting the sun go down upon your wrath. Now we'll have a cup of cocoa to seal the treaty. [*Calls*] Nona!

NONA: [*Off*] Yes.

UNCLE HARRY: [*Crosses to kitchen door and calls out*] Would you care to make a little cocoa for the family by way of a nightcap?

NONA: [*Off*] I will.

UNCLE HARRY: Thank you.

NONA: [*Off*] How's the fire in there?

UNCLE HARRY: It's fine.

NONA: [*Off*] All right.

UNCLE HARRY: The trouble is that you need such a little thing to start you off. If it were a really big cause you'd stick together like glue, but give you a tiny reason and it's all up. [*Sits in easy chair*]

NONA: [*Entering with saucepan*] I'll have to make it in here. The kitchen stove is out.

UNCLE HARRY: Go ahead, Nona.

[NONA *does, with a good deal of fuss*]

HESTER: Put in a cup for yourself.

NONA: I have. Shall I stir it or will you?

LETTIE: I'll stir it.

NONA: Right you are.

UNCLE HARRY: Let Nona do it— And tomorrow I'll try to match that cup.

LETTIE: Why trouble? We have two dozen and—

HESTER: We *had* two dozen.

LETTIE: And we never have even a dozen people in the house.

HESTER: That's not the point. The set's supposed to be two dozen and two dozen we ought to have.

UNCLE HARRY: Make you feel happy just to know the two dozen are there, eh, Hester?

HESTER: Besides it was my mother's china.

LETTIE: *My* mother's! Do you have exclusive rights to her, too?

HESTER: I'm the oldest.

UNCLE HARRY: But Hester—

LETTIE: Do you think they're yours? I suppose you do and everything else in the house.

NONA: Share and share alike.

UNCLE HARRY: Nona's the only sensible one amongst us.

NONA: Who wants sense? If I'd only had looks!

HESTER: It's the principle of the thing that troubles me.

UNCLE HARRY: We know, Hester, two dozen or nothing.

HESTER: No, it isn't that. If Lettie had only come to me and said—

LETTIE: Said what!

HESTER: Said that it had happened and she was sorry, I'd have said—

UNCLE HARRY: Oh, Lord, we've already thrashed this out—

LETTIE: Said *what* had happened?

HESTER: Instead of sneaking out downtown like a thief in the night.

UNCLE HARRY: That was just for fun.

HESTER: [*Quite furious*] Fun! Fun!

UNCLE HARRY: Can't you take anything as a joke?

LETTIE: [*Rises*] Why should I consult you about everything I do?

HESTER: I'm not asking you to consult me about everything you do. All I ask is that you show a little consideration.

UNCLE HARRY: We try to, Hester.

LETTIE: Simply because you bullied us when we were children you think you can do it now. And you call it "showing consideration."

HESTER: Oh, I understand. You wish I weren't here at all. Then you'd be free to gallivant as you please and to let the house go to rack and ruin. Don't think I've forgotten what you said this afternoon.

NONA: The cocoa's ready. [*Starts for kitchen*]

UNCLE HARRY: [*Stopping* NONA] What *did* you say this afternoon, Lettie?

HESTER: [*Short pause*] You said I wasn't wanted. You said that one of us was enough to look after Harry.

LETTIE: And I meant it, too. [NONA *listens to this and exits*] So the cup was just an excuse for your bad temper?

HESTER: Excuse!

LETTIE: That's true. You don't need an excuse. I wish you'd stayed upstairs. I wish you weren't here. It was so peaceful till you came down.

HESTER: Yes, I'm just a nuisance, I know.

UNCLE HARRY: Why don't you break that china dog and call it quits?

LETTIE: Yes, why don't you? Heaven knows it's the only thing I can call my own.

[NONA *returns with cups and pitcher of cocoa on tray*]

HESTER: I will, too. [*She gets up and seizes a china dog from the mantelpiece*]

UNCLE HARRY: Hester—don't be a fool.

LETTIE: [*Crosses to fireplace and grabs her hand*] Put that down.

HESTER: Will you let me go?

LETTIE: Will you put it down?

HESTER: I warn you, Lettie, to let me go.

LETTIE: Harry gave me that for Christmas. You shan't touch it.

HESTER: Oh, shan't I? [*She strikes LETTIE over the face*]

LETTIE: You—you devil! [*She puts her hands over her face and sits on sofa, crying*]

HESTER: [*About to throw the dog*] You asked for it.

UNCLE HARRY: Put that down, Hester.

[HESTER *bangs it on the mantel and exits furiously upstairs*]

NONA: [*Brings tray down between sofas and puts it on coffee table*] Well, I will say this: the house doesn't lack for entertainment—of a sort.

LETTIE: I hate her! [*Begins to sob*]

[UNCLE HARRY *motions* NONA *to withdraw*. NONA *exits, obviously perturbed*]

UNCLE HARRY: [*Crosses to sofa, in back of* LETTIE] She's always been jealous of you. Do you remember when we were kids catching tadpoles in the pond in old Clark's meadow and you caught more tadpoles than she did and brought the jampot to show them to me? I was so delighted with them and said you were the best fisher in the world, and then Hester smashed your jampot. I was four and you were six and Hester was twelve so she should have known better. It's just the same now. Hester never really grew up. I don't think any of us have grown up. We're still children.

LETTIE: She is! That's evident.

UNCLE HARRY: You can't be cross with a child.

LETTIE: She isn't a child. She's a vicious, bad-tempered old woman.

UNCLE HARRY: [*Moving to table*] Do you think it's any easier for me?

LETTIE: She doesn't hate you. You're the world to her and that's why she takes it out on me. Oh, I understand.

UNCLE HARRY: Love's just as painful as hate. What was it that kept me here when I could—?

LETTIE: Oh, but I did that, too.

UNCLE HARRY: Yes, you were more opposed to Lucy than Hester ever was.

LETTIE: [*She has stopped crying and turns to him*] And you really wanted to marry her as much as all that?

UNCLE HARRY: You know I did.

LETTIE: Poor Harry!

UNCLE HARRY: Poor Uncle Harry! I do get sympathy, there's no denying it. [*Picks up poison and puts it in his pocket*] Poor Uncle Harry! Lettie, why don't you make peace with your sister?

LETTIE: Peace! There'll never be any peace with her around. [*Rises*]

UNCLE HARRY: There may be—if you do what I ask.

LETTIE: I won't apologize.

UNCLE HARRY: Why should you? All I suggest is that you should be just a little kind. It'll make you a very much bigger person than Hester is.

LETTIE: What do you want me to do?

UNCLE HARRY: [*Indicating the cups*] She hasn't had her nightcap. So if—

LETTIE: I wouldn't do it if it's the last thing I did!

UNCLE HARRY: Very well, I'll do it myself. [*Sits on sofa and pulls coffee table to him*]

LETTIE: That will only make her triumph over me.

UNCLE HARRY: That's quite likely.

LETTIE: Oh, I hate to do it!

UNCLE HARRY: But you will because you're generous—because—

LETTIE: Nonsense! I do it just to stop you from doing it.

UNCLE HARRY: Is she in bed yet?

LETTIE: [*Goes up on landing and listens*] She's in bed.

UNCLE HARRY: Probably crying her eyes out, poor soul. This will make her sleep easier. [*Pours out a cup and puts it on the tray.*]

LETTIE: [*Crosses down to* HARRY] But if you think I'm going to kow-tow to her—

UNCLE HARRY: Just ask if she'd like the cocoa. Oh, you'd better get some more sugar to put in it. She likes it sweet.

LETTIE: She likes it sweet!

UNCLE HARRY: Don't stand there muttering sarcastically. Get the sugar. [LETTIE *hesitates about bringing the sugar in to the cocoa, or taking the cocoa out to the sugar.*] Bring in the bowl— I'd like a little more myself. [LETTIE *hesitates but finally puts cup down and exits to kitchen.* UNCLE HARRY *takes package from his pocket and pours some of the poison into the cup, replacing the bottle in his pocket as* LETTIE *reenters with sugar*] Now hurry, or she'll be asleep.

LETTIE: [*Puts sugar bowl on coffee tray*] Not Hester. She'll be awake contemplating her wrongs.

UNCLE HARRY: [*Puts sugar in cocoa, stirs it, and hands her the cup*] You should do this with forgiveness in your heart.

LETTIE: [*Snorts*] I'm a Christian, I hope, but I'm a Christian within decent limits. [*Exits upstairs with cocoa*]

> [UNCLE HARRY *goes over to the window; a vicious gust of wind and rain blows into the room. He closes the window, pulls down the blind and carefully wipes his face with his handkerchief. He hears* LETTIE'*s step on the stairs and sits comfortably in the easy chair*]

LETTIE: [*Comes downstairs with cup*] She says no.

UNCLE HARRY: What!

LETTIE: She says anything I gave her would be like poison to her.

UNCLE HARRY: [*Laughs*] That's the first funny thing Hester's ever said.

LETTIE: I see nothing funny in it.

UNCLE HARRY: Don't you? You didn't persuade her enough, Lettie.

LETTIE: Really, that's asking too much.

UNCLE HARRY: What did you do?

LETTIE: I put it down and said, "You've forgotten this." [*Puts cup on tray and sits on sofa*]

UNCLE HARRY: Just like a spoilt child ordered to beg pardon. Didn't I say you weren't grown up?

LETTIE: Let her enjoy her sulks.

UNCLE HARRY: [*Sharply*] Just as you say.

LETTIE: Shall we have some of this? [*Picks up the cup*]

UNCLE HARRY: As you wish.

LETTIE: [*Offering poisoned cup*] Don't you want it?

UNCLE HARRY: Not particularly.

LETTIE: But you ordered it.

UNCLE HARRY: Not for me.

LETTIE: Of course if you don't want it— [*Puts cup on tray again*]

UNCLE HARRY: For God's sake, Lettie!

LETTIE: Now you're angry, too. [*No answer*] And with me.

UNCLE HARRY: Sulks are catching.

LETTIE: Don't you want to read that poetry?

UNCLE HARRY: Not interested.

LETTIE: Please, I'd love to hear it. [*Pause*] Would you if I went up and talked to Hester?

UNCLE HARRY: If you don't go, all the squabbling will start again in the morning. And I'm sick of your squabbles.

LETTIE: But you saw her strike me. How can you expect— [UNCLE HARRY *picks up the cup and starts for the stairs*] Where are you going?

UNCLE HARRY: Up to Hester.

LETTIE: [*Rises*] I'd rather go myself.

UNCLE HARRY: You'd fail again.

LETTIE: I wouldn't. You'll see.

UNCLE HARRY: And the peace offering will be getting cold. Well— [*Starts upstairs*]

LETTIE: [*Stops him*] I insist on going. You sit down and pour out for both of us and I'll be back in a jiffy and you'll see that everything will be all right.

UNCLE HARRY: [*Giving her the cup*] Since you insist.

LETTIE: [*Starting upstairs*] She'll drink it this time if I have to pour it down her throat.

UNCLE HARRY: [*Stops her on landing*] Lettie!

LETTIE: Yes?

UNCLE HARRY: Lettie—if it was just you and me and there was no Hester—

LETTIE: We'd be much happier.

UNCLE HARRY: And I wanted to get married—what would you say?

LETTIE: What would become of me?

UNCLE HARRY: Yes, that's what I thought you'd say.

LETTIE: Well, what else should I say? [*Exits upstairs*]

UNCLE HARRY: [*Calling*] Nona! Want your cocoa? [*Crosses to sofa and sits*]

NONA: [*Appearing*] I was wondering what had become of it.

UNCLE HARRY: [*Pouring a cup for her*] Here it is.

NONA: [*Sipping*] They say that cocoa is a sign of old age, but I don't give a hoot, do you, sir?

UNCLE HARRY: Never a hoot. Sit down, Nona.

NONA: Have they gone to bed? [*Sits on opposite sofa*]

UNCLE HARRY: Miss Hester has. Miss Lettie took a cup up to her.

NONA: After what—

UNCLE HARRY: Yes—after that.

NONA: I wish I could do a thing like that. That's the kindest thing that I ever heard of.

UNCLE HARRY: It's just what Miss Lettie would do.

NONA: H'm. It's more like what you'd do, Mr. Harry, if I may say so. Maybe you used your blarney on her.

UNCLE HARRY: No blarney at all. She seemed very anxious to do it. Simply insisted.

NONA: [*Rising and putting cup on the tray*] If things go on like this we'll have a nice house of it here— Good night, Mr. Harry. [*Starts for the stairs*]

UNCLE HARRY: Do you remember where I hid that package?

NONA: You mean the package I found in the jar?

UNCLE HARRY: Yes, I—

NONA: You didn't hide it. You were just going to. You left it there. [*Points to table*]

UNCLE HARRY: Where?

NONA: [*Crossing to table*] Right here.

UNCLE HARRY: [*Goes to table; holding up empty wrapping*] Then where is it?

NONA: Miss Lettie found me with it and did I get a bawling out. She—

LETTIE: [*Comes down the stairs*] It's all settled. You'd better go to bed, Nona. Ironing tomorrow.

NONA: I know— It's wonderful what a fuss we can make by just living. [*Exits upstairs*]

UNCLE HARRY: Did she drink it?

LETTIE: [*Sitting on sofa*] She will soon as she's finished the serial she's reading in *Leslie's*.

UNCLE HARRY: [*Crosses to easy chair and sits*] It'll get cold.

LETTIE: [*Pours two cups of cocoa*] She likes it cold. Shall we have ours now?

UNCLE HARRY: [*Takes the cup she passes him*] You've earned it, Lettie.

LETTIE: [*Sipping cocoa*] This is cozy and peaceful. Do you want to read?

UNCLE HARRY: Certainly! What would you like?

LETTIE: I don't care. No more Wordsworth though.

UNCLE HARRY: [*Rising; crossing to bookcase*] Since Hester isn't with us let's find something appropriate for her.

LETTIE: She was mighty condescending. [*Sips*] I'll never give in to her again.

UNCLE HARRY: [*Takes a book*] You won't have to.

LETTIE: Kindness is just lost on her.

UNCLE HARRY: [*Looks at the ceiling*] This will be a great moment for Hester. Imagine her reaching out for it victoriously. She's beaten you, hands down. It's at such a time that a person should be careful.

LETTIE: What things you say! [*Pause*] After all my good work you should pick a piece to suit *me*. [*Puts cup down on table*]

UNCLE HARRY: It will suit you, too. Eventually.

LETTIE: I don't see how anything could suit us both.

UNCLE HARRY: This will do. Shakespeare's "Dirge from Cymbeline." [*Reads*]

"Fear no more the heat of the sun
  Nor the furious winter's rages.

Thou thy worldly task hast done
Home art gone and ta'en the wages.
Golden lads and girls all must
Like chimney sweepers come to dust.

Fear no more the lightning flash,
Nor the all-dreaded thunder stone
Fear not slander, censure rash—
Thou hast finished—"

[There is a choked scream from above]

LETTIE: *[After a silence, rises]* That's Hester. *[Starts for the stairs]*

UNCLE HARRY: There's no need to hurry.

LETTIE: *[Turns to him]* She's ill. She may need—

[Sound of HESTER *dropping on floor]*

UNCLE HARRY: *[Throws the book on the table]* Hester needs nothing any more.

LETTIE: What do you mean? [UNCLE HARRY *takes empty poison bottle from his pocket. She takes bottle]* You've used it?

UNCLE HARRY: The cocoa *you* gave her.

LETTIE: You—murdered her!

UNCLE HARRY: She was never any use.

LETTIE: You'll be hanged for this!

UNCLE HARRY: Somehow I don't believe that I will be hanged.

LETTIE: *[Staggering back against sofa]* You, Harry, you of all people.

UNCLE HARRY: Yes. I rather depend upon that attitude. *[Starts for the stairs]*

LETTIE: Where are you going?

UNCLE HARRY: Just to see. *[Starts upstairs]*

LETTIE: *[Almost in a collapse]* I can't believe it—I can't believe it!

UNCLE HARRY: Better that two of us should die than three rot together.

LETTIE: How can I go on living now?

UNCLE HARRY: Why should you? *[Exits upstairs]*

[LETTIE *looks at bottle.* NONA *enters downstairs in nightgown and robe*]

NONA: I've been in—I heard the noise she made and I ran into her room—I saw her!

LETTIE: She's dead?

NONA: Yes. I won't ever forget her face! It was no illness that took her off and you can't tell me that it was. [*She sees the bottle in* LETTIE's *hand*] So that's why you got that stuff—that's why you said that Mr. Harry— You tried to put it all off on him. [*Becomes hysterical*] Oh God! God! I didn't think you had it in you. No, I didn't think you had it in you. [*She slumps down on chair*]

UNCLE HARRY: [*Comes down the stairs, quietly; stops and smiles down at* LETTIE] You see, Lettie, the way it is?

[LETTIE *turns to look at him in horror as:*]

THE CURTAIN FALLS

ACT THREE

SCENE 1: *The Verdict*

Parlor of the Blue Bell Tavern.

The following December. Early evening.

ALBERT *is sitting at the table sipping a beer. A pause
and* BEN *comes in, takes off his hat and throws it on the
piano.*

ALBERT: Jury returned yet?

BEN: No, they've only been out half an hour. No doubt about the
verdict, though. I bet you twenty to one in beers that it will be
guilty.

ALBERT: Catch me throwing away a good half pint. But I bet you an
even beer that the jury will be out more than an hour. You've
got to give them time to drink a cup of tea and look as if they've
been arguing pro and con.

BEN: [*Taking out his watch*] You're on. It's twenty to six now
and if they're not out by six the beer's yours. It wouldn't be
decent for them to stay too long on a case like this.

ALBERT: [*Shakes his head sadly*] Bad business hanging a woman.
If she hadn't tried to put the blame on poor Uncle Harry I'd
been sorry for her. You certainly helped to settle her hash for her
there, Ben. How did it feel to be on the witness stand?

BEN: How did I do?

ALBERT: Fine. You spoke up smart as a whip.

BEN: I wanted to do all I could to help the poor chap.

ALBERT: Where you were best was the way you laid it on about how
guilty she looked when she came in to buy the stuff.

BEN: I thought I was better where I told how Harry was upset when
he found out she bought the poison.

ALBERT: You were good there, too.

BEN: But he helped himself more than anybody without knowing he was helping himself. The prosecution didn't need to treat him as a hostile witness.

ALBERT: Every time he tried to help her he put his foot in it worse. It was a fair treat to see the way the prosecution balled him up.

BEN: We'll have to be very kind to him.

MISS PHIPPS: [*Enters from bar. She is polishing a glass*] Verdict out?

BEN: Not yet. Soon.

ALBERT: Not much doubt about the verdict.

MISS PHIPPS: I can't think that she did it. My belief is that there's more in this than meets the eye. Funny the way she keeps on saying it was Uncle Harry.

ALBERT: She's got to blame someone.

MISS PHIPPS: She may be right.

BEN: Oh, bunkum!

MISS PHIPPS: Bunkum, or no bunkum, I always felt there was something queer about Uncle Harry. He's too good to be possible. I don't have much faith in him.

BEN: I've known him for fourteen years and a man who's as good as he is for fourteen years stays good to everlasting.

MISS PHIPPS: I've seen a lot of men come in here and very free some of them, but you never can tell for true what a man is thinking.

ALBERT: Look what he's sacrificed for these two women.

MISS PHIPPS: I am looking. Perhaps he got tired of sacrificing.

BEN: And if you don't believe in him you got to believe in the facts. Look at them fair and square. [*Ticks off on his fingers*] First: those two had always hated each other. Second: as the plain evidence of that girl Nona shows, they had a real set-to on the day of the murder with slapping included. Third: Lettie said Hester would be better out of the way. Fourth: she buys the poison. Fifth: she gives the poison. It's open and shut. The only point in doubt is: Did she buy the poison to give the dog and change her mind and give it to her sister, or did she mean to give it to her sister right from the first? In any case it comes to the same thing. Tchk!— [*Makes a hanging gesture*]

MISS PHIPPS: Sounds all right—but I'm not quite easy. [*Exits to bar*]

ALBERT: That's the woman for you.

BEN: The only time they stick together is when there's a murder. The moment Lettie came in for the stuff I had my doubts that she was up to any good.

ALBERT: You said so that very night.

BEN: It's an awful responsibility to be a druggist.

[UNCLE HARRY *enters*]

ALBERT: How are you, old man?

BEN: Managing all right, Uncle Harry?

UNCLE HARRY: [*Sadly*] I am well, gentlemen, very well.

BEN: [*Consoling him*] It's not much use our talking at a time like this but we're with you, Uncle Harry. The whole town is with you.

UNCLE HARRY: [*Nodding*] People have been very kind.

ALBERT: Have they brought in the verdict?

UNCLE HARRY: Not yet. [*Eagerly*] That's a good thing, isn't it?

BEN: Very good.

ALBERT: Couldn't be better.

UNCLE HARRY: Oh, if they only understood that she couldn't have done it. [*Sits on bench behind table*]

BEN: They may yet. Care for a drink?

UNCLE HARRY: No, thank you. I'm about to order some tea.

BEN: Let me—

UNCLE HARRY: I have to meet a young lady here. It's important and I was wondering if you two chaps—

ALBERT: [*Rises, mug in hand*] By all means.

BEN: We were going anyway.

UNCLE HARRY: No hurry—she isn't here yet. Sorry to put you out like this.

BEN: No trouble. I wish I hadn't testified against her but there you are.

UNCLE HARRY: You did what you thought was right, Ben. I'm not blaming you, I'm not blaming anyone. What time is it?

ALBERT: [*Looking at watch*] It's ten minutes to six.

UNCLE HARRY: The lawyer says the longer they stay out the more hope. Ben, would you care to play something just to get my mind off?

BEN: Glad to. What would you like?

UNCLE HARRY: Anything—anything.

> [BEN *goes to the piano.* ALBERT *says "Swanee" and* BEN *begins to play.* BLAKE *comes in and crosses down to them*]

BLAKE: She's done for.

ALBERT: Guilty!

BEN: [*Motioning to* BLAKE] Hush!

BLAKE: Guilty! Yes, guilty as hell. [*Turns; sees* UNCLE HARRY] Sorry I didn't know *you'd* come in.

UNCLE HARRY: [*Rises*] I—I must go to her. Excuse me.

> [*Starts out but* BLAKE *stops him*]

BLAKE: No use, Uncle Harry. No one can see her now.

ALBERT: Not until tomorrow morning. That's the law.

BEN: They'll give her something tonight so that she'll sleep.

> [UNCLE HARRY *walks to bench and sags onto it dispiritedly*]

BLAKE: Could I send you in a drink?

UNCLE HARRY: A cup of tea if you'd be so kind. I—

BLAKE: Of course. Come on, chaps, and stop bothering him. [*Exits to bar*]

> [ALBERT *and* BEN *pat* UNCLE HARRY'S *shoulder with manly sympathy and go out murmuring*]

ALBERT: If there's anything I can do, old man— [*Exits to bar*]

BEN: All you've got to do, old man, is say the word. [*Exits to bar*]

> [*Their manner indicates that they are only too glad to get away*]

BLAKE: [*Off*] Hope he don't collapse in my bar, poor chap.

> [UNCLE HARRY *takes out a pocket mirror and combs and begins to spruce up. His manner has changed from suffering to a sort of scintillating triumph*]

MISS PHIPPS: [*Enters and looks at him suspiciously as he hastily replaces mirror*] There's a lady here to see you.

UNCLE HARRY: Ask her to come in, and serve some tea.

MISS PHIPPS: All right.

UNCLE HARRY: And could we have the room to ourselves for a little while? It's important.

MISS PHIPPS: I'll see what I can do since it's important. Wasn't she one of the witnesses against your sister?

UNCLE HARRY: So were many of my friends.

MISS PHIPPS: Thought I recognized her.

[*Exits to bar. LUCY comes in*]

UNCLE HARRY: [*Rises*] Hello, Lucy, I didn't want to bring you to my home so—

LUCY: Naturally.

UNCLE HARRY: I didn't like to send for you either until it was settled.

LUCY: Settled?

UNCLE HARRY: Have you heard the verdict?

LUCY: Guilty?

UNCLE HARRY: Yes. So it is settled, don't you see?

LUCY: How dreadful for you!

UNCLE HARRY: I can stand it.

LUCY: I think you're splendid. Splendid. That moment in the witness box when you said that if there were any justice you should be in the dock and not Lettie—well, it was the most touching thing I've ever seen.

[*MISS PHIPPS enters with the tea. LUCY comes rapidly up center and covers face*]

MISS PHIPPS: [*Putting tray on table*] I've made it strong. Hope it will suit you.

UNCLE HARRY: You spoil us, Miss Phipps. [*MISS PHIPPS exits. He sits at table*] Have some?

LUCY: No, thanks.

UNCLE HARRY: You don't mind if I do?

LUCY: No. [*He picks up the teapot, and, feigning weakness, lets it slip to the tray*] Let me pour it. [*She pours*]

UNCLE HARRY: Thank you.

LUCY: [*Crossing away from him*] So you don't blame me for testifying against Lettie? I couldn't do anything else, you know.

UNCLE HARRY: No, indeed, you couldn't.

LUCY: I want you to know, Harry, that I'm with you in your trouble. As much as anyone can be.

UNCLE HARRY: [*Sipping tea*] Thank you, my dear. You don't know how happy that makes me.

LUCY: It gives one such an inadequate feeling—a disaster like this. There's so little one can say. But there is one thing.

UNCLE HARRY: Yes?

LUCY: It may sound a bit brutal but it isn't really. Only realistic. It's this. You have your own life to lead now and you've never had that before.

UNCLE HARRY: Exactly, Lucy. Exactly. You never said a truer word.

LUCY: Not that I'd breathe a syllable against those poor women. But you're free now, and you're still young.

UNCLE HARRY: [*Rises*] Yes. [*Eagerly*] It's queer what a strange business life is. You go on for years and nothing happens and all of a sudden—bang, your old life's gone and there's a new one coming up. Nothing's eternal, thank God. I remember once getting up at dawn and catching a train and before breakfast I was a hundred miles away. I thought of my old self lying in bed doing nothing when I could always be doing that. It's like that now.

LUCY: [*Rather puzzled*] Is it? That's all I had to say. Except— whatever happens you can depend on me. [*Starts to go*]

UNCLE HARRY: [*Quickly*] Before you go, Lucy, what are we going to do about George?

LUCY: [*This surprises her*] George!

UNCLE HARRY: [*Crossing toward her*] It'll be a blow to George and it's a pity.

LUCY: What difference can it possibly make to George?

UNCLE HARRY: He seemed pretty fond of you, that's all.

LUCY: Of course he is fond of me.

UNCLE HARRY: Then we'll have to make him understand.

LUCY: Understand what?

UNCLE HARRY: That you're mine.

LUCY: Good God!

UNCLE HARRY: What's wrong, Lucy?

LUCY: But—

UNCLE HARRY: I know it's too early to talk about it. But I couldn't bear the thought of George going round with you any longer. Kissing you whenever he wanted and—

LUCY: You poor man!

UNCLE HARRY: I'm not a poor man. Not any longer.

LUCY: You're not yourself and I'm not surprised. A tragedy like yours is enough to upset anyone.

UNCLE HARRY: It isn't a tragedy to me. I'm free, Lucy. You said so yourself.

LUCY: I didn't mean it like that.

UNCLE HARRY: Sit down. [LUCY *sits on piano stool*] Now. Remember that afternoon when you came to tea with us? I asked you then would you marry me if it weren't for Hester and Lettie. Do you know what you said?

LUCY: Something. I don't know. I've forgotten whatever it was.

UNCLE HARRY: You said, "That, Uncle Harry, is a leading question." Very well. It's time to answer it now. And there's only one answer to a leading question and that's "yes." I depended on that.

LUCY: You were terribly mistaken, Harry.

UNCLE HARRY: But how could I have been?

LUCY: [*Rises*] I suppose I might have encouraged you. I was a fool, but you were so pathetic and then there was some—some nostalgia mixed up in it, too. Yes, that's what it was but I swear I never had the slightest intention of—

UNCLE HARRY: [*Advances toward her threateningly*] But you're not going to marry George as things are?

LUCY: I certainly am.

UNCLE HARRY: No.

LUCY: It's quite final, Harry.

UNCLE HARRY: [*After a pause*] After what I've done for you!

LUCY: What have you done?

UNCLE HARRY: Lucy—

LUCY: Please don't make me say horrid things to you. It'll make me feel worse than I feel already. Well—

UNCLE HARRY: So George is between us now?

LUCY: No, he isn't. Not really.

UNCLE HARRY: Then?

LUCY: It would be the same, George or no George. Don't you see?

UNCLE HARRY: No, I don't. There's nothing to stop us now.

LUCY: I couldn't.

UNCLE HARRY: But why? For God's sake why?

LUCY: Don't ask me.

UNCLE HARRY: [*He almost screams it*] Why?!

LUCY: All right. Haven't you heard that it isn't the person who gets hanged who suffers most? It's his family.

UNCLE HARRY: You mean the grief?

LUCY: No. The disgrace. They have to live with the murder.

UNCLE HARRY: It isn't my fault if Lettie—

LUCY: Do people bother about whose fault it is? How could I marry you? How could any girl marry you? How could you have the nerve to ask her? And if a woman was mad enough to do it and didn't care if she was stared at all her life, what about the children? It wouldn't be fair to them.

UNCLE HARRY: [*He has stepped back and slumps on the arm of the bench*] That's a cruel way to look at it.

LUCY: Not cruel—just the ordinary way and I'm afraid I'm a very ordinary person. Goodbye, Uncle Harry.

UNCLE HARRY: [*Rising quickly*] Can't I see you again?

LUCY: No.

UNCLE HARRY: Lucy, stay with me, Lucy! Please don't leave me alone! [*Takes her hand, lifts it up. She stares at him. In fury*] Don't look at me like that! [LUCY *drags her hand away and exits quickly.* UNCLE HARRY *looks after her.* MISS PHIPPS *looks in from the bar*] So it was all useless.

> [MISS PHIPPS *enters quietly and stares at him standing there, a beaten man, then exits as:*]

THE CURTAIN FALLS

SCENE 2: *Confession*

*Office of the Governor of the prison. It is a large, formal
room. At right, a large log-burning fireplace, with an armchair in front of it; at left the Governor's desk, with
chairs, filing equipment, et cetera. Speaking tube on desk.
A coal box below the mantel; a flag up right; a clock up
right of the door; a file cabinet against left wall. There
are windows in the rear wall left center. At rear center,
a wide door opens onto the corridor of the prison.*

About three weeks later. Afternoon. The GOVERNOR, *a
decent, unimaginative man, obviously of the military type,
sits at his desk studying some papers. In front of him sits*
BURTON, *a neat, businesslike little man, fingering a derby
hat.*

BURTON: About my assistant, sir. Young Perse Dowzeberry. He's got
a pint of whiskey with him. "Perse," I said, "you know it's
against the rules." "I got to, Mr. Burton," Perse comes back at
me, "I just got to." So I says, "Well then, Perse, one little nip
before going on duty and all you want afterwards, always provided, mind you, that the Governor is willing."

GOVERNOR: [*Preoccupied*] We might stretch a point.

BURTON: That's fine, sir. Funny about Perse. As long as it's a man
no cucumber could be cooler than Perse. But when it comes to a
woman, well, he gets rattled.

GOVERNOR: I don't blame him.

BURTON: It was the same with poor Ellis. It was a woman that
broke his nerve for him. A nice chap, too. Yes, sir, very nice.

GOVERNOR: He appears to have given every satisfaction.

BURTON: He was a model to the profession, except for his old-
fashioned notions about women. Now with me it doesn't make
the slightest difference who it is.

GOVERNOR: You're not a squeamish man, Mr. Burton?

BURTON: It's all in the game, sir. [GOVERNOR *rises, as if to end the conversation*] Well, I'll look things over if you don't mind and then turn in early.

GOVERNOR: Ask the engineer to show you the—gallows.

BURTON: Very good, sir. And don't worry about tomorrow. It's not as bad as you think. Over just like that.

GOVERNOR: Is it?

BURTON: Yes, sir. Minimum of embarrassment. [*Door opens and* UNCLE HARRY *comes in*] Just one thing, sir. This Quincey woman —is she the noisy type or the quiet?

UNCLE HARRY: The quiet.

BURTON: [*Turns in surprise*] Eh? Oh, so much the better.

UNCLE HARRY: You're the hangman, aren't you?

BURTON: [*Very much annoyed by the word*] Civil servant.

GOVERNOR: You had no right to break in here, Mr. Quincey. It's most unfortunate.

BURTON: Quincey! Good afternoon! [*Starts out*]

UNCLE HARRY: I hear you say that to all your—clients.

BURTON: No! Only good morning! [*He exits rapidly*]

UNCLE HARRY: [*Crossing to front of desk*] I'm sorry about this, Mr. Governor, but our appointment was at seven so I ventured—

GOVERNOR: Ah, yes. Well, you can see her at once.

UNCLE HARRY: Thank you but that can come later. I wished particularly to see you.

GOVERNOR: Anything we can do to comfort her—

UNCLE HARRY: It will not be necessary. Would you oblige me by looking this over? [*He takes a folded manuscript from his pocket and hands it to the* GOVERNOR]

GOVERNOR: When I have time. [*He is about to put it down*]

UNCLE HARRY: [*Restrains him*] The first page, at least, sir. The rest will look after itself.

GOVERNOR: [*Glances casually at the manuscript, then mutters*] Good Lord! [*Reading rapidly*] Extraordinary! [*He sits*]

UNCLE HARRY: I always believe in getting things down in black and white. You can't argue with black and white, can you?

GOVERNOR: [*Reading the manuscript*]
"Lettie: That's Hester.
Myself: You needn't hurry—"

UNCLE HARRY: Now you're coming to the important part. [*Sits in front of desk*]

GOVERNOR: [*Continues reading*]
"Lettie: She's ill, she may need—
Myself: Hester needs nothing any more.
Lettie: What do you mean?
Myself: She's dead. The cocoa you gave her.
Lettie: You—"

UNCLE HARRY: Murdered her!

GOVERNOR: [*Slowly looks at* UNCLE HARRY, *then continues*] "Here I gave her the little bottle. It was my hope that she would hold it until the servant found her with it. This she did. Thus I entangled my sister in a net of evidence from which escape was as impossible as for a fly in the web of a spider. No hand could unspin the painstaking lies I had drawn about her. Only the reputation of a lifetime—"

UNCLE HARRY: You realize, Mr. Governor, the implication in those last remarks.

GOVERNOR: [*Rises*] Astonishing! Why are you confessing all this?

UNCLE HARRY: There's no longer any reason why I should live.

GOVERNOR: You're not doing this to save your sister?

UNCLE HARRY: There's no point in Lettie dying any more. How long will it be before you can release her? I suppose there'll be a few formalities.

GOVERNOR: This is magnificent of you, Mr. Quincey.

UNCLE HARRY: Not at all!

GOVERNOR: And now you'd better be going.

UNCLE HARRY: [*Rising*] Why don't you arrest me? I've confessed.

GOVERNOR: It doesn't hold water, old man.

UNCLE HARRY: I killed my sister Hester and involved Lettie. That's clear enough.

GOVERNOR: [*Pushes the confession into* UNCLE HARRY'S *hands*] Too clear. You can't expect the government to hang you on your mere assertion, sir. [*Crosses to door*] This way, Mr. Quincey. We respect your attempt, we honestly do.

UNCLE HARRY: I rather expected that this might happen. Red tape seldom has much vision. Why do you think I wrote all this out?

GOVERNOR: You had your reasons, probably.

UNCLE HARRY: Excellent ones, I assure you. The proof is right here. [*Taps manuscript*] Now look. You've read all the conversation Lettie and I had on the night Hester died. It didn't come out in the trial. But Lettie will remember it. She's bound to remember it. Suppose her account agrees with what I've written here?

GOVERNOR: I wouldn't care to trouble her now.

UNCLE HARRY: But you must! It's your duty.

GOVERNOR: The whole thing is impossible.

UNCLE HARRY: The world is full of impossibilities.

GOVERNOR: It's devilish irregular. However— [*He crosses to desk, picks up speaking tube*] Bring up the prisoner from the condemned cell. Yes, bring her here. I trust this will satisfy you.

UNCLE HARRY: Thank you.

GOVERNOR: It isn't quite settled yet.

UNCLE HARRY: It will be. [*Sits in front of desk*] Tell me, Mr. Governor, have you ever obliged anyone against your better judgment?

GOVERNOR: On occasions. This, for example.

UNCLE HARRY: Not regularly, however?

GOVERNOR: I'm a government official. [*Sits back of desk*]

UNCLE HARRY: Yes, that protects you, of course. I haven't been so lucky. Obliging, always obliging. That's been my trouble.

GOVERNOR: I hear you are very well liked.

UNCLE HARRY: Thank you. I always thought of the other fellow first and nearly lost myself as a result. Nobody knows me, and why should they, since I hardly know myself?

GOVERNOR: I'm not sure that I'm doing your sister a kindness in confronting her with you. She's refused to see you for the past three weeks.

UNCLE HARRY: Why shouldn't she after what I've done to her? And Lettie never forgives a wrong. [*He rises, crosses the room nervously*] How does she look, Mr. Governor?

GOVERNOR: It'll be a shock, I warn you.

UNCLE HARRY: This waiting must have been dreadful for her.

GOVERNOR: It has told on her more than most. It is almost as if she were dead already.

UNCLE HARRY: "No motion has she now, no force,
> She neither hears nor sees."

GOVERNOR: What?

[They hear footsteps, and the door slowly opens; UNCLE HARRY *crosses to left rapidly.* LETTIE, *pale and worn by her weeks in prison, enters, followed by the* MATRON]

UNCLE HARRY: Well, Lettie.

[She ignores him]

GOVERNOR: Please sit down, Miss Quincey. *[Indicates chair in front of desk]*

LETTIE: Could I sit in the armchair, please? That one looks very comfortable.

GOVERNOR: Very well.

[She sits in armchair before fireplace. GOVERNOR *follows and stands at her left]*

LETTIE: I've almost forgotten what it's like to sit in an armchair. I was going to ask: could I have an armchair in my—room, to-night? It's true, isn't it, you can have anything you like on your last night? In reason, of course.

UNCLE HARRY: *[Crossing slightly to her]* There's going to be no last night for you, Lettie.

LETTIE: *[Turning to* GOVERNOR] Mr. Governor, you shouldn't have made me look at that man. He has been dreadful to me.

UNCLE HARRY: There's no denying that, Lettie, but—

LETTIE: Send him away, please! He's wicked. Beyond belief.

UNCLE HARRY: You see, Mr. Governor.

GOVERNOR: Quiet! *[To* LETTIE] We won't trouble you long, Miss Quincey. But there are a few questions I have to ask you first.

LETTIE: More questions! Well, I'll answer them. It's so nice to be out of that place for a bit.

GOVERNOR: You maintained during the trial that your brother was responsible for the crime for which you stand condemned?

LETTIE: Yes, but no one believed me.

UNCLE HARRY: They'll believe you now, don't worry, Lettie.

LETTIE: [*To* GOVERNOR] Can't he let me be? It isn't right he should torture me any more.

UNCLE HARRY: You wait till you hear. Mr. Governor, tell her, please.

GOVERNOR: Do you still say that your brother—?

LETTIE: Yes, but why argue about it now?

GOVERNOR: Now he agrees with you.

LETTIE: What?

GOVERNOR: He's confessed to the murder.

LETTIE: What has he done?

UNCLE HARRY: I've told them that I did it, Lettie. You're cleared.

LETTIE: Oh!

GOVERNOR: Not quite cleared. There are one or two points—

UNCLE HARRY: [*Interrupting*] You know what red tape is, Lettie. I was afraid they might not believe me, so I've written the whole business down. All you've got to do is to tell the Governor word for word what we said after Hester screamed. If what you say agrees with this, then you're free.

GOVERNOR: [*Nods*] At least, it will create a reasonable doubt.

UNCLE HARRY: Go on, why don't you tell him?

LETTIE: Let me get this straight. You say you killed Hester?

UNCLE HARRY: How many times do I have to tell you?

LETTIE: I just like to know where I stand.

GOVERNOR: Well, Miss Quincey?

LETTIE: [*Rises*] Could I speak to him alone, please?

GOVERNOR: Impossible.

LETTIE: Oh, but I must!

GOVERNOR: It's the rule.

LETTIE: But I wouldn't do any harm.

UNCLE HARRY: It's the rule, Lettie.

LETTIE: All right then. [*Sits*]

GOVERNOR: If you have anything to say to your brother it must be in our presence.

LETTIE: That wouldn't do a bit of good. [GOVERNOR *crosses rapidly to desk*] It's nice here by the fire. I've missed a fire more than any other thing.

MATRON: [*Whispers to* GOVERNOR] It might be important, sir.

GOVERNOR: There's no precedent for it.

MATRON: But it can't do any harm.

GOVERNOR: Very well. [*Crossing to* LETTIE] Miss Quincey, we'll give you five minutes.

LETTIE: Thank you, sir. I always said you were a kind man.

GOVERNOR: You will be under surveillance, you understand. [*To* MATRON] You remain here.

> [*They exit,* GOVERNOR *first.* MATRON's *shadow is seen on the wall outside the door during the following scene*]

LETTIE: [*There is a long pause, then she turns to* UNCLE HARRY] Thank you— Well, Harry, what are you up to now?

UNCLE HARRY: I'm trying to save your life.

LETTIE: H'm. It must be a bit dull for you at home these days.

UNCLE HARRY: It is a bit. With Nona gone—

LETTIE: She left, did she?

UNCLE HARRY: Right after the verdict.

LETTIE: She won't find such a good place in a hurry. I see her point though. This sort of thing does drive people away.

UNCLE HARRY: That's what Lucy pointed out.

LETTIE: Lucy! Does she come to see you?

UNCLE HARRY: [*Slowly crosses down to fireplace*] She married George last week.

LETTIE: [*With a gleam of satisfaction*] A fair weather friend. I always said so. Well, well! [*She gives a curious chuckle*]

UNCLE HARRY: We're wasting time.

LETTIE: So it was Lucy, was it, who was the cause of all this?

UNCLE HARRY: What if it was?

LETTIE: I should have seen it, the day she came. Something told me I shouldn't let her in, but— Oh, well, it doesn't matter now. Didn't get much for your trouble, did you, Harry?

UNCLE HARRY: [*Dejectedly*] I don't care very much now.

LETTIE: So that's why you're here! Can't live without her! Selfish, Harry. Selfish as ever.

UNCLE HARRY: What!

LETTIE: [*Rises*] Do you suppose I don't see through you? It's just like the little trick you had of giving your toys away when you'd broken them and you'd act so big and generous about it too, and everyone was supposed to look, oh, so grateful, and then they'd all say how fine you were. Now you've broken your life and you want to give that away. But it won't do, Harry. Not this time. [*Turns away to fireplace*]

UNCLE HARRY: You don't want to die, do you?

LETTIE: [*Staring at the fire*] In the last weeks I've died all the time. Tomorrow won't matter.

UNCLE HARRY: Lettie, I've seen the hangman. He's a vile little man.

LETTIE: He won't frighten me. Nothing could, any more.

UNCLE HARRY: But it's so much better to go on living, Lettie. Imagine, you'll have the whole place to yourself! You'll be the Lord of the Manor.

LETTIE: [*Turning to him*] What would be the good of that? What would I want to be bossing an empty house for? It would be silly. I've always been a good woman and now I've finally found peace. I'm all right. I'm not afraid and that's much better for me than trying to go back to a life that's over and done with. But you— [*He is about to interrupt*] No, be quiet a minute because this is my last word. What are you going to do, Uncle Harry? You've a nasty time ahead of you. You're a great one for company, and where your company's coming from now I'm sure I don't know. You'll walk up and down the streets and people will smile at you and cross to the other side of the road and then you'll go home and the memory of me will be there at the door to meet you and you'll sit in an empty room with only your own horror to keep you company and your loneliness will gnaw at you until your mind rots to nothing. [*He slumps into the armchair*] I wouldn't be in your shoes for anything in the world.

UNCLE HARRY: Lettie, you can't do that. You'll tell the truth! You've spoilt everything for me. Don't spoil this. Please don't spoil this!

[GOVERNOR *enters followed by* MATRON]

GOVERNOR: Now what's the matter, Mr. Quincey?

UNCLE HARRY: She won't tell the truth. I did it but she says no.

LETTIE: Of course he didn't.

GOVERNOR: Then who did?

LETTIE: You say I did. Let it stand.

GOVERNOR: Very well.

LETTIE: He's always been headstrong, sir. Full of the wildest ideas. First he wanted to go to Paris to paint pictures as if he couldn't paint all he wanted to at home. He's done some lovely ones, too, I must say. Then he wanted to marry a perfectly ordinary girl and it was hard to make him see sense about that. And now he wants to die. That's the last straw, Harry.

GOVERNOR: [Goes to desk] That will be all, Miss Quincey.

LETTIE: I hate to leave this fire. I always was like a cat about fires. You won't forget about that armchair, will you? [She crosses to door, then turns to GOVERNOR]

GOVERNOR: [Nods kindly] You shall have it. You are a brave woman to refuse to take advantage of your brother's sacrifice.

UNCLE HARRY: You're not going! You shan't go!

LETTIE: You wouldn't care to say goodbye, Uncle Harry?

UNCLE HARRY: [Pleading] You've got to delay it! Just for a little while, Mr. Governor. Then she'll break down and tell the truth. She wouldn't be so cruel as to keep on lying. You see, if she dies tomorrow I'll be alone with what I've done.

LETTIE: [With a smile] You see, Harry, the way it is. [She exits with MATRON]

UNCLE HARRY: [Rushes to GOVERNOR] She said it! That's what I said to her that night. That proves it! Look in this and you'll see. [Shows confession to GOVERNOR] I'll find it for you. I know precisely where it is. [He looks hurriedly through confession] I'm sure I put it down. Maybe I didn't think those words important. But I did say them. I swear I did. [He goes to door and shouts] Come back, Lettie! Can't I have a say in my own life? Only this once, that's all I ask. Oh, God damn you, Lettie! Don't you see what you've done to me! [He breaks down weeping, leaning against the door frame]

GOVERNOR: [Fills water glass from decanter on desk, gives it to UNCLE HARRY] Drink this.

UNCLE HARRY: [Pushes glass away; pulls himself together] Thank you.

GOVERNOR: You'll be all right?

UNCLE HARRY: Yes, I'll be fine.

GOVERNOR: [*Handing him confession*] Take this with you.

UNCLE HARRY: I don't need to. I'll tell everyone myself. I'll make you all see some day. I'll be free of her yet.

GOVERNOR: Better be on your way now, Mr. Quincey.

UNCLE HARRY: On my way— [*Laughs ironically; picks up hat from the desk*] They say murder will out! Murder will out! But not my murder! Not Harry Quincey's murder! By God! That's a good one. [*He starts out the door as:*]

THE CURTAIN FALLS

Ladies
in Retirement

EDWARD PERCY
REGINALD DENHAM

Edward Percy and Reginald Denham

The writing team of Edward Percy and Reginald Denham first came into theatrical view with the 1937 production of *Suspect,* but it was two years later that they
achieved their most rewarding success with *Ladies in Retirement.* A
powerful thriller, it not only became an immediate London hit, but
it also made theatrical history by being the first serious play to be
done in wartime. Its initial run of 311 performances in blacked-
out Britain was lauded by the Fleet Street gentry with such adulatory
phraseology as "a first class slice of eeriness" that is "a collector's
piece in murder" as well as "an extraordinarily exciting thriller."

Less than six months later, a New York presentation of the play
(with Flora Robson in a masterful interpretation of the diabolic
Ellen Creed) opened to equal critical approbation. Richard Watts,
Jr., drama arbiter for the now-vanished *New York Herald Tribune,*
termed it: "Just the sort of good, sound murder play that the dramatic season has been so insistently demanding. It is a tense, taut
and properly literate melodrama." Most of his first-night colleagues
were in gleefully eerie agreement that here indeed was "a combination of play and performance that will doubtless have the customers
shivering in happy terror for months to come."

The idea for the play sprung from an actual crime that was committed in France in 1882, recorded by H. B. Irving in *Studies of
French Criminals.* And although the shadows of war were hovering
ominously over Britain, Percy and Denham decided to write the
play. As Mr. Denham has stated: "I suppose it was more force of
habit than anything else that we should proceed with our collabora-

tion. . . . Working from dawn till dusk, we turned out this play at white heat. This temporarily banished the distant rumbling of the approaching maelstrom. Within two weeks we had finished and had sent the manuscript off to be typed."

It was a fortuitous collaboration and three decades after it initially chilled theatregoers on both sides of the Atlantic, *Ladies in Retirement* remains a favorite item with stock and repertory theatres in the United States and England. In 1941 the play was made into a film under the direction of Charles Vidor with a cast headed by Ida Lupino, Elsa Lanchester, Evelyn Keyes, and Louis Hayward.

An affluent Mincing Lane broker and later a Conservative Member of Parliament for the Ashford Division of Kent (1943–1950), Edward Percy (née Edward Percy Smith) was born in London in 1891. His considerable interest in the theatre led to his founding the Mincing Lane Dramatic Society, and it was there that he first met Reginald Denham, who was engaged to direct a production of *French Leave*. Denham describes the occasion as one that raised the curtain on his own real career (directing) and brought it down on Edward Percy Smith's as a broker. "I found this Mr. Smith a good amateur actor, a great gourmet with a Dickensian taste in vintage wines, an expert criminologist, a horticulturalist and lover of the countryside, a terrific theatre addict, an antiquarian, a playwright, a poet and an exceptionally well-read man."

A firm friendship developed, and in 1922 Denham directed the favorably received West End production of Percy's drama *If Four Walls Told*, and their later association, as coauthors, resulted in six produced plays. Edward Percy died in 1968.

Reginald Denham's special theatrical lair is the dark and sinister. Ever since *Ladies in Retirement*, which he also staged both in London and New York, his directorial skill has guided numerous murder and suspense plays to success, most notably: *Rope*; *Guest in the House*; *The Two Mrs. Carrolls*; *Dial "M" for Murder*; *Bad Seed*; and *Hostile Witness*. A quadruple man of the theatre (director, author, producer, actor), Mr. Denham was born in London on January 10, 1894, and studied music and singing at the Guildhall School of Music. He made his first stage appearance in 1913 as a walk-on in Sir Herbert Beerbohm Tree's production of *Joseph and*

His Brethren and continued to play small roles under Tree's management for the next two years. He then joined Sir Frank Benson's Shakespearean company, and, after he spent an interval serving in World War I, the West End beckoned again. His first postwar engagement was in John Drinkwater's *Abraham Lincoln*. Other roles followed until 1922 when his career changed course and he became more prominent as a director than as an actor.

Among the dozens of plays (in addition to the aforementioned) that he has since directed in London and New York are: *Fata Morgana*; *The Moon and Sixpence*; *Jew Süss*; *Topaze*; *Jupiter Laughs*; *Yesterday's Magic*; *Temper the Wind*; *Portrait in Black*; *Duet for Two Hands*; *Gramercy Ghost*; and *Janus*. Between the years 1933 and 1939, he also directed twenty-four films for Paramount, Fox, and several other companies.

Mr. Denham (whose hobby is ornithology) is married to actress-writer Mary Orr, author of the novelette *The Wisdom of Eve*, which was filmed as *All About Eve* and later converted into the musical *Applause*. The Denhams have collaborated on a number of plays, including: *Wallflower*; *Dark Hammock*; *Be Your Age*; *Minor Murder*; and a dramatic version of *The Wisdom of Eve*.

Ladies in Retirement was first produced at the Richmond Theatre, Richmond, England, on November 27, 1939. The cast was as follows:

LUCY GILHAM	*Joan Kemp-Welsh*
LEONORA FISKE	*Mary Merrall*
ELLEN CREED	*Mary Clare*
ALBERT FEATHER	*Richard Newton*
LOUISA CREED	*Margaret Watson*
EMILY CREED	*Phyllis Morris*
SISTER THERESA	*Nellie Bowman*

Directed by   Reginald Denham
Setting and Décor   by Sidney Gausden

(*Ladies in Retirement* opened in London at the St. James's Theatre on December 12, 1939, under the management of William Mollison. On August 1, 1941, it transferred to the St. Martin's Theatre under the auspices of E. G. Norman, for Austin Productions, Ltd., by arrangement with William Mollison.)

Ladies in Retirement was first presented in the United States at Henry Miller's Theatre, New York, on March 26, 1940, by Gilbert Miller. The cast was as follows:

LUCY GILHAM	*Evelyn Ankers*
LEONORA FISKE	*Isobel Elsom*
ELLEN CREED	*Flora Robson*
ALBERT FEATHER	*Patrick O'Moore*
LOUISA CREED	*Estelle Winwood*
EMILY CREED	*Jessamine Newcombe*
SISTER THERESA	*Florence Edney*
Directed by	Reginald Denham
Designed by	Raymond Sovey
Costumes by	Helene Pons

SCENE: *The living room of an old house on the marshes of the Thames estuary some ten miles to the east of Gravesend.*

ACT ONE

ACT TWO

ACT THREE

ACT ONE

SCENE 1

Estuary House is an old pre-Tudor farmhouse situated below the town of Gravesend in the Thames marshes made so famous by Dickens in his Great Expectations. *It stands at a small height above the level pastures which stretch out to the massive stone walls bounding the great river.*

It belongs, in this year 1885, to a MISS LEONORA FISKE. MISS FISKE, *as you will realize when you see her, is an uncommon type. She is a retired lady of easy virtue. She has had good friends—one or two of whom pay her small quarterly allowances—and she has saved money. She has chosen to spend the last years of her life in rural retirement; and she occupies this lovely old house with her friend and housekeeper-companion,* MISS ELLEN CREED.

The living room, which you see before you, has been made by throwing two or three rooms together. It is, therefore, a large, lofty room, with its ceiling on different levels and this has the effect, when it is evening and the room is only half-lighted, of dividing the space into mountains and valleys of lights and shadows. A pleasant enough room in daylight, but perhaps a little eerie after dark.

Facing you is a huge, inset, open hearth of red brick, where, in winter, a fire of logs is burnt, at either end of which is an old settle. In the chimney wall, between the settle to your left and the fire, is the iron door of a Kentish bake-oven. It is about two feet six inches square, and about the same distance above the floor of the hearth. It has a ring handle on the side nearest the center of the hearth, and a staple has been driven into the adjoining brickwork so that the door can be, as it now is, fastened by a padlock passing through both ring and staple.

In the hearth stands a long-handled implement of polished steel with a spadelike termination once used for lifting loaves out of such an oven when baked. This is technically termed a "slice."

To the left of the hearth is a fine old built-in dresser filled with attractive crockery and brassware.

In the center of the left-hand wall is the front door opening into the room, the hinge at the far side. It is an oak door with a bronze knocker which you can see when the door is opened. On the side of this door farthest from you is a latticed window.

In the back wall, to your right of the hearth, is an arched doorway showing a flight of oak stairs leading up and winding away out of sight round the chimney. The door opens into the room and, when open, lies against the right-hand wall.

Halfway down the right-hand wall is another door leading to the kitchen and back premises of the house, and opening outwards.

The walls are of beam and old brick which is fast changing from red to violet. The floor is stone-flagged.

The furniture is individual and rather important. MISS FISKE—*like many "moderns" of her period—is a devotee of antiques and bric-à-brac, and she has assembled a motley collection of household goods, all interesting, if a little baroque, but without any particular adherence to style or method.*

If you look round the room you will see, first of all, rather to the right, a small Early Victorian pianoforte. It is black and is decorated with panels of pink and white rose bouquets painted somewhat in the Dutch manner. On this stands a large mandarin in gay porcelain with a nodding head. Centrally there is a round, highly polished, inlaid ormolu table, and, round it and elsewhere in the room, a set of several ormolu chairs. To your left of the room stands a late Georgian sofa, its head facing the window nearest you. Behind the sofa is a little occasional table covered with knickknacks—among them a silver sweetmeat box, full, at the moment, of sugarplums, one or two little tortoiseshell and agate boxes and a silver snuff-box. Beyond that stands an Oriental gong. There is a walnut bureau between the hearth and the staircase arch-way. Beyond the door to the kitchen premises is a walnut grandfather clock with a clear, penetrating, bell-like strike.

Against the wall below this door is a half-moon mahogany table on which stands a fair-sized statue of the Virgin in a sky blue robe carrying the Child. In front of the statue are two little candles (not lighted) in little brass "religious" sticks, one or two devotional books and a rosary. In front of this domestic "altar" is a prie-dieu.

In front of the dresser stands a grandfather chair. Above the hearth is a long mantel shelf crowded with blue Oriental and Delft china in splendid confusion. There are some well-worn Persian rugs on the stone floor.

It is a hot June morning. The sun is streaming in. The front door and the windows are wide open. Through these you can see a great expanse of blue sky which suggests that the house stands slightly above the marshes.

The room is empty.

From the distance comes the call of a convent bell. It has rather a flat, ugly tone, and is more like the ticking of a giant watch than a bell.

LUCY GILHAM, *a pretty young maid, in a pink print dress and white cap and apron of the period, comes down the staircase carrying a carpetbag. She is rather a flighty type.*

ELLEN CREED'S *voice calls to her down the stairway from above. It is an arresting voice, firm and clear.*

ELLEN'S VOICE: Look down the lane and see if Bates is coming!

LUCY: Yes, miss. [*She crosses the room, sets down the bag by the front door and stepping outside looks along the lane. Then she returns and going to the stairway calls up*] Yes, miss! The trap's just passing the Priory now!

ELLEN'S VOICE: Where's Miss Fiske?

LUCY: I think she's in the wood lodge.

ELLEN'S VOICE: Tell her I shall be going in a minute.

[LUCY *comes to the kitchen door, opens it and calls*]

LUCY: Miss Fiske, miss!

LEONORA'S VOICE: [*Calling*] Yes! What is it?

LUCY: Miss Creed's just off, miss!

LEONORA'S VOICE: All right. I'm coming.

[LEONORA FISKE *enters from the kitchen door. She is wearing gardener's gloves and carries a small bunch of kingcups and a little brass "religious" vase full of water.* LEONORA *is elderly—sixty, perhaps—but she emulates all the airs, graces and gaiety of youth. She is active in her movements. She is carefully rouged and enameled, and wears a somewhat obvious auburn wig, bright and curled and scented. She is wearing a violet dress and a green silk shawl. She is a good-hearted woman with a shrewd sense of wit and a rather quick temper. She is a Roman Catholic, and—in spite of her career—genuinely devoted to her Faith*]

LEONORA: Is the trap here?

LUCY: Yes, miss. It's just here.

[LEONORA *sets the bowl and flowers down on the table, removes her gloves, and begins to arrange them*]

LEONORA: Miss Creed will have nice time for her train. [*With a twinkle*] We were almost wise, weren't we, to order the trap half an hour before she wanted it? [*Looking at the grandfather clock*] He's only twenty minutes late.

LUCY: No two clocks agree in these parts.

LEONORA: That's the charm of the estuary. Nothing to measure time by—except the tides.

LUCY: And the bell at the Priory. But you can't rely on that—because the nuns are always oversleeping themselves.

LEONORA: You shouldn't say that about the Sisters, Lucy.

LUCY: A lot of old spinsters all herded up together with nothing to think about but their thoughts! It's against nature.

LEONORA: Tch! Tch! Tch!

LUCY: [*Realizing that she is being slightly tactless*] Oh—I'm sorry, miss. I keep forgetting you're a papist.

[*There is the sound of a horse and trap drawing up outside*]

LEONORA: Ah, here's Bates. Put Miss Creed's bag in the trap. And make sure the wooden flap's bolted. They won't want it to go rolling down the hill just when they've got to the top—like last time. [LUCY *takes the bag out the front door.* LEONORA *follows her to the door*] Oh, he's got the little chestnut cob that crosses its legs! [*She hurries to the stairway and calls up*] Ellen! It's time you were going.

[*As she returns* LUCY *reenters the house carrying a pair of birds*]

LUCY: Mr. Bates has brought us some curlew. His boy shot 'em over on Cooling Marsh this morning.

LEONORA: I expect they'll want hanging.

LUCY: I'll go and put them in the dairy.

LEONORA: [*Going out the front door, speaking to* BATES] Thank you so much, Mr. Bates. It *is* kind of you.

BATES' VOICE: You're very welcome, ma'am.

[ELLEN CREED *comes down the stairway. She is wearing a bonnet and cloak. She is a tall, striking-looking woman, rather younger than* LEONORA, *dark and plainly dressed. She has considerable dignity. Her eyes are very expressive and her features clear-cut. She would even be handsome if her lips were not so thin and compressed. The perfect house-*]

keeper of the period, you would say at first glimpse. As she enters, LUCY *has just reached the kitchen door*]

ELLEN: What have you got there, Lucy?

LUCY: A couple of curlew—from Mr. Bates.

[*She goes out through the kitchen door just as* LEONORA *enters from the front door, which she closes behind her. She comes to* ELLEN]

LEONORA: I've just told Bates to stop at the brick kilns on the way. I've been counting those bricks in the yard. I believe they've sent me half a load short. And, look here, Ellen, there are a couple of things before you go. [*She crosses to the bureau and takes out a letter which she gives to* ELLEN] I want you to take this letter to my lawyer. Mr. Scott—Staple Inn. You did go there once before for me, didn't you?

ELLEN: Yes, it's by the old buildings in Holborn, isn't it?

LEONORA: Don't lose it. It's got some instructions in it about those Brazilian bonds of mine. I don't think they're as sound as they ought to be. I'm going to put the money into railways instead.

ELLEN: I think you're so brave, dear, the way you put your money into things. When I had money I was always afraid to let it out of my hands.

LEONORA: [*She has taken up the vase of kingcups. With a pleasantly superior smile*] But it got away somehow, didn't it?

ELLEN: I had so many mouths to feed.

[LEONORA *takes the vase and places it before the Virgin. When she has done so she crosses herself.* ELLEN *watches this with a suggestion of disapproval. Meanwhile—*]

LEONORA: You've certainly been a wonderful sister.

ELLEN: I've found a very kind friend.

LEONORA: Fiddle!

ELLEN: [*With deep feeling*] You can't tell what it means to me to be able to offer my sisters such a holiday. And it's so good of you to let me go up and fetch them. They'd never have faced the journey alone.

LEONORA: I'm quite looking forward to their visit. [*She takes a sugarplum from the sweetmeat box and pops it into her mouth*] You've talked so much about them, I feel they're old friends.

ELLEN: They're rather pathetic, you know, dear. But they're all I've got left.

LEONORA: [*Who is not paying much attention, darting back to the bureau*] Oh, there's one other thing, Ellen.

ELLEN: What's that?

LEONORA: [*Handing her a second letter*] I want you to call at this address. It's just off Berkeley Square—anyone will tell you. Go to the servants' entrance. Ask for Mr. Blades—he's the butler. Say you've come from me with a note for Lord Kenardington. Will he give it to his lordship privately? And wait for an answer.

ELLEN: [*Rather significantly*] What's the best time to call?

LEONORA: Let me see. Harry always used to dine at eight. Call at half-past seven.

ELLEN: Very well, dear.

LEONORA: [*Opening the front door*] And, whatever you do, don't lose the reply.

ELLEN: [*Turning suddenly, in a quiet voice*] Hasn't it come this quarter?

LEONORA: No.

ELLEN: After all you've been spending, too! Oh, dear!

LEONORA: [*Unwilling that* BATES *should hear anything of this*] Go along, Ellen, go along. Have a good journey.

> [ELLEN *goes out.* LEONORA *stands watching. You hear the trap turn and rattle away.* LEONORA *waves. By now the convent bell has stopped. She comes back into the room.* LUCY *enters from the kitchen with a parcel*]

LUCY: I've been in such a fuss this morning, what with Miss Creed getting off, I forgot to give you this. It came by the post. There was nothing else.

LEONORA: [*Taking it and undoing it*] You really must try and not be so forgetful, Lucy. [LEONORA *opens the parcel. It contains a copy of the score of* The Mikado. *She gives a little purr of pleasure*] Oh! this *is* nice!

LUCY: [*Inquisitively*] What's that, miss?

LEONORA: It's the new comic opera. I used to tour the provinces with the gentleman who's sent it to me. Look, he's signed it for me—Rutland Barrington.

LUCY: [*Reading the title*] "The Mick-a-doo . . ."

LEONORA: "The Mikado." It's been the rage of London for months. [*Giving* LUCY *the wrapper and string*] Here, run along and take this paper and string. Now we've got this room comparatively straight, I want it kept straight . . .

[LUCY *goes.* LEONORA *flutters excitedly to the piano, turns over the score at random, and then begins to play the song* "Tit-Willow." *You can see she is delighted with the music and the excuse for playing. As she is at the end of the verse you hear a man's voice outside suddenly begin to sing the words*]

THE VOICE: "Though I probably shall not exclaim as I die,
Oh, willow, tit-willow, tit-willow!"

[LEONORA *stops playing in astonishment. A young man is standing in the sunny doorway. He is a little fellow of the type for which the word "cad" was coined. He is jaunty and impudent, and in consequence, in great favor with the ladies. He has a bright lustrous eye and a little line of down on his upper lip. There is a touch of the Cockney about him, especially in his overdressiness. He wears a check cutaway coat and trousers, a brightly colored, starched shirt with collar and cuffs to match and a wide-brimmed "boater" hat. He is a second-rate clerk and looks it. His name is* ALBERT FEATHER. LEONORA *rises*]

ALBERT: Go on. Don't stop.

LEONORA: What are you doing here?

ALBERT: Listening.

LEONORA: [*Instantly responding to the male*] Well, either come in or go out.

[*He comes in with a little chuckle*]

ALBERT: I'm really looking for Miss Creed. She lives here, doesn't she?

LEONORA: Yes. She lives here. But she's just driven into Rochester. Didn't you pass her on the road?

ALBERT: No. I've just walked over from Gravesend. Along the Thames wall and up through the saltings.

LEONORA: I wonder you found your way. They're tricky—the marshes, you know.

ALBERT: Don't I half? I've been up to my knees in three jolly dikes already.

LEONORA: Hadn't you better sit down?

ALBERT: Thanks—if I shan't damage the furniture. How long shall I have to wait for my aunt?

LEONORA: [*In surprise*] Your aunt? You're not Albert, are you?

ALBERT: Albert Feather. That's me.

LEONORA: The one who works in a bank at Gravesend?

ALBERT: Did work. Yes. [*Feeling this needs some explanation*] That's rather what I've come to see Aunt Ellen about. I must get back tonight, though. How long shall I have to wait for her?

LEONORA: [*Blandly: helping herself to another sugarplum*] About a week, I think.

ALBERT: [*Staggered*] A week?

LEONORA: Yes. She's gone to London.

ALBERT: [*With something like despair in his voice*] By Jove! That's done it. That *has* done it.

LEONORA: What's the matter? Can't I help?

ALBERT: But I don't know who you are—or what you're doing in my aunt's house.

LEONORA: Who told you it was your aunt's house?

ALBERT: Well, isn't it? Aunt Ellen wrote she was living here. Aunt Ellen's a great one for keeping up with the family. You aren't a lost cousin from Australia, by any chance?

LEONORA: No. We're not related, Albert. If you want to know, Estuary House is *my* house, and your aunt's living with me—as my housekeeper-companion.

ALBERT: Well, I'm blowed. The artful old geezer! She *has* led the family up the garden path.

LEONORA: Well, don't say anything about it. I daresay it's a sense of false pride, you know. We all suffer from it. You see, the poor dear's lost most of her little bit of money. I expect she doesn't want you to know she's come down in the world.

ALBERT: [Rather eagerly] Has she lost everything?

LEONORA: Practically.

ALBERT: What happened to the old curio-shop in Bartholomew Close? I thought that was a little gold mine.

LEONORA: I'm afraid more gold went into it than ever came out. That happens to a lot of gold mines.

ALBERT: [Pondering] I say—this is a blow.

LEONORA: I used to buy things at her shop. I'm very interested in bric-à-brac. If you use your eyes, you'll see quite a lot of Bartholomew Close about the room now.

ALBERT: [Looking round] Well, well! So there is, now you mention it.

LEONORA: That was the beginning of our association. Then, when I saw she wasn't doing well and I was leaving London, I asked her if she'd like to come with me.

ALBERT: I expect you've been awfully good to her.

LEONORA: Oh, I don't know. She suits me. Besides, we've got this mutual taste in antiques. Getting this place right has been a great interest. Would you believe it? The farmers who had this before had matchboarded in these walls, and then wallpapered the matchboarding with terra-cotta roses!

ALBERT: You must have had an army of workmen here.

LEONORA: Workmen? Good gracious, no. [She takes another sugar-plum] We did it ourselves.

ALBERT: [In amazement] What? You and Aunt Ellen?

LEONORA: It's not so difficult—if you've got plenty of time. Your aunt's very clever with her hands. And we don't hurry ourselves. Time doesn't matter here, you know.

ALBERT: Well, you're lucky. Time's everything to me—just at the moment. If it's not asking . . . what's your name?

LEONORA: I'm Miss Fiske, Leonora Fiske.

ALBERT: [A little doubtfully] I wonder if you could help me.

LEONORA: I don't know till you tell me.

ALBERT: [*Putting his fingers into his collar and easing his neck*] Well, I—I hardly like to tell you.

LEONORA: [*With humor*] I see. What's the amount?

ALBERT: [*After a moment*] Twelve pounds.

LEONORA: [*A little startled: she has envisaged a "fiver"*] My goodness! That's a lot of money. And what do you want twelve pounds for, Albert?

ALBERT: I need it for a debt.

LEONORA: Won't it wait?

ALBERT: No. I must have it by tonight.

LEONORA: Why is it so urgent?

ALBERT: [*He pauses: then out it comes*] I'm short in my account at the bank. Petty cash.

LEONORA: [*Her eyes widening*] I see. That *is* serious, isn't it?

ALBERT: I've got till tomorrow to put it back—when the cashier checks up. [*He shows something of what he has been going through*] It means jug, if they find out. [*With naïveté*] I'm sure Aunt Ellen'll pay you back.

LEONORA: [*Kind but firm*] I think we'd better leave Aunt Ellen out of it. What have you been spending the money on? Cards? Racing?

ALBERT: [*He pauses again*] No. A girl.

LEONORA: Are you engaged to her?

ALBERT: No. She's not that sort.

LEONORA: [*Expressively*] Ah, the other kind. I know.

ALBERT: She's an actress. There was a company at Gravesend last week.

LEONORA: [*With interest*] At the old Grand?

ALBERT: [*Seeing her interest*] Do you know it?

LEONORA: I've played there. Years ago, of course.

ALBERT: You weren't an actress, were you?

LEONORA: [*Chuckling*] Front row of the chorus. Fourth from the right.

ALBERT: Funny! She's in the chorus, too. But you've moved up in life.

LEONORA: Perhaps I've been lucky. I suppose you took her out to supper. And then she persuaded you to go round the shops with her.

ALBERT: How do you know?

LEONORA: Imagination, Albert. She may even have let you kiss her. And I'm quite sure she promised you a great deal more.

ALBERT: [Viciously] The little cheat!

LEONORA: Oh, she probably has her point of view.

ALBERT: Anyway, she's over the hills now to some other town where I suppose she'll find some other fool to steal for her.

LEONORA: [Perhaps he has touched her on the raw] Very well, Albert. You shall have your twelve pounds. After all, I owe it to you—in a sense. Or to some other fool.

ALBERT: Do you mean that? [To her surprise he breaks down. It is half genuine relief, half the sniveling of the natural beggar]

LEONORA: Oh, my goodness! Don't do that.

ALBERT: [Wiping his eyes] It's only that I'm so grateful. I wish I knew how to thank you.

LEONORA: [With a change of tone] You're not in a violent hurry, are you?

ALBERT: [Wondering what is coming] No, not now, ma'am.

LEONORA: Tell me something about your family—about your aunts. Not Aunt Ellen. The others. Aunt Louisa and Aunt Emily.

ALBERT: Oh! You mean the potty ones?

LEONORA: [This time it is her turn to be surprised] Potty?

ALBERT: Well, queer, perhaps I should say. They're quite harmless.

LEONORA: That's a comfort. They're coming to stay here. That's why Aunt Ellen's on her way to London now. She's gone to fetch them.

ALBERT: Coming to stay here? I wish you joy! They're not quite your style, are they?

LEONORA: I don't know. I've never seen them.

ALBERT: Oh, haven't you? Then you've got a good time coming. [Realizing from her face that he may have gone too far] Of course, you may be able to handle 'em. I daresay you'll rub along all right.

LEONORA: They seem to mean a great deal to your Aunt Ellen.

ALBERT: Oh, well, they would. They've sort of taken the place of children with her. Somehow, when she's with Aunt Louisa and Aunt Emily she always makes me think of a tigress with her cubs.

LEONORA: [*Laughing*] Ellen? A tigress? You silly boy. Is your mother alive?

ALBERT: No. She's been dead a long time. Aunt Ellen brought me up. [*With a change of tone*] Well, I suppose I ought to be getting back—if you're really going to . . . to . . .

LEONORA: [*With humor*] Cough up the needful? [*They both laugh*] I'll just run up and get my keys.

ALBERT: [*As she goes to the stairway*] You *are* a lifesaver, Miss Fiske. Pity there aren't more like you.

LEONORA: [*A little grimly*] That's a matter of opinion, Albert.

ALBERT: Mind if I have a tinkle on your ivories? I never get a chance on a piano like this. We've only got an old tin kettle where I lodge.

LEONORA: No. Do.

> [*She hurries upstairs.* ALBERT *looks round for a moment. Then the pocket-Autolycus in him draws him to the table of knickknacks. He picks up the silver snuffbox and slips it quietly into his pocket. Then he hurriedly seats himself at the piano. He begins to play and sing, in a half-voice, "The Man on the Flying Trapeze."* LUCY *enters wonderingly from the kitchen. Discovering* ALBERT, *she gapes. He turns his head and sees her*]

ALBERT: Hullo!

LUCY: You did scare me! I thought I was hearing things.

ALBERT: You were.

LUCY: [*Rather coyly*] But I mean—a man's voice. [*She giggles*] So funny—here!

ALBERT: [*Becoming at once the cheap* "accapareur des femmes"] Doesn't the tide wash up many male fish, my angel?

LUCY: No. Men's as scarce here as hansom cabs. We're a covey of old women. There's only the nuns down at the Priory and us.

ALBERT: What about the butcher, the baker and the candlestick maker? Don't they call?

LUCY: Oh, yes. But they're all old. Everybody's old on the marsh. The young 'uns go off to London or to foreign parts. Soon as they can.

ALBERT: Are you going off to foreign parts?

LUCY: Depends.

ALBERT: Depends? On what?

LUCY: If anyone ever asks me.

ALBERT: I shouldn't think with eyes like them there'd be any difficulty.

LUCY: [Coquetting him] Oh, go on!

ALBERT: What's your name?

LUCY: Lucy. Who are you?

ALBERT: I'm Albert. Miss Creed's nephew.

LUCY: Funny—I've never heard about you.

ALBERT: That must be remedied. How about making the most of a
male fish, now one has been washed up? What about a smacker?

[He puts his arm round her and tries to kiss her, but she
draws away, eyeing him covertly]

LUCY: No. You mustn't. I don't know you.

ALBERT: But you don't have to know people to kiss them!

LUCY: I do.

ALBERT: [With a shrug] All right, my girl. It's your loss.

LUCY: [Going to the kitchen door with a hoity-toity air] You do
think a lot of yourself, don't you?

[There is a sound on the stairs and she flashes out just as
LEONORA appears. The old lady looks very knowing]

LEONORA: Has Lucy been entertaining you, Albert?

ALBERT: [Nonchalantly] She came in. We had a word or two.

LEONORA: Nice looker, isn't she?

ALBERT: I didn't notice.

LEONORA: Come, Albert. Don't lose your sense of humor. I hope
you're not one of those people who won't learn from experience.
Otherwise my twelve pounds may be rather wasted.

ALBERT: Don't you worry, Miss Fiske. I've had my lesson.

LEONORA: I hope so. [She goes to the hearth and unlocks the bake-
oven door] This is where we keep our hoard. [She opens the
door and you see a large dark cavity in the brickwork behind. She
takes out a big, old-fashioned cashbox] It's an old bake-oven
really.

ALBERT: [*Peering in with a whistle of astonishment*] Proper tomb, isn't it?

LEONORA: Yes. It runs the full width of the chimney. This is called a "slice." It's what they used to draw the loaves out with. Look. [*She takes up the "slice" and plunges it into the aperture which swallows it right up to the handle. Then she withdraws it and stands it again in the hearth*] Of course, we don't use it as a bake-oven. It hasn't been used for years. When I came here I found this whole hearth walled up. With a hideous little gimcrack mantelpiece and a cast-iron grate!

ALBERT: That was worth uncovering, wasn't it?

LEONORA: [*At the table, opening the cashbox*] Now then, Albert—twelve pounds, I think you said? [*She takes out a little chamois leather bag full of gold and counts out twelve sovereigns*]

ALBERT: I suppose you couldn't make it fifteen?

LEONORA: [*Very directly*] No, I couldn't, Albert. [*She hands him the money, replaces the bag, locks the cashbox and puts it back in the oven, closing the door and locking the padlock*]

ALBERT: Do I—do I give you an I.O.U.?

LEONORA: No, thank you, Albert. This isn't a loan. I shouldn't like you to incur the remorse of not paying it back.

ALBERT: Do you mean that? I say! You *are* a trump. I'll never forget your kindness. [*He takes her hand and kisses it*]

LEONORA: [*Rather intrigued, laughing*] Very prettily done, Albert. [*She slaps his face playfully*] There! Now let's forget all about it. [*By now she is ready to be rid of her visitor*] I'm sorry I can't offer you lunch.

ALBERT: Oh, I'll be able to get something at one of the farms on the way back. After all, what's one lunch—compared to bread and skilly for a couple of years?

LEONORA: And I shan't mention your call to Aunt Ellen.

ALBERT: I'd be very grateful if you wouldn't. Er—what about the girl?

LEONORA: I'll see to that, too. Good-bye, Albert.

ALBERT: Good-bye, Miss Fiske. And I'll never forget your kindness as long as I live.

LEONORA: Oh, I hope you'll live much longer than that. [*He has taken up his hat. He smiles, bows and goes jauntily. LEONORA stands*] *looking after him. She, too, smiles—a little twistedly, perhaps. He is young, he has a way with him, he is probably a rogue, but—he is a man! Then she hurries to the kitchen door and calls:* "Lucy! I want you!" *She returns to the piano and sits as if to resume her playing.* LUCY *enters*] Lucy, you met the young gentleman who's just gone, didn't you?

LUCY: Yes, miss.

LEONORA: Did you like him?

LUCY: I thought he was a very affable young gentleman, miss.

LEONORA: Yes. I think that's a very good description of him. Though "plausible" might be better. He's been in a little trouble. And I've helped him. I don't want to worry Miss Creed about it. So we'd better not say he's been here. Do you understand?

LUCY: Yes, miss.

LEONORA: That's all. Thank you, Lucy.

[LUCY *retires.* LEONORA *resumes her playing of* "Tit-Willow"]

CURTAIN

SCENE 2

It is an afternoon in the following September.

At the window a little elderly woman is standing. She is gazing out of the open casement across the marshes through a large nautical telescope. She is dressed in a worn, wide-skirted garment of rust-colored velvet, many years out of date. She is a thin, faded, shadowy personality, simple rather as a child is simple, fluttering, fretful, futile. At times, though, there is something decidedly comical about her. This is LOUISA CREED. *A knitted shawl and a large workbag lie on the armchair behind her.*

There is a brief pause. Then ELLEN *enters from the kitchen.*

ELLEN: You oughtn't to be standing by that window, darling. The wind's turning quite cold.

LOUISA: [*Rather fearfully*] Don't be cross with me, Ellen. I'm so happy—looking.

ELLEN: [*Taking up* LOUISA's *shawl and arranging it tenderly round her shoulders*] Well, put your shawl on, then.

LOUISA: Oh, but I'm strong. Much stronger than when I came. [*Looking through the telescope*] It must be quite rough on the river. Do you see the waves? They're like little white feathers blowing about.

ELLEN: Is that Emily coming over the marsh?

LOUISA: [*Altering the direction of the telescope*] Yes. Her apron's loaded. I wonder what she's picked up this time. Oh, Ellen! Isn't it exciting? She brings in such pretty things. I wish I were brave like Emily. I should like to take long walks, too, and pick up things and bring them home. Perhaps I shall be able to when I've stayed here longer.

ELLEN: I'm sure you will, darling.

LOUISA: [*Anxiously*] I shall be staying here, shan't I? You're not planning to send me away, are you, Ellen?

ELLEN: No, of course I'm not.

LOUISA: This is what you always promised us. A little house in the country and the three of us being in it together. You and Emily and me.

ELLEN: Yes, dear. That's the one thing I've schemed for—ever since we had to give up the old house.

LOUISA: I wonder who's living there now. I often think of the rhododendron hedge and the flag irises down by the river. And our copper beech tree! Do you remember how we three planted it, Ellen —with father looking on and laughing at us?

ELLEN: I expect Richmond's changed—like everything else.

LOUISA: Of course this could never be like Richmond! But it's nice here.

ELLEN: And Miss Fiske's been very kind to us.

LOUISA: [*Clouding*] Miss Fiske . . . May I tell you something, Ellen? Just one of my secrets?

ELLEN: Of course, darling.

LOUISA: I don't like Miss Fiske. I don't like her religion. Can't we send her away? Then it would be really just the three of us.

ELLEN: But I keep telling you, Louisa—it's her house.

LOUISA: [*Shaking her head*] Oh, no. You'll never make me believe that. You've always had your own house. This is yours. Here are your things. You've always had your own house, Ellen, haven't you? You're the clever one. And you'll always keep me near you, won't you? I don't want to be sent back to Kennington. To those awful ugly streets. Nothing to look at from the window.

ELLEN: Darling, I've promised you. I won't send you back.

LOUISA: I think Miss Fiske wants me to go. She wants us both to go—Emily and me. I think so.

ELLEN: You're just imagining it.

LOUSIA: No, I'm not, Ellen. I'm not imagining it.

ELLEN: But, darling, I'm sure I can persuade her to let you stay.

LOUISA: Yes, Ellen. I'm sure you can. You can do anything. [*She has wandered across the room and stands looking at the statue of the Virgin with wondering disapproval*] I wish you'd take this away. It isn't right to worship idols, is it?

ELLEN: We can't take it away. It doesn't belong to us.

LOUISA: Father always said that Roman Catholics aren't saved. I don't trust people who aren't saved.

[*The front door opens and* LEONORA *sails in. She is carrying a basket of ripe William pears. This time she is dressed in a gay blue gown. She is kind and charming to her guests, but you can see that they have begun to get badly on her nerves*]

LEONORA: [*Brightly*] I've just been down to the Priory. Look what the Reverend Mother's given me.

ELLEN: Oh, what lovely pears! Look, Louisa.

LEONORA: Yes. They're Williams. Have one, dear.

ELLEN: [*Taking one*] May I?

LEONORA: Won't you have one, Miss Louisa?

LOUISA: Did you say they came from the convent?

LEONORA: Yes.

LOUISA: [*Shrinking a little*] Oh . . . I don't think I . . .

ELLEN: [*It is almost a command*] Do, dear.

LOUISA: [*Taking one*] Thank you. May I eat it later?

LEONORA: Of course.

ELLEN: [*As though to cover* LOUSIA'S *ungraciousness*] I think I'll keep mine till supper, too.

LEONORA: [*Sitting at the table*] Well, I'm going to eat one now.

[ELLEN *goes to the dresser and fetches a dessert plate and silver knife and fork which she sets before* LEONORA. *She has laid her own and* LOUISA'S *pear on a plate on the dresser*]

ELLEN: They're beautiful pears.

LEONORA: They're from that tree by the pond.

ELLEN: The one that looks so lovely in the spring?

LEONORA: Yes.

LOUISA: [*Almost clapping her hands*] Oh, I shall like to see that!

LEONORA: [*Dryly*] I wish you could. What have you been doing all today?

LOUISA: I've been resting. And looking at things.

ELLEN: She's been watching the sailing barges going up and down the Thames.

LOUISA: There've been some big steamers passing, too. It's been the turn of the tide. They've been going up and down. I do think people are brave to go on the water in boats.

LEONORA: [*Beginning on the pear*] It doesn't strike me as particularly brave. No braver than living in a city where you might be run over or have a chimney-pot blow down on your head.

LOUISA: But I don't like living in a city. Just for that reason. And I don't care to go out. I'm not very brave. I don't go out in the streets. That's why I like being here. It's so lovely—so safe.

LEONORA: I don't know what you'll do when you go back to London, then!

LOUISA: [*Like a sly child*] Ah, but I'm not going back to London.

LEONORA: Aren't you?

ELLEN: That's just Louisa's way of telling you how much she's enjoying it here.

LOUISA: Yes. I *am* enjoying it.

ELLEN: That telescope's been such a pleasure to her. She's never had much opportunity of using it before.

[LOUISA *fetches her telescope and exhibits it to* LEONORA *while she eats.* LEONORA *eyes it with no particular pleasure*]

LOUISA: Yes. It's a beautiful instrument, isn't it? I keep it beautifully polished, don't I? It belonged to the man I was going to marry. He was the captain of a sailing ship. It was lost in a typhoon in the Indian Ocean. They were sailing from Madagascar with a cargo of raffia grass. You know, it's the thing they tie up plants with in gardens. Fancy a boatload of something you tie up plants with in gardens! Funny, isn't it? They were all drowned. He hadn't taken this with him on his last voyage. His sister gave it me. I've kept it ever since.

LEONORA: Oh, dear! What a tragic story!

LOUISA: It doesn't seem tragic to me now. You see, I've no picture of him, and it's so long ago I've almost forgotten what he looked like.

[*She takes the telescope back to the window.* LEONORA *rises, thankful to escape*]

LEONORA: How sticky these pears make one! I must go and dip my fingers.

[*She goes out through the kitchen door.* LOUSIA *picks up her workbag and slips the two pears* LEONORA *gave them into it*]

ELLEN: [*Sharply*] What are you doing? You mustn't do that!

LOUISA: [*In a whisper*] I'll burn them. Before I go to bed. In the stove in the kitchen. I'll slip in when no one's there.

ELLEN: Give them to me at once!

LOUISA: [*Handing them over like a naughty child*] You mustn't be cross with me, Ellen. They come from the nuns.

ELLEN: [*Putting them back on the dresser*] The nuns didn't make the tree, Louisa.

LOUISA: No. I suppose they didn't. I see. [*Nodding*] Yes. Yes, I was wrong.

[EMILY CREED *enters from the front door. She is a big-boned elderly woman of a gypsy type. She, like* LOUISA, *is simple and has the same sense of dependence, but, in her case, she hates her inability to fend for herself, and is often sullen and resentful. She is wearing an old-fashioned dark dress, the overskirt of which has been pinned up under an apron of dark blue cloth. The underskirt is stained with mud. Her apron, which she holds up basket-fashion, contains pieces of driftwood, a red cotton handkerchief full of shells, some seaweed and a dead bird. Her hair has been blown wild by the wind*]

EMILY: Oh, dear. I *am* tired. I've walked miles. [*She kneels on the floor and lets the contents of her apron out upon it*] That's the worst of the river. It leads you on. You always want to go round the next bend, and forget you've got to come all the way back.

ELLEN: What have you found this time, darling?

EMILY: Just driftwood. There's such a lot. But it's so heavy to carry. One wants an extra pair of arms.

ELLEN: You shouldn't tire yourself like this.

EMILY: Oh, but I enjoy it. I feel I must tidy up the river banks. But it's no good. Every tide washes up something fresh.

ELLEN: [*Smiling*] I'm afraid you've set yourself a labor of Hercules.

EMILY: Oh, I knew you'd laugh. You always do. I know it's silly. But I hate waste. And I have done something for my board and lodging, haven't I? Look at the stack of wood I've collected out there for you, Ellen.

ELLEN: Yes, and I'm sure Miss Fiske's very grateful.

EMILY: Is she? She's never said anything. Not that I want any thanks. [*She takes the handkerchief with the shells and the seaweed, and the dead bird and lays them on the table*]

LOUISA: Why should she thank you, Emily? It's Ellen who should thank you. It's Ellen's house.

ELLEN: Louisa can't get it into her head that this house doesn't belong to me.

EMILY: [*Emptying the shells on to the table*] But she's right in a way, isn't she? After all, Miss Fiske's quite dependent on you. Just as we are. She needs you. Just as we do.

ELLEN: That doesn't mean that her property belongs to me.

EMILY: I expect it will some day. She'll leave it to you. You'll see!

LOUISA: What pretty shells!

EMILY: Yes. I thought they'd be so useful. We can stick them on to boxes in patterns. You had one, d'you remember, Ellen, in your curiosity shop?

LOUISA: Oh, look, Ellen. A dead bird.

EMILY: Yes. I found it. I showed it to a shepherd. He said it was a sea swallow. That it was only just dead. It was lying on this seaweed. Isn't it a lovely thing?

[LEONORA *enters. She stands transfixed before the litter on the floor*]

LEONORA: Oh, my goodness! More wood?

EMILY: Yes. I got a nice lot today. I shan't be satisfied till I've stocked you with wood for the winter.

LEONORA: Well, it's very nice of you, Miss Emily, but I do wish you'd take it round to the back door. It makes such a mess in here.

LOUISA: Emily wanted to show us what she's found. Besides, she was very tired.

ELLEN: Don't worry about it, Leonora. I'll clear it up.

[*She kneels and proceeds to gather up the wood*]

LOUISA: [*Fluttering round her*] No, Ellen. You mustn't be put to any trouble. It's our fault. Miss Fiske, don't you think we might ask for the maid?

EMILY: [*Joining them*] No, it's my business. After all, I've carried it for more than a mile across the marsh.

ELLEN: Emily, go and sit down. You're tired.

LOUISA: No, Ellen. You do far too much as it is. Put it down, Ellen.

[*As a result of their assistance the wood falls to the floor again*]

LEONORA: Well, I don't think we need have a tug of war about it.

We'll adopt Miss Louisa's suggestion about the maid, shall we?
[*Calling*] Lucy!

LOUISA: My sister's not as strong as she thinks. And she's always do-ing things for other people.

[LUCY *enters*]

LEONORA: Take that wood through into the shed, please, Lucy.

LUCY: There's no room in the shed, miss. That's chock-full.

LEONORA: Well, I don't know what we're to do with it.

LUCY: I'll make a pile in the corner of the scullery here.

LEONORA: Very well. And bring Miss Emily a dustpan and brush.
[*Sub-acidly*] I think we should all clean up our own messes, don't you?

EMILY: That's what I wanted to do before Ellen started interfering.

LOUISA: Oh, it wasn't Ellen, dear. It was me. It was my fault.

LEONORA: Well, don't start that all over again. [*To* LUCY, *who has gathered up the offending wood*] And don't stand about, Lucy. Hurry up and fetch that dustpan.

LUCY: Yes, miss. I was only listening. [*She goes*]

[LEONORA *suddenly sees the shells scattered on the table*]

LEONORA: Oh, really, Ellen! This is too bad! My best polished table! Couldn't you have found a cloth?

ELLEN: I'm sorry. I ought to have remembered.

EMILY: Yes, you should have told me, Ellen. I'd no idea that table couldn't have things put on it.

LEONORA: But surely your common sense would tell you that shells will scratch a highly polished table!

EMILY: I didn't think.

[LUCY *enters with the dustpan and brush. She stands by the kitchen door, keenly interested in the little domestic disturbance*]

LEONORA: And what's this? Wet seaweed and a horrid dead bird! Ellen, really!

LOUISA: It's nothing to do with Ellen.

LEONORA: But, Miss Louisa, Ellen's responsible to me! No one knows better than she does how carefully an old piece must be handled. It'll take a month's hard polishing to put this right.

ELLEN: I'll put it right.

LOUISA: No. You shan't, Ellen. Let me do it. Let me. I'll polish it every day all through the winter.

LEONORA: That's very kind of you, Miss Louisa. But I'm afraid you won't be here all through the winter.

LOUISA: Oh, but we shall! We shall. Ellen says so.

ELLEN: You've made a mistake, Louisa. I said nothing of the kind.

LOUISA: But you did. You promised.

ELLEN: [*Again the sense of command*] Louisa!

EMILY: [*Her voice quivering with emotion*] Oh, please don't bully poor Louisa because of me, Ellen. And please don't be cross with Ellen, Miss Fiske. I brought in the shells and the sea bird. I picked them up. They're my treasures. They're quite harmless. They've given my sisters and me a great deal of pleasure. I know it's very simple of us. But we *are* simple. We don't understand expensive things because it's so long since we lived amongst them [*Weeping*] However, I see that my humble little finds are only starting a quarrel, so they'd better be taken away. [*With a great scraping and clatter she sweeps all the shells and objects from the table into her apron, and goes upstairs sobbing bitterly*]

> [*There is a brief pause. Then* LEONORA, *almost beside herself, sees* LUCY]

LEONORA: Oh, are you there, Lucy? Give me that. [*She takes the dustpan and brush, stoops, and in silence sweeps up the litter from the floor. Then she hands them to* LUCY] Thank you. Now get on with the supper.

> [LUCY *goes*]

LOUISA: I think I'd better go up to Emily, Ellen. I can hear her crying.

ELLEN: [*Almost curtly*] No. Let her be. Go up to your own room, if you like. But don't disturb Emily.

> [LOUISA, *after grimacing and putting out her tongue like a*

gamin at LEONORA's *back, scurries upstairs, shutting the door at the foot after her*]

LEONORA: I'm sorry I was so put out, Ellen. But there's a limit to patience, you know.

ELLEN: It's I who should have apologized.

LEONORA: Nonsense, dear. I mustn't expect you to be responsible for your sisters.

ELLEN: But I *am* responsible for them.

LEONORA: I don't want to add to your troubles, and I know what a burden they are, but . . .

ELLEN: Oh, but, Leonora, they're no burden at all. When my father was dying he made them over to me. They're a sacred trust—just as if they were my children. I've always looked after them. I've supported them. Every penny I earn goes to them.

LEONORA: My dear, you must be either a saint or a fool!

ELLEN: But what would become of them if I didn't? You see, when I had the shop and it failed, I lost their little money as well as my own. Everything they have is invested in me, and I must give them *some* dividend.

LEONORA: But you're forgetting that *I* haven't been brought up with them. They haven't been made over to *me*. And, while *you* may be used to them, *I* find them impossible to have about the house.

ELLEN: They *have* been a little naughty today, I admit. But I'll give them a good talking to, and then everything will be all right.

LEONORA: [*Firmly*] That won't do, Ellen. I'm trying to tell you, as kindly as I can, that they've got to go.

ELLEN: [*She seems stunned*] To go? When? [*There is a pause*] When do you want them to go?

LEONORA: At once. This week. I can't stand them any longer. I'm at the end of my tether.

ELLEN: I don't know how I shall break it to them.

LEONORA: [*Growing exasperated*] But, my dear Ellen, I only invited them here for a few weeks. Didn't they understand that? They've been here nearly four months.

ELLEN: Oh, no! Surely not as long as that?

LEONORA: They came at the beginning of June, and now we're well into September. And another thing. I don't think you've been quite fair to me. You never told me they were—well, what they are.

ELLEN: I told you they were rather pathetic.

LEONORA: Yes, my dear; but pathetic's not next door to insane.

ELLEN: [*Almost savagely*] They're *not* insane!

LEONORA: Naturally, you put the best side of the picture forward. They're your own flesh and blood. But, insane or pathetic or whatever you choose to call them, they've overstayed their welcome. I won't have them here any longer.

ELLEN: It's your house, I know. But you'll have to give me a little time.

LEONORA: What's time got to do with it?

ELLEN: Well, I don't quite know where I'll be able to send them.

LEONORA: But surely they've only got to get into a train and go back where they came from?

ELLEN: No. I didn't keep on their room.

LEONORA: But, my dear! You knew they weren't coming here on a visit for life!

ELLEN: I didn't want the expense. Besides, I hoped that perhaps you might have taken to them more than you have. I hoped we might be able to arrange something. It's a large house. There are several empty rooms. I was going to suggest that I should pay you something out of my wages towards their keep.

LEONORA: Oh, you were, were you? And is that why Louisa made that odd remark just now?

ELLEN: What odd remark?

LEONORA: That you'd promised her she should stay through the winter!

ELLEN: I never promised her.

LEONORA: I suspected something of the sort at the time.

ELLEN: I said I never promised her.

LEONORA: Very well. I accept that.

ELLEN: I admit I didn't realize quite how you felt. You've never given an inkling of it.

LEONORA: My dear Ellen, are you quite blind? You must have seen that I've got more and more exasperated.

ELLEN: I thought we might have gone on as we were for a little longer.

LEONORA: Well, you know how I feel now. I hope you realize we can't. This little holiday has come to an end.

ELLEN: You make me feel my position very much. I suppose you want me to go, too?

LEONORA: My dear Ellen, of course not! We got on like a house on fire before they came. I don't regard you, dear, as my servant. I think of you as my friend. You know my pillar-to-post career hasn't made me any permanent ones. Mine's a lonely existence. Terribly lonely. It's bound to be. And I've no family—no relations to fall back on. Why, if I were to disappear tomorrow no one would be any the wiser! I shouldn't make a ripple on the surface. So, you see, I value your companionship. More, perhaps, than you realize. I definitely don't want you to go.

ELLEN: I'm afraid it won't be altogether easy to forget what you think about my sisters. Or that you turned them out when they were so happy.

LEONORA: But I *haven't* turned them out! Their visit's just come to its end in the normal way. That's all.

ELLEN: Things can never be quite the same, can they?

LEONORA: Ellen! Don't tell me that you're crazy, too! For goodness sake, try to see this thing sensibly. Don't you realize that you're being frightfully unreasonable?

ELLEN: [*Sitting on the sofa*] People who've got all they want never understand how much the smallest thing means to those who haven't.

LEONORA: [*Getting very angry*] Really! I don't think this calls for a sermon on charity! I've been more than generous to you and your sisters.

ELLEN: But it's a little cruel to give with one hand only to take away with the other.

LEONORA: Oh, my goodness! You're beginning to make me wish I'd never given at all!

ELLEN: People have always been very generous to you, Leonora. You've got a home. You've got investments. You've got your one or two—allowances, haven't you?

LEONORA: Well, what of it?

ELLEN: My sisters and I—we haven't any gentlemen to send us money.

LEONORA: That's hardly my fault, is it?

ELLEN: No, but don't you ever feel that you have a special responsibility to women like us?

LEONORA: I don't know what you're talking about!

ELLEN: Don't you owe a debt to virtue? I've had to work for the money I've made. But at least I've kept my self-respect.

LEONORA: [Raging] How dare you? How dare you criticize my life? Do you think it hasn't been slavery to get the little I've got? Do you think it's cost me nothing but a few cheap embraces? How can you, a dried-up old spinster—how *can* you understand anything of what my life's been? Do you think I haven't had my torments? Do you think I don't envy women who've got respectability, who've got families, who aren't just forgotten or pensioned off when they lose their stock-in-trade?

ELLEN: Then you can't blame me for fighting for *my* family!

LEONORA: Ellen, you're a frightful hypocrite. You're worse. You're a cheat. You've pretended to be my friend. But it wasn't friendship you felt for me. You meant to batten on me and get the utmost out of me. You wanted to foist your wretched brood on me indefinitely. You wanted to maneuver me into a false position and bleed me white. And when I saw through your little scheme you had the insolence to turn on me and abuse me. But you've chosen the wrong woman! [Going to the kitchen door] I suggest you take a month's wages and go.

> [She stands looking at the seated ELLEN. She is shaking with rage. Then to her amazement ELLEN crumples up. She bursts into tears]

ELLEN: Leonora, don't go like that. Don't go, please. I'm absolutely in the wrong. I didn't mean half I said. I'm dreadfully sorry.

LEONORA: [Still quivering] I should hope you are!

ELLEN: You're quite right about my sisters. They are—peculiar. I don't wonder they've got on your nerves. I think perhaps they've got on mine, too, and that's why I said what I did. But, you see, I love them. I love them intensely—just because they are so helpless.

They're almost a religion with me. You're quite right, though, Leonora. They can't stay here. They must go. I see that. I'll send them away. I'll arrange it at once. Only don't send me away, too. I've been so happy here. And I promise everything shall be the same as before. Only don't send me away.

[LEONORA, *moved but still hurt, crosses to her and lays her hand on her arm*]

LEONORA: Well, I think we'd better both sleep on it, Ellen.

[*Then she goes quietly and quickly out into the kitchen. Almost immediately the door at the foot of the stairs opens and* LOUISA *and* EMILY *steal in. Like wicked children, they have obviously been listening. They come softly to either side of the sofa where* ELLEN *is still sitting. They look rather like three witches as they whisper together*]

LOUISA: Ellen, we've been listening. Isn't she terrible, Ellen? She's wicked. Are you going to send us away? You promised you wouldn't, you know.

ELLEN: [*Putting her arms round them*] No, I'm not going to send you away.

EMILY: She spoils everything. I wish *she* could go!

LOUISA: But, Ellen, if you're not going to send us away, what are you going to do, Ellen?

ELLEN: [*Her face is distraught*] I don't know. I shall have to think.

LOUISA: Dear Ellen! Always so clever.

CURTAIN

SCENE 3

It is late afternoon—a week later. It has been a fine, hot, autumnal day, and the light is gathering for a glorious sunset.

The room is empty, but a noise can be heard on the stairway; and almost at once LEONORA—*still in her blue dress—and* ELLEN *appear lifting down a large and battered yellow tin trunk, securely corded up.*

LEONORA: My goodness! It *is* heavy.

ELLEN: Yes. But we've managed it very well.

LEONORA: We couldn't have got it down so easily when we first came here. I expect it's moving all those bricks and things. It's got our muscles up. [*She sits down on the trunk and puts her hands to her head*] My goodness! I feel an awful sight.

ELLEN: Your hair's all crooked.

LEONORA: Why not say my wig's slipped and have done with it? We're quite alone.

ELLEN: [*Arranging the "transformation"*] Let me put it straight.

LEONORA: [*Purring*] Just like being in a dressing room again! It only wants the smell of the grease paint and a nice pair of tights! [*Drawing up her skirt and eyeing her ankles critically*] Though I don't think my ankles would run to them now.

ELLEN: [*Who has watched this little by-play disapprovingly*] There!

LEONORA: [*Rising*] Thanks, dear. Now tell me exactly what you want me to do with this.

ELLEN: Let's get it into the scullery first while they're still out.

LEONORA: [*As they take up the trunk*] You must have got half the foreshore in it! [*They carry the trunk out through the kitchen door. The convent bell starts. There is a brief pause. Then they return*] Hullo. There's the Priory bell. It must be six o'clock. Bates will be here in a minute.

ELLEN: It isn't Bates.

LEONORA: Oh?

ELLEN: No. I thought we wouldn't have Bates. He's so inquisitive. And he talks so. When I went into Rochester on Wednesday I arranged for a fly at the station to come out. It'll cost a bit more, of course; but it's rather less primitive than Bates' rickety little trap.

LEONORA: Well, what am I to do about their box?

ELLEN: Let Bates take it to the station tomorrow and have it labeled through to London Bridge. I'll pick it up there in the evening. It'll be quite handy. I've got them a room in the Borough.

LEONORA: [*Smiling*] I see. You're a regular Machiavelli, aren't you?

ELLEN: Well, isn't it much better this way? For them to think they're going for a drive round the country? And then, before they know where they are, I shall have whisked them into the train. I think it's kinder this way.

LEONORA: And when am I to expect you back?

ELLEN: I think I'd better stay over the weekend and get them settled in. They'll take a lot of settling.

LEONORA: Yes, I should. Don't hurry back on my account. I shall be quite all right.

ELLEN: I hate the idea of your being alone here. I almost wish you hadn't let Lucy go on her holiday.

LEONORA: But, my dear, it was *your* idea that she shouldn't postpone it. I wanted her to wait till they'd gone.

ELLEN: Well, you see, I was afraid that if she were here when Louisa and Emily went, we mightn't have been able to conceal our little plan from them. And then there'd have been a lot of trouble. Perhaps a scene.

LEONORA: But Lucy needn't have known anything about it.

ELLEN: You never know with these girls. They listen. They overhear things. And they will gossip.

LEONORA: I expect you're right. Ellen dear, before they come back, I want to—to give you something. [*She goes to the hearth, unlocks the oven and takes out the cashbox*] I know this is going to put you to a lot of expense. And I expect you'll have a very trying time when they find out the trick you've played on them; and they learn they're not coming back. Now, look here. Here are ten sovereigns. That'll pay for your journey and a few weeks' rent. And perhaps you'll be able to buy them one or two little comforts to make up for their disappointment.

ELLEN: [*Taking the money and kissing her, but distantly*] You're much too kind.

LEONORA: I'm so glad we've made everything up. I hate quarreling. I've got a very hot temper, but it soon evaporates.

ELLEN: I wish I was made like that.

LEONORA: [*Kissing her again affectionately*] You're a dear old stick-in-the-mud, Ellen. And I'm very fond of you. I can't think why I thought of parting from you. And I never will! So far as

I'm concerned you can stay here for the rest of my life. [*With a change of tone*] Well, as we're servantless, I'd better go and see about my supper.

ELLEN: There's nothing to be cooked. I've left everything ready.

LEONORA: [*Gaily*] Yes, but, as I'm all by myself, I think I shall get up a bottle of that champagne Lord Kenardington sent me for Christmas.

ELLEN: [*Her lips tightening*] I believe you're going to celebrate my sisters' going.

LEONORA: I don't mind telling you, Ellen—I am! This is the first time I shall have been able to call my house my own for months.

ELLEN: [*With an oblique glance*] It'll be the first time you've slept here alone, too, won't it?

LEONORA: I don't suppose even that will worry me with a pint of Cliquot inside me!

ELLEN: I've made a salad. And there's a cold partridge and some cream cheese from the convent.

LEONORA: A bird! Cream cheese! Champagne! It only wants the right setting. A private room at Kettner's—candlelight—distant music. And someone's foot pressing yours—very lightly—under the table. My goodness, Ellen! What am I talking about? Why haven't you stopped me? I'm in a crazy mood today! [*She is at the kitchen door*]

[ELLEN *is by the table on which lies the cashbox*]

ELLEN: [*Quietly*] You're leaving your money.

LEONORA: [*Darting back*] Oh, mercy! I really *am* crazy. [*She puts back the cashbox in the oven and locks the padlock*] The bell's been stopped some time. Your sisters ought to be back. [*Coming to* ELLEN] Ellen, I believe in your heart you're glad to be rid of them, too. Though, of course, you'll never admit it.

[*The front door opens and* LOUISA *and* EMILY *enter. They look very quaint and uncountrified in their outdoor attire.* EMILY *carries a large spray of autumnal "Traveler's Joy"*]

LOUISA: I hope we're back in time, Ellen, as you told us. Oh, dear! How nice it is to be indoors again!

LEONORA: What have you got there, Miss Emily?

EMILY: Lucy told me it's called "Traveler's Joy."

LEONORA: H'm—very appropriate, when you're going for a drive.

EMILY: It has white flowers in the summer. I remember when we came the hedges were full of it. Do you think, Ellen, it would keep through the winter like sea lavender and honesty?

ELLEN: I don't know, Emily.

LOUISA: Oh, but I expect you do, Ellen. Only you won't say. [*Sitting down with a little sigh*] I wish I weren't going for this drive. Do you think I need to, Ellen?

ELLEN: I particularly want you to, darling. I'm giving you a great treat.

LOUISA: Yes, dear, I know. But I'd sooner stay in the house. It's getting quite evening. And I don't like the long shadows.

EMILY: [*Letting the "Traveler's Joy" fall to the ground*] I'm very glad we're going for a drive. And I'm glad it's late. We shall be able to see the sun disappear behind the river.

ELLEN: A September evening's the most beautiful time of the year. And there's nothing to be afraid of. I'm coming with you.

LOUISA: Is Miss Fiske coming, too?

LEONORA: No. You'll be just by yourselves. [*Rather naughtily*] That'll be what you like, won't it, Miss Louisa?

LOUISA: Yes. Yes.

EMILY: I think I'll go up and get into an easier pair of boots. These pinch me rather.

ELLEN: No, you sit down. I'll run up and get them.

LOUISA: No, Emily. You mustn't let Ellen wait on you.

ELLEN: It's all right. I've got to go up in any case. I've got to get my own bonnet and cloak.

EMILY: They're in the left-hand corner of the cupboard.

ELLEN: I'll find them, Emily. [*She runs upstairs*]

LOUISA: Ellen's in one of her bossy moods today, isn't she, Emily?

EMILY: She always orders us about. She won't let us have wills of our own.

LOUISA: I think she's worried about something. I think she's got something on her mind.

LEONORA: Oh, come, Miss Louisa! I don't think that's right. *I've* noticed nothing different about her.

LOUISA: But then you wouldn't, would you? You're not one of the family. I *know* Ellen's worried about something. I can tell it.

EMILY: [*Beginning to take off her boots*] I wonder if we *are* just going for a drive. I wonder if she's sending us away.

LOUISA: [*In immediate agitation*] Don't say that, Emily! Oh, I do hope it's not true. But you'd know, Miss Fiske, wouldn't you? You're not both sending us away, are you?

LEONORA: [*Artfully*] Do you think I *should* know—not being one of the family?

LOUISA: No, no. I suppose that's true. I suppose you wouldn't. Ellen would arrange that by herself, wouldn't she?

EMILY: If Ellen tries to send me away, I shan't go.

LOUISA: Oh, but we must do what Ellen tells us, mustn't we? I don't know what would become of us if we offended Ellen.

EMILY: She might take me to the station, but I wouldn't get into the train.

LEONORA: I think you're both imagining much too much.

LOUISA: Yes. I think we are. I think you're right. I don't think Ellen would deceive us.

EMILY: [*Suddenly, looking towards the window*] What's become of your telescope, Louisa?

LOUISA: It's on the windowsill, dear.

EMILY: No, it isn't.

LOUISA: [*Rising, agitatedly*] Isn't it? Where is it? It was here when I went out! I knew I oughtn't to have gone out! I knew something would happen.

LEONORA: It's quite all right, Miss Louisa. Ellen took it out into the kitchen. I think she was going to clean it.

LOUISA: Oh, no, she wasn't. I always do that myself. Why has she taken it into the kitchen? I believe it's been broken! I must get it! I must have it!

LEONORA: I promise you it's not been broken. If you'll wait here, I'll get it for you.

LOUISA: No, *I* wish to get it.

LEONORA: [*Snapping*] I'm sorry, but you can't!

EMILY: [*Sullenly*] Why shouldn't Louisa get it herself?

LEONORA: [*Going to the kitchen door*] Because it happens to be my kitchen and Miss Louisa's my guest.

LOUSIA: [*Following her*] I'm going to get it!

> [*She feebly seizes* LEONORA *and there is an undignified little struggle at the door, which ends by* LEONORA *forcing* LOUISA *on to the piano stool*]

LEONORA: Please sit down, Miss Louisa. Don't you realize you're making the most ridiculous scene about absolutely nothing? (*She goes quickly out into the kitchen*]

> [LOUISA *sobs*]

LOUISA: It's broken! I know it's broken!

EMILY: I don't think Ellen broke it. I think *she* broke it. She wasn't really angry when she spoke like that. She was only saying it to cover up something.

LOUISA: Oh, how I hate her!

EMILY: Ellen wouldn't like you to say that. They're friends again—she and Ellen. I think they're in league together.

LOUISA: I wish you wouldn't keep saying things against Ellen, Emily!

EMILY: You think Ellen's perfect, don't you? You'll find out about her one day.

> [ELLEN *comes down the stairs. She is wearing her bonnet and cloak, and carries a pair of lady's elastic-sided boots*]

ELLEN: [*Giving* EMILY *the boots*] Here are your boots, Emily.

EMILY: Thank you, Ellen.

ELLEN: What's the matter, Louisa darling?

LOUISA: [*Tearfully*] Ellen! Someone's broken my telescope.

ELLEN: Have they, dear? Oh, no. I don't think they *can* have.

LOUISA: But why did you take it out into the kitchen.

ELLEN: I didn't.

LOUISA: [*Excitedly*] There, Emily! She was lying. She was lying.

ELLEN: Who was? Who was lying?

LOUISA: Miss Fiske! She said you'd taken it into the kitchen to clean it. She's gone to fetch it now. I *knew* you wouldn't have.

ELLEN: [*Suddenly remembering that, of course, the telescope is packed*] Oh? Oh, yes, of course. It's all right, darling. I'd forgotten. I did take it out. It's quite true.

LOUISA: You're only humoring me because you know it's broken.

ELLEN: [*Sharply*] Nonsense, Louisa. Stop being silly.

EMILY: [*Suddenly*] These are not *my* boots, Ellen. They're yours.

ELLEN: Yes, I know, dear. I'm making you a present of them. You always do have my old ones, don't you?

EMILY: Thank you. But I wish you'd brought me my own. My feet ache, and yours always take a little getting accustomed to.

ELLEN: Well, you won't have to do any walking on your drive.

[LEONORA *enters from the kitchen in triumph, with the telescope.* EMILY *begins grudgingly to put on the boots* ELLEN *has brought*]

LEONORA: Here we are! You see, Miss Louisa! It's not broken. It's as right as ninepence.

LOUISA: [*Seizing it*] Oh—thank you. I *am* glad to have it. No, it hasn't been broken. But it hasn't been cleaned.

ELLEN: I haven't had time yet.

LEONORA: [*Laughing*] Miss Louisa was so agitated I believe she thought I was going to steal it, Ellen.

ELLEN: [*To* LOUISA, *tenderly*] It was just a lot of fuss about nothing, wasn't it?

LOUISA: Yes, dear. I was very silly. But it's not nothing to me.

LEONORA: [*Going to the stairs*] Ellen, call me when the fly comes. I'd like to see you all safely off.

EMILY: [*Resentfully*] There's no need for you to trouble. We shall be back in two hours, shan't we?

LEONORA: [*With almost a wink at* ELLEN] Well, I'd like to make sure you start comfortably. [*She hurries upstairs*]

LOUISA: Emily says that we're not really going for a drive. That you're sending us away. That we're not coming back. That's not true, is it, Ellen?

ELLEN: Of course it's not true. What made you think that, Emily?

EMILY: You see, Miss Fiske doesn't like us. And she's been so different, so friendly. Almost as if she knew she was getting rid of us.

ELLEN: Well, you're both quite wrong. You *are* coming back. I promise you that. And I've always kept my promises to you, haven't I?

LOUISA: Yes, Ellen. You have—always.

EMILY: She seemed very anxious to come and say good-bye to us.

ELLEN: We may be saying good-bye to *her*.

EMILY: What do you mean, Ellen?

ELLEN: I want you to keep a little secret. Will you promise me?

LOUISA: Yes, Ellen. Of course we promise.

ELLEN: And you, too, Emily. You must promise, too.

EMILY: Very well. I promise you, Ellen.

ELLEN: [*She goes to the stairway door and closes it*] You're very happy here, aren't you? You like this place?

LOUISA: Yes, Ellen.

EMILY: Yes, Ellen. We're very happy.

ELLEN: You'd be happier still, wouldn't you, if we were here just by ourselves?

LOUISA: Oh, yes, Ellen. She spoils everything.

EMILY: But it's her house. How could we be here by ourselves?

ELLEN: That's what I want to tell you. I'm going to try and persuade her to sell it to me.

LOUISA: Oh, how clever, Ellen! Then she could go away and live somewhere else.

EMILY: But supposing she wants too much money for it, Ellen? She may want more than you're prepared to pay.

ELLEN: I'm prepared to pay quite a big price, Emily.

EMILY: I didn't think you had all that much money, Ellen.

ELLEN: Oh, I've saved quite a lot.

LOUISA: [*Trembling with excitement*] Oh, it will be lovely if it can be ours! I'm so excited, Ellen. When will you know? When will you ask her?

ELLEN: I'm going to ask her today. That's one of the reasons for the drive. I want to get you out of the place. I want to tackle her by myself.

EMILY: But you're coming out with us.

ELLEN: Only as far as the Priory. Then I shall get out and slip back. And you'll go on for your drive round.

LOUISA: Oh, I shall tell the man to hurry! We mustn't be away too long. I shall be so anxious to know.

ELLEN: That's just what I don't want. I want you to give me at least two hours. It's a complicated thing to arrange, you know. It can't be done in five minutes. I want to get it all fixed up before you come back.

EMILY: But why should you come with us at all, Ellen?

[ELLEN *does not answer*]

ELLEN: I want to call at the convent.

LOUISA: But why must you call there, Ellen? Father wouldn't have liked your calling at the convent.

ELLEN: [*After a moment*] I want to get the Reverend Mother on our side. She has great influence with Miss Fiske. I want her to help me persuade her.

LOUISA: Oh, of course. Oh, how clever you are, Ellen! I should never have thought of that.

[ELLEN *goes to the half-moon table and takes a devotional book from it*]

ELLEN: Now, look here, Louisa. Here's a Bible. I want you to put your hand on it and swear on father's memory that you'll never repeat what I've told you about buying the house as long as you live.

LOUISA: Yes, Ellen. If you wish it, Ellen. But it rather frightens me. What do I say?

ELLEN: Just say "I promise."

LOUISA: I promise.

ELLEN: You, too, Emily.

EMILY: I won't swear on the Bible. It's wicked.

LOUISA: Oh, Emily! You must do what Ellen says.

ELLEN: If you won't promise me, Emily, I shan't buy the house. And I shall send you both back to London.

LOUISA: Oh, Ellen—not that, please. Emily, do be sensible.

EMILY: Very well. But I don't like being made to do things. I promise.

[*There comes a sudden rat-tat-tat at the front door*]

LOUISA: Oh, dear! What's that?

ELLEN: [*Looking through the open window*] It's the man from Rochester with the carriage. [*Calling*] All right! We'll be out in a minute!

THE MAN'S VOICE: [*Calling back*] Very good, mum. I'll turn the 'orses. Which way d'ye want to go?

ELLEN: We'll tell you later. [*Leaving the window*] Now, come along, my darlings.

LOUISA: [*Like an excited child*] Oh, wouldn't it be lovely if, when we came back, we found that you'd bought the house and she'd gone!

ELLEN: [*Turning on her almost savagely*] Will you be quiet!

LOUISA: Oh, don't! Don't be cross with me, Ellen!

ELLEN: You've just sworn on the Bible never to mention it again!

LOUISA: [*Awed*] I'm sorry. I thought it didn't count when we were together.

ELLEN: She might have overheard you and that would have spoilt everything. It's better for us not to discuss it even among ourselves.

LOUISA: [*Meekly*] Whatever you say, Ellen.

[LEONORA *enters from the stairway door*]

LEONORA: Did I hear the carriage?

ELLEN: Yes. It's just come. We're going now.

LEONORA: I do hope you all have a nice drive.

LOUISA: I expect we shall come back very hungry.

ELLEN: Now, come along. [*As they go out the front door*]

LOUISA: Oh, it is a high step, isn't it, from the ground? You'll have to help me, Ellen.

ELLEN: The driver will lift you up.

LOUISA: Oh, that will be fun! Won't it, Emily?

[*They disappear.* LEONORA *watches their departure*]

LEONORA: Good-bye. Make the most of it! Have you told the driver which way, Ellen?

ELLEN: [*Calling back*] He knows.

LEONORA: [*Waving*] *Au revoir!* [*You hear the carriage rumble away.* LEONORA *closes the front door with obvious relief. The room is now full of the evening sunlight*] Oh, thank God for that! [*She picks up* EMILY's *pair of boots with a little grimace and then the fallen strands of creeper, exclaiming grimly as she does so:* "Traveler's Joy." *She then collects* LOUISA's *telescope and with a little laugh, shoulders it like a rifle. She marches out through the kitchen door singing:—"For he's going to marry Yum-Yum—Yum-Yum!" You hear her still singing this outside. Then* ELLEN *enters swiftly and silently by the front door. She hurries across the room to the stairway which she mounts quickly but furtively. The grandfather clock strikes six. Then* LEONORA *returns, still singing gaily to herself. She carries an open bottle of champagne and a glass and a couple of turves of peat. She puts the champagne and glass on the piano and then crosses and lays the peat on the fire. She returns to the piano and, pouring out a glass of wine, toasts herself in silent complacence. She is evidently, preparing for a cozy evening. Then she sits at the piano and opens* The Mikado *score. She begins to play "Tit-Willow." When she is halfway through the verse the stairway door opens very slowly and quietly.* ELLEN *is standing there, her face taut and tense. She has discarded her bonnet and cloak, and in her hands is the cord of a pink silk dressing gown. She advances a step or two, but* LEONORA *does not hear her and goes on with her playing*]

CURTAIN

ACT TWO

It is a wild night in mid-November. There is a violent storm of rain and wind in progress.

The room is empty. It is cozily lighted by one or two oil lamps; and a great log fire roars in the hearth. The two little candles in front of the figure of the Virgin are alight. The curtains are drawn; everything is bright and shining in the warm glow, and the whole feeling is one of snugness.

As the curtain rises there comes a rapid knocking at the front door. LUCY *enters from the kitchen, crosses the room and opens the door. She admits* SISTER THERESA, *a fat, red-faced, jolly old nun with gleaming gold spectacles.* SISTER THERESA *carries a huge, dripping umbrella and a storm lantern.*

THERESA: Is Miss Creed at home?

LUCY: Yes, Sister. They're all three at home. Which one do you want?

THERESA: Oh, Miss Ellen, please. I wonder if I could see her for a minute. Unless, of course, Miss Fiske has returned.

LUCY: No. She's still away. Let me take your umbrella into the scullery. [*She relieves her of it*] I'll stand it in the sink.

THERESA: [*Setting her lantern on the floor*] Yes. It *is* coming down. Cats and dogs. And so sudden, too. After such a beautiful afternoon.

LUCY: You sit down by the fire, Sister. I'll tell Miss Creed. She's in the kitchen.

THERESA: [*Going to the hearth*] You *have* got a roaring fire.

[LUCY *goes, just as* LOUISA *enters from the stairway*]

LOUISA: [*Starting at seeing the nun sitting there*] Oh.

THERESA: Good evening.

LOUISA: Are you waiting to see my sister?

THERESA: Yes.

LOUISA: Oh.

THERESA: I understand Miss Fiske's still away.

LOUISA: Oh, yes. She's not here.

THERESA: For the moment I thought she was back—when I saw the candles.

LOUISA: [*Turning a little shrinkingly to the altar*] Oh, the candles? Yes. Ellen's taken to lighting them. I don't quite know why. I'm sure father wouldn't have approved. But she likes to do it because she thinks Miss Fiske would have liked her to. She says it keeps her memory burning.

THERESA: What a very kind thought of your sister's!

LOUISA: Ellen's full of kind thoughts. She's so clever.

[ELLEN *enters from the kitchen*]

ELLEN: I'm sorry to have kept you waiting, Sister. But we're in the middle of making our quince jam.

THERESA: Please—you mustn't apologize. I've been chatting very happily to your sister.

ELLEN: [*With a slight reaction*] Oh? I hope she's not been tiresome. We were brought up as very strict Nonconformists, you know. And my sisters are rather apt sometimes to—well, to voice their prejudices, I'm afraid.

LOUISA: But I said nothing, Ellen! Nothing at all!

THERESA: [*Blandly*] Whatever our religions are, we can always be good neighbors, can't we?

ELLEN: [*Smiling*] Of course.

THERESA: And I'm here with a neighborly request, I'm afraid. We're rather in trouble at the Priory. Our supply of oil hasn't arrived from Rochester. They forgot it yesterday, and I suppose the storm has prevented them coming today. We've absolutely run out. I wondered if I might borrow a can over the weekend—that is, if you can spare it. We'll pay you back as soon as our supply arrives. It's sure to be here on Monday.

ELLEN: Of course I will. Louisa, go into the scullery and bring me one of those gallon cans of paraffin. They're on the floor by the copper.

LOUISA: Oh, please, Ellen, couldn't Lucy do it?

ELLEN: No, darling. Lucy's busy with the jam. Run along. Do what you're told.

> [LOUISA *goes.* ELLEN *and the nun are sitting on the two settles*]

THERESA: It's very peaceful here sitting in this lovely old chimney corner. People miss such a lot in towns.

ELLEN: Oh, yes. We're pre-Tudor. The Priory's very old, too, isn't it?

THERESA: Yes. It was a monastery at one time. It goes back to Henry the Fourth. I wish you could come and see us some day.

ELLEN: Thank you.

THERESA: I think it's a very nice thought of yours to keep Miss Fiske's candles alight while she's away.

ELLEN: [*Alertly*] Oh, did Louisa tell you about that?

THERESA: I'm afraid I asked her. I thought, when I saw them, Miss Fiske might be home.

ELLEN: Oh, no.

THERESA: When are you expecting her back? We miss her so much at the convent.

ELLEN: I don't know. I haven't heard from her quite recently.

THERESA: Is she in London?

ELLEN: She went to London to begin with. Then she was going on— elsewhere.

THERESA: The Reverend Mother was wondering what she ought to do about the rent for that little three-acre field we hire from her. It's only a few pounds; but we like to pay our debts promptly.

ELLEN: Well, I'm managing all her affairs while she is away, so if you send it to me I'll be responsible for it and forward it when I get her next address. Of course, I'll let you have a receipt for it.

THERESA: Thank you. That sounds a very good arrangement. I'll tell the Reverend Mother.

[LOUISA *enters from the kitchen with a large can of oil*]

LOUISA: I've got it, Ellen, but it's rather heavy.

THERESA: Oh, thank you so much.

ELLEN: You'll want some help, won't you?

THERESA: Oh, no. I can manage.

ELLEN: You can't carry this and your lantern and your umbrella, can you? I'll get Lucy to go down with you.

THERESA: But what about your jam? It wouldn't be very neighborly of me if I let you spoil that.

ELLEN: [*At the kitchen door: calling*] Lucy! I want you to go down to the Priory with the Sister. And bring her umbrella. You'll have to wrap up. It's still pouring. I'll watch the jam. [*Turning to the Sister*] Well, you'll excuse me if I say good night, won't you?

THERESA: Of course. And you *have* been kind. Thank you so much.

[ELLEN *goes into the kitchen*]

LOUISA: I think you're so brave going out in the dark and the wet. I hate the dark. I'm always glad when morning comes.

THERESA: [*Smiling*] I never worry about things like that. I believe we're watched over.

LOUISA: I think that, too. But I'm never quite sure who's watching us.

[EMILY *enters from the stairway. She carries a tray with a little wooden box, a pot of warm glue and a pile of seashells. She starts when she sees* THERESA, *just as* LOUISA *did*]

EMILY: I didn't know anyone was here.

LOUISA: It's all right, Emily. Ellen knows. And she's just going. [*To* THERESA] It's my sister Emily.

THERESA: Good evening.

EMILY: It isn't a very good one, is it? [*She puts her tray on the table and sets to work at once sticking the shells in patterns on the wooden box*]

THERESA: Well, it *is* wild.

EMILY: I was down by the river-wall today, and a lot of ships went out to sea.

LOUISA: In this wind? Oh, the poor sailors!

> [LUCY *enters from the kitchen. She is wearing a hooded cloak and galoshes and carries two umbrellas, the Sister's and her own*]

LUCY: I'm quite ready, Sister.

THERESA: Well, good night.

LOUISA: Good night.

THERESA: Good night, Miss Emily. [*There is a pause.* EMILY *does not reply*] What very pretty work you're doing!

EMILY: Is it? I only make them because it uses up the shells.

THERESA: [*To* LUCY] Well, now, my dear, if you're coming I think we should go. Thank you again. Good-bye.

LOUISA: Good-bye. [THERESA *takes up the lantern and the can, and she and* LUCY *go out the front door,* LUCY *opening the great umbrella as they go.* LOUISA *shuts and bolts the door after them. Then she comes and sits on the settle*] I think that nun is rather a nice old woman. She'd look like a farmer's wife if she didn't wear that horrid dress. I wonder if we're wrong in not making friends with the nuns?

EMILY: I hate them. You know what father always said about Romans.

LOUISA: Ellen was very nice to her. They were quite chatty together.

EMILY: You never can tell what Ellen's thinking. Louisa, I think Ellen's changing. I hope she's not going to get in league with the nuns—against us.

LOUISA: Ellen would never do that, Emily.

EMILY: She's taken to lighting those candles.

LOUISA: Yes, I don't think that's right, do you?

EMILY: [*Suddenly, rising*] I think I'll blow them out.

LOUISA: You mustn't do that, Emily! Ellen wouldn't like that.

EMILY: Why should Ellen have everything her own way? [*She walks boldly to the altar and blows out the candles*]

LOUISA: [*Half-admiringly, half-terrified*] Oh, Emily! What have you done?

EMILY: [*Returning to the table*] Something I wanted to do.

> [*Here there is a violent knocking at the front door*]

LOUISA: That must be Lucy. She's back soon.

[*She unbolts and opens it. To her amazement* ALBERT
FEATHER *bursts in. He is wearing an ulster and a deerstalker's
cap. He is absolutely drenched. He carries a little dark
lantern with which he has been picking his way along. He
makes a mock-dramatic entrance.* LOUISA, *not recognizing
him, recoils with a shrill scream*]

ALBERT: Why, if it isn't Aunt Emily! Or is it Aunt Louisa? All right.
Don't look so scared. I shan't eat you.

LOUISA: [*Aghast*] Who are you?

ALBERT: I'm Albert. Albert Feather.

EMILY: [*Rising*] It's Albert, Louisa. Rose's boy.

LOUISA: Oh! Albert? Rose's boy? Yes. So it is. [*Meanwhile he shuts
the door but does not bolt it*] Of course. Come in, Albert. Oh,
you *are* wet! You're wet through. We must tell Ellen. Will you tell
her, Emily—or shall I?

EMILY: You tell her.

[ELLEN *appears in the kitchen doorway. She is keyed up
and tense*]

ELLEN: I heard a man's voice. Who is it?

LOUISA: It's our nephew, Ellen. It's Albert. And we haven't seen
him for years!

ELLEN: What? Albert? What on earth are you doing here?

ALBERT: I've walked over from Gravesend.

ELLEN: [*Kissing him*] What! Tonight?

ALBERT: It was fine when I started.

ELLEN: Well, sit down by the fire and take your boots off. And
your ulster. My goodness, you are wet! You must be soaked
through.

ALBERT: I'll soon get dry. This fire'll do the trick.

[*They get him to the fire, cosseting him. They take off
his overcoat and coat.* EMILY *takes his little lantern from
him*]

ELLEN: [*Giving his clothes to* EMILY] Here, take these into the kitchen, Emily. And hang them on the clotheshorse in front of the stove. Don't put them too near the grate. And stay by the jam and see that it doesn't burn till Lucy gets back.

EMILY: [*Surlily*] Oh, very well. [*She goes, rebellious at being ordered*]

ALBERT: It's awfully good of you, Aunt Ellen, but what I really want most is a bit of grub and something nice and warm to chase it down the hatchway. I haven't had anything since breakfast.

ELLEN: Of course. I'll get you something. And, Louisa, run up to the front room and bring down that dressing gown. It's only a woman's, Albert, but it'll be better than nothing.

LOUISA: Oh, yes. You—you mean the pink one? Will it matter?

ELLEN: Why should it?

LOUISA: Supposing she sends for it one day. [*She goes upstairs without waiting for a reply*]

ALBERT: I say! It *is* a change for a bachelor. To be waited on by three lovely ladies.

ELLEN: You silly billy, why didn't you write and tell me you were coming?

ALBERT: I'll tell you all about that when I'm dry outside and not so dry in. [ELLEN *goes out into the kitchen, laughing.* ALBERT *looks round the room, at the dresser and at* EMILY's *shells. Then* LUCY *enters from the front door. At first she does not see him. She turns and bolts the door. Suddenly*] What cheer, Lucy!

LUCY: [*Jumping*] Oh! You did give me a start.

ALBERT: [*Airily*] Just a little habit of mine.

LUCY: [*Recognizing him*] Why, it's you! So you've turned up again?

ALBERT: Yes. Bad pennies do, you know. Pleased to see me?

LUCY: I'm surprised.

ALBERT: [*Jauntily*] The other'll come later. Still a shortage of male fish in the estuary, duckie?

LUCY: There's a new shepherd over at Cooling, but no one's seen him yet.

ALBERT: And he's probably eighty and a bit. [*Rather anxiously*] Here, Lucy. Tell us. Is Miss Fiske about?

LUCY: No. She's away.

ALBERT: [*Relieved*] That's a bit of luck. Listen, Lucy. Does my Aunt Ellen know I blew over last summer?

LUCY: Not that I know of. I've never heard talk of it. I've said nothing. Miss Fiske told me not to.

ALBERT: Good. Then I may be all right.

LUCY: What have you come over for this time?

ALBERT: Need you ask? To get a glimpse of your bonny, bright eyes, of course!

LUCY: I see you haven't changed. You're just as fast.

ALBERT: [*There is a noise on the stairs*] Shut up! Here's one of the old gals. We don't know each other, remember. [*Slyly*] Not that we shan't—later.

LUCY: I'm very particular who I know. [*She goes off into the kitchen, her head in the air*]

> [LOUISA *comes down the stairs with a wonderful pink silk dressing gown. This, having belonged to* LEONORA, *is slightly outré and Parisian*]

LOUISA: I've got it down for you, Albert. Oh, was that Lucy?

ALBERT: [*Innocently*] I don't know, auntie. It was the servant. Is her name Lucy?

LOUISA: No. Of course you wouldn't know, dear, would you? Now, see if this fits.

> [*He puts it on. The effect is grotesque*]

ALBERT: Whoa, my hearties! The hansom cabby's delight! [*He throws himself into an exaggeratedly feminine attitude*] I say, Aunt Louisa! Shouldn't I be a riot on the halls? Ta-ra-ra-boom-de-ay! Ta-ra-ra-boom-de-ay! [LOUISA *shouts with laughter. He takes a few dance steps and she imitates him.* EMILY *enters from the kitchen.* ALBERT *rushes to her and dances her round the room*] Ta-ra-ra-boom-de-ay!

EMILY: [*Shrilly as she struggles*] Don't do it, Albert!

ALBERT: There you are, me old cup of tea. [*He picks her up and plants her in a sitting position on the tray of shells on the table*]

EMILY: Don't do it, Albert. It's all glue!

LOUISA: [*Going into fits of laughter*] Oh, the shells are sticking to her skirt! Isn't he funny?

[ELLEN *has entered from the kitchen. She carries a tray on which are a plate of cold beef, some bread, grapes and an apple, and a bottle of cognac*]

ELLEN: Now, Albert, behave. Louisa, put Emily's tray on the piano. [LOUISA *obeys. Putting* ALBERT'S *tray on the table in place of* EMILY'S] Here's your food.

ALBERT: My word, Aunt Ellen! What a spread! Cold cow and a bottle of the best. [*He picks up the bottle with interest*] Cognac, 1830. Where did you pinch this, auntie?

ELLEN: Now, pull yourself together, Louisa; stop laughing and get him a glass. No, bring two. I think I'll have a little to keep him company.

[LOUISA *goes to the dresser and brings the glasses*]

ALBERT: And bring a couple of those egg cups. You and Aunt Emily must whet your whistles, too.

LOUISA: Whet our whistles? Oh, Albert, you *are* silly. Do you think we might, Ellen? I've never tasted cognac.

EMILY: [*Fetching the egg cups*] Of course we can, Louisa. He asked us.

ELLEN: I don't think you'd better.

ALBERT: [*Dispensing the drinks*] Oh, come on, auntie! You don't have a nephew here every night of the week! Here's your ration of grog, Aunt Ellen. And a thimbleful for the Belle of the Ball, Miss Emily Creed!

EMILY: Not so much, Albert, please.

ALBERT: [*As* LOUISA *presents her egg cup*] And what have we here? That wrecker of homes, Miss Louisa. Here's a nice drop of liquid to water your garden, me old stick of celery.

LOUISA: Oh, Ellen, isn't he funny? He's just like a play.

EMILY: You've never been to a play.

LOUISA: No, I know. But I'm sure he's just like one. Have you ever been to a play, Albert?

ALBERT: [*In shocked tones*] Oh, no, Aunt Louisa. Never. Theaters are haunts of vice. I should never lower myself.

LOUISA: [*Crushed*] Oh, I'm sorry, Albert. I always say the wrong thing, don't I?

ALBERT: Don't apologize. [*Refilling their glasses*] Now then, my Siamese twins. I give you a toast. The toast of absent friends. And, so far as I'm concerned, the longer they're absent the better.

EMILY: Absent friends.

[*All but* ELLEN *raise their glasses and drink*]

LOUISA: Absent friends. I suppose we ought to think about Miss Fiske, Ellen. But she was never exactly a friend, was she?

ELLEN: Now we've had quite enough of this nonsense. I'm going to put the bottle away. You get on with your supper, Albert. And you be off to bed, Emily and Louisa.

EMILY: [*Sullenly*] I don't want to go to bed.

LOUISA: Oh, let us stop up and talk to Albert, Ellen.

ELLEN: No, my darlings. You've had quite enough excitement. You'll be able to talk to Albert in the morning. I want to talk to him now.

ALBERT: Go on. Be good little girls. Toddle off to bye-bye.

LOUISA: Very well. I suppose we must.

EMILY: Good night, Albert.

LOUISA: Fancy! Rose's boy—at our table. After all these years—all our family under one roof. And Ellen's roof, too! It's too good to be true, Emily.

[ELLEN *is staring at the extinguished candles*]

ELLEN: [*In a strange voice*] Who put out those candles?

LOUISA: What candles, Ellen? Oh, *those!*

EMILY: It must have been the wind. [*And she goes upstairs*]

LOUISA: Good night, Albert.

ALBERT: Good night, Empress.

LOUISA: [*At the foot of the stairs, looking back slyly*] It—it wasn't the wind, Ellen. [*She follows* EMILY]

[ELLEN *relights the candles with a taper lit at the fire.* ALBERT *proceeds to attack the victuals*]

ALBERT: They're like a couple of old children, aren't they? I say, Aunt Ellen, you've not turned papist, have you?

ELLEN: No, Albert.

ALBERT: I was wondering. They'd be playing musical chairs in the family vault if you did.

ELLEN: [*The candles are now relighted*] I do this for a friend. I suppose you want to stay the night?

ALBERT: Well, I do rather. Actually I was wondering if you could put me up for a little longer.

ELLEN: Well, you'll have to shake down on the sofa in here for tonight. I've told Lucy to bring you in the carriage rug when she's finished bottling the jam.

ALBERT: I don't mind where I doss.

ELLEN: Tomorrow we can get the front room ready for you. Why have you been so long in coming to see me, Albert?

ALBERT: I never have any time, auntie.

ELLEN: Then how do you come to have it now?

ALBERT: Well, it's a compulsory holiday, as you might say.

ELLEN: [*Startled*] What? Have you lost your situation at the bank?

ALBERT: I've given it up.

ELLEN: Given it up? Oh, you foolish boy! It had such good prospects.

ALBERT: Yes, auntie. That was my trouble. It was all prospects and— er—no foreground. Not enough ready, you know.

ELLEN: But you couldn't expect to start at the top. Besides—think! A bank's so safe. You're so secure. You'd have been there for life.

ALBERT: I'm too much of a rolling stone. That's what it is.

ELLEN: Ah, like your father—horrid common little man. Have you got another job to go to?

ALBERT: 'Fraid I haven't.

ELLEN: Well, you'll have to busy yourself to find one. It's no good your staying on here. There's nothing here. We're out in the wilds.

ALBERT: I know. [*Looking at her shrewdly*] That's why I've come.

ELLEN: [*Interpreting his glance*] Albert, you haven't done anything —wrong, have you?

ALBERT: Not exactly wrong, auntie. I just helped myself to a little salary I wasn't entitled to.

ELLEN: [*With an intake of her breath*] Do you mean you've taken money?

ALBERT: Well, you see—a friend of mine's made a hobby of studying keys. And I'm afraid I took a few lessons from him.

ELLEN: Have you stolen from the bank?

ALBERT: This is rattling good brandy, auntie.

ELLEN: Albert, answer me!

ALBERT: You've got it, auntie.

ELLEN: But if you were so desperately in need of money, why didn't you come to your family?

ALBERT: I've got no family but you and the old canary birds. And I thought you were on the rocks.

ELLEN: [*A little taken aback*] I did lose my money. But I've got some of it back since. I could always have found you a few pounds.

ALBERT: A few pounds wouldn't have seen me through it.

ELLEN: [*Horrified*] Is it as bad as that? How *could* you, Albert?

ALBERT: [*Almost but not quite ashamed*] I know. I know.

ELLEN: I suppose you got into low company. Now, tell me the worst. What's happened? Can the money be put back, or have they found out?

ALBERT: They've found out. They've set the police on me.

ELLEN: [*Now thoroughly alarmed*] The police?

ALBERT: Yes. I was having breakfast in the back basement this morning when I was given the tip they were coming up the steps to the front door. So I slipped out into the yard, nipped over the wall and down the alley.

ELLEN: But they'll follow you! They'll come *here!*

ALBERT: Not they. I knew the back way out of Gravesend. And it was easy enough once I got to the marshes. They might be the edge of the world. I haven't met a soul.

ELLEN: [*Slightly reassured*] But they're bound to search!

ALBERT: Not here. No one knows I've got relations here. I'm safe here for a lifetime.

ELLEN: Well, you're certainly not going to stay here for a lifetime!

ALBERT: No, of course not. But you'll let me stay here for a week or two, won't you? Till it all blows over. They're not going to waste a lot of the rate-payer's money looking for a hundred pounds they haven't a hope of getting back.

ELLEN: A hundred pounds? What have you done with it? Have you still got it?

ALBERT: No. That burnt a hole long ago. One and ninepence is the state of my current account.

ELLEN: But what do you propose to do?

ALBERT: [*Discarding the dressing gown, which he throws on the piano stool*] I want to get out of the country and start afresh. Anywhere. America—Australia—I don't care where. I wondered if you'd let me hide here till it's safe, and then advance me my passage money. It wouldn't cost much—steerage.

ELLEN: I suppose that's the only thing I *can* do.

[LUCY *enters from the kitchen with a rug*]

LUCY: I've bottled the jam, miss; and here's the rug for the gentleman.

ELLEN: Thank you, Lucy. And now you'd better be off to bed.

LUCY: All right, miss. Will it be one more for breakfast in the morning?

ELLEN: Yes.

ALBERT: Better make it two, if not three. I get an appetite like a whale in the mornings.

LUCY: Good night, miss.

ELLEN: Good night, Lucy.

LUCY: Good night, sir.

ALBERT: [*Artfully*] Good night—Lucy, is it?

LUCY: [*Giving him a look*] Yes. Lucy. [*She goes out through the kitchen*]

[ELLEN *arranges the rug on the sofa*]

ALBERT: I shall sleep better tonight than I've slept for weeks. There's no need for you to wait on me like that, auntie. I'll tuck myself up.

ELLEN: Very well, Albert. I think I'll go up to bed, too. You'll put the lamp out, won't you?

ALBERT: [*Taking a cigar from his vest pocket*] I think I'll just have a weed first. The solitary survivor of the wreck.

ELLEN: [*As he lights it*] Oh, Albert, I hope you're not taking this too lightly. You sound so horribly callous. You *have* told me the worst, haven't you? There isn't anything else?

ALBERT: What else?

ELLEN: [*She has* LEONORA'S *dressing gown in her hand, and her voice sounds very queer as she says it*] Well, there are worse things than stealing.

ALBERT: Do you mean—have I put someone to sleep? [*He laughs*] Good Lord, no. I'm not that bad. What a funny old stick you are, auntie—thinking of such a thing even! I may be a little light-fingered, but there's no blood on my hands. Besides, I'd be too scared. Putting people out calls for real nerve, you know.

ELLEN: [*Taking up one of the lamps*] Yes. [*She goes to the foot of the stairway carrying the lamp and the dressing gown*]

ALBERT: I'm sorry to be such a bird of ill omen.

ELLEN: Never mind. I daresay it's Providence. Good night, Albert.

ALBERT: Good night, Aunt Ellen. [*She goes upstairs.* ALBERT *draws from his trousers pocket a little bunch of skeleton keys. Rather furtively he softly shuts the door at the foot of the stairway and turns the key in the lock. Then he opens the kitchen door and listens. All is quiet. He goes to the hearth and examines the padlock on the bake-oven door. After a few quick tries with his keys he deftly undoes the padlock and throws the door open. To his amazement there is no cavity there now. He is faced with a solid wall as the door swings back. The oven is bricked up. In astonishment*] Well, I'm blowed!

CURTAIN

SCENE 2

The next day—Sunday—is bright and clear after the rain. You notice, now that the curtains are drawn, that the windows are barred on the inside with iron bars. LOUISA'S *telescope is standing on the dresser.* EMILY's *shells are still on the piano. The bake-oven door is closed again. There is a small fire burning on the hearth. The candles are out.*

It is shortly after noon.

ALBERT, *in his shirt sleeves, with a towel round his neck, is busy lathering his face. Shaving materials are on the table.* LUCY *enters from the kitchen with a small wall-mirror which she brings to* ALBERT.

ALBERT: [*Taking it*] Ta. We'll prop it up here, shall we? [*He puts it on the windowsill*] Is this your mirror, Lucy?

LUCY: It's from my bedroom.

ALBERT: Sees a lot of pretty scenery—that mirror—doesn't it?

LUCY: You *are* awful, aren't you?

ALBERT: So are you—if you're honest with yourself. It's given you quite a lift-up—my coming back, hasn't it?

LUCY: It's given me a lot of extra work.

ALBERT: Nice work, though. [*He tries to kiss her but she eludes him*]

LUCY: Here! I've washed my face this morning, thank you.

ALBERT: D'ye know, Lucy, you've blossomed out since I was here last. Quite the young lady, aren't you?

LUCY: I can't say you've improved.

ALBERT: Oh, come off it. You'd better make the best of me while I *am* here. I may be going abroad shortly.

LUCY: No! Are you going abroad? Where?

ALBERT: I don't know. America probably. Or India.

LUCY: Oh, I *should* like to see India.

ALBERT: [*Stropping his razor, which is of the "cut-throat" type*] Would you? Well, if you're nice to me, I'd see if I can't find you a cozy little corner down among the boilers when I stow aboard. It might help to melt you.

LUCY: It 'ud take more than boilers to do that.

ALBERT: Don't be so full of back answers. You'll eat your words one day.

LUCY: Oh, shall I, Mr. Know-All?

ALBERT: I've a good mind to make you swallow 'em now.

LUCY: [*He advances toward her*] You'll get a black eye if you try anything with me. You keep your distance.

ALBERT: You forget I've got a razor in my hand. Just for that I think I'll have a kiss now, after all—soap or no soap.

LUCY: I'll scream the place down if you touch me.

ALBERT: [*Cheerily*] If you do I'll slit your gizzard. Now, come along, be a nice little girl. You've got to go through it, you know.

LUCY: Well, you'll have to catch me, then!

ALBERT: That's a bargain. [*He puts down the razor, chases her and corners her on the settle where he kisses her soundly*] You little devil, pretending all this time you were an iceberg.

LUCY: I oughtn't to let you do this.

ALBERT: What do you think lips were made for?

LUCY: Leading respectable young girls astray—yours were. [*He tries again*] No. You've done quite enough for one Sunday morning. [*She takes the towel from round his neck and wipes her face*]

ALBERT: [*Now shaving hard*] No, don't go. Stay and talk to me.

LUCY: I've got the breakfast things to wash.

ALBERT: That can wait. I'll come and help you wash up later.

LUCY: I don't see you doing much washing up.

ALBERT: What have you got these bars over the window for?

LUCY: Miss Creed had them put up after Miss Fiske went away.

ALBERT: Seems a funny idea.

LUCY: Your aunts are all a bit funny.

ALBERT: That's a fact. She's a nice old dear—Miss Fiske. Quite a good sport, isn't she?

LUCY: She's always finding fault. But she *is* human.

ALBERT: How long's she been away?

LUCY: Nearly two months.

ALBERT: Where's she gone?

LUCY: I don't know. I didn't know she was going even. She never said anything about it.

ALBERT: Why? Did she just walk out, then?

LUCY: I don't know. I was away on my holiday. When I came back she'd gone. Funny, wasn't it?

ALBERT: Perhaps she and Aunt Ellen had a row.

LUCY: Couldn't have been that, could it? Because then it would have been for your aunt to go. It's Miss Fiske's house.

ALBERT: Yes. You're right there. She'll turn up one day.

LUCY: Well, Miss Ellen can't be expecting her just yet. Because you're to have Miss Fiske's room as long as you're staying. I've just been getting it ready.

ALBERT: [*Wiping his face*] There, that's better. I feel a little less like the Missing Link. Good job Miss Fiske left her razor. I don't suppose my aunts could have lent me one between 'em.

LUCY: I wonder what *she* wants a razor for.

ALBERT: [*Slyly*] Corns, I don't think. [*As she turns to go*] Half a mo. Have you got a bit of black wire?

LUCY: Whatever for?

ALBERT: [*At the bake-oven*] See this padlock? I was fooling about with it last night, and it came open. I couldn't get it shut again.

LUCY: You oughtn't to have done that! That's where Miss Fiske keeps her money.

ALBERT: Oh, no, you're wrong there. Quite wrong, duckie. There's only a wall behind there.

LUCY: That's all you know. It's an old bake-oven.

ALBERT: Bake-oven my foot! [*He opens the door*] Look!

LUCY: Well, I never! It's been bricked up. I wonder when that was done? But it *was* a bake-oven. Miss Fiske used to call it her safe.

ALBERT: When did you last see it opened?

LUCY: When I was going on my holiday. Miss Fiske gave me my money out of it.

ALBERT: If that's where the money used to be kept, it wouldn't do for it to look as though I'd been playing about with it, would it? I mean, people think nasty thoughts sometimes, don't they?

LUCY: Yes. And sometimes they're right, aren't they? [*Taking her mirror and going to the kitchen*] I'll get that wire.

ALBERT: And bring a pair of pliers if you've got 'em. [*LUCY goes out. ALBERT puts on his coat and slicks his hair in front of the glass. LUCY returns with some wire and the pliers*] Ta. It only wants a small bit. I don't want it to show. [*He takes the wire and the pliers and quickly adjusts the padlock*]

LUCY: You *are* clever with your fingers!

ALBERT: [*As he works*] By the way, is there a flue from in there up into the main chimney?

LUCY: Of course not. It's a bake-oven, stupid.

ALBERT: I know it is, clever! Then it must be all airtight behind there?

LUCY: Of course it's airtight.

ALBERT: I wonder why anyone should want to brick up a place like that.

LUCY: [*Artfully*] I know why: Miss Fiske probably put her jewels in there before she went away. They were always playing about with bricks, and pulling the walls down. She didn't want to take any chances—not even with your aunt.

ALBERT: I daresay you're right. I wouldn't mind having a peep at those jewels.

LUCY: Oh, so that's why you wanted to know if it had a flue of its own? You'd have soon been on the roof with a fishing line, *I* know!

ALBERT: [*Artfully*] If I read *you* rightly you wouldn't mind the feel of some of Miss Fiske's jewels round *your* neck. A nice pair of earrings might take you and me to Australia. [*There is a sharp double knock on the front door.* ALBERT *is terrified. He tiptoes to the stairway where he stands on the bottom step in the shadow ready to make a bolt for it.* LUCY *watches him in astonishment. In a whisper*] Who's that? Don't open it. See who it is. And come and tell me first.

LUCY: [*She looks out the window and then comes to him*] It's the post.

[*At the same time a letter is thrust under the door*]

ALBERT: [*Relieved: coming forward*] Oh.

LUCY: [*Retrieving the letter*] He's gone. Here's the letter. It's for Miss Fiske—from her bank.

ALBERT: How do you know? [*He takes the letter*]

LUCY: There's the crest on the envelope. Why were you so scared?

ALBERT: I wasn't scared. I'd forgotten you had a Sunday post.

LUCY: Don't tell me you weren't scared! You were frightened out of your skin. Are you in trouble?

ALBERT: We all make mistakes, don't we?

LUCY: I believe you're hiding from the police.

ALBERT: Supposing I am? You wouldn't think any the less of me for that, would you?

LUCY: That depends. [*He takes her in his arms and kisses her again*] Look out! Someone's coming!

[*They separate hastily as* EMILY *comes downstairs.* LUCY *flies*]

ALBERT: Good morning, Aunt Emily. How is it you're not at chapel?

EMILY: I had a headache.

ALBERT: Oho! Aunt Ellen's cognac too much for you?

EMILY: It wasn't Ellen's. It was Miss Fiske's. Ellen really oughtn't to have given it to you. Unless, of course, she bought it.

ALBERT: Don't say Miss Fiske would have begrudged it to us.

EMILY: [*By the piano, at her tray*] I don't know. I never liked her.

ALBERT: By the way, there's a letter just come for her. It wants re-addressing. Shall I do it? It'll save trouble.

EMILY: You'd better not touch that, Albert. Ellen might not like it. Besides, I don't know her address. [ALBERT *puts the letter on the dresser.* EMILY *takes up her tray*] I'll just put my glue down by the fire here. It'll be ready when I come back. I'm going for a walk.

ALBERT: Where are you going?

EMILY: I'm going down to look at the floods. The dikes always overflow in these big rains.

ALBERT: Don't run away, my dear. I don't often have the chance of a *tête-à-tête* with the handsome one of the family.

EMILY: [*Sitting down*] I think you're making fun of me, Albert.

ALBERT: Now, would I do a thing like that? [*Chattily*] This is a very comfortable house you three are living in. Jolly sight better than your lodgings in Kennington!

EMILY: Yes. They were horrid.

ALBERT: What's going to happen to you when Miss Fiske comes back? Will she let you stay on?

EMILY: She isn't coming back.

ALBERT: Isn't she? Why not?

EMILY: Ellen's bought the house.

ALBERT: Go on!

EMILY: Oh, yes. It's quite true. But it's a secret. Ellen made me swear on the Bible I wouldn't tell anyone. But you're one of the family. So it's different.

ALBERT: Why did Aunt Ellen want to keep it so secret?

EMILY: I don't know. It was all done in a great hurry. Aunt Louisa and I were sent out for a long drive, and when we came back it was all over and Miss Fiske had gone. You won't tell Ellen I told you, will you?

ALBERT: No. We'll make that *our* little secret, shall we?

EMILY: Yes. It's rather fun to have a secret Ellen doesn't know anything about. She always thinks *she's* the clever one. But she isn't—not always. I'll tell you another secret, Albert. Oh, no, I won't.

ALBERT: Why not? Didn't you say I was one of the family?

EMILY: I think Ellen's done something that's not quite right.

ALBERT: Why?

EMILY: Because she's looked so worried lately. And I've heard her walking about the house very late at night.

ALBERT: That's nothing. That might be indigestion.

EMILY: Yes, it might be. But I don't think it is. When it gets dark she lights those horrid little candles. She never used to do anything like that. It's only since Miss Fiske's been gone. Do you think, Albert, she hasn't really bought the house?

ALBERT: Well, if she hasn't, it's rather a large article to steal, isn't it?

EMILY: There might be ways of getting it.

ALBERT: What sort of ways?

EMILY: [*After a pause*] I don't know, Albert. I haven't thought.

[*There is a light knock at the front door. He darts to the window*]

ALBERT: Why, it's an old nun! Where's she blown from?

EMILY: She'll be from the Priory. It's down the lane. Will you open the door to her, Albert? I don't like nuns.

[ALBERT *opens the door.* SISTER THERESA *enters. She has a gallon can of oil with her*]

THERESA: Oh, good morning. Is Miss Ellen Creed in?

ALBERT: No. I'm her nephew. She's gone over to—where was it, Aunt Emily?

EMILY: The Little Bethel at Cooling.

ALBERT: [*To the Sister*] Ah, that's it. Chapel, you know. Can I do anything?

THERESA: The Reverend Mother's sent me up to repay this oil which you lent us last night. The cart which was bringing our supply got waterlogged. They couldn't get beyond the farm. So they left it there and Mr. Braiden kindly brought it up this morning. The Reverend Mother wanted you to have it at once.

ALBERT: [*Taking it*] I'll take it through.

EMILY: [*Rising*] No. I'll go, Albert. I know where it's kept. [*She takes the can and, without a glance at* THERESA, *goes out into the kitchen*]

[THERESA *produces an envelope*]

THERESA: And, as I was coming, the Reverend Mother thought I might save a journey and bring the rent for Miss Fiske's field— if Miss Creed doesn't mind taking it on a Sunday.

ALBERT: [*Receiving it*] Oh, bless you, I've no objection. The better the day, the better the deed. I'll give it her when she comes in.

THERESA: Tell her not to trouble with the receipt till the next time someone's passing our way.

ALBERT: [*Casually*] Did you know Miss Fiske well—who owned this place?

THERESA: Oh, yes. She still does, doesn't she?

ALBERT: Oh, yes.

THERESA: We all know her at the convent. She's a dear friend of ours.

ALBERT: I've only met her once. She seemed a very agreeable lady. I suppose you've no idea when she'll be back?

THERESA: No. As a matter of fact, we didn't know she was going away. The Reverend Mother was quite surprised when she heard she'd gone. And I think she's been a little hurt that Miss Fiske hasn't written to her. But perhaps I oughtn't to say that.

ALBERT: Why not? It's a free country.

THERESA: Of course. Good morning. [*She goes, shutting the door*]

> [ALBERT *stands, shaking the envelope to his ear. He realizes there is money in it. He looks, for him, very thoughtful. It is as though a vague idea were taking shape in his mind.* LUCY *enters from the kitchen*]

LUCY: Miss Emily told me to tell you she's gone out for her walk. She went out the back way. She didn't want to meet the Sister again.

ALBERT: Narrow-minded old parrot! Here, just a minute, ducks. Got a kettle boiling out there?

LUCY: Why?

ALBERT: Never you mind. Have you got one?

LUCY: Well, perhaps I have. What do you want it for?

ALBERT: Bring it in here. Then I'll show you. [LUCY *goes into the kitchen.* ALBERT *puts the nun's letter on the bureau.* LUCY *returns with a steaming kettle. Indicating the table*] That's right. Now put it down there.

LUCY: You can't stand it on the table!

ALBERT: No. I know! [*Going to the piano and taking up a score*] This bit of music. Stand it on here.

LUCY: Oh, you mustn't do that. That's Miss Fiske's.

ALBERT: [*Reading it*] "The Mikado. From her friend, Rutland Barrington." Oh, I've seen that before. No, we'd better not use that. That's special. [*Taking up another*] Here. The *Elijah*. He'll do. He's used to heat in the desert.

LUCY: [*Putting down the kettle on Mendelssohn*] What do you want to do?

ALBERT: [*Taking the bank's letter from the dresser*] Lucy, I've got a notion something's a bit wrong and I want to have a look at something.

LUCY: What?

ALBERT: This letter that came from the bank for Miss Fiske this morning.

LUCY: Well, what about it?

ALBERT: I'm going to have a look at what's inside.

LUCY: You can't go opening other people's letters.

ALBERT: [*Slyly*] Did you like Miss Fiske?

LUCY: Yes. She's a kind lady. She's been very generous to me.

ALBERT: Yes. She was very good to me, too. She got me out of a bit of trouble, and I owe her a debt of gratitude.

LUCY: Well, it's a funny way to pay it to open her private letters!

ALBERT: It might not be. I'm a little worried.

LUCY: Oh. Hurry up, then. They'll be back from chapel soon. [*He has opened it now*] Well, what's it say?

ALBERT: [*Reading*] "Dear Madam: Re your letter instructing us to forward the amount of the enclosed check in five pound notes to the payee, your signature appears to differ from that with which we are acquainted. I shall be obliged if you will kindly confirm the same by signing it afresh in your usual manner." [*Looking at the attached check*] It's for fifty quid. [*Then he whistles*] Do you notice the date?

LUCY: [*Reading it over his shoulder*] November the fourteenth.

ALBERT: I thought she went away in September?

LUCY: But she may have written the check from wherever she is, mayn't she?

ALBERT: But why have they written back to her *here*? And do you notice who the check's made payable to?

LUCY: "Miss Ellen Creed." Well, what of it? I expect it's the house-keeping money.

ALBERT: Yes. You're probably right. Well, it's a dead end, anyhow. Now we'd better cover up our tracks, hadn't we? [*He picks up the glue pot*] Just dip your forefinger in Aunt Emily's glue, will you?

LUCY: I'm not doing anything about it. I've had no hand in this.

ALBERT: Haven't you? [*He suddenly seizes her hand and puts her finger in the glue*] Now then, seal it up.

LUCY: You *are* a filthy pig! [*She seals the envelope reluctantly*]

ALBERT: [*Standing the letter back on the dresser*] Now, we'll put it up here, and I'll hand it to Aunt Ellen later. That'll give it a chance to dry. And don't forget—you're in this as deep as me.

LUCY: I wish you'd never come here. There's something about you frightens me out of my life.

ALBERT: I don't mind telling you I frighten myself sometimes.

LUCY: I don't know what's come over me. You seem to mesmerize me. You won't give me away to Miss Creed, will you?

ALBERT: Not so long as you keep your mouth shut about *me*. [*A noise outside attracts him. He peers through the window*] Hullo! Here come the performing seals! Quick—take the kettle into the kitchen. [LUCY *picks up the kettle and hurries out.* ALBERT *respectfully opens the front door to* ELLEN *and* LOUISA *who enter. They are in their Sunday-go-to-meeting attire*] Hullo, aunts. Had a nice pray?

ELLEN: [*Grimly*] There's no need to be facetious, Albert.

LOUISA: It would have done you good to come too, Albert. It was quite exciting. The minister was telling us all about Hell. You would have enjoyed the picture he drew of fire and brimstone and the lost people burning in the pit.

ALBERT: Oh, I've had quite a good time, thanks—smelling the bit of dead bullock sizzling on the stove in Aunt Ellen's kitchen.

ELLEN: That's very irreverent. You shouldn't joke about such things.

ALBERT: I'm afraid I can't take Hell all that seriously, auntie. I don't hold with these preachers hollering themselves hoarse about eternal fire. After all, if there *is* such a place, no one's ever come back from it. So where do they get all their geographical details from?

ELLEN: [*With deep, if concealed, feeling*] Hell's like the Kingdom of Heaven. It's within.

ALBERT: [*Struck by her manner, but jauntily*] I bet you read that in a book somewhere, auntie. What's an innocent old cup of tea like you ever done to know anything about Hell?

LOUISA: But, Albert, Aunt Ellen's clever. She knows about all sorts of things. She may know about Hell, too.

ALBERT: You don't say! We'll have to christen her "Hell-Fire Ellen."

LOUISA: [*Going into fits of laughter*] Oh, he does say funny things, doesn't he? "Hell-Fire Ellen!" Ho! Ho! I must tell Emily!

ALBERT: [*He is now at the fireplace and takes up the "slice"*] Yes, of course! And that explains why she keeps a pitchfork handy. To help jolly old Lucifer turn over the fry in his oven. [*He pokes* LOUISA *playfully with the "slice."* ELLEN *turns on him in a fury and grips his wrist*]

ELLEN: Put that down! I won't have you talking like this in my house on a Sunday!

ALBERT: [*Complying in feigned surprise*] It's all right, auntie. I was only trying to bring a little sunshine into your lives. You want digging out of yourselves. You three lead such a walled-up existence here, you don't realize how the other ninety-seven people in the world live.

ELLEN: Perhaps we know a little more than you give us credit for.

LOUISA: Yes, Albert. Aunt Emily and I may be a little old-fashioned, but Aunt Ellen's very up to date.

ALBERT: [*Taking up the nun's letter*] By the way, auntie, somebody called while you were out—asking for a Miss Fiske.

ELLEN: What! Who was it?

ALBERT: One of your religious friends down the road. She gave me this.

ELLEN: What did she say?

ALBERT: She just said it was for Miss Fiske and would I give it to you. [*Rattling the letter*] It's got money in it.

ELLEN: Very well. I'll take it. [*She takes it and puts it into her bag*]

ALBERT: [*Innocently*] Who is this Miss Fiske everybody's always mentioning?

ELLEN: Oh—she's just someone who used to live here.

LOUISA: She didn't like Emily and me. She was horrid. We *were* so glad when she went away.

ELLEN: Hadn't you better go upstairs, Louisa, and take your things off?

LOUISA: Oh, but I do like being with Albert, Ellen. He does say such funny things.

ELLEN: You won't want to sit about in the house in your best all day.

LOUISA: No, I shan't, shall I, Ellen? No, of course. [*She trots upstairs*]

[ELLEN *shuts the stairway door*]

ELLEN: Albert, I don't want you to mention Miss Fiske again in front of your aunts. They quarreled; and it excites them very much to talk about her.

ALBERT: [*Mock penitently*] Oh, I wouldn't like to do that. Of course, I won't refer to the subject again, auntie. You see, nobody told me. But, I say!—how comic—your quarreling. What did you quarrel about, auntie?

ELLEN: I didn't say that *I* quarreled with her.

ALBERT: Oh, then, I suppose she's the friend you lighted those candles for last night? I see!

ELLEN: Yes. That's right. She's that friend.

ALBERT: You must have been very fond of her. When did she die?

ELLEN: Die? Who said she was dead? Who said anything about her dying?

ALBERT: I just assumed she was. You don't light candles for the living, do you?

ELLEN: Why not?

ALBERT: Well, Catholics don't, do they?

ELLEN: I'm not a Catholic. I thought candles just stood for prayers.

ALBERT: Is that so? You may be right. I'm not up in the technique. I say—it must have been a priceless quarrel. I'd love to have seen it. Fancy the old birds driving Miss Fiske out of here for good!

ELLEN: We don't know that it is for good. She's away on a holiday. She may come back.

ALBERT: Crikey! Is it her room I'm having?

ELLEN: Yes.

ALBERT: What's going to happen to me if she turns up?

ELLEN: I expect you'll be gone by then.

ALBERT: I hope so. [*Suddenly*] There! Damme, if I haven't got a memory like a sieve!

ELLEN: What have you forgotten?

ALBERT: The other letter. Now where did I put it? Oh, yes. Over here on the dresser. [*He takes down the bank's letter*] It came by the post. It's another one for Miss Fiske. From a bank. It gave me quite a turn when I saw it was from a bank. If you like to readdress it, I'll take it down to the box. I could do with a breather.

ELLEN: [*Taking it*] I'm looking after everything for her while she's away. It may be important. I think I'd better open it, don't you?

ALBERT: Why not—if she wouldn't mind? [ALBERT *wanders to the piano watching her covertly. She opens the letter, and we see her react to the contents*] That's a nice piano you've got here.

ELLEN: [*Absorbed*] What? Oh, yes. I believe it is.

ALBERT: Why, it's a Pleyel! And, by Jove, isn't it stylish?

ELLEN: [*Sitting at the bureau*] Don't worry me, Albert. I must write a note. It's rather urgent. I must concentrate.

ALBERT: Don't mind me, auntie. And you *are* up to date! I never expected to find a copy of *The Mikado* here! [*He stands turning over the pages of the score. Then he saunters over and sits on the sofa watching* ELLEN *as she writes. Suddenly he begins to whistle "Tit-Willow."* ELLEN *rises with a little cry*]

ELLEN: Don't do that!

ALBERT: Sorry, auntie. Didn't mean to interrupt.

ELLEN: It's not that. But I hate that particular tune.

ALBERT: [*As she resumes her writing*] Do you? I'll find something cheerier.

> [EMILY *enters from the front door. She is carrying some strands of bryony berries which she has torn from the hedge*]

EMILY: I couldn't get down to the marsh. The floods were too bad.

ALBERT: [*Irreverently*] That's too bad. [*She crosses the room and goes upstairs. Still reading the score*] Ha! Ha! This might be you and Emily and Louisa, mightn't it? [*He sings in a half-voice*]
> "Three little maids from school are we,
> Pert as a schoolgirl well can be.
> Filled to the brim with girlish glee,—
> Three little maids from school."

> [LUCY *looks in from the kitchen*]

LUCY: Will you be ready for dinner in ten minutes, miss?

ELLEN: [*Blotting and sealing her letter*] Make it a quarter of an hour, Lucy. I've got to run down to the letter box.

> [LUCY *retires*]

ALBERT: Let me go for you, auntie.

ELLEN: Thank you. I'd rather do it myself. [*She crosses the room and goes out the front door*]

> [ALBERT *goes over to the bureau, examines the blotter and tears a sheet from it and then crosses to the kitchen door*]

ALBERT: [*Calling into the kitchen*] Hi, Lucy! Bring us back your mirror, will you? [*She enters carrying her mirror*] Here. Hold it up—facing the light.

LUCY: I should think you'd have got sick of the sight of your face.

ALBERT: I don't want it for that. I want to read what Aunt Ellen's written to the bank. It's on her blotter—see? The other way about.

LUCY: You oughtn't to do this.

ALBERT: Hold it up. [*She stands facing the window and holding up the glass. He holds the blotting paper to it and reads in the mirror, but with some slight difficulty*] "Dear Sir: Check—something—quite correct. Owing to a sprained hand there may be a discrepancy in some of my checks lately signed. Yours—something—Leonora Fiske."

LUCY: "Leonora Fiske"? Your aunt's signed "Leonora Fiske"? What's it mean, Albert?

ALBERT: [*He lays the blotting paper thoughtfully on the table*] Shouldn't like to say.

LUCY: [*Suddenly*] I know! It means she's pretending to be Miss Fiske and stealing money from her bank!

ALBERT: That's what it looks like.

LUCY: [*Putting down the mirror casually on the table so that it covers the blotting paper*] It means she's a thief—like you.

ALBERT: Here!

LUCY: But she's taking an awful risk! There'll be the deuce to pay when Miss Fiske comes back.

ALBERT: Supposing she isn't coming back? Supposing she's died on her holiday? Supposing Aunt Ellen's the only one who knows?

LUCY: You can't die and only one person know.

ALBERT: No, you can't, can you? But somehow I don't think the old canary 'ud risk stealing from her unless she knew she wasn't coming back.

LUCY: And, I say! I've just thought of something!

ALBERT: What's that?

LUCY: When I was getting Miss Fiske's room ready for you this morning what d'you think I found tucked away in the cupboard?

ALBERT: What?

LUCY: Her best wig.

ALBERT: Oh? Did she wear a wig?

LUCY: Lord, yes. She was nearly bald. She looked a scream when you took in her morning cup of tea. Why didn't she take it with her? She rather fancies herself, you know. Why should she go away in her old one?

ALBERT: What about her clothes? Has she taken her best clothes?

LUCY: I never thought to look. But I couldn't have told. She's got chests full of dresses, and they're all locked.

ALBERT: When I get into the room we'll have a look. The locks won't worry me. And you can give me some idea what's missing.

LUCY: Why are you so curious about all this?

ALBERT: Supposing Miss Fiske *is* dead. Supposing Aunt Ellen *is* tapping the funds. It might be a lifetime before anyone finds out. Why should the old canary reap *all* the benefit? There might be some nice pickings in it for you and me. There might even be India or Australia in it—if we play our cards.

LUCY: You'd tempt Old Nick himself, wouldn't you?

ALBERT: You needn't help me if you don't want to. I can do it all on my own. But if I'm right, and I can pull it off, you might do worse than join forces with me. You don't dislike me, do you?

LUCY: I ought to.

ALBERT: But you don't. I don't dislike you either. I think you're one of the smartest little pieces I've set eyes on. [*He kisses her*]

LUCY: [*In a low voice*] I'll help.

ALBERT: Good girl.

LUCY: What do you want me to do?

ALBERT: I'll have to think out something.

LUCY: I don't want to do anything mean or underhand.

ALBERT: I wouldn't ask you, would I? But we've got to get proof.

You keep your peepers open. You watch. I'll watch. And keep your ears close to keyholes—listen.

LUCY: All right. There's plenty of chances 'cause they're always talking nineteen to the dozen.

ALBERT: Listen to Aunt Ellen. She's the one.

[A *hissing noise proceeds from the kitchen*]

LUCY: Beggar me! There's something boiling over! Come out with me. We can talk in the kitchen.

> [*They hurry off.* ELLEN *enters by the front door. She comes into the room, takes off her bonnet and lays it on the table. Then she sees the mirror. She picks it up, glances at it in a puzzled way and then sees the blotting paper.* ALBERT *and* LUCY *are heard laughing in the kitchen. She looks suspiciously toward the kitchen. Then she examines the blotting paper and, with a fierce exclamation, crumples it up and throws it in the fire*]

CURTAIN

ACT THREE

It is the following Wednesday night. The lamps are lighted and the fire is burning brightly. The curtains, however, are not drawn, and the moonlight streams through the windows. The candles in front of the Virgin are not lighted.

Sitting round the table are ALBERT, LOUISA *and* LUCY. *They are playing a game of three-handed cribbage. The cognac bottle and a glass are in front of* ALBERT. EMILY *is on the sofa with her beloved tray of shells on a little table in front of her. She is busy working.*

ALBERT: Now wait a minute, fifteen two, fifteen four, fifteen six and a pair's eight, sequence twelve and one for his nob thirteen. [*To* LOUISA] I'll have to take you down a peg, my charmer.

LOUISA: Oh, Albert, now I have caught you cheating. You've muddled up all the pegs and I've gone right down to the bottom again. I won't play any more. I don't mind a little cheating, but you mustn't cheat every time.

ALBERT: Now just one more go, my old bell of Bow.

LOUISA: Oh. What will you call me next? But I don't think we'd better play any more. Ellen will be back soon.

ALBERT: Frightened of being put in the corner? All right, you naughty girl. I'll take the blame. By the way, does anyone know where Aunt Ellen's been?

EMILY: She never tells us where she goes, we're nobody.

LOUISA: I think she's gone to Rochester on business.

ALBERT: What business?

LOUISA: I think it must be to buy something for the chickens to eat. Because there's not much left in their bin. And she said it was important.

EMILY: I don't think it had anything to do with chickens. She looked so determined.

LUCY: I should ask him for all your farthings back, Miss Louisa.

LOUISA: Albert, please give me back all my farthings.

ALBERT: [*Rattling the coppers*] All right, my darling. Here you are. I wouldn't rob you. I'll tell you what. I'll toss you double or quits.

LOUISA: I don't know what that means.

ALBERT: If you win, we're quits. If you lose, you pay me double. [*Tossing a coin*] Come on. Call.

EMILY: Don't, Louisa. He's up to no good.

LOUISA: What do I call?

ALBERT: Heads or tails.

LOUISA: Heads, then.

ALBERT: [*Looking at the coin: you can see from his face that he has really lost the toss*] Tails it is. You pay me double.

LOUISA: But I haven't got double. *You've* got all my farthings.

ALBERT: All right, auntie. We'll chalk it up. And in the meantime I'll loan you back your farthings at ten per cent per annum. [*He tips the coins into her lap*]

EMILY: You're too full of tricks, Albert. You'll be behind bars one day.

ALBERT: What's *your* name? Mrs. Job? And, as for bars, we're more or less behind 'em now, aren't we? I wonder why they're there. I suppose they've been up for hundreds of years.

LOUISA: Oh, no. They're quite new. Ellen put them there.

ALBERT: Did she, now? You don't say!

LUCY: My goodness! That reminds me. I've forgotten to shut up. [*She has risen and closes the curtains*]

EMILY: Ellen's afraid of someone breaking in.

ALBERT: [*Mock dramatically*] Perhaps she's a miser. Perhaps she comes down here in the middle of the night and counts her gold.

EMILY: She *does* come down here in the middle of the night. But I don't think she counts her gold.

LUCY: [*Still at the window*] Here's the cart. Here is Miss Ellen. I'll go and bring in her tray. [*She goes out into the kitchen. You hear the cart stopping*]

ALBERT: [*Opening the front door*] Hullo, aunt! Had a nice trip?

[ELLEN *enters. She is warmly wrapped up*]

ELLEN: It was bitterly cold.

ALBERT: Shall I take the driver out a glass of something?

ELLEN: [*Dryly*] Certainly. If it's not just an excuse for having one yourself.

ALBERT: [*Pouring out some cognac*] There's not enough for that. Aunt Louisa's swigged nearly the whole bottle.

LOUISA: Oh, Albert—you story! I haven't taken even a sip. I haven't been asked to.

ALBERT: [*Teasing her*] You wicked old gambler! [*You hear the cart begin to move away and he runs out of the front door with a tumbler*] Hi! Driver! Wait a minute!

ELLEN: [*Closing the front door*] What have you been doing?

LOUISA: Lucy came in and we played a game of crib. Of course Albert cheated. But it was rather fun watching him cheat.

ELLEN: I want you two to go up to bed. I want to speak to Albert alone.

EMILY: I don't want to go to bed.

ELLEN: Well, go up to your room anyway. [EMILY *begins to pack up her work very sullenly*] What have you been talking about while I've been out, Louisa?

LOUISA: Albert's been making us laugh.

ELLEN: He never talks to you, does he, about Miss Fiske?

LOUISA: Miss Fiske, Ellen? No! Why should he?

ELLEN: [*Searchingly*] And you've neither of you told him anything about my buying the house, have you?

LOUISA: Oh, no, Ellen! Don't you remember—you made us swear on the Bible we wouldn't?

ELLEN: [*Grimly*] I remember.

EMILY: But it wasn't the Bible, Ellen. Did you know that? It was a Roman Catholic prayer book. I found that out afterwards. So it doesn't count. We could tell who we liked, couldn't we?

ELLEN: [*Almost beside herself with nervous anger*] If I ever find out that either of you breathes a word to a soul about my buying the house I'll pack you both back to London straightaway. And I won't send you another penny!

LOUISA: [*Beginning to whimper*] Oh, Ellen!

EMILY: [*With an oblique glance*] I'm not going to tell anyone, Ellen.

[ALBERT *returns*]

LOUISA: Good night, Albert. We're going to bed. Ellen thinks it's time we went.

ALBERT: [*To* ELLEN] You've missed your vocation, auntie. You ought to have been a schoolmarm. Don't you put up with it, girls. Don't you let her bully you.

LOUISA: He *is* a tease, isn't he, Ellen?

ELLEN: [*With a direct look at* ALBERT] I'm beginning to think he's not quite so harmless as that.

EMILY: All the same, Albert's right. You *ought* to have been a schoolmarm, Ellen.

LOUISA: [*They are at the foot of the stairs now*] But it *is* nice having him here! Do you know what he called me? The old bell of Bow! [*She cackles with laughter*] It's out of that game we used to play when we were children. " 'When will you pay me?' said the bell of Old Bailey. 'I do not know,' said the old bell of Bow."

[*They disappear round the bend of the stairs.* ELLEN *comes to* ALBERT. *You can see that her manner to him has changed completely. She regards him as a dangerous enemy*]

ELLEN: You've been exciting them again. It's too bad of you. I can't trust you out of my sight.

ALBERT: [*Innocently*] Oh, auntie! What have *I* done?

ELLEN: I'm never sure *what* you may do.

ALBERT: There's not much I could do, is there? After all, this isn't a bank. You haven't got any locks to pick, have you?

[*Her lips set tightly.* LUCY *enters with a tray on which are a glass of milk and a plate of sandwiches*]

LUCY: I've brought your supper, miss.

ELLEN: Put it down on the table. And then you can go to bed, Lucy. I'm just going up to wash and take off my things. And wait here, Albert. I've got something to say to you. [*She goes brusquely up the stairs*]

ALBERT: She's on the rampage tonight. There's a nasty look in her eye.

LUCY: Wonder where she's been all day?

ALBERT: I asked the driver. He picked her up at Rochester off the London train.

LUCY: London? Has she been to London?

ALBERT: Yes. I can't understand it. She'd no call to go rushing up there seeing that that fifty pounds came through from the bank yesterday. You're sure that's what that registered letter was?

LUCY: I told you. It was a bank envelope. I took it in. I signed for it. Then I watched her through the crack of the door. She took out the bundle of notes and counted 'em twice very carefully. There were ten of them.

ALBERT: Ten five pound notes. I wonder if she means to do a bolt. There's nothing for it, Lucy. We'll have to try out that plan of mine tonight.

LUCY: But supposing it doesn't come off?

ALBERT: Then there's no harm done, is there?

LUCY: I keep telling you, Albert. I don't like it. It's risky. It might lose me my place.

ALBERT: Don't be silly. I'll see you through. I'll take all the blame. I'll say it was just a practical joke of mine to scare the old girls. There's no reason why she shouldn't swallow that. She knows I'm always codding them. I shall be with you. I'll tell you when to come in. Now, you will be a darling and go through with this for me, Lucy, won't you?

LUCY: [*Coming to him affectionately*] I can't refuse you anything —now, can I?

ALBERT: [*Lightly*] You're a daisy. You'll be all right. All you've got to do is to keep thinking of when we'll be married.

LUCY: You'll never go back on me, will you? You're not just making use of me?

ALBERT: I've told you. I'm mad about you. [*Softly*] Haven't I shown you? [*Then quickly*] Sssh. She's coming down. You get to your room. [*She scurries out.* ELLEN *comes downstairs. There is a look on her face which shows she is ready to give battle. Jauntily*] Well, auntie, where's your cane? From the way you spoke I thought you were going to take down my breeches and give me a dozen.

ELLEN: Don't you wish you *could* pay for your misdeeds that way?

ALBERT: You take me too seriously, you know. Half the time I'm only fooling.

ELLEN: One has to take a thief seriously.

ALBERT: [*With a shrug*] Oh, come, auntie! We don't want to go all over that again, do we? I'm not proud of myself. [*With a swift glance*] We're all miserable sinners, aren't we? You used to tell me that often enough when I was a little boy. I'm not going about in sackcloth and ashes for the rest of my life!

ELLEN: [*Beginning to toy with her supper*] I've been to London today.

ALBERT: [*With interest*] Have you? Why didn't you tell us? You *are* a dark horse. What, have you been on a spree?

ELLEN: No. I've been on your account. I've been to a shipping company.

ALBERT: [*Wide-eyed*] A shipping company—on *my* account?

ELLEN: Yes. I've bought your passage to Canada.

ALBERT: [*Up in arms*] But I don't want to go to Canada.

ELLEN: [*Coldly*] I don't think you've very much choice, have you?

ALBERT: [*Half-jauntily this time*] I'm quite happy here for the time being.

ELLEN: [*Very directly*] I'm not quite happy having you here.

ALBERT: But I thought we'd agreed. I was to lie low till the Gravesend business blew over. Time enough for a passage abroad in a month or so.

ELLEN: I've changed my mind.

ALBERT: Well, I think you might have discussed it with me first.

ELLEN: I didn't see any need. I'm paying the piper.

ALBERT: But what's made you change your mind?

ELLEN: Well, in the first place, you play the fool so much with

Louisa and Emily that you'll have them chattering about your being here. And you know what that'll mean. The wrong sort of word to the tradesmen or the nuns and we shall have the police down on us. And I can't do with any scandal here.

ALBERT: [*Protestingly*] Oh, but isn't that a bit thin? They're not very difficult to keep an eye on.

ELLEN: You forget Emily goes for long walks. You don't know who she talks to.

ALBERT: But surely there's more to it than that, auntie? There *must* be!

ELLEN: Yes. There's Lucy. She's even more dangerous than your aunts.

ALBERT: Oh, Lucy won't give me away.

ELLEN: [*Catching at this*] Are you in a position to be sure?

ALBERT: [*Very surprised*] What do you mean?

ELLEN: You know well enough what I mean. You wouldn't mind adding Lucy to your conquests, would you?

ALBERT: [*With exaggerated innocence*] It never so much as occurred to me. I've hardly noticed the girl.

ELLEN: Don't lie, Albert. I've watched you whispering together. I saw the way you eyed her the first evening you came. I've seen her setting her cap at you ever since. I'm not going to have that sort of thing going on under my roof!

ALBERT: Well, all I can say, auntie, is—it must be your mind. We're as innocent as the driven snow.

ELLEN: [*With suppressed rage*] You hateful little hypocrite!

ALBERT: Can't one have a joke and a bit of a lark with a girl without being accused of ruining her?

ELLEN: [*Sharply*] I never said you'd ruined her. Have you? Am I a little behindhand in sending you away?

ALBERT: [*Protesting once more*] Now, look here. If you go on talking to me like this, I shall get quite cross. I'm doing my best to keep my temper as it is.

ELLEN: [*Contemptuous*] *Your* temper! You can't pull wool over *my* eyes, Albert! Now, listen. You'll start tomorrow. I'm coming with you. Bates will be here directly after breakfast.

ALBERT: [*Now thoroughly alarmed*] But I daren't go up to London! I might be recognized.

ELLEN: You're not going to London. Bates will drive us to Maidstone. Then we'll make our way across country by coach to Southampton. There's a boat leaving for Quebec on Friday. I've got your ticket. I've got everything.

ALBERT: [*Grumblingly*] By Jove, you *are* a hard woman, auntie.

ELLEN: Perhaps I am. Perhaps circumstances have made me so. And you haven't helped to make me any softer.

ALBERT: I don't know why you're suddenly so down on me.

ELLEN: [*Quietly, but with great bitterness*] I've got to know you better. I've watched you very carefully the last few days. You're not a bit sorry for what you've done. You haven't shown a spark of gratitude to me. You're thoroughly callous. You've demoralized your aunts. Goodness knows what harm you've done to that young girl. You've nosed about the house and spied on everybody. If I hadn't put my cashbox in a very secure place I'm quite sure your light fingers would have found a way to it. And I'm saying this to my sister's son!

ALBERT: [*Half-whimpering*] You *are* full of the milk of human kindness, aren't you? I suppose you realize I've never had a chance —brought up as I was. It's not my fault if I'm ambitious.

ELLEN: [*Scornfully*] Ambitious!

ALBERT: Yes. Ambitious. I don't want to be downed all my life— with other people's footmarks all over me. I want to be on top. And I'm going to be!

ELLEN: Well, you're not going to climb there on *my* shoulders! I've made up my mind, and it's no use arguing with me. You're going out of this house before you're a day older.

ALBERT: [*Plucking up his courage*] I see. That's what you think. Does it occur to you that I may not go?

ELLEN: Well, I can't throw you out physically, but I can always send for the police.

ALBERT: Somehow I'd got the impression you didn't want the police here.

ELLEN: Does that mean you refuse to go?

ALBERT: Well, I certainly shan't go tomorrow morning. [*He sits on the settle with his pipe between his lips*]

ELLEN: I'm afraid you'll have to.

ALBERT: No. On second thoughts I'm quite content to stay for the time being. I'm getting fond of the place. The air suits me. You can't bluff me, you know.

ELLEN: [*Angrily*] I'm not bluffing you, Albert. I'm ordering you to go!

ALBERT: Order—my foot! I'll tell you what I think of your reasons for wanting me out of the house. Bunkum.

ELLEN: What do you mean?

ALBERT: There's another you haven't mentioned, isn't there? A sounder one.

ELLEN: [*Facing up to the issue*] Yes. There is.

ALBERT: Ah, now we're getting down to brass tacks! It's about Miss Fiske, isn't it?

ELLEN: Yes, it is. [*Quite naturally*] I met her in town today. She's coming back.

ALBERT: [*Absolutely staggered*] You met her in town, you say?

ELLEN: Yes. Why shouldn't I?

ALBERT: [*Nonplused*] No reason.

ELLEN: [*Watching him closely*] I had to take her some money that came for her.

ALBERT: I'd got it into my head that she'd gone for good.

ELLEN: Who gave you that idea? It's her house. There's never been any question of her not coming back.

ALBERT: Well, in that case, why spend the last half hour abusing me? Why not tell me straightaway I'd got to go because she was coming back?

ELLEN: I didn't want you to know anything about it.

ALBERT: Why not?

ELLEN: You're such a chatterbox. You'd go blurting it out to your aunts. And it would be fatal if they got to know about it now. Because—don't you see?—it means that they've got to go, too. They'll be dreadfully upset about it. You know what they are. And I shall have to break it to them very gently.

ALBERT: [*Almost convinced*] Oh, well—there's nothing for it, then.

My little country holiday has obviously come to an end. I'll have to thank you for your loving care, auntie, and kiss you good-bye. I don't know what the blazes I'll do in Canada. But I suppose one can starve there as well as anywhere else.

ELLEN: I shall give you something to start on. I can't do less—for Rose's sake. I've no doubt you'll pick up a living somehow. There's a bit of the Greek in you, Albert. He thrives where the Jew starves, you know.

ALBERT: I'll do my best to deserve your good opinion, auntie. And I suppose I ought to be grateful.

ELLEN: I'm not asking for that.

ALBERT: Well, I'd better get some sleep, hadn't I? I'm going to have a tiring day tomorrow. [*He has risen. A sudden thought strikes him, and while closely watching her, he knocks out his pipe on the bake-oven door. The tap-tap of the wood on the metal sounds extraordinarily sinister. It is as if somebody inside were knocking.* ELLEN *rises with a little shudder.* ALBERT *comes forward*] Do we kiss good night?

ELLEN: No.

ALBERT: [*Looking into her drawn face*] I say! You're looking rather played out. Hadn't you better toddle off, too?

ELLEN: [*With an effort*] I'm just coming. I've got to lock up.

[*She locks the front door.* ALBERT *goes to the stairway. Then he turns*]

ALBERT: Oh, I forgot to tell you. I had a funny dream last night, auntie.

ELLEN: [*Turning to him*] What was that?

ALBERT: I dreamt Miss Fiske was dead.

ELLEN: [*Facing him coolly*] Oh? [*He goes upstairs.* ELLEN *stands alone, her face working. Then she crosses and kneels for a moment on the prie-dieu in an attitude of agonized supplication. It is indeed the revelation of a soul in torment. She is shaken with half-suppressed sobs. After a moment she rises from her knees, turns out one lamp and takes up the other, and then goes upstairs leaving the stairway door open behind her. The only light in the room is the dim glow of the fire. The grandfather clock strikes eleven. Then* ALBERT *appears coming softly down the stairs in his stockinged feet with a lighted candle. He goes to the hearth, and you see him fiddling with the bake-oven door, though you are not quite certain what he is doing. Then he leaves it, tiptoes to the kitchen door, which he opens, and whistles softly. He comes to the piano, sits at it and plays the "Tit-Willow" tune. As he finishes he hears something, and rising from the piano, slips into the kitchen. Then* ELLEN *appears on the stairs carrying a lighted night light in a Victorian night light holder. She comes into the room, holding it up. Her face is haggard]* Albert! Was that you? *[There is no answer. She goes to the hearth and shines her light on the bake-oven door. You see that it is open and the bricked-up wall is showing. You can see, too, what an effect this discovery has upon her. She crosses the room to the front door, throws it open and the moonlight streams in. She turns toward the piano and there, as the moonlight falls across the room, she sees the figure of* LEONORA FISKE *seated at the keys; her head is bent, but her auburn wig, her violet dress and her green shawl are unmistakable. The figure makes a deliberate movement and, as it rises,* ELLEN *gives a gasping scream of "Leonora" and falls to the ground in a faint, or fit.* LUCY *advances tremblingly to the prostrate* ELLEN]

LUCY: *Albert! Albert!*

CURTAIN

SCENE 2

It is nine o'clock the next morning—a clear, sunny day. The room is empty. The bake-oven door is shut. As the curtain rises the clock is striking. A knocking at the front door breaks into this, and LUCY *crosses the room from the kitchen to open it. She goes out onto the porch.*

LUCY: Good morning, Mr. Bates. Oh, are you ordered?

BATES' VOICE: Miss Creed ordered me. It's for Maidstone.

LUCY: I don't think she's very well this morning, but I'll see. *[She returns to the room, half-closing the door]*

[ALBERT *enters from the kitchen, has napkin to his mouth*]

ALBERT: Who is it?

LUCY: It's Bates. He says he's got to go to Maidstone.

ALBERT: Oh, no, he hasn't. Tell him the order's canceled.

LUCY: But, Albert . . .

ALBERT: Do what I tell you. [*He stands listening as* LUCY *returns to the porch, and you hear—*]

LUCY: Miss Creed's very sorry, Mr. Bates, but she won't be wanting you this morning after all. She's poorly.

BATES: Nothing serious, I hope?

LUCY: Oh, no, nothing serious.

BATES: Then I'll be gettin' along. 'Tween you and me I'm not sorry. I've gotter go kill a pig.

LUCY: Good morning. [*She returns as the cart moves away*]

ALBERT: [*With a jerk of his thumb toward upstairs*] No sign of her yet?

LUCY: No. She *did* look ill when I took in her early tea. Albert, I'm scared. I wish I knew if she thought it was me dressed up.

ALBERT: Of course she didn't. She doesn't know it was you any more than the man in the moon. She thinks she saw a ghost.

LUCY: All the same, I can't help wishing we hadn't done it—now. I never thought she'd take it so badly and go and faint. She might have died. Then we'd have been responsible.

ALBERT: You pull yourself together. She didn't die. She's very much alive. And we proved what we wanted, didn't we?

LUCY: Yes. I suppose we did.

ALBERT: We've proved that Miss Fiske's dead, and she knows it.

LUCY: But what puzzles me is—how *could* Miss Fiske die and she be the only one to know it?

ALBERT: [*Cunningly*] Don't you see—Miss Fiske may have died on her holiday—in some lonely place? And Aunt Ellen may have had her buried and said nothing about it?

LUCY: [*Struck*] I see . . .

ALBERT: And don't you see—that gives us a strong pull? If I'm right, she'll have to cough up what we want.

LUCY: I can't go on with it. It frightens me.

ALBERT: You haven't got to. You've only got to help me. I'm doing it all. And, when we've lined our pockets, we'll take a little trip and have a look at the world. We two, eh? Like that, won't you?

LUCY: I shall have it on my conscience for the rest of my life.

[LOUISA *enters from the kitchen*]

LOUISA: Albert, your tea's getting cold, dear. What have you been doing?

ALBERT: Lucy and I've been having a chat with old Bates. He's been telling us all the news of the outside world.

LOUISA: [*Eagerly*] Oh, Albert, do tell me!

ALBERT: It'll tickle you to death. Weeping whiskers are coming in again.

[LUCY *goes into the kitchen*]

LOUISA: [*Laughing*] Oh, Albert! Get along with you! You're never serious. I don't know whether we ought to be laughing—with Ellen so ill upstairs.

ALBERT: Of course you oughtn't. You're very wicked, Aunt Louisa.

[EMILY *enters from the kitchen. She carries a plate of stale bread. She puts this on the piano and stands there crumbling it*]

EMILY: Aren't you going to finish your breakfast, Albert?

ALBERT: No, I've had enough. I'm a bit off my pecker this morning.

EMILY: That means it'll be wasted. You shouldn't have kept him, Louisa.

ALBERT: Don't blame the old bell of Bow, Aunt Emily. [*To* LOUISA] It's not your fault if you're so fetching, is it, my puss?

LOUISA: Isn't he ridiculous, Emily?

EMILY: He's making a fool of you, Louisa. He's making a fool of all of us. I believe he could make a fool of Ellen if he tried.

ALBERT: A fool of Aunt Ellen, Aunt Emily? Oh, no. It would take someone much cleverer than me to do that. [*At the stairs*] Well, I'm going upstairs to cut my throat. [*He goes*]

[LOUISA *follows him to the foot of the stairs*]

LOUISA: What did you say, Albert? [*To* EMILY, *in distress*] Oh, what does he mean, Emily?

EMILY: [*Crumbling her bread*] You're so simple, Louisa. He's going to shave. He thought he was being funny. Stupid boy.

LOUISA: Why are you always so against everybody, Emily?

EMILY: I'm not against everybody.

LOUISA: Yes, you are. You're against Albert. You'd be against Ellen, if you dared. I expect you're against me—only you don't say so.

EMILY: I don't take all that notice of you.

LOUISA: [*Mysteriously*] I know something about you. I know you were frightened about Ellen last night. I've never seen anyone so frightened.

EMILY: Everybody was frightened.

LOUISA: What do you think was the matter with her? Why did she faint like that? It wasn't like Ellen. Ellen doesn't faint.

EMILY: I think she was walking in her sleep. I've heard her go downstairs on other nights. I think her thoughts of Miss Fiske are at the back of it.

LOUISA: [*Nodding*] Yes, Miss Fiske. She's behind everything in this house, isn't she? I've always hated her.

EMILY: Perhaps she hates us.

LOUISA: Do you know, Emily, I'm sometimes so afraid that Miss Fiske will get the better of Ellen? I sometimes think she wants to come back and turn us out.

EMILY: I don't think she ever sold the house to Ellen. I think Ellen's deceiving us. I think Miss Fiske's here now.

LOUISA: Oh, Emily, you frighten me! Why do you say that?

EMILY: Didn't you hear it?

LOUISA: Hear what?

EMILY: The piano—last night. That was Miss Fiske's music. Her silly tune. "Tit-Willow, Tit-Willow."

LOUISA: You heard it, too? I heard it. I thought it was in a dream. In my head.

> [ELLEN *comes downstairs. She looks wan and ill. But her intense agony of mind gives her a certain fineness, almost a greatness. She carries her cloak and bonnet and a reticule*]

ELLEN: What are you two whispering about?

LOUISA: Oh, Ellen! You've come down! Do you think you're well enough?

ELLEN: It's all right, darling. I'm quite strong again.

EMILY: You'd better have the doctor.

ELLEN: A doctor couldn't do any good. It's nothing.

LOUISA: But, Ellen, you walked in your sleep last night.

ELLEN: I wasn't asleep, Louisa. I wasn't even undressed. I knew what I was doing. I thought I heard someone moving about the house.

EMILY: But then, if you were wide awake, Ellen, why did you scream?

ELLEN: I thought I saw someone. But it turned out to be nobody.

LOUISA: It's funny you should have thought you saw someone. Because Emily and I thought we heard someone.

ELLEN: Who did you think you heard?

EMILY: Miss Fiske.

LOUISA: We thought we heard her at the piano. She was playing that sad little song about the willow tree. You remember how she was always playing it?

ELLEN: I remember.

EMILY: I thought it might have been Albert up to one of his tricks. But he was upstairs all the time. Because I heard him come up and go into his room—before you.

LOUISA: It *is* strange, isn't it, Ellen?

ELLEN: [*Wearily*] There's no point in going on talking about it.

EMILY: You'd better let me sleep in your room tonight, Ellen. In case you walk in your sleep again.

ELLEN: I've told you I wasn't asleep.

EMILY: But you often walk about in the night, Ellen. Perhaps you don't know it, but you do. People don't know it when they walk in their sleep.

ELLEN: I've been a little worried since Albert's been here. He's so unreliable. Why, he might take it into his head to go for a walk in the middle of the night and leave the door open! You never know what he may do.

EMILY: But you started walking about in the night long before Albert came, Ellen.

ELLEN: Oh, no, I didn't, Emily. You know you never remember things right.

EMILY: [*Resentfully*] Very well. [*She takes up her plate of crumbled bread*]

LOUISA: Where are you going?

EMILY: I'm going down to the Priory to feed the jackdaws. I put out my crusts along the top of the wall and they come down from the tower and take them.

LOUISA: Oh, I *should* like to see them, Emily!

EMILY: They won't come if you're there. You're all chatter, chatter, chatter.

LOUISA: Oh, Emily.

ELLEN: Take her with you please, Emily. [*She is now on the sofa*] I'd like to sit here alone.

EMILY: Well, you'll have to keep very quiet. Do you understand?

LOUISA: Yes, Emily. I'll be as still as a statue. I won't move or speak at all. And, oh, Emily, I think I'll take my telescope and I'll watch the ships while you're waiting for your jackdaws and I can describe them to you.

EMILY: [*Going out the front door*] Chatter, chatter, chatter.

> [LOUISA *follows her, carrying her telescope, and the front door shuts.* LUCY *enters*]

LUCY: Oh, are you down, miss? Are you better?

ELLEN: [*Lying back on the sofa*] Yes, thank you, Lucy.

LUCY: I'm so glad. Can I get you a cup of tea or anything?

ELLEN: No. I've got to go out in a minute. Bates ought to be here now. Go and see if there's any sign of him.

LUCY: Bates? But he's been and gone, miss!

ELLEN: Been and gone?

LUCY: Yes, miss. Mr. Albert sent him away. He thought you were too poorly to get up.

ELLEN: Where is Mr. Albert?

LUCY: I don't know where he's gone, miss. He's had his breakfast.

ELLEN: Try and find him, and tell him I want him.

LUCY: Yes, miss.

[LUCY goes to stairs—motions to ALBERT to come in. She exits as ALBERT comes softly downstairs. He is carrying a wig-block on which is LEONORA's auburn wig, but he conceals it from ELLEN by keeping it on the far side of him. He closes the door very gently and, coming forward, places the wig-block on the piano. Then he stands between it and his aunt. She does not realize he is there till he speaks]

ALBERT: *[Cheerily]* Good morning, Aunt Ellen. We didn't expect you down today.

ELLEN: Well, you were wrong. Is that why you sent Bates away?

ALBERT: Partly.

ELLEN: What do you mean by interfering with my arrangements? When you said good night to me last night you'd quite accepted the idea of going to Canada.

ALBERT: You're forgetting, auntie. That was the *first* time we said good night. When we said good night a second time you weren't in any shape to be jolted to Maidstone in the morning.

ELLEN: That was nothing. Only a little faintness. Well, you'll have to get hold of Bates somehow. We'll go tomorrow instead. You're going to catch that boat. You understand that?

ALBERT: I hear what you say.

ELLEN: They tell me you were very good to me last night. I'd like to say "thank you."

ALBERT: Oh, that was only nephewly feeling. Besides, we must take care of the goose that lays the golden eggs, mustn't we?

ELLEN: What d'you mean?

ALBERT: Well, that's what you are, aren't you? You're very valuable to all of us.

ELLEN: *[Bitterly]* I suppose I am. I've always had to provide. That's been my life—in one word. Provide.

ALBERT: It was a queer turn you had. What actually happened?

ELLEN: I don't know. I must have had some kind of nervous seizure.

ALBERT: Yes, I'd noticed you seemed a bit nervy.

ELLEN: It's because I haven't been sleeping.

ALBERT: That's a thing I can't understand, you know. Not sleeping. I sleep like a top. I expect you'd say that's because I haven't got a conscience to worry me!

ELLEN: Do you imagine my not sleeping has anything to do with conscience?

ALBERT: [*Cocking his head on one side*] Hasn't it?

ELLEN: What's behind that remark, Albert?

ALBERT: Nothing. [*With a change of tone*] Auntie, I've got a little confession to make.

ELLEN: [*Startled: she is now sitting up*] What! Another?

ALBERT: Yes. I've deceived you. It's been on my mind for some time, but I've kept forgetting.

ELLEN: [*Watching him closely*] What is it?

ALBERT: Don't get cross, will you? You were away last June fetching your sisters, weren't you? Well, I called here. And I met Miss Fiske.

ELLEN: [*Her eyes never leaving him*] Oh?

ALBERT: Yes. She was very kind to me. I quite took to her. I was a bit short at the time and she lent me some ready. Out of her little safe there, you know. The one that's bricked-up now. We agreed not to tell you. We thought it might worry you. But now I think you ought to know. [*Taking out his pipe*] Do you mind if I smoke, or would it upset you?

> [*He strolls to the far side of the piano, disclosing, by doing so, the wig on the wig-block.* ELLEN *stares at it. There is a pause. It is as though the missing woman had suddenly come into the room.* ELLEN *rises, still staring at it.* ALBERT *watches her cunningly*]

ELLEN: [*With a sort of slow horror*] You know . . . ?

ALBERT: [*Lightly*] Aha.

ELLEN: It was *you* last night, too.

ALBERT: [*Nodding, laconically*] Me and Lucy.

ELLEN: Lucy?

ALBERT: It's all right. I took care she didn't know what *I* know.

ELLEN: And I gave you sanctuary!

ALBERT: [*Shrewdly*] It wasn't yours to give, was it?

ELLEN: [*Bracing herself to seem almost casual*] Well, now you know —what are you going to do?

ALBERT: Do? Nothing. You've told me nothing. I know nothing.

ELLEN: But you—you want something?

ALBERT: Oh, yes. I want something. You know, auntie, I always had a fancy to settle in the country.

ELLEN: You don't mean—*here?*

ALBERT: Why not? I could help you keep an eye on—things. I shan't lose *my* nerve. Oh—and I shall want a little wedding present. I may have to marry Lucy. We shall be a very happy little family here, shan't we? How long do you think it'll last?

ELLEN: How long will what last?

ALBERT: Her money.

ELLEN: I see. So you've come to the conclusion that it's safer to be a receiver than a thief?

ALBERT: They're both safer than being a—but don't let's call each other names, auntie. That won't get us anywhere.

ELLEN: Is there anything else you'd like?

ALBERT: No. That'll do to go on with.

ELLEN: Then I think it's about time you went out and ordered Bates—at once.

ALBERT: You're a cool one, aren't you? Barring little incidents like last night, of course. I take off my hat to you.

ELLEN: I think *you're* rather brave, too, Albert.

ALBERT: Oh, no, not brave, auntie. Just cunning.

ELLEN: You surely don't propose to go on living here—with *me?*

ALBERT: Why not?

ELLEN: [*With superb irony*] Well, for one thing, you'd never be quite sure, would you? There are more ways than one, you know.

ALBERT: [*In amazement*] You wouldn't dare—a second time.

ELLEN: What makes you so sure?

ALBERT: [*Daunted in spite of himself*] Supposing I said I'd risk it?

ELLEN: You won't. Now that I've frightened you. You've got a very good appetite, haven't you, Albert? And you'd hardly be likely to enjoy your meals.

ALBERT: Easy on, aunt. I can see through you. You're bluffing.

ELLEN: Am I? D'you think I'm going to let a little thing like you stand in my way? It takes a lot of courage to kill for the first time. [*In a whisper*] But once you've sold your soul to the devil it comes easier. [*There is a pause. He watches her, fascinated*] I think you know why I did—what I did. I did it to secure to my poor sisters a little of what the world owes them. They're all I have. They're my children. They were left in my care. I think you know what I've suffered. You've seen me in torment. You've helped to torture me. But don't think I'm going to hand over what I've . . . taken to a little whippersnapper who's repaid my kindness with cheap treachery.

ALBERT: [*Thinking better of it*] Very good. What's it worth to you if I do order Bates and clear out? When all's said, we're both after the same thing—cash—aren't we?

ELLEN: I told you last night what I'd give you.

ALBERT: I'll take five hundred. And the old girl's earrings for Lucy.

ELLEN: No.

ALBERT: Well, forget the earrings, then.

ELLEN: You're wasting your breath.

ALBERT: You wouldn't like me to suggest to the police that they come and do a bit of renovating to your chimneypiece, would you?

ELLEN: I don't quite see you going to the police.

ALBERT: Oh, they'd forget what I've done—if I went and told 'em [*He is back at the piano and fondles* LEONORA's *false curls*] that the head that wore this hasn't any more use for a wig.

ELLEN: No, Albert—you've chosen the wrong moment. It's broad daylight—now.

> [*There is a sudden quick rapping at the door. Both are electrified for a moment. Then* ALBERT *snatches the antimacassar from the sofa and adroitly flings it over the wig-block.* ELLEN *opens the door.* SISTER THERESA *enters*]

THERESA: Oh, I'm sorry if I'm interrupting, but I wanted to see you, Miss Creed, if I could; and I particularly didn't want to disturb the others.

ELLEN: Yes, Sister? Good morning. What can I do?

THERESA: [*As she sees* ALBERT] I'm glad your nephew's here. It's really no business of mine and I oughtn't to have come. But we've just had a call at the Priory—from the police. They've driven over from Gravesend.

ALBERT: [*Alert and alarmed*] Gravesend?

THERESA: [*Significantly*] Yes. I heard them talking to the Reverend Mother. They're looking for a young man who's supposed to have taken money from a bank. He's been traced to the marshes. They gave a very complete description of him, and it tallied so closely with your nephew that I thought I'd come and let you know. Of course, if I *knew* it was your nephew, it would be very wrong of me to warn you.

ALBERT: Did the Reverend Mother say I was here?

THERESA: She doesn't know. I'm the only one at the Priory who does. She told them that, at the moment, there were simply three elderly ladies living at Estuary House. And, of course, so far as she knew, that was the truth. So the officers have gone down to the marsh—to Decoy Farm. But I thought I ought to come up and tell you because Miss Fiske's such a great mutual friend. I know she would like me to.

ALBERT: Well, on her behalf, old lady, thanks for the tip.

THERESA: It *was* you? I was afraid so. I'm so sorry.

ALBERT: So am I, but we can't go into that now. I've got to look slippy. Got any cash handy, auntie?

ELLEN: Yes. [*She gives him her reticule*] You can take this. It hasn't what you wanted in it, but it's not empty.

ALBERT: Oh—thanks. If I write you can send on the rest. So long, Sister. No hard feelings, aunt. [*Significantly*] And remember—there's nothing to worry about. This sees you right.

ELLEN: You'll find your ticket in there, too.

ALBERT: Good! I'll get that boat somehow. I'd better slip out the back way and through the woods. [*As an afterthought*] Er—tell Lucy. [*He goes*]

THERESA: I had a brother rather like that. They're so easily lost, aren't they?

ELLEN: Albert was born without a conscience. That's all.

THERESA: It's very sad. Perhaps this will be a lesson to him. I hope he gets away. I'm afraid that's why I came. Was it very wrong of me?

ELLEN: I'm not a very good judge of what's right or wrong; but I'm afraid, in Albert's case, it's only postponing the evil day.

THERESA: Oh, well, you know—postponement's life.

ELLEN: Is it? Yes, I suppose, in the case of the little sinner, it is. But if one has sinned *very* deeply, postponement can be death. It can be worse than death.

THERESA: Oh? I suppose you're talking of what they call—the Death-in-Life?

ELLEN: Do they call it that?

THERESA: But it doesn't apply to your nephew. He's young. He may change. I suppose I'm rather simple-minded. We're always praying to be delivered from evil. And I find it so difficult to believe that it exists. I suppose that's why I've never got any higher in my order. I haven't enough faith. You'll please not tell anyone I came, will you?

ELLEN: Thank you for coming. Thank you for warning us. [THERESA *goes.* ELLEN *goes into the kitchen calling "Lucy, Lucy!" Lucy enters from the stairway door. Her face is white and horror-struck. You realize at once that she has been following* ALBERT'S *advice and listening. She makes for the front door.* ELLEN *returns from the kitchen*] Lucy! Where are you going? [LUCY *turns but she cannot answer. She stands facing her mistress*] Come here. I've something to tell you. [*There is a pause.* LUCY *does not move*] It's about Mr. Albert. [*Still* LUCY *does not answer. Then* ELLEN *speaks in a vibrant tone*] Have you been listening? [*She steps toward her. Then* LUCY *screams. It is a wild terrified scream. She recovers the power of movement and turns and rushes out the front door.* ELLEN *follows, calling "Lucy! Lucy!" But* LUCY *has gone like the wind.* ELLEN *comes back into the room. She has her hand to her heart. She leans on the head of the sofa for support. Then she says in a whisper*] The Death-in-Life . . . [*With an effort she begins, very deliberately, to put on her cloak and bonnet.* LOUISA *and* EMILY *enter by the front door*]

LOUISA: It's quite warm out, Ellen. You wouldn't think it was November. We fed the jackdaws. But they wouldn't come down on the wall till we went away.

EMILY: [*She has in her hand a little bunch of black feathers*] That's because Louisa would chatter.

LOUISA: [*Placing her telescope back on the dresser*] I was telling her about the ships. [*Noticing* ELLEN'S *bonnet*] Why, Ellen, where are you going?

ELLEN: Out.

LOUISA: Oh! As we were coming up the lane we met Lucy. She was running so fast. We thought there was something the matter. We really thought she must be coming to fetch us. But she climbed over the stile and ran down the path toward that farm on the marsh. [*Coming to the table where* EMILY *is toying with the feathers*] What's it called, Emily?

EMILY: I told you—Decoy Farm.

ELLEN: [*Putting on her cloak*] Decoy Farm. That's right. That's where I'm going.

LOUISA: Why are you going there, Ellen?

ELLEN: There are some gentlemen there—from Gravesend. I want to see them.

LOUISA: Gravesend? Oh, are they friends of Albert's?

ELLEN: No, darling. Nothing to do with Albert. It's a personal matter.

LOUISA: You won't bring them here, will you, Ellen? It's so nice and peaceful by ourselves.

ELLEN: No. I'll try not to bring them here. [*She stands watching the two old simpletons playing with their feathers. It is rather moving*] You *have* been happy here, haven't you?

LOUISA: We *are* happy, Ellen. Aren't we, Emily?

EMILY: It's much better than London—certainly.

LOUISA: And it's so good of you to have bought this house for us. [*Looking up gratefully*] You *have* been clever! [ELLEN *moves to the front door*] How long will you be?

ELLEN: I don't know, darling. I may be quite a time. [*She is standing in the sunlight and says with a sudden smile*] Oh—it's a lovely day.

LOUISA: We can look after ourselves. Can't we, Emily?

EMILY: Yes. We can look after ourselves.

> [ELLEN *goes out of the house. The two old ladies, happily occupied in themselves, are at the table fingering the black feathers. There is a short pause, and then:*]

THE CURTAIN SLOWLY FALLS

Seven Keys
to Baldpate

A MYSTERIOUS
MELODRAMATIC FARCE

GEORGE M. COHAN

Based on the novel by Earl Derr Biggers

George M. Cohan

One of the most prolific men in the history of the American theatre, George M. Cohan served the stage in many capacities: as author, composer, lyricist, producer, director, and performer. One of his most enduring successes was, and continues to be, *Seven Keys to Baldpate*, a mystery farce he fashioned from the novel by Earl Derr Biggers and which played for 320 performances in its initial Broadway season (1913). It not only was a substantial success in New York, but was successfully played in other cities, made into a popular film, and to this day it has been fair game for summer stock revivals and amateur societies.

While Cohan publicly acknowledged that "it stands for nothing but pure entertainment and a sort of comedy kidding of the technique of melodramatic thrillers," a number of critics and colleagues credited *Seven Keys to Baldpate* with breaking new ground in the field of playwriting. Clayton Hamilton, the distinguished author and critic, advised his *Vogue* readers in 1913 that "no student of stagecraft can afford to miss this play," a view apparently shared by George Middleton, a prominent writer of the day and one of the founders of The Dramatists Guild. On the occasion of The Players' 1935 all-star revival of the play, Middleton wrote in *The Stage* magazine: "*Baldpate*, besides being a popular mystery melodrama, marked a contribution to the technique of playmaking. It was, I believe, the first substantial stage success to apply throughout the same technique which a novelist gives to a mystery story. The audience was constantly being fooled, tricked, mocked, abused, rolled up, and finally thrown, exhausted by melodramatic thrills, into a corner, where it recovered its sanity by convulsions of laughter at the solution. Moods and tenses were mixed in as potent a cocktail as any dramatist ever shook, with added irregularities of dramatic forms and fancies. In other words, there had been nothing quite like it before. I am confident that no other play so influenced the manner of writing a mystery play—so difficult because it is all visual and can make no prose comments en route, as the novelist can, to trick the suspense or bedevil the observer."

Since 1913, of course, mystery and suspense plays have matured and in the process have taken on greater refinements and wider dimensions, notably in the area of characterizations-in-depth and credibility. Yet, in its time, according to Middleton, "Cohan's short, highly concentrated scenes, stripped to essentials, his disregard for the habitual motivations in taking people on and off the stage, and his extremely exhilarated tempos also anticipated the movies and influenced all stage writing. In fact, in the rush, tons of useless stage impedimenta were dropped forever."

One interesting episode in the history of *Seven Keys to Baldpate* could not possibly have been anticipated by Cohan: through accident, he would be the first actor to perform its principal part before the public. The occurrence took place in September, 1913, when the play was scheduled for a trial engagement at Parsons Theatre in Hartford, Connecticut. On the way to the theatre, the automobile in which Cohan and the play's star, Wallace Eddinger, were occcupants "unexpectedly argued with a farmer's wagon and all were thrown out —Eddinger out of the cast into the hospital and Cohan into the principal role, in splints." The opening, consequently, was saved by Cohan who went on for the first two performances.

Twenty-two years later, Cohan was to enact the same role for the first time in New York in the outstanding revival presented by The Players, a leading theatrical club founded in 1888 with its headquarters in the Gramercy Park home of Edwin Booth. For some years, The Players offered annual all-star revivals of the classics, but in 1935 it broke with tradition by reviving *Seven Keys to Baldpate* which, according to Cohan, "not only was the first play by a member of the club to be selected for one of their spring presentations, but it is assuredly the first, and to date, the only one in which the author, himself a Player, has appeared in the feature role which he himself has created. An opportunity never offered to Shakespeare, Sheridan, Goldsmith or Farquhar!"

Although George M. Cohan staunchly maintained that he was born in Providence, Rhode Island, on July 4th, his actual birth date was July 3, 1878. Born into a family of vaudeville performers who later appeared as The Four Cohans, he had very little formal schooling. Yet, as Brooks Atkinson has written, "He was abnormally bright, ingenious, energetic, and self-confident, and spectacular success was not his hope so much as his obsession." Indefatigable, a well as uncannily shrewd in his theatrical instincts, he created some fifty plays and musicals—beginning with *The Governor's Son* in 1901—amassed a fortune, built his own Broadway theatre, and at his death in 1942 was one of the true legends of the American theatre.

Among his other plays and musicals, in many of which he starred, are: *Forty-five Minutes from Broadway*; *Little Johnny Jones*; *George Washington, Jr.*; *Get-Rich-Quick Wallingford*; *The Tavern*; *Broadway Jones*; *The Song and Dance Man*; *The Merry Malones*; *Gambling*; and *Pigeons and People*.

Twice in his career he made notable appearances in works by other dramatists. In 1933 he appeared in the Theatre Guild's production of Eugene O'Neill's *Ah, Wilderness!* and in 1937, he impersonated President Franklin D. Roosevelt in *I'd Rather Be Right*, written by George S. Kaufman and Moss Hart, with music and lyrics by Richard Rodgers and Lorenz Hart.

In 1940 the President and his stage prototype met at The White House when Roosevelt, by a special act of Congress, presented Cohan with a Congressional medal in recognition of the national value of two of his patriotic songs: *Over There* and *You're a Grand Old Flag*. Another significant honor came to him posthumously: in 1959, a statue of George M. Cohan was unveiled in Duffy Square, New York, and he thus became the first and only American theatre personality ever commemorated by a statue on Broadway.

Earl Derr Biggers (1884–1933), author of the original version of *Seven Keys to Baldpate*, wrote a number of plays but he is chiefly remembered as a novelist and for the creation of Charlie Chan, the Chinese detective who figured prominently in a number of his stories. His novels include: *The House Without a Key*; *The Chinese Parrot*; *Behind That Curtain*; *The Black Camel*; *Charlie Chan Carries On*; and *Keeper of the Keys*.

Seven Keys to Baldpate was first produced in New York at the Astor Theatre, on September 22, 1913, by George M. Cohan and Sam H. Harris. The cast was as follows:

ELIJAH QUIMBY	*Edgar Halstead*
MRS. QUIMBY	*Jessie Grahame*
WILLIAM HALLOWELL MAGEE	*Wallace Eddinger*
JOHN BLAND	*Purnell B. Pratt*
MARY NORTON	*Margaret Greene*
MRS. RHODES	*Lorena Atwood*
PETERS	*Joseph Allen*
MYRA THORNHILL	*Gail Kane*
LOU MAX	*Roy Fairchild*
JIM CARGAN	*Martin L. Alsop*
THOMAS HAYDEN	*Claude Brooke*
JIGGS KENNEDY	*Carleton Macy*
THE OWNER OF BALDPATE	*John C. King*

Directed by   Sam Forrest

Seven Keys to Baldpate was first presented in London by Charles Hawtrey, on September 12, 1914, at the Apollo Theatre. The cast was as follows:

WILLIAM HALLOWELL MAGEE	*Charles Hawtrey*
ELIJAH QUIMBY	*Sydney Paxton*
MRS. QUIMBY	*Lydia Rachel*
JOHN BLAND	*Frank Wakefield*
MARY NORTON	*Doris Lytton*
MRS. RHODES	*Mabel Younge*
PETERS	*Henry Wenman*
MYRA THORNHILL	*Mona Harrison*
LOU MAX	*Herbert Alexander*
JIM CARGAN	*D. Mayor-Cooke*
THOMAS HAYDEN	*Edgar Payne*
JIGGS KENNEDY	*George Tully*
THE OWNER OF BALDPATE	*Hugh Gibson*

Directed by   Charles Hawtrey

Seven Keys to Baldpate was revived by The Players on May 27, 1935, at the National Theatre, New York. The cast was as follows:

FOREWORD FOR THE PLAYERS — *Otis Skinner*

ELIJAH QUIMBY, *the caretaker of Baldpate Inn*	*Francis Conlan*
MRS. QUIMBY, *the caretaker's wife*	*Josephine Hull*
WILLIAM HALLOWELL MAGEE, *the novelist*	*George M. Cohan*
JOHN BLAND, *the millionaire's right-hand man*	*Ernest Glendinning*
MARY NORTON, *the newspaper reporter*	*Zita Johann*
MRS. RHODES, *the charming widow*	*Irene Rich*
PETERS, *the Hermit of Baldpate*	*James T. Powers*
MYRA THORNHILL, *the blackmailer*	*Ruth Weston*
LOU MAX, *the Mayor's Man Friday*	*Ben Lackland*
JIM CARGAN, *the crooked Mayor of Reuton*	*Edward McNamara*
THOMAS HAYDEN, *the president of the R. and A. Suburban R.R.*	*George Christie*
JIGGS KENNEDY, *the Chief of Police of Asquewan Falls*	*James Kirkwood*
FIRST POLICEMAN	*Percy Moore*
SECOND POLICEMAN	*Allen Delano*
HAL BENTLEY, *the owner of Baldpate Inn*	*Walter Hampden*

Directed by — Sam Forrest
Setting by — W. Oden Waller

 SCENE: *The office of Baldpate Inn.*

TIME: *The present.*

PROLOGUE

At rise of curtain the stage is bare. No lights on the stage except the rays of the moon shining through glass door and the sky above. The wind is heard howling outside. The effect is that of a terrific storm taking place. Everything within the scene proves that it is a deserted, desolate spot; in fact, an inn, a summer resort on the mountains closed for the winter.

After thirty seconds, ELIJAH QUIMBY *appears at glass door upstage and is seen swinging a lantern. He does this as if guiding someone who is following; a sort of signal to* MRS. QUIMBY, *who presently appears trudging behind him. He hands her the lantern while he fumbles with a bunch of keys he has taken from his pocket. She gives him a light from the lantern while he finds the right key and unlocks the door. As the door swings open the wind is heard howling unmercifully. He holds the door open for her to enter, then follows her in, closing the door. They both stamp their feet to get them warm.* MRS. QUIMBY *goes down center, holding up lantern and peering around room, then goes to table on which she places the lantern.* QUIMBY, *after locking the door, goes slowly to table, meanwhile stamping feet, removing earmuffs and placing cap and mittens on table.* MRS. QUIMBY *removes her mittens, and they both stand rubbing their hands and ears. All this business is done without a word being spoken. The reason for it is to prove to the audience that the night is bitterly cold and that the two people are half-frozen after their climb up the mountain.*

QUIMBY: [*Shivering*] You know, mother, I think it's colder in here than it is outside.

MRS. QUIMBY: [*Shivering*] I was going to say the same thing, Elijah.

QUIMBY: Maybe we'd better open the door and let in some warm air.

MRS. QUIMBY: You'd better not; the snow'll blow all over the place. See if there's any logs over there and we'll build a fire. [*Indicates fireplace with a nod of her head*]

QUIMBY: [*Starts; stops and stamps his feet*] You know, mother, I think my feet are froze. I can't feel 'em when I walk. [*Knocks hands together*]

MRS. QUIMBY: I don't wonder, after that climb up the mountain. Lord, I'll never forget this night! I'm about perished. [*She straightens chairs, etc., while* QUIMBY *is looking for logs*] Any logs there?

QUIMBY: Yep, plenty of 'em. I got this thing all ready, anyway. I was goin' to build a fire when I was up here last week. I'll have 'em blazin' in a minute if I can find them darned matches. [*Searches through his pockets*] I can swear I put a box of 'em in my pocket before I left the house! [*Finds them*] Yep, here they are!

MRS. QUIMBY: You'd better light a lamp first, so's you can see what you're doin'.

QUIMBY: That's a good idea.

[*Clock in distance strikes eleven while he is scratching match and lighting lamp over fireplace*]

MRS. QUIMBY: [*Standing at foot of stairs*] Eleven o'clock.

QUIMBY: Yep, that's what it is—eleven o'clock. [*Goes and looks through glass door*] That train's been in over twenty minutes already. I suppose it's the storm that delays him. 'Tain't over a ten-minute walk up the mountain from the depot.

MRS. QUIMBY: Maybe the train's late on account of the storm.

QUIMBY: No; I heard it signal the crossing at Asquewan Junction a half hour ago. That feller'll be here before we know it. [*Hands her matches*] Light the other lamp, will you, mother, while I get at this fire?

[MRS. QUIMBY *takes matches and lights lamp near stairway. He builds fire in fireplace. Both are busily engaged in fixing room, heating and lighting it during following conversation*]

MRS. QUIMBY: Maybe we should have gone to the depot to meet him?

QUIMBY: No; we shouldn't have done nothin' of the kind. The tele-gram just said to come here and to open up the place and have it ready for him. Them's the instructions, and them's the only things I foller—is instructions.

MRS. QUIMBY: But what do you suppose anybody wants to be doin' in a summer hotel on the top of a mountain in the dead of winter?

QUIMBY: Mother, you know I can't figger out nothin'. [*Goes up to door, peers out, then comes down to* MRS. QUIMBY] If I could I'd 'a' been a multi-millionare years ago, instead of an old fool care-taker. . . . Dust up a bit there, will you, mother, and make the place look a little respectable? [*Goes toward fireplace*] She'll be goin' all right in a minute now.

MRS. QUIMBY: [*Dusting with cloth she has taken from foot of stairs*] What's his name again?

QUIMBY: Magee, I think the telegram says.

MRS. QUIMBY: Magee?

QUIMBY: Wait a minute, I'll make sure. [*Takes telegram from his pocket*]

MRS. QUIMBY: [*Takes telegram from him*] Give it to me; I want to read it myself. The whole thing's very mysterious to me. [*Goes to table and sits, reading by light of lantern*]

QUIMBY: Of course it's mysterious, but it's none of our business. Mr. Bentley is the owner of Baldpate Inn. If Mr. Bentley wants to per-mit some darn fool to come to this place to be froze to death by stale air and to be frightened to death by spooks, it's his concern and not ours. [*Turns and looks at fire, which is blazing*] Ah, there she goes, she's blazing up fine. That'll warm it up a little.

MRS. QUIMBY: [*Reading message slowly*] "My friend, William Hal-lowell Magee, will arrive in Asquewan Falls tonight on the ten-forty. He will occupy Baldpate Inn, so be prepared to receive him there, and turn the key over to him and do whatever you can to make him comfortable. He has important work to do, and has chosen Baldpate for his workshop. Follow instructions. Ask no questions. Hal Bentley."

QUIMBY: [*Has been listening attentively*] Sounds like them Black Hand notes they send to rich men, don't it?

MRS. QUIMBY: I can't understand it for the life of me. [*Hands telegram back to* QUIMBY]

QUIMBY: Mother!

MRS. QUIMBY: Yes?

QUIMBY: Maybe the feller's committed some crime and is comin' here to hide.

MRS. QUIMBY: Do you think so, Elijah?

QUIMBY: I don't know; I say—mebbe.

MRS. QUIMBY: Well, if that's so, why should Mr. Bentley be interested in such a man?

QUIMBY: [*Thinks*] I never thought of that. Well, whatever it is, it's none of our business, and we mustn't mix in other people's affairs.

MRS. QUIMBY: [*Thinks a moment, then comes down near* QUIMBY] Elijah!

QUIMBY: [*Looks up*] What?

MRS. QUIMBY: Do you think I'd better fix up one of them rooms?

QUIMBY: Sure; he'll have to have a place to sleep. Here—[*Gives her key*]—that opens the linen closet. You'd better fix up that first room to the left. [*Points to room on balcony*] That's the one Mr. Bentley always takes when he comes.

MRS. QUIMBY: [*As she goes toward stairs, taking lantern from table*] And you'd better put another log on the fire. He'll probably be chilled to the bone by the time he climbs that mountain. Do you think he'll find his way alone?

QUIMBY: Oh, he'll find his way all right. The station agent will most likely direct him. [*Puts log on fire, which blazes up*]

MRS. QUIMBY: [*Going up the stairs*] Occupying a summer hotel in the dead of winter! It beats all what some people will do! [*Exits, leaving door open*]

QUIMBY: [*Takes out his pipe and sits thinking near fire*] Humph! It's pretty darned mysterious, all right. [*Lights pipe and smokes*] I'll be jiggered if I can figger it out.

> [MRS. QUIMBY *remains inside room for a few seconds, then comes from room carrying linen and bed coverings in her arms. She crosses balcony to room left of balcony and exits, closing door.* QUIMBY *sits smoking and thinking.* MA-

[MAGEE *appears at door upstage and peers through. He is carrying a suitcase and typewriter case. He puts them down and knocks on window.* QUIMBY *doesn't move at first, but sits listening, to make sure he has heard a sound.* MAGEE *repeats the knocking.* QUIMBY *shifts around in his chair, looks up toward the window, sees a form there, then gets up and sneaks along until he gets to foot of stairs, then calls in suppressed tones to* MRS. QUIMBY]

QUIMBY: Mother, mother! [*No answer from* MRS. QUIMBY. *He runs halfway upstairs and calls a bit louder*] Mother!

MRS. QUIMBY: [*Appears on balcony, peers over*] Did you call me, Elijah?

QUIMBY: Hush! Don't talk so loud!

MRS. QUIMBY: [*Lowering her voice*] What's the matter? [*They both listen for a second.* MAGEE'S *third rap comes*] Good Lord, what's that?

QUIMBY: [*On stairs*] It's him—he's here! [*He points to door*]

MRS. QUIMBY: Who?

QUIMBY: The telegram—I mean the man.

MRS. QUIMBY: [*Starts down the stairs*] Where?

QUIMBY: At the door.

[MAGEE *again raps impatiently*]

MRS. QUIMBY: [*Urging* QUIMBY *down the stairs*] Why don't you let him in?

QUIMBY: [*Both come downstairs*] Do you think I'd better?

MRS. QUIMBY: Well, ain't that what the telegram said?

QUIMBY: Why, yes, of course, but——

MRS. QUIMBY: [*Shoving* QUIMBY *toward door*] You got your instructions. Go on and do as you're told!

[MAGEE *knocks again and rattles the doorknob*]

QUIMBY: [*In a loud voice as he goes up toward door*] Yes, yes; jest a minute, jest a minute!

[QUIMBY *unlocks door and swings it open. The wind howls.* MAGEE, *carrying the two cases, enters and stands bowing, first to* MRS. QUIMBY *and then to* QUIMBY, *then drops the cases in the middle of the room. Looks around the room for a moment, wild-eyed, then sees fire burning and goes over to it as fast as his half-frozen legs will allow him. He pulls chair in front of fire and sits warming himself.* QUIMBYS *stand watching him in amazement. As soon as* MAGEE *has entered* QUIMBY *has locked the door and come to* MRS. QUIMBY]

MRS. QUIMBY: [*Aside to* QUIMBY] The poor thing's half-froze.

QUIMBY: [*Approaches* MAGEE, MRS. QUIMBY *following him to fireplace*] What's the matter, young fellow, are you cold?

MAGEE: [*Smiles a sickly smile, shakes his head, laughs half-heartedly, then replies*] Humph! Am I cold! I feel pretty rocky, but I've got to laugh at that one.

MRS. QUIMBY: [*Aside to* QUIMBY] Better give him a drink of whiskey.

QUIMBY: Yes, I guess so. [*Takes flask from his pocket and hands it to* MAGEE] Here, young fellow, try a little of this.

MAGEE: [*Looks up, sees flask, and grabs it*] Thanks! [*Takes a long drink*]

MRS. QUIMBY: [*Aside to* QUIMBY] Do you suppose it's him?

QUIMBY: [*Aside*] How do I know?

MRS. QUIMBY: [*Aside*] Well, ask him and find out.

MAGEE: [*Offers flask to* QUIMBY] Thanks again, a thousand thanks.

QUIMBY: Oh, you just put that in your pocket; you might need it later on.

MAGEE: Thanks.

[MRS. QUIMBY *picks up cases from floor and takes them to table*]

QUIMBY: You're Mr. Magee, ain't you?

MAGEE: Right! What's left of me is still Magee. You expected me, of course.

QUIMBY: Oh, yes; we got Mr. Bentley's telegram all right. My name's Quimby.

MAGEE: So I surmised.

QUIMBY: This lady is my wife, Mrs. Quimby.

MAGEE: I thought as much. Delighted, Mrs. Quimby. [*Bows to* MRS. QUIMBY *without rising*]

MRS. QUIMBY: Glad to meet you, Mr. Magee.

MAGEE: You'll pardon me for not rising, but really I'm terribly cold.

MRS. QUIMBY: That's all right. You sit there and get het up. We've been living here in the mountains so long we don't mind the cold as much as strangers do, but even we felt it tonight, didn't we, Elijah?

QUIMBY: That's right, mother; this is an uncommon cold night.

MAGEE: [*Rises, removes overcoat, muffler and hat, and places them on chair*] That little trip from the railroad station to the top of the mountain has taught me to firmly believe everything Jack London ever wrote about and everything old Dr. Cook ever lied about. [*Looking at everything, very much interested, and rubbing his hands*] So this is Baldpate, is it? Well, well, well!

MRS. QUIMBY: [*Aside to* QUIMBY] Don't he talk funny?

QUIMBY: [*Aside*] Yes. Acts funny, too. Something's the matter with him, sure.

[*Both watch* MAGEE *closely*]

MAGEE: You say you received Mr. Bentley's telegram saying I would be here?

QUIMBY: Yes; it only came about an hour ago, so we didn't have much time to prepare.

MAGEE: I didn't decide to come here until four o'clock this afternoon.

MRS. QUIMBY: We was scared 'most to death gettin' a telegram in the middle of the night.

MAGEE: I'm very sorry to have taken you out on a night like this, but it was altogether necessary in order that I accomplish what I've set out to do. Let me see—the rooms above are equipped with fireplaces, I believe?

MRS. QUIMBY: Yes; I'm just fixin' up one of the rooms. I'll start the fire, too. I'll have it all ready for you inside of five minutes. [*She crosses to get wood from box*]

MAGEE: I wish you would. [*Looks around room*] Yes; this would be too big a barn to work in. [QUIMBYS *look at each other*] I'll no doubt be more comfortable up there. [*Continues to take in sur-roundings*]

QUIMBY: [*Aside to* MRS. QUIMBY] He says he's goin' to work. I wonder what he means?

MRS. QUIMBY: [*Aside*] Pump him. Try to find out. [*Aloud*] Give me the matches.

QUIMBY: Here you are. [*He hands her a box of matches*]

> [MRS. QUIMBY, *with wood in her arms, starts for stairs and goes up on balcony*]

MAGEE: This, I presume, is the hotel office.

QUIMBY: That's right.

MAGEE: [*Strolls around, looking at everything carefully.* QUIMBY *watching him closely*] Well, well! This certainly is old John H. Seclusion himself.

> [*Lights go up*]

MR. *and* MRS. QUIMBY: [*Together*] Good Lord, where did those lights come from? Good Lord, what's happened?

> [*As lights go up,* QUIMBY *darts behind desk.* MRS. QUIMBY *is leaning over balcony. Both are frightened*]

MAGEE: [*Laughs*] Don't be alarmed, Mrs. Quimby; it's all right. I think I can explain this thing. Mr. Bentley has probably had the power turned on. He knew I'd have to have some real light for this kind of work. [MRS. QUIMBY *exits into room right on balcony, closing the door.* MAGEE *goes to* QUIMBY] I suppose you're wondering what the devil I'm doing here.

QUIMBY: That's just what I was wondering, young fellow.

MAGEE: Well, I'll try to explain, although I'm not sure you'll understand. Sit down, Mr. Quimby. [QUIMBY *hesitates*] It's all right, sit down. [QUIMBY *gets chair, then sits*] Now, you are not, I take it, the sort of man to follow closely the light and frivolous literature of the day.

QUIMBY: How's that?

MAGEE: You don't read the sort of novels that are sold by the pound in the department stores.

QUIMBY: Nope.

MAGEE: Well, I write those novels.

QUIMBY: The dickens you do!

MAGEE: Wild, thrilling tales for the tired businessman's tired wife; shots in the night; chases after fortunes; Cupid busy with his arrows all over the place. It's good fun—I like to do it, and—there's money in it.

QUIMBY: You don't mean to tell me!

MAGEE: Oh, yes, considerable. Of course, they say I'm a cheap melo-dramatic ranter. They say my thinking process is a scream. Perhaps they're right. [*Moves chair out and sits*]

QUIMBY: Perhaps.

MAGEE: Did you ever read *The Scarlet Satchel?*

QUIMBY: Never.

MAGEE: That's one of mine.

QUIMBY: Is it?

MAGEE: I've come here to Baldpate to think; to get away from melo-drama, if possible; to do a novel so fine and literary that Henry Cabot Lodge will come to me with tears in his eyes and beg me to join his bunch of self-made immortals. And I'm going to do all this right here in this inn, sitting on this mountain, looking down on this little old world as Jove looked down from Olympus. What do you think of that?

QUIMBY: [*Shakes his head, affecting an air of understanding*] Maybe it's all for the best.

MAGEE: Of late I've been running short of material. [*Rises*] I've needed inspiration. A title gave me that—"The Lonesomest Spot on Earth," suggested by my very dear friend and your employer, Mr. Hal Bentley. "What and where is the lonesomest spot on earth?" I asked. "A summer resort in winter," said he. He told me of Baldpate—dared me to come. I took the dare—and here I am.

QUIMBY: [*Rising*] You mean you're goin' to write a book?

MAGEE: That's just exactly what I'm going to do. I'm going to novelize Baldpate. I'm here to get atmosphere.

QUIMBY: [*Laughs*] Lord, you'll get plenty of that, all right! When are you goin' to start in?

MAGEE: Just as soon as I absorb my surroundings and make a few mental notes. You see, I do most of my work in the dead of night. I find I concentrate more readily from midnight on. But I must have absolute solitude. The crackle of the fire, the roar of the wind, and the ticking of my watch will alone bear me company at Baldpate Inn. This all sounds very strange and weird to you, I suppose.

QUIMBY: How's that?

MAGEE: I say, you can't quite fathom me.

QUIMBY: Well, you're here of your own accord, I take it.

MAGEE: My dear Mr. Quimby, I'm here on a bet.

QUIMBY: On a bet!

MAGEE: Exactly. I have here an explanation of the thing in Bentley's handwriting. [*Takes paper from his pocket*] Do you care to look it over yourself, or would you rather I'd read it to you?

QUIMBY: Yes, go on and read it—I like to hear you talk. [*Sits*]

MAGEE: [*Smiles*] Ah, then my personality has wormed its way into your good graces.

QUIMBY: How's that?

MAGEE: I mean to say, I evidently appeal to you.

QUIMBY: Well, I don't know as you particularly appeal to me, but——

MAGEE: But what?

QUIMBY: [*Laughs, confused*] Oh, I guess I better not say it.

MAGEE: Come on, what's on your mind? Tell me.

QUIMBY: Well, to be honest with you, I can't figger out whether you're a smart man or a damn fool.

MAGEE: [*Laughs*] Would you believe it, my dear sir, I've been stalled between those two opinions of myself for years? My publishers say I'm a smart man; my critics call me a damn fool. However, that's neither here nor there. This—[*Indicating paper*]—will perhaps clear away the cloud of mystery to some extent. Oh, perhaps Mrs. Quimby would be interested enough to hear this also. Will you call her, please?

QUIMBY: [*Rises and calls*] Mother! Oh, mother!

MRS. QUIMBY: [*Appears on balcony*] Yes, I'm all through. Everything's ready up here. [*Leans over balcony*] You'd better come up, mister, and see if it satisfies you before we go.

MAGEE: It's all right, Mrs. Quimby. I'll take your word for it that everything's all right.

QUIMBY: Come on down here, mother; Mr. Magee wants to read something to you.

MRS. QUIMBY: Is that so? [*Starts downstairs*] I started the fire, so I guess the room'll be comfortable enough to sleep in by the time you get ready to go to bed.

QUIMBY: Sit down, mother.

MRS. QUIMBY: What!

QUIMBY: Go on. See, I'm sittin'. [MRS. QUIMBY *goes toward* QUIMBY] Mr. Magee's goin' to tell us why he's here.

MRS. QUIMBY: [*Sits*] Is that so? Lord, I'd love to know!

MAGEE: I have just explained to your husband that I am an author. I do popular novels, and I'm here to write a story—a story of Baldpate Mountain, laid in this very hotel, perhaps in this identical room. I am to complete this task within twenty-four hours, starting at midnight tonight.

QUIMBY: Understand, mother? He's goin' to write a book.

MRS. QUIMBY: [*To* MAGEE] Goin' to write a book in twenty-four hours!

MAGEE: That is the wager that has been made between Mr. Bentley and myself. He claimed it couldn't be done. I claimed it could. Five thousand dollars' worth of his sporting blood boiled, and he dug for his fountain pen and check book. I covered the bet, and we posted the checks at the Forty-fourth Street Club. He was to choose the godforsaken spot. [*Looks around room*] He succeeded. I ran to my apartment, placed some manuscript paper, a dozen sandwiches and my slippers in a suitcase, grabbed my faithful typewriting machine, just made the train, and here you see me, ready to win or lose the wager, as the case may be.

QUIMBY: What do you think of that, mother?

MRS. QUIMBY: [*To* MAGEE] I never heard of such a thing!

MAGEE: Here is a copy of the agreement, in which you will notice your name is mentioned, Mr. Quimby. Listen. [*Reads*] "You are to leave New York City on the four-fifty-five for Asquewan Falls, arriving at ten-forty, and go direct to Baldpate Inn, atop the Baldpate Mountain, where you will be met by my caretaker, Mr. Elijah

Quimby, who, after making you comfortable, will turn over to you the key to the inn, the only key in existence." [*To* QUIMBY] Is that correct?

QUIMBY: It's the only key I know of.

MRS. QUIMBY: There ain't no other key; I can swear to that.

MAGEE: Good! [*Continues reading*] "This will insure you against interruption, and give you the solitude necessary for concentration. You are to begin work at twelve o'clock Tuesday night, and turn over to Mr. Elijah Quimby the completed manuscript of a ten-thousand-word story of Baldpate no later than twelve o'clock Wednesday night." [*To* QUIMBY] You understand?

QUIMBY: You're to turn it over to me?

MAGEE: Precisely.

QUIMBY: What do you think of that, mother?

MRS. QUIMBY: I never heard of such a thing!

MAGEE: You know Bentley's handwriting; there's his signature—see for yourself. [*Hands paper to* MRS. QUIMBY. QUIMBYS *get up and read it together*]

[MAGEE *moves about*]

QUIMBY: It's his writin', ain't it, mother?

MRS. QUIMBY: [*Doubtfully*] Looks like it, but— [*Looks at* MAGEE *suspiciously*]

QUIMBY: [*Aside*] But what?

MRS. QUIMBY: [*Aside*] The whole thing don't sound right to me.

QUIMBY: [*Aside*] Me neither. We'd better watch this cuss.

MRS. QUIMBY: [*Aside*] I think so, too.

[*Phone rings.* MRS. QUIMBY *runs to foot of stairs, screaming.* QUIMBY *hugs the desk, frightened*]

MRS. QUIMBY: Good Lord!

QUIMBY: [*To* MAGEE] Did you hear that?

MAGEE: You mean the telephone?

MRS. QUIMBY: [*Runs to* MAGEE—QUIMBY *grabs* MAGEE *by the arms*] Spooks!

QUIMBY: Why, that thing's been out of commission all winter!

[*Phone continues ringing.* MAGEE *laughs*]

MRS. QUIMBY: Let's get out of here, Lije!

MAGEE: [*Laughs*] Don't be alarmed, Mrs. Quimby; I think I can explain. Bentley has just about had the service renewed. He probably wants to find out if I've arrived. Excuse me just a moment. [*Goes to phone*] Hello, hello! . . . Yes. Yes, right on time . . . Almost twenty minutes ago . . . Half-frozen, thank you . . . Yes, he's here now, also Mrs. Quimby . . . Oh, we understand each other perfectly well. . . . It's everything you said it was. . . . The lonesomest spot on earth is right. [*Laughs*] You still feel that way about it, eh? Well, your opinion is going to cost you five thousand, old man. [*Laughs*] All right, we'll see. . . . You want to talk to him . . . Just a second. [*To* QUIMBY] He wants to talk to you, Mr. Quimby.

QUIMBY: [*Goes over to phone*] Is it Mr. Bentley?

MAGEE: Yes, here you are. Sit right down. [*He hands* QUIMBY *receiver and goes toward staircase, taking notes.* MRS. QUIMBY *goes up and listens to phone conversation while watching* MAGEE]

QUIMBY: [*In phone*] Hello! [*Smiles as he recognizes* BENTLEY's *voice*] Hello, Mr. Bentley. . . . Yes, sir; yes, sir . . . I understand, sir . . . At twelve o'clock? . . . Yes, sir . . . Oh, I'll be right here waiting . . . Fine, thank you, sir; we're both fine . . . All right, sir. . . . Wait a minute I'll ask him [*To* MAGEE, *who is on first landing of stairs*] He wants to know if there's anything more you want to say?

MAGEE: No; just give him my regards, and tell him I'm spending his money already.

QUIMBY: [*In phone*] He says there's nothing else, sir. . . . Yes, sir, I understand. . . . Good-bye, sir. [*Hangs up receiver and crosses to* MAGEE] He wants me to be here at twelve o'clock tomorrow night to talk to him on the telephone again.

MAGEE: [*Laughs as he goes to phone and severs connection*] And it's very sad news you'll impart to him, Mr. Quimby. I'm going to win this wager! You know this whole thing wouldn't make a bad story in itself. I'm thinking seriously of using it for the ground plot. [*Points to door left*] Oh, this leads to where? [*Goes to door of dining room and opens it*]

MRS. QUIMBY: [*Going over toward door*] That's the dining room—

leads through to the kitchen. That door to the left goes to the cellar.

MAGEE: Ah, ha, I see! [*Goes toward* QUIMBY] Have you the exact time, Mr. Quimby?

QUIMBY: [*Looks at his watch*] Mine says half-past eleven.

MAGEE: Thirty minutes to get my bearings and frame up a character or two for a start.

MRS. QUIMBY: [*Picks up suitcase and typewriter case from table*] Will I put these in your room?

MAGEE: No, no; you needn't bother.

MRS. QUIMBY: Oh, it's no bother at all. [*Starts for the stairs*] I'm only too glad to do anything for any friend of Mr. Bentley. [*She climbs stairs with cases and exits into room*]

MAGEE: Now you're quite sure I won't be disturbed while I am writing?

QUIMBY: Who's goin' to disturb you here? No one ever comes within a mile of this place till around the first of April, except myself, and I only come up about once a week this kind of weather.

MAGEE: You don't suppose any of Bentley's Asquewan friends, hearing of the wager, would take it upon themselves to interrupt the progress of my work?

QUIMBY: Nobody knows you're here except me and the missus, and we ain't goin' to tell no one.

MAGEE: I have your word for that? [*Offers his hand to* QUIMBY]

QUIMBY: [*Takes* MAGEE'S *hand*] I never broke my word in my life. Guess that's why I'm a poor man. . . . The only other time I remember of anybody comin' here in the winter was the time of the reform wave at Reuton. The reformers got after a lot of crooked politicians, and they broke in here in the middle of the night and hid a lot of graft money in that safe over there.

[*He points to safe.* MAGEE *goes up to safe, opens the door, then comes down to* QUIMBY, *after closing safe door*]

MAGEE: You mean to tell me the reformers hid money in that safe?

QUIMBY: No, the politicians. Reformers never have any money.

MAGEE: [*Laughs*] Splendid!

QUIMBY: What are you laughing at?

MAGEE: Nothing; it's all right. Go on, tell me about the hidden graft.

[MRS. QUIMBY *starts downstairs, bringing lantern and placing it on table*]

QUIMBY: Oh, there's nothing much to tell. Some fellers up and gave 'em away, and the police come the next morning and found it here. Nobody claimed it, so of course they never got the gang. They threw a lot of fellers out of office, I believe. I didn't read much about it. But that's over four years ago. You needn't be afraid, you won't be disturbed here.

[*He goes to table and gets his mittens and cap.* MRS. QUIMBY *is at table putting on mittens, etc.*]

MAGEE: Grafting politicians—reformers—hidden money! Sounds like a good seller.

[QUIMBY *takes lantern from table*]

MRS. QUIMBY: Is there anything more we can do for you, Mr. Magee?

MAGEE: No, nothing I can think of, thank you. I'll be quite—— Oh, yes, of course! You've forgotten something, Mr. Quimby.

QUIMBY: Forgot what?

MAGEE: The key.

QUIMBY: Oh, Lord! Yes, the key! Here it is. [*Hands* MAGEE *the key*]

MAGEE: You're positively certain that this key is the only key to Baldpate in existence?

QUIMBY: Yes, sir; I'm sure.

MRS. QUIMBY: I can swear to it.

MAGEE: Good!

MRS. QUIMBY: What are you going to do, lock yourself in?

MAGEE: Precisely.

QUIMBY: I don't mind staying here and keepin' watch for you if you want me to.

MAGEE: No, thanks; I much prefer to be alone.

MRS. QUIMBY: I'd rather it would be you than me. Lord, I should think you'd be afraid of ghosts.

QUIMBY: Mother, I've told you twenty times there ain't no such a thing.

MRS. QUIMBY: Well, they've been seen here, just the same.

MAGEE: [Goes to QUIMBYS] Ghosts!

QUIMBY: Oh, don't mind her, Mr. Magee. We think we know what the ghost is. There's an old feller up here in the mountain by the name of Peters—he's a hermit.

MAGEE: A hermit!

QUIMBY: Yes; he's one of them fellers that's been disappointed in love. His wife run off with a traveling man. He come here about ten years ago—lives in a little shack about a mile and a half north of here; calls it the Hermit's Cave. All the summer boarders buy picture postcards from him. We figger he's the feller that's been frightening the people down in the valley by wavin' a lantern from the mountainside with a white sheet wrapped around him.

MRS. QUIMBY: But no one ever proved it was him.

QUIMBY: Well, who else could it be? There ain't no such a thing as ghosts, is there, Mr. Magee?

MAGEE: Well, I hope not. [Muses] Ghosts—hermits—not bad at all!

QUIMBY: Well, come along, mother; I guess maybe Mr. Magee is anxious to get to work. I'll say good night, sir. [Offers hand to MAGEE]

MAGEE: [Shakes QUIMBY's hand] Good night. And remember, twelve o'clock sharp for Mr. Bentley's phone call tomorrow night.

QUIMBY: I'll be here on the minute.

MRS. QUIMBY: [Shaking hands with MAGEE] And I'm comin' to see if you're still alive. Lord, I should think you'd be scared to death.

QUIMBY: Mother, he will be if you keep on like that. Well, good night, sir, and good luck. [Goes up toward door, followed by MRS. QUIMBY]

MAGEE: [Goes up to door and unlocks it] Good night. I don't envy you your trip down the mountain on a night like this. [Opens door. The wind howls]

MRS. QUIMBY: Good night, sir.

[Starts through door, followed by QUIMBY, carrying lantern]

MAGEE: Good night, Mrs. Quimby. Keep a sharp lookout for ghosts and hermits. [Laughs]

MRS. QUIMBY: [*Outside*] Lord, don't remind me, please!

MAGEE: [*Slams door quickly, locks it, waves his hand to the* QUIM-BYS, *then stands looking at key in his hand*] The only one, eh? Humph, we'll see!

> [*He puts key in his pocket, looks around room, thinks, then claps his hands as if decided on something; grabs his coat and hat from chair near fire, extinguishes lamps and bracket lights, takes a last look around room, and then exits upstairs into room on balcony*]

THE LIGHTS GO OUT

ACT ONE

The clock strikes twelve. The sound of a typewriter is heard clicking from the room occupied by MAGEE. *A short pause of absolute silence, then* BLAND *appears at door, peering into room.*

BLAND: [*Opens door, enters, locks door, then looks about, rubbing his hands and blowing on them to warm them. Sees safe, goes up to it, tries the door, opens it, and as he starts for phone he sees fire burning, and stops dead*] A log fire! Who the devil built that? [*Thinks, snaps fingers, goes to phone and puts in plugs*] 2875 West. Hurry it along, sister. [MAGEE *enters from room and stands on balcony listening, leaving door of room open. In phone*] Hello, is that you, Andy? . . . This is Bland . . . Yes, Baldpate . . . Yes, damn near frozen . . . Oh, awful! It's like Napoleon's tomb . . . I thought you said Mayor Cargan would meet me here? . . . No, no, I can't stay here all night; I'd go mad. . . . Listen, I'll hide the money here in the safe, and meet him at nine o'clock in the morning and turn it over to him then. . . . There isn't a chance in the world of anything happening. . . . The money's safer here than any spot on earth. . . . I'll lock the safe as soon as I put the package in. . . . Mayor Cargan knows the combination. . . . My advice is to let it lay here a week. It's the last place they'll look for it. Besides, how could they get in? My key to Baldpate is the only one in existence. [MAGEE, *on balcony, takes out his key and looks at it*] They don't figure we'd take the chance after the other exposure. I tell you I know best. . . . I'll be back in town by one o'clock. . . . I've got the president's machine waiting at the foot of the mountain. . . . All right; good-bye. [*Hangs up receiver, takes package of money from his pocket, looks at it and around room, then goes to safe and deposits the money therein.* MAGEE *starts slowly and stealthily downstairs.* BLAND *closes door of safe, turns the handle, tries doors to see if they are locked securely, then comes down to fireplace and warms himself. As he turns his back to the fire, he comes face to face with* MAGEE. BLAND's *hand goes to his pocket for his gun*]

MAGEE: [*Cool and collected*] Good evening—or perhaps I should say, good morning.

BLAND: [*Keeping his hand on gun as he advances toward* MAGEE] Who are you?

MAGEE: I was just about to put that question to you.

BLAND: What are you doing here?

MAGEE: I rather think I'm the one entitled to an explanation.

BLAND: Did you follow me up that mountain?

MAGEE: Oh, no; I was here an hour ahead of you.

BLAND: How'd you get in here?

MAGEE: [*Points*] Through that door.

BLAND: You lie! There's only one key to that door, and I have it right here in my pocket.

MAGEE: My dear sir, I was laboring under that same impression until a moment ago; but as your key fits the lock, and my key fits the lock, there are evidently two keys to Baldpate instead of one. [*He shows* BLAND *his key*] See?

BLAND: You mean to tell me that's a key to Baldpate?

MAGEE: Yes. That's why I became so interested in your arrival here. I heard you telephone your friend just now and declare that your key was the only one in existence. It sort of handed me a laugh.

BLAND: You heard what I said over the telephone?

MAGEE: Every word.

BLAND: [*Pulls pistol*] You don't think you're going to live to tell it, do you?

MAGEE: Have no fear on that score. I'm not a tattle-tale, nor do I intend to pry into affairs that do not concern me. But I should like your answering me one question. Where did you get your key to Baldpate?

BLAND: None of your damned business! I didn't come here to tell you the story of my life!

MAGEE: Well, you might at least relate that portion of it that has led you to trespassing on a gentleman seeking seclusion.

BLAND: Trespassing, eh? Who's trespassing, you or I?

MAGEE: My right here is indisputable.

BLAND: Who gave you that key?

MAGEE: None of your damned business! If I remember rightly, that's the answer you gave me.

BLAND: [*Goes slightly nearer* MAGEE] You've got a pretty good nerve to talk like that with a gun in front of your face.

MAGEE: Oh, that doesn't disturb me in the least. While I have never experienced this sort of thing in real life before, I've written so much of this melodramatic stuff and collected such splendid royalties from it all, that it rather amuses me to discover that the so-called literary trash is the real thing, after all. You may not believe it, but, really, old chap, I've written you over and over again! [*Laughs heartily and slaps* BLAND *on the shoulder. The latter backs away after second slap.* MAGEE *sits at table, still laughing heartily*]

BLAND: Say, I killed a man once for laughing at me!

MAGEE: That's my line—I used it in *The Lost Limousine*. Four hundred thousand copies. I'll bet you've read it.

BLAND: [*Pointing gun*] If you don't tell me who you are and what you're doing here, I'll kill you as dead as a doornail. Come on, I mean business—who are you?

MAGEE: Well, a name doesn't mean so much, so you may call me Mr. Smith.

BLAND: What are you?

MAGEE: A writer of popular novels.

BLAND: What are you doing here?

MAGEE: Trying to win a bet by completing a story of Baldpate in twenty-four hours. [*Gets up*] A few more interruptions of this sort, however, and it's plain to be seen I'll pay the winner. [*Up close to* BLAND] You can do me a big favor, old man, by leaving me this place to myself for the night. I give you my word of honor that whatever I've seen or heard shall remain absolutely sacred.

BLAND: [*Sneeringly*] You must think I'm an awful fool to swallow that kind of talk!

MAGEE: Very well, if you don't believe I'm who I say I am, and you doubt that I'm here for the reason I gave, go upstairs into that room with the open door—[*Points to room on balcony.* BLAND *looks up and backs away*]—and you'll find a typewriting machine, several pages of manuscript scattered about the floor, and a letter on the dresser from the owner of this inn to the caretaker, proving conclusively that all I've told you is the truth and nothing but the truth, and there you are.

BLAND: And you're not in with the police?

MAGEE: No. I wish I were, if the graft is as good as they say it is.

BLAND: You say you have a letter from the owner of the inn?

MAGEE: Yes. Wait a minute, and I'll get it for you. [*Starts upstairs, but is stopped by* BLAND *as he is about halfway up*]

BLAND: [*Shouts*] Come back!

MAGEE: [*Returning*] What's the matter?

BLAND: I've been double-crossed before, young fellow. I'll find it if it's there.

MAGEE: Oh, very well. If you prefer to get it yourself, why, go right along. [*He turns from* BLAND. *As he does so,* BLAND *fans him for a gun.* MAGEE *turns, surprised; then, as he understands, he laughs*] You needn't be alarmed; I never carried a gun in my life.

BLAND: But you keep one in your room, eh?

MAGEE: If you think so, search the room.

BLAND: That's just what I'm going to do. I guess I'll keep you in sight, though. Go on; I'll let you show me the way.

MAGEE: All right. [*Starts toward stairs*] If that's the way you feel about it, why, certainly.

[*He goes upstairs leisurely, followed by* BLAND, *who keeps him covered.* MAGEE *starts to exit into room.* BLAND *stops him*]

BLAND: Wait a minute; I'll peek around that room alone first. You don't look good to me; you're too damned willing. [*Goes to door of room.* MAGEE *steps out*] You wait out here. I'll call you when I've satisfied myself you're not trying to spring something.

MAGEE: Very well. If you don't trust me, go ahead.

[BLAND *exits into room, keeping his eyes fixed on* MAGEE. *The latter stands thinking for a moment, then turns and slams door quickly, locks it, and runs downstairs to phone*]

BLAND: [*Yelling and hammering on door*] Open this door! [*Hammers*] Damn you, I'll get you for this!

MAGEE: [*At phone*] Hello, I want to talk to the Asquewan police headquarters. . . . That's what I said, police headquarters.

> [BLAND *pounds on door. As* MAGEE *sits waiting for connection,* MARY NORTON *appears at door. She unlocks it and enters, closing door. The cold blast of wind attracts* MAGEE, *who jumps up and yells:*]

MAGEE: Who's there? What do you want?

MARY: Don't shoot; it's all right. I'm harmless.

MAGEE: How did you open that door?

MARY: Unlocked it with a key, of course.

MAGEE: My God!

MARY: [*Comes toward* MAGEE] If you will allow me to bring my chaperon inside, I will explain in a moment who I am and why we're here.

MAGEE: Your chaperon!

MARY: Yes; another perfectly harmless female who has been kind enough to accompany me on this wild adventure. [*Turns to* MAGEE] I have your permission?

MAGEE: [*Looks up at room, then back at* MARY, *puzzled*] Say, what the deuce is this all about?

MARY: You'll soon know. [*Opens door and calls*] All right, Mrs. Rhodes!

> [MRS. RHODES *screams offstage, then enters and runs past* MARY, *terribly frightened*]

MAGEE: What's the matter? What's happened?

MRS. RHODES: [*Shouting to* MARY] Lock the door! Lock the door!

> [MARY *hurriedly locks the door*]

MAGEE: [*Crosses to* MRS. RHODES, *speaking hurriedly*] Tell me, please, what is it?

MARY: [*Rushes to* MRS. RHODES] What frightened you, Mrs. Rhodes?

MRS. RHODES: [*Almost hysterical*] A man!

MAGEE: A man?

MARY: What man?

MRS. RHODES: I don't know. He appeared at the window above, flourishing a revolver, and then he jumped to the ground and started running down the mountainside.

MAGEE: Are you sure?

MRS. RHODES: Of course I'm sure.

MAGEE: Just a moment. [*Turns and darts upstairs, taking key from his pocket as he goes*]

MARY: Is there anything wrong?

MAGEE: I'm beginning to think I am! [*Opens room door on balcony and exits*]

MRS. RHODES: [*Still hysterical*] Why did you ever come here?

MARY: [*Coolly*] It's all right. Don't get excited.

MAGEE: [*Enters from room and comes to center of balcony*] The bird has flown, but he forgot this when he took the jump. [*Points gun at women. Screaming, they run in opposite directions*] Don't be alarmed; I'm not going to shoot—at least, not yet. [*Is on landing of stairs as he speaks*] Now might I ask why I'm so honored by this midnight visit? [*Snaps on bracket lights and comes down*]

MARY: I can explain in a very few words.

MAGEE: That will suit me immensely. My time is valuable. I'm losing thousands of dollars, perhaps, through even this waste of time. [*Looks at* MARY *intently*] Be as brief as possible, please. I— [*Stares at her*]

MARY: Why do you stare at me so?

MAGEE: Do you believe in love at first sight?

[MRS. RHODES *takes a step toward them, surprised*]

MARY: What do you mean?

MAGEE: You know, I've written about it a great many times, but I never believed in it before. It's really remarkable! [*Looks from* MARY *to* MRS. RHODES, *puzzled; then laughs in an embarrassed manner*] Oh, pardon me, you were about to explain your visit here.

MARY: Well, to begin with, I——

[*Phone rings. All turn and look at it*]

MAGEE: [*Goes to phone, stops buzzer; then to* MARY] Will you be kind enough to answer that phone? I don't care to turn my back on anything but a bolted door tonight. [*As* MARY *looks surprised*] If you please.

MARY: Certainly. [*Goes to phone*] Hello! . . . What's that? . . . Hold the wire, please, I'll see. [*Turns to* MAGEE] Did you wish to talk to police headquarters?

MRS. RHODES: [*Frightened*] Police headquarters!

MAGEE: Yes. [*Starts, then stops and looks up at room on balcony*] But, no; just say they must have made a mistake.

MARY: [*In phone*] Hello! . . . No, no such call put in from here. Must be some mistake. That's all right. [*Stands up receiver.* MAGEE *goes to phone, severs connection*] Then you did call police headquarters?

MAGEE: I did.

MRS. RHODES: Why did you call police headquarters?

MARY: Yes, why did you call police headquarters?

MAGEE: [*Looks at both, puzzled, then laughs*] You know, these are the most remarkable lot of happenings. No sooner do I get rid of one best seller, than along comes another dyed-in-the-wool "to-be-continued-in-our-next." [*To* MARY] You know there's no particular reason for my saying this, but I really believe I'd do anything in the world for you.

MARY: I don't understand.

MAGEE: But you promised to explain your presence here.

MARY: Which I fully intend to do; but first of all I should like to ask you one question.

MAGEE: Proceed.

MARY: How did you get in here without this key? [*Shows him her key*]

MAGEE: [*Laughs*] Oh, no, no! You know, I'm beginning to think this whole thing is a frame-up.

MARY: What do you mean?

MAGEE: [*Points to her key*] You have the only key to Baldpate in existence, I suppose?

MARY: So I understood.

MAGEE: Well, if it's any news to you, ladies, believe me, there are more keys to Baldpate than you'll find in a Steinway piano.

MARY: Then he lied!

MAGEE: Who lied?

MRS. RHODES: [*Quickly*] Remember your promise, Mary! [*Crosses to chair in front of fire and sits*]

MAGEE: [*Follows* MRS. RHODES *with his eyes*] Well?

MARY: I can't tell you his name.

MAGEE: Well, at least tell me *your* name.

MARY: My name is Mary Norton. I do special stories for the *Reuton Star.*

MAGEE: [*Surprised*] In the newspaper game?

MARY: That's it. And this lady—— [*Pointing to* MRS. RHODES, *who is now removing her rubbers*] —is Mrs. Rhodes, with whom I live in Reuton, and who is the only other person who knows I'm here to do this story.

MAGEE: What story?

MARY: The story of the five-thousand-dollar wager you have made with a certain gentleman that you would write a complete novel inside of twenty-four hours.

MAGEE: Who told you this?

MRS. RHODES: Remember your promise, Mary.

MAGEE: You've made many a promise, haven't you, Mary? I should certainly like to know who gave you this information.

MARY: I can tell you only that when the wager was made at the Forty-fourth Street Club this afternoon, a certain someone dispatched the news to me at once. Believing that I had the only key to Baldpate, I hurried here to let you in, and lo and behold—— I find you already at work, and as snug and cozy as you would be in a New York apartment. . . . Now that you know my story, I am going to throw myself on your mercy and ask you to allow me to stay here and get the beat. I promise you we shall not disturb you in the least. Have you any objections?

MAGEE: And you won't tell me who gave you the story?

MARY: I can't.

MAGEE: Nor where you got the key?

MRS. RHODES: Remember your promise, Mary.

MAGEE: [*Turns and looks at* MRS. RHODES *and then at* MARY] You know, I wish you hadn't brought her with you.

MRS. RHODES: What! [*Gets up and starts toward* MAGEE]

MAGEE: No offense, Mrs. Rhodes! Of course I understand that Mary is a very promising young woman, but why continually remind her of the fact. [*Laughs apologetically*] That's just my little joke. Excuse me. [*Goes to* MARY. MRS. RHODES *goes to window, looking out*] Let me get this clear. Your idea is to stop here and write the story of my twenty-four-hour task?

MARY: With your permission.

MAGEE: Well, I'll tell you. Had you put such a proposition up to me—half an hour ago, I should have said emphatically, no; but since my little experience with the gun-flourishing, window-jumping gentleman, I'm inclined to entertain the idea of a companion or two.

MRS. RHODES: Who was the man with the gun?

MARY: Why did he jump from the window?

MAGEE: You might as well ask me why he placed a package of money in that safe. [MARY *and* MRS. RHODES *go up toward safe*] Or why he telephoned the fact to someone else, who was to pass the word along to Mayor Cargan.

MRS. RHODES: [*Turns to* MAGEE, *amazed*] Mayor Cargan!

MAGEE: What seems to be the trouble?

MARY: [*To* MAGEE] Mrs. Rhodes is a widow; Mayor Cargan a widower. Perhaps you will understand why the name startled her when I tell you that Mrs. Rhodes is to become Mrs. Cargan next Sunday morning.

MAGEE: Oh, indeed! [*He crosses to* MRS. RHODES] Well, congratulations, Mrs. Rhodes. And again I say I did not mean to offend. I am not accusing Mayor Cargan of any transaction, dishonest or otherwise. I was merely trying to point out to you ladies that it has been a night of wild occurrences up to now. However, if you care to take the risk, stay here. It won't disturb me in the least, and may possibly benefit this young lady in her business. [*Looks at his watch and whistles*] I've lost half an hour already, and as every minute means money to me right now, I'll have to work fast to make up for the time I've lost. [*To* MRS. RHODES] Again I apologize for any mistake I may have made, Mrs. Rhodes.

MRS. RHODES: I assure you a more honest man than Jim Cargan never lived.

MAGEE: I sincerely trust you're right, especially for your own sake. [MRS. RHODES *sits in front of fire.* MAGEE *goes to* MARY *and takes her hand*] I hope the story proves a whale. I wish——

MARY: What do you wish?

MAGEE: Oh, nothing—I was just thinking of Sunday morning. Good night.

MARY: Good night.

MAGEE: [*As he goes up the stairs*] I'd gladly offer you ladies my room, but it's the only one cleaned and heated, and I must have some comfort for this kind of work. [*On balcony*] Good night, ladies.

MARY *and* MRS. RHODES: Good night.

MAGEE: [*Leaning over balcony*] Mary—that's the sweetest name in the world.

MARY: [*Looking up at him*] Thank you.

MAGEE: Good night.

MARY: Good night.

MAGEE: [*A long look at* MARY *and then at* MRS. RHODES] I still wish you hadn't brought her with you. Good night.

[MAGEE *exits into room on balcony, closing door*]

MRS. RHODES: [*Goes to* MARY] You don't believe Jim Cargan guilty of any treachery? Tell me you don't, Mary.

MARY: I don't know, Mrs. Rhodes. I told you of the Suburban bribe story we got last night, but I certainly hope the name of Cargan is kept clean, for both your sakes.

MRS. RHODES: I can't believe he's wrong! I won't believe it!

MARY: But if he is wrong, it's best you should know it now. The fates may have brought us here tonight to protect you; who knows?

MRS. RHODES: [*Going toward safe*] Money hidden in that safe, he said.

MARY: Yes, and that dovetails with the Suburban bribe story. I came down here to do a special. I may get two sweeps with the one broom. Wouldn't that be wonderful? I'd be made!

MRS. RHODES: [*Turns, looks toward door, and sees* PETERS] Great Heavens, Mary, look!

MARY: What is it? [*Looks up at door, sees* PETERS, *screams, and runs behind banister.* MRS. RHODES *screams and runs and hides behind chair.* MAGEE *enters on balcony after second scream*]

MAGEE: [*Looking down at women*] What's wrong down there?

MRS. RHODES: A ghost!

MAGEE: What!

MARY: A ghost! A ghost!

MAGEE: [*Laughing*] I'll bet you four dollars that's the fellow whose wife ran away with a traveling man! [*Starts to come downstairs*]

MARY *and* MRS. RHODES: [*They wave* MAGEE *back*] Ssh!

> [MAGEE *snaps out lights.* PETERS *unlocks the door, enters, locks door, then throws the sheet over his arm and comes downstage, looking from* MARY *to* MRS. RHODES, *who both come forward a trifle.* MAGEE *comes to* PETERS]

MAGEE: I beg your pardon; but have you any idea just how many keys there are to this flat?

PETERS: [*Ignores question*] What are these women doing here?

MAGEE: How's that?

PETERS: I don't like women.

> [MRS. RHODES *and* MARY *scream and run to foot of stairs*]

MAGEE: It's all right, ladies; he's not a regular ghost. I know all about him. He's in the picture-postcard business.

PETERS: [*Gruffly*] What!

MAGEE: [*To* PETERS] Just a minute, Bosco. [*To ladies*] If you ladies will kindly step upstairs into my room, I'll either kill it or cure it. [*Ladies go up and stand on balcony*]

PETERS: [*Gruffly*] What?

MAGEE: [*To* PETERS] See here, that's the second time you've barked at me. Now don't do it again, do you hear? [*To ladies*] Go right in, ladies. [*They exit into room, closing door. To* PETERS] So you're the ghost of Baldpate, are you?

PETERS: How'd you people get in here?

MAGEE: [*Laughs*] You're not going to pull that "only key in existence" speech on me, are you?

PETERS: What?

MAGEE: You know there are other keys besides yours.

PETERS: They're all imitations. Mine's the real key. The old man gave it to me the day before he died.

MAGEE: What old man?

PETERS: The father of that young scamp who wastes his time around those New York clubs. You know who I mean.

MAGEE: Then you're not particularly fond of the present owner of Baldpate?

PETERS: I hate him and all his men friends.

MAGEE: You don't like women either, you say.

PETERS: I despise them!

MAGEE: How do little girls and boys strike you?

PETERS: Bah!

MAGEE: [*Laughs*] I can understand your wife now—anything in preference to you, even a traveling man!

PETERS: Don't mention my wife's name, or I'll— [*Raises lantern to strike* MAGEE]

MAGEE: [*Pulls lantern out of* PETERS' *hand*] Now, see here, old man, if you make any more bluffs at me I'll take that white sheet away from you and put you right out of the ghost business. Haven't you any better sense than to go about frightening little children this way? Why don't you stick to your own line of work? You're a hermit by trade, if I'm rightly informed.

PETERS: Yes, I'm a hermit, and proud of it!

MAGEE: Then why don't you cut out this ghost stuff and be a regular hermit?

PETERS: I play the ghost because I love to see the cowards run.

MAGEE: Oh, they're all cowards—is that it?

PETERS: Cowards, yes! [*Laughs gruffly*]

MAGEE: And you're a brave man. I suppose?

PETERS: A cave man is always a brave man.

[*Pistol shots heard outside, then a woman's scream.* PETERS *laughs and dances up to door and peers through*]

PETERS: Ha, ha! They're shooting again! They're shooting again!

> [MARY *and* MRS. RHODES *have come out on balcony at shots*]

MAGEE: [*Rushes to door and peers through*] What's that?

MARY: What's happened?

MRS. RHODES: Is someone hurt? [*Both lean over balcony, looking down*]

MAGEE: Did you hear a woman scream?

MARY: [*Frightened*] Distinctly!

MRS. RHODES: [*Frightened*] And a pistol shot!

PETERS: [*Dramatically, as he goes toward door left, slowly*] A woman in white—a woman in white! They shot at her as they shoot at me when I play the ghost. [*Laughs*] They thought it was the ghost! [*Almost whispers*] Thought it was the ghost! [*Laughs viciously and exits*]

> [MYRA THORNHILL *appears at door and is seen unlocking it*]

MAGEE: [*Runs to foot of stairs and calls up to women*] My God, another key!

MARY *and* MRS. RHODES: What?

MAGEE: Ssh! It's a woman! [*He waves them back*] Ssh!

> [MARY *and* MRS. RHODES *go back into room.* MAGEE *crouches behind banister, unseen by* MYRA *until he speaks.* MYRA *enters, locks door, then tiptoes cautiously to dead center. She takes a sweeping glance around, then goes to fire and warms herself; comes to center again, and on making sure that no one is in the room, she goes to safe and starts working combination, first picking up lantern from desk and holding it in her left hand, while working combination with her right*]

MAGEE: [*Snapping on bracket lights*] I thought I'd give you a little more light so you could work faster. [MYRA *puts lantern on desk and throws up her hands*] You needn't throw up your hands; I'll take a chance on that quick stuff. Come on out here, please. [*Laughs, as* MYRA *comes slowly around desk*] I didn't think they did that sort of thing outside of melodrama and popular novels, but I see I was wrong, or I should say right, when I wrote it. [MYRA *continues to advance to him slowly*] Really, you're the most attractive burglar I've ever seen. That is, if you are a burglar. Are you?

MYRA: [*Coolly*] Are you one of the Cargan crowd, or do you represent the Reuton Suburban people?

[MARY *and* MRS. RHODES *enter on balcony and listen*]

MAGEE: No, I'm just an ordinary man trying to win a bet; but up to now the chances have been dead against me. Perhaps you'd like to tell me who you are?

MYRA: I will, if you'll answer me one question.

MAGEE: [*Laughs*] Of course, of course. I'll answer that one before you ask it. A friend of mine gave it to me. Of course you thought you had the only one in existence, but he lied to you. I have a cute little key of my own. Oh, there are keys and keys, but I love my little key best of all. [*Shows her his key, kissing it*] See?

MYRA: I can't understand it at all!

MAGEE: You haven't anything on me. And just about two more keys, and I'll pack up my paraphernalia, go back to New York, and never make another bet as long as I live!

MYRA: Will you please tell me your name?

MAGEE: Well, a name doesn't mean so much, so you may call me Mr. Jones. And yours?

MYRA: My name is—— [*Hesitates.* MARY *and* MRS. RHODES *lean over balcony, listening*] Listen! [*Close to him*] My husband is the president of the Reuton-Asquewan Suburban Railway Company. He has agreed to pay a vast amount of money for a certain city franchise; a franchise that the political crowd at Reuton has no power to grant. They are going to cheat him out of this money and use it for campaign funds to fight the opposition party at the next election. If he sues for his money back, they are going to expose him for entering into an agreement he knows to be nothing short of bribery. The present mayor is at the bottom of it all! [MARY *and* MRS. RHODES *start at mention of mayor's name*] I ran to my husband tonight and begged him not to enter into this deal. I warned him that he was being cheated. He wouldn't believe me, but I know it's true. He's being cheated, and will be charged with bribery besides. That's why I risked the mountain on a night like this. I must have been followed, for I was shot at as I reached the top of Baldpate. Oh, I don't know who you are, but you're a man and you can help me. [*Puts her hands on his shoulders, pleadingly*] You will help me, won't you?

MAGEE: [*Interested*] Yes. What do you want me to do?

MYRA: [*Looks at* MAGEE *for a moment without speaking, then goes up to safe and back to* MAGEE] In that safe there is a package containing two hundred thousand dollars.

MAGEE: [*Goes up toward safe*] Two hundred thousand dollars!

[MARY *and* MRS. RHODES *start downstairs very slowly*]

MYRA: [*Following* MAGEE] That's the amount. It must be there! A man named Bland was to bring it here and deposit it at midnight. Cargan was to follow later, and was to find it here.

MAGEE: Cargan coming here!

MYRA: So they've planned it. I must have that money out of there before he arrives. You'll help me, won't you? Don't you understand? My husband is being cheated, tricked, robbed, probably ruined.

MAGEE: But I don't know the combination.

MYRA: Oh, there must be something we can do! Please, please—— [*She kneels at his feet and puts up her hands imploringly*] For the sake of my children, help me, please! [MAGEE *sees women on stairs, and warns* MYRA *with a look as he helps her to her feet. She turns and faces* MARY *and* MRS. RHODES, *then turns abruptly to* MAGEE] Who are these women? What are they doing here? [*She has changed from hysteria to dignified coldness*]

MAGEE: Oh, of course, pardon me! [*Goes to women at foot of stairs*] May I introduce Miss——

MYRA: [*Cuts him off sharply*] Please don't! [*Turns to women*] Will you pardon me for a moment, ladies?

MARY *and* MRS. RHODES: Certainly.

[*They remain near stairs, keeping their eyes fixed on* MYRA *and* MAGEE. MAGEE *goes to* MYRA]

MYRA: [*Aside to* MAGEE] For God's sake, don't tell them who I am! My husband will kill me if he ever learns that I've been here on such an errand.

MAGEE: [*Aside*] I understand; you may trust me. I sympathize with you very deeply, madam, and I promise you that no one shall take that money away from here tonight unless it be yourself. And I'll get it out of that safe if I have to blow the thing to smithereens!

MYRA: You give me your word as a gentleman??

MAGEE: [*Offers his hand*] My word as a gentleman.

MYRA: [*Takes his hand*] Thank you.

MAGEE: [*Pulls down his vest and goes up to* MARY *and* MRS. RHODES] Ladies, I wish to present a girl schoolmate of mine, Miss Brown, who has become interested enough in my career to find her way to Baldpate to witness my endeavor to break all records as a speedy story-writer.

MARY *and* MRS. RHODES: Miss Brown. [*Both bow.* MYRA *returns the bow*]

MAGEE: [*Takes out his watch and looks at it*] Up to now I'm almost an hour behind myself. However, I expect to catch up with myself before the night is over. That is, of course, provided there aren't over three hundred more keys to the old front door.

MARY: [*Goes up to* MAGEE] Now, might I have a word with you alone?

MAGEE: I'd be delighted. I'd like to be alone with you forever.

MARY: [*To* MYRA] Will you pardon me for a moment?

MYRA: Certainly.

MAGEE: Go right upstairs, Miss Brown, and make yourself quite at home. [*Starts toward stairs with* MYRA] Oh, Mrs. Rhodes, will you be good enough to show her to the room? I'm sure she needs a little drop of something after that bitter cold trip up the mountain. You'll find a flask on the table.

MRS. RHODES: [*Starts up the stairs*] Come right along, miss. I know where it is; I've already tried it. [*Exits into room*]

MYRA: [*Following* MRS. RHODES *upstairs*] Well, really, I don't know what to say to all this kindness. I—— [*Stops on balcony, looks down and warns* MAGEE *to silence with finger on her lips. He reassures her, then crosses to* MARY]

MRS. RHODES: [*Appearing at door*] Right in here, miss.

MYRA: Thanks, awfully. [*Exits into room, followed by* MRS. RHODES, *who closes door*]

MARY: Who did that woman claim to be?

MAGEE: That's a secret I've promised never to reveal.

MARY: But I overheard everything she said.

MAGEE: Then you know.

MARY: I know she lied.

MAGEE: She lied!

MARY: She claimed to be the wife of Thomas Hayden, president of the Suburban Railway. She lied, I tell you. Why, I've known Mrs. Hayden all my life; was brought up and went to school with her daughters. Mrs. Hayden is a woman in her fifties. You can see for yourself that she is nothing more than a slip of a girl. There's a mystery here of some kind—someone's playing a desperate game!

MAGEE: Yes, and it's costing me five thousand dollars. I'll never get my work done tonight, I can see that right now. But what do I care? I've met you!

MARY: You're going to give this money over to that woman?

[PETERS *enters from left and hides behind banisters*]

MAGEE: Not if she lied.

MARY: Well, you believe me, don't you?

MAGEE: [*Takes her hand*] Believe you! Let me tell you something, little girl. I've written a lot of those Romeo speeches in my novels, though I never really felt this way before, but here goes: The moment you walked through that door tonight and I laid eyes on you, I made up my mind that you were the one woman in the world for me. Why, there's nothing I wouldn't do for you. Try me.

MARY: Very well, I shall. Get me that package of money out of that safe before Cargan comes to steal it. Help me to reach Reuton without being molested, and I'll annihilate the graft machine with tomorrow's edition of the *Star*. With that money to turn over to the proper authorities as proof of the deal, I'll wipe out the streetcar trust and the Cargan crowd with one swing of the pen. And just think, I'll save Mrs. Rhodes from an alliance with a thief! I know Cargan's crooked, always has been; but I must prove it before she'll break off the engagement. Great Scott! what a story I'll write! Think what it will mean to me and to the city of Reuton itself! [*Puts her hands on his shoulders pleadingly*] You will do this for me, won't you? Please, please!

MAGEE: Yes. What do you want me to do?

MARY: Come, we must hurry! Can't you think of some way to open that safe? [*She goes up toward safe,* MAGEE *following*]

MAGEE: What are we going to do? We don't know the combination, and I haven't any dynamite. But we must have that two hundred thousand dollars.

[PETERS *moves chair just enough to betray his presence*]

MARY: [To MAGEE, *frightened, placing her hand on his arm*] What was that?

MAGEE: Oh, that was nothing. It was just the wind creeping through the cracks, I fancy. [*Aside*] Go upstairs; there's someone hiding in this room. [*Aloud*] Good night, Miss Norton.

MARY: Good night. [*She hurries upstairs and exits into room*]

[MAGEE *looks around room for a moment, reaches over banisters and snaps out lights; starts whistling, and then goes upstairs to right room on balcony, opens door, slams it loudly, and then comes out and sits behind banisters, watching* PETERS. PETERS *makes sure no one is in sight, then goes quickly over to safe and starts working combination quietly, but hurriedly,* MAGEE *watching him from stairs.* CARGAN *and* MAX *appear outside, peering through into room. As the safe door flies open, they enter quickly,* CARGAN *opening the door.* MAX *quickly covers* PETERS *with gun.* CARGAN *closes door and goes quickly to* PETERS]

MAX: Get away from that safe! [PETERS *jumps away*] Put up your hands! [PETERS' *hands go up*]

CARGAN: [*Recognizes him as he goes toward safe*] Oh, it's you, is it? [*To* MAX] The ghost came near walking that time for fair! [*To* PETERS] Come out of there! [PETERS *comes in front of desk*] How did you know the combination of that safe? [*No reply from* PETERS] Who told you there was money in there? [*No reply from* PETERS] Get out of here, you vagabond! What do you mean by breaking into a man's safe in the middle of the night? Throw him in the cellar, Max.

MAX: Come on, hurry up! Get out! [*He shoves* PETERS *toward door left*]

PETERS: [*At door*] Damn you, Cargan, I hate you!

CARGAN: Get out! [*He goes up and locks front door*]

MAX: Go on, get out!

> [PETERS *exits.* MAX *follows him off and returns almost immediately*]

CARGAN: [*Goes to safe and gets package of money*] By gad, we weren't any too soon! [*Goes to table*] Another moment, and he'd have had it sure. It would be good-bye to the hermit if he ever got hold of a roll like this! [*Flips bills in his hands*] Two hundred one-thousand-dollar bills.

MAX: Is it all there?

CARGAN: I don't know; I'll see. [MAGEE *comes downstairs and goes behind desk while* MAX *and* CARGAN *are counting money*] You seem surprised that I found the money here.

MAX: What do you mean—surprised?

CARGAN: [*Rises, puts money in his pocket*] I'm going to tell you something, Max. I didn't trust you all day, and I didn't trust you tonight.

MAX: What do you mean—you didn't trust me?

CARGAN: I'll be truthful with you. I thought you were going to double-cross me. I thought you were going to beat me to the bank-roll through this woman Thornhill.

MAX: Myra Thornhill?

CARGAN: Yes, Myra Thornhill. Oh, don't play dead; you knew she was around. You've had secret meetings with her during the last forty-eight hours. I know every move you've made—I've had you watched. You've worked with her before. [As MAX *makes a motion of protest*] You've told me so. I had my mind made up to kill you, Max, if this money had been gone, and that's just what I'm going to do if you ever double-cross me, do you understand?

MAX: [*In a hangdog tone*] Yes, I understand.

[MAGEE, *who has been crouching between safe and desk, now stands up, takes aim, and fires at wall, then rushes over and turns on bracket lights. At the sound of the shot the women come out on balcony, frightened, and stand looking down at men*]

CARGAN: [*As* MAGEE *shoots*] My God, I'm shot!

[*He reels against table.* MAX *draws back*]

MAGEE: No, you're not! I just put a bullet into the wall, and I'll put one in you if you don't toss that package of money over here! Come on, hurry up! I mean business! [CARGAN *hesitates, then throws money to* MAGEE. *The latter picks it up and puts it in his pocket*] You see, being a writer of sensational novels, I'm well up in this melodramatic stuff.

MRS. RHODES: [*On balcony, watching* CARGAN] Jim Cargan!

CARGAN: [*He and* MAX *look up and see women on balcony*] What are you doing here?

[MRS. RHODES *doesn't reply, but continues staring at him*]

MYRA: [*Looking down at* MAX] Max, Max, are you hurt?

MAX: No; I'm all right.

CARGAN: [*Turning slowly to* MAX] Myra Thornhill, eh? So you were trying to cross me, you snake! [*Chokes* MAX. *Women scream*]

MAGEE: I must insist upon orderly conduct, gentlemen. No roughhouse, please! [*To* MAX] Young man, be good enough to put that gun of yours on the table. [MAX *hesitates*] Hurry now. [MAX *does as directed*] Now kindly remove that gun from Mr. Cargan's pocket—I'm sure he has one—and put it on the table also. He might want to take a shot at you, and I'm giving you the necessary protection. Hurry, please.

[MAX *takes* CARGAN's *gun and places it on table*]

MAGEE: Now, Mrs. Rhodes, will you kindly ask the streetcar president's wife to step back into that room, then lock the door and remove the key? [MYRA *goes slowly to room.* MRS. RHODES *follows her, locks the door, then comes to center of balcony*] Thank you. And now, Miss Norton, will you kindly step down here— [MARY *starts downstairs and hangs muff on chair*]—and take those two revolvers from the table and place them in the hotel safe, and then close the safe and turn the combination? [MARY *places guns in safe, turns combination*] Thank you very much. [*To men*] Now, gentlemen, I must insist that you step upstairs to the room on the right of the balcony. And, Mrs. Rhodes, will you please step over there and lock the door when these gentlemen are on the other side? [MRS. RHODES *goes to room right, unlocks door, and stands aside for the men to pass in*] I shan't keep you there long, gentlemen; I'll release you as soon as I've transacted some important business with this young lady. Lively, now, gentlemen! Lively! [*As men start upstairs slowly*] That's it! Now to your right. Correct! Now straight ahead. [MAX *exits into room.* CARGAN *stops as he gets to door, and turns and looks appealingly at* MRS. RHODES, *who ignores his outstretched hands*] Now right in. [CARGAN *exits into room*] Lock the door, Mrs. Rhodes, and bring the keys down to me. [MRS. RHODES *locks door and brings keys to* MAGEE] That's the ticket! Thanks, very much. [*To* MARY] Well, how's my work? Some round-up, wasn't it? [*To* MRS. RHODES] I'm awfully sorry about this, for your sake, Mrs. Rhodes.

MARY: [*To* MAGEE] It's best she should know. [*To* MRS. RHODES, *extending her hand*] Isn't it, dear?

MRS. RHODES: [*Moving away, after taking* MARY's *hand*] I suppose so, dear, I suppose so.

MAGEE: Well, come on, little girl! You've got to work fast. Here's the graft money. [*Takes money from his pocket and gives it to* MARY] Now what?

MARY: I've everything planned. I know just what I'm going to do. What's the time?

MAGEE: [*Looking at watch*] One-thirty. But you can't get a train out of Asquewan until five.

[MARY *crosses and gets muff; places money in it*]

MRS. RHODES: We can't sit around the station for three hours, dear.

[MARY *returns to* MAGEE]

MAGEE: Try to get a taxi, or whatever sort of conveyance they have in the darned town; but whatever you do, get out of Asquewan as soon as you can.

MARY: You leave it to me; I'll find a way. Are you going to stay here?

MAGEE: I'll have to. I want to keep guard on this crowd of lady and gentleman bandits until I'm sure you're well on your way. I'll keep them here until you phone and tell me you're out of danger, even though it's all night tonight and all day tomorrow.

MARY: But your work?

MAGEE: Never mind the work; I can write a novel any old time. So far as the bet is concerned, I can lose that and still be repaid a million times over—I've met you. [*Takes her hand, then crosses to* MRS. RHODES] Good night, Mrs. Rhodes, and God bless you both!

MRS. RHODES: Good night. [*Shakes hands with* MAGEE, *then starts for door and stands looking up at door on balcony*]

MAGEE: [*To* MARY, *near door*] I wonder if we'll ever meet again?

MARY: I live in Reuton—good night.

[MRS. RHODES *exits*]

MAGEE: Good night. [MARY *comes to door* MAGEE *is holding open. She pauses for a moment, looks at him intently, then down at floor, then exits quickly.* MAGEE *locks door, stands peering out at them for a moment, then stands thinking*] Crooked politicians —adventuress—safe robbed—love at first sight! [*Points to different rooms and at safe*] And I wanted to get away from melodrama! [*Hears* HAYDEN *at door, and backs away to foot of stairs*] And still they come!

[HAYDEN *enters, locks door, puts key in his pocket, takes off gloves, rubs his hands and nose trying to warm them, then comes down to fireplace and stands with his back to the fire. As he turns he comes face to face with* MAGEE, *who has come to center. He goes to* MAGEE *slowly*]

HAYDEN: I beg pardon, but who are you?

MAGEE: I'm Mayor Cargan's butler.

HAYDEN: Mayor Cargan!

MAGEE: Yes, he's here. Do you wish to see him?

HAYDEN: [*Importantly*] Yes. Say to him that Mr. Hayden of the Reuton-Asquewan Suburban Road is calling.

MAGEE: Oh, I see! Are you the president of that road, sir?

HAYDEN: [POMPOUSLY] I most certainly am, sir.

MAGEE: [*Looks at* HAYDEN, *and then up at room right and laughs*] Your wife's here.

HAYDEN: What!

MAGEE: Yes; locked in that room up there. [MAGEE *points to room on balcony.* HAYDEN *turns and looks up. As he turns,* MAGEE *fans him for gun.* HAYDEN *turns to* MAGEE *quickly, sputtering*] Pardon me, I just wanted to see if you had a gun on you. Just a minute; I'll tell the mayor the president has arrived. [*Starts upstairs, laughing*]

HAYDEN: Are you a crazy man, sir?

MAGEE: That's what the citics say, but I'm beginning to think they are all wrong. Sit down, Mr. Hayden. I'll tell the boys you're here. [*Unlocks door and steps aside*]

HAYDEN: The boys!

MAGEE: Come on, boys; everything's all right; the president's here. [*As men come down,* HAYDEN *steps forward toward stairs*] Watch your step. Easy, that's it; one at a time, please. Lead on, boys. I'll walk a little behind.

[CARGAN *and* MAX *come downstairs, followed by* MAGEE, *who covers them with gun. As men get to foot of stairs,* HAYDEN *backs away, thunderstruck*]

CARGAN: [*Gruffly*] Hello, Hayden.

HAYDEN: What is the meaning of this, Cargan?

CARGAN: I don't know. Ask him. [*Nods toward* MAGEE]

HAYDEN: [*To* CARGAN] Who is he?

CARGAN: I don't know, and I don't care a damn! I'm disgusted with the whole works. We're nailed, that's all I know.

[*He sits.* PETERS *enters from door left. On seeing crowd of men, he starts to back out, but is stopped by* MAGEE]

MAGEE: No, you don't! Come back here. I'll keep my eye on you, too. You'd better sit down and join the boys, Hermy.

[PETERS *sits*]

HAYDEN: [*To* MAGEE] I'd very much like to know the reason for such strange actions, young man?

MAGEE: Your wife will be down in a minute; she'll probably tell you all about it.

HAYDEN: Confound it, sir, my wife is home in bed!

MAGEE: That's what you think! You're not the first fellow that's been fooled, you know. [HAYDEN *backs away from* MAGEE. MAGEE *throws key to* PETERS] Here, Hermy; take that key and open the first door to the left on the balcony, and tell Mrs. Hayden that her husband wants to see her downstairs right away. [*As* PETERS *hesitates*] Hurry along, that's a good ghost—go on. [PETERS, *mad all through, does as he is told, picking up the key from floor and going upstairs*] Better sit down, boys, and make yourselves comfortable. We're liable to have quite a wait.

[MAX *sits*]

HAYDEN: Well, I'll be running along.

MAGEE: [*Stops* HAYDEN *as he starts for door*] Better stay a while, Mr. Hayden; I'd like to have your wife meet you. I don't think she's ever had the pleasure.

[MYRA *and* PETERS *enter on balcony and start downstairs*]

HAYDEN: [*To* CARGAN] What the devil sort of a man is this?

[BLAND *knocks on door. All jump and turn*]

MAGEE: Well, here's a novelty at last—a man without a key.

HAYDEN: It's Bland. I have his key; I'll let him in. [*Starts for door*]

MAGEE: Don't bother. I have a dandy little key of my own; I'll let him in. [*Opens door, keeping all covered*]

> [BLAND *enters as* MAGEE *unlocks door, the latter keeping him covered.* BLAND *comes down to* HAYDEN. *Men all sit as* BLAND *enters*]

BLAND: [*To* HAYDEN] What's the matter, Guv'nor?

HAYDEN: I don't know.

BLAND: [*Goes to* MAGEE, *as he recognizes him*] That's him, the man I told you about. He locked me in!

MAGEE: Oh, hello! Are you back again? I thought you jumped out of town.

BLAND: [*To* CARGAN] Did you get it all right?

CARGAN: No; he's got it.

BLAND: What? [*Rushes over to* MAGEE] Give me that money!

MAGEE: [*Covering* BLAND *with gun*] Say, I killed a man once for hollering at me. [BLAND *backs away.* PETERS *comes downstairs. To* MYRA, *as she advances slowly to center*] Ah, here we are! Mr. Hayden, although I think you are getting a shade the best of it, this young lady claims to be your wife.

HAYDEN: What! [*To* MYRA] You claim what?

MYRA: Go on, holler your head off, grandpa! [*As she strolls languidly over to fireplace*] It's music to my ears to hear an old guy squawk.

> [*She sits in chair in front of fire.* HAYDEN *goes to* BLAND]

BLAND: [*Waves* HAYDEN *away, then crosses to* MAGEE] What are you going to do with that money?

MAGEE: [*Keeping all covered*] I haven't got the money. [*All turn and look at him in amazement*] It's on its way to Reuton. Miss Norton will see that it is placed in safe and proper hands directly she arrives at the office of the *Reuton Daily Star*.

CARGAN: The *Daily Star!* We're gone! [*To* MAGEE] Where did Mrs. Rhodes go?

MAGEE: Out of your life forever, Cargan; she's got your number. [CARGAN *lowers his head without speaking. Pause, then* MAGEE *gets chair for* BLAND] Sit down there. [BLAND *pays no attention*]

Did you hear me? Sit! [BLAND *sits slowly and sulkily*] Sit down, Hermy. Come on, that's a nice ghost, go on. [PETERS *sits*. MAGEE *places chair for* HAYDEN] Sit down, Hayden.

HAYDEN: I don't care to sit down, sir.

MAGEE: Do as you're told; sit down.

HAYDEN: Confound it, sir, do you know that I'm the president of the Reuton-Asquewan Railway Company?

MAGEE: I wouldn't care if you were president of the National League. Sit down! [HAYDEN *sits, indignant*. MAGEE *sits in chair, front of switchboard, facing all and covering them with gun*] Now we're all going to stay right here till that phone bell rings and I get word that Miss Norton is safe and sound in Reuton. That may mean three hours or it may mean six hours; but we're all going to stay right here together, no matter how long it takes; so get comfortable and sit as easy as you can.

        [*All move uneasily*]

CARGAN: [*To* MAX, *after a pause*] So you tried to cross me, eh? The chances are I'll kill you for this.

BLAND: [*After a pause, looking at* HAYDEN] I'm afraid I made a mistake in bringing you up here, Guv'nor.

HAYDEN: [*After a slight pause*] You're always making mistakes, you damned blockheaded fool!

MAX: [*After a pause*] I'm sorry I got you into this, Myra. [*No reply from her*] Oh, Myra, I say I'm sorry I got you into this.

MYRA: [*Turns and looks at* MAX] Oh, go to hell!

PETERS: [*After a slight pause*] I hope to God you're all sent to prison for life!

MAGEE: [*After a pause*] This is going to be a nice, pleasant little party; I can see that right now.

                    SLOW CURTAIN

ACT TWO

The curtain rises on the same situation.

After curtain is up, there is silence for about six seconds, then the clock is heard striking two.

HAYDEN *takes out his watch and looks at it. All squirm and look at each other impatiently.*

MAGEE: Two o'clock. We've been sitting here over twenty minutes already. Say, Hermy, you'd better put another log on the fire. [PETERS *crosses to fireplace, puts a log on the fire, looks closely at* MYRA *in front of fireplace, then goes back to former position and sits*] I think someone ought to say something. Come on, let's start a conversation. Things are getting awfully dull.

HAYDEN: [*Gets up after a short pause and goes toward* MAGEE] This is all damned nonsense! I refuse to stay here another minute.

MAGEE: [*Coolly, and without moving*] Sit down, Hayden. I'm very sorry to inconvenience you in this way, but it's necessary that you should stay here and keep us company; so sit down before I shoot you down! That's a good little president. [HAYDEN *sits sulkily*] That's it. Now, let me see, what can we talk about to kill the monotony and keep things sort of lively? I have it! Let's all tell each other where we got our keys to Baldpate. [*All move uneasily*] What do you think of the idea? [*No reply*] No? Well, I'll start the ball rolling, then perhaps we'll all 'fess up. I brought a letter from the man who owns the inn to the caretaker, giving him instructions to turn the key over to me. That's how I got mine. Next? [*Pause. No one speaks*] No? Big secrets, eh? [*Laughs*] By George! that's funny. Let's see, how many keys are there? I had the first, Bland the second, Miss Norton the third, our friend the ghost the fourth, this young lady had the fifth, and, if I'm not mistaken, you had the sixth key, Mr. Cargan. Hayden doesn't count—he had Bland's key. Six keys to Baldpate so far. I wonder if there are any more.

PETERS: [*After a pause*] There are seven keys to Baldpate.

[*All turn and look at* PETERS *in surprise*]

MAGEE: Seven! How do you know?

PETERS: The old man told me the day before he died. Mine's the original—all the others are imitations.

[*All turn from him in disgust*]

MAGEE: Seven keys, eh? *More* company expected. More melodrama, I suppose. Where did you get your key, Bland?

BLAND *and* MAGEE: [*Together*] None of your damned business!

MAGEE: [*Laughs*] I knew you were going to say that. How about you, Mr. Cargan? Perhaps you'll be good enough to throw some light on the key subject. Where did you get yours?

CARGAN: I wouldn't tell you if my life was at stake.

MAGEE: Well, perhaps the young lady will be good enough to inform me where her key came from?

[*All turn and look at* MYRA]

MYRA: [*Turns and faces men*] I've no objections.

MAX: [*Pleadingly*] Myra, please!

MYRA: [*Pointing to* MAX] He gave the key to me.

[*All turn and look at* MAX]

CARGAN: [*To* MAX] Where did you get a key to Baldpate?

MAX: I can't tell you, Mr. Mayor; I've sworn never to tell.

CARGAN: [*To* MYRA] I suppose he also gave you the combination to the safe.

MYRA: He did.

MAX: [*Pleadingly*] Myra!

MYRA: Oh, shut up! You never were anything but a crybaby! You've got me into a pretty mess! Do you think I'm going to sit here like a fool and not pay you back when I've got the chance to do it? [*Gets up and faces men. They all stare at her*] I'll tell you the whole scheme. I was to come here and make off with the package, and Cargan was to follow and find it gone. We were to meet tomorrow and divide the money equally.

CARGAN: [*Turns on* MAX] You rat!

[MAX *turns from* CARGAN *in hangdog fashion*]

MYRA: His cxcuse to Cargan for the disappearance of the money was going to be to accuse Bland of never having put it there.

BLAND: [*Rises, starts*] Whatl

MAGEE: Sit down, Bland.

[BLAND *hesitates, then sits*]

BLAND: [*Turning to* HAYDEN] Do you hear that, Guv'nor? He was going to accuse me of stealing the money.

CARGAN: [*To* MAX] You mark my words, I'm going to kill you for this!

BLAND: [*To* CARGAN] Where did you get a key to Baldpate, Cargan? You told me you couldn't get in here unless I met you and unlocked the door.

[CARGAN *looks embarrassed, but does not reply*]

MYRA: I can explain that. [*All look toward her*] He was to meet you here tomorrow morning at nine o'clock. Am I right?

BLAND: That's right; I made the appointment over the phone.

MYRA: Well, the plan was to steal in here in the dead of night and take the money. He fully intended to keep his appointment here tomorrow morning, however, and appear just as much surprised as you would have been when you discovered the safe empty and the package gone. In other words, he was going to cross not only you, but Hayden and everyone else connected with the bribe. He tried to cross you—[*Points to* BLAND]—and Lou Max tried to double-cross him. [*Points to* CARGAN. *Laughs and sits*] If I hadn't been interrupted by our friend here—[*Nods her head in* MAGEE's *direction*]—I'd have gotten the money and *triple*-crossed the whole outfit!

BLAND *and* HAYDEN: What!

MYRA: Yes, that was my intention. Scruples are a joke when one is dealing with crooks.

CARGAN: [*Starts up*] Who's a crook?

MAGEE: Sit down, Cargan!

CARGAN: [*Infuriated*] Do you think I'll stand to be——

MAGEE: [*Sternly*] Sit down, I tell you! I'm the schoolteacher here. Be a good little mayor and sit down.

[CARGAN *sits*]

MYRA: [*Sneeringly, after a slight pause*] Why, you're not even clever crooks. You trusted Max, and Max trusted me. [*Laughs*] A fine chance either one of you had if ever I had gotten hold of that money!

HAYDEN: [*To* BLAND, *after thinking a moment*] Who is this woman?

BLAND: I don't know.

CARGAN: [*Turns to* HAYDEN] Her name is Thornhill. Don't believe a word she says, Hayden; her oath isn't worth a nickel. She's a professional blackmailer, pure and simple.

HAYDEN: [*To* MYRA] Is this true?

MYRA: I never heard of a pure and simple blackmailer, did you? [*Laughs*] So far as my word is concerned, I fancy it will carry as much weight as the word of a crooked politician or the word of his man "Friday," whom he knows to be an ex-convict.

MAX: [*Starts up*] What!

MAGEE: Sit down, Maxy; it's just getting good.

[MAX *slinks into his chair*]

HAYDEN: [*To* BLAND, *who looks at him*] Fine people you've introduced me to, you lunk-headed idiot!

BLAND: Well, what are you blaming me for? You wanted the deal put through, didn't you? After this you can do your own crooked work. I'm not anxious to get mixed up in a thing of this kind. You've got a fine nerve to go after me.

HAYDEN: [*Gets up*] How dare you talk to your employer in such a manner!

BLAND: Oh, sit down! [HAYDEN *sits*] What do you think I care for this job? I told you to stay out of the deal—that it was wrong. You know well enough that it's only cheating the city of Reuton out of its rights. If this thing ever comes to light, we're all lucky if we don't spend five or six years in a stoneyard! I tell you right now, if it comes to a showdown, I'm going to make a clean breast of the whole affair. I don't care who I send away, so long as I can save myself! You needn't think you can get me in a fix like this and have me keep my mouth shut. No, sir; I'm going to tell the truth, and I don't care a damn who suffers, so long as I get away.

MYRA: [*Laughs*] One of our best little squealers!

BLAND: [*To* MYRA] Well, you squealed, didn't you?

MYRA: Sure, I'm with you, cutie! I'm going to scream my head off all over the place.

[*All show alarm*]

CARGAN: [*To* MAX, *after a pause*] So you tried to cross me, eh?

MAX: Certainly I tried to cross you. Why shouldn't I? You're around crossing everybody, ain't you? [*Rises*] I've stood for your loud talk long enough, Cargan. I've been wanting to call you for the last two years. You're a great big bluff, that's all you are, and I'm going to get even for that punch you took at me, do you hear? Now you shoot any more of that killing stuff at me, and I'll go after you like a wild bear! You're never going to kill anybody, you haven't got the nerve; but I have, and the next bluff you make at me will be your last! [*Sits*] It's your fault I'm mixed up in this affair, and the best thing you can do is to get me away clean, do you understand? [*Smashes table with fist. Pause, then looks at* HAYDEN] You didn't think you were going to get that franchise for two hundred thousand, did you, Hayden? Why, this man would have bled you for half a million before the bill went through, and then held you up for hush money besides. I know what I'm talking about. He was going to rob you, Hayden, and I dare him to call me a liar!

[*All look at* CARGAN, *who swallows the insult in fear of* MAX's *attitude*]

HAYDEN: [*After a pause*] Cargan, is it true that you were going to rob me of this money?

CARGAN: [*Turns to* HAYDEN, *after a slight pause*] Well, if you want to know—yes, that's what I was going to do, rob you; just what you deserve. You were trying to rob the city, weren't you? You're just as much a thief as I am. If I'm a crook, it's your kind that has made me so—you, with your rotten money, tempting men to lie and steal! [*Settles back in his chair*] Big corporations such as yours are the cause of corrupt politics in this country, and you're just the kind of a sneak that helps build prisons that are filled with the poor devils that do your dirty work. You're worse than a crook —you're a maker of crooks! [*Turns to* HAYDEN, *leans forward and points at him*] But I promise you, Hayden, that if I go up for this, you'll go with me! It's your fault that I entered into this thing, and, by Gad! I'll get even if I have to lie over a Bible and swear your life away! [*Turns*] Rob you! Humph! You've got a hell of a gall to yell about being robbed, you have!

PETERS: [*After slight pause*] I hope the prison catches fire and you're all burned to a crisp!

MAGEE: You know, my suggestion was to start a conversation, not a roughhouse.

HAYDEN: [*After a slight pause*] This woman who took the money —who is she?

MYRA: A newspaper reporter.

BLAND: On the *Daily Star*.

CARGAN: The sheet that has fought me ever since I've been in office. They've got me this time, sure!

MAX: [*After a pause, looking nervously at* MAGEE] How much longer are you going to keep us here?

MAGEE: That's for the telephone to say. I'll release you as soon as I'm sure Miss Norton is safe and sound in Reuton.

[*All turn toward* MAGEE, *surprised*]

BLAND: Then you're not going to turn us over to the police?

MAGEE: Certainly not. Why should I?

[*Movement of relief from all*]

PETERS: [*Gets up*] Because they're a lot of crooks! [*All turn toward* PETERS] Oh, how I'd love to be on the jury!

MAGEE: Sit down, Hermy! I need a little target practice, and remember, there's no law against killing ghosts!

[PETERS *sits*]

HAYDEN: There's no train to Reuton till five o'clock. That means we must stay here till six, eh?

MAGEE: I'm afraid so, unless they make it by automobile from Asquewan. It means several hours at the best, so you might as well be patient; you've got a long wait.

[*All move uneasily*]

MYRA: [*Cuddling up in her chair*] Me for my beauty sleep! Good night.

[*Short pause, then phone rings. All start and stare at it.* MAGEE *gets up and stops buzzer*]

MAX: She couldn't have made it as quick as that. It's over an hour by automobile.

MAGEE: [*Keeps them all covered with gun*] Answer that phone, please, Miss Thornhill. [MYRA *gets up and goes to phone.* MAGEE *backs upstage*] I'm going to keep looking straight ahead of me tonight. Hurry, please. Give me the message as you get it. I'll tell you what to say if it requires an answer.

MYRA: [*At phone; in a bored tone*] Hello . . . Yes, Baldpate Inn. . . . Yes, I know who you mean. Just a moment. [*To* MAGEE] Someone wants to talk to you.

MAGEE: Get the name.

MYRA: [*In phone*] Hello, who is this, please? . . . Oh, yes. . . . Very well, I'll tell him. [*Turns to* MAGEE] Miss Norton.

MAGEE: Say that it is impossible for me to turn my back long enough to come to the phone, and that you will take the message and repeat it to me as you get it.

MYRA: [*In phone*] It is impossible for him to turn his back long enough to come to the phone. You are to give me the message and I am to repeat it to him as I get it. . . . You're talking from the Commercial House in Asquewan. . . . You missed the package of money five minutes ago. . . . [*All turn*] You either dropped it in the inn before you left, or else lost it while hurrying down the mountain. . . . Search the inn thoroughly. [*Pause, while all look around room*] Ask him whether or not you should notify the police. [*All show fear*] You're nearly crazy, and don't know which way to turn. . . . Just a moment. [*Turns and looks at* MAGEE] Well, what shall I say?

MAGEE: [*Looks around at all, then answers, after a pause*] Say to hold the wire.

MYRA: [*In phone*] Hold the wire, please. [*Gets up and goes toward chair*]

HAYDEN: The money lost!

CARGAN: Thank God, there goes their evidence!

MAX: Who ever heard of losing two hundred thousand dollars!

BLAND: Can't be done outside of Wall Street. Surest thing you know, she's holding out.

MAGEE: [*Smiles*] You're a quick thinker, Miss Thornhill.

MYRA: [*Turns to* MAGEE] What do you mean?

MAGEE: That I don't believe you got that message at all.

MYRA: [*Shrugs her shoulders indifferently*] Very well; she's on the wire—see for yourself. [*Sits in chair in front of fire*]

MAGEE: Come here, Hermy.

PETERS: My name's not Hermy; my name's Peters.

MAGEE: Well, whatever it is, come here. [PETERS *goes up to* MAGEE] I know you don't like anybody in this room any better than I do, so I'm going to take a chance on you. Take this gun and guard that door until I get this message, and you kill the first man or woman that makes a move, do you understand?

PETERS: [*Vindictively*] I'd like to kill them all!

MAGEE: Don't shoot unless you have to. [*He hands* PETERS *the gun and goes to phone*] Hello!

PETERS: Damn you, Cargan, I've got you at last!

[PETERS *goes toward* CARGAN *and is grabbed by* HAYDEN. MYRA *screams and jumps up.* BLAND *springs on* MAGEE *and struggles with him.* MAX *rushes over and the two overpower* MAGEE *at phone. When* HAYDEN *grabs* PETERS,

CARGAN *rushes over and struggles with* PETERS, *wresting gun from him*]

MAX: [*To* MAGEE] Take it easy, young fellow; you haven't got a chance!

BLAND: We've got him!

CARGAN: [*After wrenching gun from* PETERS, *he hits him a blow, knocking him down*] What do you think of that? [BLAND *and* MAX *are each holding* MAGEE *by the arms.* PETERS *is on the floor,* CARGAN *standing over him, with gun.* HAYDEN *is looking on.* CARGAN *to* PETERS] So you wanted to take a shot at me, eh? [*Kicks* PETERS] Get up! [PETERS *gets up in fear*] Put them both up in the room where he put us, and lock the door!

BLAND: They can make a getaway from the window, Cargan; I did it myself.

CARGAN: There's no window in that room; it's a linen closet. Put them up there!

[*He backs up; gun in hand.* PETERS *starts upstairs*]

MAGEE: [*To* CARGAN, *on way to stairs*] What's the idea, Cargan?

CARGAN: [*Backing up and pointing gun*] Go on, I'm the school-teacher now—do as you're told! [PETERS *and* MAGEE *go upstairs, followed by* MAX. CARGAN *speaks to* MYRA *with his back to her*] Get on that phone, Miss Thornhill, and tell that woman not to notify the police. Say that she is to return here at once, and see what she says.

[MYRA *goes to phone.* MAGEE *and* MAX *are now on landing.* PETERS *is standing at door of room on balcony*]

MYRA: [*In phone*] Hello . . . Yes . . . Why, the message is that you are not to notify the police of the loss. Say nothing to any-one, but return here at once. . . . That is the message. . . . Yes, good-bye. [*Hangs up receiver*]

CARGAN: [*To* MYRA, *still watching* MAGEE] All right.

MYRA: [*Rising from switchboard*] As quick as she can get here, she says. [*Goes to chair*]

MAGEE: [*Stops on landing as he hears phone conversation*] What are you going to do, Cargan?

CARGAN: Never mind; I'm running things now. Get in there!

[PETERS *exits into room on balcony*]

MAGEE: You harm that girl, and I'll get you if it's the last act of my life!

CARGAN: I've read that kind of talk in books.

MAGEE: I write books of that kind, but I'm talking real talk now!

MAX: [*To* MAGEE] Go on, get in there!

[MAGEE *goes into room.* MAX *locks door and comes to foot of stairs.* CARGAN *puts gun in his pocket*]

HAYDEN: Now what's the move, Cargan?

CARGAN: We're going to get that money if she's got it on her.

BLAND: You don't think she's fool enough to bring it back with her if she's trying to get away with it, do you?

HAYDEN: What are you going to do with it if you find it on her, Cargan?

CARGAN: Keep it, of course.

HAYDEN: It's my money!

CARGAN: Our agreement holds good. You people will get the franchise. Don't worry.

HAYDEN: Why, you've just openly declared that you were going to rob me of the money.

CARGAN: Oh, because I was mad clean through. Wasn't I being accused right and left? I didn't mean a word I said, Hayden. I don't even know now what I said. [*Pats* HAYDEN *ingratiatingly on the shoulder*]

HAYDEN: What do you think, Bland?

BLAND: Don't ask me; you bawled me out once tonight; that's enough!

CARGAN: I haven't forgotten what you said to me, Mr. Max.

MAX: I don't want you to forget it. I want you to remember it all your life. [*As* CARGAN *reaches for gun*] I wouldn't care if you had six guns on you! Cut out that wild talk; I ain't going to listen to it any more. Why, you're nothing but a cheap coward, Cargan! [CARGAN *looks at* MAX *a moment, then turns, cowed.* MAX *crosses to* MYRA] So you tried to double-cross me, eh?

MYRA: [*Turns and faces* MAX] Why, certainly! Who are you?

MAX: Why, damn you, I—— [*Raises his hand to strike* MYRA, *who shrinks away*]

BLAND: Here, wait a minute, Max; nothing like that while I'm around.

MAX: [*Turns to* BLAND] Maybe you want some of it? Why, I—— [*Raises his hand to strike* BLAND]

BLAND: [*Grabs* MAX's *arm and throws it back*] Now behave yourself! The same speech you just made to Cargan goes for me. I want you to cut out this wild talk. I'm not going to listen to any more of it. I'll put you on your back if you make another bluff at me!

HAYDEN: [*Goes toward* MAX *and* BLAND] Gentlemen, gentlemen, please!

> [MAX *and* BLAND *look each other in the eye for a moment, then* MAX *goes up near safe*]

BLAND: [*Turns to* HAYDEN] You keep out of this, Hayden; you'll get all you're looking for if you don't! [*Raises his hand to* HAYDEN *as if to strike*]

HAYDEN: Put it down! Put it down, do you hear me? What do you mean by raising your hand to me? Why, damn me, for two pins I'd take and wipe up the floor with you! I can whip a whole army of cowards like you! Now get away from me! Get away from me before I knock you down! [BLAND, *surprised at* HAYDEN's *attitude, goes up to door, after staring at* HAYDEN *a moment.* HAYDEN *goes to* MYRA. MAX *goes to safe and begins working combination*] Now, madam, what do you mean by claiming to be my wife? I demand an explanation!

MYRA: [*Turns quickly and angrily on* HAYDEN] Now let me tell you something, old man. You can scare these three little boys, but I don't want you to annoy me, because I've got a nasty temper; so go on, get away before I lose it!

> [HAYDEN *stares at* MYRA, *dumbfounded, then quickly moves away.* MYRA *seats herself in chair.* MAX, *by this time, has worked combination of safe, and at this point the door*

flies open. He grabs a gun from safe and slams door shut.
CARGAN, *who has been standing at foot of stairs looking up at room, turns as he hears the door slam and crosses quickly, catching* MAX *at safe door*]

CARGAN: [*Pulling his gun*] Get away from that safe! What are you doing there?

MAX: [*Flashes revolver.* MYRA *rises*] Oh, you needn't be afraid. I ain't going to do anything, only I——

[MAX *has come in front of desk and now takes deliberate aim at* MYRA *and shoots. She screams and drops into chair*]

BLAND: [*Runs to* MYRA] God!

CARGAN: What's the matter, Max? Have you gone crazy? [*Puts gun in his pocket*]

HAYDEN: Now we're in for it! Is she hurt?

MAX: I couldn't help it; it was an accident! I didn't mean it, I tell you!

[MAGEE *raps on door upstairs. All look up*]

MAGEE: [*From upstairs*] What's wrong down there? [*Raps again*] What's happened?

[*All stand rigid, staring*]

BLAND: [*In a low voice*] Put out the lights!

[CARGAN *tiptoes over and turns out bracket lights, leaving only the reflection of burning logs on* MYRA's *face, then tiptoes back*]

HAYDEN: Anything serious, Bland?

BLAND: You're a damn good shot, Max; you got her, all right! [*He is feeling* MYRA's *pulse*]

CARGAN: Don't say that!

HAYDEN: It can't be possible!

BLAND: It's all over—she's gone! [*Drops her hand, then turns her chair around*]

MAX: [*Wild-eyed*] But I didn't mean it, I tell you—it was an accident!

BLAND: You lie!

CARGAN: I saw you take aim.

HAYDEN: So did I.

MAX: [*Pleadingly*] No, no, don't say that! It isn't so! Before heaven, I swear it was an accident!

[MAGEE *pounds on door upstairs*]

HAYDEN, CARGAN *and* BLAND: [*To* MAX] Ssh!

[*All look up in direction of door*]

MAGEE: [*From room*] Tell me what the matter is down there!

CARGAN: [*Goes to foot of stairs and calls up*] Everything's all right—nothing wrong.

MAGEE: I know better! Open this door! [*Pounds on door*]

BLAND: Give me a hand, Cargan, and we'll get her out of here.

CARGAN: Where do you mean?

BLAND: [*Pointing to room left on balcony*] Up in that room! Come on, hurry up!

[CARGAN *assists* BLAND *in lifting* MYRA *to the latter's shoulders.* BLAND *starts for stairs, carrying* MYRA; CARGAN *following with her wraps, etc.*]

MAX: [*As* BLAND *passes with* MYRA] I didn't mean it, I tell you! I'm innocent! Why, I wouldn't harm a fly!

HAYDEN: [*Goes to* MAX *and silences him roughly*] Keep quiet, you damn fool! Do you want the world to hear you?

[MAGEE *resumes pounding on the door. Just as* BLAND *and* CARGAN *get to first landing,* MAGEE *kicks the door open from the inside, and in the breakaway the lock falls to the floor.* MAGEE *enters on balcony as the door flies open,* PETERS *following him out.* MAGEE *comes to first landing and follows* BLAND *and* CARGAN *up opposite stairs a few steps.* PETERS *remains outside door.* BLAND *and* CARGAN *stop only a second on first landing, and then continue on up the stairs during following lines*]

MAGEE: What's happened?

CARGAN: She's fainted, that's all.

MAGEE: Where are you taking her?

CARGAN: You'll keep out of this, young fellow, if you know what's good for you!

[BLAND and CARGAN *exit into room*, CARGAN *closing door*]

MAGEE: [*Has followed them on balcony. Watches them exit with* MYRA, *then rushes downstairs to* HAYDEN] Who fired that pistol shot?

MAX: [*Blurts out*] It was an accident!

HAYDEN: [*Quickly to* MAX] Shut up!

MAGEE: See here, Hayden, if there's anything wrong here, you can't afford to mix up in it; you're too big a man.

MAX: [*Hysterically*] I didn't mean to kill her! I'm not responsible! It was an accident!

MAGEE: Oh, we have a murder case on our hands—is that the idea?

HAYDEN: I don't know; but whatever it is, we're all in this thing together. We must frame a story and stick to it, do you understand?

MAGEE: No, I don't understand.

HAYDEN: We must claim suicide!

MAX: That's it! She killed herself! I was an eyewitness—she killed herself!

MAGEE: Do you think I'd enter into such a dastardly scheme? [BLAND and CARGAN *enter and stand on balcony, listening*] No! If it's murder, there's the murderer—[*Points to* MAX]—self-confessed. But you're all as guilty as this man—every one of you! It's the outcome and result of rotten politics and greed. I'll swear to every word that's been uttered here tonight. I've had my ear against the crack of that door for the last five minutes. I overheard every word that passed between you. I'll tell the story straight from the shoulder. You can't crawl out of it, gentlemen, with your suicide alibi! It's murder in the first degree, and I'm going to help make you pay the penalty!

[HAYDEN *and* MAX *stand staring at him.* CARGAN *and* BLAND, *after a bit of pantomime, come downstairs*]

CARGAN: [*After a pause; to* MAGEE] I'm afraid you're in wrong here, young fellow.

[PETERS *sneaks across balcony and stands listening to next few speeches, hidden behind post*]

CARGAN: I'm sorry for you. From the bottom of my heart I pity you.

[MAGEE *does not reply; simply looks at* CARGAN, *then at* BLAND]

BLAND: [*After a pause*] She's dead—you killed her, all right!

[MAGEE *looks* BLAND *in the eye, then at* CARGAN]

HAYDEN: [*To* MAGEE] Better plead insanity, old man; it's the only chance you've got.

[MAGEE *stares at* HAYDEN, *then crosses over and looks* MAX *straight in the eye.* MAX *stares back at him*]

MAX: [*After a pause*] Bad business, this carrying guns. Who was the woman—your wife?

[PETERS *exits into room on balcony, closing door*]

MAGEE: [*Turns, sees the three staring at him, smiles*] No, no, gentlemen! You can't get away with it! It's good melodrama, but it's old stuff. I know every trick of the trade. I've written it by the yard. You can't intimidate me. I won't be third-degreed. You work very well together, but it's rough work, and it isn't going to get you anything. Besides, you forget I have a witness in Peters, the hermit.

[*All turn and look up at room*]

CARGAN: [*To* BLAND] Get him! Bring him down!

[*He goes to foot of stairs as* BLAND *goes upstairs*]

BLAND: [*Runs up and looks into room, then comes out on balcony*] He's gone!

[HAYDEN *looks at* MAX, *then back to* BLAND]

CARGAN: Gone! Where?

BLAND: [*Comes quickly down the stairs*] He probably found a way; he knows the place better than we do.

CARGAN: [*Comes to* MAGEE] I saw you when you fired; you shot to kill.

BLAND: [*To* MAGEE] I tried to knock the gun from your hand, but I was too late.

HAYDEN: I didn't witness the shooting myself, but I turned just in time to grab you before you got away.

MAX: But you shouldn't have choked her; that was the brutal part of it!

MAGEE: [*Starts for* MAX, *who backs away to fireplace, frightened*] Why, you dog, I——

> [CHIEF KENNEDY *appears outside door and pounds on it three times. All stop abruptly and look toward door, holding the picture for a repeat of the pounding*]

CARGAN: [*Loudly*] Who's there?

KENNEDY: [*Yells through door from outside*] Open this door in the name of the law!

MAX: The police!

HAYDEN: [*Quickly to* MAX] Keep quiet! [*Gets behind desk*]

BLAND: [*To* CARGAN] You'd better let them in, Cargan.

MAGEE: [*Starts for door*] I'll unlock the door.

CARGAN: No, you don't; I'll attend to it!

> [*He crosses, goes up to door and unlocks it.* KENNEDY *steps in, watching* CARGAN *as the latter locks the door. As* CARGAN *is about to put key in his pocket,* KENNEDY *speaks*]

KENNEDY: [*Just inside door*] Here, wait a minute! I'll take that key. I'll take that gun I saw you stick in your pocket, too.

BLAND: [*Takes a couple of steps toward* KENNEDY] What authority have you?

KENNEDY: Close your trap! I'm Chief Kennedy of the Asquewan Falls Police Headquarters—that's my authority!

CARGAN: [*Pointing to* BLAND] It's all right, Chief; he's all right.

KENNEDY: Where's the light switch?

MAGEE: Up there to your left.

KENNEDY: [*Goes and turns on lights, then comes to* CARGAN, *recognizing him*] Hello, Mr. Mayor! What are you doing here?

CARGAN: I can explain all that.

MAGEE: [*Pointing to* MAX] That man has a gun on him also!

[HAYDEN *moves slowly away*]

KENNEDY: [*Goes over and looks* MAGEE *over carefully*] Who are you?

MAGEE: I'll tell you who I am at the proper time and place. You'd better get on your job quick here, Chief; there's something doing. Two of these men are carrying weapons, and two of them also have keys to that door. I'm telling you this to prevent a getaway.

KENNEDY: What are you trying to do, run the police department?

MAGEE: This is an important case, Chief. Thousands of dollars are involved, and a crime committed besides. I advise placing every man in this room under arrest immediately!

KENNEDY: [*To* CARGAN] What's this all about, Mr. Mayor?

[*All appear anxious*]

CARGAN: He's four-flushing, Chief. He's stalling for a chance to break away.

KENNEDY: Don't be afraid; I've got men outside; nobody'll get away. [*Crosses to* MAX *and looks at him closely*] Lou Max, eh? Quite a crowd of celebrities. [*To* MAX] You got a gun? [MAX *hands him his gun*] What are you totin' this for? [*No reply from* MAX. CHIEF *turns and fans* MAGEE] He's clean. [*Crosses to* CARGAN] I'm sorry to trouble you, Mr. Mayor, but I'll have to relieve you of that hardware. [CARGAN *hands* CHIEF *his gun*] And the key, too, please. [CARGAN *hands* CHIEF *his key*] I've come here to investigate, and I've got to do my duty. [*He crosses over to* BLAND]

BLAND: [*Holding up his hands as* CHIEF *approaches him*] There's nothing on me.

KENNEDY: [*Fans* BLAND] Who's got the other key? He said there were two.

BLAND: [*Points to* HAYDEN] This gentleman.

KENNEDY: [*Goes to* HAYDEN, *who hands the* CHIEF *his key*] Hello! Mr. Hayden. Humph! This is a real highbrow affair, isn't it? Well —— [*Smiles, and looks them all over*] Come on, somebody open up. What's the big gathering all about?

MAX: [*Pointing to* MAGEE] He's got a key. Make him give it up.

KENNEDY: [*To* MAGEE] Come on. [MAGEE *hands* CHIEF *his key*] You got anything more to say?

MAGEE: I prefer to tell my story in the presence of witnesses. I insist upon the immediate arrest of everyone here, myself included.

HAYDEN: Don't mind him, Chief; he's a madman.

KENNEDY: Well, somebody telephoned police headquarters from here about two hours ago, and when we got on the wire Central said they'd hung up. We got a new connection, and asked if they'd called, and some woman said, "No, it was a mistake." We got to thinking it over at headquarters and it didn't listen good, so we looked it up and found out that the call had been put in from Baldpate Inn; so I made up my mind to come here and investigate. Now, when I started up the mountain ten minutes ago the lights were on full blast, and all of a sudden they went out, and there was a pistol shot, too. Every one of my men heard the report, and we all agree it came from this direction. Now, what's it all about?

MAGEE: 'Twas I who called up police headquarters.

[*All look at* MAGEE]

KENNEDY: You! The Sergeant said it was a woman's voice on the wire.

MAGEE: That was the second time when you called up, but I tried to get you first.

KENNEDY: What for?

MAGEE: I don't intend to tell my story until I'm under oath. I want every word I say to go on the court records. I charge these men with conspiracy and murder!

KENNEDY: What is this, Cargan?

CARGAN: The poor devil's gone mad, I guess. He shot and killed a woman a few minutes ago, and he's accused every man here of the crime.

KENNEDY: Murder, eh?

HAYDEN: Yes, cold-blooded murder.

KENNEDY: [To MAGEE] Who was the woman you shot?

MAGEE: Don't let these men get away with this, Chief. I can prove my innocence. [Pointing to MAX] There's the real murderer. These men know it as well as I do. They're accusing me in an attempt to save their own necks. They're afraid to tell the truth because this man is a squealer, and they know that a confession from him of a scheme to steal the right of way for a streetcar franchise in Reuton will send them all to the state penitentiary. I can prove why I'm here tonight. Ask these men their reason for being here, and let's hear what they have to say.

[KENNEDY *looks from one to the other without speaking*]

CARGAN: He's been raving like that for the last ten minutes, Chief.

KENNEDY: [To MAGEE] What is your reason for being here?

MAGEE: I came here to write a book.

KENNEDY: [To CARGAN] You're right; he's a lunatic, sure. [To CARGAN] Who was the woman that telephoned to headquarters?

MAGEE: Miss Norton, of the *Reuton Star*.

KENNEDY: The *Reuton Star*, eh? [To CARGAN] Is she the woman that was killed?

CARGAN: No; her name is Thornhill.

KENNEDY: Where is she?

CARGAN: In one of the rooms upstairs.

KENNEDY: Was there anybody else here besides you people?

MAGEE: Yes; Peters, the hermit.

KENNEDY: Another crazy man, eh?

BLAND: But he's disappeared.

KENNEDY: Well, he won't go far. [Goes up and looks out of door] I've got the house surrounded. [Returning] I'll look the ground over before I send for the coroner. He won't be here till seven or eight o'clock. You people will have to stay here till he comes. What room is she in?

CARGAN: I'll show you, Chief.

[He starts toward stairs, leading the way, followed by the

CHIEF, HAYDEN, BLAND and MAX *in order named. All look back at* MAGEE *as they go upstairs*]

KENNEDY: [*To* MAGEE, *when he gets on balcony*] Take my tip and don't try to get away, young fellow. One of those cops outside will blow your head off if you do!

MAGEE: [*Goes near foot of stairs as men go up*] You needn't be afraid. I'm going to stay right here, and I'm going to make sure these other men do until we're all taken into custody.

HAYDEN: It's a sad case, Chief.

KENNEDY: We're used to that. They generally go out of their minds after they shoot. Where is she?

CARGAN: [*Goes to door of room*] In here, Chief.

[CHIEF *exits into room, followed by* HAYDEN, BLAND, MAX *and* CARGAN, *the latter closing the door. During the last few speeches* PETERS *has been peering through glass in dining room door. He now enters and goes quickly to* MAGEE]

PETERS: I carried the body from that room through the secret passage to the cellar.

MAGEE: [*Amazed*] What!

PETERS: I heard them accuse you of the crime. [*Backs toward dining room door slowly*] They'll never find the secret passage— [*Laughs*]—and they'll never find the body! [*He laughs viciously*]

MAGEE: What did you do that for, you damn fool?!

[*Door opens on balcony*]

PETERS: Hist!

[*He points up at door on balcony.* MAGEE *looks up.* PETERS *exits hurriedly.* CARGAN *enters, wild-eyed, from room, runs downstairs.* MAX *follows him down.* HAYDEN *follows* MAX. BLAND *follows* HAYDEN. *All the men show extreme fear.* MAGEE *watches them.* KENNEDY *comes out on balcony, looks at people downstairs, then back at room for a moment*]

HAYDEN: [*To* CARGAN] What do you make of this, Cargan?

CARGAN: The damn place is haunted!

MAX: She must have escaped by the window.

BLAND: How could a dead woman jump from the window? Besides the windows are closed.

[*They all stand staring up at balcony.* KENNEDY *appears from room and closes door*]

KENNEDY: [*Comes to center of balcony and stands looking down at men*] Say, what are you fellows trying to do, string me? [*Starts downstairs*] You know I was born and brought up in New York City, even if I do live in Asquewan Falls. [*He comes down and looks them all over*]

HAYDEN: I can't understand it at all.

CARGAN: She was in that room ten minutes ago, Chief.

BLAND: I'll take a solemn oath on that.

MAX: My God, I'm going insane! [*Grabs chair to steady himself*]

KENNEDY: Say, what the devil is this all about? [*Looks from one to the other*] If you people think you can make a joke out of me, you're mistaken. I won't stand for it. Now come on, what's the answer?

MAGEE: It's no joke, Chief; there has been a murder committed here.

KENNEDY: Then where's the victim?

MAGEE: In the cellar.

BLAND, CARGAN, HAYDEN *and* MAX: What!

KENNEDY: In the cellar?

MAGEE: If I'm not mistaken, that's where she was taken after the murder.

HAYDEN: You lie!

CARGAN: You know she was taken to that room. [*Points to room on balcony*]

BLAND: You saw us carry her there.

MAX: Of course he did.

KENNEDY: [*To* MAGEE] What are you trying to do, trap me in the cellar?

MAGEE: I tell you, Chief, you'll find the victim in the cellar.

Then you can judge for yourself if I'm as crazy as these men claim me to be, or whether they've suddenly gone mad themselves.

KENNEDY: [*Blows his whistle*] I'll get at the bottom of this thing pretty quick! [*Rushes up to door, unlocks and opens it. Two* COPS *enter and await orders.* KENNEDY *locks door and goes to* COPS] Search the cellar of this place, and report to me here what you find—every nook and corner. And don't leave a thing unturned, understand? [COPS *salute.* MARY *appears outside door*] Hurry up, then! [COPS *exit through dining room door*] If this thing is a practical joke, you'll all land in jail for it! I'm not going to be made the laughingstock of Asquewan Falls, I'll tell you that right now. [MARY, *who has been peering through door, opens it and enters.* KENNEDY *turns as door opens*] Hello! Who's this?

MAGEE: [*As* MARY *enters*] Miss Norton!

[MARY *locks door*]

KENNEDY: [*To* MARY] I'll take that key, please.

MARY: [*Hands* CHIEF *the key and goes to* MAGEE] Why are the police here?

MAGEE: [*Reassuring* MARY] It's all right.

KENNEDY: [*To* BLAND] Who is this woman?

BLAND: She claims to be a newspaper reporter.

MAX: She's a thief; she stole a package of money!

KENNEDY: Whose money?

HAYDEN: My money!

CARGAN: No, my money!

MAGEE: It's bribe money, Chief.

KENNEDY: Where is the money?

MARY: [*Turns and faces* CHIEF] The money's been lost.

BLAND, HAYDEN, MAX *and* CARGAN: What!

KENNEDY: Say, what the hell are you people trying to do to me, anyway?

MAGEE: [*To* MARY] Where did you lose it?

MARY: [*To* MAGEE—KENNEDY *goes over, listening*] I don't know—somewhere between here and Asquewan. I searched every inch of the way from the bottom of the mountain to the top. It's gone, I'm afraid.

MAGEE: Where is Mrs. Rhodes?

MARY: She became too hysterical to return. I left her at the Commercial House in Asquewan.

KENNEDY: How much money was it?

MAGEE: Two hundred thousand dollars.

KENNEDY: [Looks from one to the other] Come on, cut out the kidding stuff! How much was it?

HAYDEN: That's the exact amount the package contained, Chief—two hundred thousand dollars.

KENNEDY: [To MARY] Where'd you get this money?

MAGEE: I gave it to her.

KENNEDY: Where did you get it?

MAGEE: From Mayor Cargan.

KENNEDY: Where did you get the money, Cargan? (No reply from CARGAN]

MAGEE: [After a pause] He took the money from the safe.

KENNEDY: [Goes a couple of steps, looks at safe, then comes back] How'd you open the safe, Cargan?

CARGAN: I didn't open the safe.

KENNEDY: Who did?

MAGEE: Peters, the hermit.

KENNEDY: Who put the money in the safe?

MAGEE: Bland. That man to your right.

KENNEDY: [To BLAND] Where'd you get the money to put in the safe?

BLAND: From Mr. Hayden.

KENNEDY: [Looks at HAYDEN] Is this true, Mr. Hayden?

HAYDEN: I refuse to answer for fear of incriminating myself.

KENNEDY: [To MAX] What do you know about this, Max?

MAX: Don't ask me; I don't know. My brain's on fire—I'm going mad!
[He tugs at his collar, breathing hard]

KENNEDY: [Looks them all over] Huh! Hayden gave the money to Bland; Bland put the money in the safe; Peters opened the safe; Cargan took the money from Peters; this fellow took the money from Cargan and gave it to the newspaper reporter; she loses the money in the mountains; then somebody killed a woman and the corpse got up and walked away—and you expect me to believe this bunk, do you?

MARY: [*To* MAGEE] What does he mean by saying that somebody killed a woman?

MAGEE: Don't worry; it's all right.

COP: [*Offstage*] Come on, come on! Go on, get in there! [*He opens dining room door and throws* PETERS *to center of room. The other* COP *follows them on*] That's all we could find in the cellar, Chief.

KENNEDY: No dead bodies or packages of money?

COP: Nothing else, Chief.

KENNEDY: [*Looks at* PETERS *and laughs*] Oh, it's you, is it, Peters? So that's where you hide, eh? In the cellar of Baldpate? Well, you'll have a nice room in the county jail tomorrow.

PETERS: Damn the police; I hate them!

KENNEDY: [*Shoving* PETERS] Go on, get over there! [*To* COPS *as he goes up to door*] Guard the outside. [*He unlocks door. To* COPS] And question anybody who passes up or down the mountain. [*Opens door.* COPS *exit.* CHIEF *locks door and comes to* MARY] You'll have to step upstairs, miss. I've got a lot to say to these men here, and I'm not particular about my language when I'm on a case; so come on, step upstairs.

HAYDEN: I don't believe this girl lost the money, Chief.

KENNEDY: Well, I'll get the matron of the jail here and have her searched. If she's got anything on her we'll get it. [MARY *starts for stairs,* CHIEF *following her up*] Go in one of those rooms till I call you. [MARY *is now on balcony.* CHIEF *comes back*] Who is the woman this girl says she left at the Commercial House?

CARGAN: Mrs. Rhodes. She's all right.

BLAND: How do we know? Maybe they're working together.

CARGAN: That's enough, Bland!

KENNEDY: [*As he goes toward phone all back up and watch him*] I'll call up the Commercial House and see if she's there. [*In phone*] Hello! Get me 35, Central, quick. [MARY *exits into room on balcony*] Ring me when you get it. [*Hangs up receiver*] What's her name again?

MAGEE: Mrs. Rhodes. [MARY *screams offstage and rushes from room to balcony*] What's the matter?

MARY: [*Screaming*] She's dead! Someone's killed her!

ALL: Who?

MARY: [*Hysterically*] That woman there in that room! This is terrible!

> [KENNEDY *looks at* MAGEE. MAGEE *looks at* CARGAN. *All stand rigid, staring at each other for a moment; then* KENNEDY, CARGAN, BLAND, HAYDEN *and* MAX *rush upstairs on balcony and cross to room. As they pass in front of* MARY, *she backs up against windows and stands with arms outstretched against them.* PETERS *is standing, laughing*]

MAGEE: [*Goes over to* PETERS *quickly*] What did you do, bring her back to that room?

PETERS: Isn't that what you wanted me to do?

MAGEE: No, you blithering idiot! [*He turns and takes* MARY *in his arms as she runs to him*]

MARY: Tell me who did this? How did it happen?

MAGEE: It's all right; take it easy.

> [MAX, BLAND, CARGAN *and* HAYDEN *enter from room in this rotation, all wild-eyed. They line up on balcony and keep their eyes glued to door of room.* KENNEDY *enters on balcony, also keeping his eyes fixed on room. He looks at men on balcony and then down at* MAGEE *and* MARY, *who stare up at him; then at* PETERS]

KENNEDY: Say, what are you people trying to do to me? [*To men on balcony, who are still staring at door*] Go on, get downstairs where you belong. [*The four men come downstairs and go to former positions. Telephone rings.* KENNEDY *runs downstairs*] Don't touch that phone! I'll answer it! [*Looks from one to the other suspiciously*] Is this dump haunted, or is the joke on me? [*No one replies. The phone still rings*] I'll soon find out! [*Goes to phone. All back up and watch him*] Hello! . . . Yes, I called you. Say, listen, Charlie. This is Chief Kennedy talking. Is there a woman there by the name of Rhodes? She was . . . She did, eh?

How long ago? . . . I see . . . What's that? . . . She asked you to mind a package for her till she got back? [*All look at each other, startled*] Where have you got it? . . . In the safe? . . . Say, listen, Charlie. Call headquarters right away and get a man over there. Give him that package, and tell him to bring it up to Baldpate Inn as quick as he can. Understand? . . . Never mind, you do as I tell you. And listen. Tell them to guard the garage and the depot, and put all strangers under arrest, men and women . . . I know what I'm doing, Charlie! You take orders from me! And listen. Get the coroner on the phone and tell him to get up here to Baldpate Inn in a rush. This is a case for him . . . Don't lose any time now. Keep your mouth shut and get busy! [*Hangs up receiver and comes to center. All come forward*] She left the hotel a quarter of an hour ago. She put the package in the hotel safe before she went. [*He looks them all over. They stand staring at each other*] Humph! Somebody kills a woman—the victim disappears and then comes back! That's pretty good stuff!

MAGEE: [*Aside to* MARY] How do you account for this?

MARY: [*Aside to* MAGEE] She must have stolen the money from me as we were running down the mountain.

> [*Whistle is heard outside door. All turn and look toward door*]

KENNEDY: They've got somebody! [*Rushes up to door and unlocks it.* COP *enters.* CHIEF *locks door*] What is it?

COP: A woman.

KENNEDY: Shoot her in! [*Unlocks door, opens it, and closes it as* COP *exits*] Here comes the bird, I guess, that tried to fly away with the coin.

> [*He opens the door as* MRS. RHODES *appears. She enters and watches* KENNEDY *as he locks door*]

MRS. RHODES: [*Turns, takes in situation; then to* CHIEF] What is the meaning of this?

KENNEDY: That's what I'm trying to find out!

MRS. RHODES: [*Goes to* MARY] Is there any trace of the money?

[MARY *turns from her without replying.* MRS. RHODES *then turns and looks at men, who all give her a contemptuous look*]

HAYDEN: Are you going to have these women searched, Chief?

KENNEDY: Maybe it won't be necessary. [*Looks intently at* MRS. RHODES] We'll wait until we see what's in the package she left at the Commercial House. [MRS. RHODES *starts, regains her composure, then seeing all watching her, she turns and makes a dash for the door.* CHIEF *speaks as he follows her up*] No, you don't! Nobody leaves here until this whole thing has been cleared up and I find out who killed that woman.

MRS. RHODES: [*Turns, startled*] Killed a woman! [*To* CARGAN] What does he mean? [CARGAN *turns from her without speaking. She goes to* MARY]

MARY: [*To* MRS. RHODES] You stole the money from me, didn't you? [MRS. RHODES *goes to* CARGAN *without replying to* MARY]

CARGAN: [*Looks* MRS. RHODES *straight in the eye*] I'll never trust another woman as long as I live!

PETERS: They're no good—they never were!

KENNEDY: [*To* PETERS] Shut up! [*Comes to* MRS. RHODES] Well, what have you got to say, missus?

MRS. RHODES: [*After a pause*] Yes, I did steal the money.

[MARY *looks at* MAGEE; *others look at* MRS. RHODES]

MRS. RHODES: [*To* CARGAN] But I did it for you, Jim Cargan. I knew that if the story was ever made public you would be a ruined man. I knew the package of money was the evidence that would convict you. I intended to return it to Mr. Hayden and try to kill off the bribe and save you from disgrace. I did all this because I thought you cared, and what is my reward? You stand there ready to turn against me—to condemn me. Very well, now *I'll* turn! [*Turns to* KENNEDY] Officer, these men have bargained to cheat the city of Reuton. I demand their arrest on the charge of conspiracy!

HAYDEN: It's a lie!

MAGEE: It's the truth, Chief, the absolute truth. This young lady and

I will testify against these men and prove them guilty of conspiracy and murder.

MRS. RHODES: Murder!

KENNEDY: What have you got to say to this, Mr. Cargan?

CARGAN: Nothing at all—I'm through. [*Sits at table*]

MAX: So am I! I can't stand this any longer; I'm going mad! [*Goes to* CHIEF] I want you to know the real truth. 'Twas I who killed that woman upstairs. I shot her down like a dog. I know that I haven't got a chance, but I don't want to be sent to the chair. I'll confess, I'll tell the truth, I'll turn State's evidence, anything—but, for God's sake, don't let them kill me! [*Kneels at* KENNEDY's *feet*]

KENNEDY: [*To* MAX] Get up! [MAX *rises.* CHIEF *takes handcuffs from his pocket*] Come on. You'll have to wear these, young fellow. [*He puts handcuffs on* MAX]

BLAND: [*Throwing up hands*] There we go!

HAYDEN: [*To* CARGAN] What are we going to do, Cargan?

CARGAN: No less than ten years, I'm afraid.

KENNEDY: [*To* MAX] Go on, get over there!

[MAX *sits*]

MRS. RHODES: [*Goes to* MARY] Can you ever forgive me?

MARY: [*Giving* MRS. RHODES *her hand*] I didn't understand—I do now.

[*Both go to foot of stairs*]

KENNEDY: [*To* MAGEE] And you came here to write a book, eh?

MAGEE: That was the original idea.

KENNEDY: You know, I don't know yet whether you people are kidding me or not. [*All turn toward door as police whistle is heard*] They've got somebody. [*Rushes up to door and unlocks it.* COP *enters. He closes door*] Well, what now?

COP: [*Hands package to* CHIEF] A package brought to you by the police messenger. He says it's from the Commercial House.

[*All start*]

KENNEDY: Tell the messenger to hurry back and to tell the coroner to hurry up. [*Opens door.* COP *exits.* CHIEF *locks door and comes forward a bit, a sickly smile on his face*] Say, before I open this thing, I want to tell you something. If this turns out to be a bunch of cigar coupons, I'm going to smash somebody, sure. I won't stand to be strung, even if I am a small town cop. [*Opens package and sees bills*] Great Scott, it's the real thing! How much did you say was here?

MAGEE: Two hundred thousand dollars.

HAYDEN: [*Goes to* KENNEDY] I'll take that money, please; it belongs to me.

CARGAN: [*Goes to* KENNEDY] No, it doesn't; it belongs to me.

MAGEE: You hold that money, Chief; it's the only real evidence of bribery we've got.

KENNEDY: Go away! You needn't tell me what to do; I know my business. [*He puts money in his pocket and goes to phone. As he does so, all back up and watch him. In phone*] Hello! Get me 13, Central. . . . Hello! Is that you, Jane? . . . This is the Chief. I want to talk to my wife. . . . Hello! Hello! Betty. . . . Listen, Betty; get this clear. Get some things together and get the children ready and take that five o'clock train to New York . . . Never mind now, listen. When you get there, look up the railroads, and get on the first and quickest train that goes to Montreal . . . Montreal! I'll be there waiting for you Thursday morning . . . Don't ask a lot of questions; do as I tell you . . . What are we going to do there? We're going to live there. . . . Montreal . . . I don't know. [*Turns to* MAGEE] How the hell do you spell Montreal? [*No one replies*] Listen; go to Canada—any part of it. I'll find you . . . What? . . . Never mind the furniture; we're going to live in a palace . . . Canada, that's all . . . You do as I tell you. [*He gets up from phone and goes center, looking at the money. As he sees everyone staring at him, he puts it in his pocket*]

MAGEE: What do you think you're going to do?

KENNEDY: You heard me, didn't you? I'm going to Canada.

PETERS: Canada! I hope to God you freeze to death!

MAGEE: You mean you're going to steal that money?

KENNEDY: Why shouldn't I steal it from a gang of crooks like this? It's one chance in a lifetime to get this much money. You don't suppose I'm going to pass it up when I've got it right here in my kick, do you? Not me! I'm going to have one hell of a time for the rest of my life and send my two boys to college!

BLAND: [*To* KENNEDY] Do you imagine we're going to stand by and let you get away with it?

KENNEDY: [*Whips out his gun. All but* BLAND *and* MAGEE *back away from him*] That's just what you're going to do, and I'm going to have my men keep you here all night until I get a damn good start!

[BLAND *knocks the gun from the* CHIEF's *hand.* MAGEE *grabs his arms and pins them behind him.* BLAND *gets a hold on his legs. Women scream and run halfway upstairs*]

MAGEE: I've got him! Get that money!

PETERS: [*Rushes toward* KENNEDY, *yelling*] I'll get it! I'll get it!

KENNEDY: [*Yelling from the time he is grabbed*] Let me go, do you hear! Let me go!

PETERS: [*Grabs money from* CHIEF's *pocket*] I've got it!

CARGAN: [*Starts for* PETERS] Give me that money!

HAYDEN: [*Starts for* CARGAN *and grabs him by the arm*] No, you don't, Cargan; that's my money!

MAGEE: Don't let them get it, Peters!

PETERS: Let them try to get it! [BLAND *and* MAGEE *release the* CHIEF] Now let me see you get it! [*Throws money in fire, laughing viciously. All stare into fire, watching the money burn*] Watch the rotten stuff burn!

MAGEE: What have you done!

BLAND: He's burned the money!

CARGAN: A fortune!

HAYDEN: Good God!

KENNEDY: I'll have my men here and shoot you down like a pack of hounds! [*He starts, as two pistol shots are heard outside*]

MAGEE: What's that?

[*All turn and stare toward door*]

MAX: [*Looks up on balcony and yells*] Look, look!

[*All look up on balcony as he points to* MYRA, *who is walking from room to room*]

PETERS: A ghost! A real ghost!

[MARY *screams and grabs* MAGEE; MRS. RHODES *screams and grabs* CARGAN; HAYDEN *crouches in a corner*; BLAND *jumps behind desk*; MAX *huddles up in chair near fire*; PETERS *is on his knees*]

MAX: Take her away! I didn't mean to kill her! Take her away!

KENNEDY: [*Yells*] Let me out of this place! It's a graveyard!

[*He starts for door. Door flies open and the* OWNER *enters. All stare at him*]

HAYDEN: [*After a pause*] The seventh key!

BLAND: The seventh key!

[MARY *runs to* MRS. RHODES]

KENNEDY: [*To* OWNER] Who are you?

OWNER: [*Standing at door*] I'm the owner of Baldpate Inn. Two policemen refused to allow me to pass, and I shot them dead.

ALL: What!

MAGEE: This isn't true! It can't be true! I'm a raving maniac!

OWNER: [*Comes to* MAGEE] I just arrived, Billy. I motored from New York. I expected to find you alone. [*Looks around at people*] Who are these people? How did they get in here? Have they disturbed you in your work? How are you getting on with the story?

MAGEE: How am I getting on? Great heavens! man, to what sort of a place did you send me? Nothing but crooks, murderers, ghosts, pistol shots, policemen, and dead people walking about the halls! Hundreds of thousands of dollars, and keys and keys and keys! You win—I lose. Twenty-four hours! Why, I couldn't write a book in twenty-four *years* in a place like this! My God, what a night this has been!

[OWNER *starts laughing, then all join in, laughing and talking ad lib.* MAGEE *stands looking at them in utter amazement*]

OWNER: I'm not going to hold you to the wager, Billy. I just want you to know it isn't real.

MAGEE: What isn't real?

MRS. RHODES: [*Steps toward* MAGEE, *smiling*] I'm not a real widow!

CARGAN: [*Comes to* MAGEE] I'm not a real politician!

KENNEDY: [*To* MAGEE] I'm not a real policemen!

PETERS: [*Comes to* MAGEE] This isn't real hair! [*Takes off wig*]

HAYDEN: [*Goes to* MAGEE] These are not real whiskers! [*Takes off whiskers*]

BLAND: That wasn't real money that was burned!

MAX: [*Over to* MAGEE] These are not real handcuffs—see? [*Breaks handcuffs*]

MYRA: [*Appears on balcony*] I'm not a real dead one!

[*Hearty laugh from all*]

MAGEE: [*To* MARY, *after looking around in amazement*] Are *you* real?

MARY: Not a real newspaper reporter.

MAGEE: I mean a real girl.

MARY: [*Smiles*] That's for you to say.

MAGEE: [*Turns to* OWNER] Well, for heaven's sake, don't keep me in the dark. Explain, tell me what it all means.

OWNER: It means, old boy, that I wanted to prove to you how perfectly improbable and terrible those awful stories you've been writing would seem if such things really and truly happened. I left New York an hour ahead of you today. I got to Reuton at nine o'clock tonight; went directly to the Empire Theatre; told the manager of our bet; framed the whole plan; engaged the entire stock company; hired half a dozen autos; shot over to Asquewan after the performance, and we arrived at the top of the mountain at exactly twelve o'clock. Since then you know what's happened. I've been watching the proceedings from the outside, and if it were not for the fact that I'm nearly frozen stiff, I'd call it a wonderful night.

[*All laugh heartily*]

MAGEE: You did this to me?

OWNER: [*Laughs*] You're not mad, are you? Of course, if you want to go through with the bet, why——

MAGEE: No, thanks; the bet's off. I've had enough of Baldpate. Me for the Commercial House until the train is ready to start. [*To* MARY] Is your real name Mary? [*She nods affirmatively*] Well, Mary, the shots in the night, the chases after fortunes, and all the rest of the melodrama may be all wrong, but will you help me prove to this man that there is really such a thing as love at first sight?

[*All show interest*]

MARY: How can I do that?

MAGEE: Don't you know?

MARY: Well, you don't want me to say it, do you?

MAGEE: [*Whispers in her ear; she nods affirmation*] Now remember your promise, Mary.

[*Hearty laugh from all as he kisses her*]

THE LIGHTS GO OUT

EPILOGUE

*Fire is out and lock replaced on door. The stage is bare.
Typewriter is heard clicking from room on balcony. The
clock strikes twelve.* ELIJAH QUIMBY *is seen outside waving
a lantern as he did in the first act.* MRS. QUIMBY *appears,
etc. Same business, except that instead of unlocking the
door, he raps on it.* MAGEE *comes out on balcony with hat
and coat on, and carrying the suitcase and typewriter
case and a manuscript under his arm. He stops on stairs,
and as he hears* QUIMBY's *rap he comes down the stairs,
puts the cases on the table and then goes up to door and
unlocks it*]

MAGEE: [*As he opens door*] Come right in, folks. You're right on
time, I see. [*Closes door and locks it*]

QUIMBY: We've been out there ten minutes waiting for the clock to
strike.

MRS. QUIMBY: Lord, I didn't think we'd find you alive!

MAGEE: The only difference between me and a real live one is that
I'm tired, hungry and half dead.

QUIMBY: How'd you come out?

MRS. QUIMBY: Did you finish your book?

MAGEE: [*Handing* MRS. QUIMBY *the manuscript*] Allow me.

QUIMBY: What do you think of that, mother?

MRS. QUIMBY: Lord! Wrote all that in twenty-four hours!

MAGEE: Just made it. Finished work a couple of minutes ago.

QUIMBY: Were you disturbed at all?

MAGEE: Never heard a sound.

MRS. QUIMBY: No ghosts?

MAGEE: Nary a ghost, Mrs. Quimby, except those concealed in the
manuscript. . . . How about the Asquewan hotels? I'd like to get
a bath and a bite to eat before I take that train.

QUIMBY: There's the Commercial House.

MAGEE: The Commercial House! That's strange! I guessed the name.

MRS. QUIMBY: How?

MAGEE: I've got it in the story.

MRS. QUIMBY: [*Aside to* QUIMBY] What's he mean, Lije?

QUIMBY: [*Aside*] Darned if I know. [*To* MAGEE] The missus has got a fine breakfast waiting for you up at our house.

MRS. QUIMBY: And a nice feather bed for you to take a nap in. The train don't go till five.

QUIMBY: And the drummers all say the hotel's rotten.

MAGEE: Lord, I'm tired! [*Sits*] Me for the breakfast and the feather bed. Some wild and woolly scenes have been enacted in this room since you left last night, Mrs. Quimby.

MRS. QUIMBY: What happened?

MAGEE: Nothing, really—just in the story.

MRS. QUIMBY: What's he mean, Lije?

QUIMBY: How do I know?

[*Telephone rings.* QUIMBYS *start and look toward it*]

MAGEE: [*Goes to phone, stops buzzer, comes back to* QUIMBY] There's Bentley—he's pretty near on time.

QUIMBY: Will I talk to him?

MAGEE: Of course. That's the idea, isn't it?

QUIMBY: [*Goes to phone*—MRS. QUIMBY *stands watching him*] Hello! Hello! Mr. Bentley . . . Yes, sir, I've got it right here, sir. Two minutes ago, sir . . . I'll have to find that out. Wait a minute. [*To* MAGEE] What's the name of the story?

MAGEE: It's typewritten on the cover.

MRS. QUIMBY: [*Holds up script and reads by light of lantern*] "Seven Keys to Baldpate."

QUIMBY: [*In phone*] "Seven Keys to Baldpate." [*To* MAGEE] He's laughin'. [*Pause, then to* MAGEE] He says there's only one. [*In phone*] Hello! . . . What, sir? . . . Wait, I'll see. [*To* MAGEE] You want to talk to him?

MAGEE: No. Yes, just a minute. [*Goes to phone. The* QUIMBYS *stand listening*] Hello! Hello! Hal. I'm going to collect that five thousand from you, old pal. . . . Yes, some title, isn't it? And, say, some story. Wild, terrible, horrible melodrama as usual, the kind of stuff you always roast me about. Treated as a joke, however, this time. And say, Hal, listen; I've got you in the story . . . Yes, really . . . Oh, I didn't mention your name or anything . . . And, say, I'm in the story, too . . . Oh, I'm the hero! . . . Say, Hal, this thing's going to sell over a million copies. . . . The what? The critics? [*Laughs*] I don't care a darn about the critics. This is the stuff the public wants . . . Yes, I'll met you at the Forty-fourth Street Club at two-thirty tomorrow . . .

SLOW CURTAIN

STANLEY RICHARDS

Stanley Richards, a native New Yorker, is a man of varied experience in the theatre. He has written twenty-five plays, among them: *Through a Glass, Darkly; August Heat; Tunnel of Love; Sun Deck; O Distant Land;* and *District of Columbia.* He is also the editor of a number of play anthologies.

Twelve of his own plays have appeared in the annuals *The Best One-Act Plays* and *The Best Short Plays.* His plays have been widely performed on stage, television and radio, and most of them have been translated for production and publication abroad.

One of his most recent plays, *Journey to Bahia*, adapted from a prize-winning Brazilian play and film, *O Pagador de Promessas*, had its première at The Berkshire Playhouse and later was produced in Washington, D.C., under the auspices of the Brazilian Ambassador and the Brazilian American Cultural Institute. The play also had a successful engagement Off-Broadway during the 1970–1971 season.

In addition, he has been the New York theatre critic for *Players Magazine*, and a frequent contributor to *Theatre Arts; Playbill; The Theatre; Actors' Equity Magazine,* and *The Dramatists Guild Quarterly.*

As an American theatre specialist, Mr. Richards has been awarded three successive grants by the United States Department of State's International Cultural Exchange Program to teach playwriting and directing in Chile and Brazil. He taught playwriting in Canada for ten years and in 1966 was appointed Visiting Professor of Drama at the University of Guelph, Ontario. He has produced and directed plays and has lectured extensively on theatre at universities in the United States, Canada and South America.

He is now at work on a collection of *Great Musicals of the American Theatre.*